Brahma Sūtras

By

Śrīla Kṛṣṇa-dvaipāyana Vyāsadeva

With *Govinda-bhāṣya* – the commentary of Śrīla Baladeva Vidyābhūṣaṇa

Translated into English by
HH Bhanu Swami

Readers interested in the subject matter of this book are invited by the publishers to correspond at the following address:

His Holiness Bhanu Swami
ISKCON
Hare Krishna Land (off ECR),
Bhaktivedanta Swami Road,
Akkarai,
Sholinganallur,
Chennai- 600 119.

For any feedback or queries please contact the below email id.
Email: bhanuswamibooks@gmail.com
Web: www.bhanuswami.org

First Amazon paperback edition: April 2018
ISBN: 978-19-8071-071-4

Proofread by: H.G. Chaitanya Charana Dasa
Published by: Tattva Cintāmaṇi Publishing

Dedication

This book is dedicated to

His Divine Grace A.C. Bhaktivedānta Svāmī Prabhupāda

Founder-Ācārya of International Society for Krishna Consciousness

who inspired the world to take up the path of bhakti.

Śrīla Prabhupāda on Brahma Sūtras

The Vedānta-sūtra, which consists of aphorisms revealing the method of understanding Vedic knowledge, is the concise form of all Vedic knowledge. It begins with the words *athāto brahma-jijñāsā*: "Now is the time to inquire about the Absolute Truth." The human form of life is especially meant for this purpose, and therefore the Vedānta-sūtra very concisely explains the human mission. This is confirmed by the words of the Vāyu and Skanda Purāṇas, which define a sūtra as follows:

alpākṣaram asandigdhaṁ sāra-vat viśvato-mukham
astobham anavadyaṁ ca sūtraṁ sūtra-vido viduḥ

"A sūtra is a compilation of aphorisms that expresses the essence of all knowledge in a minimum of words. It must be universally applicable and faultless in its linguistic presentation." Anyone familiar with such sūtras must be aware of the Vedānta-sūtra, which is well known among scholars by the following additional names: (1) Brahma-sūtra, (2) Śārīraka, (3) Vyāsa-sūtra, (4) Bādarāyaṇa-sūtra, (5) Uttara-mīmāṁsā and (6) Vedānta-darśana.

There are four chapters (adhyāyas) in the Vedānta-sūtra, and there are four divisions [or sections] (pādas) in each chapter. [In this edition of Vedānta-sūtra, the sutras will have heading of the format '1.2.3', wherein 1 is the chapter number, 2 is the section number, and 3 is the sūtra number. Further each section contains multiple topics (*adhikaraṇas*), each topic spanning one or more sūtras. The topic number is not given in this numbering scheme.]

Therefore the Vedānta-sūtra may be referred to as ṣoḍaśa-pāda, or sixteen divisions of aphorisms. The theme of each and every division is fully described in terms of five different subject matters (*adhikaraṇas*), which are technically called *pratijñā, hetu, udāharaṇa, upanaya* and *nigamana*. Every theme must necessarily be explained with reference to *pratijñā*, or a solemn declaration of the purpose of the treatise. The solemn declaration given in the beginning of the Vedānta-sūtra is *athāto brahma-jijñāsā*, which indicates that this book was written with the solemn declaration to inquire about the Absolute Truth. Similarly, reasons must be expressed (*hetu*), examples must be given in terms of various facts (*udāharaṇa*), the theme must gradually be brought nearer for understanding (*upanaya*), and finally it must be supported by authoritative quotations from the Vedic *śāstras* (*nigamana*).

According to the great dictionary compiler Hemacandra, also known as Koṣakāra, Vedānta refers to the purport of the Upaniṣads and the Brāhmaṇa portion of the Vedas. Professor Apte, in his dictionary, describes the Brāhmaṇa portion of the Vedas as that portion which states the rules for employment of hymns at various sacrifices and gives detailed explanations of their origin, sometimes with lengthy illustrations in the form of legends and stories. It is distinct from the mantra portion of the Vedas. Hemacandra says that the supplement of the Vedas is called the Vedānta-sūtra. Veda means knowledge, and anta means the end. In other words, proper understanding of the ultimate purport of the Vedas is called Vedānta knowledge. Such knowledge, as given in the aphorisms of the Vedānta-sūtra, must be supported by the Upaniṣads.

According to learned scholars, there are three different sources of knowledge, which are called *prasthāna-traya*. According to these scholars, Vedānta is one of such sources, for it presents Vedic knowledge on the basis of logic and sound arguments. In the Bhagavad-gītā (13.5) the Lord says, *brahma-sūtra-padaiś caiva hetumadbhir viniścitaiḥ*: "Understanding of the ultimate goal of life is ascertained in the Brahma-sūtra by legitimate logic and argument concerning cause and effect." Therefore the Vedānta-sūtra is known as *nyāya-prasthāna*, the Upaniṣads are known as *śruti-prasthāna*, and the Gītā, Mahābhārata and Purāṇas are known as *smṛti-prasthāna*. All scientific knowledge of transcendence must be supported by *śruti*, *smṛti* and a sound logical basis.

It is said that both the Vedic knowledge and the supplement of the Vedas called the *Sātvata-pañcarātra* emanated from the breathing of Nārāyaṇa, the Supreme Personality of Godhead. The Vedānta-sūtra aphorisms were compiled by Śrīla Vyāsadeva, a powerful incarnation of Śrī Nārāyaṇa, although it is sometimes said that they were compiled by a great sage named Apāntaratamā. The Pañcarātra and Vedānta-sūtra, however, express the same opinions. Śrī Caitanya Mahāprabhu therefore confirms that there is no difference in opinion between the two, and He declares that because the Vedānta-sūtra was compiled by Śrīla Vyāsadeva, it may be understood to have emanated from the breathing of Śrī Nārāyaṇa. Śrīla Bhaktisiddhānta Sarasvatī Ṭhākura comments that while Vyāsadeva was compiling the Vedānta-sūtra, seven of his great saintly contemporaries were also engaged in similar work. These saints were Ātreya Ṛṣi, Āśmarathya, Auḍulomi, Kārṣṇājini, Kāśakṛtsna, Jaimini and Bādarī. In addition, it is stated that Pārāśarī and Karmandī-bhikṣu also discussed the Vedānta-sūtra aphorisms before Vyāsadeva.

As mentioned above, the Vedānta-sūtra consists of four chapters. The first two chapters discuss the relationship of the living entity with the Supreme Personality of Godhead. This is known as *sambandha-jñāna*, or knowledge of the relationship. The third chapter describes how one can act in his relationship with the Supreme Personality of Godhead. This is called *abhidheya-jñāna*. The relationship of the living entity with the Supreme Lord is described by Śrī Caitanya Mahāprabhu: *jīvera 'svarūpa' haya kṛṣṇera 'nitya-dāsa'*. "The living entity is an eternal servant of Kṛṣṇa, the Supreme God." (CC. Madhya 20.108) Therefore, to act in that relationship one must perform *sādhana-bhakti*, or the prescribed duties of service to the Supreme Personality of Godhead. This is called *abhidheya-jñāna*. The fourth chapter describes the result of such devotional service (*prayojana-jñāna*). This ultimate goal of life is to go back home, back to Godhead. The words *anāvṛttiḥ śabdāt* in the Vedānta-sūtra indicate this ultimate goal.

Śrīla Vyāsadeva, a powerful incarnation of Nārāyaṇa, compiled the Vedānta-sūtra, and in order to protect it from unauthorized commentaries, he personally composed Śrīmad-Bhāgavatam on the instruction of his spiritual master, Nārada Muni, as the original commentary on the Vedānta-sūtra. Besides Śrīmad-Bhāgavatam, there are commentaries on the Vedānta-sūtra composed by all the major Vaiṣṇava ācāryas, and in each of them devotional service to the Lord is described very explicitly. Only those who follow Śaṅkara's commentary have described the Vedānta-sūtra in an impersonal way, without reference to viṣṇu-bhakti, or devotional service to the Lord, Viṣṇu. Generally people very much appreciate this *Śārīraka-bhāṣya*, or impersonal description of the Vedānta-sūtra, but all commentaries that are devoid of devotional service to Lord Viṣṇu must be considered to differ in purport from the original Vedānta-sūtra. In other words, Lord Caitanya definitely confirmed that the commentaries, or *bhāṣyas*, written by the Vaiṣṇava ācāryas on the basis of devotional service to Lord Viṣṇu, and not the *Śārīraka-bhāṣya* of Śaṅkarācārya, give the actual explanation of the Vedānta-sūtra.

Śrī Caitanya-caritāmṛta, Ādi-līlā, 7.106 Purport
His Divine Grace A.C. Bhaktivedanta Swami Prabhupada

Table of Contents

Chapter One

Table of Contents (Chapter 1)

Section One

satyaṁ jñānam anantaṁ brahma śivādi-stutaṁ bhajad-rūpam
govindaṁ tam acintyaṁ netum adoṣaṁ namasyamaḥ
sūtrāṁśubhis tamāṁṣi yudasya vastūni yaḥ parīkṣayte
sa jayati sātyavateyo harir anuvṛtto natapreṣṭhaḥ

I offer respects to the worshipable form of Govinda, who is Brahman, identical with existence, knowledge and bliss, who is praised by Śiva and others, and who is inconceivable, without fault and the cause of all things.

May the Lord who is Vyāsa, the son of Satyavatī, who is dear to the surrendered souls and spreads himself everywhere, and who, destroying darkness by the rays of his sūtras, reveals real knowledge, remain ever glorious.

When the Vedas were destroyed in Dvāpara-yuga by false philosophies,[1] the Supreme Lord, on the request of Brahmā and others of limited knowledge, appearing as Vyāsa, recovered the Vedas and divided them up. He revealed the Brahma-sūtras in four chapters to explain the meaning of the Vedas. This is described in the Skanda Purāṇa.

It so happens that the unintelligent think that karma (prescribed actions)[2] will give the highest benefit to humanity, that Viṣṇu is an aṅga of karma,[3] that the results of karma like Svarga are eternal, that the jīva and prakṛti are independent doers, that the jīva is a fragment (*paricchinna*) of Brahman, limited by time and space, or the jīva is a reflection (*pratibimba*) of Brahman in the intelligence, or the jīva is Brahman in illusion, and that the jīva can end saṁsāra by understanding that he is the Brahman which is consciousness itself.

---

[1] These are the philosophies of Kapila, Patañjali, Kaṇāda, Gautama, Jaimini, Buddha (four types) and Cārvāka.

[2] The word karma in this commentary will usually refer to pious acts prescribed in the scriptures.

[3] The two aṅgas of karma are devatā and materials (dravya). Some people maintain that Viṣṇu is worshipped simply by worshipping devatās and that Viṣṇu is an element assisting in accomplishing sacrifices.

Taking these false arguments, Vyāsa, in the Brahma-sūtras, explains that the supreme Viṣṇu is independent, is the cause of all actions, is omniscient, and is the very form of knowledge and dharmas such as the four human goals.

The sūtras delineate five essential elements: Īśvara, jīva, prakṛti, kāla and karma. Among them the Lord (Īśvara) is the principal conscious entity. The jīva is a subordinate conscious entity. Both the Lord and the jīva have eternal qualities like knowledge and have the sense of "I". They are knowers (arising from the sense of I) of knowledge. This is not contradictory, for one sees that light reveals itself (as well as other objects).[4]

But the Lord is independent. Possessing śakti as His very nature, He supports the universe by entering it and regulating it, and bestows enjoyment and liberation to the jīvas in the material world. Though He is one, He manifests many forms and, though indivisible (with no differentiation), is perceived by the wise as an object having qualities (differentiation). Though invisible, He is revealed by bhakti. Though self-existent pleasure itself, He gives His form of knowledge and happiness to the devotees.

The jīvas however are many, in various conditions. They are in bondage because of being inimical to the Supreme Lord. When they become favorable to the Lord, they directly perceive the Lord's *svarūpa* and other components and destroy the two types of bondage-causing coverings--that which hides the Lord's form and that which hides His qualities.

Prakṛti is a state of equilibrium of the three *guṇas.* It is also called *tamas* and *māyā.* On receiving the glance of the Lord, prakṛti becomes capable of generating the variegated universe.

Kāla or time is the cause of our ability to speak of states like simultaneous, quick and slow, past, present and future. Moving like a wheel, measured in short moments and the lifetime of Brahmā *(parārdha),* time gives rise to creation and destruction of the universe. It is an unconscious substance. These four items are eternal.

nityo nityānāṁ cetanaś cetanānām: the Lord is the chief eternal and the chief conscious entity. (Śvetāśvatara Upaniṣad 6.13) *gaur anādy anantavatī:* prakṛti, resembling a cow, is without beginning and without end. (Cūlika

[4] Similarly the self, knowing itself, reveals knowledge of other things.

Upaniṣad 5) *sad eva saumyedam agra āsīt:* the eternal Lord existed before everything else. (Chāndogya Upaniṣad 6.2.1)

However the *jīva, prakṛti* and *kāla* are subservient to the Lord.

sa viśva-kṛd viśva-vid ātma-yonir
jñaḥ kāla-kāro guṇi sarva-vid yaḥ
pradhāna-ksetrajña-patir guṇeśaḥ
saṁsāra-mokṣa-sthiti-bandha-hetuḥ

He is the creator of the universe, the knower of the universe, his own source, the knower, the controller of time, the possessor of qualities, and the omniscient one. He is the master of prakṛti and the jīvas, the lord of the guṇas, and the cause of bondage, maintenance and liberation from saṁsāra. (*Śvetāśvatara Upaniṣad* 6.16)

Karma[5] is unconscious and also known as *adṛṣṭa.* It is without beginning and subject to destruction (*anādi vināśī*). Because these four (jīva, prakṛti, kāla and karma) are the śaktis of Brahman, there is agreement with the Advaita claim that there is one Brahman-- who possesses various śaktis. These topics will be revealed in their appropriate places in the four chapters, also called *lakṣaṇā.*

These topics are also described in Bhāgavatam, which explains the meaning of the sūtras.

bhakti-yogena manasi samyak praṇihite 'male
apaśyat puruṣaṁ pūrṇaṁ māyāṁ ca tad-apāśrayam

In that mind which was undisturbed because it was pure from the performance of *bhakti*, Vyāsa saw Kṛṣṇa, complete with all his energies and spiritual expansions, and also saw *māyā* who took shelter behind the Lord.

---

[5] Here karma refers to the ability of actions to create reactions in future lives. Baladeva also explains in his commentary on Gītā that karma is like *prag-abhāva* (prior non-existence). Something which has not yet existed has not existed for infinite time in the past. It has *anādi* non-existence. But this state of non-existence comes to an end if and when the object in question makes its appearance. Thus, non-existence is an example of something that has no beginning but has an end. *Karma* is like that: having no beginning, but having an ending.

yayā sammohito jīva ātmānaṁ tri-guṇātmakam
paro 'pi manute 'narthaṁ tat-kṛtaṁ cābhipadyate

Bewildered by that *māyā,* the *jīva*, though separate from the three *guṇas,* considers himself made of the three *guṇas* and takes on material existence created by the *guṇas.*

anarthopaśamaṁ sākṣād bhakti-yogam adhokṣaje
lokasyājānato vidvāṁś cakre sātvata-saṁhitāṁ

Vyāsa saw that *bhakti-yoga* to the Lord effectively destroys the *jīva's saṁsāra*. Learned Vyāsa then wrote the *Bhāgavatam* for ignorant people. (SB 1.7.4-6)

dravyaṁ karma ca kālaś ca svabhāvo jīva eva ca
yad-anugrahataḥ santi na santi yad-upekṣayā

By connection with the Lord, matter, karma, time, *svabhāva*[6] and the totality of *jīvas* can produce effects. Without his presence, they have no power to produce effect. (SB 2.10.12)

It is stated in smṛti that Bhāgavatam acts as the commentary on the sūtras. *artho 'yam brahma-sūtrānām: Śrīmad-Bhāgavatam* is the commentary on *Vedānta-sūtra*. (*Garuḍa Purāṇa)*

In the first chapter of the Brahma-sūtras it is shown that all the Vedas indicate Brahman as the highest object. In the second chapter it is shown that this conclusion is not contrary to other scriptures. In the third chapter the various methods or *sādhanas* to attain Brahman are described. In the fourth chapter the result of *sādhana,* attaining the Brahman, is described.

The qualified person (*adhikārī)* for this work is a person with pure heart, devoid of material desires, who is greedy for the association of spiritual people, who is endowed with great faith and possesses qualities such as peacefulness. The *sambandha* is that the words of this work describe the subject Brahman. The subject or *viṣaya* is the faultless supreme Lord, endowed with eternity, knowledge and bliss, possessing unlimited, inconceivable śaktis, and possessing unlimited, pure qualities. The goal or

---

[6] *Svabhāva* means the ability of action to produce effects, the cause of change in the guṇas and also impressions.

prayojana is to realize the Lord after having destroyed countless faults.[7] All this will become clear later.

There are five parts to each topic or *adhikaraṇa* (within the *pāda* or section of the chapter): *viṣaya* (subject), *saṁśaya* (doubt), *pūrvapakṣa* (objection), *siddhānta* (conclusion), and *saṅgati* (agreement with other scriptures).[8] The subject is a statement of something worthy of discussion. *Saṅgati* means that the various statements found in various scriptures do not contradict the conclusion. On understanding the subject, knowledge should spontaneously arise. [9]

Topic 1 (Sūtra 1)

Brahma-jijñāsādhikaraṇam - Inquiry into Brahman

The work starts with the topic called Inquiry into Brahman. (This is the subject or *viṣaya.)*

yo vai bhūma tat sukhaṁ nānyat sukham asti
bhūmaiva sukhaṁ bhūmā tveva vijijñāsitavyaḥ

That which is great is happiness. There is no other happiness. That great Brahman is happiness. One must know this great Brahman. (Chāndogya Upaniṣad 7.25.1)

ātmā vā are draṣṭavyaḥ śrotavyo mantavyo nididhyāsitavyo maitreyi

One should see this Brahman, hear about it, and think of it. O Maitreyī! One should know this Brahman. (Bṛhad-āraṇyaka Upaniṣad 2.4.5)

nidhidyāsitavyaḥ means "it should be known."

The doubt (*saṁśaya*) is as follows. Is inquiry into Brahman necessary or not for a person who has studied the Vedas and who knows dharma?

(*pūrva-pakṣa*) It is said *apāma somam amṛtā abhūma:* we have attained immortality by drinking the soma-juice. (*Ṛg Veda* 8.18.3) *akṣayyaṁ ha vai*

---

[7] These four – *adhikārī, sambandha, viṣaya* and *prayojana* – are called the four anubandhas.
[8] The viṣaya or subject is often a specific passage from the Upaniṣads. The adhikaraṇa may be only one sutra or may extend over many sutras.
[9] From studying the Brahma Sūtras, one should develop realization of the Lord.

cāturmāsyājinaḥ sukṛtaṁ bhavati: those who follow the vow of *cāturmāsya* attain eternal credit. (*Āpastamba Śrauta Sūtra, Kṛṣṇa Yajur Veda* 8.1.1)

Thus, by following dharma one attains immortality and unending happiness. Inquiry into Brahman is therefore unnecessary.

Hearing this objection the Lord Vyāsa raises this first sūtra at the beginning of the work (*siddhānta*).

Sūtra – 1.1.1

|| athāto brahma-jijñāsā ||

After attaining association with devotees, one begins the inquiry concerning the Lord.

Atha indicates sequence and *ataḥ* indicates cause. The meaning is "Therefore, after this, one should inquire about Brahman." After a person has studied the Vedas according to the rules, has understood the meaning, and has been purified by following his *āśrama* duties and tenets like truthfulness, he attains the association of persons who know the truth. After attaining that association, he then realizes that the karmas performed to fulfill material desires give limited, temporary results. He understands that Brahman is attained through knowledge, that it is eternal, infinite spiritual bliss, that it produces qualities like eternal knowledge in the self and that it causes eternal happiness in the self. With this understanding, he rejects rituals for material results (*kāmya-karma*) and begins to inquire about the topics in the Brahma-sūtras.

(*saṁśaya*) "By study of the Vedas, one can understand all about Brahman, since, by studying, one will understand the meaning. From that, the mind will then reject karma and worship Brahman. What is the necessity of studying the Brahma-sūtras?"

Due to understanding the meaning of the Vedas superficially, one's intelligence can be destroyed by doubt and can take the opposite meaning of its statements. By studying the sūtras, one can understand the conclusions of the Vedas and then can overcome doubt and mistaken meanings. One can thus become fixed in the highest truth. This will certainly happen by studying these sūtras.

The meaning is this. The duties of the *āśramas* become limbs (assistants) of knowledge because they purify the heart. Thus it is said *etaṁ vedānuvacanena brāhmaṇā vividisanti yajñena dānena tapasānaśanena:* the seekers of Brahman try to know him by study of the Vedas (*brahmacārī),* by sacrifices, by acts of charity (*grhastha*), by austerities (*vanaprastha*) and by fasting (*sannyāsī*). (Bṛhad-āraṇyaka Upaniṣad 4.4) Actions such as telling the truth, austerities and *japa* also lead to Brahman. *satyena labhayas tapasā hy eṣa ātmā samyak jñānena brahmacaryeṇa nityam:* one can realize the Lord by truthfulness, austerity, knowledge and celibacy. (Muṇḍaka Upaniṣad 3.1.5)

It is not only the śrutis who say this; even the smṛtis say the same thing.

japyenaiva ca saṁsiddhyad brahmaṇā nātra saṁśayaḥ
kuryād anyan na vā kuryān maitro brāhmaṇa ucyate

Without doubt, a brāhmaṇa will attain perfection by *japa* alone. Whether he performs other duties or not, he, the friend to all beings, is called a brāhmaṇa. Manu-smṛti 2.87

Association with a person who knows the truth is the cause of *jñāna.*[10] For instance Nārada began his inquiry about Brahman by association with Sanat-kumāra. The smṛtis state this:

tad viddhi praṇipātena paripraśnena sevayā
upadekṣyanti te jñānaṁ jñāninas tattva-darśinaḥ

Know the Lord by surrender, questioning and service. The seers of truth, the *jñānīs*, will teach you this knowledge. BG 4.34

Kāmya-karmas (as opposed to karmas of the *āśramas* or *japa*) bear temporary results. *tad yatheha karma-cito lokāḥ kṣiyante evam evāmutra puṇya-cito lokaḥ kṣīyate:* just as places attained in this life as a result of actions in this life perish, places in a future life attained by pious acts of this life are also destroyed. (Chāndogya Upaniṣad 8.1.6) Brahman however is attained only by jñāna.

parīkṣya lokān karma-citān brāhmaṇo
nirvedam ayan nāsty akṛtaḥ kṛtena

---

[10]Jñāna in the commentary does not mean the sādhana to attain impersonal Brahman, but rather bhakti to attain realization of Bhagavān.

tad-vijñānārtham sa gurum evābhigacchet
samit-pāṇiḥ śrotriyaṁ brahma-niṣṭham

After examining all the worlds attained by karmas, the brāhmaṇa should become indifferent. One cannot attain freedom from karma by acts of karma. In order to realize the Brahman, a person, carrying fuel in his hands, must approach a learned teacher fixed in Brahman. (Muṇḍaka Upaniṣad 1.2.12)

This Brahman is eternal, indestructible bliss. *satyaṁ jñānam anantaṁ brahma; Brahman is* eternal, filled with knowledge and infinite. (Taittirīya Upaniṣad 2.1.1) *ānando brahmeti vyajanāt:* he understood that Brahman is bliss. (Taittirīya Upaniṣad 3.2)

Brahman is endowed with qualities like eternal knowledge and other qualities:

na tasya kāryaṁ karaṇaṁ ca vidyate
na tat-samaś cābhyadhikaś ca dṛśyate
parāsya śaktir vividhaiva śrūyate
svā-bhāvikī jñāna-bala-kriyā ca

He has no body and no senses. No one is equal to him or higher. His supreme power is manifold. His actions are naturally revealed with knowledge and strength. (Śvetāśvatara Upaniṣad 6.8)

sarvasya śaraṇam suhṛt

He is the shelter of all and the friend. (Śvetāśvatara Upaniṣad 3.7)

bhāva-grāham anīḍākhyam

Brahman, attained by prema, has no material body. (Śvetāśvatara Upaniṣad 3.17)

The Lord bestows eternal bliss.

taṁ pīṭha-sthaṁ ye tu yajanti dhīrās
teṣāṁ sukhaṁ śāśvataṁ netareṣām

Those wise men who worship Govinda situated in his abode attain eternal bliss and not others. (Gopāla-tāpanī Upaniṣad 1.5)

The inferior nature of *kāmya-karma* will be discussed in the Third Chapter. One who has studied the Vedas with their *aṅgas* and the Upaniṣads, understanding their meaning generally, becomes disgusted with the temporary and begins to study the Brahma-sūtras by distinguishing the eternal from the temporary through association with knowers of truth, in order to realize the particulars of the eternal. This does not happen simply after learning all about karma, since one does not see a person begin inquiry about Brahman without first having spiritual association. And on the other hand, those who do not know about karma but have become purified by pure acts and have associated with spiritual persons begin the inquiry about Brahman.

Nor should one say that after practicing the four *sādhanas* starting with distinguishing the eternal from the temporary[11] that inquiry about Brahman begins. These *sādhanas* are difficult to attain before attaining association and are easy to attain after receiving teachings from the association of devotees.

Those who attain knowledge are of three types, according to the nature of their teacher. The *sa-niṣṭhā d*evotee performs bhakti along with performing karmas (duties of dharma) with faith in them. The *pariniṣṭhita* devotee performs bhakti along with the same karmas to teach others. The *nirapekṣa* devotee performs only meditation on the Lord (without performance of duties). All of these attain the supreme Brahman by *brahma-vidyā* (knowledge of Brahman), according to their *bhāva.* This will be explained later.

"But *atha* merely indicates auspiciousness. It is said in the smṛti:

omkāra cātha-cābdaś ca dvāv etau brahmaṇaḥ purā
kaṇṭhaṁ bhittvā vinirjātau tena māṅgalikāv ubhau

The words *oṁ* and *atha* came from the throat of Brahmā in ancient times. They thus indicate auspiciousness.

The wise employ these words at the beginning of scriptures to destroy all obstacles."

This is not so. One should not worry about obstacles in relation to the Lord. Vyāsa is the Lord, for it is said *kṛṣṇa-dvaipāyana-vyāsaṁ viddhi nārāyaṇaṁ prabhum:* know that Vyāsadeva is the Lord Nārāyaṇa. (Viṣṇu Purāṇa 3.4.5)

---

[11] The other three are detachment from enjoyment in this world and the next, attainment of six qualities (mind control, sense control, withdrawing from sense objects, tolerance, faith, and tranquility) and desire for liberation.

However, because *oṁ* is auspicious, it may also function in this way, denoting auspiciousness like the sound of conch (besides indicating the necessity of good association). This is how it is accepted in the ordinary world.

Therefore when a person has attained association with devotees (*atha*)-- after that-- he will inquire about Brahman.

Topic 2 (Sūtra 2)

Janmādyādhikaranam - Definition of Brahman

Since the word *bhūma* indicates the jīva, the word Brahma in the previous verse[12] should refer to the jīva also since the jīva is the subject in the discussion of husband, wife and others in the Chāndogya Upaniṣad (8.23.6) and the dictionary meaning of *brahman* is "something great, the jīva, Brahmā and sacred words." This misconception is now refuted.

It said in the Taittirīya Upaniṣad 3.1.1:

bhṛgur vai varuṇir varuṇaṁ pitaram upasasāra adhīhi bho bhagavo brahma...
yato vā imāni bhūtāni jāyante yena jātāni jīvanti yat prayānty abhisaṁviśanti tad brahma tad vijijñāsasva

Bhṛgu asked his father Varuṇa, "O great one! Please teach me about Brahman." Varuṇa said, "One should know Brahman, from which all entities arise, by which they live and into which they enter at death."

The doubt is this: is the Brahman that is the subject of inquiry, the jīva or the Lord?

(Pūrva-pakṣa)

vijñānaṁ brahma ced veda tasmāc cen na pramadyati
śarīre pāpmāno hitvā sarvaṇ kāmān samāśnute

If a person knows *vijñāna* to be Brahman, and if he does deviate from that understanding, giving up all sin in the body, he enjoys all desirable objects. (Taittirīya Upaniṣad 2.5) This must refer to the jīva since *vijñāna* refers to the jīva, and jīva is the subject of meditation, and since the jīva can become the cause of creation and destruction by some good karmas according to

---

[12] *bhūmā tveva vijijñāsitavyaḥ:* one should inquire about bhumā.

scripture (which was mentioned in the previous quotation from Taittirīya Upaniṣad: yato va imāni bhūtāni).

(Siddhānta) In reply, the characteristic of Brahman which is the subject of inquiry is stated.

Sūtra – 1.1.2

|| janmādy asya yataḥ ||

From that Brahman arise creation, maintenance and destruction of this universe.

The compound *janmādi* is a *bahuvrihī* called *tad-guṇa-samvijñāna* (implied qualities are perceived along with the object itself.) Thus it means creation, maintenance and destruction. *Asya* refers to the universe consisting of varieties inconceivable to the jīva, made of the fourteen worlds and to the doers and enjoyers from Brahmā down to the immovable beings, undergoing the results of various karmas. The meaning is one should inquire about Brahman, the supreme, endowed with inconceivable śaktis, who is both the creator (efficient cause) and the material cause, from whom there arises (*yataḥ*) creation, maintenance and destruction (*janmādi*) of the worlds and beings from Brahma to immovable plants (*asya*).

The words *bhūmā* and *ātmā* refer primarily or directly (*mukhya-vṛtti*) to the Lord since etymologically they mean "all-pervading." This is also the conclusion of sūtras 1.3.7 and 1.4.19.

The word Brahman applies to the Lord only, because etymologically it means "someone possessing unlimitedly great qualities." The Vedas say *atha kasmād ucyate brahmeti bṛhanto hy asmin guṇā*: why is he called Brahman? In him are infinitely expanding qualities (bṛh=to make big).[13] Therefore the word Brahman primarily signifies the Lord. The word is also employed to refer to others, since they possess the qualities of the Lord in part, just as the word "king" sometimes is used for the kingly person. For their highest benefit, the jīvas inundated by the three miseries should inquire about the supreme Lord, who is endowed with an ocean of compassion for those who surrender to him. The supreme Lord alone is the object of inquiry.

---

[13] This is śruti quoted by Madhva in his commentary.

One cannot say that the qualities are imposed on the Lord, since the inquiry is concerning Brahman, who really has these qualities.

Inquiry (*jijñāsa*) means the desire to know. Knowledge is of two types: *parokṣa* and *aparokṣa. vijñāya prajñāṁ kurvīta*: knowing him, realize him. (Bṛhad-āraṇyaka Upaniṣad 4.4.42) The latter, *aparokṣa*, is to achieve him. The first, *parokṣa,* is the means. This will be made clear later. It is also said *vijñānaṁ brahma*: know the jīva as Brahman. This means that knowing the *svarūpa* of the jīva is helpful to understanding the Lord. One should not accept that the jīva and Brahman are the same, since the scriptures insist on the different of the jīva and the Lord as explained in sūtras 1.1.16, 1.1.17, 1.3.15, 1.3.21, and 1.3.41. It is concluded there that even in the state of liberation the two remain separate.

Topic 3 (Sūtra 3)

Śāstra-yonitvādhikaraṇam - Scripture is the basis of knowledge

upakramopasaṁhārāv abhyāso'pūrvatā phalam |
artha-vādopapattī ca liṅgaṁ tātparya-nirṇaye ||

In understanding the meaning of a particular passage, the means are *upakrama* (beginning)*, upasaṁhāra* (conclusion)*, abhyāsa* (repetition)*, apūravatā* (uniqueness)*, phalam* (fruit)*, artha-vāda* (praise) and *upapatti* (proof). Bṛhat-saṁhitā (quoted by Madhva in his BS commentary 1.1.47)

Using these six methods, the conclusion is that the jīva and the Lord are different.

dvā suparṇā sayujā sakhāyā
samānaṁ vṛkṣaṁ pariśaṣvajāte
tayor anyaḥ pippalaṁ svādv atty
anaśnann anyo 'bhicakāśīti
samāne vṛkṣe puruṣo nimagno
'nīśāya śocati muhyamānaḥ
juṣṭaṁ yadā paśyati anyam īśam
asya mahimānam iti vīta-śokaḥ

For instance in Śvetāśvatara Upaniṣad *dvā suparṇā* (two birds) is the *upakrama* (beginning), *anyam īśam* (the Lord is different) is the *upasaṁhāra* (conclusion), *tayor anyo' naśnann anyo 'nyam īśam* (the other person does not eat) is the *abhyāsa* (repetition). The *apūrvata* (uniqueness) is that, without scripture, the difference between the Lord and jīva could not be known. *Vīta-śoka* is the *phalam* (result). *Asya mahimānam* (he sees the Lord's greatness) is the *artha-vāda* (praise). *Anyo 'naśnan* (the other does not eat) is the *upapatti* (proof). One can find other examples elsewhere.

(Pūrva-pakṣa) "Because the aim of scripture is to teach something unknown and yielding great results, the meaning of this passage is non-difference of jīva and the Lord. Difference is not the meaning since that fact is already known and useless. Non-difference is the meaning of this statement."

This is not so. The great result (*phalam*) of understanding difference is stated in Śvetāśvatara Upaniṣad 1.12:

pṛthag-ātmānaṁ preritaṁ ca matvā
juṣṭas tatas tenāmṛtatvam eti

Understanding his difference from the Lord, favored by the Lord, the jīva then attains immortality.

Understanding that the Lord and the jīva are different because of different qualities is a unique result because people in general do not understand this.

Advaita (non-difference of the Lord and the jīva) however does not give any great results. Advaita cannot be known since it is not accepted by common sense, because it is non-existent, like the horns of a rabbit. Those texts which speak of the non-difference of everything from the Lord are spoken by Vyāsa to indicate that everything is pervaded by the Lord and is under his control. That is the meaning of sūtra 1.1.30

Now, the author wishes to say that the Supreme Lord, being the cause of the universe, cannot be known by argumentation but only by the Vedānta.

sac-cid-ānanda-rūpāya kṛṣṇāyākliṣṭa-kāriṇenamo vedānta-vedyāya gurave buddhi-sākṣiṇe

I offer respects to Kṛṣṇa, the form of eternity, knowledge and bliss, who performs actions without fatigue, who is to be known by the conclusion of the Vedas, who is the guru of all knowledge, and who reveals himself by guiding the intelligence of the jīva. Gopāla-tāpanī Upaniṣad 1.1

taṁ tv aupaniṣadaṁ puruṣaṁ pṛcchāmi

I inquire about the Lord who is known in the Upaniṣads. *Bṛhad-āraṇyaka Upaniṣad* 3.9.26

The doubt is this. Can the worshipable Lord be known by inference or by the Upaniṣads?

(Pūrva-pakṣa) Since Gautama and others say that the Lord can be understood by reason (*mantavyaḥ*) according to Bṛhad-āraṇyaka Upaniṣad 4.5, on this śruti evidence one can conclude that he can be known by reasoning.

Sūtra – 1.1.3

| | śāstra-yonitvāt | |

The Lord cannot be known by reasoning because the source of understanding the Lord is the Upaniṣads.

The word "not" should be added at the start of the sutra. No, those desiring liberation cannot understand Brahman by inference. Why? Because of the principle that the cause of understanding the Lord (*yonitvāt*) is the Upaniṣads (*śāstra*)-- because it is said that the Lord is to be understood through scriptures. Otherwise, if the Lord could be understood by inference, it would contradict words like *aupaniṣadam* (the Lord who is understood through the Upaniṣads). Logic which follows after the scriptures can be used to understand the Lord. That is the sense of the word *mantavyaḥ* (to be reasoned). Śruti[14] says:

pūrvāpara-virodhena ko 'rtho 'trābhimato bhavet
ity ādyam uhanaṁ tarkaḥ śuṣka-tarkaṁ vivarjayet

Reasoning which determines the meaning by resolving all contradictions with previous and later statements is correct argumentation. Argumentation should reject dry logic. Kūrma Purāṇa

The futility of dry reasoning of Gautama (*nyāya*) and others is stated in *tarkāpratiṣṭhānāt.* (Brahma-sūtra 2.1.11) Therefore, knowing the Lord from the Vedānta, one should meditate upon him. This is an authoritative statement without fault. *Śrutes tu śabda-mūlatvāt*: there is no defect because scripture declares it and scripture is the root of all knowledge. (BS 2.1.17)

---

[14] Baladeva says this is śruti but Vasu attributes it to Kūrma Purāṇa and Mahābhārata.

It will be known from scripture that the Lord has his own form, that he is the cause of the experience of all knowledge, that he is the basis of his own qualities, that he is the cause of the universe and that he is without change. After learning this from the scriptures, one can worship him properly.

(objection) In that case, the statements of the Vedānta would be impractical. They would be devoid of use, since they reveal what is already known to exist. They are like the statement, "The earth has seven continents." Statements which reveal actions to be performed or avoided are practical since they are useful: for example, "The man desiring money should go to the king" or "A person with weak digestion should not drink water." Or, in the Vedas it is said *svarga-kāmo yajeta*: a person with desire for Svarga should perform sacrifice. It is said *surāṁ na pibet:* one should not drink liquor. Statements are not made without indicating a goal. They are either positive statements to attain a desired goal or negative statements to avoid a certain result.

Brahman however is an already existing object. Statements like *satyaṁ jñānam anantam* which describe Brahman are not practical for application since they are devoid of statements of action. If someone wants to use these statements about Brahman, one could make them useful by making them statements of a goal. One should utter those statements in this manner. By describing a sacrifice, *devatā* or the performer of sacrifice, statements can become useful in performing sacrifice. Jaimini explains this.

āmnāyasya kriyārthatvād anārthākhyam atad-arthanam tasmād anityatvam ucyate.

Since scriptural statements which enjoin action are useful, statements which do not enjoin action are useless. *Pūrva-mīmāṁsa* 1.2.1

tad-bhūtānāṁ kriyārthena samāmnāyo 'rthasya tan-nimittatvāt

A group of words is used with a verb. The meaning arises from the combination of these words.

This is not so. It is a mistaken belief. Though not containing orders to perform or refrain from certain actions, by teaching the existence of Brahman as the highest human goal, there is utility in statements. It is like a statement which reveals existence of wealth. From hearing an authoritative statement that you have wealth in your house, finding that treasure becomes the goal of your live. Similarly by statements declaring the existence of Brahman who is one's source, Brahman who has a form of knowledge and bliss, who is the excellent friend of all, and who gives himself to his devotees, one gains conviction in the existence of Brahman. Thus it is not unlike the statements enjoining action. It may be seen that such statements yield results in the form of giving happiness and removing fear in the manner of statements like "A son has been born to you" and "That is not a snake but a rope."

The usefulness of the statements is clearly stated in the texts themselves.

satyaṁ jñānam anantaṁ brahma yo veda nihitaṁ guhāyāṁ so 'śnute sarvān kāmān

One who knows that Brahman residing within is eternal existence and eternal knowledge attains all desires. Taittirīya Upaniṣad 2.1

One should not claim that by such explanations of results, the Vedānta texts teach action, since the topic of Vedānta is different, since it condemns seeking results of actions (*karma kāṇḍa)* and since by such claims one negates what is actually stated in the scripture and adds something that is not stated.[15] Nor can one make into something else the scripture dedicated to Brahman, who is source of all universes, who has an eternal spiritual body, who is an ocean of auspicious qualities, who is the abode of Lakṣmī, since the work culminates in that object with authoritative proof.

Nor should one even claim that Jaimini maintained the path of karma alone, as quoted above, since he was also fixed in Brahman. Giving up the literal meanings of some statements (which do not teach action) in the sections dealing with karma, he merely established that section in terms of karma. Therefore it is clear that the texts of Vedānta are concerned with Brahman alone and not karma.

Topic 4 (Sūtra 4)

Samanvyādhikaraṇam - Reconciliation of texts

In order to strengthen the previous statement it is now said that the Brahman or the Lord is to be known by all the Vedas. Gopāla-tāpanī 2.21 says *yo'sau*

[15] The phrase *śruta-hāny-aśruta-kalpana* used by Baladeva to state this point is used in Śārīka-bhāṣya.

sarvair vedair gīyate: he is praised in all the Vedas. *Sarve vedā yat padam āmananti*: all the Vedas honor the Lord's feet. (*Kaṭha Upaniṣad* 1.2.15)

The doubt is this. Is it correct to say that Viṣṇu is to be known by the Vedas or not?

(*Purva-pakṣa*) It seems that he is not to be known since it is generally seen that karma is prescribed. It is observed that the Vedas proclaim that karmas with their *aṅgas* -- such as *kāriri* sacrifice for rain, the *putra-kāmyeṣṭi* sacrifice for obtaining sons or *jyotiṣṭoma* sacrifice for going to Svarga -- are prescribed. By such statements, the topic of karma is seen to be the prominent subject. Therefore it is not possible to conclude that Viṣṇu is the conclusion.

Sūtra – 1.1.4

|| tat tu samanvayāt ||

But Viṣṇu is the conclusion because of the agreement of other scriptures as well.

The word *tu* (but) is used to refute the objection about karma. It has been said that Viṣṇu is to be known by all the Vedas. Why? Because of correlation, logical connection (*samanvayāt*), bringing about a conclusion. *Samanvaya* means to consider the meaning very carefully. Viṣṇu is to be known in the Vedas, because that is the conclusion of the scriptures, by careful consideration, after using the six elements (*upakrama* etc.) previously mentioned. Otherwise how are scriptural statements such as "The Lord is praised in all the Vedas" in *Gopāla-tāpanī* possible? The lotus-eyed Lord also says:

vedaiś ca sarvair aham eva vedyo
vedānta-kṛd veda-vid eva cāham

I alone am to be known in all the Vedas. I have made the Vedānta and am the knower of the Vedas. BG 15.15

kiṁ vidhatte kim ācaṣṭe kim anūdya vikalpayet
ity asyā kṛdayaṁ loke nānyo mad veda kaścana
māṁ vidhatte 'bhidhatte māṁ vikalpyāpohyate hy aham

What do the Vedas instruct as action? What is the final meaning of the Vedas? What alternatives do the Vedas raise? No one except me or my dear devotee knows the intended meaning of the Vedas. The Vedas indicate *bhakti* as the action and indicate me as the meaning. SB 11.21.42-43

The following should be said. The Vedas indicate Brahman both indirectly and directly.

Directly, the *jñāna-kāṇḍa* delineates the form and qualities of the Lord. Indirectly *karma-kāṇḍa* delineates the Lord by recommending pious acts which are a limb of *jñāna* (which will lead to *jñāna*). It is also said:

tam tv aupaniṣadaṁ puruṣam pṛcchāmi

I ask about the Lord who is described in the Upaniṣads. *Bṛhad-āraṇyaka Upaniṣad* 9.21

tam etam vedānuvacanena brāhmaṇa vividiśanti

The brāhmaṇas desire to know the Lord by reciting the Vedas. *Bṛhad-āraṇyaka Upaniṣad* 4.4.22

Prescriptions for actions to attain rain, sons or Svarga are described in the Vedas only to produce a taste in men for Brahman. By seeing results like rain produced by sacrifice, they develop taste for the scriptures. From that taste, they begin to consider the meaning of the texts about Brahman and learn to discriminate between the eternal and the transitory. They develop thirst for Brahman and disgust with the material world. Thus all the scriptures are dedicated to Brahman.

One will not develop desirelessness when performing sacrifices if one desires only results such as rain. But when the same acts are performed with the desire to produce knowledge, the intelligence becomes purified. Worship of *devatās* (without desire), becoming a part of the cultivation of Brahman, is then worship of Brahman. The result of that worship is purity of the heart. That is the sense of the above text *tam etam vedānuvacanena brāhmaṇa vividiśanti:* the brāhmaṇas desire to know the Lord by reciting the Vedas.

Topic 5 (Sūtras 5 – 11)

Īkṣater adhikaranām - What is seen in scriptures

The idea that Brahman cannot be described is now rejected in order to show the consistency of texts previously cited and those to be cited later. It is said *yato vāco nivartate aprāpya manasā saha:* words cannot describe him and the mind cannot attain him. *(Taittirīya Upaniṣad* 2.4.1) It is also said:

yad vacānabhyuditaṁ yena vāg abhyudyate tad eva brahma tad viddhi nedaṁ yad idam upāsate

Know this Brahman who is not described by words but by whom words manifest. Brahman is not that which people worship.[16] *Kena Upaniṣad* 1.5

The doubt is this: can Brahman be expressed by words or not?

(*Pūrvapakṣa*) It cannot be expressed by words because this is stated in the śrutis as quoted above. If Brahman were expressible by words, then its self-revealing nature would be lost (since it would be revealed by words, not by itself). Smṛti confirms this.

yato 'prāpya nyavartanta vacaś ca manasā saha
ahaṁ cānya ime devās tasmai bhagavate namaḥ

I offer respects to that Supreme Lord whom words, along with mind, the *devatās* such as Bṛhaspati, Rudra, and others, could not understand and gave up trying to understand. SB 3.6.40

This proposition is now refuted.

Sūtra – 1.1.5

|| īkṣater nāśabdam ||

Brahman is not inexpressible because scriptural statements to the contrary are seen in the Upaniṣads.

The word *aśabdam* means that which cannot be expressed by words. Brahman is not of that nature. Rather it is expressible by words. Why? Because that is seen (*īkṣateḥ*) in the Upaniṣads. It is said *tat tv aupaniṣadaṁ puruṣaṁ pṛcchāmi*: I ask about the Lord who is described in the Upaniṣads. (Bṛhad-āraṇyaka Upaniṣad) The Lord in question is seen to be described in the Upaniṣads. The form *īkṣateḥ* from *īkṣati* (instead of *īkṣa*), with a passive meaning (being seen) is poetic license. The same fact is expressed by *sarve vedā yat-padam āmananti:* all the Vedas describe the Lord's feet. (Kaṭha Upaniṣad 2.15) The Lord is called *aśabdam* or inexpressible by words because

[16] Brahman is to be conceived by a material mind.

he cannot be *completely* described by words, just as Meru is called invisible because it cannot be completely seen. If this explanation is not accepted, statements like *yad vacānabhyuditaṁ ... tad eva brahma tad viddhi:* "know Brahman to be that which cannot be expressed by words" would be meaningless (for Brahman could not be known at all if not describable a little by words). The Lord is known by the Vedas, but the Vedas are his very self. Thus, this does not contradict the self-revealing nature of the Lord. That the Vedas are his self will be explained later. The conclusion is that Brahman is expressible by words.

Let that be. But the Brahman describable by words that you mention is the *saguṇa* Brahman, Brahman covered by material *guṇas* or material *śakti.* The Vedas conclude that Brahman is pure and complete, and can be expressed only indirectly.

Sūtra – 1.1.6

|| gauṇaś cen nātma-śabdāt ||

If you argue that Brahman described by words is Brahman covered by material guṇas, the answer is no, because the text mentions the word *ātmā* in relation to Brahman.

That Brahman which is describable is not Brahman covered by *sattva-guṇa (gauṇaḥ).* Why? Because of the word *ātmā* seen in the following texts. *ātmaivedam agra āsīt puruṣa-vidhaḥ:* the Lord, *ātmā,* a type of person, existed before creation. (*Vājasaneya-saṁhitā*) *ātmā vā idam eka evāgra āsīt nānyat kiñcanam iṣāt sa īkṣata lokān nu sṛja:* before the material world was manifest, the Supreme Lord, *ātmā,* alone existed; nothing else existed; he then thought,"Let me create the material planets." (*Aitareya Āraṇyaka)* Before the creation, the Lord is described by the word *ātmā* (non-material, not belonging to the material *guṇas*). It was previously explained that the word *ātmā* primarily applies to the perfect Brahman.

Smṛtis say:

vadanti tat tattva-vidas tattvaṁ yaj jñānam advayam
brahmeti pāramātmeti bhagavān iti śabdyate

The knowers of truth call this truth *advayam-jñānam*, the supreme conscious being, who is called Brahman by the *jñānīs*, Paramātmā by the *yogīs* and Bhagavān by the devotees. SB 1.2.11

śuddhe mahā-vibhūtākhye pare brahmaṇi śabdyate
maitreya bhagavac-chabdaḥ sarva-kāraṇa-kāraṇe

O Maitreya, the word Bhagavān means the pure, most powerful Supreme Brahman, the cause of all causes. *Viṣṇu Purāṇa*

Thus the smṛtis also declare that this pure Brahman can be described by words. That which cannot be described by words could not be discussed in the scriptures.

Sūtra – 1.1.7

|| tan-niṣṭhasya mokṣopadeśāt ||

The Lord is not a manifestation of *sattva-guṇa* because the scriptures teach that the person who worships the Lord attains liberation from the *guṇas*.

The word *na* (not) should be added to this and the three sūtras following.

asad vā idam agra āsīt tato vai sad ajāyata tad ātmānaṁ svayam akuruta. . . yadā hy evaiṣa etasminn adṛśye anātmye anirukte 'nilayane abhayaṁ pratiṣṭhaṁ vindate 'tha so 'bhayaṁ gato bhavati yadā hy evaiṣa etasminn ud aram antaram kurute atha tasya bhayaṁ bhavati

The world existed previously in a subtle form. From that, the visible world became manifest. The Lord produced himself. .... When the jīva becomes established in this Lord who is invisible, without material body, indescribable, and independent, heī becomes fearless. When the jīva deviates a little from Brahman, he becomes fearful. Taittirīya Upaniṣad 2.7

Because it is said that a person fixed in the supreme Brahman, who is beyond matter, who is described in the Vedas, and who is the creator of the universe, attains liberation, Brahman cannot be subject to the guṇas. If Brahman were covered by the guṇas, the text would not say that a person devoted to Brahman could get liberation.

The supreme *ātmā* is without guṇas and by worshipping him one attains liberation.

harir hi nirguṇaḥ sākṣāt puruśaḥ prakṛteḥ paraḥ
sa sarva-dṛg upadraṣṭā taṁ bhajan nirguṇo bhavet

The Lord, however, has no connection with the material modes. He is the Supreme Lord, the all-seeing eternal witness, who is transcendental to material nature. One who worships him becomes similarly free from the material modes. SB 10.88.5

Sūtra – 1.1.8

|| heyatva-vacanāc ca ||

The Lord does not have material qualities because statements to that effect would make the Lord an inferior object.

If the creator of the universe was characterized by material *guṇas* (to give him qualities), the scriptures would also mention, in teaching sādhana, that this Lord (the object of their worship) is inferior, like the men and women of this world. But the scriptures do not say this. Rather, he is glorified as worthy of worship by persons desiring liberation, so that they can rid themselves of material *guṇas*. The scriptures describe the Lord to be different from entities covered by the *guṇas. anyā vāco vimuñcātha:* give up speaking of everything except Brahman. (*Muṇḍaka Upaniṣad 2.2.5*) The Lord, though the creator of the universe, maintains his purity. This quality of the Lord – like his truthfulness and other qualities – is also the subject of meditation for those desiring liberation. Therefore the Lord is described as being devoid of the material *guṇas* (but endowed with spiritual qualities.)

Sūtra – 1.1.9

|| svāpyayāt ||

The Lord is not covered with material qualities because he merges into himself, not into something else.

It is said in the Vājasaneya portion of the Yajur Veda:

oṁ pūrṇam adaḥ pūrṇam idaṁ pūrṇāt pūrṇam udacyate
pūrṇasya pūrṇam ādāya pūrṇam evāvaśiṣyate

The unmanifest Brahman is perfect. The manifested Brahman is perfect. From the unmanifest Brahman appears the manifest Brahman as various *avatāras.*

When the manifested forms emerge from the unmanifest Brahman, the unmanifest Brahman remains. *Vājasaneya Yajur Veda*

Since the complete Lord merges into himself (*svāpyāt),* who is the complete Lord, his quality of being complete is not *aśabda,* inexpressible. If the Lord were made of material *guṇas* (and therefore inferior), then the sūtra should state that the Lord merges into something else (without material qualities), not himself. The inferior Lord with material qualities would also not be described as complete (*pūṛṇa*) as mentioned in the *Yajur Veda* verse.

The meaning of the above verse is as follows. The root form (*adaḥ*) is complete. The manifested form (*idam*) is complete. Both are complete or perfect. From the root form (*pūrṇāt*) the manifested form (*pūrṇam)* appears (*udacyate)* for activities like *rāsa-līlā.* Uniting *(ādāya)* the manifested form into the complete (root) form, the root form remains elsewhere, without merging.

The smṛti also describes the Lord who is devoid of material qualities.

sa devo bahudhā bhūtvā nirguṇah puruṣottamaḥ
ekī-bhūya punaḥ śete nirdoṣo harir ādi-kṛt

The Lord, without material qualities, the supreme person, becomes many, and again, the creator, without fault, becoming one, takes rest. *Padma Purāṇa*

(Pūrvapakṣa) "But Brahman has two forms, *saguṇa* and *nirguṇa.* The *saguṇa* form is Brahman covered by *sattva-guṇa.* This form is omniscient, endowed with all powers and creates the universe. The *nirguṇa* Brahman is existence alone, perfect and pure. The *saguṇa* Brahman is how Brahman is expressed through words of the Vedas. The *nirguṇa* Brahman is the final essence realized through the Vedas."

This idea is refuted in the following sūtra (siddhānta).

Sūtra – 1.1.10

|| gati-sāmānyāt ||

The Lord is not covered by the *guṇas* because all the scriptures describe the Lord as having qualities beyond the material *guṇas.*

Gati means conception. The Lord is not covered by the guṇas because there is conformity (*sāmānyāt*) in Vedic statements concerning conceptions (*gati*) of the Lord--that he is knowledge, omniscient, endowed with all powers, perfect, pure, the supreme *ātmā*, the cause of the universe, worthy of worship and the giver of liberation. The Lord is not covered by material *guṇas* because all the Vedas define *one* Brahman in this way. Brahman does not have two forms, *saguṇa* and *nirguṇa.* Smṛti also says *mattaḥ parataraṁ nānyat kiñcid asti dhanañjaya:* there is nothing superior to me, O Arjuna! (BG 7.7)

The Vedas clearly describe the Lord as *nirguṇa.*

Sūtra – 1.1.11

|| śrutatvāc ca ||

The Lord has no material *guṇas* (but has spiritual qualities) because that is the statement of the scriptures.

In the Black Yajur Veda it is said:

eko devaḥ sarva-bhūteṣu gūḍhaḥ
sarva-vyāpī sarva-bhūtāntarātmā
karmādhyakṣaḥ sarva-bhūtādhivāsaḥ
sākṣī cetā kevalo nirguṇaś ca

The Lord alone has entered all beings. He is all-pervading. He is the *antaryāmī* of all beings. He is the controller of karma. He is the basis of all beings. He is the witness and the giver of consciousness. He is the possessor of *śakti.* He is beyond the *guṇas. Śvetāśvatara Upaniṣad* 6.11

The *nirguṇa* Lord is specifically described in the above verse. He is thus without material qualities but capable of being described (having spiritual qualities). The claim that, "The conception of the *nirguṇa* Brahman can be indicated only indirectly (*lakṣaṇā*) and not directly with words, since Brahman is supposedly devoid of signification by those terms" is false, for *lakṣaṇā* cannot be applied to something that words cannot describe. And furthermore, the Lord without material qualities, can still be the cause of creation just as someone, though invisible, can still create things.

"To say the Lord is without *guṇas* but is endowed with qualities is a contradiction." That is not so. That misconception arises only from inability to understand the real meaning. Negative words like *nirguṇa* indicate that the Lord has no *material* qualities. Words like "omniscient" affirm his positive qualities. This means he is devoid of qualities like *sattva* and endowed with qualities related to his *svarūpa.* There is no doubt about this. The smṛtis describe this.

sattvādayo na santīśe yatra ca prākṛtā guṇāḥ |
sa śuddhaḥ sarva-śuddhebhyaḥ pumān ādyaḥ prasīdatu ||

The material qualities such as *sattva* do not exist in the Lord. May the preeminent Lord who is purer than all pure beings be pleased with me! *Viṣṇu Purāṇa* 1.9.43

samasta-kalyāṇa-guṇātmako 'sau

The Lord is full of unlimited, auspicious qualities. Viṣṇu Purāṇa

Therefore the Lord who is perfect and pure is describable by the Vedas. When the scriptures say the Lord has no name, such statements mean that he is beyond *complete* description. He also cannot be completely described because the Lord is supremely unique. And he cannot be completely described because he is infinite. A person who insists on the literal meaning of the words *nirguṇa* etc. should be asked, "Can one understand Brahman by those words or not?" If he says "Brahman can be understood by words like *nirguṇa*," then Brahman can be described. If he says "Brahman cannot be understood by words like *nirguṇa*" then the descriptions of Brahman in scripture would amount to being useless.

Topic 6 (Sūtras 12 – 19)

Ānandamayādhikaraṇam - The Lord is composed of bliss

Let us have faith in the powerful, pure Lord, full of bliss and knowledge, in reference to whom words like "endowed with bliss" become truly significant.

Brahman was established to be expressible through words, so that Brahman could be shown as the conclusion of the Vedas (expressed in words). Now that fact is demonstrated in the rest of the first chapter (in all its four pādas). In the first section (*pāda*), words generally thought of as indicating other objects are shown to indicate Brahman.

(viṣaya, subject) In the section beginning *brahma-vid āpnoti param* and *sa vā eṣa puruso 'nna-rasamayaḥ*, there are sequential descriptions of *annamaya, prāṇamaya, manomaya,* and *vijñānamaya* stages of existence. Then this passage occurs:

tasmād vā etasmād vijñānamayād anyo 'ntarātmānandamayas tenaiṣa pūrṇaḥ. sa vā eṣa puruṣa-vidha eva tasya puruṣa-vidhatām anvayaṁ puruṣa-vidhaḥ. tasya priyam eva śiraḥ. modo dakṣiṇaḥ pakṣaḥ. pramoda uttaraḥ pakṣaḥ. ānanda ātmā. brahma-pucchaṁ pratiṣṭhā

Higher than the *vijñānamaya* puruṣa is the *ānandamaya* puruṣa. This puruṣa is filled with bliss. The *ānandamaya* existence is a person. Like the former, this has the shape of a human. His head is pleasure (*priya*), his right side is joy (*moda*), his left side is delight (*pramoda*), and his ātmā is bliss (*ānanda*). Brahman is situated as the basis. Taittirīya Upaniṣad 2.5.

(doubt) Is the *ānanda-maya puruṣa* a jīva or the Supreme Lord?

(Pūrva-pakṣa) It refers to the jīva, because it is described as an embodied self (*śarīra ātmā*). This puruṣa is related to a material body.

Sūtra – 1.1.12

|| ānanda-mayo'bhyāsāt ||

Ānandamaya purusa is the Lord, because of repetition (at the beginning and the end).

The ānanda-maya puruṣa is the supreme Brahman. Why? Because of repetition (*abhyāsāt*). After the section previously quoted the following is found.

asann eva sambhavati asad brahmeti veda cet asti brahmeti ced veda santam enaṁ tato viduḥ

If one knows that Brahman to be non-existent, he becomes not-existent. If one knows the Brahman to be existent, that person we know to exist. (Taittirīya Upaniṣad 6.1)

The word Brahman is repeated. Because of that repetition (*abhyāsāt*) the *ānanda-maya puruṣa* is Brahman, the Lord, not the jīva. *Abhyāsa* means to repeat, without modification. This repetition of the word is found in that concluding verse. It does not refer to *brahma* in the phrase *brahma puccha* in the section quoted above.

There are four verses mentioning the *annamaya, prāṇamaya, manomaya, vijñanamaya puruṣas (jīva).* After that there is one verse concerning the *ānandamaya purusa,* who is superior to those. Ātmā is the support of the *annamaya puruṣa.* Earth is the support for the *prāṇamaya puruṣa,* Atharvaṅgiras is the support for the *manomaya purusa.* Intellect (*mahas*) is the support for the *vijñānamaya purusa.* Brahman is the support for the *ānandamaya purusa,* which occurs last. (There is no repetition of the word *brahman* in this instance. Brahman is mentioned only as the support of the *ānandamaya purusa.*)

Each passage is followed by a verse referring to the whole of that purusa. Thus, the whole of the *ānandamaya purusa* is the Brahman (and not just the support). This description will be further discussed in 3.3.13.

"Since the *ānandamaya puruṣa* is described in a series of puruṣas, such as the *annamaya puruṣa,* referring to jīvas, who are filled with misery, the *ānandamaya puruṣa* as Brahman does not have a superior position." There is no fault if Brahman is mentioned with the jīva, since Brahman is within everything. This is a method of teaching the ignorant, so they can easily understand. The Veda, the supreme benefactor, begins teaching a person desiring to know the *ātmā* by pointing out what is not Brahman and finally showing what *is* Brahman, in the manner of showing the small star Arundhatī by first showing a big star near it.

"If that is the case here, then what is the main subject elsewhere: Brahmanor something else?" Brahman is the principal subject taught elsewhere also. In the next chapter of the Taittirīya Upaniṣad, Varuṇa teaches Brahman, the cause of the universe, to his son who is desirous to know Brahman. Varuṇa then explains that food, *prāṇa,* mind and intellect (*vijñāna*) are all Brahman, for his son's understanding. Finally he concludes by showing that the *ānandamaya puruṣa* is Brahman. The section concludes by stating that his knowledge is based on Brahman (*parame vyoman pratiṣṭhatā*). In the conclusion it is said:

sa ya evaṁ-vid asmāl lokāt preyta etam anna-mayam ātmānam upasaṅkrāntya etaṁ prāṇamayam ātmānam upasaṅkrāntya etaṁ manomayam ātmānam upasaṅkrāntya etaṁ vijñanamayam ātmānam upasaṅkrāntya etam ānandamayam ātmānam upasaṅkramya imān lokān kāmāni kāma-rūpy anusañcarann etat sama gāyann āste

He who knows this, after departing from this world, after attaining the *annamaya* person, *prāṇamaya* person, *manomaya* person, *vijñānamaya* person, and finally the *ānandamaya* person, assumes a form according to his desire, and sings this *sāma* concerning Brahman, while moving above the worlds. Taittirīya Upaniṣad 3.10.5

The smṛti also describes this *ānandamaya puruṣa:*

puruṣa-vidho 'nvayo 'tra caramo 'nnamyādiṣu yaḥ
sad asataḥ paraṁ tvam atha yad eṣv avaśeṣāmṛtam

Among the manifestations known as *annamaya* and so forth, you are the ultimate one, entering within the material coverings along with the living entity and assuming the same forms as those the jīva takes. Distinct from the gross and subtle material manifestations, you are the reality underlying them all. SB 10.87.17

It is not contradictory to say that Brahman has a body (*tasyaiva eva śarīra ātmā*) for it is also said *yasya pṛthivī śarīram*: the earth is his body. (Bṛhad-āraṇyaka Upaniṣad 3.7.3) The Vedānta is also called *śārīraka* (relating to the body of the Lord). Those who explain that the *brahma-puccham* is *ānandamaya* are foolish. It goes against the natural flow of the text which has a proposition and conclusion and it destroys the intention of Bādarāyaṇa and Varuṇa.

Since the suffix *maya* means transformation, the word *ānandamaya* means "transformation of bliss" and thus refers to the jīva, not Brahman, which is bliss itself. This idea is refuted by the next sūtra (siddhānta).

Sūtra – 1.1.13

|| vikāra-śabdān neti cen, na prācuryāt ||

If one argues that the suffix *maya* means transformation, that argument is not correct since the suffix means "inherent abundance."

Ānandamaya does not mean transformation of *ānanda.* Why? Because the suffix *maya* means abundance (*prācuryāt*). It does not mean transformation. According to the rule *dvyacaś chandasi* (Pāṇini 4.3.150) the suffix *maya* cannot mean transformation when present in a word with more than two syllables.

Ānandamaya also does not mean absence of sorrow. (It is a positive attribute. Absence of suffering is mentioned separately as in the following examples.) *eṣa sarva-bhūtāntarātmāpahata-pāpmā divyo deva eko nārāyaṇaḥ:* the one shining Lord Nārāyaṇa, devoid of sin, is the soul of all beings. (Subāla Upaniṣad) *paraḥ parāṇāṁ sakalā na yatra kleśādayaḥ sānti parāvareśaḥ:* the Supreme Lord, supreme among the excellent, is without any suffering. (Viṣṇu Purāṇa) The word *pracura* indicates intensity of the word it describes. For instance, the phrase *pracura-prakāśo ravi* means "The sun has an abundance of light as its very nature." Thus *ānandamaya* does not refer to the jīva.

Sūtra – 1.1.14

|| tad-dhetu-vyapadeśāc ca ||

***Ānandamaya* does not refer to the jīva because the text says that the *ānandamaya puruṣa* causes bliss for the jīva.**

It is said:

ko hy evānyat kaḥ prāṇyāt yady eṣa ākāśa ānando na syāt. esa evānandayati

If the infinite Lord did not exist, who could inhale or exhale? The Lord alone is the cause of bliss for the jīva. (Taittirīya Upaniṣad 2.7)

Because the above statement says that the Lord, full of bliss, is the cause of the jīva's bliss (*tad-dhetu-vyapadeśāt*), the *ānandamaya puruṣa* is not the jīva. The cause of bliss for the jīva is different from the jīva. In the above quotation, the word *ānanda* means *ānandamaya.*

Sūtra – 1.1.15

|| māntra-varṇikam eva ca gīyate ||

Ānandamaya* does not refer to the jīva because the Brahman glorified in the mantra section is the same *ānandamaya puruṣa.

In the mantra section of the same Upaniṣad it is said *satyam jñānam anantaṁ brahma*: Brahman is infinite existence and knowledge. (Taittirīya Upaniṣad

2.13) The Brahman of this text is glorified as *ānandamaya* later. It is thus not the jīva.

The meaning is this. The section begins with *brahmavid āpnoti param*: the knower of Brahman attains the supreme. The worshipping jīva attains the Brahman. Brahman is the described with the words *satyam jñānam anantaṁ brahma*. Here also the phrase *ānandamaya* can be applied to Brahman because, following this section, is the section describing the various puruṣas ending with the *ānandamaya puruṣa.* That Brahman, to be achieved by the jīva, is different from the jīva who attains him. Thus the *ānandamaya puruṣa* is not a jīva.

Though Brahman mentioned in the mantra is different from the jīva, the doubt that the jīva is Brahman is not removed simply by proving that the Lord is *ānandamaya*. From inspecting the mantra, it should be concluded that when the jīva becomes free of ignorance and its effects, the jīva not different from the *ānandamaya* Brahman. In answer it is said:

Sūtra – 1.1.16

|| netaro'nupapatteḥ ||

The jīva is not the subject of the mantra because that is impossible by the context.

The jīva, even in a liberated state, is not the Brahman mentioned in the mantra *satyam jñānam anantam brahma.* Why? Because it is not possible in the context.

satyam jñānam anantam brahma yo veda hinitaṁ guhāyaṁ parame vyoman
so 'śnute sarvān kāmān saha brahmaṇā vipaścitā

He who knows that Brahman who is *satyam jñānam* enjoys all pleasures along with the all-knowing Brahman. Taittirīya Upaniṣad 2.1.2

If the jīva enjoys all pleasures with Brahman, he cannot be identical with Brahman. *Vipaścitā* means "with that person whose mind sees or experiences various types (*vividhā)* of enjoyment." *Paśya* (seeing) becomes *paś* like *pṛṣodara.* (Pāṇini 6.3.109) The jīva enjoys all pleasurable objects along with the Lord who is skilful at enjoyment (*vipaścitā*). The verb *aś* means "to enjoy." Instead of the form *aśnāte* the form *aśnute* is used in the *ātmanepada* according to the rule *vyatyayo bahulam* (Pāṇini 3.1.84) concerning Vedic usage.

By mentioning that the jīva enjoys along with the Lord, the jīva is given more prominence, though usually prominence is given to the Lord, not to the devotee. However it is said:

mayi nirbaddha-hṛdayāḥ sādhavaḥ sama-darśanāḥ
vaśe kurvanti māṁ bhaktyā sat-striyaḥ sat-patiṁ yathā

As chaste women bring their gentle husbands under control by service, the pure devotees, who see others' suffering as their own and are completely attached to me in the core of the heart, bring me under their full control. SB 9.4.66

Sūtra – 1.1.17

|| bheda-vyapadeśāt ||

The subject of the mantra is not the jīva because of statements indicating the opposite.

raso vai saḥ rasaṁ hy evāyaṁ labdhvānandī bhavati.

The Lord is rasa. Attaining the Lord as rasa, the jīva becomes blissful. Taittirīya Upaniṣad 2.7.1

The subject of the mantra is not the jīva but the Lord, since the above statement shows that the *ānandamaya* Lord described in the mantra, endowed with rasa, who is to be attained by the jīva, is different from the jīva, receiver of the bliss, even in the liberated condition. Even statements like *brahmaiva san brahmāpnoti*: becoming Brahman, the jīva attains Brahman (*Bṛhad-āraṇyaka Upaniṣad* 4.4.6) do not show that the jīva becomes non-different from Brahman. Becoming Brahman (*brahmaiva san*) means "becoming like Brahman," because of having attained qualities of Brahman. Attaining that state of likeness, one then attains Brahman (*brahmāpnoti*). Thus it means to become like Brahman. *nirañjanaḥ paramaṁ sāmyam upaiti:* the pure soul attains likeness to the supreme Lord. *(Māṇḍukya Upaniṣad* 3.1.31) *idaṁ jñānam upāśritya mama sādharmyam āgatāḥ:* taking shelter of *jñāna,* they attain similarity to me. (BG 14.2) The word *eva* in the text also means "similar." The rule says that *vāva, yathā, tathā, eva* and *iva* mean "similar."

Since pradhāna (prakṛti) is the cause of bliss in sattva-guṇa, prakṛti should be ānandamaya.

Sūtra – 1.1.18

|| kāmāc ca nānumānāpekṣā ||

One cannot infer that *prakṛti* is the *ānandamaya puruṣa* because the text states that this *puruṣa* has desire.

so 'kāmayata bahu syāṁ prajāyeya

The Lord desired "May I become many, may I produce offspring." (Taittirīya Upaniṣad 2.6.1)

From this statement describing how Brahman creates the universe, it can be inferred that *prakṛti* or *pradhāna* is not the *ānandamaya puruṣa* in the text, since *prakṛti* is insentient and cannot desire anything.

Sūtra – 1.1.19

|| asminn asya ca tad-yogaṁ ca śāsti ||

***Prakṛti* is not the *ānandamaya puruṣa* because scriptures teach that the jīva attains fearlessness by fixing himself on this puruṣa and becomes fearful when detached from him.**

The scriptures teach *(śāsti)* that the jīva has fearlessness when fixed in the *ānandamaya puruṣa (asmin)* and fear when not fixed in him. This is mentioned in Taittirīya Upaniṣad 2.7.2

yadā hy evaiṣa etasminn adṛśye anātmye anirukte 'nilayane abhayaṁ pratiṣṭhaṁ vindate 'tha atha so 'bhayaṁ gato bhavati gato bhavati yadā hyaisa etasmin ud aram antaram kurute atha tasya bhayam bhavati

When the jīva becomes established in this Lord who is invisible, without material body, indescribable, and independent, in order to become fearless, the jīva becomes fearless and when he deviates a little he becomes fearful.

This teaching of the scriptures can never apply for *prakṛti*, because for *prakṛti*, the opposite holds true: by detachment from prakṛti one becomes fearless and by contact with it one becomes fearful.

Therefore it is concluded that the *ānandamaya* Lord is not a *jīva* or *prakṛti.*

Topic 7 (Sūtras 20 – 21)

Antar-adhikaraṇam - The person within the sun

atha yā so 'ntar āditiyo hiraṇmayaḥ puruśo dṛśyate hiraṇya-śmaśrur hiraṇya-keśa aprāṇakhāt sarva eva suvarṇas tasya yathā kapyasaṁ puṇḍarīkam evam akṣiṇī tasyod iti nāma sa eṣa sarvebhyaḥ pāpmābhyah udita udeti hā vai sarvebhyaḥ pāpmābhyo ya evaṁ veda tasya ṛk sāma ca gesnau tasmād udgithas tasmāt tv evodgātaitasya hi gāthā sa eṣa ye cāmuṣmat parāṇco lokās teṣāṁ ceṣṭe deva-kāmānāṁ cety adhidaivatam

He who is to be seen in the sun is a golden person, having a glowing mustache, glowing hair, glowing from the tip of his nails, and having eyes like a blossoming red lotus. He is called Ut. He has risen above all sins. He who knows this rises above all sins. The Ṛg and Sāma produce a song concerning this person. Thus the song is called Udgītha, and thus the singer of that song is called Udgātā. He is the ruler of all worlds above the sun and of all the objects of enjoyment in those worlds. This is the meditation on the Lord. Chāndogya Upaniṣad 1.6.6-8

athādhyātmam atha ya eṣo 'ntar-akṣiṇi puruṣo dṛśyate saiva ṛk tat sāma tad ukthaṁ tad yajus tad brahma tasyaitasya tad eva rūpaṁ yad amuṣya rūpam. yāv amuṣya gesnau tau gesnau yan nāma tan nāma.

Now let us discuss the body. The person seen within the eye is Ṛk. He alone is Sāma. He alone is the Uktha. He is the Yajus. He alone is Brahman. The form of this person is the form in the sun. The forms of song concerning the person in the sun are the forms of song for the person in the eye. Chāndogya Upaniṣad 1.7.5

(Doubt) Is the person in the sun and in the eye some jīva who has attained a high position because of great knowledge and piety, or is he the Paramātmā?

(Pūrvapakṣa) This person is a jīva because he has a body. He has attained a position of being worshipped because of great knowledge and piety and because he bestows results such as rulership or objects desired by people.

Sūtra – 1.1.20

|| antas tad-dharmopadeśāt ||

Paramātmā is the person in the eye and the sun, because the teachings describe the Lord's qualities.

The person within the sun and eye is Paramātmā, not the jīva. Why? Because the section teaches qualities that belong only to the Lord such as *apahata-pāpma. Apahata-pāpma* means having no karma. Only the Lord is never under the control of karma. This cannot be said about the jīva who is subject to karma. The jīva cannot give results such as fulfilling the desires of all people by his nature nor is he the principal giver of results. Nor is the jīva the object of worship.

The argument that because he has a body he must be a jīva is not true, for the *puruṣa-sūkta* says:

vedhāham etaṁ puruṣaṁ mahāntam
āditya-varṇaṁ tamasaḥ parastāt

I know that great person, shining like the sun, above darkness.

Such statements show that the Lord has an attractive spiritual body.

Sūtra – 1.1.21

|| bheda-vyapadeśāc cānyaḥ ||

The person mentioned is the Lord because of statements showing the difference between the jīva in the sun and the Lord in the sun.

One must accept that the Paramātmā is necessarily different from the jīva who presides over the sun or other objects.

ya āditye tiṣṭhann ādityād antaro yam ādityo
na veda yasyādityaḥ śarīraṁ ya ādityam antaro
yamayaty eṣa ta ātmāntaryāmy amṛtaḥ

He who resides in the sun deity, who is different from that deity, whom the deity of the sun does not know, who has the sun deity as his body, who controls the sun deity from within, is the eternal Lord within (*antaryāmī*). Bṛhad-āraṇyaka Upaniṣad 3.7.9

Because of the distinction made between the sun deity (*jīva*) and the Lord (*antaryāmī*), the text in the Chāndogya Upaniṣad refers to the Lord. That is because the texts of the Chāndogya and Bṛhad-āraṇyaka Upaniṣads should be correlated.

Topic 8 (Sūtra 22)

Ākāsādhikaraṇam - The Topic of Ether

asya lokasya kā gatir iti ākāśa iti hovāca/ sarvāṇi hā vā imāni bhūtāny ākāśād eva samutpadyante/ ākāśaṁ pratyastaṁ yānty ākāśaḥ parāyanam

"What is the goal of the people?" He said, "It is *ākāśa.* All elements arise from *ākāśa.* They all merge into *ākāśa. Ākāśa* is the goal. Chāndogya Upaniṣad 1.9.1

The doubt is this. Does the word *ākāśa* refer to the ether or Brahman?

(Pūrvapakṣa)

The word *ākāśa* means the element ether. From ether, which is the common meaning of *ākāśa,* comes air. Ether is said to be the cause of the other material elements. Therefore *ākāśa* refers to the ether, not Brahman.

Sūtra – 1.1.22

|| ākāśas tal-liṅgāt ||

The word *ākāśa* refers to Brahman because Brahman's qualities are mentioned in the verse.

Ākāśa refers to Brahman, not ether. Why? Because qualities such as giving rise to all elements are the qualities of Brahman, not ether. The following should be mentioned.

The word "all" indicates that all elements including ether arise from this *ākāśa.* Everything (including ether) cannot arise from ether, since something cannot be the cause of itself. The word *eva* indicates that only from this *ākāśa* does everything arise. There is no other cause of everything. Ether is not the sole cause of the elements, just as earth is not the sole cause of pots; pots have other causes as well. However Brahman is the sole cause of everything, since Brahman possesses all *śaktis* and all forms. Though the common meaning of *ākāśa* is ether, Brahman has precedence as the meaning here, because that meaning makes more sense.

Topic 9 (Sūtra 23)

Prāṇādhikaraṇam - Concerning Prāṇa

katama sa devateti/ prāṇa iti hovāca/ sarvāṇi hā vai imāni bhūtāni prāṇam evābhisamviśanti prāṇam abhyujjīhate

Who is the deity? He answered, "It is *prāṇa.* All beings arise from *prāṇa* and merge into *prāṇa.* Chāndogya Upaniṣad 1.11.4-5

The doubt is this. Is this prāṇa the chief air within the body or the supreme Lord?

(Pūrva-pakṣa)

Taking the common meaning, it means air, since *prāṇa* is the cause of all beings. That is the meaning of "arising from *prāṇa* and merging into *prāṇa*" mentioned in the verse.

Sūtra – 1.1.23

|| ata eva prāṇaḥ ||

The prāṇa is Brahman, for the same reason.

Prāṇa means the Supreme Lord, not the transformation of air. Why? Because the quality of Brahman--giving rise to all beings and destroying them-- is mentioned.

Topic 10 (Sūtras 24 – 27)

Jyotiścaraṇādhikaraṇam - Concerning Light described as Feet

It is said in the Upaniṣad:

atha yad ataḥ paro divo jyotir dīpyate viśvataḥ pṛṣṭheṣu sarvataḥ pṛṣṭheṣv anuttameṣūttameṣu lokeṣu idaṁ vāva tad yad idam asminn antaḥ puruṣe jyotiḥ

That light which shines above heaven, higher than everything in the highest worlds beyond which there are no other worlds, is the same light which is within man. Chāndogya Upaniṣad 3.13.7

The doubt is this. Is this *jyoti* fire or Brahman?

(Pūrva-pakṣa) It is the light of the sun since Brahman is not mentioned previously in the verse.

Sūtra – 1.1.24

|| jyotiś caraṇābhidhānāt ||

Light refers to Brahman, because of the mention of Brahman's feet in a previous verse.

The *jyoti* or light means Brahman. Why? Because of the mention of feet. Previously it was said:

etāvan asya mahimato jyāyāṁs ca puruṣaḥ pado 'sya sarva-bhūtāni tri-pad asyāmṛtaṁ divi

Such is the greatness of *gāyatrī.* Greater than this is the Lord. All entities are one of his feet. His three feet are nectar in the sky. Chāndogya Upaniṣad 3.12.6

In this previous verse, the living entities comprising one foot are mentioned in relation to the spiritual sky. The meaning is this. The verse describes Brahman as having four feet. Brahman is indicated by the word *yat* in the verses following that, including 3.13.7. (*atha yad ataḥ...*) Though the verses occur at a distance from each other, the connection between them remains. Also the passages are connected since sky is mentioned in both verses. Therefore "light" refers to the Lord endowed with all effulgence. It does not refer to the sun.

(Pūrva-pakṣa) "The word Brahman is greatly separated from the verse describing light. Therefore light cannot refer to Brahman."

This is refuted by the following sūtra.

Sūtra – 1.1.25

|| chando'bhidānān neti cen, na,
tathā ceto'rpaṇa-nigadāt tathā hi darśanam ||

If one objects that the feet are in reference to the *gāyatrī* meter mentioned previously in the same section of the Upaniṣad, the answer is no, since that section teaches concentration of one's heart on Brahman in the form of *gāyatrī.* That is consistent with the meaning.

"It is said *gāyatrī vā idaṁ sarvaṁ bhūtaṁ yad idaṁ kiñcit:* everything that exists is *gāyatrī. (Chāndogya Upaniṣad 3.12.1)* After that it is explained that *gāyatrī* is all living beings, the earth, speech, the body and the heart. Then it is said *caiṣa catuṣ-padā ṣaḍ-vidhā gāyatrī tad etad ṛcābhyuktam etāvan asya mahimā: gāyatrī* has four feet and six varieties; this is described in a verse;

such is its greatness. With this description, how can the mantra suddenly refer to Brahman with four feet? The word *jyotis* does not refer to Brahman because the four feet refer to the *gāyatri* (*chandaso abhidānāt*)."

That is not so. Why? The sūtra answers. Because the verses teaches (*nigadād)* about meditation in the heart (*ceto 'rpaṇa*) on Brahman, which appears in the form of *gāyatrī*. That is why it says that *gāyatrī is* everything (since *gāyatrī* indicates Brahman). The word *darśaṇam* means consistency. If the *gāyatrī* were to be accepted as merely a meter, then the meaning would be lost. (How can a meter be all beings?) Thus, that *gāyatrī* refers to Brahman has been shown to be correct.

Another reason is given to show that *gāyatrī* is Brahman, not the meter.

Sūtra – 1.1.26

|| bhūtādi-pāda-vyapadeśopapatteś caivam ||

Brahman alone should be considered *gāyatrī* because living beings, earth, body and heart are mentioned as its four feet.

Brahman alone should be considered *gāyatrī*. Why? Because living beings, earth, body and heart are mentioned as the four feet of *gāyatrī*. If *gāyatrī* did not mean Brahman, then it would be meaningless to say that a meter has four feet consisting of living beings, earth, body and heart. Therefore the first statement of the section indicates that Brahman is everything. Thus the word *jyotis* refers to Brahman because of *yat* in the next section concerning *jyotis* (light) and the reference to the sky in both passages.[17]

Someone may object that the sky means the same thing in the two verses.[18] The *siddhānta* is given in the next sūtra.

Sūtra – 1.1.27

|| upadeśa-bhedān neti cen, nobhayasminn apy avirodhāt ||

---

[17] tripādasyāmṛtaṁ divi (Chāndogya 3.12.6) and paro divo jyotir dpiypate (Chāndogya 3.13.7)

[18] Three feet of the Lord are nectar in the sky (divi). The light which shines above the sky (divaḥ) is also within man.

If one argues that the statements have different meaning in relation to the sky, that is not so, since there is no contradiction in the two statements.

(Pūrva-pakṣa) "*Tripādasyāmṛtaṁ divi* (three feet of the *gāyatrī* are nectar in the sky) has sky in the locative case. The sky acts as the support. In the other sentence *paro divaḥ* (the light is above the sky) sky is in the ablative case. Thus *gāyatrī* and light cannot refer to the same object since they are differently placed according to the teachings (*upadeśa-bhedāt*)."

That is not so. Why? The sūtra answers by saying that there is no contradiction (*avirodhāt*) in the two teachings *(ubhayasmin)* since both mean the locative case. A parrot sitting on top of a tree is said to be in the tree and above the tree. (So the Lord is in the sky (on top) and above the sky. Though the teachings look different, the meaning is the same. Thus there is no contradiction.

Topic 11 (Sūtras 28 – 31)

Pādānta-prāṇādhikaraṇam - Another reference to *prāṇa*

In the Kauśītaki-brāhmaṇa 3.2 it is said *pratardano ha vai daivodāsir indrasya priyaṁ dhāmopajagāma*: Pratardana, son of Divodāsa went to the favorite abode of Indra because of his valor. After this, Indra spoke to Pratardana. Pratardana inquired about what was most beneficial. Indra gave the following instruction. *prāṇo 'smi prajñātmā taṁ māṁ āyur-amṛtam upasasva*: I am *prāṇa*, the intelligent *ātmā*; meditate on me as that *prāṇa,* the nectar of life.

(Doubt) "Whom is Indra referring to as the *prāṇa*: the *jīva* (Indra) or Paramātmā?"

(Pūrvapakṣa) "Since Indra is well known to be a *jīva,* the word *prāṇa* also refers to a *jīva.* The jīva Indra asked by Pratardana says that worship of himself is most beneficial."

Sūtra – 1.1.28

|| prāṇas tathānugamāt ||

Prāṇa indicates the Lord, not the jīva, since this is understood by the context.

Indra indicates Paramātmā when he speaks of *prāṇa.* He is not referring to the jīva. Why? Because this is understood from the concerned passage (*tathānugamāt*). *sa eṣa prāṇa eva prajñḷatamāndo 'jaro 'mrtaḥ*: the *prāṇa* is the intelligent *ātmā,* without old age, without death. (*Kauṣītaki-brāhmaṇa* 3.9) Because these words refer to Brahman, not the jīva, the *prāṇa* that Indra mentions is also Brahman.

(Pūrva-pakṣa) "What you say is not correct, because Indra, the speaker, a *jīva,* describes himself. Indra says, "Know that I am *prāṇa.* (*Kauṣītaki-brāhmaṇa* 3.2)He says *tri-śirṣāṇaṁ tvaṣṭram ahanam aruṇmukhān ṛṣīn śalavṛkebhyaḥ prayacchan:* "I killed Vṛtrāsura, the three-headed son of Tvaṣṭā, and I gave the Aruṇmukha sages to the wolves." This shows that he teaches worship of himself as a *jīva.* Thus the concluding passage mentioning nectar or bliss of life etc. also refers to a *jīva* even though mention is made of bliss, because of the previous statements. When Indra says "I am *prāṇa*" he teaches worship of himself, a jīva. It means "Worship me as *prāṇa,*" just as it is said elsewhere "Worship speech as a cow." (*Bṛhad-āraṇyaka Upaniṣad* 5.4.1) Indra teaches worship of himself as *prāṇa* to indicate that he is the deity controlling strength, for it is said *prāṇo vai balam*: *prāṇa* is indeed strength. (*Bṛhad-āraṇyaka Upaniṣad* 4.14.4) Therefore *prāṇa* refers to a *jīva.*"

This proposition is refuted in the following sūtra.

Sūtra – 1.1.29

| | na vaktur ātmopadeśād iti ced
adhyātma-sambandha-bhūmā hy asmin | |

If one says that the passage teaches about Indra, the reply is no. In that section of the Upaniṣad there are plenty of references to the Paramātmā.

In this section *(asmin)* there are plenty (*bhūmā*) of references to the Paramātmā (*adhyātma-sambandha*). Because that is seen, the *prāṇa* refers to Paramātmā.

Firstly, Pratardana asked what was most beneficial. That means he asked about the method of attaining liberation. The answer given is, "Worship me as *prāṇa.*" Only the Lord can give liberation.

Secondly, the same Upaniṣad contains other statements concerning *prāṇa*. *eṣa eva sādhu karma kārayati: prāṇa* makes a person perform pious acts. (Kauṣītaki Upaniṣad 3.8) Only the Lord is the cause of all action.

Thirdly, the same Upaniṣad says this about *prāṇa*:

tad yathā rathasyāreṣu nemir arpitā nābhavara arpita evam evaita bhūta-mātraḥ prajñā-mātrāsv arpitaḥ. prajñā-mātrāḥ prāṇe 'rpitaḥ

Just as in a chariot wheel the rim rests on the spokes, and the spokes on the hub, in the same way the material elements rest on *prajñā* (intelligence), and *prajñā* rests on *prāṇa*.

Only the Lord is the support of all sentient and insentient things.

Fourthly, the Upaniṣad also says this about *prāṇa*:

sa eṣa prāṇa eva prajñātmānando 'jaro 'mṛtaḥ. eṣa lokādhipatir eṣa sarveśvaraḥ

Prāṇa is the self of the jīva, it is bliss, it is without old age and without death. It is the Lord of all worlds and the controller of everything.

The Lord is the principal being having bliss and other items mentioned as his nature.

Therefore, because *prāṇa* is described as having all these qualities, it actually means Brahman and nothing else.

"If that is so, why does Indra speak about himself?" The sūtra answers.

Sūtra – 1.1.30

|| śāstra-dṛṣṭyā tūpadeśo vāma-devavat ||

Indra gives the teachings of identity from the point of view of scriptural insight as is the case of Vāmadeva.

The word *tu* (but) indicates refutation. When Indra, who is a jīva, which is understood by descriptions in the Upaniṣad, gives instruction (*upadeśaḥ*) to worship himself as the Lord, it is done only from the viewpoint of scripture (*śāstra-dṛṣtyā*) and nothing else. Scripture teaches identity of the dependent function with its source. Thus it is said:

na vai vāco na cakṣūmsi na śrotrāṇi na manāṁsīty ācakṣate prāṇa ity evācakṣate prāṇo hy evaitāni sarvāṇi bhavanti

These are not called voices, eyes, ears or minds. They are called *prāṇa. Prāṇa* is all these things. Chāndogya Upaniṣad 5.1.15

In this statement the senses are called *prāṇa* because their functions are dependent on *prāṇa.*

Similarly, wise Indra, desiring to teach his obedient student his knowledge, says "I am *prāṇa*" to teach the student that Indra's functions depend on Brahman.

An example is given of Vāmadeva (*vāma-devavat*). It is said in Bṛhad-āraṇyaka Upaniṣad:

tad vaitat paśyann ṛṣir vāmadevaḥ pratipade ahaṁ manur abhavaṁ sūryaś ca

Seeing this, the sage Vāmadeva constantly repeated, "I have become the moon and the sun."

Vāmadeva identifies himself as the moon and sun, to indicate that Brahman is the cause of his functions as well as the functions of the moon and sun. Identity with the Lord, because he pervades everything, is also found in the smṛtis:

yo 'yaṁ tavāgato deva-samīpaṁ devatā-gaṇaḥ
sa tvam eva jagat-sraṣṭā yataḥ sarva-gato bhavān

The *devatās* who have come before you are identical with you, the creator of the universe, since you pervade everything. Viṣṇu Purāṇa 1.9.69

sarvaṁ samāpnoṣi tato 'si sarvam

You are all-pervading, and thus you are everything. *Bhagavad-gītā* 11.40

Common people also speak of oneness when two entities are situated in the same place or are of the same opinion. For instance, one may say, "The cows become one in the evening" or "The quarrelling kings became one in opinion." The oneness of Indra and Brahman is to be understood in this way.

(Pūrva-pakṣa)

"Though there are many words indicating the qualities of Brahman in the passage, it is not possible to conclude that it indicates Brahman since there are also many words indicating the jīva. It is said:

na vācaṁ vijijñāsitā vaktāraṁ vidyāt

Do not try to understand words. Try to know the speaker. *Kauṣītaki Upaniṣad* 3.8

Here, the speaker is clear:

tri-śirṣāṇaṁ tvaṣṭram ahanam

I killed the son of Trastṛ.

There are also statements describing *prāṇa* as the life force in the jīva:

yāvad asmin śarīre prāṇo vasati tāvad āyur atha khalu prāṇa eva prajñātma idaṁ śarīraṁ parigṛhyotthāpayati

As long as *prāṇa* remains within it, the body is alive. *Prāṇa* is the conscious self. *Prāṇa,* taking hold of this material body, makes it rise up. *Kauṣītaki Upaniṣad* 2.2-3

yo vai prāṇaḥ sa prajñā yā prajñā sa prāṇaḥ. sa hā hy etāv asmin śarīre vasataḥ. sahotkramate

What is known as *prāṇa* is *prajñā* and what is known as *prajñā* is *prāṇa*. The two live in the body and together they leave. *Kauṣītaki Upaniṣad*

These statements indicate that *prāṇa* can mean the jīva and the life force, but ultimately the jīva, for the two are names of one object in its inactive and active state. Therefore all three--Brahman, *prāṇa* and jīva should be worshipped."

The sūtra refutes this.

Sūtra – 1.1.31

| | jīva-mukhya-prāṇa-liṅgān neti cen, na, upāsā-traividhyād, āśritatvād, iha tad-yogāt | |

If one claims that jīva and *prāṇa* should be worshipped, and not just Brahman because of indications in the text, the answer is no, because then there would be three types of worship, because Brahman is described elsewhere as a jīva and prāṇa, and because there are explicit indications to indicate Brahman.

If one claims that jīva and *prāṇa* should also be worshipped, and not just Brahman, because of indications in the text (*jīva-mukhya-prāṇa-liṅgāt*), the answer is no. Why? Because then there would be three types of worship. It is not possible to accept that instruction in one statement, since that one statement would then represent many statements.

The meaning is this. Because of indications of jīva and prāṇa, are we to apply the qualities of Brahman to these two? Or should the three be treated separately? Or should we apply the characteristics of the jīva and prāṇa to Brahman? The first option was already refuted (for jīva cannot have Brahman's qualities). The second option is spoiled by indicating three types of worship. The third option is accepted because elsewhere (*āśritatvāt*) also Brahman is described in terms of jīva and *prāṇa.*

(Doubt) "Other texts may be interpreted in this way because of explicit indications in those particular cases. But what are the explicit indications for this kind of interpretation here?"There are explicit indications in this particular text also in the form of Pratardana's question about the activity most beneficial for man. This appropriate indication (*tad-yogāt*) allows the interpretation of jīva and *prāṇa* as Brahman.

(Doubt) "*etāv asmin śarīre vasataḥ. sahotkramate: prāṇa* and *prajñā* live together in the body and exit together. Can these be applied to Brahman?"

No. Actually this means that the *kriyā-śakti* and *jñāna-śakti* representing Brahman dwell together in the body and leave together.

(Doubt) "Words like *prāṇa* and jīva denote substance. How can they indicate qualities?" That is not so. Though they are used as qualities, they also indicate the object since there is non-difference of the quality and object. When Indra says "I am *prāṇa* and *prajñā*" he praises the qualities of the two and the Lord indicated by the qualities of these two śaktis. *Yo vai prāṇaḥ sa prajñā:* what is *prāṇa* is *prajñā.* This means that Brahman alone is indicated by the words Indra, *prāṇa* and *prajñā.*

(Doubt) "This *adhikaraṇa* which explains identification of *prāṇa* with Brahman is unnecessary since *prāṇa* has already been shown to be Brahman in an earlier *adhikaraṇa* (1.1.23)."

That is not so. Previously the doubt was only about the meaning of the word *prāṇa*. Here the doubt is about the proper object of meditation. Because in a section of the Upaniṣad related to bliss there are words describing jīva and *prāṇa*, the *sādhaka* might meditate on jīva or *prāṇa* and not Brahman to attain bliss. To prevent this mistake, this *adhikaraṇa* is given separately.

Section Two

Topic 1 (Sūtras 1 – 8)

Sarvatra-prasiddhādhikaraṇam - The Lord is famous everywhere

mano-mayādibhiḥ śabdaiḥ svarupam yasya kīrtyate
hṛdaye sphuratu śrīmān mamāsau śyāmasundaraḥ

May Śrī Śyāmasundara, whose form is glorified by words like *manomaya*, appear in my heart.

In the first pāda, it was stated that one should inquire about the supreme Brahman called the supreme person, from whom all universes arise. Certain words which generally mean something else were shown to indicate Brahman. In the second and third pādas other words which do not seem to clearly indicate Brahman are shown to indicate Brahman.

The following is found in the Śāṇḍilya-vidyā section of the Chāndogya Upaniṣad:

sarvaṁ khalv idaṁ brahma taj jalān iti śānta upāsīta. atha khalu kratumayaḥ puruṣaḥ. yathā kratur asmin loke puruṣo bhavati tathetaḥ pretya bhavati. sa kratuṁ kurvīta. manomayaḥ prāṇa-śarīro bhā-rūpaḥ satya-saṅkalpa ākāśātmā sarva-karmā sarva-kāmāḥ sarva-gandhaḥ sarva-rasaḥ sarvam idaṁ abhyāto avākyan ādaraḥ.sa ātmāntar-hṛdaya etad brahma

Everything is Brahman. The peaceful person should worship Brahman as the creator and destroyer. The worshipper then develops faith. As a person develops according to his faith in this world, so he attains in the next life. One should cultivate faith. That Brahman is understood by the mind (*manomayaḥ*). He is the controller of *prāṇa*. He is effulgent, and his every desire is fulfilled. He is all pervading, performs attractive pastimes, and is endowed with all enjoyment, all fragrance and all rasa. He encompasses everything. He is silent. He is the support. That Brahman is in the heart. Chāndogya Upaniṣad 3.14.1-2

Here is the doubt. Is the object described by qualities like *manomaya* the jīva or the Lord?

(Pūrvapakṣa) It must be the jīva since mind and *prāṇas* belong to the jīva. These are not present in the Paramātmā. *aprāṇo hy amanāḥ śubhraḥ*: the Lord is without *prāṇas* or mind and is pure. (Muṇḍaka Upaniṣad 2.1.2) In the statement *sarvaṁ khalv idaṁ brahma* at the beginning of the passage, one should not take the word *brahman* to mean supreme Brahman. It is a means of creating peacefulness, which is useful in worship: one is instructed to think of everything as Brahman in order to become peaceful. Since the words in the passage describe the jīva, the word *brahma* at the end of the passage (Chāndogya Upaniṣad 3.14.4) also means the jīva.

Sūtra – 1.2.1

|| sarvatra-prasiddhopadeśāt ||

The word *manomaya* refers to Brahman because teachings of these qualities which belong to the Lord are found everywhere in the scriptures.

Manomaya refers to Paramātmā, not the jīva. Why? Because teachings concerning famous qualities unique to the Lord, such as his being the cause and destruction of the universe, stated everywhere in the Vedānta, are found in the phrases like *taj-jalān* in the passage. Though the introductory phrase *sarvam khalv idaṁ brahma* is for the purpose of creating peacefulness, and is not meant to define Brahman primarily, Brahman is indicated by the words starting with *manomaya*. *Kratu* means worship. *Manomaya* means "he who is comprehended by the pure mind" for śruti says *manasaivānudraṣṭavyaḥ*: the Lord is to be perceived by the mind. (Bṛhad-āraṇyaka Upaniṣad 4.4.19) Of course, some statements also indicate the opposite. *yato vacā nivartante aprāpya manasā saha:* the Lord cannot be expressed by words, not being comprehended by the mind. Such statements however mean that the low-minded cannot comprehend the Lord at all and that the knowers of truth cannot know the Lord completely.

Moreover, the Lord is called *prāṇa-śarīraḥ* (possessing a body of *prāṇa*) because he controls *prāṇa.* Others say that he is so called because his body is as dear to the devotees as their lives. Statements like *aprāṇo hy amanā*: the Lord is without *prāṇa* or the mind (Muṇḍaka Upaniṣad 2.1.2) mean that his knowledge does not depend on a mind, or that he has no material mind because it is also said *manovān*: the Lord has a mind[19] and *anīd avātam*: he breathes without material breathing. (Ṛg Veda 10. 129.2) Others say that since the word *manomaya* means the Lord in many famous Vedic texts, therefore in this text also it should refer to him.

manomayaḥ prāṇa-carīra-netā

Possessing a mind, he is the guide for the body and senses. *Muṇḍaka Upaniṣad* 2.2.7

sa eṣo 'ntar-hṛdaya ākāśas tasminn ayaṁ puruṣo manomayo 'mṛtamayo hiraṇmayaḥ

There is ether in the heart. In that the *manomaya* Lord resides, immortal and effulgent. *Taittirīya Upaniṣad* 1.6.1

hṛdā manīṣā manasābhiklpto ya etad vidur amṛtas te bhavanti

Those who understand that the Lord is conceived by the heart, intellect and mind, become immortal. *Kaṭha Upaniṣad* 7.9

prāṇasya prāṇaḥ

He is the life of the *prāṇa*. Bṛhad-āraṇyaka Upaniṣad 4.4.18

Sūtra – 1.2.2

|| vivakṣita-guṇopapatteś ca ||

***Manomaya* refers to Brahman because of other qualities in the passage which refer to Brahman.**

Manomaya refers to Brahman because the other qualities mentioned in the same passage apply to the Supreme Lord, not the jīva. For instance *prāṇa-śarīro bhā-rūpaḥ:* he is the controller of *prāṇa;* he is effulgent.

---

[19] *buddhi-mano 'ṅga-pratyaṅgavattāṁ bhagavato lakṣayāmahe buddhimān mano-vān aṅga-pratyaṅgavān:* we describe that the Lord is endowed with limbs, subsections, mind and intelligence. He has intelligence, mind, limbs and subsections. This is quoted in Baladeva's commentary on BG 13.15 and in Jīva's Sarva-saṁvādinī.

Sūtra – 1.2.3

|| anupapattes tu na śārīraḥ ||

***Manomaya* does not refer to the jīva because the qualities mentioned cannot refer to the jīva, who is like a glow-worm.**

It is impossible for the qualities mentioned to refer to the jīva, since he is insignificant like a glow-worm.

Sūtra – 1.2.3

|| karma-kartṛtva-vyapadeśāc ca ||

Manomaya does not refer to the jīva since the text later says that the jīva (subject) meets the manomaya Lord (object) after death.

At the end of the section dealing with the *manomaya puruṣa* it is said *etam itaḥ pretyābhisaṁbhavitāsmi:* I will attain him after death. The *manomaya puruṣa* is the object of the sentence. The jīva is the subject of the sentence. The *manomaya* Lord, the object, is distinguished from the jīva, the subject. *Abhisambhavati* means "the jīva meets the Lord as a river meets the ocean."

Sūtra – 1.2.5

|| śabda-viśeṣāt ||

***Manomaya* is the Lord because the Lord and jīva are distinguished by words in different cases, indicating the worshipped and the worshipper.**

In the sentence *eṣa me ātmāntar hṛdaye*: he is within my heart (Chāndogya Upaniṣad 3.14.3, the next verse), the word *me* in the genitive case indicates the jīva, who is the worshipper and the subject *esaḥ* which indicates the *manomaya* Lord, who is to be worshipped. The two words in different cases indicate two different entities. Thus the object worshipped, *manomaya,* is different from the jīva, the worshipper.

Sūtra – 1.2.6

|| smṛteś ca ||

This is supported by the statements of smṛti.

īśvaraḥ sarva-bhūtānāṁ hṛd-deśe 'rjuna tiṣṭhati
bhrāmayan sarva-bhūtāni yantrārūḍhāni māyayā ||

O Arjuna, the Lord is situated in the heart of all living entities. He engages in action all living entities, who are mounted on a machine made of *prakṛti.* BG 18.61

This smṛti statement shows that the jīva is different from the Lord.

(Pūrvapakṣa) *"eṣa ma ātmāntar-hṛdaye 'ṇīyān brīher vā yavād vā:* this *ātmā,* smaller than a grain of rice or barley, resides in my heart. (Chandogya Upanisad 3.14.3) This śruti text shows that the *manomaya* refers to the jīva, not the Lord, since it describes the *manomaya* as inhabiting a small place (the heart) and being miniscule in size (which can apply only to the jīva, not to the Lord)."

This is refuted in the next sūtra.

Sūtra – 1.2.7

| | arbhakaukastvāt tad-vyapadeśāc ca neti cen na nicāyyatvād evaṁ vyomavac ca | |

If one argues that *manomaya* cannot refer to the Lord, because the *manomaya puruṣa* is stated to dwell in small place and be very small, the answer is "No" because that description is given for meditation and the Lord is also described in the same passage as being larger than the sky.

One cannot say that *manomaya* does not refer to the Lord because the Lord is described as inhabiting a small place and being small in size, since in the same text the Lord is described as being huge, by comparing him to the sky. *Jyāyān pṛthivī jyāyān antarikṣāt*: the Lord is greater than the earth and greater than the sky. How can the contrary statements (being small and huge) be reconciled? By the understanding that the Lord is described as small only because he is to be worshipped (*nicayyatvāt*) in the heart.

The point is this. Sometimes the Lord is described as small in a figurative way and sometimes because it is actual. The Lord is figuratively described as small for the convenience of the devotee who remembers him within the heart (which is small). He actually *becomes* small out of mercy to his devotee by applying his inconceivable energy. The one form of the Lord appears variously to the devotees. *Eko 'pi san bahudhā yo 'vabhāti:* one Lord appears as many. (Gopāla-tāpanī Upaniṣad) Though the Lord is large, he becomes small by his *acintya-śakti.* This topic is also discussed in *vaiśvānarādhikaraṇa* (Brahma-sūtra 1.2.25). The small-sized Lord is also described as huge because he has the power to appear simultaneously everywhere.

(Pūrvapakṣa) "The Lord, due to residing within the body like the jīva, will establish a relationship with it, and thus will experience its suffering in the same manner."

This is refuted in the next sūtra.

Sūtra – 1.2.8

| | sambhoga-prāptir iti cen, na, vaiśeṣyāt | |

If one objects that the Lord will share the experiences of the jīva if he resides in the body, the answer is "No" because the relationship of the Lord with the body is different.

The word *sam* in *sambhoga* means "along with" as in the word *saṁvāda* (discussion with another person). The Lord does not enjoy and suffer along with the jīva (*sambhoga-prāptiḥ)*. Why? Because of difference.

The meaning is this. Relationship with the body is not the cause of enjoying and suffering in the body. Being under the control of karma is the real cause. The Lord is not under the control of karma since it is said *anaśnann anyo 'bhicākaśīti*: one bird eats the fruit and the other does not. (Muṇḍaka Upaniṣad 3.1.1.) Smṛti also says *na māṁ karmāṇi limpanti na me karma-phale spṛhā:* I am not touched by karma and I have no desire for the results of karma. (BG 4.14)

Topic 2 (Sūtras 9 – 10)

Attādhikaraṇam - The eater

It is said in Kaṭha Upaniṣad:

yasya brahma ca kṣātraṁ ca ubhe bhavataḥ odanaḥ
mṛtyur yasyopasecanaṁ ka itthā veda yatra saḥ

Brāhmaṇas and kṣatriyas are his food and death is the topping sprinkled on the food. Who knows where this person dwells? Kaṭha Upaniṣad 1.2.25

The words *odana* and *upasecana* indicate an eater. The doubt is this. Is the eater the fire of digestion or the jīva or the Lord?

(Pūrva-pakṣa) Because the descriptive terms do not clearly specify any of the three, and because of the nature of the questions and answers, fire seems to be the eater. Śruti says *agnir annādaḥ*: fire eats the food. (*Bṛhad-āraṇyaka Upaniṣad* 1.4.6) Or the eater is the jīva since eating requires action, appropriate to the jīva, and not to the Lord, who performs no action. The śruti indicates who eats and does not eat in the following. *Tayor anyaḥ pippalam:* of the two, the jīva eats the fruit of the tree. (*Muṇḍaka Upaniṣad* 3.1.1) Therefore the eater is the jīva.

Sūtra – 1.2.9

|| attā carācara-grahaṇāt ||

The Lord is the eater because he devours all moving and non-moving entities.

The Lord is the eater. Why? Because he takes the moving and non-moving entities as his food. He accepts the whole universe, represented by brāhmaṇas and kṣatriyas, sprinkled with death, as his food. No one except the Lord can devour the universe. The sprinkled sauce (*upasecanam*) causes one to eat other foods when a portion of it is eaten. The eater of the whole universe sprinkled with death can refer only to the destroyer of the universe. The Paramātmā is well known for this. Though the scriptures say that the Lord does not eat, what is denied in such a statement is his accepting the results in the form of karma, because being unaffected by karma is his very nature. Therefore it is correct to conclude that the Lord is the eater in the passage cited.

Sūtra – 1.2.10

|| prakaraṇāc ca ||

The eater refers to the Lord, because the Lord is the subject.

In the same section of the Kaṭha Upaniṣad it is said *aṇor aṇīyān mahatomahīyān*: the Lord is smaller than the small and greater than the great. (*Kaṭha Upaniṣad* 1.2.20) This indicates that the Lord is the topic of discussion. The word *ca* indicates that smṛti confirms this. *attāsi lokasya carācarasya*: you are the eater of all moving and non-moving beings.[20]

Topic 3 (Sūtras 11 – 12)

Guhādhikaraṇam - The person in the heart

In the same Upaniṣad it is said:

ṛtaṁ pibantau sukṛtasya loke
guhāṁ praviṣṭau parame parārdhe
chāyā-tapau brahma-vido vadanti
pañcāgnayo ye ca trināciketāḥ

The knowers of Brahman, who tend the five fires and perform the three *nāciketa* sacrifices, say that the two entities, one dark and one light, having entered the space in the heart, enjoy the results of karma in the body. Kaṭha Upaniṣad 1.3.1

The doubt is this. Is the person mentioned in this verse, who enjoys the results of karma with the jīva, the intelligence, or *prāṇa* or the Supreme Lord?

(Pūrva-pakṣa) The person who enjoys the results of karma can be the intelligence or *prāṇa,* since they accompany the jīva. But the person cannot be the Lord since he does not experience karma.

Sūtra – 1.2.11

|| guhāṁ praviṣṭāv ātmānau hi tad-darśanāt ||

The two beings in the space within the heart are the jīva and the Lord because that is described elsewhere.

The two entities in the space within the heart are the jīva and the Lord, not the jīva and intelligence or the jīva and prāṇa. Why? Because this description is also seen elsewhere.

yā prāṇena sambhavaty aditir devatāmayī
guhāṁ praviśya tiṣṭhantī yā bhūtebhir vyajāyata

---

[20] *pitāsi lokasya carācarasya* (you are the father of all moving and non-moving beings in the world) occurs in BG 11.43, and in that chapter Kṛṣṇa is described as devourer of the worlds.

The jīva, endowed with senses, who appears with various powers, entering the heart along with the *prāṇa*, remains there. Kaṭha Upaniṣad 2.1.7

taṁ durdarśaṁ gūḍham anupraviṣṭam
guhāhitaṁ gahvareṣṭaṁ purāṇam
adhyātma-yogādhigamena devaṁ
matvā dhīro harṣa-śokau jahāti

The sage who understands by means of meditation, the shining, eternal Lord, hard to perceive, who has entered the heart, and remains hidden there in its very depths, gives up joy and sorrow. Kaṭha Upaniṣad 1.2.12

These verses from the same Upaniṣad describe the jīva and the Lord entering the heart. Because of this description (*tad-darśaṇāt*), the other person must be the Lord. *Hi* indicates that the Purāṇas also confirm this. Both are described as the experiencers (*pibantau*) of the fruits of karma only to indicate the experience of karma in a general way. The Lord is the controller of the experience and the jīva is the actual experiencer. Or the above statement is similar to the statement "The umbrella carriers go" to indicate a crowd in which the umbrella carriers are conspicuous and numerous, in which persons not carrying umbrellas are also present. The jīva and the Lord are described as dark and light to indicate their degrees of knowledge or to show that the jīva is trapped in *saṁsāra*, whereas the Lord is not.

Sūtra – 1.2.12

|| viśeṣaṇāc ca ||

The Lord is the person accompanying the jīva because of distinctive qualities.

In this section of the Upaniṣad, the jīva and the Lord are to be known particularly by their positions, described as meditator (jīva) and object of meditation (the Lord). In the Kaṭha Upaniṣad text quoted earlier *tam durdarśam* describes the jīva as the meditator and the Lord as the object of meditation ("they known the Lord who is hard to know"). In the text under discussion, dark and light describe the jīva as ignorant and the Lord as full of knowledge. The following verse distinguishes the jīva as the attainer from the Lord as the object of attainment:

vijñāna-sārathir yas tu manaḥ-pragrahavān naraḥ
so 'dhvanaḥ pāram āpnoti tad viṣṇoḥ paramaṁ padam

The person, who has good intelligence as his charioteer and who holds firmly the reins of the mind, reaches the end of the path, the supreme abode of Viṣṇu. *Kaṭha Upaniṣad* 1.3.9

Topic 4 (Sūtras 13 – 17)

Antarādhikaraṇam - The person in the eye

It is said in Chāndogya Upaniṣad:

ya eṣo 'ntar-akṣiṇi puruṣo dṛśyate sa eṣa ātmeti hovāca. etad amṛtam ayam etad brahma tad yad yad asmin sarpir vodakaṁ vā siñcati vartmani eva gacchati. etaṁ sampad-dhāma ity ācakṣate etaṁ hi sarvāṇi kāmāny abhisaṁyanti

The person seen within the eye is the ātmā. He is immortal, he is Brahman. Because of his presence, if one sprinkles ghee or water on the eye, it runs off. He is called Sampad-dhāma (most pleasurable) because all desired objects enter him. Chāndogya Upaniṣad 4.15.1-2

The doubt is this. Is the person in the eye a reflection, a *devatā*, the jīva, or the Lord?

(Pūrva-pakṣa) It is merely a reflection of the jīva since the text states that the eye is the support for the reflection, and that this figure is visible. Or it can be the *devatā* of the eye, for Bṛhad-āraṇyaka Upaniṣad 5.5.2 says *eṣo'smin pratiṣṭhitaḥ*: the sun resides in the eye. Or the person in the eye can be the jīva for when the jīva sees an object using the eye, the jīva momentarily appears in the eye. The person in the eye could be any of these three, but not the Lord.

Sūtra – 1.2.13

|| antara upapatteḥ ||

The person in the eye is Paramātmā because of the evidence in the passage.

The person in the eye (*antara*) is Paramātmā. Why? Because of the evidence (*upapatteḥ*). This conclusion is proved in the passage itself by mention of qualities, indicated through words like *ātmā*, immortality, Brahman, being uncontaminated by water or ghee, and having all desirable objects in him.

Sūtra – 1.2.14

|| sthānādi-vyapadeśāc ca ||

The person in the eye is the Lord because of the scriptural statement that the Lord is situated there.

It is also stated in Bṛhad-āraṇyaka Upaniṣad 3.7.18 that Paramātmā is situated in the eye as its controller. *Yaś cakṣuṣi tiṣṭhan*: the Lord is situated in the eye.

Sūtra – 1.2.15

|| sukha-viśiṣṭābhidhānād eva ca ||

The person in the eye is the Lord because the description of the Lord endowed with bliss at the beginning of the topic should be applied to the later description of the person in the eye.

Prāṇo brahma kaṁ brahma khaṁ brahma: the Lord is *prāṇa,* the Lord is bliss, and the Lord is ether. (Chāndogya Upaniṣad 4.10.5) This statement, which says that the Lord is endowed with complete bliss, occurs at the beginning of the topic. This should also refer to the person in the eye who is described later. What is previously mentioned should be applied to the present topic. Though the topic of Agni-vidya comes between the description of the Lord as happiness and the description of the person in the eye, the intervening topic of Agni-vidyā is actually a sub-topic of Brahma-vidyā (which occurs previous to and after it). The word *viśiṣṭa* (endowed with) indicates that the Lord is endowed with attributes like *jñāna* as his very nature.

Sūtra – 1.2.16

|| śrutopaniṣatka-gaty-abhidhānāc ca ||

The person in the eye is Paramātmā because of other descriptions which indicate that the person who hears the Upaniṣads attains the Lord.

In another śruti, it says that one who knows the Upaniṣads and understands their meaning attains the Lord in the spiritual realm. Upakośala says *arciṣam abhisambhavanti*: persons who know the person in the eye go by the path of light (and attain liberation). (Chāndogya Upaniṣad 4.15.1) The person in the eye must therefore be the Lord in the spiritual realm.

Sūtra – 1.2.17

|| anavasthiter asambhāvāc ca netaraḥ ||

The person in the eye is not a reflection, prāṇa or the jīva because none of these reside permanently in the eye, and none have the qualities mentioned in the verse that describe that person.

It is not possible that the person in the eye is a reflection of the jīva, is the *prāṇa* or is the jīva because none of these permanently reside in the eye (*anavasthiteḥ*), and because all of them lack qualities (*asambhavāt*) like unconditioned immortality which are present in the person in the eye. Therefore the person in the eye is Paramātmā.

Topic 5 (Sūtras 18 – 20)

Antaryāmy-adhikaraṇam - The antaryāmī

Bṛhad-āraṇyaka Upaniṣad 3.7.18 says:

yaḥ pṛthivyāṁ tiṣṭhan pṛthivyā antaro yaṁ pṛtivī na veda yasya pṛthivī śarīraṁ yaḥ pṛthivīm antaro yamayaty eṣa ta ātmāntaryāmy amṛtaḥ

He who resides in the earth, he whom the earth does not know, he whose body is the earth and who, dwelling within, rules the earth, is the eternal *ātmā* within.

The doubt is this. Is the controller situated within the earth *pradhāna (prakṛti)*, the jīva or the Lord?

(Pūrva-pakṣa) It is *pradhāna* because *pradhāna* dwells in the earth and conforms to the other characteristics mentioned. The cause is necessarily connected with the effect. The cause is thus the controller of the effect. Thus *pradhāna* is the controller of the earth. *Pradhāna* may be called the *ātmā* figuratively because it gives pleasure (like the self). Because it is universally present or because it is eternal, *pradhāna* may be called *amṛta.*

The person dwelling in the earth may also be some yogī who is a jīva. Through yoga, by the power of entering everything, a jīva can become a controller, and by his power of being invisible, he can become invisible (earth does not know him). Being a jīva, he is naturally called ātmā and is eternal.

Thus the person dwelling in the earth is either *pradhāna* or a jīva.

Sūtra – 1.2.18

|| antaryāmy adhidaivādiṣu tad-dharma-vyapadeśāt ||

The *antaryāmī* is the Lord because the qualities mentioned in the passage are suitable to the Lord.

He who is known in the scripture quoted above as *antaryāmī* is the Supreme Lord. Why? Because the qualities mentioned there, such as dwelling within everything like earth, being unknown, being the controller, being all-pervading, being a knower, being filled with bliss and being immortal, belong to the Lord.

Sūtra – 1.2.19

|| na ca smārtam atad-dharmābhilāpāt ||

The *antaryāmī* is not *pradhāna* because qualities are mentioned that do not belong to *pradhāna*.

Because of the reasons mentioned, *pradhāna (smārtam)* cannot be called the *antaryāmī.* Why? Because of mention of qualities that do not belong to *pradhāna (atad-dharma).*

adṛṣṭo draṣṭā aśruto śrotā amato mantā avijñāto 'āto vijñātā nānyato 'sti draṣṭā nānayto 'sti śrotā nānyato 'sti mantā nānyato 'sti vijñātaiṣa ta ātmāntaryāmy amṛta ito 'nyat smārtam

Though unseen, he is the seer. Though unheard, he is the hearer. Though unthinkable, he is the thinker. Though unknown, he is the knower. There is no other seer, no other hearer, no other thinker and no other knower. He is your ātmā, the *antaryāmī,* and immortal. He is different from the *pradhāna* mentioned in the smṛtis. Bṛhad-āraṇyaka Upaniṣad 3.7.23

It is impossible for pradhāna to have these qualities.

Sūtra – 1.2.20

|| śārīraś cobhaye'pi hi bhedenaivanam adhīyate ||

The *antaryāmī* is not a yogī. Both versions of the text indicate that the yogī is different from the *antaryāmī.*

The word *na* should be added to the sūtra from the previous sūtra. For the reasons already given, the yogī (*śārīraḥ*) cannot be the *antaryāmī* of earth.

Why? Because (*hi*) both recensions (*ubhaye*), Kānva and Madhyandina, say that the yogī is different from the *antaryāmī*. The Kāṇva recension reads *yo vijñānam anataro yamayati*: he who is within the jīva controls the knower. The Mādhyandina ṛecension reads *ya ātmānam antaro yamayati*: he who is within the ātmā controls the ātmā. Both versions indicate that there is a difference, one person being the controlled and the other being the controller. Therefore the *antaryāmī* is the Supreme Lord. Subāla Upaniṣad mentions that Nārāyaṇa is the *antaryāmī* of the earth and the other elements, the *antaryāmī* of *pradhāna (avyakta),* the *antaryāmī* of the jīva (*akṣara*) and finally the antaryāmī of destruction (*mṛtyu*).[21] One of these verses spoken by the brāhmaṇa is as follows:

antaḥ-śarīre nihito guhāyām aja eko nityaḥ yasya pṛthivī śarīraṁ yaḥ pṛthivīm antare sañcaran yaṁ pṛthivī na veda

He who is one, unborn, and eternal, residing within the heart in the body, has the earth as his body, spreads within the earth. The earth does not know him. Subāla Upaniṣad 7.1

Topic 6 (Sūtras 21 – 24)

Adṛśyādhikaraṇam - The unseen person

The *Muṇḍaka Upaniṣad* (1.1.5-6) says:

atha parā yayā tad akṣaram adhigamyate. yat tad adṛśyam agrāhyam agotram avarṇam acakṣuḥ-śrotraṁ tad apāṇi-pādaṁ nityaṁ vibhuṁ sarva-gataṁ su-sūkṣmaṁ tad avyayaṁ yad bhūta-yoniṁ paripaśyanti dhīrāḥ

This is the spiritual knowledge by which the Lord *(akṣara)* can be understood. The wise see the Lord who cannot be seen or grasped, who is without name, without color, without eyes and ears, without hands and feet, who is eternal, powerful, all-pervasive, the smallest, unchangeable, and the source of all beings.

Later *Muṇḍaka Upaniṣad* (2.1.2) also says:

divyo hy amūrtaḥ puruṣah sa-bāhyābhyantaro hy ajaḥ aprāṇo hy amanāḥ śubhro 'kṣarāt parataḥ paraḥ

---

[21] The commentary text says nectar or immortality (*amṛta*), but the common version of the Upaniṣad has death (*mṛta*).

The attractive person is without form, is inside and outside, is unborn, without *prāṇas,* without mind, pure, and superior to the *akṣara (prakṛti).*

The doubt is this. Do these two statements speak of *prakṛti* and the *jīva (puruṣa)* or the Lord?

(Pūrva-pakṣa) The first quotation speaks of *prakṛti* called *akṣara* because qualities of a conscious being such as being a seer are not mentioned and the source *(yoni)* refers to the material cause of the universe. The second quotation describes the jīva since it is described as being superior to the akṣara or prakṛti, which undergoes transformations.

Thus the first quotation refers to prakṛti and the second refers to the jīva. The *siddhānta* follows.

Sūtra – 1.2.21

|| adṛśtvādi-guṇako dharmokteḥ ||

The verses refer to the Lord full of qualities like invisibility because they mention particular qualities appropriate to the Lord.

Both verses refer to Paramātmā, who has qualities such as invisibility (*adṛśtvādi-guṇakaḥ*). Why? Because the verses mention the Lord's qualities (*dharmokteḥ*).

The *Muṇḍaka Upaniṣad* (1.1.9) says:

yaḥ sarvajñaḥ sarvavid yasya jñānamayaṁ tapaḥ. tasmād etad brahma nāma-rūpam annaṁ ca jāyate

From Brahman, who is omniscient, knowing everything, whose austerity is filled with knowledge, arose Brahman as food, which has name and form.

The passage refers to the Lord because appropriate qualities are mentioned and because the section deals with *para-vidyā*, superior knowledge.

Sūtra – 1.2.22

|| viśeṣeṇa bheda-vyapadeśāc ca netarau ||

The verses do not refer to *prakṛti* or the jīva because words distinguish the Lord from prakṛti in the first passage and words distinguish the Lord from the jīva in the second.

The other two *(itarau)*, *prakṛti* and jīva, cannot be indicated by the verses because the words such as omniscience in the first verse distinguish the being from prakṛti and because the words like *divya* in the second verse distinguish the being from the jīva. Thus both verses refer to the Supreme Person who is the cause of everything.

Sūtra – 1.2.23

|| rūpopanyāsāc ca ||

And the two passages indicate the Lord because of other passages which specifically describe the form of Lord, using the same description.

The Lord is indicated because other passages describe (*upanyāsāt*) the form (*rūpa*) of the Lord, called akṣara, as the source of all beings (*brahma-yonim*).

yadā paśyaḥ paśyate rukma-varṇaṁ
kārtāram īśaṁ puruṣaṁ brahma-yonim
tadā vidvān puṇya-pāpe vidhūya
nirañjanaḥ paramaṁ samyam upaiti

When the perceiver sees the Lord *(īśam)* a golden person, the source of Brahmā, the cause of the universe, that person, full of knowledge, washed of piety and sin, spotless, attains a form similar the Lord's. Muṇḍaka Upaniṣad 3.1.3

The form is Paramātmā, not jīva or *prakṛti.*

Sūtra – 1.2.24

|| prakaraṇāc ca ||

The texts refer to the Lord because of the context.

The meaning is clear.

The *smṛti-śāstra* also confirms that this text refers to Lord Viṣṇu. The *Viṣṇu Purāṇa* (6.5.65-70) says:

dve vidye veditavye iti cātharvaṇī śrutiḥ
parayā tv akṣara-prāptiḥ ṛg-vedādi-mayī aparā

The Muṇḍaka Upaniṣad of the Atharva Veda says there are two types of knowledge to be known: *parā vidyā* to attain the Lord, akṣara, and *aparā vidya*, consisting of the Ṛg Veda and other *saṁhitās.*

yat tad avyaktam ajaram acintyam ajam avyayam
anirdeśyam arūpaṁ ca pānipādādy-asaṁyutam

This akṣara, the Lord, is invisible, without old age, inconceivable, without birth, without decay, indefinable, without material form and without hands or feet.

vibhuṁ sarva-gataṁ nityaṁ bhūta-yonim akāraṇam
vyāpy-avyāpyaṁ yataḥ sarvaṁ tad vai paśyanti sūrayaḥ

He is powerful, all-pervasive, eternal, the cause of all beings, without cause, pervading everything but unpervaded, from which everything arises. The wise know this Lord.

tad brahma paramaṁ dhāma tad dhyeyaṁ mokṣa-kāṅkṣiṇām
śruti-vākyoditaṁ sūkṣmaṁ tad viṣṇoḥ paramaṁ padam

The supreme abode is Brahman. It is the object of meditation for persons desiring liberation. What is described in the scriptures is this most subtle, supreme abode of Viṣṇu.

tad eva bhagavad-vācyaṁ svarūpaṁ paramātmanaḥ
vācako bhagavac-chabdas tasyādyasyākṣarātmanaḥ

He is called Bhagavān, the form of the supreme ātmā. The word Bhagavān denotes the first, imperishable being.

evaṁ nigaditārthasya sat-tattvaṁ tasya tattvataḥ
jñāyate yena taj-jñānaṁ param anyat trayīmayam

This is the highest truth concerning Bhagavān, as explained. By this truth, one truly realizes the highest knowledge. It is superior to everything else in the three Vedas.

Topic 7 (Sūtras 25 – 33)

Vaiśvānarādhikaraṇam – The meaning of Vaiśvānara

ko nu ātmā kiṁ brahmeti

Who is the ātmā? Who is Brahman? Chāndogya Upaniṣad 5.11.1

ātmānam evaṁ vaiśvānaraṁ sampraty adhyeṣi tam eva no bruhi

You know about the ātmā, Vaiśvānara. Please describe him. Chāndogya Upaniṣad 5.11.6) *yas tv enam evaṁ prādeśa-mātram abhivimānam ātmānaṁ vaiśvānaraṁ upāste sa sarveṣu lokeṣu sarveṣu bhūteṣu sarveṣu ātmasu annam atti etasya ha vā etasyātmano vaiśvānarasya mūrdhaiva su-tejāś cakṣur viśvarūpaḥ prāṇaḥ pṛthag-vartmā sandeho bahulo vastir eva rayiḥ pṛthivy eva pādāv ura eva vedir lomānir bahir hṛdayaṁ gārhapatyo mano 'nvāhāryapacana āsyam āhvanīyaḥ*

One who meditates on the ātmā Vaiśvānara, who is limitless but the size of the distance between the thumb and forefinger, eats food in all worlds, in all elements, and in all hearts. Suteja (heaven) is the head of Vaiśvānara, Viśvarūpa (sun) is his eye, pṛthagvartmā (air) is his prāna, Bahula (ether) is his trunk, Rayi (water) is his abdomen, the earth is his feet, the sacrificial altar is his chest, the sacrificial grass is his hair, the *gārhapatya* fire is his heart, the *anvāhāryapacana* fire is his mind, and the *āhavanīya* fire is his mouth. Chāndogya Upaniṣad 5.18.1-2

The doubt is this. Is the *vaiśvānara* the fire of digestion, the *devatā* Agni, the element fire or Viṣṇu? Since the word is used for all these four, it is inconclusive which one it is.

Sūtra – 1.2.25

|| vaiśvānara-sādhāraṇa-śabda-viśeṣāt ||

The word refers to Viṣṇu because words mentioned particularize the general meaning of Vaiśvānara.

Vaiśvānara is Viṣṇu alone. Why? Because of descriptive words that apply only to the Lord (*sādhāraṇa-śabda-viśeṣāt*). The meaning is this. Even though the word *vaiśvānara* is used for all four objects, in this passage it is described in conjunction with words such as heaven and head, which apply to Viṣṇu only. By this, one can understand that Viṣṇu is meant. The beginning of the passage mentions *ātmā* and Brahman.[22] These words also indicate that Viṣṇu is Vaiśvānara. The result of knowing Vaiśvānara at the end of the passage -- sins are burned up like a reed (*yatheṣika-tulam*) -- is also the result ascribed only to knowing Viṣṇu. Etymologically the word "Vaiśvānara" means Viṣṇu for it is composed of *viśva* (all) and *nara* (men) which means "he who is the shelter of all men." Therefore Vaiśvānara refers to Viṣṇu.

---

[22] *ko nu ātmā kiṁ brahmeti*

Sūtra – 1.2.26

|| smaryamāṇam anumānaṁ syād iti ||

Vaiśvānara is Viṣṇu because one can infer the same from smṛti passages.

The word *iti* denotes a reason.

ahaṁ vaiśvānaro bhūtvā prāṇināṁ deham āśritaḥ

Becoming Vaiśvānara, I take shelter in the bodies of all beings. BG 15.14

In this smṛti passage Vaiśvānara is identified with Viṣṇu. Thus one may infer that the Vaiśvānara-vidyā is in reference to Viṣṇu. Because of this, Vaiśvānara is Viṣṇu.

Vaiśvānara cannot mean the digestive fire.

Sūtra – 1.2.27

|| śabdādibhyo'ntaḥpratiṣṭhānāc ca neti cen na,
tathā-dṛṣṭy-upadeśāsambhavāt,
puruṣa-vidham api cainam adhīyate ||

If one argues that the Vaiśvānara is the fire of digestion because it is described in many places as the fire dwelling within, the answer is "no" because such descriptions of Vaiśvānara as the fire in the heart are for the purpose of meditation on Viṣṇu and because descriptions of heaven and head are impossible to apply to the digestive fire. Furthermore other texts describe this fire as having the form of a man.

(Pūrva-pakṣa) "Vaiśvānara is not Viṣṇu. For it is said in the text *ayam agnir vaiśvānaraḥ*: the fire is Vaiśvānara. It is also said that the heart is the *gārhapatya* fire. It is situated in the heart and other places as fire while being designated as three fires. It is also explained in the text that oblations are offered into this fire in the form of offerings to the *prāṇas*. It is said in other śrutis as well that the fire is situated in the heart: *puruṣe 'ntaḥ-pratiṣṭhitaṁ veda* (Śatapatha-brāhmaṇa 10.6.1.11) Thus Vaiśvānara in this text refers to the digestive fire."

The answer is "No." Why? Because such descriptions of Vaiśvānara as the fire in the heart are for the purpose of meditation on Viṣṇu (*tathā dṛṣti*) and because descriptions of heaven and head are impossible to apply to the digestive fire.

Moreover, it is said in another śruti that this fire has the shape of a man. *sa yo hy etam evāgniṁ vaiśvānaraṁ puruṣa-vidhaṁ puruṣe 'ntaḥ pratiṣṭitaṁ veda:* he who knows this fire of Vaiśvānara with the form of a man, situated within man, conquers death. *(Śatapatha Brāhmaṇa* 10.6.1.11) If one takes the Vaiśvānara as the digestive fire, it certainly resides within man, but it does not have the shape of a human. Both descriptions however apply to Viṣṇu.

The next sūtra refutes the idea that this fire is the *devatā* Agni or the element fire.

Sūtra – 1.2.28

|| ata eva na devatā bhūtaṁ ca ||

Because of the reasons mentioned above, Vaiśvānara is not the *devatā* Agni or the element fire.

(Pūrva-pakṣa) "Because the *devatā* Agni, being endowed with great power, has the heavens as his head, the passage can refer to the *devatā* Agni or to the element fire. The following description is found in the Vedas. *yo bhānunā pṛthivī dyām utemām ātatāna rodasī antarīkṣam:* Agni, in the form of the sun, is spread through the earth, heaven, and everything between. *Rg Veda* (10.88.3)"

The answer is no. Why? Because of what has been stated already (*ata eva*). Vaiśvānara is not the *devatā* fire or the element fire. The above mantra quoted is mere praise (and not to be taken literally.)

According to Jaimini and others, the word *agni,* like the word Vaiśvānara, primarily denotes Viṣṇu. This is explained in the next sūtra.

Sūtra – 1.2.29

|| sākṣād apy avirodhaṁ jaiminiḥ ||

According to Jaimini there is no contradiction in saying that Vaiśvānara is Agni because the etymological meaning of the two words is the same.

Vaiśvānara means "he who is the shelter of all men" because he is the leader of all beings in the universe or because he is the cause of everything. Similarly Agni means Viṣṇu. Etymologically it means "he who leads in front (*agre nayati*)." Thus there is no contradiction in saying Vaiśvānara is Agni because the meaning depends on the particular qualities expressed by the words. This is the opinion of Jaimini.

"How can the Lord be limited to a small size--the distance between the thumb and forefinger?" That is answered in the next sūtra.

Sūtra – 1.2.30

|| abhivyakter ity āśmarathyaḥ ||

Āśmarathya says that Viṣṇu appears in this size for the devotees.

Āśmarathya says that Viṣṇu becomes this size for the worshippers who meditate on the Lord in the heart which is that size.

Sūtra – 1.2.31

|| anusmṛter iti bādariḥ ||

According to Bādari, the Lord is described as being this size simply for meditational purposes.

Bādari says that the Lord is described with this size because the worshipper meditates in his mind on the Lord being situated in the heart, which is this size.

Sūtra – 1.2.32

|| sampatter iti jaiminis tathā hi darśayati ||

Jaimini says the Lord can be the size of a *pradeśa* because he has inconceivable powers, since this is stated in many texts.

Jaimini says that the powerful Lord can be the size of a *pradeśa* because he has a form with inconceivable *śakti.* That size is, therefore, not a limitation on the Lord. Why? Because (*hi*) texts show this power.

tam ekaṁ govindaṁ sac-cid-ānanda-vigraham

He is the one Govinda, who has a form of eternity, knowledge and bliss. Gopāla-tāpanī Upaniṣad 1.33

eko 'pi san bahudhā yo 'vabhāti

Though he is one, he is also many. Gopāla-tāpanī Upaniṣad 1.19

These śruti texts show that the Lord has contrary qualities within him by his inconceivable *śakti.* Though he is knowledge itself, he has a form, and though he is one he is many. This will be explained in detail later. Thus, though he is the all powerful Lord, he is also of medium size.

Sūtra – 1.2.33

|| āmananti cainam asmin ||

The followers of the Atharva Veda describe the inconceivable powers in the Lord.

The followers of the Atharva Veda describe (*āmananti*) this quality of inconceivable śakti (*enam*) in the Lord (*asmin*). *apāṇi-pādo 'ham acintya-śaktiḥ:* endowed with inconceivable *śakti,* I have no hands or feet. (Kaivalyopaniṣad 21)[23] Smṛti says *ātmeśvaro 'tarkya-sahasra-śaktiḥ:* you are endowed with thousands of inconceivable energies. (SB 3.33.3)

As regards the opinions of the other sages cited here, it should be understood that there is no contradiction between their opinions and the opinions of Vyāsa.

vyāsa-citta-sthitākāśād avicchinnāni kānicit
anye vyavaharanty etad urī-kṛtya gṛhādivat

Other sages accept and use some of Vyāsa's individual conclusions, which are like houses which separate into parts the vast sky situated in Vyāsa's heart. Skanda Purāṇa.

[23] This Upaniṣad actually belongs to the Kṛṣṇa Yajur Veda, not the Atharva Veda.

Section Three

viśvaṁ bibharti niḥsvaṁ yaḥ kāruṇyena devarāṭ |
mamāsau paramānando govindas tanutāṁ ratim ||

May Govinda, who is full of the highest bliss, who is the ruler of the *devatās,* and who maintains the destitute world by his mercy, bestow prema to me.

Topic 1 (Sūtras 1 – 7)

Dyu-bhv-ādy-adhikaraṇam - Abode of Heaven and earth

In the third pāda, some statements which seem to indicate jīva and prakṛti are shown to refer to Brahman. In Muṇḍaka Upaniṣad it is said:

yasmin dyauḥ pṛthivī cāntarikṣam
otaṁ manaḥ saha prāṇaiś ca sarvaiḥ |
tam evaikaṁ jānatha ātmānam anyā
vāco vimuñcathāmṛtasyaiṣa setuḥ ||

Know the one *ātmā* within whom heaven, earth*, antarikṣa* and mind are woven along with all the *prāṇas.* Give up all other words. He is the bridge of immortality. Muṇḍaka Upaniṣad 2.2.5

There is a doubt in this statement. Is the abode of heaven, earth etc. *pradhāna,* the jīva or Brahman?

(Pūrva-pakṣa) It refers to *pradhāna* since it is the abode of everything, because *pradhāna* is the cause of all transformations. *Pradhāna* can be called the bridge to immortality because it arranges for liberation of humans, just milk produces nourishment of the calf. The word *ātmā* is used to describe *pradhāna* figuratively, since it gives joy to the jīvas, or because it pervades everything *(ātmā* means that which spreads out).

Or it refers to the jīva because the jīva is the abode of heaven, earth etc. which are enjoyed, since he is the enjoyer. Also it is well known that the jīva is endowed with mind and *prāṇas.*

Sūtra – 1.3.1

|| dyu-bhv-ādy-āyatanaṁ sva-śabdāt ||

The Lord is the abode of the heavens and earth because he is the bridge to immortality.

Brahman is the abode of all these. Why? Because of the unusual words mentioned in the statement: he is the bridge to immortality. The word *setu* comes from the verb *sinoti* (he binds but in this case he increases). Thus "bridge to immortality" means "he who causes the jīva to attain immortality." Or the Lord is like a bridge, for crossing *saṁsāra* to gain liberation just as one uses a bridge to cross a river to get to the other bank. Therefore the word refers to the Lord only. Śruti says *tam eva viditvāimṛtyuma eti*: knowing him one surpasses death. (Śvetāśvatara Upaniṣad)

There is another reason.

Sūtra – 1.3.2

|| muktopasṛpya-vyapadeśāt ||

It refers to the Lord because he is attained by liberated souls.

Later in the same Upaniṣad it is *said yadā paśyaḥ paśyate rukma-varṇam... nirañjanaḥ paramaṁ sāmyam upaiti:* when the seer sees the golden person, he, being pure, attains a form similar to the supreme. (Muṇḍaka Upaniṣad 3.1.3) He who is attained by the liberated souls can only be Brahman.

Sūtra – 1.3.3

|| nānumānam atac-chabdāt ||

***Pradhāna* cannot be meant because some of the words refer to a conscious entity.**

The proposed *pradhāna* cannot be meant in the passage. Why? Because the passage does not contain any words that refer to the unconscious *pradhāna (atac-chabdāt)*, whereas it contains words like omniscience that refer to a conscious being.

Sūtra – 1.3.4

|| prāṇa-bhṛc ca ||

The abode of heaven and earth is not the jīva because there are no words describing the jīva in the passage.

Na and the cause, *atac-cabdha*, should be understood from the previous sūtra. The passage does not refer to the jīva because it does not contain any words referring to the jīva. The word *ātmā* cannot be mean the jīva in this passage because etymologically *ātmā* means that which spreads out (*ātati*) and Brahman is the principal entity which does so, being all -pervading. And all other words such as *yaḥ sarva-jñāḥ sarva-vit:* he is all-knowing (Muṇḍaka 2.7) apply to Brahman, not the jīva. Thus, since there are no words describing the jīva, the jīva should not be accepted as the abode of heaven and earth.

There is another reason why the passage does not refer to the jīva.

Sūtra – 1.3.5

|| bheda-vyapadeśāc ca ||

The passage does not refer to the jīva because of indications of difference.

The passage says "Know this one entity (*tam evaikam*)" shows that something different from jīva is meant (since jīvas are many, and the entity that the jīva is being told to know has to different from the jiva himself).

Sūtra – 1.3.6

|| prakaraṇāt ||

It does not refer to the jīva because of the context.

The Upaniṣad begins with a question about Brahman. *kasmin nu bhagavo vijñate sarvam idam; vijñātam bhavati:* what is that by which, being known, all things are known? (Muṇḍaka Upaniṣad 1.1.3). (Therefore, this passage which follows after this initial question should also refer to Brahman.)

Sūtra – 1.3.7

|| sthity-adanābhyāṁ ca ||

It does not refer to the jīva because of a later statement concerning birds in a tree in which one bird eats the fruit.

Later, concerning the abode of heaven and earth, it is said:

dvā suparṇā sayujā sakhāyā
samānaṁ vṛkṣaṁ pariṣasvajāte |
tayor anyaḥ pippalaṁ svādv atty
anaśnann anyo abhicākaśīti ||

Two beautiful birds associate in the same tree as friends. Of the two, one relishes eating the fruit. The other, not eating, shines. Muṇḍaka Upaniṣad 3.1.1

In the above verse whom does he who shines (*abhicakāśiti*) refer to? If previous to this verse, the abode of heaven and earth (referring to Brahman) had not been mentioned, then the sudden mention of Brahman in this verse (one who shines) would be meaningless. Then, one who shines would have referred to the jīva. But this phrase does not refer to the jīva because it repeats a phrase which is well known as a description of the Lord[24]. Thus, the previous reference to the abode of heaven and earth must also mean Brahman.

Topic 2 (Sūtras 8 – 9)

Bhūmādhikaraṇam - The great one

Being asked by Nārada, Sanatkumāra instructed him concerning the name.

bhūmā tv eva vijijñāsitavya iti bhūmānaṁ bhagavo vijijñāsa iti | |
yatra nānyat paśyati nānyac chṛṇoti nānyad vijānāti sa bhūmā |
atha yatrānyat paśyaty anyac chṛṇoty anyad vijānāti tad alpam

You should inquire about *bhūmā.* He said, "Teach me about *bhūmā,* O saintly one!" *Bhūmā* is where one sees nothing else, hears nothing else, and knows nothing else. Where one sees something else, hears something else, or knows something else, one knows something insignificant or small. Chāndogya Upaniṣad 7.23.1-24.1

Here *bhūmā* does not refer to numerical quantity (many) but to great pervasiveness, or largeness of form. This can be inferred from the statement that seeing something else is insignificant or small. Therefore an object possessing the quality of largeness is indicated because it must be the opposite of a small object.

Here is the doubt. Is *bhūmā* the *prāṇa* or Viṣṇu?

(Pūrva-pakṣa) Because previously in the same text it was said *prāṇo vā āśāyā bhūyān*: *prāṇa* is better than hope (7.15.1) and there was no question or

---

[24] Two birds in a tree is also described in Śvetāśvatāra Upaniṣad. The other bird is described as īśam (the Lord.)

reply, *bhūmā* must be *prāṇa. Prāṇa* refers to the jīva who is accompanied by *prāṇa.* It does not mean the modification of air element called *prāṇa.* The section begins with *tarati śokam ātmavit*: the knower of ātmā surpasses lamentation (7.1.3) and ends with *ātmataḥ evedaṁ sarvam*: all of this is from ātmā. Therefore the word *bhūmā* in the middle of the section means the jīva. The description of "where one sees nothing else" fits the jīva for there is elimination of seeing etc. during deep sleep when the senses enter *prāṇa.* It is said *yo vai bhūmā tat sukham: bhūmā* is bliss. (7.23.1) This is not contrary to the jīva for the jīva says "I slept happily in deep sleep." After discerning that *bhūmā* refers to the jīva, the remaining descriptions of *bhūmā* can be made to align favorably to this.

Sūtra – 1.3.8

|| bhūmā samprasādād adhyupadeśāt ||

Bhūmā refers to the Lord because the text states that he has a form of bliss and this teaching comes at the end as the highest teaching.

Bhūmā is Viṣṇu, not the jīva endowed with *prāṇa.* Why? Because it is said in the text that he has a form of great bliss. *Yo vai bhūmā tat sukham*: he who is Bhūmā has happiness. (7.23.1) and because among all the teachings, this is the highest, coming at the end. Or *samprasāda* can refer to the jīva. *Evam evaiṣa samprasādo 'smāc charīrāt samutthāya*: the object of mercy rises from this body. (Chāndogya Upaniṣad 8.12.3) Thus the meaning can also be "Bhūmā means Viṣṇu because the Lord has qualities greater than the jīva who is called *samprasāda.*"

The meaning is this. Previously, after teaching about the name, Sanat-kumāra says *sa vā eṣa evaṁ paśyann evaṁ manvāna evam; jijānann ativādī bhavati:* he, seeing this *prāṇa,* being aware of this *prāṇā,* and understanding this, becomes an *ativādī.* (Chāndogya Upaniṣad 7.15.4) Then the word *tu* is used to make a distinction from becoming an *ativādī* by worshipping of *prāṇa,* which was being discussed. The word *satya* is used to indicate Viṣṇu. Knowing him, one becomes a true *ativādī.* He is distinct from *prāṇa* and can be equated with *bhūmā.* If *prāṇa* were *bhūmā,* then it would not be possible to say in the text that higher than *prāṇa* is *bhūmā.* Various objects are considered higher than the previous one mentioned. Higher than name is speech. Higher than *prāṇa* is *satya* or *bhūmā.*

As well, *satya* is well known to indicate Viṣṇu, the supreme Brahman. *Satyam jñānam anantaṁ brahma:* the unlimited Brahman is *satyam* and knowledge. *Satyam param dhīmahi*: let us meditate on the supreme *satya,* Viṣṇu.

He is the true *ativādī* because of the supreme Brahman (*satyena*). Meditation on *prāṇa* is superior to meditation on name, etc up to hope. Compared to those who do not know *prāṇa,* the worshipper of *prāṇa* is superior or *ativādī.* But meditation on Viṣṇu is superior. Thus such a person is the chief *ativādī.* The *ativādī* of Satya is better than the *ativādī* of *prāṇa.* The pupil asks *so'haṁ bhagavaḥ satyenātivadāni:* may I be an *ativādī* because of Satya. The guru responds *satyaṁ tv eva vijijñasitavyam*: one should desire to known Satya (Chāndogya Upaniṣad 97.16.1)

One cannot say that because there is no question and answer about something greater than *prāṇa,* being an *ativādī* of *prāṇa* is the same as being an *ativādī* of the Lord. The reason is that there is no instruction to equate *prāṇa* with *satya.* One may ask why the disciple does not ask about something higher than *prāṇa.*

The answer is this. In the list of unconscious items starting with name and ending with hope, it is taught that the latter item is superior to the former. The knower of these is not called an *ativādī* by the teacher. He then teaches about *prāna,* which means the jīva. The knower of jīva is called an *ativādī.* The pupil thinks that this is the final teaching. Therefore he does not ask about anything higher. The teacher, not accepting that idea, teaches about Satya, with the understanding that the highest knowledge is the form of Viṣṇu. The pupil, being taught that Viṣṇu is the best, and desiring to learn the nature of Viṣṇu's form and method of his worship, requests that he also should become an *ativādī* of Viṣṇu with the words *so 'haṁ bhagavaḥ satyenātivādāni.* (Chāndogya Upaniṣad 7.26.1)

One cannot say that the word *ātmā* refers to the jīva accompanied by *prāṇa,* using the argument that the word *ātmā* is mentioned at the beginning and also at the end. The word *ātmā* applies etymologically (all pervading) primarily to the Lord, not to the jīva. Later also it is said *ātmanaḥ prāṇaḥ:* the jīva arises from ātmā. (Chāndogya Upaniṣad 7.26.1) Accepting that *bhūmā* means Viṣṇu, there is harmony with the statement "*Bhūmā* exists where nothing else can be seen." This defeats the idea that *bhūmā* means the jīva.

When one experiences the Lord, the experiencer, completely absorbed in him, cannot see or hear anything else.

Since the happiness experienced during deep sleep is meager, it is ridiculous to say that the jīva in deep sleep is what is referred to by the term *bhūmā*. Thus *bhūmā* refers to Viṣṇu alone.

Sūtra – 1.3.9

|| dharmopapatteś ca ||

Bhūmā refers to Viṣṇu, because of the evidence--qualities appropriate to Viṣṇu are mentioned in the text.

The qualities mentioned in relation to *bhūmā* are applicable to the supreme Brahman and to no one else. *yo vai bhūmā tad amṛtam*: he who is *bhūmā* is immortal. (Chāndogya Upaniṣad 7.24.1) This shows that the Lord is naturally eternal. *sa bhagavaḥ kasmin pratiṣṭhita iti sve mahimni*: what is the basis of *bhūmā*? He is fixed in his own glory. (Chāndogya Upaniṣad 7.24.1) This indicates a person who has no other shelter than himself (being independent). He alone is thus the shelter of everything else. *Ātmataḥ prāṇaḥ:* from him arises the jīva. This indicates that he is the cause of everything.

Topic 3 (Sūtras 10 – 12)

Akṣarādhikaraṇam - The imperishable

It is said in Bṛhad-āraṇyaka Upaniṣad 3.8.7-8:

kasmin nu khalv ākāśa otaś ca protaś ceti |
etad vai tad akṣaraṁ gārgi brāhmaṇā abhivadanty asthūlam anaṇv
ahrasvam adīrgham alohitam asneham acchāyam

In what is this *ākāśa* woven? O Gārgī, the brāhmaṇas say that this *akṣara* is not big or small, it is not short or long, it is without blood, without fat and without shadow.

This is the doubt. Is this *akṣara* the *pradhāna,* the jīva or Brahman? Among the three, none of them are clearly defined because the word *akṣara* is used for all three.

Sūtra – 1.3.10

|| akṣaram ambarānta-dhṛteḥ ||

***Akṣara* refers to Brahman because Brahman supports everything up to ether.**

Akṣara is Brahman. Why? Because this *akṣara* supports everything including the *ākāśa* according to the text *tasmin nu khalv akṣare gārgy ākāśa otaś ca protaś ca*: O Gārgī, the ether is woven in that *akṣara*. (Bṛhad-āraṇyaka Upaniṣad 3.8.12)

"That could mean *pradhāna,* since p*radhāna* is the cause of all transformation. That could mean the jīva, since the jīva is the shelter of all unconscious objects, useful for his enjoyment." In response it is said:

Sūtra – 1.3.11

|| sā ca praśāsanāt ||

Brahman is the akṣara because only Brahman commands.

Brahman supports everything including the ether. Why? Because commanding can be done only by Brahman, and not by *pradhāna* or the jīva.

etasya vā akṣarasya praśāsane gārgi dyāv-āpṛthivyau vidhṛte tiṣṭhataḥ |
etasya vā akṣarasya sūryā-candramasau vidhṛtau tiṣṭhataḥ

By the command of *akṣara,* heaven and earth remain in their place. By the command of *akṣara*, the sun and moon remain in their place. Bṛhad-āraṇyaka Upaniṣad3.8.9

Commanding and supporting everything is impossible for unconscious pradhāna, and for the jīva, either conditioned or liberated.

Sūtra – 1.3.12

|| anya-bhāva-vyāvṛtteś ca ||

Both jīva and *pradhāna* are excluded because of the qualities of *akṣara* mentioned in the text.

Other statements in the text indicate that Brahman is the *akṣara,* not *pradhāna* or the jīva.

tad vā etad akṣaraṁ gārgy adṛṣṭaṁ draṣṭṛ, aśrutaṁ śrotṛ: this *akṣara* is the seer but unseen, and is the hearer but not heard. (Bṛhad-āraṇyaka Upaniṣad 3.8.11) *Pradhāna* is excluded because, being unconscious, it cannot see or hear. Because the text says that the *akṣara* cannot be seen by anyone but sees everything, it cannot be the jīva.

Topic 4 (Sūtra 13)

Īkṣati-karmādhikaraṇam - The person seen

It is said in Praśna Upaniṣad:

etad vai satyakāma paraṁ cāparaṁ ca brahma yad oṁkāras tasmād vidvān etenaivāyatanenaikataram anveti

O Satyakāma! This higher and lower Brahman is oṁkāra. Therefore by this means, the knower attains one of these. Praśna Upaniṣad 5.2

yaḥ punar etaṁ trimātreṇaiva om ity etenaivākṣareṇa paraṁ puruṣam abhidhyāyīta, sa tejasi sūrye sampannaḥ / yathā pādodaras tvacā vinirmucyata evaṁ ha vai sa pāpmanā vinirmuktaḥ sa sāmabhir unnīyate brahma-lokaṁ sa etasmāj jīva-ghanāt parāt-paraṁ puriśayaṁ puruṣam īkṣate.

He who by the three syllables of oṁ meditates on the supreme person attains the bright sun. As a snake becomes freed from its old skin, this person becomes freed of sin. He rises to Brahmaloka by chanting the Sāma verses. He sees that person in his abode, that person who is superior to the mass of jīvas. Praśna Upaniṣad 5.5

The doubt is this. Is the person seen and meditated upon Brahmā or the Supreme Lord?

(Pūrva-pakṣa) It is explained that the worshipper of one syllable of oṁ reaches the world of men. The worshipper of two syllables reaches *antarikṣa.* The worshipper of three syllables attains Brahma-loka. According to the sequence of planets, Brahma-loka must mean the planet of Brahma, Satyaloka. Going there, a person sees Brahmā. Thus the person mentioned is Brahmā, not the Lord.

Sūtra – 1.3.13

|| īkṣati-karma vyapadeśāt saḥ ||

This person seen is Viṣṇu because the qualities described refer to Viṣṇu.

The Supreme Lord is who is seen *(īkṣati-karma)*. Why? Because the person seen is described (*vyapadeśāt*) as having the qualities of Brahman.

tam oṁkāreṇaivāyatanenānveti vidvān yat tac chāntam ajaram amṛtam abhayaṁ paraṁ ceti

The knower attains by oṁkāra the person who is peaceful, ageless, immortal, fearless and supreme. Praśna Upaniṣad 5.7

Having discerned this, the word Brahma-loka must mean the planet of Viṣṇu. Brahma-loka means the planet which *is* Brahman, not the planet *of* Brahmā, just as *niśāda-sthapati* means the leader who is a Niṣāda, not the leader of the Niṣādas.

Topic 5 (Sūtras 14 – 23)

Daharādhikaraṇam - The space in the heart

It is said in Chāndogya Upaniṣad:

atha yad idam asmin brahma-pure daharaṁ puṇḍarīkaṁ veśma
daharo'sminn antarākāśas tasmin yad antas tad anveṣṭavyaṁ tad vāva
vijijñāsitavyam

In the city of Brahman there is a small lotus dwelling. That dwelling is small. In that place, there is an inner space. Within that space is that which should be sought, and which should be known. Chāndogya Upaniṣad 8.1.1

The doubt is this: is the small space situated within the lotus of the heart the element ether, the jīva, or the Lord?

(Pūrvapakṣa) Because the term is well known, it means material ether. Or it means the jīva because it is described as the master of the city (body).

Sūtra – 1.3.14

|| dahara uttarebhyaḥ ||

The space is Viṣṇu because of subsequent statements.

The small space is Viṣṇu. Why? Because of subsequent statements. That which is compared to ether but free of all sins and supports everything cannot be material ether or the jīva. The city of Brahman is the body of the worshipper according to the text. The lotus of the heart is a limb of the body. It is called the abode of Brahman. Within that abode is the small *ākāśa,* the object of meditation. In that one should seek the supreme Brahman free of all sin.

There is another reason why the small space is Viṣṇu.

Sūtra – 1.3.15

|| gati-śabdābhyāṁ tathā dṛṣṭaṁ liṅgaṁ ca ||

The space in the heart is Viṣṇu because it is seen that all beings go to the Lord during deep sleep, and the word Brahma-loka indicates Viṣṇu.

This passage is found a little later in the same chapter:

yathāpi hiraṇya-nidhiṁ nihitam akṣetrajñā upary upari sañcaranto na vindeyur evam evemāḥ sarvāḥ prajā aharahar gacchantya etaṁ brahma-lokaṁ na vindanty anṛtena hi pratyūḍhāḥ ||

Just as people ignorant of the whereabouts of a buried treasure wander on the ground above it, but do not know it is there, so all beings covered by ignorance day after day go to that world of Brahman, but do not know it. Chāndogya Upaniṣad 8.3.2

That space in the heart is here called "that (*enam*)" and is described as the goal of all beings and is called Brahma-loka. For these reasons the space is discerned to be Viṣṇu only. Elsewhere it is stated *satā saumya tadā sampanno bhavati*: O gentle one, one attains the Lord (during sleep.) It is seen (*dṛṣṭam*) that the living beings go to the Lord during sleep. It should be understood (*gamakam*) that the word Brahma-loka means Viṣṇu. And, on the other hand, all beings do not go daily to Satyaloka.

Sūtra – 1.3.16

|| dhṛteś ca mahimno'syāsminn upalabdheḥ ||

The space in the heart is Viṣṇu because this great person alone is observed to be the maintainer of the universe.

After the words *daharo'sminn anarākāśa*, this *dahara* or space is compared to *ākāśa.* It is then described as spreading everywhere, is called *ātmā* and is said to be free of sin. It is then said *atha ya ātmā sa setur vidhṛtir eṣāṁ lokānāṁ asambhedāya*: that ātmā is a dike, a boundary, for preventing destruction of the worlds. It is thus understood that this space (*dahara*) has greatness, in that it maintains the universe. Thus the space refers to Viṣṇu. In other Upaniṣads also Viṣṇu is glorified in this way. Bṛhad-āraṇyaka Upaniṣad 4.4.22 says *eṣa setur vidhāraṇa eṣāṁ lokānāṁ asambhedāya*: the Lord is like a supporting dike so that these worlds do not disintegrate.

Sūtra – 1.3.17

|| prasiddheś ca ||

The space in the heart is Viṣṇu also because he is often described as space.

It is also well known that the word *ākāśa* is often used to mean Brahman in passages such as *ko hy evānyāt kaḥ prāṇāt yad eṣa ākāśa ānando na syāt*: who could breathe if *ākāśa* were not bliss? (Taittirīya Upaniṣad 2.7)

(Pūrva-pakṣa) "But within the same passage concerning the space in the heart, the jīva is mentioned.

atha ya eṣa saṁprasādo'smāc charīrāt samutthāya paraṁ jyotir upasampadya svena rūpeṇābhiniṣpadyata eṣa ātmeti hovācaitad amṛtam abhayam etad brahma

The liberated soul rises from the body, reaches the supreme light and becomes endowed with his own form. That is the immortal fearless Brahman. Chāndogya Upaniṣad 8.3.4

Thus the space in the heart must be the jīva."

Sūtra – 1.3.18

|| itara-parāmarśāt sa iti cen nāsambhavāt ||

If one says that the space refers to the jīva because of reference to the jīva in the text, the answer is no, because it is impossible for the jīva to have the qualities mentioned.

Just because of a reference (*paramarṣāt*) to jīva *(itara)* in the middle of the passage it cannot be claimed that the space in the heart is the jīva. Why?

Because it is impossible (*asambhavāt*) since the eight attributes of that space mentioned (starting with being free of sin)[25] are not applicable to the jīva.

(Pūrva-pakṣa) Let that be. After the teachings about the space in the heart where the eight qualities are mentioned, Prajāpati speaks about the jīva. Thus the qualities mentioned in the section concerning the space in the heart can be applied to the jīva. Thus the space in the heart must be the jīva.

This idea is refuted in the next sūtra.

Sūtra – 1.3.19

|| uttarāc ced āvirbhāva-svarūpas tu ||

If one argues that later passages show that jīva has the eight qualities, and is thus the space in the heart, the answer is "No," because the jīva's qualities manifest through *sādhana*.

The word *tu* (but) indicates a refutation. The word *na* should be understood. In Prajāpati's speech, he teaches that these eight qualities arise in the jīva by *sādhana*. But it is not possible to say that the space in the heart develops the eight qualities by *sādhana*. It is to be understood that the space in the heart has the eight qualities eternally. However Prajāpati states that the jīva's qualities arise from *sādhana*, for it is said *sa evam avaiṣam prasādo 'smāc charīrāt samutthāya:* the liberated soul rising from the body appears in its own form. (Chāndogya Upaniṣad. 8.12.3) Thus there is great difference between the jīva and the Lord. Even though the jīva attains these qualities by *sādhana*, the qualities like supporting the world and acting as a dike show that the Lord is the space in the heart.

If that is so, then why talk about the jīva at all within that section?

Sūtra – 1.3.20

|| anyārthaś ca parāmarśaḥ ||

The jīva is mentioned for another purpose.

---

[25] Chāndogya Upaniṣad 7.7.1 (in relation to the Lord) and 8.7.3 (in relation to the jīva): the eight qualities are freedom from sin, freedom from old age, freedom from death, freedon from sorrow, freedom from hunger, freedom from thirst, satyakāma and satyasaṅkalpa.

The jīva is mentioned in the passage in order to teach about Paramātmā. Attaining the Lord, the jīva attains a form endowed with those eight qualities.

Sūtra – 1.3.21

|| alpa-śruter iti cet tad uktam ||

Because the space is small, it must refer to the jīva. This argument has already been refuted.

This objection has between answered (*tad-uktam*) in 1.2.7: *nicāyyatvād evaṁ vyomavac ca.* The Lord is said to be the size of a *pradeśa* only because that size is convenient for meditation in the heart which is of that size. The Lord possessing inconceivable powers is described as that size for the convenience of meditation.

There is another reason also.

Sūtra – 1.3.22

|| anukṛtes tasya ca ||

The jīva cannot be Brahman because the jīva develops similarity to Brahman.

The space in the heart is eternally endowed with the eight qualities. Prajāpati explained that the eight qualities appear in the jīva by *sādhana*. Thus the jīva's qualities follow after those of the space in the heart. Therefore the jīva is different from the space in the heart. Previously the jīva's *svarūpa* was covered by falsity (*anṛta*). The covering is later removed by worship of Brahman. Then the jīva manifests the eight qualities. Prajāpati says that the jīva becomes "like" the space in the heart. The jīva is a replica or likeness of the space in the heart. The original object and the object which imitates are different, as in the statement, "Hanuman imitates the wind." Similarly, the statement that the liberated jīva becomes like Brahman indicates that the jīva is different from the Brahman. Moreover, a similar statement is found in another śruti *nirañjanaḥ paramaṁ sāmyam upaiti*: the pure jīva attains similarity to the Lord. (Muṇḍaka Upaniṣad 3.1.3)

Sūtra – 1.3.23

|| api smaryate ||

The smṛtis also say that the jīva becomes like Brahman.

idaṁ jñānam upāśritya mama sādharmyam āgatāḥ |
sarge'pi nopajāyante pralaye na vyathanti ca ||

Those who have attained qualities similar to mine, by realizing this knowledge through *guru,* do not take rebirth in this world, and do not experience pain at the time of death. BG 14.2

The smṛtis say that the liberated souls show qualities similar to the Lord's. Therefore the space in the heart is the Lord, not the jīva.

Topic 6 (Sūtras 24 – 25)

Pramitādhikaraṇam - The person the size of a thumb

In the Kaṭha Upaniṣad it is said:

aṅguṣṭha-mātraḥ puruṣo madhya ātmani tiṣṭhati
īśāno bhūta-bhavyasya na tato vijugupsate

The person the size of a thumb resides within the ātmā. He is in control of past and future. After knowing him one is not disturbed. Kaṭha Upaniṣad 2.1.12

The doubt is this. Is the person the size of a thumb the jīva or Viṣṇu?

(Pūrvapakṣa) The Śvetāśvatara Upaniṣad says *prāṇādhipaḥ sañcarati sva-karmabhir aṅguṣṭha-mātro ravi-tulya-rūpaḥ:* the master of the *prāṇa,* the size of a thumb, with a form like the sun, moves by his karmas.

Therefore this confirms that the person who is the size of a thumb is the jīva.

Sūtra – 1.3.24

|| śabdād eva pramiteḥ ||

The person is Viṣṇu because of appropriate words in the text describing the person who is the size of a thumb.

The person the size of a thumb *(pramiteḥ*) is Viṣṇu only. Why? Because of the words in the text (*śabdāt*) *īśāno bhūta-bhavyasya*: he is the master of past and future. It is not possible for the jīva who is under the control of karma to have this power.

"But how can the Lord be the size of a thumb?"

Sūtra – 1.3.25

| | hṛdy apekṣayā tu manuṣyādhikāratvāt | |

The Lord is said to be the size of a thumb because that is the size of the heart of humans, who are qualified for meditation in the heart.

The word *tu* (but) indicates a limited instance. The Lord is the size of a thumb only because the devotee meditates on him in the heart which is that size. The Lord is said to be figuratively this size because the heart is this size. Or the Lord actually appears in the heart with that size by his inconceivable power in response to the devotee's devotion. This was explained previously.

"It is impossible to argue in this way because in different species the heart is of a different size." This objection is answer by mentioning that this is in reference to humans (*manuṣya*). Though the scriptures are applied generally they are meant for humans since only humans have the capacity to worship. Since human bodies are of one type, there is nothing wrong in giving one size for the heart. Though animals like elephants, horses and snakes may have similar sized hearts, they do not have the capacity for worship. Thus they are excluded by the word *manuṣya.*

It is also said that the jīva is the size of a thumb. This is said only because the jīva is situated in the heart and so it is metaphorically said to be of that size. Actually, the jīva is atomic in size because scriptures state that.. *balāgra-cāta-bhāgasya:* the jīva's size is one ten thousandth of the tip of a hair. (Śvetāśvatara Upaniṣad 5.9) Therefore the person who is the size of a thumb is Viṣṇu alone.

Topic 7 (Sūtras 26 – 32)

Devatādhikaraṇam - Concerning devatās' qualification for worship

For proving that Brahman is the size of the thumb it was mentioned that men are qualified for scriptures dealing with this description. By that statement it seems that humans alone can worship the Lord. To refute this, the next *adhikaraṇa* begins. Bṛhad-āraṇyaka says:

tad yo yo devānāṁ pratyabudhyata, sa eva tad abhavat |
tatha ṛṣīṇāṁ tathā manuṣyāṇām

All the *devatās* who meditated on the Lord attained him and likewise did all the sages and humans. Bṛhad-āraṇyaka Upaniṣad 1.4.10

tad devā jyotiṣāṁ jyotir āyur hopāsate'mṛtam

The *devatās* meditate on the Lord who is the light of lights, who is life and immortality. Bṛhad-āraṇyaka Upaniṣad 4.4.16

The doubt is this. Is worship of Brahman possible for *devatās* as it is for men, as mentioned in the scripture?

(Pūrvapakṣa) That worship is not possible for the *devatās* since they do not have bodies and senses. They are made of mantra, and do not have bodily senses. Lacking senses, they cannot meditate nor can they hanker for renunciation of material enjoyment.[26]

Sūtra – 1.3.26

|| tad-upary api bādarāyaṇaḥ sambhavāt ||

It should be accepted that devatās, who are above men also worship Brahman, because they have bodies. That is Lord Bādarāyaṇa's opinion.[27]

It should be accepted that devatās, who are above men (*tad-upari*) also worship Brahman. That is Lord Bādarāyaṇa's opinion. Why? Because they are capable (*sambhavāt*), since they have bodies. This is recognized by humans, the Purāṇas, Itihāsas, Upaniṣads and the mantra portion of the Vedas. They are capable of worship because they have celestial bodies and senses. They can also renounce their state of power because they realize that their powers are insignificant and temporary. Smṛti says:

na kevalaṁ dvija-śreṣṭha narake duḥkha-paddhatiḥ
svarge 'pi yāta-bhītasya kṣayiṣṇor nāsti nirvṛtiḥ

O best of the twice-born! Suffering exists not only in hell, but also in Svarga. There is no cessation of fear of destructible objects. Viṣṇu Purāṇa 6.5.50

Because of this, the *devatās* hanker for Brahman as well, for they have heard that Brahman is pure, eternal bliss. It is also said that the *devatās* accept

---

[26] The Pūrva-Mimāsakās hold that the devatās are not embodied beings, but are just the creations of the sages who chant the Vedic mantras corresponding to those devatās

[27] Bādarāyaṇa is the author of the Brahma-sūtras.

brahmacārya in order to gain knowledge. *tatra yāḥ prājāpatyāḥ prajāpatau pitari brahmacaryam ūṣur devā*

manuṣyā asurāḥ: the offspring of Prajāpati, *devatās,* humans and demons practiced *brahmacārya* with their father Prajāpati. (Bṛhad-āraṇyaka Upaniṣad 5.2.1) *eka-śataṁ ha vai varṣāṇi maghavā prajāpatau brahmacaryam uvāsa:* Indra practiced *brahmacārya* with Prajāpati for a hundred years. (Chāndogya Upaniṣad 8.11.3) Since the *devatās* are capable, they also are qualified for worshipping Brahman.

"If it is accepted that *devatās* have bodies, there will be a contradiction in performing sacrifice. It is not possible for one *devatā* with his limited body to be present at many sacrifices performed simultaneously by humans."

Sūtra – 1.3.27

|| virodha-karmaṇīti cen nāneka-pratipatter darśanāt ||

If one argues that there is contradiction in regard to sacrifices, the answer is no, since it is seen that the *devatās* can expand their forms into many.

In accepting that devatās have bodies, there is no contradiction. Why? Because it is seen that persons possessing great powers can expand their forms into many (*aneka-pratipatter darśanāt*) as in the case of Saubhari.

"Using that reasoning, if you say that *devatās* have bodies, there will be no problem in doing sacrifices for *devatās.* But then their names should not be mentioned in the Vedas. Since they are born and later meet with destruction, their names in the Veda will have no meaning after they disappear, just as the phrase "son of a barren woman" has no meaning. Moreover, a Pūrva-mīmāṁsa text says *autpattikas tu śabdenārthasya sambandhaḥ*: the relation of an object denoted with a specific word is eternal. There is thus a contradiction (for if *devatā's* names exist without the *devatā* being present, the relationship is not eternal.)"

Sūtra – 1.3.28

|| śabda iti cen nātaḥ prabhāvāt pratyakṣānumānābhyām ||

If one argues that the words of the Vedas denoting devatās are not eternal, the answer is no, since beings are created from eternal words. This is shown in śruti and smṛti statements.

There is no contradiction in Vedic words (*śabda*), though the *devatās* are not eternal. Why? Because beings are created from the eternal words *(ataḥ prabhavāt*). The words denoting objects in the Vedas denote the eternity of those particular forms. The material forms arise by remembrance of those eternal forms expressed by the particular words. The forms are eternal because they exist previous to their manifestation. In Viśvakarmā's book, these forms are described --for instance Yama has a staff in his hand or Varuṇa has a noose in his hand. Others then paint the picture. Words in the Vedas describing Indra are indications of a particular form, like the word "cow." They do not describe a specific individual like the word "Caitra." Since the words of the Veda express eternal forms, they are not without authority. Nor are they contrary to the Mīmāṁsa statements. Why is that? Because of śruti and smṛti statements (*pratyakṣānumānabhyām)*. Śruti describes the creation with words.

eta iti ha vai prajāpatir devān, asṛjatāsṛgram iti manuṣyān, indava iti pitèṁs, tiraḥ pavitram iti grahān, āśva iti stotraṁ, viśvānīti mantram, abhisaubhagety anyāḥ prajāḥ

Brahmā created the *devatās* by uttering "Ete." He created men by uttering "Āsṛgram." He created the Pitṛs by uttering "Indavaḥ." He created planets by uttering "Tiras pavitram." He created verses of praise by uttering "Āśuva." He created mantras by the word "Viśva." He created all other beings by uttering "Abhisaubhaga." Pañcaviṁśati-brāhmaṇa 6.9.13.22, 6.12.1.3

Smṛti says:

nāma rūpaṁ ca bhūtānāṁ kṛtyānāṁ ca prapañcanam
veda-śabdebhya evādau devādīnāṁ cakāra saḥ

From the words of the Vedas Brahmā created names and forms of all beings, of the devatās and of the development of rituals. Viṣṇu Purāṇa 1.5.63

Sūtra – 1.3.29

|| ata eva ca nityatvam ||

Therefore the Vedas are eternal.

The eternity of the Vedas is proved since the words indicate eternal models and remind Brahmā how to create those forms. Names like Kāṭhaka (referring to the speaker Kaṭha) should be understood to indicate the name of not a sage who created the mantras but a person who uttered the verses which are eternal.

(Pūrva-pakṣa) Let that be. After the daily destruction, Brahmā creates the forms of *devatās* by remembering their forms contained in the words of the Veda. At the time of final devastation, however, everything other than *prakṛti* (including the Vedas) is destroyed. How can another creation take place and how can the Vedas be eternal?

Sūtra – 1.3.30

|| samāna-nāma-rūpatvāc cāvṛttāv apy avirodho darśanāt smṛteś ca ||

There is no contradiction because after *pralaya* things are created with the same names and forms. This is confirmed in śruti and smṛti.

The word *ca* is used to destroy doubt. At the time of a new creation after the *pralaya* (*āvṛttau*) there is no contradiction about the words of the Vedas being eternal *(avirodhaḥ*). Why? Because things exist in the new creation with the same names and forms (*samāna-nāma-rūpatvāt*). At the time of the great destruction, the Vedas and the various forms expressed in their words, which are eternal objects, reside within the Lord endowed with *śaktis,* having become one with him. When the Lord desires to create the universes, these forms again appear. The creation will be manifested by the Lord and four headed Brahmā while reflecting on the various forms described in the Vedas. Just as a potter considers the forms of previous pots through the word "pot" and then produces similar pots, so the later creation is similar to the previous creation. The creation takes place after the great destruction just as it does after the destruction following the day of Brahmā.

How is this known? It is known from the śrutis (*darśanāt*) and smṛtis (*smṛteḥ*). Some śrutis are as follows:

ātmāvā idam eka evāgra āsīn nānyat kiṁcanam iṣat sa īkṣata lokān nu sṛja

The Lord was alone in the beginning. Nothing existed at all. He glanced and created the worlds. Aitareya Upaniṣad 1.1

yo brahmāṇaṁ vidadhāti pūrvaṁ yo vai vedāṁś ca prahiṇoti tasmai

He first created Brahmā and gave the Vedas to him. Śvetāśvatara Upaniṣad 6.18

sūryācandramasau dhātā yathā-pūrvam akalpayat

The creator made the sun and moon as he did previously Ṛg Veda 10.190.3

The following are some smṛtis that describe this:

nyagrodhaḥ su-mahān alpe yathā bīje vyavasthitaḥ
samyame viśvam akhilam bīja-bhūte yathā tvayi

Just as a huge banyan tree is situated in a small seed, the whole universe is situated in you at the time of destruction. Viṣṇu Purāṇa 1.13.66

nārāyaṇaḥ paro devas tasmāj jātaś caturmukhaḥ

The Supreme Lord is Nārāyaṇa. From him was born Brahmā. Varāha Purāṇa

tene brahma hṛdā ya ādikavaye

The Lord transmitted the Vedas to Brahmā. SB 1.1.1

The main point is this. After the great destruction, the Supreme Lord Bhagavān, contemplating the universe as it existed previously and deciding to expand himself into many, separates from himself all the enjoyers and enjoyed objects which had merged into him in subtle from and creates the universe made of elements starting with mahat-tattva, and also creates Brahmā as previously. He manifests the Vedas also as they previously existed. He teaches the Vedas to Brahmā mentally and engages him in creating the universe with forms like *devatās* as previously. He also remains within the universe as the inner controller. Brahmā, being given powers of omniscience by the mercy of the Lord, after contemplating the forms of the beings through the words of the Vedas, creates them as replicas of previous beings like *devatās*, humans etc.

Because the Vedas containing words like Indra express eternal archetypes such as Indra, the Vedas remain perfect. The relationship of word to the object is eternal. Thus the objection that the Vedas express temporary objects is countered. And thus the *devatās* (having bodies) are capable of worship, since they are qualified to worship Brahman. There is no contradiction in *devatās* meditating on the Lord who is the size of a thumb since they conceive the Lord's size according to the size of their thumbs.

Are the *devatās* qualified for methods of worship (*vidyā*) of which they are the objects of worship? This should be considered. *asau vā āditya deva-madhu tasya dyaur eva tiraścīna-vaṁśaḥ:* the sun is honey for the *devatās* and his heaven is the rafter. (Chāndogya Upaniṣad 3.1.1) In this verse, the sun is considered to be honey for the *devatās.* Different rays of the sun are considered to be honey comb cells. The Vasus, Rudras, Ādityas, Maruts and Sādhyas (*devatās*), seeing the nectar, become satisfied through the medium of chief *devatās.* The sun becomes honey by possessing *rasa* in the form of cells represented by rays, and is produced by performing acts described in the Ṛg and other Vedas (represented by bees who make the honey).[28] Other types of worship are described elsewhere involving meditation on *devatās.* In the next sūtra, Jaimini's opinion is given.

Sūtra – 1.3.31

|| madhv-ādiṣv asambhavād anadhikāraṁ jaiminiḥ ||

Jaimini says that the *devatās* cannot perform this *madhu-vidyā* since it is impossible to be both the object of worship and the worshipper, and it is meaningless to attain what is already attained.

Jaimini says that the *devatās* are not qualified for this meditation on honey. Why? Because it is impossible. One who is the object of worship cannot be the worshipper. One person cannot be both. Also it would be meaningless for a Vasu to attain the result of *madhu-vidyā*, which is becoming a Vasu.

Sūtra – 1.3.32

|| jyotiṣi bhāvāc ca ||

The *devatās* are not qualified for this worship, because they are supposed to worship the supreme light, the Lord.

They are not qualified because they have a position (*bhāvāt*) of worshipping the supreme Brahman in the form of light (*jyotiṣi*). Śruti says *tad devā jyotiṣāṁ jyotiḥ āyur upāsate*: the *devatās* worship the Lord, the light of all lights, the essence of life. (Bṛhad-āraṇyaka Upaniṣad 4.4.16) Though *devatās* and humans can both worship Brahman, the worship of the light of all lights is the particular worship for the *devatās*. It is suggested that they should not do other types of worship. The response comes in the next sūtra.

---

[28] By knowing this vidyā one can become a Vasu, Ādiya etc.

Topic 8 (Sūtra 33)

Bhāvādhikaraṇam - Position of the devatās

Sūtra – 1.3.33

| | bhāvaṁ tu bādarāyaṇo'sti hi | |

Bādarāyaṇa says that the *devatās* are qualified for this meditation because they perform the meditation in a certain way.

Tu indicates a refutation of the doubt. Lord Bādarāyaṇa considers that the *devatās* are in a position (*bhāvam*) for *madhu-vidyā* and other types of worship, because Āditya, the Vasus etc. may desire to attain Brahman after having attained a similar form of a *devatā* again by worshipping Brahman in a devatā form. This is worship of Brahman as cause and effect[29]. At the present moment as Ādityas and Vasus, they worship Brahman as Āditya, Vasu etc. and in the next *kalpa,* becoming Āditya, Vasu etc again, by worshipping the *antaryāmī* of Āditya etc. as the cause, they become liberated. One should not think that the words Āditya, Vasu etc do not mean Brahman, for it is said at the conclusion of this section of the Upaniṣad *ya etam evaṁ brahmopaniṣadaṁ veda sakṛd-divā haivāsmai bhavati:* he who knows this Upaniṣad concerning Brahman has continuous day. (Chāndogya Upaniṣad 3.11.3)

Nor should one think that it is meaningless for *devatās* to desire through this *vidyā* to attain a position that they already have, for it is seen that people who have sons desire sons in the next life also. And the worship prescribed is actually worship of Brahman.

That the *devatās* are qualified to worship Brahman rather than *devatās* (*tad devā jyotiṣām jyotiḥ*) is actually described in this *vidyā.* Other śruti texts also show that *devatās* are qualified for sacrifices and worship. It is not contrary for them to do so, since they do this by the order of the Lord to set an example for common people.

---

[29] Worship of the devatās is worship of the Brahman through its effects and worship of the Brahman directly (the antaryāmī of the devartās) is worship of the Brahman as the cause.

prajāpatir akāmayata prajāyeyeti sa etad agnihotraṁ mithunam apaśyat | tad-udite sūrye'juhot

Prajāpati desired: may I create offspring. He saw a pair of sacrificers. When the sun rose he performed sacrifice. Taittirīya-brāhmaṇa 2.1.2.8

devā vai satram āsata

The devatās conducted a sacrifice. Taittirīya-brāhmaṇa

"If *devatās* tolerate delay for many *kalpas* while practicing *madhu-vidyā* as described above, how could they be desirous of liberation, since they must give up taste even for Satyaloka in order to gain liberation?" That is true. But one must accept that such candidates (a type of *sa-niṣṭhā* devotee) are possible because the scriptures describe them and they are under the control of various karmas.

This *adhikaraṇa* shows that the humans described in the previous *adhikaraṇa* must make even greater endeavor.

Topic 9 (Sūtras 34 – 38)

Apaśūdrādhikaraṇam - Śūdra's lack of qualification

Since *devatās* and humans have the capacity, they are both qualified to worship Brahman. But this worship is not possible without studying the Vedas, for it is said *aupaniṣadaḥ puruṣaḥ*: the Lord is known through the Upaniṣads. (Bṛhad-āraṇyaka Upaniṣad 1.1.2) As śudras are not qualified to study the Vedas, are they qualified to worship Brahman? This section answers.

In the Chāndogya Upaniṣad there is the story of Jānaśruti. Hearing about Rainka from some swans, Jānaśruti approached Rainka who was with his horses. Offering gold, cows and horses to Rainka, Jānaśruti asked him which *devatā* he worshipped. Seeing Jānaśruti Rainka spoke *ahaha hāre tvā śūdra tavaiva saha gobhir astu:* "O śudra, let your cows, chariots and necklace remain with you."

Though called a śūdra, Jānaśruti again came, bringing cows, gold, chariots and young girls as gifts. Rainka spoke. *tam ājahāremāḥ śūdrānenaiva mukhenālāpayiṣyathāḥ:* "You have brought these gifts. O śūdra, by these you have made me speak." Rainka then taught him *saṁvarga-vidyā.*

The doubt is this. Is a śūdra qualified for knowledge of the Vedas or not?

(Pūrva-pakṣa) The śūdra is qualified for Vedic knowledge because firstly no distinction is made while stating that humans are qualified; secondly the śūdra has a capacity for knowledge; thirdly the text mentions the word śūdra, and he was taught the Vedas; and fourthly the Purāṇas tell us that Vidura and others who were śūdras had knowledge of Brahman.

Sūtra – 1.3.34

|| śug asya tad-anādara-śravaṇāt tadādravaṇāt sūcyate hi ||

The śūdra is not qualified to study the Vedas because in the story, Jānaśruti is called a śūdra only because he was grief stricken (śu) by the swan's disrespectful words and then approached (dra) Rainka.

The word *na* should be understood from a previous sūtra. The śūdra is not qualified to study the Vedas. Why? Because (*hi*) Jānaśruti, ignorant of Brahman, heard the disrespectful words of the swans: "Can this person be compared to Rainka with his horses?" In grief (*śuk)* he went (*dravati*) to Rainka who had knowledge of Brahman. Because Jānaśruti was filled with grief at the swans' words and went to Rainka, he was called a śūdra by Rainka, even though he was not a śūdra, because Rainka knew of his condition by his omniscience. He is not called śūdra due to being born in the fourth *varṇa.*

If Jānaśruti was not a śūdra, who was he? One can infer that he was a kṣatriya.

Sūtra – 1.3.35

|| kṣatriyatvāvagateś cottaratra caitrarathena liṅgāt ||

Jānaśruti was not a śūdra because the description indicates that he was a kṣatriya and Abhipratāri, a kṣatriya, received the same instructions from a brāhmaṇa.

It is understood that Jānaśruti was a kṣatriya since he had immense wealth and ruled a population. *śraddhādeyo bahudāyī*: he had faith and was charitable. (Chāndogya Upaniṣad 4.1.1) Also he sent a chamberlain to find Rainka and gave Rainka cows, gold, chariots and his daughter. This is not possible for anyone except a kṣatriya. Because of having qualities of a kṣatriya, it is understood from the beginning of the story that he was a kṣatriya. At the conclusion of the story, this is also understood. At the end of the description of *saṁsarga-vidyā*, he is understood to be a kṣatriya by mention of Caitraratha, and Abhipratāri (descendent of Kakṣasena).

atha śaunakaṁ kāpeyam abhipratāriṇaṁ ca kākṣaseniṁ pariviśyamānau brahmacārī bibhikṣe

A brahmacārī begged food from Śaunaka and Abhipratāri. Chāṇdogya Upaniṣad 4.3.5

"But it is not stated in this section that Abhipratāri was a *caitraratha* and kṣatriya."

It is known from characteristics (*liṅgāt*). The hint is that he was in the company of Śaunaka Kāpeya. In another place it is said that the sons of Kapi made Caitraratha perform sacrifices. Thus Caitraratha was related with the Kāpeyas. Caitraratha was a kṣatriya for it is said *tasmāt caitrarathir nāma kṣatra-patir ajāyata*: from him Caitrarathi, a kṣatriya, was born. Therefore Abhipratāri, a descendent of Caitraratha was a kṣatriya. Thus Saunaka, a Kāpepya, and Abhipratāri, a Caitrarathi, were a brāhmaṇa and a kṣatriya, worshippers of *saṁsarga-vidyā*. Since they were related as guru and disciple, Rainka and Jānaśruti were related in the same way. Therefore Jānaśruti was a kṣatriya.

Therefore a śūdra is not qualified to study the Vedas. By logic this has been proved. The truth is shown by śruti reference in the next sūtra.

Sūtra – 1.3.36

|| saṁskāra-parāmarśāt tad-abhāvābhilāpāc ca ||

The śūdra is not qualified for the Vedas because the study of the Vedas depends on *saṁskāras* and the scriptures say that śūdras do not undergo *saṁskaras*.

Brāhmaṇas are qualified according to śruti statements, because *saṁskāras* are considered necessary for study.

aṣṭa-varṣaṁ brāhmaṇam upanayīta tam adhyāpayed ekādaśe kṣatriyaṁ dvādaśe vaiśyam

One should initiate the brāhmaṇa child at the age of eight and have him study. For the kṣatriya his *upanayana* should take place in the eleventh year and for the vaiśya in the twelfth year. Pāraskara-gṛha-sūtra 2.1.1

The śūdra is not qualified because it is said that he lacks *saṁskāras. nāgnir na yajño na kriyā na saṁskāro na vratāni śūdrasya*: the śūdra does not light fire, does not perform sacrifice or rituals, and does not undergo *saṁskāras* or vows. Thus the śūdra is not qualified for studying the Vedas, which depend on *saṁskāras,* because he lacks *saṁskāras,* being outside the three upper *varṇas.*

Sūtra – 1.3.37

|| tad-abhāva-nirdhāraṇe ca pravṛtteḥ ||

In the case of Jābala, he was taught because the guru determined that he was not a śūdra and arranged for his saṁskāra.

The śūdra's lack of *saṁskāras* is here emphasized. In the Chāndogya Upaniṣad 4.4.4 Jābala spoke the truth by saying *nāham etad vede bho yad gotro 'ham asmi*: "I do not know to which *gotra* I belong." Because he told the truth, Gautama determined that he was not a śūdra. *naitad abrāhmaṇo vivaktum arhati samidhaṁ saumyāhara tvopaneṣye*

na satyād agāḥ : Gautama then said, "A non-brāhmaṇa would not speak in this way. Gentle one, bring the fire wood. I will accept you. You did not deviate from the truth." Thus Jābala was taught the Vedas because Gautama made arrangement for the *saṁskāra.* It should be understood that brāhmaṇa qualification is representative of any of the three higher *varṇas.* They all accept *saṁskāra.* Thus the śūdra is not qualified for the Vedas.

Sūtra – 1.3.38

|| śravaṇādhyayanārtha-pratiṣedhāt smṛteś ca ||

The śūdra is not qualified for the Vedas because hearing and studying it and performing its actions are forbidden for the śūdra, and the smṛtis also forbid the śūdra to do this.

pady u ha vā etat śmaśānaṁ yac chūdras tasmāc chūdra-samīpe nādhyetavyam

One should not recite the Vedas in front of a śūdra, since he is like a moving cremation ground. Therefore the śūdra, like an animal, is unfit for sacrifices.[30]

---

[30] Quoted in Śārīrīka-bhāṣya also.

The śūdra is not qualified for studying the Vedas because he is forbidden to hear the Vedas. Without hearing, performing actions like sacrifices, gaining knowledge of the meaning and study cannot take place. Thus these three are also forbidden.

The smṛtis also state the same:

nāgnir na yajñaḥ śūdrasya tathaivādhyayanaṁ kutaḥ |
kevalaiva tu śuśrūṣā tri-varṇānāṁ vidhīyate ||

A śūdra cannot attend the fire, perform sacrifices, or study the Vedas. He can only serve the three upper *varṇas.*

vedākṣara-vicāreṇa śūdraḥ patati tat-kṣaṇād

By trying to understand the syllables of the Veda, the śūdra immediately degrades himself.[31]

Because Vidura and others had perfected realization, their case cannot be considered. Śūdras can be liberated by gaining knowledge from hearing the Purāṇas and other texts. However, there will be some difference in the resulting liberation.

Topic 10 (Sūtras 39 – 40)

Kampanādhikaraṇam - Cause of Trembling

Completing an incidental topic, the main topic now continues. It is said in the Kaṭha Upaniṣad:

yad idaṁ kiṁ ca jagat sarvaṁ prāṇa ejati niḥsṛtam |
mahad bhayaṁ vajram udyataṁ ya etad vidur amṛtās te bhavanti ||

The universe emerges from prāṇa. It is a raised thunderbolt (*vajram*), which causes great fear. Those who know it become immortal. Kaṭha Upaniṣad 6.2

The doubt is this. Is the *vajram* a thunderbolt or Brahman?

(Pūrvapakṣa) The word *vajra* means a thunderbolt because it causes trembling and because liberation is caused by knowing it. It is called *prāṇa* because it gives protection. From the context it is not possible to take the

[31] *vedākṣara-vicāreṇa śūdraś cāṇḍālatāṁ vrajet* - Parāsara-smṛti 1.67

word to mean Brahman. *udyam vajram*, a raised thunderbolt, cannot indicate Brahman, since Brahman is without motion.

Sūtra – 1.3.39

| | kampanāt | |

The thunderbolt is Viṣṇu because he causes the world to tremble.

Because the trembling of the whole universe is mentioned along with the *vajra,* the *vajra* must be Brahman. In the smṛti scriptures it is said:

cakraṁ caṅkramaṇād eṣa vajanād vajram ucyate |
khaṇḍanāt khaḍga evaiva heti-nāmā hariḥ svayam | |

The Lord is called cakra because he moves like a wheel. He is called vajra because he

goes everywhere. He is called khaḍga because he cuts. Thus the Lord is named because of his weapons. Brahma-vaivarta Purāṇa.

The meaning is this. It is well known in the śrutis that Paramātmā is called *prāṇa* and the cause of fear. Thus *vajra* means Paramātmā who is glorified by this word.

Sūtra – 1.3.40

| | jyotir-darśanāt | |

The thunderbolt refers to Brahman because of contiguous passages describing the Lord as light and fire.

Previous to the description of the thunderbolt the following statement is found. *na yatra sūryo bhāti na candra-tārake*: he is not illuminated by the sun, the moon or stars. (Kaṭha Upaniṣad 5.15) Later it is said *bhayād asyāgnis tapati:* fire burns out of fear of him. (Kaṭha Upaniṣad 6.3) In these two cases, Brahman is equated with light and fire. Thus the statement between these two describing the thunderbolt must also refer to Brahman.

Topic 11 (Sūtras 41 – 43)

Arthāntarādhikaraṇam - The jīva is not the Lord

ākāśo ha vai nāma-rūpayor nirvahitā te yad antarā tad brahma tad amṛtaṁ sa ātmā

The *ākāśa* which supports name and form and which exists without these is Brahman and immortality. He is ātmā. Chāndogya Upaniṣad 8.14.1

The doubt is this. Does the word *ākāśa* (ether) refer to the jīva released from bondage, or Paramātmā?

(Pūrva-pakṣa) It means the liberated *ātmā* because he is also described in a condition previous to liberation. *aśva iva romāṇi vidhūya pāpam*: he is like a horse, shaking off all sin. The present quotation describes the *ātmā* liberated from names and forms. Previous to liberation the *ātmā* supports names and forms. Furthermore the word *ākāśa* (open space) can indicate the unrestricted splendor of the liberated *ātmā.* It is called Brahman and immortality because it has reached that state.

Sūtra – 1.3.41

|| ākāśo'rthāntaratvādi-vyapadeśāt ||

***Ākāśa* refers to Paramātmā because the text describes qualities of a person other than the jīva and the word Brahman means the greatest.**

Ākāśa is Paramātmā only not the liberated jīva. Why? Because of other indications. The meaning is this. The *ākāśa* is described as something other than the jīva in a liberated state (*arthāntaratvādi*) since it accomplishes (*nirvāhitā*) names and forms. In the state of bondage, the jīva partakes of names and forms under the control of karma. Due to his bound nature the jīva cannot produce names and forms. And in a liberated state the jīva gives up worldly actions (and thus would not produce names and forms).

The scriptures say that Paramātmā has the ability to create the universe (what to speak of names and forms). *anenajīvenātmanānupraviśya nāma-rūpe vyākaravāṇi* : entering with the jīva let me separate names and forms. (Chāndogya Upaniṣad 6.3.2) Therefore *ākāśa* refers to Paramātmā. The word *ādi* indicates the characteristic of the word Brahman mentioned in the quotation, expressed by its etymology: unconditional greatness. The previous description of the horse shaking off sin refers to the liberated jīva but the passage says that the person attains the world of Brahman (Paramātmā). Thus the subject of the present text is Paramātmā. The word *ākāśa*, meaning all-pervading, is inapplicable for the jīva, but is well known to apply to Paramātmā.

(Pūrva-pakṣa) "Let that be, but it is not proper to say that Brahman refers to something other than the liberated jīva, since that is impossible to tolerate."

The jīva in a state of bondage is described in the following.

katama ātmeti yo'yaṁ vijñānamayaḥ prāṇeṣu hṛdy antar-jyotiḥ puruṣaḥ |
puruṣaḥ sa samānaḥ sann ubhau lokāv anusaṁcarati

Who is the *ātmā*? Yājñavalkya said, "The person who is full of knowledge, who is internal light in the heart within the *prāṇas,* remaining the same, wanders in the two worlds." Bṛhad-āraṇyaka Upaniṣad 4.3.7

But later, the jīva is described as Brahman. *sa vā ayam ātmā brahma vijñānamayaḥ*: this jīva is Brahman, full of knowledge. (Bṛhad-āraṇyaka Upaniṣad 4.4.5) Elsewhere, the jīva's liberated state is described as *athākāmayamāna* (devoid of desire) and then the jīva is described as Brahman. *brahmaiva san brahmāpyeti*: becoming Brahman, jīva attains Brahman. (Bṛhad-āraṇyaka Upaniṣad 4.4.6) At the end, in describing the result, it is said, *abhayaṁ vai brahma bhavati ya eva veda*: whoever knows this becomes fearless Brahman. (Bṛhad-āraṇyaka Upaniṣad 4.4.25)

Though sometimes distinctions are made between jīva and Brahman, that distinction is like the distinction between air in a pot and air in the sky, created by *upādhi.* When the *upādhi* is destroyed, the limited jīva becomes great (Brahman), just as when the pot is destroyed, the air in the pot merges with the air in the sky. Because the jīva can attain powers to create universes, Brahman does not refer to something other than jīva."

To this pūrva-pakṣa argument the next sūtra responds.

Sūtra – 1.3.42

|| suṣupty-utkrāntyor bhedena ||

The jīva is not Brahman because of descriptions showing that the jīva differs from the Lord while in deep sleep and while leaving the body.

The word *vyapadeśāt* (because of descriptions) from the last verse should be understood here also. It is not possible that the liberated jīva can be Brahman in these statements. Why? Because Brahman is described (*vyapadeśāt*) as different (*bhedena*) from the jīva, either when he is in deep sleep or going out of the body at death (*suṣpty-utkrāntyoḥ*). Concerning the state of sleep it is said *prājñenātmanā sampariṣvakto na bāhyaṁ kiñcana veda nāntaram:* the jīva, embraced by the omniscient ātmā (Brahman) does not know anything outside or inside. (Bṛhad-āraṇyaka Upaniṣad 4.3.21) Concerning his going out of the body it is said *prājñenātmanā anvārūḍha utsarjan yāti:* mounted upon the omniscient *ātmā,* the jīva goes out of the body while groaning. (Bṛhad-āraṇyaka Upaniṣad 4.3.35) *Utsarjan* means groaning. It is impossible that the jīva, with meager knowledge, when sleeping or going out of the body, could be embraced or ride upon itself. Nor can the other person be another jīva since no jīva is omniscient *(prajñātmā)* as described in the text.

(Pūrva-pakṣa) "This argument does not prove that the jīva cannot become Brahman. It only shows difference between jīva and Brahman when the jīva is conditioned by *upādhis.*" The next sūtra replies.

Sūtra – 1.3.43

|| paty-ādi-śabdebhyaḥ ||

The jīva is not Brahman because words like "master" show difference between the Lord and the jīva even in liberated state.

In latter sections the word *pati* (master) is used several times (This word is applicable only to Brahman not the jīva).

sa vā ayam ātmā...sarvasya vaśī sarvasyeśānaḥ sarvasyādhipatiḥ sarvam idaṁ praśāsti yad idaṁ kiñca

This ātmā is the controller of all, the ruler of all, the master of all. He rules everything. Bṛhad-āraṇyaka Upaniṣad 5.6.1

sa na sādhunā karmaṇā bhūyān no evāsādhunā kanīyān eṣa sarveśvara eṣa bhūtādhipatir eṣa lokeśvaraḥ loka-pāla eṣa setur vidharaṇa eṣāṁ lokānām asaṁbhedāya

He does not become greater by good actions, nor less by bad actions. He is the lord of all, the master of all beings, the lord of all people, the protector of all people, a dike, a separator, so that people will not be confused. (Bṛhad-āraṇyaka Upaniṣad 4.4.22)

These passages show that the Brahman is distinct even from the liberated jīva (who is under the Lord in the liberated state). As well, one cannot call the liberated jīva the master of all or ruler of all, since actions involved with the material world are forbidden for the liberated jīva. *jagad-vyāpāra-varjyam*: the liberated jīva is free from dealing with the world. (Brahma-sūtra 4.4.17)

Brahman however fits this description. *antaḥ praviṣṭaḥ śastā janānām:* the Lord enters all and is the ruler of men. (*Taittirīya Āraṇyaka* 3.11)

One cannot argue that the difference between jīva and Brahman is due to *upādhi* since the Lord and the jīva exist separately even when the jīva is free of *upādhis*. The conclusion will be further strengthened in Brahma-sūtra 2.3.41. Though it is said *ayam ātmā brahma*: this *ātmā* is Brahman (Bṛhad-āraṇyaka Upaniṣad 4.4.5), there it is explained that the jīva is called Brahman because he possesses a portion of Brahman's qualities. *Brahmaiva san* (the jīva becomes Brahman) actually means that the jīva becomes *like* Brahman because of manifesting the eight qualities, for it is said *paramaṁ sāmyam upaiti:* the jīva attains similarity (not identity) with Brahman. (Muṇḍaka Upaniṣad 3.2.3)

It was previously explained (1.1.17) that becoming Brahman did not mean merging, since after "becoming Brahman" it is mentioned that one then attains Brahman (and thus Brahman remains separate from the jīva.) Thus it is proved that in conditioned and liberated state the jīva remains separate from Brahman. The liberated jīva is not the producer of names and forms. Only Paramātmā is described in the text.

As well, in Brahma-sūtra 1.1.16-17 difference was also taught. To remove any remaining doubt, the present sūtra again states the fact. Repetition is not a fault, since this time it states that difference from the Lord exists even in the liberated jīva.

Section Four

tamaḥ sāṅkhya-ghanodīrṇaṁ yasya go-gaṇaiḥ
taṁ samvid-bhūṣaṇam kṛṣṇa-pūṣaṇaṁ samupāsmahe

I worship Kṛṣṇa, the sun, whose ornament is knowledge, and who, by his rays, has extinguished the darkness caused by many Sāṅkhya arguments.

Topic 1 (Sūtras 1 – 7)

Anumānādhikaraṇam - Pradhana, the inferred

It has already been concluded that the supreme Brahman is the subject of inquiry as a means to liberation, and that it is the cause of the universe, that it is distinct from the matter and the jīvas, that it is endowed with auspicious qualities like omniscience and inconceivability, that it possesses unlimited *śaktis*, that it is devoid of all bad qualities, and that it has unlimited powers. In this section there is a reconciliation of statements in some Upaniṣads, which are filled with words about matter and jīva that seemingly support Kapila's philosophy.

indriyebhyaḥ parā hy arthā
arthebhyaś ca paraṁ manaḥ
manasas tu parā buddhir
buddher ātmā mahān paraḥ
mahataḥ param avyaktam
avyaktāt puruṣaḥ paraḥ
puruṣān na paraṁ kiñcit
sā kāṣṭhā sā parā gatiḥ

Superior to the senses are the sense objects. Superior to the sense objects is the mind. Superior to the mind is intelligence. Superior to intelligence is the great ātmā. Superior to great ātmā is *avyakta.* Superior to *avyakta* is the *puruṣa.* There is nothing superior to the *puruṣa.* That is the final goal. Kaṭha Upaniṣad 1.3.10-11

Here is the doubt. Does *avyakta* mean *pradhāna* or the body?

(Pūrvapakṣa) The sequence of *mahat-tattva, avyakta* and *puruṣa* is well known in the smṛtis, and in the śrutis it is similarly recognized. Because of this, the word *avyakta* is traditionally recognized as independent *pradhāna* in this passage.[32]

Sūtra – 1.4.1

|| ānumānikam apy ekeṣām iti cen, na,
śarīra-rūpaka-vinyasta-gṛhīter darśayati ca ||

Though some say that *avyakta* refers to *pradhāna*, it is not so, because the *avyakta* represents the body in the previous metaphor of body representing a chariot, and the text shows this.

Some followers (*ekesām*) of the sage Kaṭha refer to *pradhāna* as *ānumānikam*, inferred, since it is not visible (*vyakta*). If one claims that *avyakta* refers to *pradhāna,* the inferred, the answer is "No." Why? Because the text shows this (*darśayati*), because it gives a simile of a chariot compared to the body with the *ātmā* as the passenger (*śarīra-rūpaka-voyasta-gṛhīteḥ*). This is mentioned before the present text:

ātmānaṁ rathinaṁ viddhi
śarīraṁ ratham eva ca
buddhiṁ tu sārathiṁ viddhi
manaḥ pragraham eva ca
indriyāṇi hayān āhur
viṣayāṁs teṣu gocarān
ātmendriya-mano-yuktaṁ
bhoktety āhur manīṣiṇaḥ

"Know the ātmā to be the passenger, the body to be the charioteer, the intelligence to be the driver and the mind to be the reins. The senses are called the horses and the sense objects are the field of action. The wise say that *ātmā* joined with senses, and mind is the enjoyer."

The worshipper desiring to attain the feet of Viṣṇu is compared to the passenger seated in the chariot of the body. When he controls the chariot and other factors mentioned, he attains the feet of the Lord after traversing the path. The passage in question thus indicates lesser or greater importance in regard to controlling the body and other factors, represented by the chariot and its elements. For instance *indreybhyaḥ parā hy arthā*: more

[32] In Sāṅkhya philosophy *pradhāna* and *puruṣa* (jīva) are the final causes.

important than the senses are the sense objects. The senses, equated with the horses in the analogy, should be equated with the senses and other factors mentioned in the passage in question, because the words are generally the same. The remaining factor to equate with *avyakta* is the body (since senses, sense objects, mind, intelligence and *ātmā* have been correlated). Also the context indicates this. It does not refer to the Sāṅkhya philosophy since it contradicts their theory of elements. (In that philosophy sense objects are not higher than senses, and intelligence is not an element).

"Since the body is visible, how can it be called invisible (*avyakta*)?" The next sūtra answers.

Sūtra – 1.4.2

|| sūkṣmaṁ tu tad-arhatvāt ||

Avyakta can refer to the body since the subtle body is invisible.

The word *tu* (but) indicates a removal of the doubt. Body here means the subtle body, as the causal body (the seed of the gross body). Why? Because the meaning of the word *avyakta* is suitable to describe the subtle body, since it is invisible to our eyes. *taddhedaṁ tarhy avyākrṭam āsīt*: the world was unmanifest. (Bṛhad-āraṇyaka Upaniṣad 1.4.7) This indicates that gross world was unmanifest but existed previously as *śakti* in seed form. (This is its causal form). The subtle and gross bodies bear a similar relationship.

Sūtra – 1.4.2

|| tad-adhīnatvād arthavat ||

***Pradhāna* is useful, since it produces the world under the Lord's direction.**

Since *pradhāna* is dependent on the supreme cause, Brahman, it has a use (*arthavat*) or is capable of producing effects. It produces effects by the glance of the Lord. It cannot do this independently, since it is inert.

māyāṁ tu prakṛtiṁ vidyān
māyinaṁ tu maheśvaram

Know that *prakṛti* is *māyā* and the Lord of *māyā is* the supreme lord. Śvetāśvatara Upaniṣad 4.10

asmān māyī sṛjate viśvam etat

From *pradhāna* the Lord created this universe. Śvetāśvatara Upaniṣad 4.9

ya eka varṇo bahudhā śakti-yogād
varṇān anekān nihitārtho dadhāti

The one Lord with his own purpose, by his *śakti* produces many forms of great variety. Śvetāśvatara Upaniṣad 4.1

sa eva bhūyo nija-vīrya-coditṁ
sva-jīva-māyāṁ prakṛtiṁ sisṛkṣatīm
anāma-rūpātmani rūpa-nāmanī
vidhitsamāno 'nusasāra śāstra-kṛt

The Lord, after manifesting the scriptures, and desiring to make names and forms for the *jīvas*, then pursued *prakṛti*, who desired to create the universe, but who moves only by his power, and who by his will alone bewilders the *jīvas*. SB 1.10.22

pradhānaṁ puruṣaṁ cāpi
praviśyātmecchayā hariḥ
kṣobhayām āsa samprāpte
sarga-kāle vyayāvyayau

By his will the Lord enters *pradhāna* which is subject to change and also enters the jīva who is not subject to change, and agitates both of them at the time of creation. Viṣṇu Purāṇa

mayādhyākṣeṇa prakṛtiḥ
sūyate sa-carācaram
hetunānena kaunteya
jagad viparivartate

By my direction, *prakṛti* gives rise to the universe of moving and non-moving entities. By this cause, O son of Kuntī, the universe appears again and again. BG 9.10

Because of this, we do not entertain the Sāṅkhya view, since they hold that *pradhāna* is independent.

For another reason also, *avyakta* does not refer to *pradhāna* in the text.

Sūtra – 1.4.4

|| jñeyatvāvacanāc ca ||

***Avyakta* does not mean *pradhāna* because it is not indicated as an object of knowledge in the text.**

The followers of Sāṅkhya say that liberation is caused by distinguishing *pradhāna* from the jīva (*puruṣa*). Thus they say that *pradhāna* is an object of knowledge for gaining certain powers. Because no words in the text establish *avyakta* as the object of knowledge, it does not mean *pradhāna* in this text.

Sūtra – 1.4.5

|| vadatīti cen na prājño hi prakaraṇāt ||

If one argues that *avyakta* is described as the object of knowledge, the answer is no, because the context shows the object of knowledge is the Lord.

"You cannot say that *avyakta* is not mentioned as the object of knowledge. Later it is indicated that *avyakta* is the object of knowledge (that which is beyond *mahat* or *mahat-tattva*) with the word *nicāyya* (worship):

aśabdam asparśam arūpam avyayaṁ
tathā-rasaṁ nityam agandhavac ca yat
anādy anantaṁ mahataḥ paraṁ dhruvaṁ
nicāyya taṁ mṛtyu-mukhāt pramucyate

Meditating on that which has no sound, no touch, no form, without decay, without taste, eternal, without smell, without beginning, without end, greater than *mahat*[33], and fixed, one becomes freed from the mouth of death. Kaṭha Upaniṣad 2.3.15"

If you claim this *(vadati*), the answer is no. Why? Because (*hi*) Paramātmā or *prajña* is being described, since he is the subject of discussion:

puruṣān na paraṁ kiñcit
sā kāṣṭhā sā parā gatiḥ
eṣa sarveṣu bhūteṣu
gūḍhātmā na prakāśate

There is nothing higher than the *puruṣa* (Paramātmā). That is the highest goal. The secret *ātmā* is not visible in all beings. Kaṭha Upaniṣad 1.3.11-12

For another reason also *avyakta* does not mean *pradhāna.*

---

[33] *Mahat* actually refers to the ātmā by reference to the previous verses (*mahān ātmā)* not to *mahat-tattva*, to which *pradhāna (avyakta)* is superior.

Sūtra – 1.4.6

| | trayāṇām eva caivam upanyāsaḥ praśnaś ca | |

Only three subjects are introduced in response to three questions.

The word *ca* indicates destroying the doubt. In the three sections of the Kaṭha Upaniṣad knowledge concerning pleasing his (Naciketas') father, the fire of Svarga and the *ātmā* is given, in response to only these three questions. There is no question concerning any other object. Thus the answer cannot be taken to be *pradhāna* in this passage.

Sūtra – 1.4.7

| | mahadvac ca | |

Since *mahat* does not refer to *mahat-tattva, avyakta* cannot refer to *pradhāna*.

The text says *buddher ātmā mahān paraḥ*: the great ātmā is higher than intelligence. *Mahat* modifies ātmā and cannot mean *mahat-tattva* element of Sāṅkhya philosophy. After mentioning atmā, *avyakta* cannot mean *pradhāna* (since in Sāṅkhya *pradhāna* follows *mahat-tattva.*)

Topic 2 (Sūtras 8 – 10)

Camasādhikaraṇam - The Cup

Another Sāṅkhya conclusion is refuted. In Śvetāśvatara Upaniṣad it is said:

ajām ekāṁ lohita-śukla-kṛṣṇāṁ
bahvīḥ prajāḥ sṛjamānāṁ sarūpāḥ
ajo hy eko juṣamāno 'nuśete
jahaty enāṁ bhukta-bhogām ajo 'nyaḥ

One unborn entity, satisfied, follows another unborn entity--a female entity who is red, white and black and who produces many offspring of similar nature. Another male gives up this female who has been enjoyed. Śvetāśvatara Upaniṣad 4.5

The doubt is this. Is the unborn (*ajā)* the material *prakṛti* of the Sāṅkhya philosophy or is it something related to the Brahman mentioned in the Upaniṣads?

(Pūrva-pakṣa) Because it creates independently (creates many offspring) and is the unborn, not an effect but a cause, the unborn is *prakṛti.*

Sūtra – 1.4.8

|| camasavad aviśeṣāt ||

The unborn cannot be *prakṛti* because no particulars support that conclusion in the context, just as *camasa* does not mean cup according to context in another Upaniṣad.

The word *na* from the sūtra 1.4.5 should be added. It cannot be *prakṛti* of the Sāṅkhya philosophy. Why? Because of lack of clear reason (*aviśeṣāt*) to accept this conclusion. The only evidence is that *ajāḥ* means unborn (which could apply to other things). And example is the word *camasa* used in Bṛhad-āraṇyaka Upaniṣad 2.2.3. The word means a cup used for drinking during sacrifice, that which is used to sip (*cam*). But in the context of that passage, it cannot mean a cup.[34] One cannot determine the exact meaning of word using the etymological method without considering the context. Therefore in this mantra the unborn cannot mean *prakṛti* of the Sāṅkhya philosophy because of lack of support for this in the context. Nor can one conclude that this female produces independently from the description given. It merely says that she creates many offspring

The unborn should be accepted as the *śakti* of Brahman because of particular reasons.

Sūtra – 1.4.9

|| jyotir ūpa-kramā tu tathā hy adhīyata eke ||

Brahman is certainly the cause of *ajā* by context. As well, some branches of the Vedas have texts stating that Brahman produces *prakṛti*.

The word *tu* indicates certainty of the conclusion. The word *jyotiḥ* means Brahman, for it is well known in statements like *tad devaḥ jyotiṣāṁ jyotiḥ*: the Lord is the light among all lights. (Bṛhad-āraṇyaka Upaniṣad 4.4.16) *Upakramā* means cause. Brahman is the cause of the unborn female. The

---

[34] A metaphor is used, and the head is called a cup in that particular passage.

literal meaning "unborn," meaning "without a cause" or "independent," cannot be taken, as in the case of *camasa,* because of the special understanding derived from the context. *Arvāg-bilaś camasa ūrdhva-budhna*: the cup has its mouth downwards and its bottom upwards. (Bṛhad-āraṇyaka Upaniṣad 2.2.3) By this description the cup must actually be a head.

In the first and fourth chapters of Śvetāśvatara Upaniṣad there is mention of *ajā* with the word *śakti*. Thus *ajā* means a *śakti* of Brahman.

te dhyāna-yogānugatā apaśyan
devātma-śaktiṁ sva-guṇair nigūḍhām

Devoted to meditation, they saw the *śakti* of the Lord, hidden in its *guṇas*. Śvetāśvatara Upaniṣad 1.3

ya eka-varṇo bahudhā śakti-yogāt

The one became many by means of *śakti.* Śvetāśvatara Upaniṣad 4.1

Therefore *ajā* does not mean independent *prakṛti* of the Sāṅkhya philosophers.

Another proof is shown. The word *hi* indicates a reason. Because some schools of the Vedas teach in this way. They say that *prakṛti* arises from the Lord.

tasmād etad brahma nāma rūpam annaṁ ca jāyate

From the Lord this brahman (*prakṛti),* name, form and food were born. Muṇḍaka Upaniṣad 1.1.9

In the above verse, *brahma* means *pradhāna*, made of three *guṇas*, as in the smṛti statement *mama yonir mahad brahma*: the great *prakṛti* is my womb. (BG 14.3)

"How can *prakṛti* be called unborn and at the same time arise from Brahman?" This doubt is answered in the next sūtra.

Sūtra – 1.4.10

|| kalpanopadeśāc ca madhv-ādivad avirodhaḥ ||

There is no contradiction in saying that *prakṛti* is unborn and created because there are statements saying that *prakṛti* is created. *Prakṛti* has dual characteristics like *madhu* in the sun.

The word *ca* indicates destroying the doubt. *Prakṛti* can be both unborn and created. Why? Because scripture teaches that it is created (*kalpana*) from the *śakti* of Brahman. *Kalpana* means creation as in the phrase *yathāpūrvaṁ akalpayat*: as previously he created the universe. (Taittirīya Āraṇyaka)

The truth is this. There is a *śakti* of the Lord called *tamas* which is eternal and very subtle.

tama āsīt tamasā gūḍham agre praketaṁ yadā tamas tan na divā na rātriḥ

Before the creation, there was *tamas* covered by ignorance. When there was *tamas*, there was no day and no night. Ṛg Veda 10.1.20.3

gaur anādy-antavatī

Tamas is like a cow, without beginning or end. Cūlika Upaniṣad

At the time of universal destruction, this *śakti* unites with the Lord, but remains without merging into him. *Pṛṭhivy apsu pralīyate*: earth merges into water. Each element from earth up to *akṣara* merges into the next higher element and *akṣara* merges into *tamas.* However *tamas* does not merge into the Lord but rather "unites with him." Uniting with the Lord means it is impossible to separate it from the Lord because of its subtle nature and nothing else. *Tama ekī bhavati* (*tamas* becomes one with the Lord) means this alone. *Avyaktam (prakṛti)* with three *guṇas* arises from the śakti of *tamas* when the Lord desires to create. *mahān avyakte līyate avyaktam akṣare akṣaraṁ tamasi: mahat-tattva* merges into *avyakta* and *avyakta* merges into *akṣara*[35] and *akṣara* merges into *tamas.* Smṛti says

tasmād avyaktam utpannaṁ tri-guṇaṁ dvija-sattama: "O brāhmaṇa, from *tamas* arose *prakṛti* with the three guṇas. From *prakṛti* arise *mahat-tattva* and other elements." Thus it can be said that by saying *pradhāna* was created (*pradhāna-kalpanopadeśa*) it indicates *pradhāna* as a cause (producing mahat-tattva etc.) and as an effect (coming from or created from *tamas*).

pradhāna-puṁsor ajayoḥ kāraṇaṁ kārya-bhūtayoḥ

The Lord is the cause of *pradhāna* and the jīva, both of whom are without creation, but are also effects of the Lord. Viṣṇu Purāṇa 1.9.37

---

[35] According to Śṛī-sampradāya *avyakta* has *guṇas* manifest and *akṣara* state has no *guṇas* manifest.

At the time of creation, this *tamas,* with the name of *pradhāna* or *avyakta,* takes the form of red, white and black, or manifests three guṇas, and divides into various names and forms. Thus it is said that *prakṛti* arises from Brahman.

An example is given. Its dual nature is like *madhu* in the *madhu-vidyā*. The sun as a cause is one, and as an effect the sun becomes honey enjoyed by the Vasus and others, and seems to rise and set. Thus though *prakṛti* is created, this does not contradict other statements which say *prakṛti* is unborn.

Topic 3 (Sūtras 11 – 13)

Saṅkhyopasaṅgrahādhikaraṇam - Grouping the five of five

In Bṛhad-āraṇyaka Upaniṣad it is said:

yasmin pañca-pañca-janā ākāśāś ca pratiṣṭhitāḥ tam eva manya ātmānaṁ vidvān
brahmāmṛto 'mṛtam

Since I am in knowledge as the nectar of Brahman, I consider that to be the eternal *ātmā,* in which the five of five beings and ether reside. Bṛhad-āraṇyaka Upaniṣad 4.4.17

The doubt is this. Does the term "five of five beings" refer to the twenty-five categories in Sāṅkhya philosophy or five other things?

(Pūrva-pakṣa) Since it is a *bahuvrīhi* compound (*pañca-jana*) modified by *pañca,* it becomes a *karmadhārya,* meaning twenty-five elements as described by Kapila. *Ātmā* and ether though mentioned separately (making twenty-seven) should be ignored as separate from the twenty-five. The word *jana* also means *tattva* (element) in some instances.

Sūtra – 1.4.11

|| na saṅkhyopasaṅgrahād api nānā-bhāvād atirekāc ca ||

Though it is possible that the phrase means twenty-five, in this case it is not so, because the elements do not group themselves into five groups of five in the living beings, and there are two extra elements ātmā and ether in the list.

The word *api* admits this possibility. Even though the phrase may mean twenty -five elements, in this case it does not mean that. Why? Because it is impossible to group those elements in five groups of five. They do not occur in that grouping in various living beings *(nāna-bhāvāt).* And because with *ātmā* and ether listed separately there would be twenty-seven elements *(atirektāt).* One should not be mistaken by hearing *pañca-pañca.* What is the conclusion? *Pañca-jana* refers to the name of a whole group, like the name of the constellation called seven sages. This follows the rule *dik-saṅkhye sañjñāyām* (Pāṇini 2.1.50) Each one of the stars of the constellation is addressed as seven sages and when we mention the seven *saptarṣis*, we mean the one constellation. Similarly, five *pañca-janas* means one group of five members each of which is called *pañca-jana*. Thus "five *pañca-janas*" means "the five of the five elements."

What are these five?

Sūtra – 1.4.12

|| prāṇādayo vākya-śeṣāt ||

The five are *prāṇa*, the eye, the ear, food and mind because of the final statement in the particular section of the Upaniṣad.

prānasya prāṇam uta cakṣuṣaś cakṣur uta śrotrasya śrotram annasyānnaṁ manaso ye mano viduḥ

Those who know the *prāṇa* of the *prāṇa,* the eye of the eye, the ear of the ear, the food of food, and the mind of the mind know Brahman, ancient and primeval. Bṛhad-āraṇyaka Upaniṣad 4.4.18

The five should be understood to be the *prāṇa*, eye, ear, food and mind (each of which is called *pañca-jana*).

"That is possible by taking the Mādhyandina version of the text. However, the Kāṇva recension omits food from the list (and thus there are only four items.)" To allay this doubt it is said:

Sūtra – 1.4.13

|| jyotiṣaikeṣām asaty anne ||

Though the word "food" is missing in the Kānva recension, the word *jyotiṣ* is added to make the total five.

Though the word "food" is missing in the Kāṇva recension, the word light (*jyotiḥ*) is found there to make a total of five items. Before the description of *pañca-jana* is found the phrase *tad devā jyotiṣāṁ jyotiḥ:* the Lord is the light of lights. (Bṛhad-āraṇyaka Upaniṣad 4.4.16) Though this phrase about light occurs in both recensions, it is included to make five in the Kāṇva recension since food is omitted there, and it is omitted while counting five in the Mādhyandina recension.

Topic 4 (Sūtras 14 – 15)

Kāraṇatvādhikaraṇam - The cause of everything

The followers of Sāṅkhya raise another doubt. The Vedas do not say that Brahman is the sole cause of creation. There are texts like *tasmād vā etasmād ātmana ākāśaḥ sambhūtah*: from the *ātmā* arose ether. (Taittirīya Upaniṣad 2.1.3) In this statement, creation arises from the *ātmā.* Another texts says that *asat* is the cause. *asad vā idam agra āsīt tato vā sad ajāyata tad ātmānaṁ svayam akuruta: asat* existed previously; from *asat* rose the *sat*; it made itself. (Chāndogya Upaniṣad 6.2.1) Elsewhere, ether is said to be the cause of creation. *asya lokasya kā gatir ity ākāśa iti hovāca*: "What is the origin of the world?" "It is ether," he said. (Chāndogya Upaniṣad 1.9.1) Elsewhere, *prāṇa* is said to be the cause. *sarvāṇi hā vā imāni bhūtāni prāṇam evābhisamviśanti*: all beings enter into *prāṇa.* (Chāndogya Upaniṣad 1.11.5)

Asat is mentioned as the cause. *asad evedam agra āsīt tat sad āsīt tat samabhavat*: Previously *asat* existed; it was *sat;* it became that.(Chāndogya Upaniṣad 3.19.1) But *sat* is also said to be the cause. *sad eva saumyedam agra āsīt*: *sat* existed previously, O gentle one! And *avyakta* is said to be the cause. *tad dhedaṁ tarhy avyākṛtam āsīt tan-nāma-rūpābhyāṁ vyākriyata*: this was *avyakta*; it transformed with name and form. (Bṛhad-āraṇyaka Upaniṣad 1.4.7)

Thus there are many causes. Since one cause alone is not delineated, one cannot ascertain that Brahman alone is the cause of the universe. But it is possible to determine that *pradhāna (avyakta)* is the cause, as mentioned in the last quotation. As well, to support this assertion, one can say that effect and cause are similar. (*prāṇa*, ether etc which are effects, represent *pradhāna,* the cause). *Pradhāna* may be called *ātmā* (spreading out), ether (vast like the sky) or Brahman (that which is great) because of its pervading nature. *Pradhāṇa* can be called *asat* because it is the shelter of temporary transformations and it is called *sat* because it is eternal. It is called *prāṇa* metaphorically since it produces *prāṇa. Pradhāna* can be said to "glance" etc to express beginning of action. Therefore the Vedānta says that *pradhāna* alone is the cause of the universe. The following sūtra refutes this.

Sūtra – 1.4.14

|| kāraṇatvena cākāśādiṣu yathā-vyapadiṣṭokteḥ ||

Brahman alone can be determined as the cause of the universe since Brahman is stated to be the cause of ether and other items mentioned, according to the descriptions of Brahman in the texts.

The word *ca* indicates removing the doubt. It is possible to determine that Brahman alone is the cause of the universe. Why? Because it is the cause of ether and other items mentioned, since it is described as such in the texts. Brahman is described in some passages as having qualities like omniscience and the power to do as he wishes (*satya-saṅkalpa*). Brahman alone is described as the cause of ether and other items in all the Vedānta texts. Brahman's qualities like omniscience are described in *satyaṁ jñānam anantam*: Brahman is unlimited existence and knowledge. Following this, it is said that *ātmā* gives rise to ether. This indicates Brahman as the cause (not the individual *ātmā*). When it is said that everything arises from *sat,* this statement is followed *by tad aikṣata bahu syāma tat tejo 'sṛjata:* he thought, "Let me be many;" then he created light. Thus *sat* indicates Brahman (since he can think, whereas *pradhāna* cannot.) Other texts can be treated similarly.

The argument of similarity of effect and cause can be used to support the case for Brahman as the sole cause. (*Prāṇa* and ether are effects, but represent Brahman.) In the literal sense, *ātmā* means pervading, ether means effulgent (*kāś*), *prāṇa* means full of life, *sat* means essence and Brahman means great. These terms describe Brahman aptly. And words like "thinking" literally apply to Brahman and not to *pradhāna.*

The words *asat* and *avyākṛta* are now explained.

Sūtra – 1.4.15

|| samākarṣāt ||

Taking all the passages together, *asat* and *avyākṛta* mean Brahman.

The word *asat* refers to the subject of the previous passage starting with *so'kāmayata,* dealing with Paramātmā. Brahman was described with phrases like *asad vā* and *āditiyo brahma* (Chāndogya Upaniṣad 3.19.1) Thus *asad evedam* refers to the supreme Brahman by taking all the passages together (*samākārṣāt*).

The word *asat* (non-existence) refers to Brahman because before creation, name and form did not exist, and thus Brahman was not related to them. This alone can be the meaning, for there is a later statement *sad eva saumya: "sat* alone existed, O gentle one!" This shows that *asat* is not the real cause since another cause exists. Also it is impossible to relate non-existence to time by the verb *āsīt* (non-existence existed). The text itself also refutes the idea of *asat* being the cause. Thus *asat* means Brahman in possession of invisible *śaktis*.

The word *avyākṛta* also refers to Brahman in intermediate state. This can be deduced by taking the later statement *sa eṣa iha praviṣṭa*: he entered it. Brahman with his *śaktis* (from undeveloped state *avyākṛta*) then developed with name and form by his own decision. Otherwise, to take *avyākrṭa* as *pradhāna* would contradict the conclusion established by Vedānta-- which concludes that the Lord is ultimate (*gati samānyāt*: all scriptures describe the Lord in sūtra 1.1.27). Therefore the texts determine that one Brahman is the cause of the universe.

Topic 5 (Sūtras 16 – 18)

Jagad-vācitvādhikaraṇam - The creator of the world

Sāṅkhya is again refuted. In the Kauṣītaki-brāhmaṇa, Bālāki says to the king named Ajātaśatru, "I will teach you about Brahman." After he explained sixteen persons such as Āditya to be Brahman, Ajātaśatru rejected this explanation. *yo vai bālāka eteṣāṁ puruṣānāṁ kartā yasya caitat karma sa veditavya:* O Bālāki! He who is the cause of these persons, who performs action, should be known.

The doubt is this. Does this teach that the person to be known is the enjoyer and controller of *prakṛti (puruṣa* or jīva) of the Sāṅkhya philosophy or does it teach Viṣṇu, the supreme Lord?

(Pūrvapakṣa) It is the *puruṣa* of Sāṅkhya because it is understood that jīva is the enjoyer since it is stated that he performs actions. He is also described as the enjoyer later on. *tau ha suptaṁ puruṣam ājagmatuḥ:* the two went to a sleeping person. *tad yathā śreṣṭhaiḥ svair bhuṅkte*: a person enjoys with his best men. The word *prāṇa* (life) is used because the jīva supports life.

Therefore this is the meaning. *yo vai bālāka eteṣāṁ puruṣānāṁ kartā yasya caitat karma sa veditavya:* one should know, distinct from *prakṛti,* that person (*jīva*) who is the cause (*kartā*) of human bodies used for enjoyment and who produces karma of sin and piety which cause the enjoyment.

Thus one should know that this passage refers to the jīva as described in Sāṅkhya. And the Brahman that was promised in the teachings is the jīva only, since there is no controller other than the jīva. Thinking and other attributes of the senses are suitable to the jīva. *Prakṛti* creates the universe and the jīva is its controller.

Sūtra – 1.4.16

|| jagad-vācitvāt ||

The passage does not refer to the jīva because the word *karma* means "creation of the universe."

Here the insignificant jīva of Sāṅkhya is not discussed. The passage speaks of the Supreme Lord to be known as the sole object of worship in the Vedas. Why? Because the words *etat-karma* used in describing the person means "the universe made of matter and jīvas." The Lord is the creator of this universe. Here is the meaning. The word karma in the context means the universe--that which is made (*kriyate*).

The passage speaks of the Lord who has this (*etat*) action (*karma*), creating the universe-- which was attributed to sixteen other persons. Accepting this explanation, the word *etat* becomes meaningful (emphasized, being the action of the Lord not sixteen other persons mentioned). It also removes the problem of the jīva being the creator (*karṭa* in the verse), since even the followers of Sāṅkhya do not accept the jīva as the creator. (Sāṅkhyites say *prakṛti* is the creator.) The jīva cannot be the creator by superimposition (*adhyāsa*), since the jīva does not associate with *prakṛti* at all according to Sāṅkhya. Therefore the creator (*kartā*) is the supreme Lord.

This explanation avoids the implication that Ajātaśatru told a lie when he promised, "I will speak to you about Brahman." When Bālāki spoke of the seven *puruṣas,* Ajātaśatru said that those statements were all false. When Ajātaśatru desired that he speak of Brahman, if Bālāki then spoke of the jīva, he would similarly be speaking falsely. Thus the person discussed is Brahman, not the jīva. One should know the Supreme Lord, who is the creator of the persons who were falsely explained to be Brahman and who is the supreme cause of all the universe.

"One should accept the jīva as the subject of the passage since the passage states characteristics of the jīva and the chief *prāṇa.*"

Sūtra – 1.4.17

|| jīva-mukhya-prāṇa-liṅgān neti cet tad vyākhyātam ||

If one argues that the passage does not refer to the Lord because of references to the jīva and chief prāṇa, the answer is no. The reasons were explained previously in sutra 1.1.31.

In the analysis of the story of Indra and Pratardhana (1.1.31), it was concluded that, because Brahman was the topic of discussion in the beginning and ending passages, any words in the intermediate passages that might denote the jīva were actually describing Brahman. The same principle applies to this discussion. In the present case also, the beginning of the discussion is, "I will speak to you about Brahman." The end of the discussion says, "He who knows this surpasses all sins and becomes the best leader among all beings." Because of this, all other words that seem to refer to the jīva should be taken as references to Brahman. Why is the same topic discussed here again? The topic is not redundant, though it was delineated in the discussion about Pratardana, since the new topic is the interpretation of the word *karma.*

"Though it is possible to conclude that Brahman is the subject of the discussion because of the word *karma* modified by *etat* and because of the word *prāṇa,* it is finally not possible to make this conclusion because of the glorification of the jīva in the same passage. And it is not possible to conclude that Brahman is different from the jīva from the questions and answers in the passage, because the subject is clearly the jīva. The question about the sleeper relates to the jīva. Only jīva is described as having the *nādīs* as his place of sleep. The senses merge into the jīva called *prāṇa* during sleep. It is the jīva who awakens. Since all this refers to the jīva, the subject is jīva (who is also called Brahman.)" The next sūtra replies to this doubt.

Sūtra – 1.4.18

|| anyārthas tu jaiminiḥ praśna-vyākhyānābhyām api caivam eke ||

According to Jaimini the discussion about the jīva has another purpose. From the questions and answers it can be concluded that the jīva is distinct from Brahman. The Vājasaneya recension also makes the difference clear.

The word *tu* indicates destruction of this doubt. The discussion of the jīva has another purpose (*anyārthaḥ)*. It is for the purpose of indicating that Brahman is different from jīva. This is the opinion of Jaimini. Why? The question itself indicates that the jīva is different from the *prāṇa* since the jīva awakens with enlivened *prāṇa* and emerges from something (later explained as *prāṇa). kvaiṣa etad bālāke puruṣa śayiṣṭa kva vā etad abhūt kuta etad agāt:* O Bālāki, where does this person rest while he sleeps, and from where does he come when he wakes? (Kauṣītaki Upaniṣad 4.18)

The answer also shows the difference of jīva from Brahman. *yadā suptaḥ svapnaṁ na kañcana paśyati tathāsmin prāṇa evaikadhā bhavati:* when he sleeps without seeing a dream, he becomes one with the *prāṇa. etasmād ātmanaḥ prāṇā yathāyatanaṁ vipratiṣṭante prāṇebhyo devā devebhyo lokāḥ*: from that *ātmā* comes the breath of life and from the breath of life comes the *devatā* and from the *devatās* come the planets. From this it is understood that Brahman is different from the jīva. *Prāṇa* refers to Paramātmā since Paramātmā is well known as the support of the jīva during deep sleep. The jīva goes into and comes out of Paramātmā. The *nāḍīs* serve as the gates for going to the place of sleep. One should understand in this verse that the jīva, tired from staying awake, enters Paramātmā and goes to sleeps and again comes out of Paramātmā on waking for enjoyment.

In the Vājasaneya version of the Upaniṣad, during the discussion of Bālāki and Ajātaśatru, the word *vijñāna-maya* is used to denote the jīva. Thus this version also declares that the jīva is different from Brahman. The question is *ya eṣa vijñānamayaḥ puruṣaḥ kvaiṣa tadābhūt kuta etad āgāt*: O Bālāki, where does this person full of knowledge rest while he sleeps and from where does he come when he wakes? The answer is *ya eṣo 'ntar hṛdaya ākāśas tasmin śete*: he sleeps in the *ākāśa* (Brahman) within the heart. Therefore the text teaches that the Supreme Lord alone should be known.

Topic 6 (Sūtras 19 – 22)

Vākyānyādhikaraṇam - By context the Lord is understood

In Bṛhad-āraṇyaka Upaniṣad, Yājñavalkya instructs his wife Maitreyī.

na vā are patyuḥ kāmāya patiḥ priyo bhavati
na vā are sarvasya kāmāya sarvaṁ priyaṁ bhavati ātmanas tu kāmāya sarvaṁ priyaṁ bhavati
ātmā vā are draṣṭavyaḥ śrotavyo mantavyo nididhyāsitavyo maitreyy ātmano vā
are darśanena śravaṇena matyā vijñānena idaṁ sarvaṁ viditam

The husband is dear to the wife not for loving the husband, but for loving the *ātmā*.

Everything is dear not for loving those objects, but for loving the *ātmā*. O Maitreyī, ātmā should be seen, heard, contemplated, meditated upon. By seeing, hearing, contemplating and realizing *ātmā,* everything becomes known. Bṛhad-āraṇyaka Upaniṣad 2.45, 4-6

There is a doubt in this passage. Is the *ātmā* which is to be seen and heard the jīva of Sāṅkhya philosophy, or is it Paramātmā?

(Pūrva-pakṣa) It is jīva because the commencement of the passage describes love between a husband and wife. Also in the middle of the passage, going from body to body with production and destruction of bodies is described:

etebhyo bhūtebhyaḥ samutthāya tāny evānuvinaśyati na pretya-saṁjñāsti

When he rises from the elements, he vanishes with them. When he departs, there is no consciousness.

At the conclusion, the jīva is indicated as the knower. *vijñātāram are kena vijānīyāt*: by what should the knower be known? "Knowing that *ātmā* everything becomes known" cannot literally be applied to the jīva but metaphorically it can, for when the jīva is known as the enjoyer, he understands all things as objects of enjoyment.

At the beginning of the passage, the subject of immortality is indicated. *Amṛtatvasya tu nāśāsti vettena:* there is no hope for being immortal by attachment to wealth. Therefore the topic is discussed in order to attain immortality. How then can the topic be about knowing the jīva if the purpose is to attain immortality? According to Sāṅkhya however immortality is possible by jīva realizing he is distinct from *prakṛti*. Therefore qualities which may be ascribed to Brahman in this passage are not valid. The jīva is taught in this passage. *Prakṛti* which the jīva rules creates the universe.

This is refuted in the next sūtra.

Sūtra – 1.4.19

|| vākyānvayāt ||

The subject is Paramātmā because of the context.

Paramātmā alone is taught in this passage, not the jīva of the Sāṅkhya philosophy, since that is the conclusion after reviewing all passages before and after.

This meaning of the statement as an answer to a promise is confirmed by the opinions of three sages.

Sūtra – 1.4.20

|| pratijñā-siddher liṅgam āśmarathaḥ ||

Āśmaratha concludes that the *ātmā* refers to Paramātmā because of indications in the promise that by knowing *ātmā* all things are known.

The promise is that knowing this *ātmā* everything becomes known. Āśmaratha considers this indicates Paramātmā. It is not taught in scriptures that by knowing the jīva one knows everything. In other places, it is said that by knowing the supreme cause everything becomes known. It is not possible to say that the statement is metaphorical, for it is explained that this same *ātmā* is the form of everything, the shelter of brāhmaṇas, kṣatriyas and the universe. And the *ātmā* cannot be the jīva, for other statements following that indicate only the Lord. Nor is it possible to say that *ātmā* is the jīva controlled by karma, since this *ātmā* is said to be the cause of the whole universe. *tasya vā etasya mahato bhūtasya niḥśvasitam:* everything arose as the breathing of the great being. Nor would a teacher speak about the jīva instead of Brahman to his wife Maitreyī, who asked about the means of liberation after renouncing wealth, since knowledge of jīva would not produce liberation. On the other hand, it is said in scriptures that knowledge of Brahman leads to liberation. Therefore ātmā means Paramātmā.

"*Ātmā* refers to the jīva because there is proof of rebirth in mentioning affection of the wife for husband. Nor should one explain that *ātmā* is Paramātmā on the promise that by knowing him everything becomes known and that, by worshipping Paramātmā, the jīva becomes dear to all and shows compassion to all. It is true that smṛti says:

yenārcito haris tena tarpitāni jaganty api
rajyanti jantavas tatra sthāvarā jaṅgamā api

One who worships the Lord is pleasing to all the worlds. And all moving and non-moving creatures are pleasing to the devotee. Padma Purāṇa

However this is mere exaggeration, since it has never been seen that by worshipping the Lord the devotee becomes dear to all and they become dear to him."

Sūtra – 1.4.21

|| utkramiṣyata evam-bhāvād ity auḍulomiḥ ||

Auḍulomi says that *ātmā* means Paramātmā because the person who approaches Paramātmā becomes dear to all.

Auḍulomi says that *ātmā* means Paramātmā because the wise man, who practices and approaches (*utkramiṣataḥ*) realization of Paramātmā, becomes dear to all (*evam bhāvāt*). The meaning of the statement is as follows. The husband is not a loving husband if he thinks, "I will love for my own purposes (*patyuḥ kāmāya*)." He becomes a loving husband when he thinks, "I will be affectionate to her for satisfying the Lord-- engaging her for the Lord's worship." *Kāmā* here means desire. Therefore *ātmanaḥ kāmāya* would mean "to satisfy the Lord." *kriyārthopapadasya ca karmaṇi sthāninaḥ*: dative case can stand in place of an infinitive. (Pāṇini 2.3.14) The Lord worshipped by bhakti makes all things pleasing for the devotee.

akiñcanasya dāntasya
śāntasya sama-cetasaḥ
mayā santuṣṭa-manasaḥ
sarvāḥ sukhamayā diśaḥ

One who does not desire anything within this world, who has controlled his senses, who has fixed his intelligence on me, who regards heaven and hell equally, and whose mind is completely satisfied in me finds only happiness wherever he goes. SB 11.14.13

Or satisfying the husband does not make him a good husband but satisfying the Lord makes him dear:

prāṇa-buddhi-manaḥ-svātma
dārāpatya-dhanādayaḥ
yat-samparkāt priyā āsaṁs
tataḥ ko 'nyaḥ paraḥ priyaḥ

It is only by contact with the Paramātmā that one's vital breath, intelligence, mind, friends, body, wife, children, wealth and so on are dear. Therefore what object can possibly be dearer than Paramātmā? SB 10.23.27

Kāma means happiness in this verse. Dative case is used as previously in this meaning. Someone becomes dear from relationship with (and consequently the will of) the Lord. The Lord alone is dear.

The word *ātmā* cannot mean the jīva since the etymology of the word refers to the all-pervading Lord (ātmā =pervading). Otherwise the word *ātmā* used in the beginning would be contrary to the statement *athā ātmā vā* used later, which definitely refers to the Lord. If that were the case, the fault of the same word having a different meaning in proximity would take place. If ā*tmā* refers to the jīva in the first instance, we see no use at all in the first statement referring to jīva, since the later passage says that the *ātmā* should be seen (*draṣṭavyaḥ)* as a means of gaining liberation. Nor can both statements concerning *ātmā* refer to the jīva because the qualities of the Lord only are shown in both statements.

Auḍulomi is a propounder of *nirguṇātmā* since it will be said later *citi tan-mātreṇa tad-ātmakatvād ity auḍulomiḥ:* the liberated jīva is pure intelligence because that is the essence of the statement, according to Auḍulomi. (4.4.6) However, he maintains that the Lord must be worshipped in order to destroy *avidyā* and reveal the ātmā. This is revealed later in this work. *ārtvijyam ity auḍulomis tasmai hi parikrīyate*: the Lord sells himself to the devotee, like the priest to the sponsor, according to Auḍulomi. (3.4.45) Thus bhakti will enable one to attain all desires (even according to him).

Let that be. However, the following is stated:

sa yathā saindhava-khilya udake prāptam udakam evānulīyate na hāsyodgrahaṇāyaiva syād yato yatas tv ādīta lavaṇam evaivaṁ vā. are idaṁ mahad bhūtam anantam apāraṁ vijñāna-ghana evaitebhyo bhūtebhyaḥ samutthāya tāny evānuvinaśyati

Whenever salt is placed in water, it merges with it and cannot be taken out. Whenever we taste water, we taste salt. The great, unlimited, infinite being emerges from the elements and disappears in them. Bṛhad-āraṇyaka Upaniṣad 2.4.12

How can this statement in the middle of the dialogue be reconciled with the proposition that only the Lord is the subject? It is more suitable that the subject is the jīva as described by Sāṅkhya philosophy.

Sūtra – 1.4.22

|| avasthiter iti kāśa-kṛtsnaḥ ||

Kāsa-krṭsna says that the great being is the Lord because of the teachings concerning the great being who is full of knowledge.

This text in the middle of the section teaches that Paramātmā is the great element, distinct from the jīva. Paramātmā is described by the word *vijñāna-ghanaḥ* (full of knowledge), represented by a lump of salt, and unites with the jīva who is like water. Because of the distinction made between the superior *ātmā* and inferior *ātmā,* the great, unlimited object (*idaṁ mahad bhūtam anantam apāraṁ)* who is full of knowledge, cannot be the jīva. This is the opinion of Kāśakrṭsna.

The meaning is this. The sage is asked about the method of liberation. *Yenāhaṁ nāmṛtaḥ syāṁ kim ahaṁ tena kuryām:* what do I have to do with things which obstruct my being immortal? (Bṛhad-āraṇyaka Upaniṣad 4.5.4) The sage explains the method of liberation, worship of Paramātmā, with the words *ātmā vā are draṣṭavyaḥ śrotavyo mantavyo nididhyāsitavyo maitreyy ātmano vā are darśanena śravaṇena matyā vijñānena idaṁ sarvaṁ viditam* (previously translated). He then mentions some of the qualities of the object of worship with the words *ātmani khalv are dṛṣṭe:* having seen the Lord, all things are known (4.5.6). He then indicates the method of worship to include sense control with *sa yathā dundubheḥ:* when a drum is beaten (4.5.8).

After this general description, he then explains in more detail about the method and object of worship with *sa yathā 'rdraidhāgenḥ:* just as smoke arises from wet fire wood (4.5.11) and *sa yathāsarvāsaṁ apā:* just as the ocean is the goal of water (4.5.12). Then to excite the listener to practice the method of liberation, he describes the intimate contact of jīva with the object of worship by giving the example of salt being inseparable from water.

But then he describes the confusion of a person who does not worship the Lord and who identifies with the body which is subjected to birth and death, through the metaphor of leaving the body and disappearing (*etebhya eva bhūtebhyaḥ sumutthāya* 4.5.13). The person who worships the Lord however attains final separation from the material body and no longer identifies with the names of this world. That is described with *na pretya saṁjñāstiti:* he gains liberation. The liberated person, having merged the elements, does not identify himself with bodies of humans or devatās, because of manifesting his natural knowledge of himself. He then teaches that Paramātmā is the shelter of the liberated person with *yatra hi daivatam iva bhavati:* where the two exist. He states that the Lord is difficult to understand. *yenedaṁ sarvaṁ vijānatī taṁ kena vijāniyāt*: how can one know the person by knowing whom everything is known? He ends with *vijñātāram are kena vijānīyāt:* how should one know the knower?

Can one know the omniscient Lord, without his mercy produced by worshipping him? Not at all. He concludes by saying that this worship is the method of gaining immortality. Attaining Paramātmā is immortality. Thus Paramātmā is delineated in this section, not the jīva or *prakṛti* ruled by the jīva of Sāṅkhya philosophy.

Topic 7 (Sūtras 23 – 27)

Prakṛty-adhikaraṇam - Prakṛti as the material cause

Having refuted the atheistic proponents (*nirīṣvara*-not acknowledging the Lord) of *pradhāna* as the cause of everything, now the author refutes the concept of *seśvara* (acknowledging the Lord, but not completely) by taking statements concerning the cause of the world and showing that they indicate the supreme Brahman.

The following statements occur in the śrutis.

tasmād vā etasmād ātmana ākāśaḥ sambhūtaḥ

From ātmā the sky was manifested. Taittirīya Upaniṣad 2.1.1

yato vā imāni bhūtāni jāyante

From that, these creatures were born. Taittirīya Upaniṣad 2.1.1

sad eva saumyedam agra āsīd ekam evādvitīyaṁ tad aikṣata bahu syām prajāyeya

O gentle one, in the beginning was the Supreme, who was one without a second. He thought: let me become many, let me produce progeny. Chāndogya Upaniṣad 6.2.1

sa aikṣata lokān nu sṛjā

He thought: now I shall create the worlds. Aitareya Upaniṣad 1.1.2

(doubt) Do the statements indicate Brahman as the *nimitta* (efficient cause) or as both the *nimitta* and *upādāna* (material cause)?

(Pūrva-pakṣa) Though the Upaniṣads say that the supreme Brahman is the cause of the universe with statements like *tasmād vā etasmād ātmana ākāśaḥ sambhūtaḥ* (above) Brahman should be considered to be the efficient cause only, since there are statements that the Lord glanced or thought (*sa aikṣata, tad aikṣata*) in order to cause creation. We see the creator, such as the potter, who is the efficient cause of pots. The material cause of the universe is *prakṛti* only, for we see resemblance between the material cause, *prakṛti* and the effects, the world. And it is impossible to say that the efficient cause is itself the material cause since we see difference between the material cause, clay, and its efficient cause, the potter, who is conscious. And it is seen that there are many causes which combine to produce one effect. Ignoring ordinary experience, one cannot say that one object is both the efficient and material cause. *Prakṛti,* transformed by its controller, unchanging Brahman, is the material cause of the universe, which is the transformed product. Brahman is only the efficient cause. This is not only a logical conclusion. Śruti also supports this:

vikāra-jananīm ajñāṁ
aṣṭa-rūpām ajāṁ dhruvam
dhyāyate 'dhyāsitā tena
tanyate preritā punaḥ
sūyate puruṣārthaṁ ca

tenaivādhiṣṭhitā jagat
gaur anādy-antavatī sā
janitrī bhūta-bhāvinī
sitāsitā ca raktā ca
sarvakām adhunā vibhoḥ
pibanty enām aviṣamām avijñātāḥ kumārakāḥ
ekas tu pibate devaḥ
svacchando 'tra vaśānugām
dhyāna-kriyābhyāṁ bhagavān
bhuṅkte 'sau prasabhaṁ vibhuḥ
sarva-sādhāraṇīṁ dogdhrīṁ
pīyamānāṁ tu yajvabhiḥ
catur-viṁśati-saṅkhyākaṁ avyaktaṁ vyaktam ucyate

The Lord meditates on the mother of transformation, ignorance, having eight forms, unborn, and permanent. Being the object of meditation, inspired, she produces.

Controlled by him, the mother, like a cow, with no beginning or end, producing all beings, gives birth to the universe for the jīvas. She is white, black and red, makes no distinctions among them and fulfills the desires of the Lord. One person, the Lord, however drinks by his will, since she is under his control. By meditation and action the powerful Lord strongly enjoys the cow who serves all beings, who is drunk by the sacrificers. The invisible becomes visible as twenty-four elements. Cūlika Upaniṣad

Smṛti also says:

yathā sannidhi-mātreṇa
gandhaḥ kṣobhāya jāyate
manaso nopakartṛtvāt
tathāsau parameśvaraḥ

Just as a fragrance by its mere proximity to mind produces mental agitation without directly contacting the mind,similarly the Lord also agitates *prakṛti* without contacting it.

sannidhānād yathākāśa- kālādyāḥ kāraṇaṁ taroḥ
tathaivāpariṇāmena viśvasya bhagavān hariḥ

Just as space and time by their very presence are causes of a tree , though they themselves don't change, so the Lord by his very presence creates the universe without transforming himself.

nimitta-mātram evāsau
sṛṣṭānāṁ sarga-karmaṇi
pradhāna-kāriṇī bhūtā
yato vai sṛjya-śaktayaḥ

In the actions of creation the Lord is the efficient cause of everything created. *Pradhāna* is the material cause, endowed with powers for creation. Viṣṇu Purāṇa

Those texts which say that Brahman is the material cause should be explained in another way.

The following sūtra refutes this.

Sūtra – 1.4.23

|| prakṛtiś ca pratijñā-dṛṣṭāntānurodhāt ||

The Lord is also the material cause because of correlation of the proposition and the example.

Brahman is the material cause *(prakṛtiḥ*) of the universe. Why? Because only then is there harmony between the propositions and the examples. There is the following proposition about knowing something which provides all knowledge:

śvetaketo yan nu saumyedaṁ mahā-manā anūcāna-mānī stabdho
'sy uta tam ādeśam aprākṣīr yenāśrutaṁ śrutaṁ bhavaty amataṁ
matam avijñātaṁ vijñātam

Gentle Śvetaketu! You are very proud, praised, thinking yourself a scholar. Have you asked about the ruler by which the unheard becomes heard, the inconceivable becomes conceived and the unknown becomes known? Chāndogya Upaniṣad 6.1.3

This proposition becomes possible if the ruler is also the material cause because the Brahman as *prakṛti* is non-different from the effects (universe). An efficient cause alone however is not non-different from the effect, as we see in the case of the potter and the pot. There is an example given. *yathā somyaikena mṛt-piṇḍena sarvaṁ mṛnmayaṁ vijñātaṁ syāt*: by knowing one portion of earth, all things made of earth are known. (Chāndogya Upaniṣad 6.1.4) The subject of this statement is knowing the material effects by knowing the material cause. This is not possible by knowing only the efficient cause. If one knows the potter, the pot is not known. For harmony between the proposition and the example, Brahman is the material cause, and from the explicit statements of scripture Brahman is also the efficient cause.

Sūtra – 1.4.24

|| abhidhyopadeśāc ca ||

Brahman is both the efficient and material cause because of teachings about his desire.

The word *ca* indicates inclusion of unspoken elements.

so 'kāmayata bahu syāṁ prajāyeya sa tapo 'tapyata tapas taptvā idaṁ sarvam asṛjat. yad idaṁ kiñcana tat sṛṣṭvā tad evānuprāviśat. tad anupraviśya sac ca tyac cābhavat

He desired, "Let there be many. May I produce progeny." He performed penance, and having done penance, created all this. Having created this, he entered it. Entering it, he became *sat* (jīva*)* and *tyat* (matter). Taittirīya Upaniṣad 2.6.1

The Lord is both the efficient and material cause because of teachings about the will of the Lord to become many, as matter and jīvas (thus indicating that he is the efficient cause), and because of the teaching that he created many things which are himself (thus indicating that he is the material cause).

Sūtra – 1.4.25

|| sākṣāc cobhayāmnātāt ||

The Lord is the efficient and the material cause because of a direct statement to that effect.

The word *ca* indicates certainty.

kiṁsvid vanaṁ ka u sa vṛkṣa āsīt yato dyāvā-pṛthivī niṣṭatakṣuḥ
maṇīṣiṇo manasā pṛcchataitat yad adhyatiṣṭhad bhuvanāni dhārayan
brahma vanaṁ brahma sa vṛkṣa āsīt yato dyāvā-pṛthivī niṣṭatakṣuḥ
manīṣiṇo manasā prabravīmi vo brahmādhyatiṣṭhad buvanāni dhārayan

What was the forest and what was the tree, from which he made heaven and earth? O wise men! Ask with your mind, "What person, supporting the worlds, ruled over it?" The forest and tree from which he made heaven and earth were Brahman. O wise men! I say to you with my mind that Brahman supporting the worlds ruled over it. Taittirīya Brāhmaṇa 2.8.9.6

The Lord is the efficient and material cause because of the above statement which directly indicates the Lord as both causes. From the tree, which arises from the material cause (*prakṛti*), the Lord made heaven and earth, representing the universe. The plural form of the verb is a Vedic usage. What is the tree and what is the forest, its support? Who is it that, supporting the worlds, stood? In answer to these worldly questions, Brahman is the material cause (forest and tree--effects) and the efficient cause (the ruler). This is possible because Brahman is non-worldly. Thus the Lord is both the material and efficient cause according to this direct statement.

Sūtra – 1.4.26

|| ātma-kṛteḥ pariṇāmāt ||

The Lord is the material and efficient cause of the universe because scripture states that he is the maker of himself (the world) and because he can modify himself through his *śaktis*.

so 'kāmayata: he desired may I become many. (Taittirīya Upaniṣad 2.6) This desire for creation can refer only to Paramātmā. Another statement is *tadāmānaṁ svayam akuruta:* he made himself. (Taittirīya Upaniṣad 2.7) The person who acted as creator is also the object created. This indicates that the Lord is agent and the object acted upon.

"How can one entity already existing as the doer be acted upon to become something created?" This takes place by transformation (*pariṇāmāt*). There is no contradiction in the Lord, because his position of being changeless is not in conflict with a particular type of modification.

Here is the truth of the matter. Brahman has three *śaktis* according to śruti and smṛti.

pradhāna-kṣetrajña-patir guṇeśaḥ

The Lord is master of the *guṇas,* master of *prakṛti* and the *jīva*. Śvetāśvatara Upaniṣad 6.16

parāsya śaktir vividhiava śrūyate
svābhāvikī jñāna-bala-kriyā ca

The Lord is glorified as having various intrinsic śaktis of *jñāna, bala and kriya.* Śvetāśvatara Upaniṣad 6.8

viṣṇu-śaktiḥ parā proktā
kṣetrajñākhyā tathāparā
avidyā-karma-saṁjñānyā
tṛtīyā śaktir ucyate

The Lord has a superior energy, another energy called the *jīva* and a third energy, the material energy, called *avidyā-karma. Viṣṇu Purāṇa*

It is described in scriptures that Brahman is both the efficient cause and the material cause. He is the efficient cause by being the possessor of the *parā śakti*. He is the material cause by his other two *śaktis: aparā* (jīva) and *avidyā (prakṛti).* There is a rule *sa-viśeṣaṇe vidhi-niṣedhau viśesaṇam upasaṁkrāmataḥ sati viśeṣye bādhe:* statements of affirmation and denial change the meaning of their particular descriptive elements if there is a contradiction to the principal subject. (*Nyāya-vartika-tātparya* by Vacaspati Miśra). (It is a contradiction to assert that the Lord can transform, since he is changeless. Thus he transforms via his *śaktis* related to matter and jīva.) It is also said *ya eko 'varṇo bahudhā śakti-yogād:* the Lord is one but many by the application of *śakti.* (Śvetāśvatara Upaniṣad 4.1)

Thus as the efficient cause, Brahman is without change. As material cause he is subject to change. As the doer, he has a subtle nature and as the object acted upon, he has a gross nature. In this way both qualities apply to the one Brahman because of the scriptural example of a lump of clay (Chāndogya Upaniṣad 6.1.1) and the present sūtra.

This conclusion defeats the theory of *vivarta* in which the world exists as a false imposition on Brahman (and not as a transformation of Brahman's *śakti*). It is impossible to have a false imposition of the world upon Brahman, like imposing the concept of silver on a shell, since no person can stand in front of Brahman to make this mistaken imposition-- since Brahman is the greatest. Brahman is not like *ākāśa* (which is great and colorless but can have imposition of color) since Brahman cannot be perceived or understood like material *ākāśa.* Moreover, the appearance of illusion means the existence of something called illusion. That is not possible without reverting to another cause, more illusion, something other than Brahman. Thus the theory becomes an endless cycle of illusion.

Sometimes the world is called an illusion to induce detachment from it. This is the opinion of the knowers of truth. If the world was actually an illusion, there would be scarcity or excess of the elements and sense objects, since there would be no laws governing the workings of the world. One would see irregular change in the state of objects, whereas we see that their natures are actually regulated. Therefore *pariṇāma,* actual modification of Brahman (through *śakti*), is the teaching of scripture.

Sūtra – 1.4.27

|| yoniś ca hi gīyate ||

The Lord is the material cause because the Lord is described as the womb of created beings in the scriptures.

It the śrutis, the Lord is called the *yoni* (material cause) or source and the creator (efficient cause). Therefore Brahman is both material and efficient cause. *Yad bhūta-yoniṁ paripaśyanti dhīrāḥ:* the wise see the Lord who is the womb of all beings. (Muṇḍaka Upaniṣad 1.2.6*) kartāram īśaṁ puruṣaṁ brahma yoniṁ*: one sees the person who is the creator, the Lord, Brahman and womb. (Muṇḍaka Upaniṣad 3.1.3) The word *yoni* (womb) indicates that the Lord is the material cause as in the phrase "the earth is the womb of herbs and trees."

"In the ordinary world and in scriptures, the efficient and material causes are different and it is usually necessary for many factors to be involved to produce one effect. Thus one cannot say that one person could function in both ways." However, this is possible for Brahman because of the statements to this effect in the scriptures.

Topic 8 (Sūtra 28)

Sarva-vyākyātādhikaraṇam - The Lord is all names

This section's purpose is to destroy the doubt, "Can the conclusion already shown be accepted or not?" It is said in Śvetāśvatara and other Upaniṣads:

kṣaraṁ pradhānam amṛtākṣaraḥ haraḥ

Pradhāna is subject to change. *Hara* is immortal and unchanging. Śvetāśvatara Upaniṣad 1.10

eko rudro na dvitīyāya tasthuḥ

Only Rudra existed and no one else. Śvetāśvatara Upaniṣad 3.2

yo devānāṁ prabhavaś codbhavaś ca
viśvādhiko rudraḥ śivo maharṣiḥ

He who is the creation and power of the *devatās* is the controller of the universe, Rudra, Śiva, the great sage. Śvetāśvatara Upaniṣad 3.4

yadā tamas tan na divā na rātrir
na san na cāsac chiva eva kevalaḥ

When there is darkness, there is no day or night, no *sat* or *asat*. Only Śiva exists. Śvetāśvatara Upaniṣad 4.18

pradhānād idam utpannam
pradhānam adhigacchati
pradhāne layam abhyeti
na hy anyat kāranaṁ matam

From *pradhāna* this world arises and into *pradhāna* it goes. The world merges into *pradhāna.* There is no other cause.

jīvād bhavanti bhūtāni
jīve tiṣṭhanty acañcalāḥ
jīve ca layam icchanti
na jīvāt kāraṇaṁ param

All entities arise from the jīva. Without movement they remain in the jīva. They merge into the jīva. There is no cause other than the jīva.

Here is the doubt. Do the names like Hara and Rudra in these verses refer to Śiva or the supreme Brahman, and do *pradhāna* and jīva mean *pradhāna* and jīva or the supreme Brahman?

(Pūrva-pakṣa) They mean Śiva, *pradhāna* and jīva since these are the normal meanings of those words.

Sūtra – 1.4.28

|| etena sarve vyākhyātā vyākhyātāḥ ||

By the conclusion already reached in this section, all other names indicate the Supreme Lord if the context indicates this.

All the names like Hara mentioned (*sarve vyākyātā*) should be taken to mean Brahman by considering the conclusion already reached in this section (*etena*) since all names are the Lord's names.

The Bhāllaveya-śruti explains:

nāmāni viśvāni na santi loke
yad āvirāsīt puruṣasya sarvam
nāmāni sarvāṇi yam āviśanti
taṁ vai viṣṇuṁ paramam udāharanti

All the names do not belong to the people since all of them refer to the Lord. The wise say that it is the supreme Viṣṇu whom all names indicate.

Vaiśampāyana also says that all names are the names of Kṛṣṇa. Also it is said *śrī-nārāyaṇādīni nāmāni vinānyāni rudrādibhyo harir dattavān*: except for the names like Nārāyaṇa, the Lord gave the other names to Śiva and others. (Skanda Purāṇa)

The principle, however, is as follows. Where there is no contradiction to other statements, in that case the names refer to the other deities. Where there is a contradiction, then the names must refer to Viṣṇu. The last word *vyākhyātāḥ* is repeated to indicate the end of the chapter.

Chapter Two

Table of Contents (Chapter 2)

Section One

duryuktika-droṇaja-bāṇa-vikṣataṁ
parīkṣitaṁ yaḥ sphuṭam uttarāśrayam |
sudarśanena śruti-maulim avyathaṁ vyadhāt
sa kṛṣṇaḥ prabhur astu me gatiḥ ||

May Lord Kṛṣṇa, who, by his Sudarśana cakra, protected extraordinary Parīkṣit in the womb of Uttarā when he was wounded by the devious Aśvatthāma's arrows, be my refuge.

May Vyāsa who protected the most excellent, crown jewel of the Vedas (Upaniṣads), pertaining to the Uttara Mīmāṁsa, which is examined by the Vedānta-sūtras, which had been misinterpreted by arrows from envious scorpions, be my refuge.

Topic 1 (Sūtras 1 – 2)

Smṛty-adhikaraṇam - Sāṅkhya smṛti

In the first chapter, it was concluded that the Lord is free of all faults, endowed with unlimited inconceivable *śakti*, endowed with unlimited attractive qualities, dwells within all beings, is different from all other beings, is both the efficient and material cause of the universe, is the controller of all beings, and is to be known by Vedānta (Upaniṣads).

In the second chapter, by presenting the truth, the author rejects contrary views presented in logical treatises. The fallacious reasoning of those who advocate *pradhāna* as the highest cause and unified conclusions concerning creation, as expressed in Vedānta, are described. First opinions contrary to the śruti are refuted.

The doubt is this. Is the conclusion that Brahman is the cause of everything contrary to the Sāṅkhya smṛtis or not? If Brahman is accepted as the cause, this will make the Sāṅkhya smṛtis useless.

Kapila is mentioned in Śvetāśvatara Upaniṣad: ṛṣim prasūtaṁ kapilam (the sage Kapila was born). The great sage Kapila, desiring liberation, having accepted the actions of sacrifice described in karma-kāṇḍa, composed a smṛti text to promote the meaning of jñāna-kāṇḍa. He has concluded that unconscious *pradhāna* is the independent cause of the universe in statements like *atha trividha-duḥkhātyanta-nivṛttir atyanta-puruṣārthaḥ | na dṛṣṭārtha-siddhir nivṛtter apy anuvṛtti-darśanāt*: the highest goal is to extinguish the three miseries but this is not attainable by material arrangements, since after extinguishing the suffering, it returns. (Sāṅkhya-kārikā 1.1-2)

vimukta-mokṣārthaṁ svārthaṁ vā pradhānasya

Pradhāna creates the world for liberating the jīva, who is by nature liberated. (Sāṅkhya-kārikā 2.1]

acetanatve'pi kṣīravac ceṣṭitaṁ pradhānasya

Though unconscious, *pradhāna* creates the world, like milk turning to yogurt. Sāṅkhya-kārikā 3.60

If one accepts Brahman as the cause, then the content of Kapila's smṛti becomes useless, since the smṛti's aim is to establish doctrine it propounds. Therefore one should explain Vedānta so that it is not contrary to the authority Kapila's smṛti. Doing this will not make other words like Manu-smṛti useless, since the subject of those works is promotion of karma-kāṇḍa by propounding dharma (which Kapila also accepts).

Sūtra – 2.1.1

|| smṛty-anavakāśa-doṣa-prasaṅga iti cen nānya-smṛty-avakāśa-doṣa-prasaṅgāt ||

If one argues that refusing the conclusions of Sāṅkhya smṛti would make that scripture useless, the answer is no, for accepting it would render the conclusions of other smṛtis useless.

Anavakāśa means "having no opportunity for use" or "having a useless subject." There would arise a fault of making the Sāṅkhya smṛtis useless by concluding that Brahman is the cause of the world in Vedānta. Therefore one should explain those Vedānta texts in an opposite way (to make Sāṅkhya texts useful). The answer is no. Why? By doing so, one would make useless other smṛtis like Manu, which agree with Vedānta and say that Brahman is the sole cause. This would be a greater fault. The smṛtis state that the supreme Lord is the cause of creation and destruction of the universe. They do not agree with the theory enunciated by Kapila.

Manu says:

āsīd idam tamo-bhūtam aprajñātam alakṣaṇam
apratarkyam avijñeyaṁ prasuptam iva sarvataḥ

This universe was dark, unperceived, without qualities, inconceivable, unknown, in all ways, as if sleeping.

tataḥ svayaṁbhūr bhagavān avyakto vyañjayann idam
mahā-bhūtādi vṛttaujāḥ prādurāsīt tamo-nudaḥ

Then the self born, invisible Lord, having the power of all elements, manifesting the universe, dispelling the darkness, became visible.

yo 'sāv atīndriya-grāhaḥ sūkṣmo 'vyaktaḥ sanātanaḥ
sarva-bhūta-mayo 'cintyaḥ sa eva svayam udbabhau

He who is beyond the senses, who is subtle, invisible and eternal, who consists of all beings and is inconceivable, appeared by his own will.

so 'bhidhyāya śarīrāt svāt sisṛkṣur vividhāḥ prajāḥ
apa eva sasarjādau tāsu vīryam avāsṛjat

Desiring to create various offspring from his own body, he first created water and impregnated that water with his semen.

tad aṇḍam abhavad dhaimaṁ sahasrāṁśu -sama-prabham
tasmin jajñe svayaṁ brahmā sarva-loka-pitāmahaḥ

That became a golden sphere shining like the sun. In that egg, Brahmā, the grandfather of all planets was born. Manu 1.5-9

Parāśara says:

viṣṇoḥ sakāśād udbhūtaṁ jagat tatraiva ca sthitam
sthiti-saṁyama-kartāsau jagato' ṣya jagac ca saḥ

The universe arises from Viṣṇu and remains in him. He is the creator, maintainer and destroyer of the universe. He is the universe. Viṣṇu Purāṇa 1.1.31

yathorṇanābhir hṛdayād ūrṇāṁ santatya vaktrataḥ
tayā vihṛtya bhūyas tāṁ grasaty evaṁ maheśvaraḥ

Just as the spider from within himself expands thread through his mouth, plays with it for some time and eventually swallows it, similarly, the Supreme Lord produces the universe and then withdraws it. SB 11.9.21

There are other statements in scripture also. These smṛtis do not only promote karma-kāṇḍa (action). They also promote purification of the heart.

This is true of the śrutis as well. *tam etaṁ vedānuvacanena*: the brāhmaṇas try to know the Lord through studying the Vedas. (Bṛhad-āraṇyaka Upaniṣad 1.5.4.22) Even in the Vedas one will sometimes see descriptions of material results like rain, sons or Svarga. And one can experience the results also. However that is for the purpose of producing faith in the scriptures. The conclusion of scriptures is that the Lord is the creator. *sarve vedā yat padam āmananti*: all the Vedas praise him. (Kaṭha Upaniṣad 1.3.15) *Nārāyaṇa-parā vedāḥ*: the Vedas conclude that Nārāyaṇa is supreme. (SB 2.5.15)

One cannot promote the meaning of the Vedas by reliance on Sāṅkhya smṛtis, since those smṛtis promote a meaning contrary to the śruti. The Sāṅkhya smṛtis do not do promote clarity by producing a unified meaning of the Vedas. Thus the Sāṅkhya smṛti, which is contrary to the Vedas, being manufactured in someone's head, is without authority. One should not fear that those scriptures would then have the fault of being meaningless. One should not show favor to that smṛti on the basis that it was produced by some authority, for if one were to favor the many explanations of truth in various smṛtis with various opinions, the real truth would be inconclusive.

When there is a contradiction between smṛtis, there is no recourse except referring to śruti. Only those smṛtis which concur with the śrutis should be respected. One may think "I can refute those who argue on the strength of smṛtis, by the strength of the smṛtis themselves."[36] But this would lead to the fault of making other smṛtis useless.

One may argue that Kapila is a recognized authority because he is mentioned in Śvetāśvatara Upaniṣad 5.2: *ṛṣīm prasūtam kapilam yas tam agre jñānair bibharti*: he endowed the sage Kapila born before the creation with knowledge. But this refers to another Kapila and cannot be the founder of Sāṅkhya philosophy, since the founder of Sāṅkhya spoke against the meaning of the Vedas.

However, Manu is said to be authoritative. *yad vai kiṁ ca manur avadat tad-bheṣajam:* whatever Manu has declared is a cure. (Taittirīya-brāhmaṇa) It is also said that Parāśara attained spiritual knowledge worthy of a *devatā* by the mercy of Pulastya and Vasiṣṭha. The Kapila who produced a smṛti contrary

[36] The smṛtis are all inferior in nature to śrutis and thus should not be accepted.

to the Vedas, was a jīva born in the Agni dynasty, and was bewildered by *māyā*. He was not Vāsudeva, the Lord, born from the sage Kardama.

kalipo vāsudevāṁśas tattvaṁ sāṅkhyaṁ jagāda ha
brahmādhibhyaś ca devebhyo bhṛgv-ādibhyas tathaiva ca
tathaivāsuraye sarva-vedārthair upabṛṁhitam
sarva-veda-viruddhaṁ ca kapilo 'nyo jagāda ha
sāṅkham āsuraye 'nyasmaikutarka-paribṛṁhitam

Kapila, the expansion of Vāsudeva, spoke Sāṅkhya philosophy, promoting the meaning of all the Vedas, to Brahmā, *devatās,* Bhṛgu and others and to Āsuri. Another Kapila spoke Sāṅkhya which was contrary to the Vedas and full of faulty logic to another person named Āsuri. Padma Purāṇa

Thus there is no fault in discarding Sāṅkhya smṛti, which was written by a person without authority, since it is contrary to the Vedas.

Sūtra – 2.1.2

|| itareṣāṁ cānupalabdheḥ ||

Sāṅkhya cannot be accepted because other ideas that it propounds are not found in the Vedas.

Because other things stated in the Sāṅkhya smṛtis are not based on the Vedas, they cannot be accepted as authority. They claim that the jīvas pure consciousness alone and all-pervading and that *prakṛti* produces both bondage and liberation for the jīva.[37] Bondage and liberation are aspects of *prakṛti.* There is no supreme Lord. Time also does not exist as a principle. The *prāṇas* are merely forms of functions of the senses.

Topic 2 (Sūtra 3)

Yoga-pratyuktyādhikaraṇam - Refutation of Yoga

"It is not proper to explain Vedānta by Sāṅkhya smṛti since it is contrary to the Vedānta. Vedānta should be explained by yoga-smṛtis, since it is said that they follows the conclusions of the Vedas. It is a *śrauta* philosophy, following the Vedas, since there are many descriptions of yoga in the śrutis. *tām yogam iti manyante srhirām indriya-dhāraṇām:* the sages consider yoga to be firm

---

[37] Prakṛti by itself works for liberation of the puruṣa.

control of the senses. (Kaṭha Upaniṣad 6.11) *vidyāṁ etāṁ yoga-vidhiṁ ca krtṣnam*: know this method of yoga completely. (Kaṭha Upaniṣad 6.18) The yoga *āsanas* are also described there. *trir unnataṁ sthāpya samaṁ śarīram*: one should sit with the body straight with chest, neck and head raised. (Śvetāśvatara Upaniṣad 2.8) The great authority Patañjali wrote the yoga smṛti for those desiring to give up suffering in the world using this yoga.

atha yogānuśāsanam yogaś citta-vṛttti-nirodhāh

Now yoga will be explained. Yoga is cessation of functions of *citta*.

If the Vedānta is explained by non-contrary correlation of the meaning of śruti alone (without reference to yoga) this smṛti will be useless, since it deals only with knowledge of yoga, whereas Manu and other smṛtis have scope in Vedānta since they teach about dharma. Therefore the Vedānta should be explained according to yoga-smṛti and not according the method of *samanvaya* (correlation of Vedic śruti) just explained.

Sūtra – 2.1.3

|| etena yogaḥ pratyuktaḥ ||

Yoga is refuted for the same reasons.

By refutation of Sāṅkhya smṛti, yoga smṛti is also refuted since it is similarly contrary to Vedānta. By interpreting the Vedānta according to yoga-smṛtis, Manu and other smṛtis following the Vedas would be useless. Therefore the texts should not be explained by yoga-smṛtis. One cannot say that the yoga-smṛtis are not contrary to Vedānta for, according to those smṛtis, *pradhāna* is the independent cause of the universe. The Lord and the jīva are mere consciousness. They are all pervading. From yoga arises destruction of suffering and this is called liberation. These are all contrary to the Vedānta conclusions.

As well, things not mentioned in the Vedas are mentioned. According to yoga, *pramāṇa* is one of the five functions of *citta*.[38] These things are found only in the yoga smṛtis. Therefore one should not be frightened from the fault of making yoga-smṛti useless by not using it to interpret Vedānta, since that

---

[38] The five *vṛttis* (fluctuations) of *citta* are *pramāṇa* (means of knowledge), error, conceptualization, sleep and memory.

smṛti contradicts Vedānta. The arguments against Sāṅkhya hold good for yoga as well. The real nature of *īśvara* and *jīva* and the method and goal known through Vedānta, will be discussed later.

Though postures are mentioned in the śruti and understanding the supreme cause by Sāṅkhya and yoga is mentioned as well in śruti, those terms refers merely to meditation (yoga) and knowledge (sāṅkhya). The Sāṅkhya and yoga philosophies however are very different from the Vedic conclusions. One cannot attain liberation by knowledge of the difference between prakṛti and puruṣa or by yoga. (One attains liberation by knowing the Lord, as in the following statements.)

tam eva viditvātimṛtyum eti: knowing the Lord one surpasses death. (Śvetāśvatara Upaniṣad) *vijñāya prajñāṁ kurvīta*: knowing him one should meditate. (Bṛhad-āraṇyaka Upaniṣad) *etad yo dhyāyati rasati bhajati so 'mrto bhavati*: he who meditates on the Lord, chants his name and worships him attains immortality. (Gopāla-tāpanī Upaniṣad)

However, we do not hate those portions of Sāṅkhya and yoga which are not contrary. But the contrary portions must be rejected. It seems that Patañjali was a theist for he says *īṣvara-praṇidhānād vā*: one may attain concentration by meditating on God and *kleśa-karma-vipākāśayair aparāmṛṣṭaḥ puruṣa-viśeṣa īśvaraḥ*: there is a special person, the Lord, who is not touched by suffering caused by ripened karma. But they say that he uttered these sūtras out of bewilderment.

Gautama and other also, bewildered, produced theories contrary to Vedānta. These theories will be refuted. Bewilderment of such intelligent men should be understood to be the Lord's *māyā*, who became angry at their pride in their knowledge, or the Lord's will, for his own purpose. Since yoga is theistic, and thus different from Sāṅkhya, a new section (*adhikaraṇa*) has been started to refute that philosophy separately. The yoga smṛti made by Hiraṇyagarbha (Brahmā) is also rejected for the same reasons. [39]

Topic 3 (Sūtras 4 – 6)

Vilakṣaṇatvādhikaraṇam – Special quality of the Vedas

---

[39] Before Patañjali, Hiraṇyagarbha taught yoga.

Some followers of Sāṅkhya, in opposition, will object to even the Vedas, which take Sāṅkhya and yoga smṛtis as unauthoritative since they oppose the Vedas. This adhikaraṇa refutes that objection.

The doubt is this. Are the Vedas themselves unauthoritative or not?

(Pūrvapakṣa) It is said *kārīryā yajeta vṛṣṭi-kāmaḥ:* one desiring rain should perform the *kārīrī* sacrifice. Though one performs the sacrifice, the result is not obtained. This proves that the Vedas are unauthoritative.

Sūtra – 2.1.4

|| na vilakṣaṇatvād asya tathātvaṁ ca śabdāt ||

No, the Vedas are not unauthoritative, since they are special. They are eternal because of śruti statements to that effect.

The Vedas are not unauthoritative like Sāṅkhya and other smṛtis. Why? The Vedas have the special quality (*vilakṣaṇatvāt*) of being devoid of defect of having an author with the four defects. Their eternal nature (*tathātvam*) is understood from śruti itself (*śabdāt*). The Sāṅkhya and other smṛtis on the other hand have the four faults, since they are made by jīvas. *Tathātvam* in the sūtra means "being eternal." Śruti says *vācā virūpa nityayā vṛṣne codasva:* O sage Virūpa, offer praise to the Lord using the eternal word. (Ṛg Veda 8.75.6)

Smṛti says:

anādi-nidhanā nityā vāg utsṛṣṭā svayambhuvā
ādau vedamayī divyā yataḥ sarvāḥ pravṛttayaḥ

In the beginning the self-born Lord produced the beginnningless receptacle, the eternal word consisting of the divine Vedas, from which all this came. Mahā-bhārata 12.231.56-57

Smṛtis like Manu-smṛti are also authoritative since they are based on the Vedas. Previously the Vedas were established as eternal by reasoning (1.3.29). Here the Vedas are shown to be eternal by śruti evidence. That is the difference in the sūtras.

"It is stated in *puruṣa-sūkta*:

tasmād yajñāt sarva-hutaḥ ṛcaḥ sāmāni jajñire
chandāṁsijajṇire tasmād juastasmād ajāyata

From the Lord were born all sacrifices, the Ṛg and Sāma mantras. From him were born the meters and the Yajur mantras. Ṛg Veda 10.90.9

In the *puruṣa-sūkta* it is stated that the Vedas were born. Since that which is born must perish, the Vedas are not eternal."

That is not so. The word "birth-- *jan*" actually means "manifest." It is said:

svayambhūr eṣa bhagavān vedo gītas tvayā purā
śivādyā ṛṣi-paryantāḥ smartāro 'sya na kārakāḥ

The great Veda, self-born, was sung by you previously. Śiva and the sages recollect and teach it. They are not its creator.

One cannot say that because results do not appear that it is unauthoritative, since one sees results according to qualification of the performer. If results are not seen, that simply means that the performer of sacrifice was unqualified. Sāṅkhya and similar smṛtis are not authoritative because they contradict the Vedas.

Let that be. The Vedas make statements with absurd meaning. For instance:

tat teja aikṣata bahu syām ta āpa aikṣante bahvyaḥ syāma

Fire then willed "Let me be many." The water desired "Let me be many." Chāndogya Upaniṣad 6.2.3-4

te heme prāṇā ahaṁ śreyase vivadamānā brahma jagmuḥ ko naḥ viśiṣṭa

These *prāṇas* quarreled saying "I am the best." They went to Brahmā and asked "Which of us is the best?" Bṛhad-āraṇyaka Upaniṣad

These statements are like the son of a barren woman. They have no authority at all. Since one part of the Vedas is with authority, the other parts must also be without authority. Thus Brahman as the cause of the world is not proved.

Sūtra – 2.1.5

|| abhimāni-vyapadeśas tu viśeṣānugatibhyām ||

The Vedas are not unauthoritative since words referring to inanimate objects that act as if conscious refer to their presiding deities, because subsequent passages describe *devatās* entering the elements and because the adjective *devatā* is used.

The word *tu* indicates refuting this doubt. The terms fire and water refer to the presiding deities of those elements (*abhimāni-vyapadeṣaḥ*), not to the unconscious elements. Why? Because of fire, water and food are qualified (*viśeṣa*) by the word *devatā. hantāham imās tisro devatā:* I have entered these three deities (fire, water etc.) (Chāndogya Upaniṣad 6.3.2) The prāṇas (senses) are also described as *devatās.*

sarvā ha vai devatā ahaṁ śreyase vivādamānās.... te devā prāṇe
niḥśreyasaṁ viditvā...asmāl lokād uccakramuḥ

All the *devatās* of the senses quarreled, saying "I am the best." These *devatās,* knowing *prāṇa* to be the best, left the world.

It is also said that the presiding deities entered into (a*nugatibhyām*) the voice and other organs. *Agnir vāg bhūtvā mukha prāviśad ādtiyaś cakśur bhūtvākṣiṇī prāviśat*: fire, becoming voice entered the mouth, and the sun, becoming the eye, entered the two eye balls. (Aitareya Āraṇyaka 2.4.2.4) As well smṛti says:

pṛthivy-ādy-abhimāninyo devatāḥ prathitaujasaḥ
acintyāḥ śaktayas tāsāṁ dṛśyante munibhiś ca tāḥ

The sages see the presiding deities of earth and other elements, who display great power and they also see the devatās' inconceivable energies. Bhaviṣya Purāṇa

It is said *grāvāṇaḥ plavante*: stones float.[40] This is praise to increase the power of the stones present in special rites of sacrifices (for extracting soma). The bridge built by Rāma is of that type of stone (so it is not impossible literally). Thus the Vedas are never unauthoritative and thus it is correct that Brahman is the sole cause of the universe.

To attack the proposition that Brahman is the material cause of the world, again the follower of Sāṅkhya takes shelter of argumentation. In matters related to *ātmā,* argumentation must be given up for it is said *śruti-viordhāt*

---

[40] This phrase is found in Sabara's commentary 1.1.5 on Jaimini Mīmāṁsa sūtra 1.135. The expression is commonly used to indicate something impossible. In Mahābharata Vidura says this in relation Dhṛtarāṣṭra taking his advice. Jīva Gosvāmī in Sarvasamvādini also gives the same example of something seemingly impossible that must be accepted because it is in the Vedas.

na kutarkāpasadasyātma-lābhaḥ: a low person who resorts to bad logic cannot attain *ātmā* since it is opposed to the śruti. (Sāṅkhya-smṛti 6.35) However he uses logic to find fault in his opponent.

Here is the doubt. Does the world arise from Brahman as the material cause or not?

(Pūrvapakṣa) How can Brahman be the material cause since the world is completely different in nature from Brahman? Brahman is said to be omniscient, all-controlling, and pure and joyful. The universe is directly seen to be full of ignorance, lack of control, contamination and suffering. The difference cannot be disputed. It is seen that the effect has the very nature of the material cause: pot and clay, crown and gold, cloth and thread. Since it is impossible for the world to be the effect of Brahman because of such difference, one must search out a different material cause having similar qualities to the world. That material cause is *pradhāna* alone since it has qualities (*tamas, rajas, sattva*) similar to the world, which is full of bewilderment, sorrow and joy.

"But there is in that pure, omniscient Brahman, as the material cause, two very subtle *śaktis,* consisting of consciousness and matter, to make it similar to the effect, the material world."

By this argument, the problem is not removed, since the difference still exists. From the subtle material cause with subtle *śaktis* arises a gross effect. Other differences can also be seen. Therefore the universe cannot arise from Brahman as a material causes because of its difference from Brahman. Scriptures must depend on logic since the meaning of its topics must be determined through logic sometimes.

Sūtra – 2.1.6

|| dṛśyate tu ||

Difference between cause and effect is seen in the material world also.

The word *tu* indicates a refutation of the doubt. The word *na* is understood from sūtra 2.1.4. It is not true that Brahman cannot be the material cause because of difference, since we see there is difference of cause and effect in this world. We see appearance of qualities different from the original substance. We see worms arising from honey and elephants and horses arising from a desire tree. We see gold arising from *cintāmaṇi.* The Ātharvaṇikas give the following example to illustrate this.

yathorṇa-nābhiḥ sṛjate gṛhṇate ca
yathā pṛthivyāṁ oṣadhayaḥ sambhavanti
yathā sataḥ puruṣāt keś-lobhāni
tathākṣarāt sambhavatīha viśvam

Just as a spider produces and withdraws its threads, just as the herbs arise from the earth, just as hairs arise from a man, so the universe arises from the imperishable Lord. Muṇḍaka Upaniṣad 1.1.7

Topic 4 (Sūtras 7 – 11)

Asadity-adhikaraṇam - Proposition that the effect is not in the cause

"If the world is different from its material cause, it means that the effect, the world, must have not previously existed in Brahman, the material cause, before the creation of the universe. Because everything was previously one entity, Brahman, this gives rise to the world being *asat,* or non-existent in the cause. But this goes against your theory that the effect is existent in the cause (*sat-karya-vāda*)."

Sūtra – 2.1.7

|| asad iti cen na pratiṣedha-mātratvāt ||

If you claim the effect is not in the cause, the answer is no, because there was denial of likeness of cause and effect in regards to some qualities.

This is not a fault. Why? In the previous sūtra likeness of cause and effect was denied. But it did not deny difference in the very substance of the material cause and effect. Brahman transforms as the form of the universe which is different from itself.

The meaning is this. When you criticize Brahman as the material cause because of lack of similarity to the effect, do you mean that the world does not have all of Brahman's qualities or that it does not have any of its qualities at all? You cannot mean the first, because then there would be no material cause and effect (since there must be some difference in cause and effect). The lump of clay does not have exactly the same qualities or form as the pot, the effect. You cannot mean the second, because that is without foundation. The world has qualities of Brahman, such as real existence.

"You cannot consider similarity of all qualities in cause and effect, for then everything could be the cause of everything. Therefore the qualities that distinguish a particular object form others should be present in the effect. The qualities that distinguish gold from thread should be present in a bracelet, the effect. That must be considered."

This is not so, since we see an exception to that rule when worms arise from honey. And gold and the bracelet are not identical in qualities since their situations are different. Thus, though there is difference between the world and Brahman like that between the gold and *cintāmaṇi*, the effect is not non-existent in the cause (*asat*) since the two exist as one substance like gold and the bracelet.

The opponent again attacks with logic.

Sūtra – 2.1.8

|| apītau tadvat prasaṅgād asamañjasam ||

At the time of destruction, Brahman would be like the world. Because of contact with the world that merged into Brahman, there would be contradiction to the pure Brahman declared in the scriptures.

If Brahman endowed with subtle śaktis is the material cause of the universe of matter and jīva, undergoing various changes unbeneficial to the soul, then, at the time of *pralaya,* Brahman would also have the same faults. *Tadvat* means "like that." Brahman would be like the material effect, having transformations not beneficial for the soul since at the time of destruction everything of the world becomes one with Brahman. There would thus be a contradiction (*asamañjasam*) to all the statements of the Upaniṣads since they say that Brahman, the material cause, has qualities like omniscience and complete absence of fault.

This objection is refuted.

Sūtra – 2.1.9

|| na tu dṛṣṭānta-bhāvāt ||

There is no contradiction because there are examples of separateness even when in contact.

The word *tu* refutes the possibility of objection. There is no contradiction at all. Why? Because there are examples (*dṛṣānta-bhāvāt*) to shot that Brahman as the material cause remains pure even when in contact with the world as effect. Just as blue, yellow and other colors remain in their particular place on one picture canvas, and do not mix, so in Brahman the universe remains but does not mix with Brahman. Similarly in a living being, the qualities of the body such as childhood are discerned in the body, and not in the ātmā, or having one eye and other qualities of the senses are discerned in the senses and not in the ātmā. Thus the qualities of Brahman's śakti, a transformation not beneficial for the jīvas, remain within his śakti, and do not contaminate the pure Brahman.

Not only is Brahman as material cause is acceptable because of being faultless, but pradhāna as the material cause cannot be accepted because of those very faults.

Sūtra – 2.1.10

|| sva-pakṣe doṣāc ca ||

Sāṅkhya is not accepted, for even in the Sāṅkhya theory the same objections apply.

The faults that you as a follower of Sāṅkhya have attributed to our view can be seen in your proposition since these have been refuted elsewhere by us. According to Sāṅkhya, there will be difference between the material cause and the effect. For instance you accept that the world which has sound arises from pradhāna which has no sound. Because of this difference you have the same problem with the effect that you oppose in our proposition. Since you accept that everything merges into pradhāna at destruction, your objection to our proposition in sūtra 2.1.8 is also an objection to yours. The production of the universe also is impossible in the theory of pradhāna as the ultimate cause (since there is no will in pradhāna). That will be discussed in a detailed examination of the theory.

"The meaning of scripture can be deduced by taking the said scripture and applying logic." That is refuted in the next sūtra.

Sūtra – 2.1.11

*| | tarkāpratiṣṭhānād apy anyathānumeyam
iti ced evam apy anirmokṣa-prasaṅgaḥ | |*

If you think otherwise, when we say that logic is not solid proof. It would lead to the impossibility of liberation.

Because of varieties in men's intelligence, arguments are without finality, since one argument is demolished by another. Therefore, not giving regard to those arguments, one should accept that Brahman mentioned in the Upaniṣads to be the object of worship. Argumentation does not produce finality even for the great sages, for one sees disagreement among great sages like Kapila and Kaṇāda.

"I think otherwise, so that logic will not be useless (*apratiṣṭha*). One cannot say that logic has no finality, since logic was even used to deduce that logic is non-final. If all logic was useless, then all worldly actions would come to an end. One sees that people attain pleasure or avoid pain in the future based upon experiences of the present and past (logically classified as favorable or unfavorable)."

But this would lead to absence of liberation. When you depend on logic based on human intelligence, it is possible that your conclusion will be refuted by a more skillful logician from another place or at another time. By the inconclusiveness of logic you cannot be liberated. Though logic is final in particular worldly matters, in regards to Brahman, logic is not given respect since it is useless regarding what is inconceivable and contrary to the śruti. And it is contrary to your own words. (*śruti-virodhān na* Sāṅkhya smṛti 6.35)

Śruti says that Brahman is beyond logic:

naiṣā tarkeṇa matir āpaneyā proktānyenaiva sujñānāya preṣṭha

This knowledge cannot be achieved by logic. O dear one! It should be taught by another person in order to be understood properly. Kaṭha Upaniṣad 1.2.9

*ṛṣe vidanti munayaḥ praśāntātmendiryāśayāḥ
yadā tadaivāsat-tarkais tirodhīyeta viplutam*

O sage! The contemplative sages know that peaceful form of the Lord when they have controlled their mind, senses and body. That form disappears when assailed by false logic. SB 2.6.41

Therefore śruti is the proof for Brahman as it is for dharma.

Logic which supports śruti is given regard, for śruti says *mantavyaḥ*: Brahman is the object of reasoning. (Bṛhad-ārāṇyaka Upaniṣad 4.5) Smṛti says:

pūrvāpara-virodhena ko 'rtho 'trābhimato bhavet
ity ādyam uhanaṁ tarkaḥ śuṣka-tarkaṁ vivarjayet

Reasoning which determines the meaning by resolving all contradictions with previous and later statements is correct argumentation. Argumentation should reject dry logic. Kūrma Purāṇa

Therefore Brahman is the material cause of the universe.

Topic 5 (Sūtra 12)

Śiṣṭāparigrahādhikaraṇam - Rejection of remaining philosophies

The contrary views made by the smṛtis of Sāṅkhya and yoga and their logical arguments have been refuted. Now the views of Kāṇḍa and others along with their arguments will be refuted.

The doubt is this. Should Brahman be rejected as the material cause by these philosophers? This question is important for them because if Brahma is the material cause, their smṛtis become useless.

(Pūrvapakṣa) Brahman as the material cause should be rejected since everything arises from combination of two, three and more very small particles and thus Brahman is unsuitable as the material cause because Brahman is all-pervading.

Sūtra – 2.1.12

|| etena śiṣṭā parigrahā api vyākhyātā ||

By the refutation of Sāṅkhya and yoga, the remaining philosophies which do not accept the Vedas are refuted.

Śiṣṭāḥ means "those remaining." *Aparigrahāḥ* means "those who do not accept the Vedic actions." The compound is *karmadhāraya.* By refuting Sāṅkhya and yoga which contradict the Vedas, it should be understood that the philosophies of Kaṇāda, Akṣapada (Gautama) and others, those remaining, are refuted since the reasons for rejecting them are the same.

There is no rule that the larger entities must arise from the smaller particles, since even in *ārambhavāda* this is contradicted by the fact that ether (not one particle) gives rise to sound and woven cloth arises from long threads.

This *adhikaraṇa* deals with an additional argument--everything should arise from small particles--raised to oppose the author's proposition that logic is useless in regard to the cause of everything. It is now refuted on grounds of being useless dry logic.

As well, the Buddhists and others describe the smallest particles differently. Some (Vaibhāṣika Buddhists) say these particles are temporary but actually existing. Others (Yogācāra Buddhists) say that the particles are only in the mind (*jñāna-rūpa*). Others (Mādhyamika Buddhists) say the particles do not exist at all (*śūnya-rūpa*). Others (Jains) say the particles are both existing and non-existing (*sad-asad-rūpa*). All of these are opposed to permanent particles.

Topic 6 (Sūtra 13)

Bhoktṛ-āpatty-adhikaraṇam - Oneness with the jīva

Again a doubt is raised and resolved.

Sūtra – 2.1.13

|| bhoktr-āpatter avibhāgaś cet syāl lokavat ||

If one argues that because the jīva as *śakti* is non-different from Brahman, there will be no distinction seen between them at all, this argument is rejected. Distinction in oneness is seen in the ordinary world.

Brahman as the possessor of subtle *śakti* is the material cause and as the possessor of gross *śakti* is the effect. The doubt is this. Is this true or not?

(Pūrva-pakṣa) Because of oneness of Brahman with the jīva (*bhoktṛ*), there is no distinction between them (*avibhāgaḥ*) since there is non-difference between the *śakti* and the possessor of *śakti,* Brahman."

That proposition would make meaningless the difference expressed in śruti in passages such as the following. *dvā suparṇā... juṣtaṁ yaḍa paśyaty anyam īṣam:* there are two birds in a tree.... when one bird sees the other, the Lord. Therefore this proposition is not correct. This should be rejected (*syāt*) from what we see in ordinary life (*lokavat*). In the world, though we make no distinction between a man holding a stick and that very person, there is difference essentially between the stick and the man. Similarly though Brahman is non-different from its *śakti,* there is an essential difference between the *śakti* and Brahman. There is no harm in this.

Topic 7 (Sūtras 14 – 20)

Ārambhaṇādhikaraṇam - Transformation by word

Accepting that Brahman is different from the world, it was concluded that Brahman was the material cause. If you then conclude that the effect is not in the cause (*asat*), this must be opposed. The author now raises an argument for the claim of *asat* and resolves it.

(Doubt) Is the world, the effect, different or non-different from Brahman, the material cause?

(Pūrvapakṣa) The material cause is different from the effect because the words "material cause" and "effect" are different; because of difference in use--for instance, clay being used to make a pot but a pot being used to bring water; because the forms are different-- as in the case of the shape of lump of clay and the effect, the shape of a pot with a neck; and because of difference in time--the material cause exists previous to the effect such as a pot.

There is difference between the material cause and the effect since otherwise the actions of the maker of the effect would be useless. One may argue that if the material cause and effect are the same, still, by actions of the doer, the effect, though already existing, becomes manifest . But this is not correct. The argument is invalid, as follows.

Does the effect exist previous to the action of the doer or not? It cannot have existed previously to the action, because then there would be no need of an action to make it appear, and there would be eternal perception of the effect. The distinction (that we perceive) between eternal and non-eternal objects would disappear. If you argue that for manifesting an effect another manifestation is necessary you end up with endless regression of manifestations. If you argue that effect does not exist previous (*asat*) to the action of the doer, it is not possible, because you end up with *asat-kāryavad*, which is our philosophy, and which you originally denied.

For producing the effect which is *asat* (not inherent in the cause) the doer is unnecessary. The Vaiśeṣikas and other Nyāyikas say that the effect, which is different, arises from the material cause which is *asat* (devoid of effect within it). This is refuted in the next sūtra.

Sūtra – 2.1.14

|| tad ananyatvam ārambhaṇa-śabdādibhyaḥ ||

From the Brahman arises the world which is non-different from it. This is proved by statements starting with *vācārambhaṇa.*

From that (*tat*), from Brahman, endowed with *jīva-śakti* and *prakṛti-śakti,* from Brahman which is the material cause of the world, arises the effect, the universe, which is non-different from Brahman (*ananyatvam*). How is this known? By statements in scripture starting with the word *ārambhana (ārambhana-śabdādibhyaḥ).* This refers to statements found in various places in the Chāndogya Upaniṣad.

vācārambhaṇaṁ vikāro nāma-dheyaṁ mṛttikety eva satyam

Clay takes on a name as it undergoes transformation by actions initiated by words. But clay alone is proven by authority. Chāndogya Upaniṣad 6.1.4

sad eva saumyedam agra āsīd ekam evādvitīyam

Sat, which is one without a second, existed in the beginning, O gentle one! Chāndogya Upaniṣad 6.2.1

tad aikṣata bahu syāṁ prajāyeya

He willed, "May I become many. May I produce offspring." Chāndogya Upaniṣad 6.2.3

san-mūlāḥ saumyemāḥ prajāḥ sadāyatanāḥ sat pratiṣṭhāḥ

All these being are based on *sat. Sat* is their support and receptacle. Chāndogya Upaniṣad 6.8.6

aitadātmyam iḍaṁ sarvam

Everything has the property of *sat.* Chāndogya Upaniṣad 6.8.7

These texts state the non-difference of the world composed of dull matter with the superior Brahman, which is related to it. Accepting in the heart that the whole world comes from Brahman as material cause and is thus non-different from Brahman, the teacher promises that one can have knowledge of the whole world, the effect, by knowing Brahman which is the material cause. *Stabdho 'sy uta tam ādeśam aprākṣyaḥ yenāśrutaṁ śrutaṁ bhavati:* you are proud--have you asked that knowledge by which what is unheard becomes heard? (Chāndogya Upaniṣad 6.1.3) The student, ignorant of the teacher's intentions, thinks, "Knowledge of one thing is impossible by knowing something else." He asks, *kathaṁ nu bhagavaḥ sa ādeśaḥ*: what is that instruction? The teacher explains that Brahman is the material cause of the world and shows non-difference of material cause and effect by giving examples of things perceived in this world, by saying, "Just as with one lump of clay..." All pots and objects made from their material cause, a lump of clay, are known by knowing the clay, since those objects are non-different from the clay. Thus by knowing Brahman, the material cause of everything, the whole world, the effect, is known. That is the meaning of the instruction.

"Because of differences in intelligence, words, use, form, and time (mentioned above in the *pūrva-pakṣa*), the effect will be different from the cause." In answer to this, the author replies that there are statements saying the opposite, starting with the words *vācārambhaṇam*. The word *ārambhana,* meaning "taking hold of" or "beginning," is formed with a *kṛt* affix, which functions in many ways according to *kṛtya lyuṭo bahulam* (Pāṇini 3.3.113)

The name of an object has been initialized by the doer, when there is a transformation of a lump of clay into a form with a neck. Why? Because of actions (*ārambhaṇam*) connected with words. For instance "Bring water using a pot." The instrumental case here indicates cause.

In order to accomplish the action expressed in words, the substance clay becomes a particular aggregate of knowledge (round with a neck) and takes a name like "pot." The pot is ultimately what is called clay. That is founded on evidence (*satyam*). The pot, being made of clay substance, is also real, but it is not another substance. According to different situations of the substance clay, different conceptions and words arise. For instance, a person named Caitra in different situations undergoes childhood, youth and different conceptions of himself and different descriptions in words. In the material cause such as clay, *sat* manifests as pot or stick by being non-different from that cause. The effect is not *asat.* The effect is non-different from the material cause.

If the cause and effect were different, the final weight after transformation should be double: the weight of cause plus weight of effect. For other reasons also there must be non-difference.

This effect is not an illusion like the illusion of silver on seeing a sea shell. Nor is there a completely separate substance like silver situated elsewhere from the sea shell (cause). That is indicated by the words *iti eva* (it is this alone). Thus the idea that the word *iti* is useless is refuted.

One cannot say that the concept of manifestation (*abhivyakti*) is without basis. This is proven by the following:

kalpānte kāla-sṛṣtena yo 'ndhena tamasāvṛtam
abhivyanak jagad idaṁ svayaṁrociḥ svarociṣā

At the end of the *kalpa* the self-effulgent Lord, by his light, manifested (*abhivyanak*) this universe covered with dense darkness created by time. SB 7.3.26

This proposition does not have the fault of accomplishing what is already accomplished or the fault of infinite regression (*anavasthā),* for we do not accept that the manifestation existed prior of the action of the doer, and the manifestation does not depend on another manifestation.

"This becomes *asat-kāryavada*. That which did not exist appeared because of action."

That is not so, for what is manifested is not an effect as you know it. You say that an effect manifests on its own. But that is not the case, for this effect is accomplished only because of the manifestation of the substrate. The manifestation of a particular form by the doer is regulated. Thus there is no fault in its production.

Those who say that an effect arises from what was previously non-existent are foolish, since there is no solid proof of that claim. If the effect were totally absent before the action, everything could arise from everything else, since everything would be non-existent in all places. Milk could arise from sesame seeds. Things would arise without cause since the effect was previously totally non-existent.

One cannot say that there is some *śakti* fixed in the cause to regulate production of a certain effect because a relationship of a *śakti* could not be established with something non-existent.

Does the very manifestation cause manifestation or not? If manifestation causes manifestation, it must require a further manifestation etc. This is an infinite regression. If it does not cause the manifestation, nothing could arise since the effect is non-existent and temporary. Both these alternatives are faulty, since in the first case there would be a constant perception of the effect and in the second no perception of effect at all.

"The manifestation of an object happens as a manifestation of itself. Why imagine another manifestation as cause?" If you say this, it is the same as our proposition: manifestation of something that was previously existing.

Further arguments are given to show that the effect is non-different from the material cause.

Sūtra – 2.1.15

|| bhāve copalabdheḥ ||

The effect is non-different from the cause because we see the qualities of the cause in the effect.

In the state of being an effect like pot or crown (*bhāve*), we can see the cause, since we perceive (*upalabdheḥ*) clay and gold, the material cause, present there and recognize the pot or crown by the presence of clay or gold.

"We cannot recognize the desire tree from the elephant or horse that comes from it." We recognize earth as the material cause. "Though smoke is caused by fire we do not see fire in the smoke." The cause of smoke is damp fuel contacting fire. That is detected in the smoke by the similar smell of the fuel and the smoke.

Sūtra – 2.1.16

|| satvāc cāvarasya ||

The effect is non-different from the cause because the effect exists in the cause even before manifesting.

The effect is non-different from the cause, because of the previous existence (*satvāt)* in the material cause of the effect which manifests later (*avarasya*) by non-difference. Śruti says *sad va saumyedam agra āsīt*: O gentle one, *sat* (the effect) existed in the beginning (Chāndogya Upaniṣad 6.2.1) Smṛti says:

brīhi-bīje yathāmūlaṁ nālaṁ patrāṅkurau tathā
kāṇḍaṁ kośas tu puṣpaṁ ca kṣīraṁ tadvac ca taṇḍulaḥ
tuṣāḥ kaṇāś ca santo vai yāntyāvirbhāvam ātmanaḥ
praroha-hetu-sāmagrīm āsādya muni-sattama
tathākarma-svanekeṣu devādhyāḥ samavasthitāḥ
viṣṇu-śaktim; samāsādya praroham upayānti vai.

O best of sages! Just as the root, stalk, leaves, buds, branches, seed vessels, flowers, sap grains, husk and seeds, existing in the barley seed, manifest when there are causes for growth, so *devatās* and others situated in many karmas, meeting with the *śakti* of Viṣṇu, begin to manifest. Viṣṇu Purāṇa 2.7.37-39

Oil comes from sesame because it existed in the seeds. Oil does not come from sand because it is never present there. One spiritual substance exists in cause and effect. It was already proved that even after the effect appears, it is one with the material cause. Even after destruction of the effect, the effect is non-different from the cause in another place. That is stated in the next two sūtras.

Sūtra – 2.1.17

| | asad vyapadeśān neti cen na, dharmāntareṇa vākya-śeṣāt | |

If you say that scripture says that *asat* (non-existence of effect in the cause) existed in the beginning, the answer is no, because the last sentence indicates a different quality, non-manifestation.

"Let that be. Previously it was said *asad vā idam agra āsīt.* (Taittirīya Upaniṣad 2.6.1) Thus the effect was *asat,* non-existent in the beginning. The effect was not present in the material cause."

That is not so. The word *asat* does not mean total non-existence but existing in a different way (*dharmāntareṇa*). The words *sat* and *asat* refer to the gross and subtle states of one substance as effect and material cause. Here the word refers to the subtle quality different from the gross quality of the object. Why? Because of the sentence at the end of the passage (*vākya-śeṣāt*).

tadātmānaṁ svayam akuruta: that made itself by itself. (Taittirīya Upaniṣad 2.6.1) This statement removes doubt about the statement in the beginning (*asad vā idam agra āsīt*). Something non-existent (*asat*) could not make itself by itself. As well, something non-existent cannot be expressed in time and it is impossible to speak of a non-existent entity doing something (making itself).

Asat refers to a different quality. The cause is shown in the next sūtra.

Sūtra – 2.1.18

|| yukteḥ śabdāntarāc ca ||

The meaning of *asat* and *sat* are derived by reasoning and by scriptural statements.

The lump of clay assuming the form with a neck is the cause of saying, "This is a pot." The cause of saying "This is not a pot" is the clay assuming another form like a fragment. Smṛti says *mahī ghaṭatvaṁ ghatātaḥ kapālikā kapālikāc cūrṇa-rajas tato' ṇuḥ*: the clay becomes a pot, from the pot a fragment, and from the fragment, dust, from that dust, particles. (Viṣṇu Purāṇa) It does not happen that the pot is absolutely non-existent and total non-existence is not perceived. That is what is deduced by reasoning *(yukteḥ)*.

Since the word *asat* was previously explained, *sat* means the opposite. That is found in the passage *sad eva saumyedam*: *sat* alone existed in the beginning. Thus by logic and scripture (*śabdāntarāt*) the meaning of *asat* is "a subtle manifestation." It does not mean something imaginary like a rabbit's horn--something completely false. The universe after destruction enters a most subtle condition and merges into Brahman. Because it is very subtle it is called *asat.* Since it exists in the body of the material cause previous to manifesting, that effect is non-different from its cause. One may say "The world is not *asat* since it is impossible (for non-existence to exist) and the world cannot be *sat* because actions of the doer would be uselessness (since it already exists). It is indescribable." That is foolish since it comes from bad argumentation by mistaking the meanings of *sat* and *asat.*

Examples of *sat-kāryavada* are given.

Sūtra – 2.1.19

|| paṭavac ca ||

The universe is non-different from Brahman as cloth is non-different from threads.

Cloth at first exists as threads only and then manifests from the threads by particular joining together. Similarly the universe exists as Brahman which is endowed with subtle *śaktis* and then manifests from the Lord when he desires to create. The word *ca* indicates that there are other examples like the seed and the banyan tree.

Sūtra - 2.1.20

|| yathā ca prāṇādiḥ ||

The effect is non-different from the cause just as the *prāṇas* are modifications of the chief *prāṇa.*

The five *prāṇas,* controlled by *prāṇāyāma,* become only the chief *prāṇa*, and at the time when the body again begins functioning, with the chief *prāṇa* occupying various places like the heart, the *prāṇas* again manifest from the chief *prāṇa* with their own conditions. Similarly the universe, dissolving at the time of destruction, becoming one with Brahman endowed with subtle *śaktis*, at the time of creation, when the Lord desires to create, again manifests as *pradhāna, mahat-tattva* etc. from Brahman. The word *ca* indicates that this sūtra combines with the previous one to show examples.

There are no examples given to illustrate *asat-kāryavada*. One does not see the son of a barren woman being born nor a flower in the sky. Therefore the one Brahman endowed with *śaktis* of *jīva* and *prakṛti* is the material cause of the world. The effect, the universe, is non-different from him. That has now been proved. And though manifesting as the effect, Brahman remains in its previous, complete state because of its inconceivable qualities.

oṁ namo vāsudevāya tasmai bhagavate sadā
vyatiriktaṁ na yasyasti vyatirikto' khilasya yaḥ

I constantly offer respects to the Lord Vāsudeva from whom nothing is different and who is different from everything. Viṣṇu Purāṇa 1.19.78

Topic 8 (Sūtra 21)

Itara-vyapadeśādhikaraṇam - Jīva as creator

In sutra 1.4.23 it was proved that the Lord is the material cause and the efficient cause of the universe. Doubts raised concerning Brahman as the material cause have been refuted in sūtra 2.1.6, and in other sūtras the point is strengthened. Now, after refuting the idea that a jīva is the creator of the universe, the author strengthens the proposition that the Lord is the efficient cause, though some other statements appear to support the idea that the jīva is the creator.

Some say that the Lord is the creator of the universe using statements like *kartāram īśam:* the Lord is the creator. (Muṇḍaka Upaniṣad) Others say that a jīva with good karma is the creator of the universe using statements like *jīvād bhavanti bhūṭāni*: from the jīva all beings arose. They say that the creator is a jīva because if the Lord were the creator it would contradict his quality of perfection (since the world is full of imperfection and as a perfect person he does not need a world at all.) Because of the two opposing śruti statements, can the question be resolved?

Sūtra - 2.1.21

|| itara-vyapadeśād dhitākaraṇādi-doṣa-prasaktiḥ ||

The proposition that the jīva creates the universe has the fault that the jīva creates something unbeneficial for himself.

Some other learned persons (*itara*) who accept the idea (*vypadeśāt*) that a jīva is the maker of the world, or some who accept the teaching of creation of the universe (*vyapadeśāt*) by some jīva *(itara)*[41] end up with the fault (*doṣa-prasaktiḥ*) of the jīva producing something not beneficial to himself (*hitākaraṇādi*). He produces something unbeneficial because in the world that he produced he experiences labor and faults. No intelligent person by his own choice would make a prison for himself and then enter it, like a silk worm making a cocoon. Nor would someone who is by nature clean accept a very unclean body. Nor has any jīva produced a universe, an effect made of

---

[41] *Itara* can be taken to refer to some persons holding the opinion or to some jīva creating the world.

pradhāna, mahat-tattva, ahaṁkāra, ether, air and other elements. He would become exhausted just thinking about such a creation. Therefore the theory that jīva creates the world, which is contrary to the perfection of the Lord as creator, is rejected.

Topic 9 (Sūtras 22 - 26)

Adhikādhikaraṇam - Greater powers of Brahman

"Even Brahman creates the universe with effort and without benefit for himself, since it is said that he wills the creation into existence and then enters it."

Sūtra - 2.1.22

| | adhikaṁ tu bheda-nirdeśāt | |

Brahman has greater powers than the jīva since the difference is stated in the scriptures. Thus Brahman cannot be influenced by the world though he creates it.

The word *tu* indicates a refutation of the doubt. Brahman is much greater (*adhikam*) than the jīva because he possesses great powers. Why? Because the difference between them is stated in scriptures (*bheda-nirdeśāt*). Muṇḍaka Upaniṣad says:

samāne vṛkṣe puruṣo nimagno' nīśayā śocati muhyamānaḥ
juṣṭaṁ yaḍ paśyaty anyam īśam asyamahimānam iti vīta-śokaḥ

Though dwelling within the same tree, the jīva, bewildered, laments because of not recognizing the Lord. When he sees the glorious Lord who is different, he gives up lamentation. 3.1.2

This verse distinguishes the Lord as different from the jīva afflicted by lamentation and illusion since the Lord has unrestricted powers. Smṛtis also describe this.

dvāv imau puruṣau loke kṣaraś cākṣara eva ca |
kṣaraḥ sarvāṇi bhūtāni kūṭastho 'kṣara ucyate | |

uttamaḥ puruṣas tv anyaḥ paramātmety udāhṛtaḥ |
yo loka-trayam āviśya bibharty avyaya īśvaraḥ | |

There are two conscious beings mentioned in the *Vedas*: the conditioned *jīvas* and the liberated *jīvas*. The bound *jīvas* are all these living entities with destructible bodies. The liberated *jīvas* are fixed with one form for all time. The highest person is different from this. He is described in the scriptures as the Paramātmā, who, by entering the three worlds, supports the living entities, as the unchanging controller. BG 15.16-17

pradhāna-puruṣa-vyakta-kālānāṁ paramaṁ hi yat
paśyanti sūrayaḥ śuddhaṁ tad viṣnoḥ paramaṁ padam

The wise see the pure, supreme abode of Viṣṇu which is superior to *pradhāna,* the *jīva,* the universe and time. Viṣṇu Purāṇa 1.2.16

viṣṇoḥsvarūpāt parato hi te 'nye
rūpaṁ pradhānaṁ puruśaṣ ca vipra
tasyaiva te 'nyena dhṛte viyukte
rūpena yad tad dvija-kāla-saṁjñām

O brāhmaṇa! The *svarūpa* of Viṣṇu is different from time, from *pradhāna* and the jīva. That form by which *pradhāna* and the jīva are joined and then separated is called time. Viṣṇu Purāṇa 1.2.24

etad īśanam īśasya prakṛti-stho 'pi tad-guṇaiḥ |
na yujyate sadātma-sthair yathā buddhis tad-āśrayā ||

This is the power of the Lord: though he is situated in *prakṛ*ti, he is not affected by the *guṇas* which are situated in him, just as the intelligence of the devotee remembering the Lord is not affected by the *guṇas.* SB 1.11.39

That the Lord is not contaminated by the world has also been concluded in the sūtra 1.2.8. Thus, the Lord endowed with great inconceivable *śakti* creates the universe by his will alone and, entering, plays there, and when it grows old he withdraws it, just a like a spider. He is not influenced by the faults of the world mentioned.

"The Lord is greater than the jīva only in the sense of the ether being greater than the space in a pot." That is not so, for it cannot be accepted that Brahman can be divided up like sky being divided by a pot. Nor are jīva and Brahman related like the reflection of the moon in water and the moon in the sky since the all-pervading Lord does not have material form that can be reflected. Nor can the jīva be compared to a prince who did not know he was born as a son of a king and later finds out, for this is contrary to the śruti statements concerning the Lord's omniscience and it makes Brahman into a jīva under illusion.

Sūtra - 2.1.23

|| aśmādivac ca tad-anupapattiḥ ||

The jīva is unsuitable as the creator of the universe since he is dependent, like stone.

The jīva fails as an independent creator, because even thought the jīva is conscious, he is not independent. He is like a stone, piece of wood or lump of clay. *antaḥ praviṣṭaḥ śāstājanānām*: the Lord is within all jīvas and controls them all. (Taittirīya Āraṇyaka 3.11.10) *īśvaraḥ sarva-bhūtānām*: the Lord controls all beings. (BG 18.61)

Sūtra - 2.1.24

|| upasaṁhāra-darśanān neti cen na kṣīravad dhi ||

If you argue that the jīva can create a universe because we see him perform actions, the answer is no, since the jīva is dependent in his actions just as a cow is dependent in producing milk.

"The jīva is not inert or inactive like a stone since we see the jīva accomplish (*upasamḥāra*) actions. It is seen that the jīva initiates and completes action. This is not an illusion, since there is nothing to refute this condition. So the jīva can create the universe, with dependence on the Lord."

That cannot be. The Lord, though not seen, must be inferred. He sets in motion the jīva's actions, since he is more powerful.

If one then proposes that the jīva is the doer since the action is practically done by him, not the Lord, the answer is still no. Why? Because (*hi*) the jīva completes actions in the manner of the cow producing milk (*kṣiravat*). The suffix *vat* indicates similarity of action. *tena tulya-kriyā ced vatiḥ* (Pāṇini5.1.116)

Smṛti says

gavi dṛṣyamānam api kṣīraṁ prāṇad evajāyate
annam ṛasādi-rūpeṇa prāṇaḥ pariṇamayaty asau

Milk that is seen in the cow arises from *prāṇa. Prāṇa* transforms food into the form of nourishing juices etc.

Thus, though accomplishment of acts is seen in the jīva, he accomplishes because of the Lord, not independently. This will be explained in sūtra 2.3.39.

One cannot say that the agency of the Lord cannot be seen. That is explained in the following sūtra.

Sūtra - 2.1.25

|| devādivad iti loke ||

In this world results of *devatā's* actions are seen though they themselves are invisible.

The suffix *vat* here indicates the possessive case: of the *devatās* and others. Though Indra and other *devatās* are not visible, it is seen that they produce rain etc. in this world. Thus though the Lord is not seen, it can be concluded that he is the creator by seeing things in the world.

There is another fault in ascribing the creation of the world to the jīva.

Sūtra - 2.1.26

|| kṛtsna-prasaktir niravayava-śabda-vyākopo vā ||

The jīva would have to absorb himself completely in the action. Otherwise it would violate statements that the jīva has no parts.

Since it is well known that the jīva's svarūpa is without parts, as the doer, the jīva must engage himself totally (not partly) in an action (*kṛstsna-praśaktiḥ*). But it is unreasonable to say this, because in ordinary life see that one uses only a finger to lift a blade of grass. Exertion produces a need for use of full strength using the whole *svarūpa.* In lifting a heavy rock, such exertion is necessary whereas in lifting a blade of grass only a portion of strength is necessary. One cannot say that a portion of the *svarūpa* is used for lesser action, since the jīva is without parts. If one maintains that the jīva is divisible, it contradicts scriptures which say that the jīva is without parts (*niravayava-śabda-vyakopāt*). *eśo 'ṇur ātmā:* the ātmā is a small particle.

Where scripture says that the jīva creates all beings (*jīvād bhavanti bhūtāni*), jīva there means Brahman. That was explained previously. Therefore only the foolish propose that the jīva is the creator.

Are these two faults -- being without parts and putting forth all effort—also present in the proposition of Brahman as creator? It is not possible. If he uses all his *svarūpa* in all activities, then he would use all powers to lift a blade of grass. But that is not possible. He must therefore have parts by which he does it. If he does actions through his parts, this would violate statements of scripture like *niṣkalam niṣkriyam:* the Lord is without parts and without action.

Topic 10 (Sūtras 27 - 29)

Śabda-mūlādhikaraṇam - Scripture is the source of knowledge

Sūtra - 2.1.27

|| śrutes tu śabda-mūlatvāt ||

The defects of the agent do not apply to Brahman because of scriptural statements, which are the only proof concerning inconceivable subjects.

The word *tu* indicates refuting the doubt. The word *na* (not) is understood, taken from sūtra 2.1.24. The faults seen in the world do not apply to Brahman as the doer. Why? Because of scriptural declarations about the Lord (*śruteḥ*). He is beyond this world, inconceivable. Though he is the very form of knowledge, he possesses a form and is the possessor of knowledge. Though one entity, he appears as many, and though without parts, he possesses parts. Though measurable, he is immeasurable. Though the performer of all actions, he is without change. This Brahman is described in the scriptures.

He is inconceivable. *bṛhac ca tad-divyam acintya-rūpam*: he has a great, shining, inconceivable form. Muṇḍaka Upaniṣad.

He is knowledge itself but possesses knowledge. *tam ekaṁ govindaṁ sac-cid ānanda-vigraham*: this one Govinda is a form of eternity, knowledge and bliss. (Gopāla-tāpanī Upaniṣad 1.36) *barhāīḍābhirāmāya rāmayākuṇṭha-medhase*: I offer respects to Govinda, with peacock feather ornament, most attractive in form, with unlimited intelligence. (Gopāla-tāpanī Upaniṣad 1.37)

(Though one he is many). eko 'pi san bahudhā yo vibhāti: though one, he appears as many. (Gopāla-tāpanī Upaniṣad 1.19)

He possesses parts, though without parts. *amātro 'nanta-mātraś ca dvaitasyopaśamaḥ śivaḥ:* he is auspiciousness, with lack of duality, without parts, and with unlimited parts. (Māṇḍūkya Upaniṣad)

Though measurable his is immeasurable. *āsīno dūraṁ vrajati śayāno yāti sarvataḥ*: while sitting he goes far away and while sleeping he goes everywhere. (Kaṭha Upaniṣad.)

Though the doer of all actions he is without change. *dyāv ābhūmī janayan deva ekaḥ:* the one lord produced heaven and earth. (Śvetāśvatara Upaniṣad 3.3) *eṣa devo viśva-karmā mahātmā*: this Lord is the great soul, maker of the universe. (Śvetāśvatara Upaniṣad 4.7) *sa viśva-kṛd viśva-vid ātma-yoniḥ*: he is the maker of the universe, the knower of the universe, the source of the *ātmā.* (Śvetāśvatara Upaniṣad 6.16) *niṣkalam niṣkriyam śāntaṁ niravadyaṁ nirañjanam*: the Lord is without parts, without action, peaceful, without fault, without blemish. (Śvetāśvatara Upaniṣad 6.19)

All these qualities are accepted according to scripture, and not to be rejected by logic (though seemingly contradictory).

"How can we understand a scriptural statement which is a contradiction?" We can accept the statement because scripture is the only authoritative proof (*śabda-mūlatvāt*) for describing the inconceivable. We see similar inconceivable powers in gems and mantras. Then what to speak of inconceivable powers in the Lord!

Here is the point. The proofs are senses perception, inference and scripture. Sense perception is seen to be unreliable. On seeing a head by some magician's trick, one may think that it is a real person's head. A fire extinguished by a shower may give up double the smoke on a mountain. One may think there is still a fire there, because of that smoke. This is the problem with inference. Words from reliable authorities however are not liable to mistake. Statements like "There is snow in the Himalayas and there are jewels in the ocean" are always true. Such statements confirm perception and reason, are completely independent of perception and reasoning, and gives knowledge of things that cannot be understood by senses and logic.

(Examples are given.) A person may not believe it when he sees a head, since he has been subject to a magician previously to see an illusory head. But a voice from the sky, some authority, may say "This is a real head." "O traveller afflicted with cold! Do not think that to be a fire. We have seen that the fire was extinguished by a shower. It appears like that because the mountain is spouting smoke." Verbal testimony can thus clarify perception and logic.

"You have the gem on your neck." This knowledge (to a person who cannot find his gem) is independent of the person's perception and inference.

Śabda also produces knowledge of things that cannot be ordinarily understood, such as eclipses.

Since *śabda* is the best knowledge, *śruti-śabda* allows us to understand Brahman. *nāvedavin manute taṁ bṛhantam*: a person cannot conceive of Brahman without knowing the Vedas. This is because scripture is without fault, since it is self-proved.

This is understood through an example.

Sūtra - 2.1.28

|| ātmani caivaṁ vicitrāś ca hi ||

As various marvelous creations arise from desire trees or cintāmaṇi according to authorities, so we can believe from scripture that various creations arise from the Lord. The Purāṇas confirm this.

Through authoritative sources we learn about and believe in marvelous creations (*victrāḥ*) like elephants and horses which arise from the desire tree or *cintāmaṇi*, due to the inconceivable powers arising from the Lord's *vibhūtis*. Therefore we should believe in the wonderous creations of *devatās,* men and animals by the Supreme Lord Viṣṇu (*ātmani)*. We should not logically ask if these things are created by the whole *svarūpa* of the desire tree or by a part of it, since the only way we obtain knowledge of the nature of inconceivable objects is authoritative sources. Similarly we should not question about the Lord. The statements should be accepted as they are in the scriptures. The locative case is used (*ātmani*--in the desire tree etc.) to indicate that the Lord is the support for various objects. The second *ca* indicates that if we accept the case of inconceivable productions from desire trees, how much more we should accept the productions of the Lord. The word *hi* indicates that this is confirmed by Purāṇas. Therefore one should accept that Brahman is the creator.

This proposal alone should be accepted.

Sūtra - 2.1.29

|| sva-pakṣe doṣāc ca ||

Your proposal cannot be accepted because the fault of a whole jīva being involved with creation cannot be answered by you.

In your *(sva)* proposal that the jīva is the creator, there is also the fault of the whole *jīva* being involved in the creation rather than a part (which you cannot refute). This fault is eliminated when Brahman is the creator.

Topic 11 (Sūtra 30)

Sarvopetādhikaraṇam - Endowment of all śaktis

Other doubts are raised and resolved. The doubt is this. Is the Lord suitable as a creator or not, since false claims have been made?

(pūrvapakṣa) He is not suitable because scriptures say the Lord does not have *śaktis. satyaṁ jñānam anantaṁ brahma*: Brahman is unlimited existence and knoweldge. *sad eva saumyedam agra āsīt*: O gentle one, only *sat* existed in the beginning. (Chāndogya Upaniṣad 6.2.1) It is seen that only a person who possesses *śakti,* like a carpenter, can perform wonderful actions. Something without *śakti* (Brahman) cannot do this.

Sūtra - 2.1.30

|| sarvopetā ca tad-darśanāt ||

The Lord is endowed with all *śaktis,* because that is seen in the scriptures.

The word *ca* is used for emphasis. The supreme Lord alone is endowed with all *śaktis. upetā* comes from *upetṛ* (one who is endowed). Paramātmā is endowed with all *śaktis.* Why? That is seen (*tad-darśanāt*) in many śruti statements.

apaśyan devātma-śaktiṁ sva-guṇair nigūḍhām

They saw the Lord's own *śakti,* hidden by his qualities. Śvetāśvatara Upaniṣad 1.3

ya eko 'varṇo bahudhā śakti-yogāt

He is of one type, but is many because he is endowed with *śaktis.* Śvetāśvatara Upaniṣad 4.1

parāsyaśaktir vividhaiva śrūyate

It is said that the Lord has various *śaktis.* Śvetāśvatara Upaniṣad 6.8

The smṛtis also describe the Lord's *śaktis. viṣṇu-śaktiḥ parā proktā:* one *śak*ti of Viṣṇu is said to be supreme. (Viṣṇu Purāṇa) These *śaktis* are inconceivable. *apāṇi-pādo 'ham acintya-śaktiḥ:* I am without hands and feet and have inconceivable *śakti.(*Kaivalya Upaniṣad) *ātmeśvaro 'tarkya-sahasra-śaktiḥ*: the Lord has thousands of inconceivable *śaktis.* (SB 3.33.3) The Lord is an agent or doer through his inconceivable *śaktis.*

The Lord's *svarūpa* is described with words like *satyaṁ jñānam anantam.* His *śaktis* are described with phrases like *devātmā –śakti. (*Śvetāśvatara Upaniṣad 1.3) Thus the *svarūpa* of Brahman possesses *śaktis.*

Because of this, his decision to act is described in varous texts. *so 'kāmayata*: he desired. *tad aikṣata:* he glanced. Both types of statements--concerning his *svarūpa* and his *śaktis*--are valid since they are all śruti.

Topic 12 (Sūtras 31 - 32)

Vikaraṇatvādhikaraṇam - Is the Lord without senses?

Again doubts are put forth and resolved. Brahman cannot be the creator since he has no senses. Though *devatās* have *śakti,* they also have senses that allow them to perform actions. Brahman is without senses. How can Brahman then create the universe? The śrutis such as Śvetāśvatara state that Brahman is without senses.

apāṇi-pādo javano grahītā
paśyaty acakṣuḥ sa śṛṇoty akarṇaḥ |
sa vetti vedyaṁ na ca tasyāsti vettā
tam āhur agryaṁ puruṣaṁ mahāntam ||

Without feet he moves and without hands he grasps. He sees without eyes and hears without ears. He knows what is to be known but he is not the knower. They say he is the chief, great person. Śvetāśvatara Upaniṣad 3.19

Sūtra - 2.1.31

|| vikaraṇatvān neti cet tad uktam ||

If one objects that the Lord cannot be the creator because he has no senses, the answer has already been stated.

If one argues that Brahman cannot be the creator since he has no senses, the answer has already been given in the verse you quoted showing that he had no senses. The same passage later shows that the Lord has natural supreme *śaktis.* It is said:

tam īśvarāṇāṁ paramaṁ maheśvaraṁ
taṁ devatānāṁ paramaṁ ca daivatam |
patiṁ patīnāṁ paramaṁ parastād
vidāma devaṁ bhuvaneśam īḍyam ||

We know the worshipable Lord, ruler of the world, the great Lord, supreme among controllers, supreme *devatā* among *devatās,* the master of masters, greater than the great.

na tasya kāryaṁ karaṇaṁ ca vidyate
na tat-samaś cābhyadhikaś ca dṛśyate |
parāsya śaktir vividhaiva śrūyate
svābhāvikī jñāna-bala-kriyā ca ||

He has no body and no senses. No one is equal to him or higher. His supreme power is manifold. He has intrinsic knowledge, strength and action.

na tasya kaścit patir asti loke
na ceśitā naiva ca tasya liṅgam |
sa kāraṇaṁ karaṇādhipādhipo
na cāsya kaścij janitā na cādhipaḥ ||

He has no master or ruler in this world. He has no mark to distinguish him. He is the cause, the rulers of the senses. He has no father or ruler. Śvetāśvatara Upaniṣad 6.7-9

In the original verse quoted, it was stated that, though the Lord has no feet and hands (senses), he is still capable of actions like moving and grasping. In response to doubters these verses reiterate the truth. He is in the position of the great person because he controls all persons. He does not have a *material* body or *material* senses. This is understood through the use of the word *ca* in the phrase *na tasya kāryaṁ karaṇaṁ ca vidyate.* He has superior or spiritual *śakti* (*parāsya śaktiḥ*). That *śakti* is natural (*svabhāvikī*), related to his *svarūpa*. His knowledge, strength and action are also related to his *svarūpa*. Because others lack such qualities, no one is his equal. No one is superior to him. Thus, though devoid of material senses, since he is endowed with senses related to his *svarūpa*, there is not obstacle to his performing actions.

Others explain the verses as follows. The verses do not really say that the Lord does not have senses, since it is stated that he can still move and grasp. The statement merely denies that each sense is restricted to a particular function (eg. foot for moving, hand for grasping etc.) since the following is also said:

sarvataḥ pāṇi-pādaṁ tat sarvato'kṣi-śiro-mukham |
sarvataḥ śrutimal loke sarvam āvṛtya tiṣṭhati ||

Everywhere are his hands and feet. Everywhere are his eyes, head and mouth. Everywhere are his ears. Extending everywhere he stands. Śvetāśvatara Upaniṣad 3.16

It is also said in smṛti *aṅgāni yasya sakalendriya-vṛttimanti*: all his limbs perform the functions of all senses. (*Brahma-saṁhitā*) This is also seen when Kṛṣṇa ate food with his friends in the forest. *na tasya kāryam karaṇam* in this interpretation means that the Lord has no goal to accomplish (*kāryam*) since he is complete and thus performs no actions *(karaṇam)* to accomplish that goal. The rest of the verse has the same meaning.

Is the behaviour of Brahman in creation suitable or not to him? The *pūrva-pakṣa* is the next sūtra.

Sūtra - 2.1.32

|| na prayojanavatvāt ||

The Lord is not suitable for creation because he has no goal.

The word *na* (not) is carried from the last sūtra. The sūtra is the compound *na-prayojanavvatvāt* instead of the usual *aparyojanavatvāt.* The action to create is not suitable to the Lord. Why? Because he has no goal in doing that, since he is complete already. In this world we see that people act for themselvs and others. In the case of the Lord he cannot act for himself, since this would contradict the śruti statements that the Lord is fully satisfied. He cannot create the world on behalf of others since he should act to show mercy to others, not to give various pains such as birth and death. If the Lord creates the world without any goal, it would mean he acts without consideration. This would contradict śruti which says he has all knowledge. Therefore Brahman is not suitable to create the world.

Topic 13 (Sūtra 33)

Līlā-kaivalyādhikaraṇam - Action because of līlā

The objection is resolved with the following sūtra.

Sūtra - 2.1.33

|| lokavat tu līlā-kaivalyam ||

The objection is unfounded. The Lord's creation of the world is an act without motive, as we see in an ordinary person's conduct.

The word *tu* indicates a refutation. The conduct of the complete Lord in creating the world is pastime only (*līlā-kaivalyam*), not to gain some result for himself. There is an example. The suffic *vat* indicates a possessive case: it is like the activities of people in this world (*lokavat*). A person, overcome with joy, becauseof intense joy, is seen to perform actions such as dancing, without regard for any result (*līlā*). This is the case of the Lord also. He has such actions (*līlā*) because of the spontaneous bliss in his *svarūpa.*

devasyaiva svabhāvo'yam ātma-kāmasya kā spṛhā

The action of creation is the nature of the Lord. For a person who is satisfied in himself what desire is there? Māṇḍukya Upaniṣad

sṛṣṭy-ādikaṁ harir naiva prayojanam apekṣya tu |
kurute kevalānandād yathā mattasya nartanam ||
pūrṇānandasya tasyeha prayojana-matiḥ kutaḥ |
muktā avyāpta-kāmāḥ syuḥ kim utāsy akhilātmanaḥ ||

Without a goal, the Lord carries out creation out of bliss alone, like a mad man dancing. What is the question of a goal for the Lord who is complete bliss? Persons who are liberated have no desires to be fulfilled. What then to speak of desires in the Lord, the soul of all beings? Nārāyaṇa-saṁhitā

Taking this example, it does not mean that the Lord has ignorance (like a mad man) since it is accepted that without seeking results, out of intense bliss, a person performs certain actions called *līlā.* The example of a person inhaling and exhaling during deep sleep to illustrate līlā, raised by the Kevalādvaitins is subject to the objection that the Lord does not sleep. The example of a king playing ball raised in Viśiṣṭādvaita philosophy is not accepted because the king has a goal of gaining happiness from his playing.

Topic 14 (Sūtra 34)

Vaiṣamya-nairghṛnyādhikaraṇam - Partiality and cruelty in the Lord

Another objection is raised and refuted. Is maintaining that Brahman is the creator correct or not? It is not correct since there would be inquality or harshness (*vaiṣamya*) in Brahman, since he would have created *devatās* and humans who are subject to happiness and suffering. This contradicts śrutis which say that Brahman is without fault.

Sūtra - 2.1.34

|| vaiṣamya-nairghṛṇye na sāpekṣatvāt tathā hi darśayati ||

The Lord is neither prejudiced nor cruel because bodies are created according to karma. Scripture shows this.

Brahman as the creator does not have the fault of inquality (*vaiṣamya)* and cruelty (*nairghṛnye*). Why? Because the creator carries out creation according to the jīva's karma (*sāpekṣatvāt*). There is proof. Scripture shows this.

eṣa eva sādhu-karma kārayati taṁ yam ebhyo lokebhya unninīṣate |
eṣa evāsādhu karma kārayati taṁ yam adho ninīyate

The Lord makes him do good actions whom he wants to raise to higher planets. He makes him do bad actions who he wants to lead to hell.[42] Bṛhad-āraṇyaka Upaniṣad

This śruti shows *(darśayati)* that the Lord is the indirect cause for jīvas attaining the status of *devatās* etc. The Lord considers their karma while doing this.

[42] The idea here is not that the jīva has no free will, but that the Lord is the ultimate agent. See commentary on 2.3.39.

Topic 15 (Sūtra 35)

Na karmāvibhāgādhikaraṇam - No divisions of karma

Sūtra - 2.1.35

|| na karmāvibhāgād iti cen nānāditvāt ||

If you argue that in the beginning there was no division of karma, the answer is no, since karmas are without beginning.

"The fault of inequality and cruelty is not removed by saying it is karma that puts jīvas in different bodies. Why? Because there was no distinction of karmas (*karmāvibhāgāt*). *sad eva samyedam:* only *sat* existed, O gentle one!" Before the creation, karma divided up by Brahman was not visible. "

This is not true. Why? Because we accept that karma and the jīvas are without beginning, like the Lord. There is no fault because later karmas proceed according to previous karmas. Smṛti says:

puṇya-pāpādikaṁ viṣṇuḥ kārayet pūrva-karmaṇā |
anāditvāt karmaṇaś ca na virodhaḥ kathañcana ||

Viṣṇu will make jīvas experience the effects of piety or sin (enjoyment and suffering) according to previous karma. Because karmas are without beginning there is no inconsistency. Bhaviṣya Purāṇa

There is no fault of infinite regress if we say that karma is without beginning, because there is proof in this world (as in the case of the seed and the sprout).[43] Nor can it be said that the Lord is not independent, since he depends on karma (to create bodies for the jīvas) for karma, time and the elements are all dependent on the Lord. It is said:

dravyaṁ karma ca kālaś ca svabhāvo jīva eva ca
vāsudevāt paro brahman na cānyo 'rtho 'sti tattvataḥ

O *brāhmaṇa*! The elements, *karma,* time, *svabhāva* and the jīva are not different from Vāsudeva. Nothing but he exists in truth. SB 2.5.14

---

[43] The seed produces a tree which produces a seed, which produces another tree. There is no beginning to this sequence.

Nor can one say that this is "dawn in the hut at the landing place."[44] The Lord assigns jīvas their karma according to its condition which has no initial state. Though the Lord is capable of making its nature otherwise, he does not do that for anyone, since he is equal to all.

Topic 16 (Sūtra 36)

Bhakti-pakṣa-pātādhikaraṇam - The Lord favors his devotees

Injustice in Brahman was refuted. The author now accepts Brahman's favortism towards the devotee. The doubt is this. Does the Lord show unequal treatment by protecting the devotee and destroying his material desires?

(pūrva-pakṣa) It is not inquality since the Lord's protection of the devotee is also is dependent on karma.

Sūtra - 2.1.36

|| upapadyate cābhyupalabhyate ca ||

It is suitable that the Lord favors his devotees. This is seen in scripture.

Favoritism of the Lord, who is affectionate to his devotees, is suitable *(upapadyate*) since his protecting the devotee depends on the devotee's bhakti, which arises from the function of the *svarūpa-śakti*. This does not conflict with the Lord being without fault, since such partiality of the Lord in relation to his devotee is praised as a good quality. Śrutis says that these qualities are his decoration. Without this quality all the other Lord's qualities would not be attractive to the people. This is found in the śrutis also.

yam evaiṣa vṛṇute tena labhyas tasyaiva ātmā vivṛṇute tanuṁ svām

The Lord can be attained by the person whom the Lord chooses. To him the Lord reveals his form. Muṇḍaka Upaniṣad 3.2.3

Also it is found in the smṛtis:

---

[44] Some merchants try to avoid the tax at the toll gate. But they get lost in the night, and end up at the same toll gate at dawn. In order to defend the Lord from the accusation of cruelty the opponent ends up making the Lord cruel since the Lord enacts suffering through karma.

priyo hi jñānino'tyartham ahaṁ sa ca mama priyaḥ

This *jñānī* loves only me, and I love only him. BG 7.17

samo 'haṁ sarva-bhūteṣu na me dveṣyo 'sti na priyaḥ |
ye bhajanti tu māṁ bhaktyā mayi te teṣu cāpy aham ||29||

I am equal to all living beings. I do not hate anyone nor do I favor anyone. But those who worship me with devotion are in me, and I am in them.

api cet su-durācāro bhajate mām ananya-bhāk |
sādhur eva sa mantavyaḥ samyag vyavasito hi saḥ ||30||

If the most sinful person worships me with no other desire than to please me, I still consider that person to be my devotee, since he has fixed himself completely in me.

kṣipraṁ bhavati dharmātmā śaśvac-chāntiṁ nigacchati |
kaunteya pratijānīhi na me bhaktaḥ praṇaśyati ||31||

Very quickly, he becomes a righteous person, and becomes completely devoid of contamination. O son of Kuntī, you should declare to all that my devotee never perishes. BG 29-31

Topic 17 (Sūtra 37)

Sarva-dharmopapatty-adhikaraṇam - Endowment of all qualities

Sūtra - 2.1.37

|| sarva-dharmopapatteś ca ||

The Lord favors the devotee because the Lord is endowed with all qualities.

The wise acknowledge the quality of favortism to the devotee because the Lord, with inconceivable *svarūpa,* is endowed (*upapatteḥ)* with all contrary and non-contrary qualities. Similarly theLord is *jñana* itself and the possessor of knowledge. He is colorous but blackish, and though equal, has great affection for his devotees. Thus contrary qualities and non-contrary qualities like tolerance and honesty exist in the Lord. Smṛti says:

aiśvarya-yogāt bhagavān viruddhārtho'bhidhīyate |
tathāpi doṣāḥ parame naivāhāryāḥ kathañcana ||
guṇā viruddhā apy ete samāhāryāḥ samantataḥ ||

By his powers, the Lord is said to have contrary qualities. Thus one cannot find fault in the Lord at all. Though contrary qualities exist in him they are all to be accepted. Kūrma Purāṇa

Thus it is proved that though impartial, the Lord is the friend of the devotee.

Section Two

kṛṣṇa-dvaipāyanaṁ naumi yaḥ sāṅkhyādy-ukti-kaṇṭakān |
chittvā yukty-asinā viśvaṁ kṛṣṇa-krīḍā-sthalaṁ vyadhāt ||

I offer respects to Vyāsa who, having refuted the thorny declarations of Sāṅkhya and other philosophies with the sword of logic, established the universe as the place of pastimes of Kṛṣṇa.

Topic 1 (Sūtras 1 – 10)

Racanānupapatty-adhikaraṇam - Creation from Pradhāna

In the first pāda of the second chapter, faults raised by objectors to Vyāsa's views were refuted. In the second pāda, Vyāsa directly attacks the objectors' opinions. If he were not to do so, people would give up the path of the Vedas and end up with misfortune. In this section he refutes the Sāṅkhya philosophy.

Kapila, the *ācārya* of Sāṅkhya, assembled the sūtras that explain the elements (*tattvas*). According to his sūtras, *prakṛti* is the static state of *sattva, rajas* and *tamas.* From *prakṛti* arises *mahat-tattva*, and from *mahat-tattva* arises *ahaṅkāra.* From *ahaṅkāra* arises the five *tan-mātras* (sense objects), the two types of senses (eleven) and the gross elements (five). With the *puruṣa* (jīva), the total is twenty-five *tattvas.* When all three *guṇas* are situated in equilibrium it is called *prakṛti. Sattva* has the quality of joy, *rajas* has the quality of suffering and *tamas* has the quality of delusion. All this is understood because, in, its effect, the universe, things are described in terms of joy, suffering and delusion. A young woman gives joy to the husband because of love. This is the aspect of *sattva.* She gives suffering to the same person when she is angry with him. This is the aspect of *rajas.* She creates bewilderment when he is separated from her. This is the aspect of *tamas.* All of these are seen from the conditions of this world.

There are two types of senses: ten external senses and one internal sense, the mind. Thus there are eleven senses. *Prakṛti* is eternal and all-pervading. *mūle mūlābhāvād amūlaṁ mūlam:* It is the root without a further root since a root can have no further root (Sāṅkhya-sūtra 1.67*) aparicchinnam sarvopādānam*: it is unlimited and the material cause of everything. *sarvatra* *kārya-darśanāt vibhutvam*: *prakṛti* is all-pervading because we see its effects everywhere.

Mahat-tattva, ahaṅkāra, and the five *tan-mātras* are both the cause of something and an effect. These are effect or products of *pradhāna,* but are also causes. For instance *mahat*-tattva is the cause of *ahaṅkāra.* The eleven senses and five gross elements are effects only (and not causes). *Puruṣa* is neither cause nor effect since it does not transform. Īśvara-kṛṣṇa says:

mūla-prakṛtir avikṛtir mahad-ādyāḥ prakṛti-vikṛtayaḥ sapta /
ṣoḍaśakaś ca vikāro na prakṛtir na vikṛtiḥ puruṣaḥ / / iti / /

The root *prakṛti* is not an effect. The seven from *mahat-tattva* are causes and effects. The other sixteen are effects only. The *puruṣa* is neither a cause nor an effect.

Prakṛti is eternally the cause of effects. It is itself unconscious, but is the cause of many conscious beings enjoying and becoming liberated. Though completely imperceptible, *prakṛti* is inferred from its effects. Though it is one, when the *guṇas* become disturbed, it gives rise to the universe made of *mahat-tattva* and other elements by transformation of *śakti. Prakṛti* is the efficient and material cause of the universe. The *puruṣa* is without action, without qualities, all-pervading and conscious, and different in different bodies. It is inferred from the fact that the whole body works for the benefit of another entity. Because *puruṣa* is devoid of change and action, it is not a doer or enjoyer. This being the case, by proximity of *prakṛti* and *puruṣa,* there appears to be an exchange of qualities between them. There is *adhyāsa* of the *puruṣa* being the enjoyer and doer, and of *prakṛti* being conscious. Thus, because of lack of this discrimination, the *puruṣa* enjoys in the world, and because of discrimination, the *puruṣa* attains liberation. Liberation is the *puruṣa's* indifference to *prakṛti.* Kapila composed these points using sūtras filled with proofs.

In this system he accepts three proofs: sense perception, inference and scripture. *trividhaṁ pramāṇaṁ tat-siddhau sarva-siddher nādhikya-siddhiḥ*: these three are proof; there is nothing further to be known, because by these means all is known. (Sāṅkhya-sūtra 2.2.14 and 1.88) There is not much disagreement with things proved by sense perception and scripture. But in certain sūtras he infers that *pradhāna* is the cause of the world.

parimāṇat

Because of limited size, these are the products of *prakṛti* (unlimited).

samanvayāt

Because they are similar to *pradhāna* in qualities, the other elements are its products.

śaktitaś ca

Because if its inherent *śakti, prakṛti* can be the efficient cause. (sūtra 1.130,131,132)

These points must be refuted since by refuting them his whole philosophy is refuted.

The doubt is this. Is *pradhāna* the material cause and efficient cause of the world or not?

(Pūrva-pakṣa) *Pradhāna* is the material and efficient cause because it can be inferred that the *guṇas* of the material world arise from the *guṇas* of the *pradhāna* as the material cause. It is seen that the qualities in the effect like a pot are similar to the qualities in the cause. Though unconscious, *prakṛti* can be the doer, as is the case with trees giving fruit and water flowing. Therefore *pradhāna* is the material cause of the world and the maker (efficient cause) of the world.

Sūtra - 2.2.1

|| racanānupapatteś ca nānumānam ||

It cannot be inferred that *pradhāna* is the material and efficient cause since creations do not take place without a sentient agent, and similarity of qualities in objects do not necessarily indicate a cause-and-effect relationship between them.

It cannot be inferred (*anumānam)* that insentient *pradhāna* is the material cause of the universe nor the efficient cause. Why? Because the variegated creations within the universe *(racana*) cannot be accomplished *(anupapatti*) by something insentient. In the world it is seen that building cannot be produced just by bricks, which have no consciousness. The word *ca* indicates that there is a fault in connection of cause and effect. Thus simply because *sattva* (quality) is seen in the world and *prakṛti* also has *sattva,* that does not mean that *prakṛti* is the material cause of the world.

An external object like a pot is not endowed with intrinsic joy, since joy is an internal experience that occurs on seeing the pot. Furthermore, one does not perceive the pot as joy itself. (Kapila maintains that joy, sorrow and bewilderment appear in *prakṛti* and are also observed in the world.)

Sūtra - 2.2.2

| | pravṛtteś ca | |

***Pradhāna* is not the cause of the world because even *pradhāna* cannot act without a conscious agent.**

Pradhāna is not the cause because action (*pravṛtteḥ*) of the insentient cannot take place without a conscious director. *Pradhāna* begins to produce when there is an agent to invoke the insentient matter, just as a chariot driver is necessary to make the chariot move. This is applicable to the argument that trees, though insentient, bear fruit. Trees bear fruit because of a controlling conscious entity, Brahman, as the *antaryāmī.* This will be clarified elsewhere. The word *ca* is for emphasis. Or it indicates "because we see the inclination to do something such as "I do this" only in conscious entities, insentient *pradhāna* cannot be the cause."

(Pūrva-pakṣa) "The cause of producing the world comes from superimposition of qualities exchanged between *puruṣa* and *prakṛti* by proximity."

Is the proximity, which is the cause of superimposing qualities, inherent in them (*sad-bhāva*)? Or is it a transformation within *puruṣa* and *prakṛti*? It cannot be something inherent in them since then even the liberated souls would develop superimposition. It cannot be some transformation within *prakṛti,* since then *prakṛti* would be the cause of superimposition, whereas you argue that *prakṛti* takes up the superimposition as an effect, in order to appear conscious and thus create the world. And it cannot be a transformation of *puruṣa* (jīva) since, according to your philosophy, jīva does not undergo any transformation.

"Milk changes into yogurt by itself. Water released from a cloud, having one taste, develops sweet taste if it falls on a mango tree, or sour taste if it falls on a different tree. *Pradhāna* also transforms into different bodies and earth planet because of the various karmas of the jīvas."

Sūtra -2.2.3

|| payo'mbuvac cet tatrāpi ||

If you say that *pradhāna* changes by itself just as milk becomes yogurt or water develops various flavors, there must be a conscious regulator in that case also.

Even in milk or water, there is conscious controller causing action. The transformation does not take place by itself as can be inferred from the case of a moving chariot (which must have a driver, though not seen). That milk and water have a controller is proven by the śruti describing *antaryāmi-brāhman* (Bṛhad-āraṇyaka Upaniṣad).

Sūtra – 2.2.4

|| vyatirekānavasthiteś cānapekṣatvāt ||

You cannot say that *pradhāna* alone is the cause of its changes, just because there was no cause except *pradhāna* existing before creation, and because *pradhāna* is independent.

The word *ca* means "moreover." Just because there was no other cause *(anavasthitheḥ)* before creation except for *pradhāna (vyatireka),* because of its independence (*anapekṣatvāt*), you cannot conclude that *pradhāna* caused its own transformation. You say that except for *pradhāna* itself, there is no instigator or inhibitor before the creation, but there is dependence even there, for you accept another cause--the proximity of the conscious *puruṣa* (jīva). Thus the theory of insentient *pradhāna* being the sole creator of the universe is defeated. Moreover, without any other cause, and with the continued proximity of the jīva during destruction of the universe, creation should arise even at that time. One cannot say that creation does not take place at that time because the karmas of the jīva are not active, since even at that time those karmas could be aroused.

(Pūrva-pakṣa) "Creepers, grass and buds turn into milk spontaneously, without another cause. *Pradhāna* changes into *mahat-tattva* and other elements without another cause also."

Sūtra - 2.2.5

|| anyatrābhāvāc ca na tṛṇādivat ||

Grass transforming naturally into milk is not a sound argument since milk will not be produced in other circumstances.

The word *ca* is for emphasis. This is not a reasonable argument either, for the transformation does not take place in other circumstances *(anyatrābhāvāt)*. If a bull eats grass the grass does not turn into milk. If grass turned into milk by itself, grass which falls in the yard should turn into milk. But that does not happen. Therefore grass transforms, not because of its own nature, but because of contact with a particular being, the cow. The will of the Lord then makes the transformation happen.

It has been concluded that *pradhāna*, being insentient, cannot initiate activity for creation on its own. Even if, to satisfy you, we accept that *pradhāna* can initiate the action on its ownthis will not help you prove your theory.

Sūtra - 2.2.6

|| abhyupagame'py arthābhāvāt ||

Even if it is accepted that *pradhāna* can initiate creation on its own, the proposal does not stand, since *pradhāna* would have no purpose in creating the universe.

The word *na* (not) should be supplied in this and the next three sūtras. You claim that *pradhāna* acts for the enjoyment and liberation of the jīva by thinking in the following manner: "The jīva, having enjoyed me and consequently realizing my faults, will attain liberation in the form of detachment from me." *pradhāna-pravṛttiḥ parārthā svato'py abhoktṛtvād uṣṭra-kuṅkuma-vahanavad*: *pradhāna's* action (as agent) is for the sake of another, spontaneously, because *pradhāna* is not an enjoyer, like a camel's carrying a load of *kuṁkuma* (for the sake of another, its master). (Sāṅkhya sūtra 3.58) The jīva is not the agent but the enjoyer. *Akartur api phalopabhogo 'nnadyavat*: the jīva is just like a person who eats rice though he does not cook it. (Sāṅkhya sūtra 1.105)

This activity cannot be accepted. Why? Because in accepting it, there is absence of purpose *(arthābhāvāt)*. You claim that the goal of *pradhāna's* action is jīva's enjoyment in the form of seeing *prakṛti,* and liberation in the form of detachment from *prakṛti.* But the goal of the action cannot be the jīva's enjoyment, because before the action of creation, the jīva (according to your definition) was not an agent, but conscious being alone, without modification. Thus there was no necessity for the jīva to change, in order to see *prakṛti,* and no need to be liberated, since the jīva previous to creation was liberated. If you argue that the cause of the jīva modifying itself for enjoyment is proximity to *prakṛti,* that would also be the case of the jīva in his state of liberation, since proximity of *pradhāna* and *puruṣa* is eternal.

(Pūrva-pakṣa) "If a lame man incapable of walking and a blind man incapable of seeing come in proximity, the blind man, though without sight, is capable of moving about. Similarly, by the proximity of iron and a magnet, the inert iron moves. *Prakṛti,* though insentient, by proximity with the jīva who has consciousness, acts as if conscious, as jīva's shadow, to create the universe for the jīva." In response to this is the following sūtra.

Sūtra - 2.2.7

|| puruṣāśmavad iti cet tathāpi ||

If you give the example of the blind and lame man, or the iron and magnet, there is still no reason to accept *pradhāna* as the creator of the universe.

Even accepting such an analogy, insentient *prakṛti* could not act on its own. Even if a lame man cannot walk, he can give instructions where to walk because he can see and the blind man can accept those instructions even if he cannot see. (Both are conscious beings.) In the case of the iron and magnet, there must be someone to bring the two together. The jīva however, eternally without action and without qualities, can undergo no transformation. If you say that proximity of jīva and *prakṛti* causes change in *prakṛti,* their proximity is eternal. Therefore this would mean that creation would be eternal. And this would mean liberation is impossible. Since the lame man and the blind man are both conscious and the iron and magnet are both unconscious, (whereas jīva is conscious and *prakṛti* is unconscious), the examples are clearly disparate (and so inapplicable to the context).

The followers of Sāṅkhya say that the universe is created by the appearance of principal and secondary guṇas, caused by predominance or subordination among the three *guṇas.* This idea is refuted in the next sūṭra.

Sūtra - 2.2.8

|| aṅgitvānupapatteś ca ||

This argument cannot be accepted because there is no cause of one *guṇa* becoming prominent.

Pradhāna is a condition of equilibrium of the *guṇas.* One among the *guṇas*, neutral by nature in that state, cannot be principal (*aṅgitvānupapatteḥ*) since the other two cannot become subordinate, since all three are in a state of equilibrium. Therefore one of the *guṇas* cannot become principal, making the others secondary. The cause of disruption of equilibrium cannot be the Lord or time, since you do not accept them as agents capable of doing this. Kapila says:

īśvarāsiddheḥ mukta-baddhayor anyatarābhāvān na tat-siddhiḥ

God is not accepted because there is no proof of his existence. He has to be either liberated or bound up (and in both cases he can't be capable of initating creation). (Sāṅkhya-sūtra 1.92-93)

dik-kālāv akāśādibhyaḥ

Space and time arise from ether. (Sāṅkhya-sūtra 2.12)

Jīva cannot be the cause of disturbing equilibrium because jīva is indifferent to *prakṛti.* (Sāṅkhya -sūtra 1.1.63) Even accepting that the equilibrium of *guṇas* is disturbed without any cause at the beginining of every creation, there would be no cause of the *guṇas'* disturbance at the very first creation.

"One can infer that the *guṇas* have remarkable natures because of seeing their effects. Thus the faults you enumerate are not valid."

Sūtra - 2.2.9

|| anyathānumitau ca jña-śakti-viyogāt ||

Arguing that *guṇas* are remarkable has no foundation since the *guṇas* are without consciousness.

Even if you infer that the *guṇas* have remarkable powers (*anyathānumitau*), this does not take away the faults. Why? Because the *guṇas* are incapable of considering (*jñātṛtva-viyogāt*) "I will create the world." *Pradhāna,* devoid of consciousness, cannot create. Bricks cannot create a house without a conscious controller.

The author concludes [in the next sutra].

Sūtra - 2.2.10

|| vipratiṣedhāc cāsamañjasam ||

Because Kapila's philosophy is inconsistent, it is unfit.

Because of thorough contradictions, Kapila's philosophy is inconsistent (*asamañjasam*) – and thus to be disregarded by those desiring the highest good.

Because he says that *prakṛti* acts for other's benefit and is visible, the jīva is the enjoyer, seer and controller of *prakṛti*. *śarīrādi-vyatiriktaḥ pumān*: the jīva is separate from the body and other things. *saṁhata-parārthatvāt*: *pradhāna* is a combination which exists for others. But he also says that the jīva is without change, without qualities, devoid of knowing, acting, and enjoying, a being in isolation. *jaḍa-prakāśāyogāt prakāśaḥ:* the jīva is conscious and matter is not consciousness. *nirguṇatvān na cid-dharmā:* because it has no qualities, the jīva has no quality of consciousness. (Sāṅkhya-sūtra 1.145-146)

In one place Kapila says that the jīva is in bondage because of non-discrimination of the *guṇas,* and becomes liberated by discriminating the *guṇas.* However, in another place he says that bondage and liberation belong to the *guṇas* not to the jīva. *naikāntato bandha-mokṣau puruṣasyāvivekād ṛte, prakṛter āñjasyāt sasaṅgatvāt paśuvat:* bondage and liberation do not belong to the jīva and only arise because the jīva lacks discrimination; they belong to *prakṛti* by association, like an animal in association with a rope. In this way one can find many contradictions in the philosophy.

Topic 2 (Sūtras 11 - 17)

Mahad-dīrghādhikaraṇam - Triple Atoms

Now *ārambha-vāda (asat-kārya-vāda* of the Vaiśeṣikas and Nyāyikas) is refuted. These logicians speculate that there are four types of atoms: earth, water, fire and air. These are without parts, have form and are spherical. At the time of destruction they are in the state of not starting effects. At the time of creation however with the jīvas' karmas in front of them, they begin creation of the world, which is gross, with parts, by combining into two particles and more. Two atoms, having action dependent on the jīva's karma, conjoin by that and produce a double atom called *hrasva* (small). Thus the causes are two atoms (*samavāyī*), the conjunction (*asamavāyī*) and the karma of the jīva (*nimitta*, efficient cause). Three double atoms combine in the same way to produce a triple atom called *mahat* (big). Two single atoms cannot produce a triple atom, for a greater product must be produced by a greater cause. Four triple atoms combine to make a quadruple atom. From these four atoms other grosser atoms arise, and from those, still grosser atoms arise. In this manner, great earth, water, fire and air arise. Form etc in the effect arises from form etc. in the cause, the *samavāyī* or atoms, which are the quality's shelter. Qualities in the cause produce qualities in the effect. When the Lord wants to destroy earth and other product, by separating the action (*kriyā)* from the atoms, by destruction of *saṁyoga*, the double atom is destroyed. Without any shelter, the triple atom is destroyed. Step by step, earth and other products are destroyed. In destruction of cloth, by destroying the shelter, the threads, there is destruction of form and other qualities. This is how the universe is destroyed.

The atom (smallest particle) is called a *parimaṇḍala.* Its size is called *pārimāṇḍalyam*. The double atom is called *aṇu* and its size is *hrasva* or small. The triple atom is called *mahat* or *dīrgha* (big).

The doubt is this. Does the universe arise from *parimaṇḍalas* or not?

(Pūrvapakṣa) Yes, because the creation arises gradually by their combination into the double atom, from single atoms, with initial action caused by contact with the jīva with his karma.

Sūtra - 2.2.11

|| mahad dīrghavad vā hrasva-parimaṇḍalābhyām ||

The formation of the triple atom from single and double atoms is untenable.

The word *vā* indicates "and." The word "unfit" from the last sūtra is understood. Their whole theory, with single atoms and double atoms (*hrasva-parimaṇḍalābhyām*) forming into the triple atom (*mahad dīrghavat*), is untenable. Like the appearance of earth and other elements from a combination of single atoms into double atoms, double atoms into triple atoms, and triple atoms into quadruple atoms, their other procedures are also contradictory. It is not logical to say that the double atoms with parts arise from atoms with no further divisible parts, for one sees a cloth with parts formed from combination of threads with parts and with six sides. Therefore, atoms must have parts (divisibility). Otherwise, even by combining a thousand atoms, double or triple atoms of bigger size could never form because they would have no size, since the atom is without dimension in their theory.

Larger effects do not necessarily arise from larger material causes. That idea is mental speculation. Even if this idea were accepted, (still, for the double atoms to have parts) the atoms would need to have different parts, and those parts would need to have further parts. And those parts too would need to have parts to infinity. As each object would have unlimited atoms, Meru and the mustard seed would be the same size. Thus, the idea that large triple atoms arise from small double atoms which in turn arise from dimensionless single atoms is empty talk.

This sūtra should not be explained as a refutation of objections concerning the author's own propositions since this section of the chapter deals with refuting others points of view.

What else is untenable?

Sūtra - 2.2.12

|| ubhayathāpi na karmātas tad-abhāvaḥ ||

In either case, initial action in the atom cannot take place. Thus creation cannot take place.

These logicians maintain that the world arises from combination of two atoms and more by the action of the single atoms. Is the action generated in the single atom due to karma within the atom or due to karma in the *ātmā*?

It cannot be from karma within the atom because it is impossible for the karma generated by sin and piety of the *ātmā* to reside within the atom. It cannot come from karma in the *ātmā* since it is impossible for action to arise within the atom by something within the *ātmā*. The action cannot arise from the atom in contact with the *ātmā* since part-less atoms cannot join with partless *ātmā*.[45] In either case, karma cannot generate the first action in the atom. It was already concluded that an insentient object cannot on its own initiate action since it is inert. Nor can the *ātmā* cause the first action in the atom because after universal destruction, the *ātmā,* devoid of consciousness, is also inert. Nor can the desire of the Lord according to the jīva's karma be the cause of the atom's initial action, since the action would be eternal, because the Lord's will is eternal. One may argue that the Lord's will is absent during destruction since the karmas of the jīvas are not awakened. But that is not acceptable, because if the ingredients are present, then creation should occur. Because there is absence of a definite cause for the atom's initial action, the first action cannot take place. Because of absence of action in the atoms, their coming together will not take place. Without that initial coming together, the double atom will not form. Without those combinations, creation cannot take place (*tad-abhāvaḥ*).

Sūtra - 2.2.13

|| samavāyābhyupagamāc ca sāmyād anavasthiteḥ ||

The theory is not valid because of acceptance of the principle of *samavāya*, which entails infinite regress.

Their theory is invalid. Why? Because it accepts *samavāya* (inherence) (as an eternal *padārtha*). The logicians accept relationship (*samavāya*) of atoms with double atoms as a basic principle. That cannot be, because that relationship requires a similar relationship (*sāmyāt*) in order to exist. *Samavāya* would depend on another *samavāya.* This would cause an infinite regression *(anavastitheḥ*).

The principle of *samavāya* produces awareness of quality, action and class (*jāti*), or a relationship with those items. If it does more that than, it becomes excessive. Another *samavāya* would have to be accepted, causing infinite regression. If you maintain that the relationship is the essential nature of *samanvāya* (not requiring another *samavāya*), that same relationship would have to exist everywhere. Thus one cannot agree with this principle of *samavāya,* since all qualities would be everywhere if this *samavāya* were

---

[45] For them to join, they would need to have a point of contact, which in turn would require them to have parts.

inherent in the object. For those who proclaim *samavāya* to be a common principle, fragrance would be in the air, sound in earth, form in the *ātmā,* and intelligence in fire, since the relationships would be present in every object.

One cannot argue, "This is not so because *samavāya* does not operate in relation to the particular object. *Samanvāya* operates as an essential principle (*svarūpa)* in relation to the state of the object being defined." It is impossible to have an additional factor (the state of the object) operating in a theory with a fixed number of *padārthas* (categories of existence). Therefore the whole logic is contradictory.

Sūtra - 2.2.14

|| nityam eva ca bhāvāt ||

Because of *samanvāya,* which is eternal, the universe would be eternal.

Since you accept that *samavāya* is eternal, then the universe would be eternal (since atoms would always relate to each other). But this (the eternality of the universe) is not accepted in Vaiśeṣika philosophy.

Sūtra - 2.2.15

|| rūpādimatvāc ca viparyayo darśanāt ||

Since you maintain that atoms have qualities such as form, from seeing these qualities in temporary objects with parts, the atoms will have to be temporary and have parts.

Since you accept that atoms of earth, water, fire and air have form, taste, fragrance and touch *(rūpādimatvāt*), they would become opposite (*viparyaya*)-- non-eternal and endowed with parts--since we see (*darśanā*t) that pots with form and other qualities are temporary and have parts. But this is the opposite of your doctrine of eternal, partless atoms. Thus your philosophy is not valid.

Sūtra - 2.2.16

|| ubhayathā ca doṣāt ||

In both cases, because of fault, the theory is untenable.

If you do not accept that atoms have form and other qualities, then earth and other elements should also not have them (which is not true.) In order to remove that fault, if you do accept that atoms have form and other qualities, the previous fault occurs (atoms would be temporary and have parts). In both cases, the theory fails because its weak points cannot be defended.

Sūtra - 2.2.17

|| aparigrahāc cātyantam anapekṣā ||

Because the theory of atoms is not accepted by the sages, it should be completely ignored.

Manu and other authorities give some regard to Kapila's ideas by accepting some of its portions. But persons desiring the highest benefit should not give regard *(anapekṣā)* to the idea that atoms are the cause of the universe, which is contrary to the Vedas, since the authorities do not accept *(aparigrahāt)* any portion of that theory and since it is incoherent.

Topic 3 (Sūtras 18 - 27)

Samudāyadhikaraṇam - Everything arises from internal and external objects

Now Buddhist doctrine is refuted. Buddhism had four offshoot schools of thought: Vaibhāṣikas, Sautrāntikas, Yogācāras and Mādhyamikas.[46] Among them the Vaibhāṣikas hold that all external perceived objects are real. Sautrānikas hold that the objects can only be inferred by various ideas, so the ideas are real, whereas the objects may or may not be real. Yogacāras hold that objects are not real at all; only thought faculty is real and external objects are like a dream. Mādhyamikas hold that all things – objects and thoughts – are unreal. These are their various ideas. All of them hold that all existing

[46] Baladeva calls them disciples (*śiṣya*), but this must be taken in a general sense as far as historical Buddhism goes. The names refer to schools of Buddhism that evolved over time, long after Buddha's demise. The sūtras of Vyāsa predate many of the schools of philosophy it discusses, according to modern chronology of the philosophies. However, the principles of these philosophies existed long before they were codified in the philosophical works presently existing.

objects are temporary. The first two groups (Vaibhāṣikas and Sautrāntikas) hold that all objects are divided into two categories:

1. Physical, further divided into two sub-categories: *bhūta* and *bhautika* and

2. Mental, further divided into two sub-categories: *citta* and *caitya.*

There are five *skandhas* (constituent elements): form (*rūpa*), consciousness (*vijñana*), perception (*vedanā*), names (*saṁjñā*) and mental impressions (*saṁskāra*). The atoms are of four types: earth, water, fire and air, with natures of hardness, liquidity, hotness and mobility. These atoms join together and become earth, water, fire and air. These elements become bodies, senses and sense objects. This is the first *skandha* called *rūpa,* consisting of the elements *(bhūta)* and its derivatives *(bhautika*), and it includes all external objects.

Vijñana-skandha is the continuous flow of consciousness, giving the sense of "I". This is the agent or doer, the enjoyer and the *ātmā. Vedanā-skandha* is the perception of happiness and suffering. *Saṁjñā-skandha* consists of names such as Devadatta. The *saṁskāra-skandha* consists of mental qualities like attachment, repulsion and delusion. These last four *skandhas* are *citta* and *citta* derivatives. Inner nature is composed of these and is the seat of all actions. All internal objects are included in the last four *skandhas.* Thus, the unlimited world is made of these two only: internal and external objects. Anything else, like ether, is non-existent.

The doubt is this. Is the concept of internal and external objects valid or not?

(Pūrvapakṣa) Yes, because it explains how actions in the world arise.

Sūtra - 2.2.18

|| samudāya ubhaya-hetuke'pi tad-aprāptiḥ ||

If everything arose from internal and external objects, still the universe could not arise.

Even if one accepts this theory of two types of *skandhas* causing all objects (*samudāya ubhaya-hetuke),* still it does not explain everything in the world (*tad-aprātiḥ*), since everything in this theory is unconscious, and there is no permanent conscious entity to bring about the combination. If one proposes that the inclination to come together is intrinsic to the *skandhas,* then the world would be eternal (since the *skandhas* are eternal). However, this contradicts this philosophy, which holds that everything is temporary. Thus this idea is not logical.

(Purva-paksa) "In Buddhist doctrine, it is said that *avidyā* (ignorance) and the *skandhas* mutually give rise to cause and effect. No one has refuted this. Since these *skandhas* and ignorance revolve continuously like a waterwheel in sequence, the combination of these is valid because, without it, the other factors could not accomplish anything. These factors are *avidyā, samskāra, vijñāna, nāma, rūpa,* the body, touch, perception, thirst, clinging to existence, birth, class, old age, death, grief, lamentation, suffering and depression."

Sūtra - 2.2.19

|| itaretara-pratyayatvād iti cen notpatti-mātra-nimittatvāt ||[47]

If you say that combination arises from mutual cause and effect of *avidyā* and other factors, that cannot be, because those factors give rise to each other but not the combination that makes the world.

Pratyaya means cause. If you say that combination arises from mutual causes (*intaretara-pratyayatvāt)* of *avidya* etc. the answer is no. Why? The previous cause explains that the later object arises but does not explain the combination of *skandhas.* Moreover, a combination arises for the purpose of enjoyment, but there can be no enjoyment for the *ātmās,* since they are momentary. Since they are momentary, they cannot produce sinful or pious acts causing enjoyment or suffering. You cannot say that the karma to enjoy is produced by a continuity of *ātmā* because this would contradict your theory that everything is momentary. If you maintain that everything is momentary, then that is subject to the faults previously mentioned. Thus the Buddhist theory is untenable.

Next the theory of mutual causation (*avidyā* etc.) is criticized.

Sūtra - 2.2.20

|| uttarotpāde ca pūrva-nirodhāt ||

---

[47] The Ramanuja reading of this sutra is *itaretara-pratyayatvād iti cet, na, saṅghāta-bhāvānimittatvāt |*

The theory of causation is invalid because, when the effect arises, the cause is destroyed.

The word *na* should be added from the previous sūtra. The Buddhists argue that everything in existence vanishes in the next instant. When an effect arises in a later moment, its cause in the previous moment has already been destroyed. This cannot produce the cause and effect cycle of *avidyā* etc. mentioned previously because the cause of the effect at the later moment could not arise since the cause of the previous instant disappeared completely into nonexistence. It is seen that the cause actually carries on into the effect.

The Buddhists maintain that existing objects arise from non-existence and that without the destruction of the cause, the effect cannot appear. This view is refuted.

Sūtra - 2.2.21

|| asati pratijñoparodho yaugapadyam anyathā ||

Destruction of the cause destroys the theory of causation by skandhas. If the effect arises from a material cause, then cause and effect would exist simultaneously.

If the material cause is non-existent *(asati)*, then the claim that everything arises from the *skandhas* by cause and effect is false (*pratijñoparodhaḥ*). Everything would give rise to everything else at all times and anything that arose would be non-existent. If the effects arise from the material cause (*anyathā*), they would exist simultaneously (*yaugpadyam*), which is against your theory, since the effect would be connected with the cause. Thus the theory of momentary existence is refuted. Thus effects cannot arise from non-existence.

The Buddhists claim that there is absolute destruction of a pot similar to destruction of a lamp flame. This view is refuted.

Sūtra - 2.2.22

|| pratisaṅkhyāpratisaṅkhyā-nirodhāprāptir avicchedāt ||

Total destruction by volition or otherwise is impossible because objects cannot be totally destroyed.

Destruction of objects by intention is called *pratisaṅkhyā-nirodha.* Destruction without intention is called *apratisaṅkhyā-nirodha. Ākāśa* is non-existence of coverings. These three are called absolute non-existence (*nirupākhyaṁ śūnyam*). Everything else has momentary existence. It is said *buddhi-bodhyam trayād anyat saṁskṛtaṁ kṣaṇikaṁ ca*:

except for these three, everything else which is perceived by intellect is a momentary impression. This theory of *ākāśa* will be refuted elsewhere. Here the other two types of destruction will be refuted.

These two types of destruction are impossible *(aprāptiḥ*). Why? Because total destruction of an existing object is impossible (*avicchedāt).* Creation and destruction of an object mean simply that the object changes condition. The substance (*dravyam*), the shelter of the condition, remains one. One cannot say that the flame is totally destroyed everywhere on seeing it extinguished here, because it can be verified by principles that it has no total destruction because the flame simply changed state. The other state of the flame is not seen because it is very subtle. If there were total destruction of objects, then you would see the momentary universe as totally non-existent. You also would not exist. But this is not so. Therefore, this theory is invalid.

Next the Buddhist concept of liberation is refuted.

Sūtra - 2.2.23

|| ubhayathā ca doṣāt ||

In both ways their concept of liberation fails because of fault.

The word *na (*not) from sūtra 19 is understood, in this and three following sūtras. Buddhists say that liberation is destruction of *avidyā* and the rest of the cycle, which is the cause of rebirth. Does liberation arise from knowledge of the truth or does it arise on its own? It cannot arise from knowledge because then the acceptance of the concept of causeless destruction (*apratisaṅkhyā-nirodha*) would be useless. It cannot arise on its own, since then the practices prescribed in Buddhist teachings would be useless. Therefore, their concept of liberation is invalid since it cannot stand up to scrutiny either way *(ubhayathā*).

The concept of *ākāśa* as complete non-existence is refuted.

Sūtra - 2.2.24

|| ākāśe cāviśeṣāt ||

Postulating non-existence as *ākāśa* is invalid because it has qualities like any other substance.

It is impossible that they define *ākāśa* (space) as non-existence. Why? By perceiving "A hawk flies in the space" one infers that *ākāśa,* with the quality of sound, is a real entity, the shelter of real objects, just as it is seen that earth, because of actually existing, is the shelter of real fragrance, water is the shelter of taste, fire, of form and air, of touch. Since you admit that air exists within ether, you contradict yourself by saying that ether does not exist. It is not possible to say that *ākāśa* is mere absence of coverings (objects within it), since that is not reasonable. *Ākāśa* is neither previously non-existing, non-existing because of destruction, nor totally nonexistent.

The universe should be without *ākāśa* because it cannot be perceived, since there would be objects like earth, water etc. covering it (since the definition of *ākāśa* is "no covering.") Moreover, by the presence of *ākāśa* (space), earth and other elements would not be perceived. It cannot be mutual non-existence (no objects in space and no space in objects) because one would then not perceive space between the various objects. If you maintain that *ākāśa* exists when there is the absence of coverings, then it becomes a real object since it can be distinguished by lack of coverings. Thus *ākāśa,* like earth and other elements, has real existence. It is not something non-existent.

The concept of momentary existence is criticized.

Sūtra - 2.2.25

|| anusmṛteś ca ||

Objects are not momentary because of recollection.

Recollection is cognition of things previously experienced. It is also called recognition. One recognizes what was previously experienced as "This is that very object." The object is not a momentary condition (it existed earlier and exists now). When we say "This is that Gaṅgā" or "This is that flame," it indicates similarity with a previous object, since one cannot say it is exactly the same object. But this recognition could not take place in the absence of the same permanent person experiencing similarity of the river or the flame at different times. There may sometimes be doubt whether an object is the same as that seen previously, but there can be no such doubt about the self, the experiencer; the previous experience cannot be that of another person, since it is impossible to have another person's memories.

One cannot propose a continuous "oneness" of all impressions since, in accepting something permanent and pervading over all time, one must accept the *ātmā,* which is against your theory. If one does not accept this proposition, then recollection cannot be explained, since the idea that one can have another's experience has already been rejected.

Further, what does momentariness mean? Does it mean something related to momentariness or something which appears and disappears in a moment? It cannot mean something related to momentariness, since even a permanent object is also related to moments of time. It cannot mean instant appearance and disappearance of an object because that is never experienced. Thus the theory of *dṛṣṭi-sṛṣṭi,* creation of objects by seeing, has also been refuted. It can also be rejected because it is based on momentary existence, which has already been rejected. Therefore, existence of objects is not momentary.

Though an object actually disappears, it is inferred by cognition to have yellow color etc, from having deposited that form with yellow in consciousness. Thus recognition of variety in objects creates variety in cognition. This is Sautrāntika's opinion.

Sūtra - 2.2.26

|| nāsato'dṛṣṭatvāt ||

Destroyed objects do not transfer their qualities to another object, because this is never seen.

It is not possible that the yellow form in cognition is that of a yellow form that disappeared completely (*asataḥ*).[48] Why? Because it is not seen (*adṛṣṭatvāt*). When an object with qualities is destroyed, one does not see those qualities

---

[48] This is an attempt to explain of how momentarily manifested objects appear to be long lasting.

establishing a relationship with another object (in the mind). Nor can you say that an object like a pot was only an inference and not actually perceived externally. That is refuted by the awareness, "I know by directly seeing." This is the particular fault of Sautrāntika's philosophy. Therefore, the perceived pot is not merely inferred by a form held in cognition.

Now a common fault of both Vaibhāṣika and the Sautrāntika is shown.

Sūtra - 2.2.27

|| udāsīnānām api caivaṁ siddhiḥ ||

With this philosophy one could attain all goals without effort.

By accepting creation of objects from nothing, with momentary existence, goals would be achieved by persons who do not have any method *(udāsīnām)*. People would attain goals without employing any means, because if things were created and then destroyed in a moment, there would be no motive for attaining desired objects or avoiding undesired objects. Even if a person desired a certain object, he would not undergo any method for attaining it. No one would endeavor for liberation or Svarga. But this is not so.

It is seen that all people, desiring objects, accept some method and attain their goal. Thus these two schools of thought tend to delude the universe. Believing that everything arises from *skandhas* that actually exist, they also speak of real objects arising from nothing. And then they teach methods for the momentary *ātmā* to attain Svarga or liberation. These philosophies are insignificant.

Topic 4 (Sūtras 28 - 31)

Abhāvādhikaraṇam - Non-existence of objects

Though Vaibhāṣika's and Sautrāntika's philosophy has been refuted, Yogācāra remains ready to fight. According to Yogācāra, Buddha, conceding to disciples absorbed in external objects, made a system concerning external objects. This was not his intention, since his conclusion is that only *vijñāna-skandha* (cognition) exists. Thus awareness of an object like a pot is mere cognition. Cognition takes the form of an object. You cannot say that action cannot be accomplished without real objects since action is accomplished in dreams without real objects. Even those who consider external objects real accept that cognition has the quality of taking the form of the object. How else can awareness of a pot or cloth arise? As actions can be accomplished in this manner, what is the need of external objects?

"How does internal cognition take the form of a pot or mountain?" This does not happen. Cognition is a revealer. Cognition has a form since it is impossible for a formless entity to reveal anything.

"Why does the mind assume various forms, if external objects are unreal?" This happens because of variety of impressions (*vāsanā*). One can understand that the variety in the mind arises because of a variety of impressions since one sees forms in the presence of impressions and senses an absence of forms in the absence of impressions. Since knowledge and the object of knowledge consistently accompany each other, the object of knowledge is not separate from the cognition of it. The object is actually only cognition.

The doubt is this. Is it correct to conclude that everything is mere cognition or not?

(Pūrvapakṣa) Because one can accomplish actions by cognition without objects, as in dreams, and because, by accepting this proposition, another element (external objects) becomes unnecessary, it is proper to say everything is mere cognition.

Sūtra - 2.2.28

|| nābhāva upalabdheḥ ||

One cannot claim external objects do not exist, because of experience.

One cannot claim that external objects do not exist *(na abhāvaḥ)*. Why? Because of experience (*upalabdheḥ*). We are aware of an object different from cognition when we have knowledge of a pot. The wise do not accept statements that are opposed to awareness. One cannot say, "It is not that I am not aware of objects, but rather I am not aware of anything except knowledge." By the force of awareness alone, one must conclude the existence of the external object.

When people make the statement "I know the pot," they are aware that there are three factors: an agent, an object and the act of knowing expressed by a verb "to know." And they make others believe this also. If you claim that only knowledge exists, you become the object of scorn. Objects are different from cognition (knowledge).

"If there is something like a pot separate from cognition, how does that object appear in knowledge? Everything is revealed in one object of knowledge since all 'otherness' is included in one object of knowledge." That is not so. In cognition there is a relation established in making a particular thing an object of knowledge and excluding other objects. As different forms arise in the knowledge of a person looking at yellow or red objects as his subject, this difference within one's knowledge demonstrates the actual existence of differences in external objects, and thereby the actual existence of those objects.

You argue that because knowledge and its object accompany each other, objects are mere cognition. This is wrong since the two things – knowledge and object of knowledge – coming together indicates their difference.

Knowledge and object of knowledge go together because one (knowledge) is the result and the other (the object of knowledge) is the cause. Though Buddha denied external objects, he also accepted their separate existence. *yat-tad-antar jñeyaṁ rūpaṁ tad bahirvad avabhāsate*: the form known internally appears like an external object.[49] If external objects were not real, he would not use the word *vat* (like) for comparison. No one gives an object of comparison which does not exist, such as "son of a barren woman."

"Without recourse to external objects, everything in the waking world arises by *vāsanā* alone, by variety of cognition, just as one carries on activity in a dream." This idea is refuted in the next sūtra.

Sūtra - 2.2.29

|| vaidharmyāc ca na svapnādivad ||

One cannot claim that objects are only cognition as in dreams, since there is difference in the dream object and object of waking perception.

The word *ca* is for emphasis. It is not possible to say that just as in a dream or imagination *(svapnādivat)* one can conceive of objects like pots through

---

[49] This is apparently from *Ālambana-parīkṣa* by Dinnāga, and quoted by Saṅkaṛa.

cognition, the same happens in waking sate. Why? Because there is a difference *(vaidharmyāt)* between the objects of dream and waking state. In a dream, objects are remembered from previous experience. In waking state, however, they are experienced directly. Objects realized in dreams change continually with the moment and are negated as false by waking. Objects experienced in waking state, however, have the same quality even after a hundred years. That objects are remembered in dreams was stated only as an argument. Actually, the opinion of the author (Vyāsa) is that the Lord creates situations in a dream according to what the individual should experience. This is explained further in sūtra 3.2.1.

Now the idea that varieties of cognition occur because of varieties of impressions, without any external objects, is refuted.

Sūtra - 2.2.30

|| na bhāvo'nupalabdhe ||

In your theory, there will be no impressions, since there is no contact with external objects.

Existence of impressions cannot occur according to your theory. Why? Because, according to your theory, there is no contact with external objects (*anupalabdhe*). The necessity of external objects is proved by the fact that in the presence of objects, impressions arise, whereas in their absence, there are no impressions. Since you do not accept external objects, no impressions should arise.

Moreover, an impression *(vāsanā)* is a particular mental formation. It cannot exist without a permanent basis. That is explained in the next sūtra.

Sūtra - 2.2.31

|| kṣaṇikatvāc ca ||

In your theory, there can be no permanent basis of the impressions, since everything is momentary.

The word *na* (not) is carried over from the previous sūtra. According to your philosophy, there can be no permanent basis for the impression. Why? Because you claim that everything – including individual and aggregate (*ālaya*) cognition – is momentary (*kṣaṇikatvāt*). In the absence of a conscious entity, which is permanent in past, present and future, the actions of recollection, reflection and impressions depending on time and place will not occur. Because of lack of a shelter, impressions cannot exist. Because there are no impressions, there can be no variety in cognition. The theory of cognition as the only existence is thus insignificant.

Topic 5 (Sūtra 32)

Sarvathānupapatty-adhikaraṇam - Totally Illogical

With the Yogācāra defeated, the Mādhyamika, propounding complete voidism, comes forward to argue. His philosophy is as follows: Accepting external objects and *vijñāna* (cognition), Buddha created the concept of momentariness etc. as a ladder for raising the intelligence of his disciples. But those disciples did not ascend the path. Voidness is the only truth and liberation is attaining that. This is the secret teaching.

It is a correct teaching because it is self-proved, since voidness needs no cause for its existence and its origin needs no explanation--since only existing objects require explanation of cause. But an existing object cannot arise from an existing object for we do not see a sprout arising unless the seed is destroyed. The existing object can also not arise from an non-existing entity, since this would mean the sprout arises from a nonexistent seed. An existing object cannot arise on its own, since it is meaningless to say that it produced itself. An existing object cannot arise from some other entity since then anything could arise from anything, since "anything" includes all things. Since there is no origination, there is no destruction. Therefore origination, destruction, existing object and non-existing object all arise from illusion. The only truth is voidness.

The doubt is this. Is it correct or not to say that the only truth is voidness?

(Pūrva-pakṣa) Voidness is correct because it needs no proof and all objects are nonexistent, since they are produced from illusion.

Sūtra - 2.2.32

|| sarvathānupapatteś ca ||

The voidness doctrine is refuted because it is totally illogical.

The word *na* (not) is understood. Do you, in speaking of voidness, propose its existence, its non-existence or its existence-non-existence? Your doctrine cannot be proved at all. Why? Because it is illogical (*anupapatteḥ*). If you admit that voidness is an existing entity (*bhāvam*), then you defeat yourself (since nothing should exist in your doctrine). If you say it is a non-existing entity *(abhāvam)* your doctrine of complete voidness is destroyed due to the fact that you exist as the propounder of the theory and the logic you use also exists. If you say that the voidness is both existing and non-existing, it is a self-contradictory statement, and is therefore useless.

Moreover, if the proof by which you conclude voidness is non-existent, the doctrine of voidness is destroyed. If the proof exists, then everything exists. Thus, the theory of voidness is defective.

Thus, in teaching three mutually contradictory theories (objects are real, cognition is real, nothing is real) Buddha deluded the world. It should be understood that Vyāsadeva does not refute Lokāyata teachings (Cārvaka) since they are most unworthy of discussing. By defeating Buddhist doctrine, the author has also defeated a similar doctrine proclaiming the world is illusion (*māyāvāda*). It is similar to Buddhism in that it proposes voidness, because it also holds that the creation is mental (*dṛṣṭi-sṛṣṭi*), taking shelter of momentariness, and it defines the world as illusion.

Topic 6 (Sūtras 33 - 36)

Ekasminn asambhavādhikaraṇam - Impossibility of contrary qualities

Now Jain doctrine is refuted. They say that there are two types of objects (*padārthas)*: jīva and non-jīva. The jīvas are conscious, the size of the body, and with limbs. Non-jīvas are of five types: *dharma, adharma*, the body, time and *ākāśa.* Dharma causes motion. *Adharma* causes lack of motion. Both are all-pervading. The body (*pudgala*) has color, smell, taste and touch. The body is of two types: atoms and their combinations. The combinations are air, fire, water, earth, bodies and planets.

The atoms which are the cause of earth, fire, water and air are not of four types but one type. By transformation of that one nature, they become earth etc. Time, which is the cause of past, present and future, is atomic. *Ākāśa* however is one substance with unlimited space. These six objects are substances (*dravya*). The world is made of these.

Among these, with the exception of atoms, five substances (excluding time) are called *astikāya: jīvāsti-kāya, dharmāsti-kāya, adharmāsti-kāya, pudgalāsti-kāya and ākāsāsti-kāya. Asti-kāya* means a substance which occupies various spaces. The Jains describe seven things which should be understood so that the jīva can attain liberation: *jīva, ajīva, asrava, saṁvara, nirraja, bandha and moksa.* Among them, jīva was previously described. It has qualities such as knowledge. *Ajīva* are objects of jīva's enjoyment. *Āsrava* are the collection of senses, by which the jīva flows (*āsravati*) to sense objects. *Saṁvara* is lack of discrimination and other qualities which cover *(saṁvṛnoti*) discrimination. *Nirjara* is penance such as plucking body hairs or sitting on hot stones, by which lust and anger etc. are finally worn away (*jīryati*). *Bandha* is the continuous cycle of birth and death inflicted by eight types of action. There are four *ghāti-karmas* which are sinful: those obstructing natural knowledge, wisdom, seeing, strength and happiness. There are four *aghāti-karmas*[50] consisting of piety, which creates identity with the body and consequent experience of happiness, distress, attachment to body and detachment from body.

Liberation is jīva being situated in *ākāśa* beyond the worlds or going upwards after being freed from the eight actions, by methods indicated in the scriptures, and manifesting his natural form as *ātmā.* Their practice is called three jewels and comprises, correct knowledge, correct vision and correct conduct.

They establish the *padārthas* by the logic of seven-fold refutation. 1. somehow it may be. 2.somehow it may not be. 3. somehow it maybe or may not be. 4. somehow it is beyond words. 5. somehow it may be, but it is beyond words. 6. somehow it may not be, but it is beyond words. 7. somehow it may be and may not be, but it is beyond words. *Syāt* is an indeclinable meaning "somehow or somewhat." *Sapta-bhaṅgī* means a system to refute seven rules. These are seven rules concerning *padārthas* in various theories: 1 .existence, 2.nonexistence, 3. existence and non-existence, 4. something

---

[50] These are pious actions which create happiness, body, status and longevity.

different from existence and non-existence, 5. though something exists, it is different from it, 6. though there is non-existence, it is different from it. 7. while there is existence and non-existence, it is different from it. The seven principles are used to refute these seven theories. They are necessary because of qualities of existence, non-existence, eternality, non-eternality, difference and non-difference among all objects.

If an object exists absolutely, it will exist everywhere at all times, completely, and no one will desire or reject it at any place, any time or in any way since one does not strive to attain what is already attained and since it is impossible to reject or avoid it.

If an object does not exist absolutely however, but exists sometime, somewhere, somehow, then someone by some means will try to attain or avoid it, since it is capable of being achieved or avoided.

All objects are either substances *(dravya)* or its derivative (*paryāya*). Those which are substances are real. Those which are derivatives are unreal. *Paryāya* is a particular condition of the substance. Thus, from them there is manifestation of real by the existing and manifestation of unreal by the non-existing.

The doubt is this. Is the Jain theory of jīvas and *padārthas* correct or not?

(Pūrva-pakṣa) It is correct because it uses the process of refuting seven propositions.

Sūtra - 2.2.33

|| naikasminn asambhavāt ||

The categories cannot be accepted because of the impossibility of contrary qualities existing in one object.

These categories proved by their logic cannot be accepted. Why? Because it is impossible that contrary qualities reside in one object (*eksasmin*) simultaneously. One never sees an object which is cold and hot at the same time. Moreover, the *sādhana* for attaining Svarga, liberation or avoiding hell is useless because everything is uncertain, and Svarga, hell and liberation are thus mutually confused. Since a pot would have uncertain elements, a person wanting water would use fire instead of a pot or a person wanting to build a house would use air instead of wood. One cannot say that because of the difference, the person desiring water will avoid fire--because there is also non-difference between them and thus he would use fire to get water.

There are categories defined, a means of defining, using the seven fold logic. There is the definer, the jīva. And there is the result of defining. However, all these become uncertain by the contrivance of "it may somehow be" with qualities of existence and non-existence. The logic is as delicate as a spider's thread. What is the need to examine it further?

The idea that the *ātmā* is the size of the body is refuted.

Sūtra - 2.2.34

|| evaṁ cātmākārtsnyam ||

The ātmā would lose its completeness (due to not fitting properly in various bodies).

Just as it is a fault that contrary qualities inhere in one substance in their theory, it is a fault that the *ātmā* is incomplete (*akārtsnyam*) in their theory. They say that the jīva is the size of the body. Thus the size of the *ātmā* in an infant would not fit properly in the body of young man. If the *ātmā* the size of a human body entered an elephant body by his karma, he would not be able to experience happiness and pain in all limbs (since the soul would not extend to all parts of the elephant's body). And if the human *ātmā* obtained a mosquito body, it would not fit in that body at all.

Sūtra - 2.2.35

|| na ca paryāyād apy avirodho vikārādibhyaḥ ||

The problem of ātmā's size cannot be removed by proposing that the *ātmā* changes its size, because then it would be subject to change.

"The *ātmā* has unlimited parts. In occupying an infant or youth body or an elephant body, its size would not be different from the particular body because it can decrease or increase its parts." This cannot be. Why? Because then the *ātmā* would be subject to transformation (*vikārādibhyaḥ*). But you say that the *ātmā* is without change. Because karmas for acts already performed would be destroyed and new ones created without having acted,[51] the theory is useless. You may claim that the jīva has no transformation because, when he is liberated, the size of the body in liberation and the jīva would be the same (and this state would be eternal). This is a foolish argument since, according to your own theory, the jīva in liberation can have no permanence at all, because it must also be created and uncreated, existing and non-existing.

The Jain theory of liberation is criticized.

Sūtra - 2.2.36

|| antyāvasthiteś cobhaya-nityatvād aviśeṣāt ||

The Jain theory is untenable because liberation is like bondage, which is eternal.

The word *na* (not) is understood from the last sūtra. The Jain philosophy is incorrect because of the nondescript condition (*aviśeṣāt*) of liberation (*anyāvasthiteḥ*). It is not distinguishable from the state of bondage. Why? Because of the description of both types of liberation. Liberation is described as continuously going upwards or being situated in the *ākāśa* without a planet. Both these states of liberation are eternal. But no one can be happy by moving upwards continually, or remaining without a shelter. (In both conditions of liberation, they would suffer as in bondage.) One cannot argue that there is no suffering of a person in that condition as there would be for a person with a body, since even in liberation the *ātmā* would have heaviness because of limbs of the ātmā. One cannot say that both conditions are eternal since anything created must be destroyed.

Therefore the Jain doctrine is insignificant and the object of scorn. The Jains in teaching what is contrary to the Vedas--that the universe is existent and non-existent, and that Brahman mentioned in the Upaniṣads cannot be described-- and Māyāvadīs who teach similar theories, are hereby refuted.

---

[51] By accepting a body too big, one could not experience all the limbs, and by accepting a body too small, the jīva would extend beyond the body and experience karmas of other bodies.

Topic 7 (Sūtras 37 - 41)

Paty-adhikaraṇam - The Paśupatas

Now the author refutes the ideas of the Pāśupatas and others. Pāśupatas say that there are five categories (*padārtha*): cause, effect, yoga, discipline (*vidhi*) and the end of pain. These were taught by Śiva, the Supreme Lord, for liberating the *paśu (jīva)* from bondage (*pāśa*). Pāśupati or Śiva is the efficient cause, *mahat-tattva* and other elements are the effect, yoga means meditation while uttering *oṁ*, discipline means bathing three times a day etc., and the end of suffering is liberation. The followers of Ganeśa and Sūrya say that Ganeśa or Sūrya is the efficient cause, and from them the universe is created through *prakṛti* and time. By worshipping these *devatās* respectively the jīva attains cessation of suffering or liberation at the time of death.

The doubt is this. Are these doctrines of the followers of Śiva, Ganeśa and Sūrya correct or not?

(Pūrvapakṣa) Their doctrines are correct because liberation is possible by their *sādhanas,* since it is seen that God is only the efficient cause just as the potter is the maker of a pot.

Sūtra - 2.2.37

|| patyur asāmañjasyāt ||

The conclusions of Pāśupati are incorrect because they contradict the Vedas.

The word *na* is understood from 2.2.35. The conclusions of Pāśupati *(patyuḥ)* are not correct. Why? Because they contradict the Vedas (*asāmañjasyāt).*

The Vedas define Nārāyaṇa alone as the sole cause of the universe and all others like Brahmā and Śiva are his effects. Liberation is caused by offering *varṇāśrama, dharma, jñana* and bhakti to him. In the Atharva Veda it is said:

tad āhur--eko ha vai nārāyaṇa āsīn na brahmā neśāno nāpo nāgnīṣomau neme dyāv-āprthivī na nakṣatrāṇi na sūryo na candramāḥ sa ekākī na ramate tasya dhyānāntaḥ sthasya yajña-stomam ucyate tasmin puruṣāś caturdaśa jāyante ekā kanyā daśendriyāni mana ekādaśaṁ tejaḥ dvādaśo 'haṅkāraḥ trayodaśakaḥ prāṇaḥ caturdaśa ātmā pañcadaśī buddhiḥ bhūtāni pañca tan-mātrāṇi pañca mahā-bhūtāni tasya dhyānāntasthasya lalāṭātryākṣaḥ śūlapāṇiḥ puruṣa jāyate bibhrac chriyaṁ satyamṁ brahmacaryaṁ tao varāgyam tatra brahmā caturmukho 'jāyata

The sages explained. Only Nā*rāyaṇa* existed. Brahm*ā*, *Ś*iva, water, fire, Soma, sky and earth, constellations, the sun and the moon did not exist. Being alone, he did not enjoy. When he meditated, sacrifice and hymns arose. Fourteen males and one daughter were born: the ten senses and the brilliant mind, ahaṅkāra (twelfth), prāṇa (thirteenth), ātmā (fourteenth), and the intelligence (fifteenth, a daughter). The five sense objects and five gross elements also arose. When Nārāyaṇa meditated, three-eyed Śiva with trident, possessing beauty, truth, celibacy, austerity and renunciation, was born. Four-headed Brahma was born from him. Mahā Upaniṣad (1-2)

atha puruṣo ha vai nārāyaṇo'kāmayata prajāḥ sṛjeya ity ārabhya, nārāyaṇād brahmā jāyate nārāyaṇād rudro jāyate nārāyaṇāt prajāpatiḥ prajāyate nārāyaṇād indro jāyate nārāyaṇād aṣṭau vasavo jāyante nārāyaṇād ekādaśa-rudrā jāyante nārāyaṇād dvādaśādityā jāyante ity ādi |

The puruṣa Nārāyaṇa desired "Let me produce progeny." From Nārāyaṇā, Brahmā was born. From Nārāyaṇa, Śiva was born. From Nārāyaṇa, Prajāpati was born. From Nārāyaṇa, Indra was born. From Nārāyaṇa, the eight Vasus were born. From Nārāyaṇa, the eleven Rudras were born. From Nārāyaṇa, the twelve Ādityas were born. Nārāyaṇa Upaniṣad

ahaṁ rudrebhir vasubhiś carāmy aham ādityair uta viśvadevaiḥ
yaṁ kāmaye taṁ tam ugraṁ kṛṇomi tam brahmāṇaṁ tam ṛṣiṁ taṁ sumedhām
ahaṁ rudrāya dhanur ā tanomi brahma-dviṣe śarave hantavai u
ahaṁ janāya samadaṁ kṛṇomy aham dyāv āpṛthivī āviveśa

I travel with the Rudras, the Vasus, the Ādityas and Viśvadevas. I make the person I love a strong person, a brāhmaṇa, a sage, and intelligent person. I bend the bow for Śiva so that his arrows will slay the enemies of the Lord. Ṛg Veda 10.125.1, 6-7

In Yajur Veda it is said *tam etaṁ vedānvacanena*: they study the Vedas to understand him. (Bṛhad-āraṇyaka Upaniṣad 4.4.22) *vijñāya prajñāṁ kurvīta:* after understanding him, one should meditate on him. (Bṛhad-āraṇyaka Upaniṣad 4.4.21) *ātmā vā are draṣṭavyaḥ*: *ātmā,* the Lord, is to be seen. (Bṛhad-āraṇyaka Upaniṣad 4.5.6) The smṛtis which follow after the Vedas state the same many times.

When the Vedas use words Śiva or Ganeśa as referring to the Supreme Lord and cause of everything, those words are used not to refer to the particular deities, but to indicate Nārāyaṇa in an etymological sense, as in the auspicious one (Śiva) or the Lord of the ganas (Ganeśa). This understanding ensures that these statements are not contrary to the śrutis just mentioned and agree with the greater context of scripture. Thus everything is clear.

These philosophers contrary to the Vedas conclude that the Lord is merely the efficient cause. In using inference (reasoning) they speak only in relation to the material point of view. Intolerance of their false notions is expressed in the next sūtra.

Sūtra - 2.2.38

|| sambandhānupapatteś ca ||

The philosophy is not valid because the Lord's relationship with the world cannot be established.

Since in their philosophy the Lord does not have a body, a relationship with the world *(sambandha)*--his being creator of the world--cannot be accomplished since we see that only a potter with a body has a relationship with clay.

Sūtra - 2.2.39

|| adhiṣṭhānānupapatteś ca ||

And this is because in their theory the Lord does not have a body.

The theory is invalid because the Lord has no body. It is seen that a person with a body (*adhiṣṭhāna),* like a potter, does activities.

"Just as the jīva without a body has a body and senses as his support, so the Lord also can have *pradhāna* as his support." The next sūtra replies.

Sūtra - 2.2.40

|| karaṇavac cen na bhogādibhyaḥ ||

If you argue that *pradhāna* is like the Lord's senses, this cannot be accepted because then the Lord would suffer and enjoy like ordinary jīvas.

You cannot say that the Lord creates the world, taking support of *pradhāna* which exists at *pralaya,* which assists like the senses (*karaṇavaṭ)* in a body. Why? Because the Lord's position would be destroyed by experiencing happiness and suffering (*bhogādibhyaḥ*) through birth and death, by accepting and rejecting *pradhāna,* representing his senses.

"We can suppose that the Lord accepts a body because of karma. One sees a king with very good karma gets a body, control and rules a country. A person with bad karma does not get that result." This idea is refuted.

Sūtra - 2.2.41

|| antavatvam asarvajñatā vā ||

If the Lord had karma, he would be subject to death and lack omniscience.

If the Lord had karma, he would have a body and be subject to death. He would be like a jīva, and would also not be omniscient, for a person subject to karma cannot be omniscient.

"But you also claim that the Lord is without destruction and is omniscient."

There is no fault in saying that Brahman is the creator, since it is based on śruti. This was shown in *śabda-muṭlatvāt* (2.1.27). Independence of *devatās* is refuted, but they are respected as the Lord's servants. These five sūtras are for the purpose of refuting three groups--worshippers of Śiva, Ganeśa and Sūrya, since the reasons for refutation are the same for all of them. Thus the word *pati* is used to indicate all of them. The five sūtras also serve to refute establishing the Lord as the cause by logical means.

Topic 8 (Sūtras 42 - 45)

Utpatty-asambhavādhikaraṇam - Śakti is impossible as the cause

The author now refutes *śakta* theories. According to them, *śakti,* endowed with omniscience and omnipotence, is the cause of the universe.

The doubt is this. Is this possible or not?

(Pūrva-pakṣa) It is possible because the universe arises by *śakti.*

Sūtra - 2.2.42

|| utpatty-asambhavāt ||

Śakti is not the cause of the world because it is impossible that śakti creates the world.

The word *na* (not) is understood. Because this philosophy is contrary to the Vedas, the idea that *śakti* is the cause arises by using inference only. The logic is established by material means only. Thus *śakti* is not the cause of the universe. Why? Because *śakti* by itself cannot create the universe. We do not see that sons are born from women without the mercy of a man. *Śakti* cannot be accepted as omniscient since we do not see in this world.

"There is a male who gives mercy to *śakti.* By his mercy *śakti* creates."

Sūtra - 2.2.43

|| na ca kartuḥ karaṇam ||

This is not valid since the *puruṣa* has no senses.

If you say that the *puruṣa* gives mercy to *śakti,* he cannot give mercy because he does not have senses and body suitable for creating the universe. And if you say that he does have senses and body, he would be subject to karma.

"But the Lord is endowed with qualities like eternal knowledge and will."

Sūtra - 2.2.44

|| vijñānādi bhāve vā tad-apratiṣedhaḥ ||

There is no objection if you say the Lord is endowed with knowledge and other qualities.

If you say that the *puruṣa* has eternal knowledge and will, we have no objection since that is included in our proposal of Brahman. We accept that the *puruṣa* with eternal qualities is the creator of the universe.

Those who maintain that *śakti* alone is the cause of the world cannot be respected by those desiring the highest good. This is the conclusion.

Sūtra - 2.2.45

|| vipratiṣedhāc ca ||

Śaktivāda cannot be accepted because it contradicts scripture.

Śakti-vāda is insignificant because it contradicts all śruti and smṛti.

śrutayah smṛtayaś caiva yuktayaś ceśvaraṁ param
vadanti tad-viruddham yo vadet tasmān na cādhamaḥ

Śruti, smṛti, and logic say that the Lord is supreme. There is no one lower that he who says something contrary to this. Padma Purāṇa

The word *ca* indicates cause-- because *śakti* cannot create the world. The path of Vedānta, devoid of the thorny faults adopted by Sāṅkhya and other philosophies, should be followed by those desiring the highest good.

Section Three

May the sun of Kṛṣṇa who destroyed with his rays the misconceptions about ether and other subjects destroy my material attachments.

Topic 1 (Sūtra 1)

Viyad-adhikaraṇam - Ether

In the second pāda of the second chapter, the fallacious nature of arguments of philosophers concerning *pradhāna* and other subjects was shown. In the third pāda, the creation of various elements from the Supreme Lord and their merging with him are presented. Also the author shows that the jīva is not created, that the jīva is the shelter of knowledge and has a body made of knowledge, that the jīva is atomic and spreads out by its knowledge, that the jīva is an agent or doer and is an *aṁśa* of Brahman, that the *avatāras* are directly the Lord, and that jīvas' variety is caused by karma, while refuting contrary statements about them.

The sequence of creation --*pradhāna, mahat, ahaṅkāra, tan-mātras,* senses, and the gross elements starting with ether--is chiefly proven in śrutis like Subāla Upaniṣad. The order of creation mentioned in Taittirīya Upaniṣad, starting with ether will be discussed in order to resolve contradictions. This will be made clear later.

In Chāndogya Upaniṣad the following statements are found:

sad eva samyedam agra āsīt.. tad aikṣata bahusyāṁ prajāyeyeti tat tejo 'sṛjata
tat teja aiksāta bahu syām prajāyeyeti, tad-apo 'sṛjata tā āpa aikṣanta bahvyaḥ syāma prajāyemahīti tā annma asṛjanta

Only *sat* existed in the beginning. The *sat* willed, "Let me be many, may I produce offspring." *Sat* produced fire. Fire willed, "May I be many, may I produce offspring." Fire produced water. Water willed, "May I be many, may I produce offspring." Water produced food. (Chāndogya Upaniṣad 6.2.1-3)

There it says that fire, water and food were produced. One must consider this. The doubt is whether ether is produced or not, that is, whether it has an origin or whether it is eternal.

(Pūrvapakṣa) Because it is not mentioned in śruti, ether is not produced. That view is presented in the following sutra.

Sūtra - 2.3.1

|| na viyad aśruteḥ ||

Ether is not produced because it is not mentioned in śruti.

Ether is eternal. It is not produced. Why? It is not mentioned in the section dealing with the production of elements in Chāndogya Upaniṣad. That section mentions the production of fire, water and food but not of ether. Therefore it is not produced.

Topic 2 (Sūtras 2 - 4)

Viyad-utpatty-adhikaraṇam - Creation of Ether

This statement is now refuted.

Sūtra - 2.3.2

|| asti tu ||

Ether also has an origin.

The word *tu* indicates a removal of doubt. Ether has *(asti)* an origin. Though it is not mentioned in Chāndogya Upaniṣad, ether's creation is mentioned in Taittirīya Upaniṣad.

tasmād vā etasmād ātmana ākāśa ṣambhūtaḥ ākāśād vāyur, vāyor agnir, agner āpo 'dhbhyo mahatī pṛthivīti

From Brahman came ether. From ether came air, from air came fire, from fire came water and from water came the great earth.

Another doubt is raised.

Sūtra - 2.3.3

|| gauṇya-saṁbhavāc chabdāc ca ||

Ether is not created because the meaning is figurative only, and because there is a statement in the text saying ether is eternal.

(This sutra gives the argument of the pūrva-pakṣa, which is explained below)

"It is not possible to imagine that ether is created, as sages like Kaṇāda and Gautama have shown. Just as people in a crowd make statements like "Make space" that are figurative, similarly the śruti statements about creation of ether are also figurative. Why? Because it is not possible to create ether or space, since it is all pervading and without form, and because śruti says that ether is without any ingredient for a cause. *vāyuś cāntarīkṣaṁ caitad amṛtam:* air and ether are eternal. (Bṛhad-āraṇyaka Upaniṣad) Therefore one should consider that ether does not have a creation."

An objection is presented to the opponent's argument:

"If the scripture speaks the word "produced" in relation to fire and other elements, in the literal sense, how can that word be taken figuratively with ether in the same passage?"

The opponent replies in the next sūtra.

Sūtra - 2.3.4

|| syāc caikasya brahma-śabdavat ||

Words can have a figurative meaning as well as a literal meaning in one passage, just as the word Brahman has literal and figurative meanings in a passage in Taittirīya Upaniṣad.

Take the phrase *tapasā brahma vijijñāsasva tapo brahma:* try to know Brahman by austerity; austerity is Brahman. (Taittirīya Upaniṣad 3.2.1) In this statement (*ekasya*) the word Brahman is taken in the second part figuratively to mean a method for understanding Brahman, and in the first part literally to mean Brahman. The same can be said of the word "produced." Since Chāndogya Upaniṣad does not mention creation of ether, other statements (for instance in Taittirīya Upaniṣad) concerning ether's creation are negated.

Topic 3 (Sūtras 5 - 6)

Pratijña-hāny-adhikaraṇam - Rejection of the proposal

This argument is rejected.

Sūtra - 2.3.5

|| pratijñāhānir avyatirekāc chabdebhyaḥ ||

Ether is produced from Brahman, for the promise made at the beginning of the passage is fulfilled if everything is non-different from Brahman (and

thus everything comes from Brahman including ether), and other statements in the same Upaniṣad state this.

Preceding this passage, the promise (*pratijñā*) is made in the Chāndogya Upaniṣad to teach that by which what is not heard becomes heard etc. This promise is fulfilled *(ahaniḥ)* if Brahman alone is everything *(avyatirekhāt).* If everything were not Brahman, knowing Brahman would not produce knowledge of everything. Brahman being non-different from everything means that Brahman is the material cause. Thus by knowing one thing, all things are known. Accepting that Brahman is the cause of everything, one must accept that ether is created. It is also known because of other statements in the same Upaniṣad *(śabdebhyaḥ). sad eva somyedam agra āsīd ekam evādvitīyam aitadātmyam idaṁ sarvam:* O gentle one, in the beginning only *sat* existed: it was one without a second, and one with everything. (Chāndogya Upaniṣad 6.2.1) One should accept from such statements that before creation there is one Brahman and after creation there is oneness of Brahman with everything described.

"How can you say this without a specific statement in the Upaniṣad?"

Sūtra - 2.3.6

|| yāvad-vikāraṁ tu vibhāgo lokavat ||

Since all transformations come from Brahman, any object not specifically mentioned must also come from Brahman, just as in ordinary life.

The word *tu* indicates refutation of the doubt. *aitadātmyam idaṁ sarvam*: everything is one with him. Whatever transformations exist *(yāvad-vikākam)*-- all the varieties (*vibhāgaḥ*)-- are in him. *Pradhāna, mahat-tattva* and all other transformation and their divisions described in Subāla and other śrutis are indicated by this statement to be one with him. An example is given. If a person after saying, "All these are Caitra's sons" glorifies one of those sons as being born of Caitra, it is understood that all of them are born of Caitra. Thus the Upaniṣad says "Everything is one with Brahman." After it stated that *pradhāna, mahat-tattva* etc. arose from Brahman, in describing how fire, water and food arose from Brahman, it should be understood that all the elements arose from Brahman. Thus, though the Upaniṣad does not specifically mention ether arising from Brahman, that arising of ether is understood implicitly. That is the meaning of *vibhāga* in the sūtra (all divisions are included even if not mentioned specifically.)

If one argues (3.3.3) that origination of ether is figurative since ether cannot be created, it is also said that the Lord has inconceivable powers for creating everything. Though there are statements in scripture saying that ether is eternal, those statements are figurative, since scripture also says that ether is subject to creation and destruction. We can determine that ether has an origin and destruction from inference also. Ether is created because it is an element and elements like fire have the quality of being created and destroyed. This is the positive argument. The negative argument is: ether is not like the *ātmā* and therefore cannot be eternal.

The objection raised in sūtra 3.3.4, that a word can have two meanings in one sentence, is also refuted by this sūtra. Thus accepting the origin of ether is not a new concoction (but instead is authoritative).

Topic 4 (Sūtra 7)

Mātariśvādhikaraṇam - Air

The next sūtra shows that previous conclusions about ether apply to air as well.

Sūtra - 2.3.7

|| etena mātariśvā vyākhyātaḥ ||

By this explanation it is also explained that air has an origin.

By explaining that ether has an origin *(etena)* it is explained that air (*mātariśvā*), which takes shelter of ether, is also an effect (having an origin). The steps of the argument are as follows. "Air is not produced because it is not stated in Chāndogya Upaniṣad." It has an origin since air arises from ether according to Taittirīya Upaniṣad. "This is a figurative statement since air is stated to be eternal in the śrutis." Because the promise in the Upaniṣad to teach one thing by which everything is known---everything is one with Brahman--must not be contradicted , it must be concluded that everything is the effect of Brahman. Thus the conclusion of Chāndogya Upaniṣad is that air also has an origin in Brahman. Saying that air is eternal is figurative.

The present sūtra is separated from the previous sūtra to ensure that sūtra 2.3.9 concerning fire would refer only to air, and not to air and ether.

Topic 5 (Sūtra 8)

Asambhavādhikaraṇam - Brahman has no origin

There is a doubt concerning the statement *sad eva saumyedam*: only *sat* existed in the beginning. Is *sat* or Brahman also produced or not?

(Pūrva-pakṣa) Since causes like *pradhāna* and *mahat-tattva* are produced, Brahman is also produced since it is also a cause like the others.

Sūtra - 2.3.8

|| asambhavas tu sato'nupapatteḥ ||

Brahman has no origin because it is unbefitting its definition.

The word *tu* indicates a refutation of the doubt or it is used for emphasis. There is no origin *(asambhavaḥ)* of Brahman *(sataḥ).* Why? Because it is unsuitable (*anupapatteḥ*) for that which is without cause. Thus the śruti says:

sa kāraṇaṁ karanādhipādipo na cāsya kaścij janitā na cādhipaḥ

Brahman is the cause, the Lord of the lords of causes. He has no cause or ruler over him. Śvetāśvatara Upaniṣad 6.9

One cannot infer that Brahman has an origin because it is a cause (and every cause must have another cause), since this is contradicted by śruti and reasoning. Brahman is accepted as the root cause (final cause), and without any other root cause, because otherwise causes would go on in an infinite regression. That which is the root cause has no cause, since a root cannot have another root. By refuting that Brahman has a cause, it is also understood that Brahman alone is without cause or origin since it is the ultimate cause, and everything like *avyakta* and *mahat-tattva* arises from Brahman alone. The origin of ether and air are used as examples of this.

Topic 6 (Sūtra 9)

Tejo 'dhikaraṇam - Fire

The digression about origin of Brahman completed, now ideas about fire which are contrary to the Vedas are refuted. It is said in śruti that Brahman created fire: *tat tejo 'śṛjata*. It is also said fire came from air. Since the ablative cause (*vayoḥ*) can mean "after" this śruti statement can mean, "After creating air, Brahman created fire." In response it is said:

Sūtra - 2.3.9

|| tejo'tas tathā hy āha ||

Fire comes from air because śruti says this.

The meaning of the śruti statement is "From air fire was produced." The principal meaning of the ablative case is "from." This principal meaning should be taken here. The meaning "after" is secondary. The principle is to take the principal meaning wherever possible. By taking this meaning, Brahman as the cause is not contradicted.

Topic 7 (Sūtra 10)

Ab-adhikaraṇam - Water

The origin of water is discussed. If scripture says that water came from fire and also says that water came from Brahman, because of these two contradictory statements, the statement that water came from fire cannot be accepted. The next sūtra refutes this.

Sūtra - 2.3.10

|| āpaḥ ||

Water comes from fire for scripture explicitly states this.

The phrase *tathā hy āha* are understood from the last sūtra. Water arises from fire because (*hi*) śruti says this (*tathā āha*). *tad apo 'sṛjata:* fire created water. *Agner āpa:* water came from fire. One should not use logic to interpret the direct meaning. Chāndogya Upaniṣad also gives the reasoning about how fire produced water. *tasmāt yatra kva ca śocati svedate vā puruṣas tejasa eva tad adhy āpo jāyante*: therefore when a man perspires or laments, water is produced from fire.

Topic 8 (Sūtra 11)

Pṛthivy-adhikaraṇam - Earth

The following statement should be considered.

tā āpa aiksānta bahvyaḥ syāma prajāyemahīti tā annam asṛjanta

Water desired, "Let me become many. May I produce offspring." Water produced *anna.*

Does the word *anna* in that statement refer to grains or earth?

tasmāt yatra kvacana varṣati tad eva bhūyiṣṭham annaṁ bhavaty adbhya eva tad-adhyan nādyaṁ jāyata

When it rains anywhere, that becomes grains. From water alone food and other things are produced. Chāndogya Upaniṣad 6.2.4

From this evidence and from the direct meaning of the word, it can be inferred that *anna* means grains.

Sūtra - 2.3.11

|| pṛthivy-adhikāra-rūpa-śabdāntarebhyaḥ ||

The word *annam* means earth because of the topic of discussion, because of the color mentioned and because of other śruti statements.

Annam means earth, not grains. Why? Because the topic being discussed *(adhikāra)* is the origin of the gross elements, of which earth is one, whereas grains are not an element. As well, anna means earth because of the word "black" in reference to *anna,* since earth has black color (*rūpa*). There are also similar statements in other śrutis (*śabdāntarebhyaḥ*). The statement concerning grains arising from water indicates that there is oneness between the cause (earth) and its effect (grains).

Topic 9 (Sūtras 12 - 14)

Tad-abhidhyānādhikaraṇam - The desire of the Lord

The Upaniṣad presented considers the creation of elements, with the order of elements from ether, to remove doubt. The discussion proves that Brahman is the cause of everything (*janmādyasya yataḥ*). Now a detailed description of the elements is given. In Subāla Upaniṣad it is said:

kim tadāsīt tasmai sahovāca na san nāsan na sad asad iti tasmāt tamaḥ sañjāyate tasmād bhūtādir bhūtāder ākāśaṁ ākāśād vāyur vāyor agnir agner āpo 'dbhyaḥ pṛthivī tad-aṇḍam abhavat

What existed in the beginning? The teacher said to him, "There was no sat. There was no *asat*. There was no *sat* or *asat.* From this arose *tamas,* from *tamas* came *bhūtādi,* from *bhūtādi* came ether, from ether came air, from air came fire, from fire came water and from water came earth. This became the egg."

Between *tamas* and *ākāśa* there should be added *akṣara, avyakta* and *mahat-tattva, bhūtādi, tanmātṛas* and senses, for there should be agreement with a later statement describing destruction.

sandaghdhā sarvāṇi bhūtāni pṛthivy-apsu pralīyate āpas tejasi līyante tejo vāyau vlīyate vāyur ākāce vlīyate ākāśam inriyeṣu indiryāṇi tan-mātreṣu tan-mātrāṇi bhūtādau vilīyante bhūtadir mahatī vilīyate mahān avyakte viliñate avyaktam akṣare viliyate akṣaraṁ tamasi viliyate tama ekībhavati parasmin parasmāt na san nāsan na sad asat

All elements are destroyed. Earth merges into water. Water merges into fire. Fire merges into air. Air merges into ether. Ether merges into the senses. The senses merge into the sense objects. The sense objects merge into *ahaṅkāra. Ahaṅkāra* merges into *mahat-tattva. Mahat-tattva* merges into *avyakta. Avyakta* merges into *akṣara. Akṣara* merges into *tamas. Tamas* merges into the Lord. There is nothing gross or subtle or a combination of both that is higher than this.

The word *bhūtādi* means *ahaṅkāra,* which has three types. From *sāttvika ahaṅkāra* arise *devatās* and mind. From *rājasic ahaṅkāra* arise the senses. From *tamasic ahaṅkāra* arises the sense objects and through them the gross elements. There are many statements to confirm this.

The Gopāla-tāpanī Upaniṣad says:

pūrvaṁ hy ekam evādvitīyaṁ brahmāsīt tasmād avyaktam avyaktam evākṣaraṁ
tasmād akṣarāt mahat tattvaṁ mahato vai haṁkāras tasmād evāhaṁkārāt pañca tan-mātrāṇi

Before creation there was only one Brahman. From that Brahman arose its *śakti,* which was *avyakta akṣara oṁ*. From *oṁ* arose *mahat-tattva*. From *mahat-tattva* arose *ahaṅkāra.* From *ahaṅkāra* arose the five *tanmātras* and from them arose the gross elements. The *akṣara* became covered by them.

The doubt is this. Do the elements arise from the previous element or directly from the Supreme Lord?

(Pūrvapakṣa) They arise from the previous element, as is evident from the direct meaning of the words.

Sūtra - 2.3.12

|| tad-abhidhyānād eva tu tal-liṅgāt saḥ ||

The elements arise from the Lord because he alone has the quality of desiring to create.

The word *tu* refutes the doubt. The Supreme Lord, possessor of *śaktis* like *tamas,* is the direct cause of all effects starting with *pradhāna* and ending with earth. Why? *so 'kāmayata bahu syāṁ prajāyaya:* He desired, "Let there be many, may I produce offspring." The Lord alone can have the quality (*liṅgāt*)--a desire *(abhidhyānāt)* to produce the elements, since he possesses all powers. Brahman enters successively into the elements starting with *tamas* and transforms them to *pradhāna* etc. This is understood from śrutis like *yasya pṛthivī śarīram:* his body is the earth. (Bṛhad-āraṇyaka Upaniṣad 2.7.3)

Sūtra - 2.3.13

|| viparyayeṇa tu kramo'ta upapadyate ca ||

Different order of elements described in the śrutis arises because the Lord is within everything.

The word *tu* is used for emphasis.

etasmāj jāyate prāṇo manaḥ sarvendriyāṇi ca
khaṁ vāyur jyotir āpaś ca pṛthivī viśvasya dhāriṇī

From him *prāṇa,* mind, all the senses, ether, air, fire water and earth, support of everything, arose. Muṇḍaka Upaniṣad

Though the order of the elements (*kramaḥ)* is given differently *(viparyayena*) in these śrutis, this indicates that the Lord is within everything like *prāṇa* and earth. From the Supreme Lord *(ataḥ*), the producer of *śakti* in the various elements, the creator of effects, everything comes (*upapadyate*). Otherwise the direct meaning of the words would be lost. If it were not so, it would contradict the fact that the Lord is the material cause of all things, the creator of all things and the statement that by knowing him all things are known. The word *ca* indicates that from insentient *pradhāna* and the rest, transformations are impossible on their own. Therefore it can be concluded that the Lord is directly the cause of everything in all cases.

Another doubt is refuted.

Sūtra - 2.3.14

|| antarā vijñāna-manasī krameṇa tal-liṅgād iti cen nāviśeṣāt ||

If one argues that everything does not come directly from the Lord because a specific succession of elements with sense organs and mind between the elements and *prāṇa* is given, the answer is no, because all elements without distinction arise from the Lord.

Vijñāna means the senses. The manifestation of everything from the Lord is understood because of the indication-- that he alone desired. This is confirmed by śruti. "But this is not possible because śruti itself specifies a certain order of creation of elements *(tal-liṅgāt)*. The order of ether and other elements is confirmed by the order mentioned in other śrutis. Thus the order should be understood with senses and mind between the elements and prāṇa. Therefore you cannot insist that creation of these elements arises directly from the Lord by quoting your śruti."

This is not true. Why? Because all the elements are not any different (*aviśeṣāt*). They all are born from the Supreme Lord. *Etasmāt* means "from him" came the elements from *prāṇa* to earth. This is the meaning. The Lord desired to be many. From him *prāṇa,* mind and senses were born. Smṛtis say the same. *ahaṁ sarvasya prabhavo mattaḥ sarvaṁ pravartate*: I am the source of everything; from me everything arises. (BG 10.9)

tatra tatra sthito viṣṇus tat tac chaktiṁ prabodhayet
eka eva mahā-śaktiḥ kurute sarvam añjasā

Viṣṇu, situated everywhere, awakes the power in everything. The one great power does everything easily. Vāmana Purāṇa

One should understand that all the elements starting with *pradhāna* arise from the Supreme Lord. And this is not contrary to the order seen in Subāla Upaniṣad. The intention of the Chāndogya Upaniṣad (though not mentioned explicitly) is to state that the Lord, endowed with the power of *tamas* and other items, is the cause of the effects starting with *pradhāna.* Thus both Upaniṣads are complete. That being the case, the phrase *tat tajosṛjata (*it created fire) means the Lord endowed with the powers of *tamas* and other elements, having created elements from *pradhāna* to air, then created fire. In the Taittirīya Upaniṣad it is said *tasmād vā ātmanaḥ ākāśaḥ sambhūtaḥ:* from the *ātma* arose ether. This means "From the Lord (*ātmānaḥ*), endowed with the energies of *tamas* and other items, having produced *pradhāna* and the rest (down to *ahaṅkāra*), arose ether." In this way there is a unified meaning.

Topic 10 (Sūtra 15)

Carācara-vyapāśrayādhikaraṇam – The meaning of moving and non-moving entities

(Pūrva-pakṣa) "If the Supreme Lord alone is the ātmā of all beings, then all words denoting moving and non-moving entities actually indicate the Lord. But this is not so because primarily those words denote those beings. Therefore, by taking the primary meaning, the words refer to the Lord secondarily."

Sūtra - 2.3.15

|| carācara-vyapāśrayas tu syāt tad-vyapadeśo'bhāktas tad-bhāva-bhāvitatvāt ||

Words denoting moving and non-moving beings primarily denote the Lord because in the future one will understand from scripture that the Lord is primarily denoted.

The word *tu* indicates a refutation. Words denoting bodies of moving and non-moving beings (*carācara-vyapāśrayaḥ)* primarily (*abhāktaḥ*) refer to the Lord. Why? Because by increase in intelligence, in the future this will be understood *(bhāvitatvāt*), by hearing from scriptures that all words mean the Lord (*tad-bhāva*). Śruti says *so 'kāmayata bahu syām*: the Lord desired, "May I become many." *sa vāsudevaona yato 'nyad asti*: there is nothing other than Vāsudeva. (Gopāla-tāpanī Upaniṣad) Smṛti says:

kaṭaka-mukuṭa-karṇikādi-bhedaiḥ
kanakam abhedam apīṣyate yathaikam
sura-paśu-manujādi-kalpanābhir
harir akhilābhir udīryate tathaikaḥ

Just as one piece of gold appears separately as bracelets, crowns, and earrings, the one Lord appears as products like *devatās,* animals, and humans. Viṣnu Purāṇa 3.71.6

The meaning is this. Words denoting power ultimately refer to the person possessing the power since the *śaktis* are non-different from him.

Topic 11 (Sūtra 16)

Ātmādhikaraṇam - The jīva

Paramātmā who has no origin because he is the first cause and from whom everything arises has been discussed. Now the description of the jīva begins. Jīva's having an origin is also refuted. In Taittirīya Āraṇyaka it is said:

yataḥ prasūtā jagataḥ prasūtī
toyena jīvān vyasasarja bhūmyām

From the Lord was born the female creator of the universe. She created the jīvas on earth using water.

san-mūlāḥ saumyemāḥ sarvāḥ prajāḥ

All beings are rooted in the Lord, O gentle one!

The doubt is this. Does the jīva have an origin or not?

(Pūrva-paksa) Jīva has an origin because it is understood that the universe composed of jīvas and matter is an effect and if jīvas had no origin, then the promise of the Chāndogya Upaniṣad that by knowing the Lord all things become known would be broken (since jīvas would not be created from the Lord).

Sūtra - 2.3.16

|| nātmāśruter nityatvāc ca tābhyaḥ ||

The jīva is not born because of śruti statements and because its eternal nature is understood from śruti and smṛti.

The jīva *(ātmā)* is not produced. Why? Because of śruti (*śruteḥ*).

na jāyate mriyate vā vipaścin
nāyaṁ kutaścin na babhūva kaścit
ajo nityaḥ śāśvato 'yaṁ purāṇo
na hanyate hanyamāne śarīre

The knower is not born and does not die. The jīva never came into being. Jīva is unborn, eternal, continuous, and ancient. Jīva is not destroyed though the body is destroyed. Kaṭha Upaniṣad 1.2.18

Śvetāśvatara Upaniṣad also says the jīva is without birth. *jñājñau dvāv ajāv īśānīśāu:* the two--the knowing Lord and the ignorant jīva--are unborn. It is without origin because its eternal nature is seen in śruti and smṛti (*nityatvāt tābhyam*). The word *ca* means that jīva's conscious nature is also described. *nityo nityānāṁ cetanaś cetanānām:* the Lord is the chief eternal and the chief conscious entity. (Kaṭha Upaniṣad 2.2.13) *ajo nityaḥ śāśvato 'yaṁ purāṇaḥ*: the jīva is eternal, continuous and ancient. (BG 2.20)

This being the case when people in the world say "Yajñadatta, who was born, has died" and when they speak of a birth ceremony connected with a person, this refers to the jīva which has taken shelter of a body.

sa vā ayaṁ puruṣo jāyamānaḥ śarīram abhisampadyamānaḥ sa utkraman mriyamāṇaḥ

Being born the jīva enters a body and on dying leaves the body. Bṛhad-āraṇyaka Upaniṣad 4.3.8

jīvopetam vāva kiledaṁ mriyate na jīvo mriyate

The body which the jīva accepts dies, but the jīva does not die. Chāndogya Upaniṣad 6.11.3

How does one reconcile this with the promise that by knowing Brahman everything becomes known? This promise requires that the jīva be an effect of Brahman and so should have an origin. Brahman, possessing two subtle *śaktis* (jīvas and *pradhāna*) is also the effect, after simply changing his condition. This is now explained. *Pradhāna,* unconscious, to be enjoyed by the jīva, becomes different essentially when it becomes manifest as an effect. The jīva, the enjoyer, expands his contracted knowledge on becoming manifest. In both cases, because of oneness of cause and effect, there is no contradiction. (Everything can be known by knowing Brahman.) The śrutis are thus harmonized and it is concluded that the jīva has no origin.

Topic 12 (Sūtra 17)

Jñādhikaraṇam – The jīva is a knower

Now the author discusses the *svarūpa* of the jīva. It is said in śruti *yo vijñāne tiṣṭhan vijñānād antaro yaṁ vijñānaṁ ne veda yasya vijñāṁ śarīraṁ:* the jīva is situated in knowledge and is within knowledge, whom knowledge does not know, and who has knowledge as his body. (Bṛhad-āraṇyaka Upaniṣad 3.7.22) Śruti also says *sukham ahaṁ svāpsaṁ na kiñcid avediṣam*: I slept happily and did not know anything. The doubt is this. Is the jīva's *svarūpa* knowledge itself, (first śruti quotation) or is his *svarūpa* to be a knower of knowledge (second śruti quotation)?

(Pūrva-pakṣa) The jīva is knowledge itself (*jñāna-mātra*) because that is proved by the quotation from Bṛhad-āraṇyaka Upaniṣad. Knowing is a quality of intelligence. By relationship with intelligence, "I slept happily" is attributed wrongly to the jīva.

Sūtra - 2.3.17

|| jño'ta eva ||

The jīva is a knower because of śruti statements.

Jña means the jīva. Though the jīva is the form of knowledge (*jñāna-rūpa*), jīva's *svarūpa* is a knower (*jñātṛ-svarūpa*). The word *eva* indicates that this is because of śruti. *eṣa hi draṣṭā spraṣṭā śrotā rasayitā ghrātā mantā boddhā kartā vijñānātmā puruṣaḥ:* the jīva is the seer, the toucher, the hearer, the taster, the smeller, the thinker, the comprehender, the doer, and the knower. (Praśna Upaniṣad 4.9) This is concluded on the strength of śruti, not logic. Our position is *śrutes tu śabda-mūlatvāt*: scripture alone is the basis of all authoritative knowledge. Smṛti says *jñātā jñāna-svarūpo 'yam*: the jīva is a knower and has a *svarūpa* of knowledge. One cannot say that the jīva is only knowledge itself, because this contradicts śrutis stating that jīva is a knower. As well, the argument that the intelligence causes the conception of a knower is unproven.

Topic 13 (Sūtras 18 - 25)

Utkrānti-gaty-adhikaraṇam – The jīva's coming to and going from the body

Now the author considers the size of the jīva. *eṣo 'ṇur ātmā cetasā veditavyo yasmin prāṇaḥ pañcadhā samviveṣa:* the atomic *ātmā* in which the *prāṇa* in five forms rests is known by the mind.

The doubt is this. Is the jīva all-pervading or atomic?

(Pūrvapakṣa) The jīva is all-pervading because śruti says jīva is large (*mahān*) and even opponents should accept this. It is called atomic figuratively for gaining an intellectual grasp.

Sūtra - 2.3.18

|| utkrānti-gaty-āgatīnām ||

The jīva is atomic because scriptures describe how the jīva exits and enters bodies.

The word *aṇuḥ (*atomic) is understood here, in relation to the pūrvapakṣa-sūtra in 2.3.20. The possessive case (*āgatīnām*) has an ablative meaning (because of entering). The jīva is atomic, not all-pervading. Why? Because it leaves and enters the body (*utkranti-gati-agatīmām*).

tasya haitasya hṛdayasyāgraṁ pradyotate. tena pradyotenaiṣa ātmā
niṣkrāmati cakṣuṣo vā mūrdhno vānyebhyo vā śarīra-deśebhyaḥ

A point in his heart lights up. By that light, the jīva leaves through the eyes, head or other parts of the body. Bṛhad-āraṇyaka Upaniṣad 4.4.2

anandā nāma te lokā andhena tamasāvṛtāḥ
tāṁs te pretyābhigacchanti avidvāṁso 'budhā janāḥ

These worlds are without bliss, covered by deep darkness. The ignorant without knowledge go to these worlds. Bṛhad-āraṇyaka Upaniṣad 4.4.11

prāpyāntaṁ karmaṇas tasya yat kiñcedam karoty ayam tasmāt lokāt punar
etya yasmai lokāya karmaṇe

Having attained the end of his karmas that he did on this earth, from that world he comes to this world of karma. Bṛhad-āraṇyaka Upaniṣad 4.4.6

The Bṛhad-āraṇyaka Upaniṣad describes the jīva's exiting and entering the body. All this would be impossible if the jīva were all-pervading (since he would be everywhere already). Smṛtis confirm this.

aparimitā dhruvās tanu-bhṛto yadi sarva-gatās
tarhi na śāsyateti niyamo dhruva netarathā

O shelter of everything! If the *jīvas* were unlimited and eternal, and all powerful, the scriptures would not say that they are under your control. But the *jīvas* are not so, and thus are under your control. SB 10.86.30

The Lord, however, can move about though he is all-pervading, since he has inconceivable powers.

"Though all-pervading and thus without movement, the jīva's leaving the body can mean that he just gives up bodily conceptions just as a ruler gives up ownership of a village. Thus 'going and coming' is possible for a non-moving jīva."

Sūtra - 2.3.19

|| svātmanā cottarayoḥ ||

The jīva' coming and going is not figurative because going and coming refer to the jīva's actions.

The word *ca* is for emphasis. A relationship is expressed of going and coming (*uttarayoḥ*) with the *ātmā (svātmanā)*, because action is situated in an agent. Since the jīva is the agent and the action is real, one must accept that the jīva leaves the body. This is concluded by the śruti which says *tena pradyotena*: the jīva leaves by a ray of light. (Bṛhad-āraṇyaka Upaniṣad 4.4.2)

śarīraṁ yad avāpnoti yac cāpy utkrāmatīśvaraḥ
gṛhītvaitani samyāti vāyur gandhān ivāśayāt

Whenever the *jīva* accepts or leaves a body, he takes these senses with him in the subtle body, just as air takes fragrances from objects and goes elsewhere. BG 15.8

To say that going from and entering a body is simply giving up and accepting identity with the body is foolish. Kauṣītaki Upaniṣad refutes this by using the word "with":

sa yadāsmāt śarīrāt samutkrāmati sahaivaitaiḥ sarvair utkrāmati

When the jīva leaves this body, it leaves with all the senses and sense objects.

This "with" indicates one action with a principal and secondary agent as in "The father eats with the son." The senses actually leave secondarily, and the jīva actually leaves primarily. The senses cannot leave figuratively since they cannot give up an identity. And this figurative meaning would be inconsistent with the Gītā statement of the ātmā taking with it the senses and leaving the body. In this way the theory of jīva and Brahman being like air in a pot and the air in the sky separated by false identity (and thus the theory that the jīva, being Brahman, is all-pervading and only has a false idea of leaving the body) is refuted as a childish argument.

Sūtra - 2.3.20

|| nāṇur atac chruter iti cen netarādhikārāt ||

If you argue that the jīva is not atomic because of the statement that it is large, the answer is no, because the *ātmā* described as large is actually Paramātmā by context.

"The jīva is not atomic because Bṛhad-āraṇyaka Upaniṣad says the opposite: it is great in size. *sa vā eṣa mahān aja ātmā:* the *ātmā* is great." This is not so. Why? Because this statement refers to Paramātmā, which is the subject of discussion in that text. The topic starts with a description of the jīva. *yo 'yaṁ vijñānamayaḥ prāṇeṣu:* the jīva consisting of knowledge is surrounded by the *prāṇas.* In the middle of the passage however the topic is not the jīva but the Supreme Lord, since it describes his greatness, such as *yasyānuvittaḥ pratibuddha ātmā:* knowing him, one becomes enlightened.

Sūtra - 2.3.21

|| sva-śabdonmānābhyāṁ ca ||

And because of two texts with words which describe the jīva as atomic, [it can be concluded that] the jīva must be atomic.

The word indicating atomic (*sva-śabda*) is stated in the scriptures. *eṣo ṇur ātmā*: the *ātmā* is atomic. (Muṇḍaka Upaniṣad 3.1.9) It is compared in size to an atom (*unmānam*). To describe the jīva, it is compared in size to something else.

bālāgra-śata-bhāgasya śatadhā kalpitasya ca
bhāgo jīvaḥ sa vijñeyaḥ sa cāntantyāya kalpate

The jīva is known to be a hundredth part of a hundredth part of the tip of a hair and is qualified for liberation. Śvetāśvatara Upaniṣad 4.9

These two texts show that the jīva is atomic. *Ānantya* means refers to liberation--not being subject to death (*anta*).

"If the jīva is atomic, it could not spread throughout the body."

Sūtra - 2.3.22

|| avirodhaś candanavat ||

There is no contradiction because the jīva can spread throughout the body like sandalwood.

A drop of sandalwood oil placed in one part of the body gives joy to the whole body. Similarly, the jīva can spread its awareness throughout the body. Smṛti says:

aṇu-mātro 'py ayaṁ jīvaḥ sva-dehaṁ vyāpya tiṣṭhati
yathā vyāpya śarīrāṇi haricandana-vipruṣaḥ

Just as a drop of sandalwood oil spreads throughout the body, the atomic jīva spreads throughout the body and remains there. Brahmāṇḍa Purāṇa

Sūtra - 2.3.23

|| avasthiti-vaiśeṣyād iti cen nābhyupagamāt hṛdi hi ||

If you argue that the sandalwood spreads because it is located in one place in the body but the ātmā does not have a particular location in the body from which to spread, the answer is no, for the ātmā is situated in the heart.

"It is seen that a drop of sandalwood is situated in a particular place on the body (from which to spread out). But the jīva is not seen nor inferred to be situated in a particular place. Using the example of sandalwood is therefore not appropriate. So one can infer that the ātmā, because it is all-pervading, spreads throughout the body like ether." That is not true. Why? Because we accept descriptions (*abhiyupagamāt*) that the jīva has a particular location in one place in the body. "Where does the jīva reside?" In the heart *(hṛdi)*. *hṛdi hy eṣa ātmā:* the ātmā is in the heart. (Praśna Upaniṣad 3.6)

Though the jīva is proven to be atomic there is no contradiction to its spreading throughout the body. The author gives the best opinion.

Sūtra - 2.3.24

|| guṇād vā ālokavat ||

The jīva spreads throughout the body because of its quality of consciousness, just as the sun spreads its light in the sky.

Though the jīva is atomic, it spreads throughout the whole body because of its quality (*guṇāt*) of consciousness, because the jīva is endowed with consciousness, just as the sun or another body (*ālokavat*) spreads all over the sky by its light. The Lord himself says this:

yathā prakāśayaty ekaḥ kṛtsnaṁ lokam imaṁ raviḥ |
kṣetraṁ kṣetrī tathā kṛtsnaṁ prakāśayati bhārata ||

Just as one sun lights up the whole world, this *ātmā* illuminates the whole body, O descendent of Bharata. BG 13.34

You cannot say that the effulgence of the sun is atoms spread from the sun. If that were so, then it would mean that the sun would decrease. It is seen that rubies and other gems light up the surrounding area by their effulgence and one cannot say that atoms stream forth from them because if that were so, the weight of the gems would decrease. Thus, light is their quality.

The manifestation of a quality in a place devoid of that quality was explained. This is made clear by an example.

Sūtra - 2.3.25

|| vyatireko gandhavat tathā hi darśayati ||

Jīva spreads consciousness just as fragrance spreads to a place without fragrance. The Upaniṣads show this.

Just as the flower's quality of fragrance manifests in a place without fragrance, the jīva's quality of consciousness manifests in places outside the heart such as the head and feet. The Kauṣītaki Upaniṣad shows this (*tathā hi darśayati*). *prajñayā śarīraṁ samāruhya sukha-duhkhe āpnoti*: the jīva, having taken possession of the body by consciousness, experiences happiness and pain. Though fragrance spreads far, it is not separate from its source, just as the light of a gem is not separate from the gem. Smṛti says:

upalabhyāpsu ced gandhaṁ kecid brūyur anaipuṇāḥ
pṛthivyām eva tam vidyād apo vāyuṁ ca saṁśritam

Foolish people, on smelling a fragrance in water, will say fragrance belongs to water. One should know that fragrance belongs to earth alone, and has taken shelter of air or water.[52]

---

[52] Quoted by Śaṅkara in his commentary, attributed to Vyāsa.

Topic 14 (Sūtras 26 - 29)

Pṛthag-upadeśādhikaraṇam – Other statements concerning the jīva

It is said that the jīva is the seer (*eṣa hi draṣṭā*). Here is the doubt. Is the knowledge which is manifest as a quality (*dharma-bhūta-jñāna*) of the jīva eternal or temporary?

(Pūrva-pakṣa)

"Knowledge arises when the jīva, which is like a stone by nature, is joined to the mind, because it is said "I slept happily."[53] The quality of the jīva having knowledge is understood from a relationship with knowledge (in the mind) just as the qualities of fire manifest in iron by relationship with fire. If knowledge were eternal, then the jīva could not have deep sleep without any consciousness and it would not need the senses for acquiring knowledge."

Sūtra - 2.3.26

// pṛthag upadeśāt //

Knowledge in the jīva is eternal because of teachings in the scriptures, other than the statement that the ātmā is a seer.

Knowledge as a quality of the jīva is eternal. Why? Because other than the statement (*pṛthag)* that the jīva is the seer, there are teachings of the jīva having eternal knowledge, in Bṛhad-āraṇyaka Upaniṣad 4.5.14. *avināśī vā are 'yam ātmānucchitti-dharmā:* the jīva is indestructible and has indestructible qualities. Knowledge does not arise in the jīva by contact with the mind, because contact cannot take place between two items having no parts. This knowledge becomes covered by turning away from the Lord and it manifests by turning towards the Lord when aversion towards him is destroyed. Smṛti says:

yathā na kriyate jyotsnā mala-prakṣālanān maṇeḥ
doṣa-prahāṇān na jñānam ātmanah kriyate tathā

[53] Without the mind functioning, in deep sleep (symtomized by "I slept happily"), the jīva is completely inert like a stone.

Just as light is not created in a jewel by washing away dirt, so knowledge is not created in the jīva by destroying faults.

yathodapāna-khananāt kriyate na jalāntaram
sad eva niyate vyaktim asataḥ sambhavaḥ kutaḥ

Just as water is not created by digging a well, an existing thing simply becomes manifest. How can something not existing appear?

tathā heya-guṇa-dhvaṁsād avarodhādayo guṇāḥ
prakāśyante na jānyante nitya evātmano hi te

Similarly by destruction of bad qualities, the obscured qualities, which are eternal in the ātmā, manifest. They are not created. Viṣṇu-dharma

The meaning of the śruti statement *yo vijñāne tiṣṭhati* is explained.

Sūtra - 2.3.27

|| tad-guṇa-sāratvāt tad-vyapadeśa-prājñavat ||

The jīva is knowledge itself, just as the Lord is so designated, because the quality of knowledge is his essence.

Though the jīva is a knower, it is designated *(vyapadeṣa)* as knowledge itself *(jñāna-svarūpa)*. Why? Because it has the quality (*guṇa*) of knowledge as its essence (*sāratvāt*). "Essence" means that which, without any modification, defines an object's very nature. For example, the Lord who is omniscient (*prajñavat*), whose omniscience is described by statements like *yaḥ sarvajñah sarvavit* (Muṇḍaka Upaniṣad), is designated as the essence of knowledge, *jñāna-svarūpa*, in statements like *satyaṁ jñānam*. Similarly, the jīva, a knower, is designated as knowledge itself.

Having shown that the jīva is both a knower and knowledge, the author speaks again.

Sūtra - 2.3.28

|| yāvad ātmābhāvitvāc ca na doṣas tad-darśanāt ||

It is not a fault that the jīva is both knower and knowledge itself, since these exist with the jīva eternally. This is seen in the case of the sun also, which is both light and illuminator.

It is not a fault (*na doṣaḥ*) that the jīva who is knowledge itself is also designated as the knower. Why? It is not contrary, because it is seen that the condition of being both a knower and knowledge coexists with *ātmā* as long as it exists (*yāvad ātmābhāvitvāt*). It is acknowledged that the *ātmā* exists without beginning or end in time. This is understood from seeing (*tad darśanāt*) that the sun, though a form of light, gives off light. (Similarly, the ātmā, a form of knowledge, also knows, or is a knower.) As long as the sun exists, these designations (as light and illuminator) are to be given. The wise say that though there is one object, there is an appearance of it being two objects because of the principle of *viśeṣa.*

(Pūrva-pakṣa)

"Knowledge as an attribute of the *ātmā* (*guṇa-bhūtam jñānam* or *dharma-bhūta-jñāna*) is not eternal, since the jīva does not know anything during deep sleep and the ingredients of knowledge appear only on waking."

Sūtra - 2.3.29

|| puṁstvādivat tv asya sato'bhivyakti-yogāt ||

You cannot say that the jīva's knowledge is not eternal, because it exists during deep sleep and simply manifests on waking. It is like maleness which is unmanifest in a child but appears when he grows up.

The word *tu* indicates refutation of the doubt. The word *na* is understood from the previous sūtra. If you say that knowledge is absent during deep sleep and is created on waking, the answer is no. Why? Because the knowledge (*asya*) exists (*sataḥ*) during deep sleep and simply manifests on waking (*abhivyakti-yogāt*). An example is given. It is like being a man (*puṁsavtādivat*). Though maleness is present with the jīva during childhood, it manifests only during adolescence.

The objection concerning knowledge during deep sleep is refuted by śruti. Concerning deep sleep, it is said in Bṛhad-āraṇyaka Upaniṣad 4.3.30:

yad vai tan na vijānāti vijānan vaitad vijñeyam na vijānāti na hi vijnātur vijñānāt viparilopo vidyate avināśitvān na tu tad dvitīyam asti tato 'nyad vibhaktaṁ yad vijānīyāt

When the jīva who knows does not know in deep sleep, he does not know the object of knowledge. The knower is never separate from knowledge since that is indestructible. But at that time, there is no second object other than himself which he can know.

Knowledge which is present during deep sleep does not manifest as an object of perception because of lack of an object. The combination which acts as a cause, in the form of contact with the senses, manifests the knowledge. If knowledge did not exist during deep sleep, it could not manifest later, just as a eunuch cannot manifest maleness later on if maleness were not present in in him in an unmanifest state. Thus it is proved that the atomic jīva, the form of knowledge, has knowledge (awareness) as his eternal attribute.

Topic 15 (Sūtra 30)

Nithyopalabdhi-prasaṅgādhikaraṇam – The jīva's being eternally aware and unaware

Now the author refutes the opposing views of Sāṅkhya philosophers. Is it proper or not to say that the *ātmā* is knowledge alone and all-pervading?

(pūrvapakṣa) It is correct to say that the jīva is all-pervading because its effects are realized everywhere. If the jīva were atomic, it could not experience happiness and suffering in all its limbs. If the jīva were of medium size, it would not be eternal and karmas due to it would be destroyed, while undeserved karmas would be received (since jīva would be too big for some bodies and too small for others).

Sūtra - 2.3.30

|| nityopalabdhy-anupalabdhi-prasaṅgo'nyatara-niyamo vānyathā ||

The proposition of an all-pervading jīva would mean that it would be eternally aware and unaware; or eternally aware; or eternally unaware.

According to the idea (*anyathā*) that jīva is knowledge alone, all -pervading, it would mean that there would be eternal awareness and unawareness concerning objects or there would be a restriction of one or the other (*anyatara-niyamaḥ*). The meaning is this. It is observed in the world that there is awareness and lack of awareness. If the *ātmā*, being consciousness alone, and all-pervading, were the cause of these two, they should eternally exist simultaneously and this would be perceived by all people. If the *ātmā* were the cause of only awareness and not unawareness, unawareness would not exist anywhere in anyone. If the *ātmā* were the cause of only unawareness, then awareness would not exist anywhere in anyone.

One cannot say that awareness and unawareness depend on contact with the senses, since the all-pervading *ātmā* would always be in contact with all the senses. Moreover, according to this idea, since all ātmās are all-pervading, they would contact all bodies. Thus they would obtain all enjoyment (and suffering) of all bodies. The proposition that enjoyment comes from individual karma, and individual karma comes from individual desires, will be defeated (by the fact that the all-pervading ātmā would have all desires of all other ātmās.*)* In other philosophies (those of Gautama and Kaṇāda) there is a similar fault.

But there is no fault in our philosophy because in it the atomic jīva is different in each body. Since the jīva is atomic, it exists and experiences everywhere but with results experienced sequentially, not simultaneously. Thus this proposition is faultless. The jīva experiences happiness or suffering in all limbs because it spreads out by its quality of consciousness.

Topic 16 (Sūtras 31 - 40)

Kartr-adhikaraṇam – The jīva as a doer

Now, the following text is discussed. Taittirīya Upaniṣad says *vijñānaṁ yajñaṁ tanute karmāṇi tanute 'pi ca*: knowledge performs sacrifice and performs actions.

The doubt is this. Is the jīva who is knowledge, the doer (agent) or not?

(Pūrva-pakṣa) The following śruti denies that jīva is an agent. The jīva cannot be an agent. *Prakṛti* is the agent.

hantā cen manyate hantuṁ hataś cen manyate hatam
ubhau tau na vijānītau nāyaṁ hanti na hanyate

One who thinks the jīva is the killer and one who thinks that he is killed, both do not know. The jīva does not kill nor is killed. Kaṭha Upaniṣad 1.2.19

Smṛtis also confirm this:

prakṛteḥ kriyamāṇāni guṇaiḥ karmāṇi sarvaśaḥ
ahaṅkāra-vimūḍhātmā kartāham iti manyate

The person bewildered by pride thinks that he is the doer of actions which are being done completely by the body, senses and *prāṇas* made of *prakṛti.* BG 3.27

kārya-kāraṇa-kartṛtve hetuḥ prakṛtir ucyate
puruṣaḥ sukha-duḥkhānāṁ bhoktṛtve hetur ucyate

Prakṛti is said to be a cause, instrumental in producing the body and senses. The *jīva* is said to be a cause, being the enjoyer of happiness and distress. BG 13.21

Therefore the jīva is not the doer or agent. It is *prakṛti.* This is understood from discerning the truth. The jīva falsely attributes himself to be the agent and becomes the enjoyer of the fruits of his actions.

This argument is refuted in the following sutra.

Sūtra - 2.3.31

|| kartā śāstrārthavattvāt ||

The jīva is the agent, because this gives meaning to the scriptures.

The jīva is the agent, not the guṇas. Why? Because only the jīva's being agent gives meaning to scriptural injunctions (*śāstrārthavattvāta*). *svarga-kāmo yajeta*: desiring Svarga one should perform sacrifice. (Āpastamba Śrauta Sūtra 19.10.14) *ātmānam eva lokam upāsīta*: one should worship the visible Lord. (Bṛhad-āraṇyaka Upaniṣad 1.4.15) Scriptures have meaning only if we accept a conscious agent. They would be meaningless if the guṇas were the agent. The scriptures inspire the intellect by promising results and engaging the person in action to enjoy the result. They cannot inspire the intellect of insentient guṇas.

The jīva is actually the agent.

Sūtra - 2.3.32

|| vihāropadeśāt ||

The jīva is the agent because the scriptures describe that even the liberated jīva plays.

The jīva is the agent because the scriptures describe that even the liberated jīva plays (*vihāropadeśāt*). *sa tatra paryeti jakṣan krīḍan ramamāṇaḥ*: in the spiritual world the jīva moves, laughs, plays and enjoys. (Chāndogya Upaniṣad

8.12.3) There, though the jīva is an agent, the action does not accrue suffering. Here, the agent related to the *guṇas* accrues suffering since he has made his *svarūpa* debilitated.

Sūtra - 2.3.33

|| upādānāt ||

The jīva is the agent because he is so described in the scriptures.

In the śruti it is said:

sa yathā mahā-rājaḥ... evam evaiṣa etān prāṇān gṛhītvā sve śarīre yathā-kāmaṁ parivartate

Like a king moves with his subjects in his kingdom, the *ātmā*, taking the *prāṇas* with him, moves about in his body. Bṛhad-āraṇyaka Upaniṣad 2.1.18

śarīraṁ yad avāpnoti yac cāpy utkrāmatīśvaraḥ |
gṛhītvaitāni samyāti vāyur gandhān ivāśayāt

Whenever the *jīva* accepts or leaves a body, he takes these senses with him in the subtle body, just as air takes fragrances from objects and goes elsewhere. BG 15.8

These texts indicate that the jīva is the agent and the *prāṇas* are used by him. The conscious jīva is the agent, just as a magnet is the agent that draws iron. In grasping objects, the *prāṇas* (and senses) are the cause but none other than the jīva is the grasper of the *prāṇa.*

Another reason is given.

Sūtra - 2.3.34

|| vyapadeśāc ca kriyāyāṁ na cen nirdeśa-viparyayaḥ ||

The jīva is an agent because he is designated as such in actions. If it were not so, the sentence would be constructed differently.

vijñānaṁ yajṇaṁ tanute: the intelligence (jīva) performs sacrifice. (Taittirīya Upaniṣad 2.5) The jīva is the agent because of this teaching, with the jīva as the chief agent in actions both Vedic and secular. If the word *vijñānam* did not mean the jīva, but rather the intelligence, it would be stated differently. *Vijñānam* is in the nominative case to indicate the agent. The instrumental cause would be used to indicate intelligence since it is merely an instrument of action. But the sentence is not constructed in this manner. Moreover, if intelligence were the agent, one would have to image another instrument of action since one sees that actions are carried out with instruments. Thus the dispute is in name only because in this case one accepts the agent as identical with the instrument.[54]

"If the jīva were an agent, its creations would be beneficial for itself and not unbeneficial for itself, since it is an independent agent." That is not so. Though the jīva desires to produce something beneficial, sometimes he performs unbeneficial acts because of various karmas accompanying him. Therefore it can be concluded that the jīva is an agent. That being so, when the scriptures talk of the jīva not being an agent, it simply means that the jīva is not independent in his actions.

"The conclusion of scripture cannot be that the jīva is the agent, because we see suffering related to the jīva." Such bad arguments are refuted by the fact that they would make meaningless instructions for a person to perform *darśa-paurṇamasa* sacrifice.

The faults in ascribing agency to *prakṛti* are shown.

Sūtra - 2.3.35

|| upalabdhivad aniyamaḥ ||

***Prakṛti* cannot be the agent, since there would be unrestricted experience in all humans, since *prakṛti* is all-pervading.**

It was previously shown that if the jīva were all-pervading awareness would be unrestricted. Similarly, because *prakṛti* is all-pervading and thus common to all humans, actions would not be restricted to an individual. All actions would be for all to enjoy or one person not acting would mean no jīva would not enjoy. You cannot avoid this problem by saying that there would be lack of common experience for all jīvas because some jīvas would be distant and thus not have contact with *prakṛti.* In your philosophy all jīvas are constantly in contact with all of *prakṛti,* since all jīvas are all-pervading.

---

[54] The jīva as agent, being intelligent, uses his intelligence to perform his acts.

Sūtra - 2.3.36

|| śakti-viparyayāt ||

If *prakṛti* were the agent, then there would be a reversal of the capacity to enjoy; it would have to be -taken from the jīva and given to *prakṛti.*

If *prakṛti* were the agent, there would be a reversal of the capacity of being the enjoyer, which is fixed in the jīva. It would mean that *prakṛti* should be the enjoyer of its acts. But this would contradict the Sāṅkhya doctrine *puruṣa' asti bhoktṛ-bhāvāt*: the jīva exists because it is an enjoyer. (Sāṅkhya-kārikā 27) Since it is impossible for the enjoyer to be anyone other than the performer of the act, one must accept that the capacity to enjoy would reside in *prakṛti* if *prakṛti* is the agent.

Sūtra - 2.3.37

|| samādhy-abhāvāc ca ||

Prakṛti* cannot be the agent because then there could be no *samādhi*--the conception of being different from *prakṛti.

The doctrine of *prakṛti* as the agent is useless because then there could be no *samādhi,* the gof liberation. *Samādhi* means understanding, "I am different from *prakṛti*." That would not be possible because it would be impossible to separate oneself from oneself (*prakṛti* the agent from *prakṛti*) and because *prakṛti* is insentient, incapable of thinking such a thing. Therefore it is proved that the jīva is the agent.

The author shows by example that the jīva is the agent by its own *śakti,* assisted by its instruments.

Sūtra - 2.3.38

|| yathā ca takṣobhayathā ||

Like a carpenter, the jīva is the doer in two ways.

The carpenter in doing his carpentry is an agent in two ways-- by using his own *śakti* in holding his axe and through the instruments like the axe. The jīva is the agent by his own *śakti* in grasping the *prāṇas* and by using the *prāṇas* to grasp other things. Though the action originates from the pure jīva, it is said figuratively that the material body is the agent because of the strong influence of the *guṇas*. Thus it is said:

puruṣaḥ prakṛti-stho hi bhuṅkte prakṛti-jān guṇān |
kāraṇaṁ guna-saṅgo 'sya sad-asad-yoṇi-janmasu

The *jīva*, identifying with *prakṛti* in the form of his body, experiences happiness and distress which are born from *prakṛti*, by taking birth in various bodies of *devatās* and animals. This is caused by his desires for objects made of the *guṇas*. BG 13.22

This explains why there are statements in scripture calling the *guṇas* the agent. One who sees the jīva as the sole agent is called a fool (BG 3.27) because, though action depends on five factors, the person thinks of himself as the only factor. One cannot take a superficial meaning of these statements, since such a meaning would contradict the statements concerning jīva's methods of action for liberation in the same work. The statement "He does not kill and is not killed" simply indicates that the result of killing, being cut, is an impossible act to perform on the *ātmā,* since this would contradict the eternal nature of the *ātmā.* The statement does not deny that the *ātmā* is an agent, since that was previously proved.

That action which the devotees perform in this life and the next--worship of the Lord--is without *guṇas,* because their actions predominated by bhakti, which is a function of the *cit-cakti,* has destroyed the *guṇas* in this life and because the devotee attains liberation (goes beyond the *guṇas*) in the next life. With this intention the Lord speaks:

sāttvikaḥ kārako 'saṅgī rāgāndho rājasaḥ smṛtaḥ
tāmasaḥ smṛti-vibhraṣṭo nirguṇo mad-apāśrayaḥ

A performer of action who is free of attachment is in *sattva*, a performer of action overcome by sense objects is in *rajas*, and a performer of action who is devoid of inquiry is in *tamas.* But a performer of action who has taken shelter of me alone is beyond the *guṇas.* SB 11.25.26

The experience of enjoyment or suffering belongs to the pure jīva. Smṛti says:

puruṣaḥ sukha-duḥkhānāṁ bhoktṛtve hetur ucyate ||

The jīva is said to be a cause, being the enjoyer of happiness and distress. BG 13.21

Although the perception of the jīva takes place when in association with the guṇas, the jīva, which has a conscious form, takes prominence, not the *guṇas*, because it is contrary to the guṇas' nature to be the enjoyer (being insentient). The jīva's desire to be an enjoyer becomes the cause of its experience of happiness and distress because it has self-awareness as its nature. Therefore it can be concluded that the jīva is the agent with the help of the *guṇas* and by its own *śakti.* The śruti also says *eṣa hi draṣṭā spraṣṭā śrotā*: the jīva is the seer, the toucher, the hearer. Using the example of the carpenter, the idea that the jīva as a perpetual agent is refuted (since he decides when to work).

Another doubt arises in relation to this. Is the jīva's agency independent or dependent?

(pūrva-pakṣa) The jīva is an independent agent since injunctions and prohibitions in the scripture take on meaning if this is true. Examples are as follows. *svarga-kāmo yajeta*: a person desiring Svarga should perform sacrifice. (*Āpastamba Śrauta Sūtra, Kṛṣṇa Yajur Veda*, 10.2.1) *tasmād brāhmaṇaḥ surāṁ na pibet pāpmanotsaṁsṛja:* therefore the brāhmaṇa should not drink liquor and not commit sin. He who is ordered by scriptures is he who can perform or not perform the action using his own intelligence.

Sūtra - 2.3.39

|| parāt tu tac-chruteḥ ||

The jīva's ability as an agent arises from the Supreme Lord, since this is stated in the śruti.

The word *tu* indicates a refutation of the doubt. The jīva's ability to act arises from the Supreme Lord (*parāt*). Why? Because śruti says so. *antaḥ praviṣṭaḥ śāstā janānām*: the controller has entered within all people. (Taittirīya Upaniṣad 3.1.10*) ya ātmani tiṣṭhann ātmānam antaro yamayati:* he who resides in the jīva controls the jīva from within. (Bṛhad-āraṇyaka Upaniṣad 3.7.22) *eṣa eva sādhu karma kārayati*: the Lord makes the jīva perform good actions. (Kauṣītaki Upaniṣad 3.8)

Let that be. If the jīva's agency depends on the Supreme Lord, then the injunctions and prohibitions (for humans) in scriptures would be useless, since the scriptures apply to a person who can do or not do according to his intelligence.

Sūtra - 2.3.40

|| kṛta-prayatnāpekṣas tu vihita-pratiṣiddhāvaiyarthyādibhyaḥ ||

No, because the Lord acts after considering the jīva's efforts, the injunctions and prohibitions are not useless and the Lord is not liable to the charge of cruelty.

The word *tu* indicates refutation of the doubt. Considering the effort that the jīva makes in terms of dharma and adharma, the Supreme Lord makes him act. Therefore the fault raised does not apply. And because of the differences in dharma and adharma in the acts jīva, the Lord, being the efficient cause only, gives different results just as rain gives different fruits to different trees. The rain is the general cause of trees and creepers which arise from their particular seeds. If there is no rain, there will be no variety of flowers and taste in the trees. And if there were no seeds, there would be no flowers and taste. Therefore, it can be concluded that the Lord considers the actions of the jīvas and gives good or bad results. Moreover, though the jīva as agent acts under the inspiration from the Lord, the agency of the jīva is not removed.

"Why do you say this?" Because then the injunctions and prohibitions of scripture would not be meaningless (*vihita-pratinisīddhāvaiyarthyādibhyaḥ*). The word *ādibhyaḥ* (and other reasons) indicates "and also because in this way the Lord avoids prejudice in awarding mercy and punishment." Only in this way will scripture with its injunctions not be useless. If the Supreme Lord ordered the jīva as if he were a piece of stone, the authority of the Lord's words would be destroyed, since the words would be directed to something most inferior.

It is said "Wishing to lead the jīva up, the Lord makes him do good actions." This expresses the Lord's mercy. "Wishing to lead the jīva down, the Lord makes him do bad actions"[55] expresses the Lord's punishment. However, that

---

[55] The real meaning would be "The Lord permits the jīva to do bad action according to his propensity, and then awards him punishment according to that act."

mercy and punishment cannot be applied to a jīva who is like a stone because that would make the fault of cruelty on the part of the Lord unavoidable. Therefore it can be concluded that the jīva is the dependent agent and the Lord is the causal agent. Without the Lord's permission the jīva cannot act. Thus everything is clear.

Topic 17 (Sūtras 41 - 43)

Aṁśādhikaraṇam - Jīva as an aṁśa

To strengthen the previous conclusion, jīva is described as an *aṁśa* of Brahman.

In śruti it is said *dvā suparṇā:* there are two birds in a tree (Muṇḍaka Upaniṣad 3.1.1) It appears that one is the Lord and the other is the jīva.

The doubt is this. Is the jīva the Lord himself, limited by *māyā*? Or, is the jīva an *aṁśa* of the Lord, like the ray of the sun, separate from the Lord, depending on his relationship to the Lord? What is the conclusion?

(Pūrva-pakṣa) The jīva is the Lord limited by *māyā*. It is said in śruti:

ghaṭa-samvṛtam ākāśaṁ nīyamāne ghaṭe yathā
gato līyeta nākāśaṁ tadvaj jīvo nabhopamaḥ

Just as space covered by a pot does not disappear when the pot is removed and though the pot disappears, so the jīva, like space, remains when the covering is removed. Brahma-bindu Upaniṣad 8

Furthermore statements like *tattvam asi (*you are Brahman) should be accepted.

This is refuted in the next sutra.

Sūtra - 2.3.41

|| aṁśo nānā-vyapadeśād anyathā cāpi dāsa-kitavāditvam adhīyata eke ||

The jīva is a part of the Lord because of many scriptural statements. Other statements giving descriptions of oneness of jīva and the Lord, such as the fisherman and the gambler being Brahman, are also taught. but they do not indicate absolute oneness.

The jīva is an *aṁśa* of the Lord, just as a ray of the sun, is different from the sun, follows after it, and is dependent on its relationship to the sun. "Why?" Because of many statements in śruti and smṛti.

udbhavaḥ sambhavo divyo deva eko nārāyaṇo mātā pitā
bhrātā nivāsaḥ śaraṇaṁ suhṛd gatir nārāyaṇaḥ

One Lord Nārāyaṇa is creation and destruction. Nārāyaṇa is the mother, the father, the brother, the abode, the shelter, the friend and the goal. Subāla Upaniṣad 6

gatir bhartā prabhuḥ sākṣī nivāsaḥ śaraṇaṁ suhṛt

I am the method to attain the goal, the master, the controller, the witness, the abode, the shelter, and the friend.[56] BG 9.18

These statements teach various relationships: creator and created, controller and controlled, support and supported, master and servant, friend and object of friendship *(sakhitva)*, the object of attainment and the attainer.

And in a different way (*anyathā*) other śrutis describe the jīva as one with the Lord by the Lord's pervasion. *brahma dāsā brahma dāsā brahmaiveme kitavāḥ*: these slaves are Brahman, these fishermen are Brahman, these gamblers are Brahman. (Ātharvaṇikā brahma-sūkta, Atharva-saṁhitā, Paippalada sākhā 8.9.11)[57] Such statements would not be possible if the *svarūpa* of the Lord and jīva were exactly the same. If the Lord and the jīva were the same, one who is the creator cannot be what one has created or one who is the pervader cannot be pervaded. The Lord with full consciousness cannot be the slave. If there was complete identity, this would negate teachings that one should become detached from the material world. Nor could the Lord be limited or separated by *māyā* since the Lord is never

---

[56] From Baladeva's Gita commentary: *Gati* means the method or path by which a goal is achieved, literally "that by which something is attained (*gamyate*)." *Bhartā* means a protector. *Prabhu* means controller. *Sākṣī* means the seer of all sinful and pious acts. *Nivāsa* means a place of enjoyment, literally, where one resides. *Śaraṇa* means He who takes away the suffering of the person who approaches Him. The derivation of the word is "that in which suffering will be destroyed (*duḥkham śīrṣyate asmin*)." *Suhṛt* is one who does beneficial activities for someone else because of that person's qualifications.

[57] Cited as such by Śaṅkāra, Rāmānuja and others.

subject to *māyā*. The jīva is not a piece of the Lord, broken off from the Lord, like a piece of stone cut off with a chisel, because this contradicts scripture which states the Lord cannot be cut and this would amount to the Lord being changeable. Thus the jīva, being different from the Lord, having a relationship as the created etc., is called the Lord's *aṁśa* or part because of being subordinate to the Lord. This condition is accomplished because the jīva is the *śakti* of the Lord. *viṣṇu-śaktiḥ parā proktā kṣetrajñākhyā tathā parā*: the Lord has a superior energy, another energy called the *jīva. (*Viṣṇu Purāṇa) This is similar to the statement that the planet of Venus is a hundredth part (*aṁśa*) of the planet moon (Venus is subordinate to the moon).

This does not contradict the definition of *aṁśa* being a part of one substance. Brahman, possessor of *śaktis,* is one substance. The *śakti* of Brahman is the jīva. Jīva is an *aṁśa* of Brahman because it is a part of Brahman (being his *śakti).* Thus the jīva's subordination to Brahman is established.

The example of the pot and the sky is resolved by saying that when the *upādhis* on the jīva cease, the two (who are different) meet together. "You are that (*tat tvam asi*)" means that the functions of the jīva (*tvam*), who is mentioned after mentioning the Lord, are dependent on the Lord (*tat*), who is mentioned first. This is not different from the meaning of previously quoted texts also.

Thus, because of deducing the qualities of controller and controlled, all-pervading and atomic size in the Lord and the jīva, it can be concluded that there is difference between the jīva and the Lord. This cannot be known from sense perception. It is known only by scripture.

The author quotes from the Vedas.

Sūtra - 2.3.42

|| mantra-varṇāt ||

The jīva is an *aṁśa* because this is stated in a Vedic mantra.

pādo 'sya viśvā bhūtāni: all beings are one quarter *(aṁśa*) of Viṣṇu. (Ṛg Veda 10.90.3) This wording of the mantra (*mantra-varṇa*) says that the jīva is an *aṁśa* of Brahman. The word *pāda* is synonymous with *aṁśa.* In this Vedic mantra, the plural *sarva-bhūtāni* is used (to indicate that there are many jīvas) whereas the word *aṁśa* is in the singular in the previous sūtra to indicate a class. This is the case in other texts as well.

Sūtra - 2.3.43

|| api smaryate ||

Smṛtis also confirm this.

mamaivāṁśo jīva-loke jīva-bhūtaḥ sanātana:

The jīvas are my part and eternal in the world of jīvas. BG 15.7

By saying that the jīva is eternal (*sanātanaḥ*), the Lord refutes the idea that the jīva arises as an *upādhi*-- Brahman under limiting conditions. Thus, it can be concluded that the jīva is an *aṁśa* of the Lord, dependent on a relationship with him. His role as an agent is dependent on the Lord. The smṛtis also give details of the *svarūpa* of the jīva:

jñānāśrayo jñāna-guṇaś cetanaḥ prakṛteḥ paraḥ
na jāto nirvikāraś ca eka-rūpaḥ svarūpa-bhāk

The jīva is knowledge itself, has the quality of knowledge, is conscious, is superior to prakṛti, is not born, does not change, is similar to others of its class, and has its individual form.

aṇur nityo vyāpti-śīlaś cid-ānandātmakas tathā
aham artho 'vyayaḥ sākṣī bhinna-rūpaḥ sanātanaḥ

The jīva is atomic, eternal, pervasive, composed of knowledge and bliss, has a sense of I, does not diminish, is a witness, is separate from other jīvas, and is permanent.

adāhyo 'cchedyo 'kledyo 'śoṣyo 'kṣara eva ca
evam-ādi-guṇair yuktaḥ śeṣa-bhūtaḥ parasya vai

The jīva cannot be burned, cannot be cut, cannot be moistened, cannot be dried up, cannot be destroyed. The jīva is endowed with these and other qualities. It is an *aṁśa,* a servant of the Lord.

ma-kareṇocyate jīvaḥ kṣetra-jñaḥ paravān sadā
dāsa-bhūto harer eva nānyasyaiva kadācana

The syllable *ma* of *oṁ* denotes the jīva, who knows his body, and is always dependent on the Lord. The jīva is a servant of the Lord and of no one else ever. Padma Purāṇa Uttara-khaṇḍa 226.34-37

The phrase *evam-ādi-guṇaiḥ* (endowed thus with other qualities) means that the jīva is also the agent, enjoyer, and self-luminous (aware of himself). *Prakāśa* (illumination, knowledge) is of two types: concerning quality and substance. The first, concerning quality, is the ability of a quality to manifest its shelter. (A quality manifests the object in which inheres.) The second is a particular substance which is the cause of manifesting itself and other things: this is the *ātmā.* A flame reveals the eye and reveals its own form by itself. It is not like the illumination of a pot, which depends on the flame to reveal its form. Thus, the flame illuminates itself or is self-illuminating (*svayam prakāśa*). However, the flame does not reveal itself *to itself.* (It is not aware of itself, but reveals its form to a person with consciousness), since it is unconscious of itself. *Ātmā* reveals others and also reveals itself *to itself.* Therefore, that which reveals itself to itself is the *ātmā,* which is *cid-rūpa,* a form of consciousness.

Topic 18 (Sūtras 44 - 48)

Matsyādy-adhikaraṇam – The nature of Matsya and other avatāras

Incidentally, the following is considered.

eko vaśī sarva-gaḥ kṛṣṇa iḍya eko 'pi san bahudhā yo 'vabhāti

Kṛṣṇa is supreme, all-pervading, most worthy of praise. Though he is one, he is also many. Gopāla-tāpanī Upaniṣad 1.19

Viṣṇu Purāṇa 1.2.3 also says *ekāneka-svarūpāya sthūla-sūkṣmātmane namaḥ*: I offer respects to the Lord who has unlimited forms, and who is both subtle and gross. It appears that the one Lord as the *aṁśī* appears as many *aṁśa* or parts of *aṁśas.*

The doubt is this. Is an *aṁśa* like Matsya different from the jīva who is also an *aṁśa*?

(Pūrvapakṣa) The *avatāras* are not different from the jīvas since all *aṁśas* are the same.

Sūtra - 2.3.44

|| prakāśādivan naivaṁ paraḥ ||

The *avatāras* are not like jīvas but are the Lord, just as the sun and the firefly are called light but are different.

Though Matsya and other *avatāras* are called *aṁśas,* theyare not like jīvas. Two examples are given. Though both the sun and the firefly, being *aṁśas* of light, are called light they do not have the same type of light. Though both nectar and liquor, being *aṁśas* of water, are called water, they are not the same.

Sūtra - 2.3.45

|| smaranti ca ||

The smṛtis confirm this.

svāṁśaś cātha vibhinnāṁśa iti dvedhāṁśa iṣyate
aṁśino yat tu sāmarthyaṁ yat-svarūpaṁ yathā sthitiḥ
tad eva nāṇumātro 'pi bhedaḥ svāṁśāṁśino kvacit
vibhinnāṁśo 'lpa-śaktiḥ syāt kiñcit sāmarthya-mātra-yuk
sarve sarva-guṇaiḥ pūrṇāḥ sarva-doṣa-vivarjitāḥ

There are two types of *aṁśas: svāṁśa* and *vibhinnāṁśa.* The *svāṁśa* does not differ at all from the *aṁśī* in powers, nature and position. The *vibhinnāṁśa* has little power and only some ability. The *svāṁśa* forms are all devoid of all faults and perfect. Mahā-varāha Purāṇa.

The meaning is this. *ete cāṁśa-kalāḥ puṁsaḥ kṛṣṇas tu bhagavān svayam*: all are *aṁśas* or *kalās*, but Kṛṣṇa is bhagavān svayam. (SB 1.3.28) Matsya and other forms are considered *aṁśas* of the *svayamrūpa* entity called Kṛṣṇa. They do not differ from the Lord, as do the jīvas. Kṛṣṇa is like the *vaidūrya* gem (which manifests various colors at various times) since he manifests the various forms of the *avatāras (*while still remaining in his form). They are given their various designations depending on whether they are manifesting or not manifesting all of the Lord's *śaktis.* Kṛṣṇa is the *aṁśī,* manifesting six qualities completely. *Aṁśas* manifest those qualities incompletely and *kalās* manifest just one or two qualities.

An example is given. A person who speaks on the six scriptures is called most learned. Sometimes he does not speak completely on the six scriptures and sometimes he speaks on one or two of them. He is then called a learned or somewhat learned person (though he is the same person).

It is said in Puruṣa-bodhini-śruti that Rādhā and others are his complete *śaktis.* The Tenth Canto of Bhāgavatam describes Kṛṣṇa's qualities. He has followers filled with the highest prema, has a sweetness in his flute that astonishes the most learned like Śiva, and a sweetness of form which astonishes everyone including himself. He has intense compassion. These qualities appear eternally in Kṛṣṇa, who drinks the milk of Yaśodā. But those qualities do not appear in Matsya and others. Nonetheless, because these forms manifest some of his various qualities, they are not like the jīvas, who are of another category (*tattva*). Rather, these forms are non-different from him.

The author shows the difference by a different logic.

Sūtra - 2.3.46

|| anujñā-parihārau deha-sambandhāt jyotir-ādivat ||

Because of relation with a body, the jīva is subject to actions permitted by the Lord and liberation arranged by him, just as the eye is dependent on the sun.

Though the jīva is an *aṁśa* of Brahman, the scriptures say that the Lord gives permission and rejection of works to the jīva, because the jīva is related with a body (*deha-sambandhāt*), manifested because of beginningless (*anādi*) *avidyā.* These rules are not for Matsya and other forms, for it is stated in scriptures that they are devoid of relationship with material bodies and are directly the Supreme Lord. These forms are greatly different from the jīva. Permission (*anujñā*) means the Lord inspires the jīvas to do good or bad acts (according to their desires). *eṣa eva sādhu-karma kārayati*: the Lord alone makes them do good acts. (Kauṣītaki Upaniṣad 2.9) Rejection (*parihārau*) means that the Lord inspires them to give up these actions and thereby grants them liberation. *tam eva viditvā* atimṛtyum eti*:* knowing him alone one surpasses death. (Śvetāśvatara Upaniṣad 6.15)

An example is given. The eye (*jyotir-ādivat*), though an *aṁśa* of the sun, because of relation with the body, takes on various forms in different bodies and depends on the mercy of the sun. It acts or ceases to act depending on the sun. This is not so for the sun's rays because, though the rays are also *aṁśas* of the sun situated in the sky, they are one with the sun.

The jīvas are like the eyes and the *avatāras* are like the sun's rays.

Sūtra - 2.3.47

|| asantateś cāvyatikaraḥ ||

Because the jīva is incomplete, he cannot compare with the *avatāras.*

Because the jīva is incomplete (*asantateḥ*), he has no resemblance (*avyatikaraḥ*) with the *avatāras* who are complete. The śrutis state the jīva's incompleteness. *bālāgra-śat-bhāgasya:* the jīva is the size of a part of a hundredth part of a tip of hair. (Śvetāśvatara Upaniṣad 4.9) The *avataras,* however, are complete. *Pūrṇam adaḥ pūrṇam idam*: the Lord is complete and from him comes the complete *avatāras. (Vājasaneya Yajur Veda)*

The author criticizes the reasoning that equates the *avatāras* and jīvas.

Sūtra - 2.3.48

|| ābhāsa eva ca ||

There is a logical fallacy in equating the *avatāras* with the jīvas.

One may equate the jīva with the a*vatāras* because they are both called *aṁśas*. This, however, is a fallacy (*ābhāsa*). The faulty reasoning (*hetvābhāsa*) in this case is called *sat-pratipakṣa,*[58] since an opposite conclusion can be reached by citing a different reason. The word *ca* indicates other examples. The earth and ether are both substances, but one cannot say they are completely the same. Or though existence and non-existence are both categories, they are not the same. Thus the word *aṁśa* applied to *avatāras* like Matsya refers to the Lord in a form not manifesting all the qualities. On the other hand, the same word applied to the jīva refers to his dependence on the Lord.

Topic 19 (Sūtras 49 - 51)

Adṛṣṭāniyamādhikaraṇam - Difference in karma

---

[58] *Sat-pratipakṣa* means existence of the opposite argument. This is an argument in which there is a contrary reason which may prove the opposite conclusion. *Avatāras* are the same as jīvas because they are *āṁśas.* Avatāras are not the same as jīvas because the *avatāras* are complete.

Having completed the digression, the author considers the main topic of the jīva.

Such statements as the following are found in the Upaniṣads like Kaṭha:

nityo nityānāṁ cetanaś cetanānām
eko bahūnāṁ yo vidadhāti kāmān

The Lord is the chief eternal among eternals, and the chief conscious being among conscious beings. The one fulfills the desires of many. Kaṭha Upaniṣad 2.2.13

In the passage, it says that there are many jīvas with eternal consciousness. The doubt is this. Are all of them same (in their experience)?

(Pūrvapakṣa) Because no differences are recognized, they are the same.

Sūtra - 2.3.49

|| adṛṣṭāniyamāt ||

All jīvas are not the same because of differences in karma.

The word *na* is understood from sūtra 2.3.44. The jīvas are not all the same (in their experience). Why? Though their *svarūpa* is the same, they are not the same because they are having different karmas. Their karma (*adṛṣtam)* is without beginning *(anādi*).

One may argue that the differences occur because of difference in desires and hatreds. This is refuted in the next sūtra.

Sūtra - 2.3.50

|| abhisandhyādiṣv api caivam ||

Though desires and some temporary differences may be accepted as a cause, they must also have a cause.

Though the desires and hatreds are accepted as causes for variety in jīvas (*api*), these desires and hatreds arise from karma alone, since one must find a cause of those desires and hatreds (*evam*). The word *ca* indicates that this includes the temporary differences as well.

"The jīvas have variety because of being in different places such as Svarga or earth."

Sūtra - 2.3.51

|| pradeśād iti cen nāntarbhāvāt ||

If one proposes that difference in place gives rise to variety in jīvas, the answer is no, because attaining those places depends on karma.

The answer is no, because attaining different places is included in karma, since attaining those particular places depends on karma.[59] One also sees variety in jīvas who are in the same place.

[59] Desire and hatred arise from the jīva's perception in situations in a certain place in a certain body, all endowed with a variety of guṇas. The place, body and circumstances are dictated by karma.

Section Four

tvaj-jātāḥ kalitotpātāḥ mat-prāṇāḥ santy amitrabhit |
etān śādhi tathā deva yathā sat-patha-gāminaḥ ||

O Lord! O killer of enemies! My senses, arising from you, have gone astray. Make them follow the path of bhakti.

Topic 1 (Sūtras 1 - 5)

Prāṇotpatty-adhikaraṇam – Origin of the prāṇas

In the third pāda, the author refuted various misconceptions about the elements described in the śrutis. In the fourth pāda, he refutes misconceptions concerning the *prāṇas*. There are two types of *prāṇa*: secondary and primary. The secondary ones are the eleven senses starting with the eye. The primary *prāṇas* are the five *prāṇas* such as *prāṇa* and *apāna.*

The eleven senses are now examined. *etasmāj jāyate prāṇo manaḥ sarvendriyāṇi*: from this was born *prāṇa,* the mind and all senses. (Muṇḍaka Upaniṣad 2.1.3)

The doubt is this. Do the senses and mind arise like the jīva (with no creation) or like ether?

asad vā idam agra āsīt tad āhuḥ kiṁ tad āsīd iti ṛṣāyo vāva te asad āsīt tad āhuḥ ke te ṛṣayaḥ iti prāṇā vāva ṛṣayaḥ

Asat existed in the beginning. "What was that? *Asat* was these sages. Who were these sages? The *prāṇas* were the sages. Śatapatha-brāhmaṇa 6.1.1

(Pūrva-pakṣa) Here, since it is said that the *prāṇas* or sages, meaning the senses, existed previous to the creation, the senses must be like the jīva (with no creation).

Sūtra - 2.4.1

|| tathā prāṇāḥ ||

The senses are created like other elements.

Just as ether and other elements arise from the Supreme Lord, *prāṇas* or senses also arise from him since the śrutis say that before the creation only one entity existed, and from him the mind and senses arose. *manaḥ sarvendriyāṇi caitasmāt jāyanta:* the mind and senses arose from the Lord. (Muṇḍaka Upaniṣad) One cannot say that the senses arise like the jīva, since the jīva is not subject to the six transformations. Thus the creation of jīvas is figurative only. Because the senses are material, their creation is literal. The sages and the *prāṇas* mentioned in the quotation from Śatapatha-brāhmaṇa actually mean the Lord, since the sage indicate someone with all knowledge and the *prāṇa* refer one who gives life.

"But that cannot be, because sages and *prāṇas* are in the plural."

Sūtra - 2.4.2

|| gauṇy-asambhavāt ||

The plural is figurative since only the Lord existed.

The plural is figurative only *(gauṇi)*. Why? Because it is impossible (*asambhavāt*) to have many entities, since there was no distinction of forms at that time. Moreover, with the desire to manifest, he would be many in the future (and thus the plural may be used). The Lord is like a single *vaidūrya* gem or like an actor. He appears as many. Śruti says *ekaṁ santaṁ bahudhā dṛśyamāna*: he is on but appears to be many. *ekāneka-svarūpāya*: I offer respects to the Lord who is many. (Viṣṇu Purāṇa 1.2.3)

Sūtra - 2.4.3

|| tat prāk śruteś ca ||

And the plural is only figurative because before creation only the Lord existed according to śruti.

There could be no objects during *pralaya (prāk)*. One cannot speculate that there were many entities existing then, since at that time everything was merged in the Lord. Therefore the plural is figurative.

The logic is given for why *prāṇa* means the Lord.

Sūtra - 2.4.4

|| tat pūrvakatvād vācaḥ ||

Before the creation of names and elements, only Brahman was present.

Because Brahman existed previous to the creation of *pradhāna, mahat-tattva* (*tat pūrvakatvāt*) and names (*vacah*) of all objects other than Brahman, because of the absence of instruments, the senses, the word *prāṇa* means Brahman. *tad dhedaṁ tarhi avyaktam āsīt:* at that time, all this was unmanifest. (Bṛhad-āraṇyaka Upaniṣad 1.4.7) Before the creation names and forms were absent. Therefore the senses arise like ether and other elements.

Having refuted ideas about the senses which are contrary to the śruti, the author now refutes wrong ideas about the number of senses.

sapta prāṇāḥ prabhavanti tasmāt
saptārciṣaḥ samadhiḥ sapta-homāḥ
sapteme lokā yeṣu sañcaranti
prāṇā guhāśayā nihitā sapta sapta

From the Lord come the seven *prāṇas* (senses), the seven fires, the seven sacrifices, and the seven planets, in which the seven *prāṇas* move. These groups of seven reside in the heart. Muṇḍaka Upaniṣad 2.1.8

However, Bṛhad-āraṇyaka Upaniṣad (3.9.4) says *daśeme puruṣe prāṇā ātmaikādaśaḥ*: there are ten senses and the mind, the eleventh.

The doubt is this. Are there seven senses or eleven? The *pūrva-pakṣa* is stated in the next sūtra.

Sūtra - 2.4.5

|| sapta gater viśeṣitatvāc ca ||

There are seven senses, since this is described in the scriptures.

There are seven senses only. Why? Because scripture says in all cases that seven senses leave (*gateḥ*) the body with the jīva.

yadā pañcāvatiṣṭhante jñānāni manasā saha
buddhiś ca na viceṣṭeta tām āhuḥ paramāṁ gatim

The sages say that the supreme goal is attained when the five knowledge senses are at peace and with the mind intelligence is no longer active. Kaṭha Upaniṣad 2.3.10

There are seven senses because the knowledge senses are particularly described in the state of yoga. The jīva has seven senses: ear, eye, nose, skin and tongue, intelligence and mind. Because the scriptures do not say that the voice, hands, feet, genital and anus leave with the jīva, they are called senses only secondarily, since they help the other senses to a small degree.

Topic 2 (Sūtra 6)

Hastādayādhikaraṇam – Limbs like the hands are classed as senses

The conclusion is given.

Sūtra - 2.4.6

| | hastādayas tu sthite'to naivam | |

The hands, feet, voice, anus and genital are also senses, for while the jīva is in the body they assist the jīva in his enjoyment. There are not seven senses.

The word *tu* indicates refutation of the proposal. The hands and other action senses (*hastādayaḥ*) should be considered senses along with the other seven. Why? Because, while the jīva is in the body, they assist the jīva in getting his enjoyment, and perform different functions.

hastau vai grahaḥ sarva-karmaṇābhigraheṇa gṛhītāḥ hastābhyāṁ karma karoti.

One grasps with the hands. It is fond of action. With the hands one performs actions. Bṛhad-āraṇyaka Upaniṣad 3.2.8

Because more than seven are listed in scriptures, one cannot consider only seven *(naivam*). One should accept five knowledge senses, five action senses and the inner sense, making eleven. The *ātmā* mentioned in Bṛhad-āraṇyaka Upaniṣad is the inner sense, understood from the context. This should be understood. There are five sense objects, five types of awareness: sound, touch, form, taste and smell. For these, there are five knowledge senses: the ear, skin, eyes, tongue and nose. There are five actions: speaking, receiving, moving, excreting and pleasure. There are five senses for these actions: voice, hands, feet, anus and genital. The *antaḥkaraṇa,* existing in all phases of time, with diverse functions, is one, and has all the above as its objects. This is designated sometimes as mind, when it desires; as intelligence when it apprehends; *ahaṅkāra* when it identifies with itself; and *cittam* when it contemplates.

Topic 3 (Sūtra 7)

Prāṇāṇutvādhikaraṇam - Atomic Senses

The size of the senses is now considered. Are the senses pervasive or minute?

(Pūrvapakṣa) They are pervasive because we experience that one can see and hear over a great distance.

Sūtra - 2.4.7

|| aṇavaś ca ||

The senses are atomic.

The word *ca* is used to express certainty. The senses are minute for certain. Hearing at a great distance is accomplished by the spreading of qualities from the objects. Only the jīva spreads, from head to foot. Thus the Sāṅkhya doctrine of pervading senses is refuted.

Topic 4 (Sūtra 8)

Prāṇa-śreṣṭhādhikaraṇam - The Chief Prāṇa

Now the chief *prāṇa* is examined in the passage *etasmāj jāyate prāṇaḥ*: from him arose *prāṇaḥ*. (Muṇḍaka Upaniṣad 2.1.3) Does the chief *prāṇa* arise like the jīva or like ether?

Śruti says *naivaprāṇadeti nāntam eti*: the *prāṇa* is not born nor does it die. Smṛti says:

yat-prāptir yat-parityāga utpattir maraṇaṁ tathā
tasyotpattir mṛtiś caiva kathaṁ prāṇasya yujyate

Birth and death mean acceptance and rejection of a body. How can prāṇa have birth and death?

Therefore the *prāṇa* is like the jīva.

Sūtra - 2.4.8

|| śreṣṭhaś ca ||

Even the chief prana is created.

Even the chief *prāṇa (śreṣṭhaḥ)* arises like ether and the other elements since śruti says *jāyate prāṇaḥ*: the *prāṇa* is born. (Muṇḍaka Upaniṣad 2.1.3) And the declaration should not be contradicted. *sa idam sarvam asṛjata*: he created all this. (Taittirīya Upaniṣad 2.6.1) This being the case, statements that *prāṇa* is not created are relative. The scriptures call this the chief *prāṇa* because it is the cause of maintaining the body. This sūtra is separated from the previous one in order to give continuity to the next sūtra, which also concerns the chief *prāṇa.*

Topic 5 (Sūtra 9)

Vāyu-kriyādhikaraṇam – The chief prāṇa is not air element

Now the essential nature (*svarūpa*) of *prāṇa* is examined. Is *prāṇa* just air or an active vibration or air that goes to other places (wind)? What is it?

(Pūrva-pakṣa) It is external air only, for śruti says *yo 'yaṁ prāṇaḥ sa vāyuḥ*: that which is *prāṇa* is air. (Bṛhad-āraṇyaka Upaniṣad 3.1.5) Or *prāṇa* is activity of air, since the word *prāṇa* is well known for denoting inhalation and exhalation and since *prāṇa* is not generally known as simply air.

Sūtra - 2.4.9

| | na vāyu-kriye pṛthag-upadeśāt | |

The chief *prāṇa* is not air or its vibration, because they are designated separately in the scriptures.

The chief *prāṇa* is not air or its vibration. Why? Because of statements of difference between *prāṇa* and air. *etasmāj jāyate prāṇaḥ*: from him was born *prāṇa.* (Muṇḍaka Upaniṣad 2.1.3) If *prāṇa* were merely air, then that statement would not be made separately. If *prāṇa* were a vibration of air, then also a statement about *prāṇa* which was a vibration of air would not be made separately. One does not see separate statements about fire along with its activities. The statement *yo 'yaṁ prāṇāḥ sa vāyuḥ(prāṇa* is air) means that a slight modification of air becomes *prāṇa.* It is not a separate element like light. The followers of Sāṅkhya say *sāmānya-karaṇa-vṛttiḥ prāṇādyā vāyavaḥ pañca*: the five airs or *prāṇas* are all the sense functions. The *prāṇa* is merely action of the senses according to them. This is not true, because it is impossible for one *prāṇa* to act as a variety of differing senses.

Topic 6 (Sūtras 10 - 11)

Jīvopakāraṇatvādhikaraṇam - Instrument of the Jīva

It is said:

supteṣu vāg-ādiṣu prāṇa eko jāgarti. prāṇa eko mṛtyunānāptaḥ. prāṇaḥ samvargo vāg-ādīn samvṛṅkte.

When the senses like voice are sleeping, the *prāṇa* is awake. The one *prāṇa* does not die. *Prāṇa* controls the senses such as the voice. Chāndogya Upaniṣad[60]

prāṇa itarān prāṇān rakṣati māteva putrān

The *prāṇa* protects the other senses just as a mother protects her sons. Bṛhad-āraṇyaka Upaniṣad[61]

The doubt is this. Is the chief *prāṇa* in the body the jīva and thus independent, or does it assist the jīva?

(Pūrva-pakṣa) The *prāṇa* is independent since it is said that it is very powerful.

Sūtra - 2.4.10

|| cakṣur-ādivat tu tat saha śiṣṭy-ādibhyaḥ ||

The *prāṇa* is an instrument of the jīva like the eye, since it is mentioned with the senses in scriptural passages.

The word *tu* indicates a destruction of the doubt. Like the eye, it is a sense of the jīva. Why? Because *prāṇa* is mentioned in the scriptures (*śiṣṭādibhyaḥ*) along with the senses of the jīva (*tat-saha*) such as the eye (*cakṣur-ādivat*) in talking about the *prāṇa*. It is appropriate to discuss together things of the same nature, just as the Bṛhad and Rathāntara songs are grouped together as Brhad-rathāntara because of a similar nature. The word *ādi* indicates that prāṇa is an instrument as well because it means "sense."

yatra vāyaṁ mukhyaḥ prāṇaḥ sa evāyaṁ madhyamaḥ prāṇaḥ

---

[60] prāṇo vāva saṁvargaḥ sa yadā svapiti prāṇam eva vāgapyeti prāṇaṁ cakṣuḥ prāṇaṁ śrotram prāṇaṁ manaḥ prāno hyevaitān sarvān saṁvṛṅkta iti

[61] māteva putrān rakṣasva śrīś ca prajñāṁ ca vidhehi naḥ is found in Praśna Upaniṣad 2.13

Wherever the chief *prāṇa* exits, it is the central *prāṇa* (sense). Bṛhad-āraṇyaka Upaniṣad 1.5.22

It is grouped with the senses in order to deny its independence.

"If the chief *prāṇa* is accepted as an assistant to the jīva like the eye, it should have activity to assist the jīva like the senses. But such a function does not exist. Then scriptures should mention twelve senses (instead of eleven). Therefore *prāṇa* is not like the senses."

Sūtra - 2.4.11

|| akaraṇatvāc ca na doṣas tathā hi darśayati ||

You cannot say that the chief *prāṇa* has the fault of no action. Its action is described in the śruti.

The word *ca* indicates a refutation of the objection. The fault (*na doṣaḥ*) that may arise because it does not perform activities (*akaraṇatvāt*) in assisting the jīva does not exist, because it does the greatest service in functions such as supporting all the senses. This is shown (*tathā hi darśayati*) in Chāndogya Upaniṣad 5.7. *atha ha prāṇā ahaṁ śreyasi vyūdire:* the senses argued "I am the best." (In this passage it is concluded that the chief *prāṇa* is the best sense.) From this it is understood that the chief *prāṇa* assists the jīva. The senses are like ministers in helping the jīva as the agent and enjoyer. The chief *prāṇa* however is like the prime minister, the chief assistant in accomplishing all the jīva's goals. It is not independent.

Topic 7 (Sūtra 12)

Pañca-vṛtty-adhikaraṇam – The functions of prāṇa

It is said:

yaḥ prāṇaḥ sa eṣa vāyuḥ pañca-vidhaḥ prāṇo 'pāno vyāna udānaḥ samānaḥ: *prāṇa* is air of five types: *prāṇa, apāna, vyāna, udāna and samāna.* (Bṛhad-āraṇyaka Upaniṣad 1.5.3)

Are the four others different from *prāṇa* or just its functions?

(Pūrvapakṣa) Because of being mentioned separately by name and because they perform different actions, they are separate.

Sūtra - 2.4.12

|| pañca-vṛttir manovad vyapadiśyate ||

It is stated in the scriptures that the chief *prāṇa* has five functions, like the mind.

The one *prāṇa* has five functions. The five exist in various places like the heart and carry out different functions. The one *prāṇa* thus is designated by different names. Therefore the five are functions of the chief *prāṇa* and are not separate. Because of different functions they are named separately. The *svarūpa* however is not different. Therefore the word *prāṇa* is used to designate all five. *prāṇo 'pāno vyāna udānaḥ samāna iti etat sarvaṁ prāṇa eva: prāṇa, apāna, vyāna, udāna and samāna* are all *prāṇa.* (Bṛhad-āraṇyaka Upaniṣad 1.5.3) The chief *prāṇa* is compared to the mind, which is described as follows:

kāmaḥ saṅkalpo vikalpo vicikitsā śraddhā dhṛtir adhṛtir hrīr dhīr bhīr ity etat sarvaṁ mana eva

Desire, determination, indecision, doubt, faith, lack of faith, memory, forgetfulness shame, reflection and fear are all mind. Bṛhad-āraṇyaka Upaniṣad 1.5.3

Just as desire etc., though given different names according to function, are not separate from the mind, so, though it is given different names according to different functions, the chief *prāṇa* is one. In yoga scriptures also the mind is described as having five functions. That is the meaning of the sūtra according to some.

Topic 8 (Sūtra 13)

Śreṣṭāṇutvādhikaraṇam – Atomic nature of the chief prāṇa

Is the chief *prāṇa* all-pervading or atomic?

(Pūrvapakṣa) The chief *prāṇa* is all-pervading according to śruti. *sama ebhis tribhir lokaiḥ:* the *prāṇa* is equal to the three worlds. (Bṛhad-āraṇyaka Upaniṣad 1.3.23)

Sūtra - 2.4.13

|| aṇuś ca ||

The chief *prāṇa* is atomic.

Even the chief *prāṇa* is atomic, according the śruti, which says that it passes out of the body. Statements that it is all-pervading mean that it is situated in all living beings like *pradhāna.*

Topic 9 (Sūtras 14 - 16)

Jyotir-ādy-adhikaraṇam - Brahman is the ruler of *prāṇa*

The chief *prāṇa* action is described as being awake while the senses like voice are sleeping. The secondary *prāṇas'* actions are described with *sapta ime lokā yeṣu caranti prāṇāḥ:* the *prāṇas* move about in the seven worlds. (Muṇḍaka Upaniṣad 2.1.8) Do the senses with the *prāṇas* act on their own in their activities or do they have a separate instigator of their actions. Is the instigator some *devatās,* the jīva or the Lord?

(Pūrvapakṣa) The senses and the *prāṇas* act on their own because they are endowed with powers to act. Or the *devatās* act as instigators since it is said *agnir vāg bhūtvā mukhaṁ prāviṣad:* fire, becoming speech, entered the mouth. (Aitareya Upaniṣad 2.4) The jīva may be the mover of *prāṇa* and the senses, because the *prāṇa* and senses help the jīva attain his enjoyment.

Sūtra - 2.4.14

|| jyotir-ādy-adhiṣṭhānaṁ tu tad-āmananāt ||

The Lord is the ruler of the senses and *prāṇas* since this is described in the śruti.

The word *tu* removes the doubt. Brahman alone (*jyotiḥ*) is the chief instigator *(ādy-adhiṣṭhānam). Adhiṣṭhānam* comes from a verb meaning "to govern." This means that it is ruler of the *prāṇas.* Why? Because this is understood from the scriptural description of the *antaryāmi-brāhman* that the Lord is the mover of the *prāṇas* and senses. That *devatās* and jīvas are also movers for attaining their goals is not excluded, since there are texts like *yaḥ prāṇeṣu tiṣṭhan yaḥ prāṇam antaro yamayati*: the jīva remains with the *prāṇas* and controls the *prāṇas* from within. (Bṛhad-āraṇyaka Upaniṣad 3.7.16) The *prāṇas* and senses cannot act alone, since they are insentient.

The jīva however rules the senses and *prāṇas* for his enjoyment.

Sūtra - 2.4.15

|| prāṇavatā śabdāt ||

The senses and *prāṇas* are controlled by the jīva, because that is mentioned in the scriptures.

The senses and *prāṇas* are controlled by the jīva (*prāṇavatā*) for his enjoyment. Why is this said? Because of scripture. It is said in śruti:

sa yathā mahā-rājo jānapadān gṛhītvā sve janapade yathā-kāmaṁ parivartate evam evaiṣa etat prāṇān gṛhītvā sve śarīre yathā-kāmaṁ parivartate

Just as a king taking his subjects goes about at his will among the population, the jīva taking the senses moves about his body by his will. Bṛhad-āraṇyaka Upaniṣad 2.1.8

The meaning is this. The jīvas and *devatās,* ruled by Paramātmā, rule over the senses. The *devatās* rule the senses only to make them act. The jīvas rule the senses for their enjoyment. All that takes place by the Lord's will.

There is no deviation from this.

Sūtra - 2.4.16

|| tasya ca nityatvāt ||

Jīvas and *devatās* are controllers because of the eternal will of the Lord who is the chief controller.

They are able to rule only because of the constant will (*niytātvāt*) of the Lord who is the ruler of all actions. From the *antaryāmi-brahmaṇa* it is understood that the Lord alone is the chief ruler or mover.

Topic 10 (Sūtras 17 - 19)

Indriyādhikaraṇam - The Senses

There is another doubt on this subject. Are all the *prāṇas* senses, or is the chief *prāṇa* an exception?

(Pūrvapakṣa) All the *prāṇas* are senses because they all assist the jīva and are known by the name *pṛāṇa (*sense).

Sūtra - 2.4.17

|| ta indriyāṇi tad-vyapadeśād anyatra śreṣṭhāt ||

Other than the chief *prāṇa,* the others designated by *prāṇa* are senses, because of the statements in śruti.

Those known by the name *prāṇa,* except the chief *prāṇa,* are senses. Why? Because of scriptural statements showing that other than the chief *prāṇa,* all others are senses, like the ear etc. *etasmāj jāyate prāṇo manaḥ searvendriyāṇi ca*: from the Lord arose the *prāṇa,* the mind and all the senses. (Muṇḍaka Upaniṣad 2.3) The smṛti says *indriyāṇi daśaikaṁ ca:* the eleven senses. (BG 13.5) Another śruti says *prāṇo mukhyaḥ sa tv anindriyam*: the chief *prāṇa* is not a sense.

"It is said *hantāsyaiva sarve rūpam asāmety etasyaiva sarve rūpam abhavat*: they said, "Let us all assume *praṇa's* form" and they all became his form. (Bṛhad-āraṇyaka Upaniṣad 1.5.21) We understand from this that the senses all have the same functions as the chief *prāṇa.* How can this be, since it differs from your conclusion?"

Sūtra - 2.4.18

|| bheda-śruteḥ ||

They are different, because of śruti statements of difference.

prāṇo manaḥ sarvendriyāṇi: the *prāṇa,* mind and all senses arose from the Lord. This indicates the *prāṇa* is a different *tattva* from the senses and the mind. One should not doubt that the mind is a sense because it is said *manaḥ ṣaṣṭhīndiyāni*: the mind is the sixth sense. (BG 15.7) Also smṛti also says *indriyāṇāṁ manaś cāsmi*: I am the mind among the senses. (BG 10.22)

Sūtra - 2.4.19

|| vailakṣaṇyāc ca ||

The chief *prāṇa* is not a sense because its characteristics are different.

It is ascertained that *prāṇa* functions during sleep but the senses do not. The *prāṇa* maintains the body and senses, but the senses accomplish knowledge and action for the jīva. Because of difference in essential nature (*svarūpa*) and actions, *prāṇa* is different from the senses. "Becoming the form of *prāṇa*" indicates that the senses in their functioning depend upon the *prāṇa*, just as it is said the jīvas have the form of Brahman. This means the *jīvas* depend upon Brahman for their functioning.

Topic 11 (Sūtras 20 - 22)

Saṁjña-mūrti-kḷpty-adhikaraṇam – Dividing names and forms

It has been said that the total creation (*samaṣṭi*) of all the elements and senses and the agency of the jīva arise from the Lord. Now, the person who gives rise to the individual creation within a universe (*vyaṣṭi)* will be examined. In Chāndogya Upaniṣad, after speaking of the creation of fire, water and earth, the following is taught.

seyam devataikṣata hantāham imās tisro devatā anena jīvenātmanānupraviśya nāma-rūpe vyākaravāṇīti tāsāṁ tri-vṛtam ekaikaṁ karavāṇīti. seyaṁ devatemās tisro devatā anena jīvenātmanānupraviśya nāma-rūpe vyākarot tāsāṁ tri-vṛtaṁ tri-vṛtam ekaikām akarot

The Lord desired "Let me enter these three *devatās* (fire, water and earth) with the jīva and divide name and form. Let me divide each of these threefold." The Lord entered the three *devatās* with the jīva and divided name and form. He made each of the elements three fold. Chāndogya Upaniṣad 6.3.2-4

Does the jīva manifest name and form or does the Lord?

(Pūrvapakṣa) Jīva produces name and form, because it says "entering by means of the jīva he divided them." The meaning is not "with the jīva" since it is improper to use an auxiliary word with a declension (*saha*--with the jīva) where it is possible to take the meaning of instrument (eg. by the jīva).

(Objection) It cannot mean "by the jīva" because there is no jīva present to do the work which the Lord accomplishes by his will. The passage cannot mean "entered by the jīva the Lord divided names and forms" since the structure using the form "having entered" must have the same subject as the person who mixed. Furthermore the first person (meaning the Lord) is used (*vyākaravāṇi*--let me divide).

(reply) A king can say, "I will enter the opposing army by means of a spy and estimate that army." This is not a concoction, for another śruti says *viriñco vā idaṁ virecayati vidadhāti brahmā vāva viriñca etasmād dhīme rūpa-nāmanī*:

Brahmā (called *viriñca* because he organizes-- *virecayati)* organizes the universe and from him these names and forms arose. Smṛti says *nāma-rūpaṁ ca bhūtānām*. Brahmā made the names and forms and all beings. (Viṣṇu Purāṇa 15.63) Therefore a jīva, Brahmā, is the creator.

Sūtra - 2.4.20

|| saṁjñā-mūrti-kḷptis tu trivṛt kurvata upadeśāt ||

The Lord mixes the names and forms after making the elements threefold, because that is the direct statement.

The word *tu* dismisses the objection. The actions of dividing the elements three fold and dividing names and forms (*saṁjña-mūṛti-kḷptis*) belong to the Supreme Lord, not the jīva. Why? Because of the statement that the Lord alone did this: he divided the elements threefold and divided the names and forms. Dividing the elements threefold is described:

trīṇy ekaikaṁ dvidhā kuryāt try-ardhāni vibhajed dvidhā
tat-tan-mukhyārdham utsṛjya yojayec ca tri-rūpatā

Divide each of the elements in two and divide one of each half in two. Mix two smaller parts of the other elements with the larger part of the third element. (Eg. one part fire and half part of earth and half part of water.)

This is also stands for *pañcīkaraṇa* (five elements dividing into parts, since there are actually five elements, not three). One cannot say that Brahmā made the threefold elements since he himself is born within the universe *after* it is constructed of those threefold elements. Smṛti says *tasminn aṇḍe 'bhavad brahmā sarva-loka-pitāmahaḥ:* Brahmā, the grandfather of all planets, appeared in that universe. (Manu-samḥitā 1.9) The passage indicates that one person acted as the agent in creating the threefold elements and then in dividing names and forms. The order in the text (first dividing names and forms and the dividing the elements threefold) cannot be taken literally as that nullifies the real meaning. First the Lord made the elements threefold and then he divided (distinguished) names and forms.

The universe cannot be made of fire, water and earth without combining in the threefold manner since it is impossible for them to act in an uncombined state. Smṛti says:

yadaite 'saṅgatā bhāvā bhūtendriya-mano-guṇāḥ
yadāyatana-nirmāṇe ne śekur brahma-vittama
tadā saṁhatya canyonyaṁ bhagavac-chakti-coditāḥ
sad-sattvam upādāya cobhayaṁ sasṛjur hy adaḥ

O best of the *brāhmaṇas*! As long as the gross elements, senses and mind were not mixed together, it was not possible for them to produce material bodies. Coming together by the impulse of the Lord's energy, accepting primary and secondary forms, they created the body of the whole universe and the individual bodies in it. SB 2.5.32-33

Pañcī-karaṇam was just mentioned. It is understood in this way. Each of the five elements is divided in two. One of those halves of each element is divided into four and these are mixed with the remaining half of each element. There are phrases like *annam aśitaṁ tridhā vidhīyate:* food when eaten divides in three. (Chāndogya Upaniṣad 6.5.1) This describes the transformation of earth into three but this is not the threefold elements.

Though the text say the Lord entered with the jīva, this does not mean that the jīva divided the names and forms. *Ātmanā* and *jīvena* refer to the same person. The meaning is "by Brahman himself *(ātmanā*), who has the *śakti* of jīva, who pervades the jīva," he entered. This explains statements about Brahmā creating names and forms (Brahmā in this case being a secondary creator). Therefore the literal meaning of the passage should be accepted. The Lord entered and made the elements threefold and distinguished names and forms. The subject is the same for all the verbs. Thus the Lord is the cause of dividing names and forms. *sarvāṇi rūpāṇi vicitya dhīro nāmāni kṛtvābhivadan yad āste*: I know the Lord who exists, who made all forms, and having named them, uttered those names. (Taittirīya Āraṇyaka)

Now the physical body called *mūrti* is examined. Śruti says *śarīraṁ pṛthivīm apy eti:* the body goes to earth (at death). (Bṛhad-āraṇyaka Upaniṣad 3.2.13) *adbhyo hīdam utpadyate āpo vāva māṁsam asthi ca bhavanty āpaḥ śarīram āpa evedaṁ sarvam*: the material body is created from water: water becomes flesh and bones; the entire body is water. (Kauṇḍinya-śruti) *saḥ agner deva-yonyāḥ*: the body is made of fire. The doubt is this. Is the body made of earth, water or fire, or of all three?

(Pūrvapakṣa) This cannot be determined, since there are three different versions in śruti.

Sūtra - 2.4.21

|| māṁsādi-bhaumaṁ yathā-śabdam itarayoś ca ||

The solid portions of the body are made of earth. Other parts are made of water and fire. This is according to śruti.

The body of flesh (*māṁsādi*) is the product of earth *(bhaumam)*. The products of the other two *(itarayoḥ)*, water and fire, are blood, bones and other things in the body. This is according to the śruti statements (*yathā-śabdam*). *yat kaṭhiṇaṁ sā pṛthivī yad dravaṁ tad āpo yad uṣṇaṁ tat tejaḥ*: the solid parts of the body are made of earth, the liquid parts are made of water and the warm parts are made of fire. (Garbha Upaniṣad) Therefore the body is composed of all three.

"If all things made of elements are actually made of threefold elements, why are the bodily parts still designated as earth, water and fire?"

Sūtra - 2.4.22

|| vaiśeṣyāt tu tad-vādas tad-vādaḥ ||

The combined elements are called by their name because of predominance of that element.

The word *tu* destroys the doubt. Though it is true that all the elements contain all the other elements, it is named (*tad-vādaḥ*) because of the predominance of a particular element (*vaiśeṣyāt*). *Tad-vādaḥ* is repeated to indicate the end of the chapter.

vardhasva kalpāga samaṁ samantāt
kuruṣva tāpa-kṣatim āśritānām |
tvad-aṅga-saṅkīrṇikarāḥ parāstā
hiṁsrā lasad-yukti-kuṭhārikābhiḥ ||

O desire tree! Flourish equally all around. Give shade to those who take shelter of you. The destructive plants which limit the growth of your limbs have been defeated by shining axe of your logic.

Chapter Three

Table of Contents (Chapter 3)

Section One

na vinā sādhanair devo jñāna-vairāgya-bhaktibhiḥ |
dadāti sva-padaṁ śrīmān atas tāni budhaḥ śrayet ||

The Lord does not give his feet without *sādhanas* of *jñāna,*[62] *vairāgya* and bhakti. Thus the intelligent take shelter of these methods.

Topic 1 (Sūtras 1 - 7)

Tad-anantra-pratipatty-adhikaraṇam - On attaining another body

The previous two chapters have established the *svarūpa* of Brahman from sūtras which show that all the Vedānta texts establish that the supreme Lord, composed of eternity, knowledge and bliss, who is an ocean of faultless qualities and the sole cause of the universe, is the objection of meditation for those desiring liberation, and that all texts agree with this conclusion.

Now, in the third chapter, methods of attaining the Lord are described. The first two parts deal with perfecting the chief of these means: disgust with anything other than the Lord and thirst for the Lord.

In the first pāda, taking shelter of *pañcāgni-vidyā* (knowledge of five fires), the faulty nature of the jīva in various conditions wandering because of transferring himself to different planets is revealed, in order to create detachment from the world. In the second pāda, the causes of attraction for the Lord--the qualities of the Lord like his majesty--are discussed.

Pañcāgni-vidyā is discussed in the Chāndogya Upaniṣad. *śvetaketur hāruṇeyaḥ pāñcālānāṁ samitim iyāya*: Śvetaketu Aruṇeya went to the assembly of Pāñcālas. (5.3.1) There is a clear description of how the jīva goes to another planet and then returns to this planet.

The doubt is this. Does the jīva go to the other planet separated from his subtle elements or with the elements?

(Pūrvapakṣa) The jīva goes while being separated from his subtle elements since these are easily available in other planets.

---

[62] *Jñāna* in this case does not mean cultivation of impersonal *jñāna.*

Sūtra - 3.1.1

|| tad-anantara-pratipattau raṁhati sampariṣvaktaḥ praśna-nirūpaṇābhyām ||

On attaining another body after death, the jīva goes, surrounded by subtle elements.This is understood from the questions and answers.

The word *tat* means the body since it refers to the word *mūrti* in sūtra 2.4.20. The jīva goes (*raṁhati*) surrounded by (*sampariṣvaktaḥ*) the subtle elements, in attaining another body after leaving the previous body (*tad-anantara*). Why? Because of the question (*praśna*) such as *vettha yathā* and the answer *asau vāva* (*nirūpābhyām*).

Here is the story. A kṣatriya named Pravāhaṇa, king of Pañcāla, asked five questions to Śvetaketu, a young brāhmaṇa who had come to the king. The questions topics are: the destination of those who perform karmas, the method of coming back, the people who do not attain that world, difference between d*evayāna* and *pitṛyāna,* and why the fifth oblation of water is called "man." (Chāndogya Upaniṣad 5.3.3) Not knowing the answer to the questions, the boy, depressed, went to his father Gautama and lamented. The father also did not know.

With a desire to know, his father went to the king. The king desired to give him wealth after welcoming him. The father then begged answers to the five questions. The king answered the last question by saying *asau vāva loke gautamāgniḥ*: O Gautama, in this world there are five things famous as fire. (Chāndogya Upaniṣad 5.4.1) He described heaven, rain, earth, man and woman. In these five fires are offered oblations of faith, soma, rain, food and semen respective. The priests are the *devatās* in all the sacrifices. The sacrifice is throwing the jīva surrounded by subtle elements into various worlds like heaven made by the *devatās,* in order that he may enjoy in Svarga etc. The senses of the jīva after death are called *devas*.

These senses or *devas* offer faith in the fire of heaven. That faith turns into a celestial body called *somarāja* capable of enjoying Svarga. After enjoyment, that body is offered into the fire composed of rain by the senses and becomes rain. The rain body is offered into the fire composed of earth by the senses and becomes food. The food body is offered into the fire composed of man by the senses and becomes semen. The semen is offered into the fire composed of woman by the senses and becomes an embryo. Then it is said *iti tu pañcamyām āhutā vāpaḥ puruṣa-vacaso bhavanti:* for this reason water offered in the fifth oblation is called man.

The meaning is this. When the fifth oblation in the form of semen has been offered, water (which previously was faith, soma, rain, food and finally semen) becomes the body of a man. Endowed with that water, the jīva went to heaven, and in the manner described above, enters woman and become the form of a man. Thus man goes with the subtle elements.

"The text says that the jīva goes with water. How can you say the jīva goes with all the elements?"

Sūtra - 3.1.2

|| try-ātmakatvāt tu bhūyastvāt ||

All the elements go with the jīva because water is composed of three elements, and it is called water because of predominance.

The word *tu* indicates removal of the doubt. Because water has three forms (elements) since it is a threefold element (*try-ātmakatvāt*), when water accompanies the jīva, it is accepted that the three elements also go (being within the water). The word "water" is used because of its predominance (*bhūyastvāt*), as seen in the predominance of liquid substance in the seed of the body formed of semen and blood. Smṛti says *tāpāpanodo bhūyastvam ambhaso vṛttayas tv imā:* the nature of water is to extinguish heat and being plentiful. (SB 3.26.43) The visible elements are so called because of predominance of a particular element (in this case water).

Sūtra - 3.1.3

|| prāṇa-gateś ca ||

The elements go because it is mentioned that the *prāṇas* also go.

It is said that the *prāṇas* go with the jīva when it leaves to take another body. *tam utrkāmantam; prāṇo 'nūtkrāmati prānām anūtkrāmantaṁ sarve prāṇā anūtkrāmanti:* when the jīva leaves the chief *prāna* leaves and all the *prāṇas* leave with that *prāṇa.* (Bṛhad-āraṇyaka Upaniṣad 4.4.2) The *prāṇas* cannot exist without a shelter. Therefore, it is accepted that the elements which act as the shelter of the *prāṇas* also go.

Sūtra - 3.1.4

|| agny-ādi-gati-śruter iti cen, na, bhāktatvāt ||

If one argues that the śruti says that the senses merge into various elements, and thus do not accompany the jīva, it is not so, since those statements are figurative only.

"It is said:

yatrāsya puruṣasya mṛtasyāgniṁ vāg apy eti, vātaṁ prāṇaś, cakṣur ādityaṁ, manaś candraṁ, diśaḥśrotraṁ, pṛthivīśarīram, ākāśam ātmauṣadhīr lomāni, nvamaspatīn keśā, apsu lohitam; ca retaś ca nidhīyate kvāyaṁ tadā puruṣo bhavati

When the speech of the dead person enters fire, when *prāṇa* enters air, when the eye enters the sun, when the mind enters the moon, when the ear enters the directions, when the body enters earth, when the self enters ether, when the body hairs enter herbs, when the head hairs enter the trees, when blood and semen enter water, where is the man? Bṛhad-āraṇyaka Upaniṣad 3.2.13

The śruti passage says that the speech and other bodily parts enter into fire etc. It does not say that they go with the jīva. Thus this śruti gives another conclusion."

That is not so. Why? Because this is taken in a secondary sense (*bhāktatvāt).* Since it is never seen that body hairs enter herbs though this is mentioned in the śruti, when the śruti says that speech enters fire etc., that also must be taken figuratively, since the description of the series of senses is taken as one unit. One does not see body hair jumping into the herbs when a person dies. Therefore at the time of death, speech merging into fire simply means that the senses lose their functions, since śruti also says that the senses go with the jīva.

Sūtra - 3.1.5

|| prathame'śravaṇād iti cen na tā eva hy upapatteḥ ||

If one argues that water is not mentioned in the first oblation, the answer is no, because of the conclusion reached by studying the question and its answer.

"Though water is the fifth oblation, one cannot say that the jīva goes with water during all oblations, since only the fifth oblation mentions water. Also the conclusion is wrong since water is not mentioned in the first oblation offered into the fire (*prathame aśravaṇāt*). Faith only is mentioned. *tasminn agnau devāḥ śraddhāṁ juhvati*: into fire the *devas* offered faith. (Chāndogya Upaniṣad 5.4.2) *Śraddha* cannot mean water at all, since faith is well known as a mental function. Soma, rain food and semen however have some water in them. Thus from the sentence, one cannot say that the jīva goes with the element water when the jīva dies."

It is not so, because *(hi)* faith means water (*tā*) in the first oblation into fire. Why? Because of proof *(upapatteḥ):* the question and answer. The question was "Do you know why the fifth oblation is called water?" But this means "Why are the oblations into the five fires called water?" At the beginning of the answer, it is said that faith is offered into the first fire. If faith does not mean water, the question and answer would not correspond.

The relation of water in the fifth oblation must indicate a relationship with the other four oblations. Soma, rain, food and semen, with predominance of water, are the gross effects of *śraddha*. The effects share the qualities of the cause (*śraddha*). Therefore it is logical to say that faith means water. Thus in the text, water is indicated by the word "faith." Śruti also says *śraddhā vā āpa*: water is faith. (Kṛṣṇa Yajur Veda 1.1.6.8) In the text, faith is not a mental function since it would be improbable to make oblations of faith by extracting it out of the mind. Therefore the jīva is accompanied by water.

"The passage says that water goes, but it does not say that the jīva goes with water." This doubt is removed in the next sūtra.

Sūtra - 3.1.6

|| aśrutatvād iti cen na iṣṭādi-kāriṇāṁ pratīteḥ ||

If one argues that the text does not mention the jīva explicitly, and thus the jīva does not go accompanied by the elements, the answer is no, because it is stated that the jīva goes to the moon by doing sacrifices.

If one argues that the text does not prove that the jīva goes with water (*āśrutatvāt*), the answer is no. Because also in the Chāndogya Upaniṣad it is said that the performer of sacrifices goes to the moon. *atha ya ime grāma iṣṭā-pūrte dattam ity upāsate te dhūmam abhisambhavanti:* those who undertake charity and sacrifices go to the smoke.

(Chāndogya Upaniṣad 5.10.3) *ākāśāc candramasam eṣā somo rājā*: from there they go to the moon, and become soma-rājā. (Chāndogya Upaniṣad 5.10.4) Those who do sacrifices go the moon and are known as *soma-rājā*. In offering faith into the fire of heaven, it is said *devāḥ śraddhāṁ juhvati tasyāḥ āhuteḥ somo rājā sambhavati*: the *devas* offer faith; from the oblation arises *somarājā*. Here also the meaning is the same. Therefore, the person endowed with a body of faith is the person endowed with a body of soma. This person is the jīva since the body takes shelter of the jīva by its nature. Thus it is concluded that the jīva goes, surrounded by the subtle elements.

"It is said *eṣa somo rājā devānām annaṁ taṁ devā bhakṣayanti*: this *somarājā* is food of the *devatās*: they eat this *somarājā*. (Chāndogya Upaniṣad 5.10.4) *Somarājā* cannot be the jīva because the *devatās* eat him. It is impossible to eat the jīva."

Sūtra - 3.1.7

|| bhāktaṁ vānātmavittvāt, tathā hi darśayati ||

No, the meaning is not that *somarājā* is eaten. The statement is figurative because the jīva is the object of enjoyment of the *devatās*, since he does not know *ātmā*. That is shown in the scriptures.

The word *vā* indicates destruction of the doubt. Calling the jīva food of the *devatās* is only figurative (*bhāktam*) because the jīva is a cause of enjoyment for them like food. The reason for their delight is that the jīva serves them. And this is because the jīva does not know *ātmā (anātmavittvāt)*. Śruti shows how the jīva who does not know *ātmā* serves the *devatās*. *atha yo'nyāṁ devatām upāste anyo'sāv anyo'ham asmīti na sa veda, yathā paśur eva sa devānām*: if a man worships some other *devatā* and thinks "The *devatā* is one person and I am another" he does not know; he is like an animal for the *devatās*. (Bṛhad-āraṇyaka Upaniṣad 1.4.10)

The meaning is this. The jīva is metaphorically called food for the *devatās* because the jīva cannot be eaten like food and the jīva becomes enjoyment for the *devatās*. One sees metaphorical statements like "The *vaiśya* is food for the king and animals are food for the *vaiśya*." If the passage were taken literally, it would make the injunction to perform the sacrifices like *jyotiṣtoma* meaningless. If the *devatās* ate those person who go to the moon, why would men go there? Why would they undertake sacrifices to attain the moon? Therefore the jīva goes accompanied by the subtle elements.

Topic 2 (Sūtras 8 - 13)

Kṛtātyayādhikaraṇam - Exhaustion of Karmas

The Chāndogya describes how a person dedicated to pious karmas attains Svarga by the path of smoke and then returns. *tasmin yavāt saṁpātam uṣitvāthaitam evādhvānaṁ punar nivartante*: remaining on the moon until their good results are exhausted they return by the same path. (Chāndogya Upaniṣad 5.10.5)

The doubt is this. Does this jīva return without a remainder of karmas or with karmas remaining (*anuśaya*).

(Pūrvapakṣa) Because the passage says that they remain on the moon as long as their good works last (*yavāt sampātam*), they descend without karmas. Another text says *prāpyāntaṁ karmaṇas tasya*: the jīva whose karmas have come to an end returns. (Bṛhad-āraṇyaka Upanisād 4.4.6) The word *sampāta* means karma, by which people reach (*sampatanti*) Svarga. *Anuśaya* means a remainder of karma to be experienced, that which adheres closely (*anuśete)* to the performer for enjoying results. Since the jīva experiences all the results, there is no remainder.

Sūtra - 3.1.8

|| kṛtātyaye'nuśayavān dṛṣṭa-smṛtibhyām ||

When the jīva exhausts all his karmas which allowed for his enjoyment on Svarga, he returns with the remaining karmas, because this is seen in the same scripture and is noted in smṛti also.

When the results of karmas such as sacrifices performed for enjoying happiness on the moon are exhausted completely by enjoyment there, the jīva returns accompanied by his remaining karmas, because his body of enjoyment on the moon is burned up by the fire of grief arising from destruction of enjoyment. Why is this said? Because it is seen (*dṛṣṭa*) in the text.

tad ya iha ramaṇīya-caraṇā abhyāśo ha yat te ramaṇīyāṁ yonim āpadyeran brāhmaṇa-yoniṁ vā kṣatriya-yoniṁ vā vaiśya-yonim; vātha ya iha kapūya-caraṇā abhyāśo ha yat te kapūyaṁ yoniṁ āpadyerañśva-yoniṁ vā sūkara-yonim vā cāṇḍāla-yoniṁ vā

When those who had done good acts return, they obtain a pleasant birth as brāhmaṇa, kṣatriya or vaiśya. When those who have done bad acts return they will obtain inferior birth as dogs, pigs or *cāṇḍalas.* Chāndogya Upaniṣad 5.10.7

Ramaṇīya-caraṇā means persons having good acts, having pious acts which, after enjoying some, have a remainder which is ready to bear fruit. *Abhyāsa* means a person who arrives, from the root as with *abhi* and ā prefixed and *kvip* suffix. The word *ha* means "clearly." *yat* means *yadā* (when). *tadā* should be supplied. Smṛti says *iha punar bhave te ubhaya-śeṣābhyāṁ niviśanti:* they enter into this world with remainders of good and bad karmas. (SB 5.26.37) Therefore the words *yāvat sampātam* mean he stays on Svarga until exhaustion of karmas for particular acts which allowed the person to enjoy heavenly results.

The particular method of descent is described.

Sūtra - 3.1.9

|| yathetam anevaṁ ca ||

The descent of the jīva is partly the same as the ascent and partly different.

Descending from the moon, the jīva, with his karmas, proceeds on the path by which he came (*yathā itam*) and also differently *(an-evam).* In descending, the jīva goes by smoke and ether, as that is mentioned in the text. This is the same path as the ascent. However the descent does not mention night etc. which are on the path of ascent, and mentions rain and other items, not on the path of ascent. Thus the path is not identical *(anevam*).

Sūtra - 3.1.10

|| caraṇād iti cen na tad-upalakṣaṇārtheti kārṣṇājiniḥ ||

If one objects to the jīva returning with remaining karma because the meaning of *caraṇa* is not "remaining karmas" but "good conduct," the answer is no, because the meaning of the word is figurative and Kāṛṣṇājini agrees.

"It is not correct to say that the jīva attains birth because of remaining karma on falling from Svarga. Since the word *caraṇā* means conduct, it cannot mean "remaining karma." The meaning of the words is different, as in Bṛhad-āraṇyaka Upaniṣad. *yathākārī yathācārī tathā bhavati:* as one acts according to scripture and as one conducts (*ācārī*) oneself in general, one takes birth."

Though *anuśaya* means "remaining karma" and *caraṇa* means "conduct" it is not a fault to equate the two because the passage mentioning *caraṇa* represents remaining karma according to the sage Kārṣṇājini, since it is well known in the scriptures that actions are the cause of all things.

Sūtra - 3.1.11

|| ānarthakyam iti cen na tad-apekṣatvāt ||

If one argues that if acts determines all results, then good conduct would be useless, the answer is no, because action is dependent on conduct.

"If actions are the cause of everything, then good conduct is useless and scriptural injunctions are useless (*ānarthakyam*)." That is not so. Why? Because even those acts depend on conduct (*tad-apekṣatvāt*). A person devoid of good conduct is not qualified for sacrificial acts. Smṛti says *sandhyā-hīno'śucir nityam anarhaḥ sarva-karmasu*: a person who does not perform *sandhyā* rites daily is impure and is unqualified for all acts enjoined in scripture. Because only actions performed by a person of good conduct bear good fruit, good conduct (*caraṇa)* represents (*upalakṣaṇa*) in this case actions (which lead to Svarga), according to Kārṣṇājini.

Sūtra - 3.1.12

|| sukṛta-duṣkṛte eveti tu bādariḥ ||

According to Bādari, *caraṇa* means both good and bad deeds.

The word *tu* indicates a refutation of Kārṣṇājini's opinion. According to Bādari, *caraṇa* means good *and* bad deeds. *puṇyam karma ācarati* means "He does a pious act." The words karma and *caraṇa (ācarati)* are used in the same sentence with a similar meaning. If it is possible to take the direct meaning, secondary meaning *(upalakṣaṇa*) should be avoided. *Caraṇa, anuṣṭhānam* and *karma* means the same thing. *Ācāra* or behavior is a particular type of action. Their difference is like that of Kurus and Pāṇḍavas (Pāṇḍavas are a particular group of Kurus). The word *eva* indicates that this is the author's opinion. Because the word *caraṇa* denotes a particular action (ie. good conduct as opposed to sacrifices), the meaning is that the jīva endowed with its remainder of karmas, descends to earth.

It was said that the jīva goes to the moon after doing sacrifices and then returns with his remaining karmas. Now the ascent and descent of the person who does not do such sacrifices, the sinful person, is examined.

asūryā nāma te lokā andhena tamasāvṛtāḥ
tāṁs te pretyābhigacchantihe ke cātma-hano janāh

The planets attained by the demons are certainly covered with deep darkness. Those who kill themselves by wasting their lives in worldly pursuits enter those planets after death. Īśopaniṣad 3

Do these sinful people go to the moon or Yama's abode?

The *pūrvapakṣa* is the next sūtra.

Sūtra - 3.1.13

|| aniṣṭādi-kāriṇām api ca śrutam ||

Śruti says that even the sinful go to the moon.

One can go to the moon by sacrifices and even by not performing those acts, for it is said *ye vai ke cāsmāl lokāt prayanti candramasam eva te sarve gacchanti*: those who go from this world all go to the moon. (Kauṣītaki Upaniṣad 1.2) Since this passage says that all people go without distinction, those who do not perform sacrifice also go. Thus the words of the Īśopaniṣad are meant to make a person desist from bad actions. "Then the pious and sinful would get the same results." That is not so. The sinful go there but cannot enjoy.

Topic 3 (Sūtras 14 - 22)

Saṁyamanādhikaraṇam - Abode of Yama

The conclusion is given.

Sūtra - 3.1.14

|| saṁyamane tv anubhūyetareṣām ārohāvarohau tad-gati-darśanāt ||

The sinful go to Yama's abode and experience suffering. That is their coming and going, since it is described in scripture.

The word *tu* refutes the *pūrva-pakṣa*. The others (*itareṣām*), those who do sinful acts, go to the abode of Yama (*saṁyamane).* Experiencing (*anubhūya*) the punishment of Yama they again come here. Their ascent and descent (*teṣām ārohāvarohau*) is in this manner. Why? Because their going is described in scripture (*tad-gati-darśanāt*).

na samparāyaḥ pratibhāti bālaṁ
pramādyantaṁ vitta-mohena mūḍham
ayam loko nāsti para iti mānī
punaḥ punar vaśam āpadyate me

Thoughts of the other world do not appear to the childish person inattentive and intoxicated with illusions of wealth. Thinking "There is nothing beyond this world" he repeatedly falls under my control. Kaṭha Upaniṣad 1.2.6

Sūtra - 3.1.15

|| smaranti ca ||

Smṛtis confirm this.

tatra tatra patan chrānto mūrchitaḥ punar utthitaḥ
pathā pāpīyasā nītas tarasā yama-sādanam

Falling down here and there with fatigue, fainting and being pulled up repeatedly, he is quickly brought along the path of sinners to the abode of Yama. SB 3.30.23

sarve caite vaśaṁ yānti yamasya bhagavan: O Lord, all these come under the control of Yama. (Viṣṇu Purāṇa 3.7.4) Thus the sages say that the sinful are subject to Yama's punishment.

Sūtra - 3.1.16

|| api sapta ||

The sinful go to seven hells and others also.

In Mahābhārata it is said:

rauravo'tha mahāṁś caiva vahnir vaitaraṇī tathā |
kumbhīpākaḥ iti proktāny anitya-narakāni tu ||

tāmisraś cāndha-tamisro dvau nityau samprakīrtitau |
iti sapta pradhānāni balīyastūttarottaram ||

The temporary hells are *raurava, mahā-raurava, vahni, vaitaraṇī,* and *kumbhīpāka*. The eternal hells are *tāmisra* and *andha-tamisra*. There are the seven principal hells. Those later in the list have more intense pain.

These seven hells are described as the places where the sinful experience the results of their actions. The sinful go to these seven hells (*saptaḥ*). The word *api* means that other hells listed at the end of Bhāgavatam Fifth Canto are included.

"If you accept Yama as the punisher then what happens to the proposition that everything is controlled by the Lord?"

Sūtra - 3.1.17

|| tatrāpi ca tad-vyāpārād avirodhaḥ ||

Yama and others carrying out punishment is not contradictory to the Lord being the supreme controller.

The word *ca* is for emphasis. If Yama and others carry out punishment *(tatrāpi)* this statement does not contradict the actions (*vyāpārāt*) done by the Lord. Yama and others, engaged by the Lord, punish the sinful. This is proven by the Purāṇas.

"The sinful, after being punished by Yama, should ascend to the moon since the śruti says that all go there." This objection is set aside in the next sūtra.

Sūtra - 3.1.18

|| vidyā-karmaṇor iti tu prakṛtatvāt ||

Others cannot go to the moon because the text states that those cultivating knowledge go by the *devayāna* path and only those cultivating sacrifices go by the *pitṛyana* path (to the moon).

The word *tu* sets aside the objection. The word *na* is understood from sūtra 3.1.11. The sinful do not go to the moon. Why? Because it is mentioned that only two types of person doing acts of knowledge and karma go by the *devayāna* and *pitṛyāna* paths. In Chāndogya Upaniṣad 5.10.1, it is said that by knowledge a person attains to the *devayāna* path but those who do karma (acts of sacrifice) attain the *pitṛyana* path. That being the case, the word "all" means all those who are qualified.

"If the sinful do not go to the moon, they will not attain a body on earth, since it is impossible for them to partake of the fifth oblation, which causes birth on earth. The fifth oblation is only possible if one goes to the moon. It is necessary that everyone goes to the moon in order to get a body suitable for earth."

Sūtra - 3.1.19

|| na tṛtīye tathopalabdheḥ ||

Taking birth in the third place (as a low creature) does not require a fifth oblation because of scriptural statements.

Those who go to the third place (*tṛtīye)* do not need the fifth oblation on the moon. Why? Because this is seen in the śruti (*tathā upalabdheḥ*). The meaning is this. In śruti it is said:

athaitayoḥ pathor na katareṇa ca tānīmāni kṣudrāṇy asakṛd avṛttīni bhūtāni jīvanti jāyasva mriyasvety etat tṛtīyaṁ sthānam tenāsau loko na sampūryate

On the other hand those small creatures who do not go by either of these paths live here repeatedly. The third state is indicated by "Be born and die." Therefore that world does not become full. Chāndogya Upaniṣad 5.10.8

The meager creatures such as flies, mosquitoes and other insects repeatedly take birth and die. This is the third place. Those with bodies of insects are people who performed sins. It is called a place because such bodies are related to a place. It is called "third" because previously indicated places were *brahmaloka* and *dyuloka* (Svarga). Thus those feeble creatures who are not qualified for the *devayāna* path by knowledge or the *pitṛyāna* path by sacrifices go on the third path of continual birth as insects etc. Thus heaven never becomes full. Since it is stated that heaven never becomes full, they do not ascend there. The fifth oblation is not necessary for taking a body in the third place.

Sūtra - 3.1.20

|| smaryate'pi ca loke ||

The smṛtis also describe that the fifth oblation is not always necessary in this world.

It is seen in the smṛtis that it is not necessary for persons like Droṇa and Dhṛṣṭadyumna[63] to receive the fifth oblation to get a body in this world. The words *api* ca indicate "as well."

Sūtra - 3.1.21

|| darśanāc ca ||

The fifth oblation is not necessary because various types of birth are seen that rise from water alone.

yeṣāṁ khalv eṣāṁ bhūtānāṁ trīṇy eva bījāni bhavanti |aṇḍajaṁ jīvajam udbhijjam

There are three origins for the living beings: eggs, directly from other beings (wombs) and germination of seeds. Chāndogya Upaniṣad 6.3.1

Since it is mentioned that birth from seeds or perspiration takes place without the oblations, birth does not always depend on the fifth oblation. Thus those who ascend to the moon and descend start their bodies with the fifth oblation. Others take birth without the fifth oblation, by water alone, since this is not denied in scriptures.

"Only three types of birth are mentioned. Birth by perspiration is not mentioned." The next sūtra resolves this issue.

Sūtra - 3.1.22

|| tṛtīya-śabdāvarodhaḥ saṁśokajasya ||

Germination birth includes entities arising from perspiration.

The third type of birth from germination (*udbhijjam*) includes (*avarodhaḥ*) those arising from perspiration (*saṁśokajasya*) since both germinate, one from earth and the other from water. They are denoted differently in the world by taking the difference between non-moving and moving. Thus it is proved that the sinful do not attain the moon.

---

[63] Droṇa was born from semen in a pot, without a mother. Dhṛṣṭadyumna was born from fire.

Topic 4 (Sūtra 23)

Tat-sābhāvyāpatty-adhikaraṇam - Similarity with Ether

It has been shown that a person who performs sacrifices, endowed with subtle elements and residual karmas, descends to earth. The method is as follows.

athaitam evādhvānam punar nivartante yathetam ākāśam ākāśād vāyuḥ bhavati vāyur bhūtvā dhūmo bhavati dhūmo bhūtvā abhraṁ bhavaty abhraṁ bhūtvā megho bhavati megho bhūtvā pravarṣati

They return by the same path and become ether. From ether they become air. Having become air, they become smoke. Having become smoke, they become mist. Having become mist, they become clouds. Having become clouds, they shower down. Chāndogya Upaniṣad 5.10.5

The word *yathetam* means that the path is also different (*anevan*) from the ascent. In descending it appears that the jīva becomes ether and other things. Does this mean the jīva becomes ether or just becomes like ether?

(Pūrvapakṣa) The jīva becomes ether and other things because, taking the meaning as similarity only, one would have to take an indirect meaning (*lakṣaṇā*) whereas direct meaning is preferable.

Sūtra - 3.1.23

|| tat-sābhāvyāpattir upapatteḥ ||

The passage means that the jīva attains similarity with ether because of logical reasons.

The passage indicates similarity only *(tat-sābhavyāpattiḥ)*. Why? Because of reasons (*upapattteḥ*). The body of water attained on the moon planet for enjoyment melts with destruction of enjoyment and the sudden fire of grief, like ice in the harsh rays of the sun, and becomes subtle like ether. Then it falls under control of air, then mixes with smoke etc. since one substance like a jīva cannot become a different one like ether, and since it would be impossible to descend to earth as ether.

Topic 5 (Sūtra 24)

Nāticcireṇādhikaraṇam - Quick Descent

Does the jīva descend slowly from ether to rain or quickly.

(Pūrvapakṣa) It descends slowly since there is no restricting reason to do otherwise.

Sūtra - 3.1.24

|| nāticireṇa viśeṣāt ||

The jīva passes the stages quickly, because of details in the description.

The jīva descends quickly (*na aticireṇa*). Why? Because of descriptions (*viśeṣāt*). After descending to rain, the jīva enters grains and finds it difficult to be released from that state. *ato vai khalu durniṣprapataram*: the jīva finds it difficult to come out of the grains (*durniṣprapataram*). Since coming out of the grains is difficult, it should be inferred that passing through ether and other states is quick. *durniṣprapataram* instead of *durniṣprapatataram* is poetic license.

Topic 6 (Sūtras 25 - 28)

Anyādhiṣṭhitādhikaraṇam - Becoming Plants

After rain it is said *ta iha vrīhi-yavā auṣadhi-vanaspatayas tila-māṣā jāyante*: the jīvas are born as rice, barley, herbs, trees, sesame and beans. (Chāndogya Upaniṣad 5.10.6)

The doubt is this. Do the jīvas with residual karmas actually take birth as plants or merely contact the plants?

(Pūrvapakṣa) The jīvas are born as plants because the phrase "they are born" is used.

Sūtra - 3.1.25

|| anyādhiṣṭhite pūrvavad abhilāpāt ||

The jīvas do not become plants, since other jīvas are in those bodies as their karma. They merely contact the plants just as previously they contacted ether and rain, and attaining such a body by karma is described using other words.

The jīvas only contact the plants, since other jīvas inhabit these bodies as enjoyers. These jīvas do not appear there for enjoying those plant bodies.

Why? Because of what was previously stated (*pūrvavat):* just as the jīvas become like ether, they become like plants. When the jīvas pass through ether until rain, it is not described as karma for enjoying there. Similarly when they enter plant life it is not described as karma for enjoyment. When such enjoyment is permitted, it is described (*abhilāpāt*) with words like "pleasant karmas (*ramaṇīya-caraṇā*)." Therefore the jīva simply contacts the plants but is not born as those plants.

Sūtra - 3.1.26

|| aśuddham iti cen na śabdāt ||

If one argues that the jīva has some bad karma to experience by being born as a plant because of violence in the sacrifice, it is not so, because Vedic statements allow that violence.

"It is not correct to say that the jīvas only contact the plants without a purpose of enjoying karma, by saying that there is another jīva in the plant by karma and the jīva has no karma for enjoying there. There is karma to cause this. There is some impurity in the sacrifices for going to Svarga since the sacrifices are mixed with violence to animals. Violence is a sin since there is the prohibition *mā hiṁsyāt sarva-bhūtāni*: do not harm any living being.[64] The pious portion gives Svarga and the sinful part gives birth as plants. *śarīra-jaiḥ karma-doṣair yāti sthāvaratāṁ naraḥ*: man becomes a plant by bad karma committed in the human body.[65] (Manu-saṁḥitā 12.9) Thus, the jīva actually takes birth as rice or barley."

This is not so. Why? Because of Vedic statements such as *agniṣomīyaṁ paśum ālabheta*: one should sacrifice an animal sacred to Agni and Soma. There is a general rule (*utsarga*) of non-violence which must be accepted because only through the Vedas do we understand dharma and adharma. But the animal killed during sacrifice is an exception (*apavāda*). There can be no objection at all to animal sacrifice because of the differing scopes of the general rule and exceptional rule. Therefore "birth" simply means contact with the plants.

---

[64] *Ahiṁsan sarva-bhūtāni* is found in the *Chāndogya Upaniṣad*, 8.15.

[65] By verbal sin he becomes an animal and by mental sin he becomes a low class human.

What happens later is described.

Sūtra - 3.1.27

|| retaḥ sig-yogo'tha ||

Then the jīva contacts a man who impregnates a woman.

After entering the rice or other plant, the jīva with residual karmas joins with a man who impregnates a woman. That is stated in the same Upaniṣad. *yo yo 'nnam atti yo retaḥ siñcati tad bhūya eva bhavati:* the jīva, becoming the person who eats the food and semen which impregnates, is born. (Chāndogya Upaniṣad 5.10.6) The jīva does not literally become the impregnator since it is impossible for one form to change into another's form, and since then it would not be possible to take another body. Therefore, "becoming the impregnator" means that the jīva contacts the impregnator. This being so, it is also the same as the previous state in rice and barley, since there is no cause for taking such a birth.

Sūtra - 3.1.28

|| yoneḥ śarīram ||

Entering a womb, the jīva accepts a body.

Yoneḥ means "entering a womb" though it is in the ablative case. The verb should be supplied. From the body of the father, the jīva enters the womb of the mother (*yoneḥ*) and attains a body *(śarīram*) to enjoy residual karmas, for it was said *tad ya iha ramaṇīya-caraṇāḥ:* the jīva with good karmas attains a good birth. (Chāndogya Upaniṣad 5.10.7) Thus it has been proved that the jīva attains the plant form just as it attains the ether.

It is implied here that the intelligent person will meditate upon the Lord filled with bliss while renouncing this world filled with misery.

Section Two

vittir viraktiś ca kṛtāṇjaliḥ puro
yasyāḥ parānanda-tanor vitiṣṭhate
siddhiś ca sevā-samayaṁ pratīkṣate
bhaktiḥ pareśasya punātu sā jagat

May the Supreme Lord's bhakti, which is endowed with a body of the highest bliss, in front of whom wealth, detachment stand with folded hands, and *siddhis* wait for service, purify the world.

Topic 1 (Sūtras 1 - 3)

Sandhy-adhikaraṇam - Dream Objects

In the second pāda, bhakti, which is the cause of attraction to the Lord, is described. In order to qualify a person for bhakti towards the object to be attained, namely Brahman, the Lord's various qualities are described: the greatness of his form while acting as the creator of dreams, the oneness of his *avatāras* with him, his form, the difference between the Lord and the devotee, his dwelling within as *antaryāmī,* his nature of being attained only by bhakti, his appearing as both *dharmī* and *dharma* by *viśeṣa*, his possession of the highest bliss, his manifestation according to the *bhāva* of the devotee, his superiority to all, and his acting as the benefactor of all.

The person desiring bhakti begins bhakti when he understands these qualities and not otherwise.

First, the Lord's agency in creating dreams is discussed. If someone else caused dreams, Brahman's nature as the supreme agent would be contradicted. Bhakti will not arise if the Lord is a partial creator. Therefore, by being the creator of dreams, the Lord's glory is shown.

In Bṛhad-āraṇyaka Upaniṣad 4.3.10 it is said:

na tatra rathā na ratha-yogā na panthāno bhavanty atha rathān ratha-yogān pathaḥ sṛjate. na tatrānandā mudaḥ pramudo bhavanty athānandān mudaḥ pramudaḥ sṛjate. na tatra

veśantāḥ puṣkariṇyaḥ sravantyaḥ sṛjate sa hi kartā

In that place, there are no chariots, no horses, and no roads. He creates the chariots, horses and roads. In that place, there are no bliss, no pleasures, and no joy. He creates bliss, pleasure and joy there. In that place there are no tanks, lotus pool or rivers. He creates them.

The doubt is this. Is the creator of dream objects the jīva or the Lord?

(pūrvapakṣa) The jīva is the agent because Prajāpati says that the jīva has the power to create according to his will (*satya-saṅkalpatva*).

Sūtra - 3.2.1

|| sandhye sṛṣṭir āha hi ||

The Lord creates objects in dreams because that is stated in the text.

Sandhya means dream for it is said *sandhyaṁ tṛtīyaṁ svapna-sthānam*: the third state is the place of dreams. (Bṛhad-āraṇyaka Upaniṣad 4.3.9) and as well the dream state is the mid-point (*sandhya*) between waking and deep sleep. The creation (*sṛṣṭiḥ*) of chariots and other objects in dreams (*sandhye*) is done by the Paramātmā. Why? Because (*hi*) it is said he is the creator in the śruti quoted. *sa hi kartā*: he is the creator. The meaning is this. Paramātmā creates temporary objects like chariots which are experienced by a human dreamer in order that the person enjoys results due to small karmas. Therefore the Lord is creator of dreams. It is only possible that he, endowed with inconceivable *śakti* to create whatever he wills, can be the creator of dreams. Another text also says this.

svapnāntaram jāgaritāntam cobhau yenānupaśyati
mahāntaṁ vibhum ātmānam matvā dhīro na śocati

Thinking of the great pervading Lord by whom one sees within dreams and in waking state, the wise man does not lament. Kaṭha Upaniṣad 2.1.4

The jīva attains the power of *satya-saṅkalpa* at liberation. Thus the normal jīva cannot create dreams.

Sūtra - 3.2.2

|| nirmātāraṁ caike putrādayaś ca ||

The Lord is the creator of dream objects because the Kaṭhas say that the Lord is the creator of dream objects such as sons.

And because one group *(eke)*, the Kaṭhas, say that Paramātmā is the creator (*nirmātāram*) of all desires of the dreamers. *ya eṣu supteṣu jāgarti kāmaṁ*

kāmaṁ puruṣo nirmimāṇa: the Lord creates the desires while sleeping and in waking state. (Kaṭha Upaniṣad 5.8) These "desires (*kāma*)" are the dream objects such as sons within the jīvas, not just desires, for the word *kāma* is used to indicate dream objects in the following passage. *sarvān kāmān chandataḥ prārthayasva śatāyuṣaḥ putra-pautrān vṛṇīṣva:* ask for whatever you want (*kāmān*); choose a hundred sons and grandsons. (Kaṭha Upaniṣad 1.1.23) In smṛti it is said *etasmād eva putro jāyate. etasmād bhrātā. etasmād bhāryā yad enaṁ svapnenābhihanti:* from the Lord arises the son, the brother, the wife when he overpowers the jīva with sleep. (Gaupavana-śruti) Smṛtis also confirm this conclusion.

The cause of the Lord being the creator of dream objects is described.

Sūtra - 3.2.3

|| māyā-mātraṁ tu kārtsnyenānabhivyakta-svarūpatvāt ||

The cause is the Lord's *māyā* because the dreams by nature are not revealed to everyone.

Inconceivable *māyā* is the cause of objects created in dreams. It is not five elements mixed with each other and it is not Brahmā. Why? Because the dreams do not become manifest (*anabhivyakta*) to all (*kārtsneyena)* who are capable of perceiving them. Thus it is proved that the Paramātmā is the creator of objects in dreams.

Topic 2 (Sūtras 4 - 5)

Svapnādhikaraṇam - Reality of Dreams

Are the dream objects real or false?

(Pūrva-pakṣa) They are false because they are negated on waking.

Sūtra - 3.2.4

|| sūcakaś ca hi śruter ācakṣate ca tad-vidaḥ ||

Because the dream objects indicate future results, because śruti describes the truth of dreams and because knowers of dreams predict results, dream objects are real.

Because (*hi*) the dream object indicates (*sūcakaḥ*) things auspicious or inauspicious or indicates a mantra, the creations in dreams are real. How is that indicated? That is indicated in śruti (*śruteḥ*).

yadā karmasu kāmyeṣu striyaṁ svapne 'bhipaśyati
samṛddhiṁ tatra jānīyāt tasmin svapna-nidarśane

If, when performing *kāmya-karmas*, one sees a woman in a dream, he should know that the rites were successful. Chāndogya Upaniṣad 5.2.9

atha svapne puruṣaṁ kṛṣṇaṁ kṛṣṇa-dantaṁ paśyati sa enaṁ hanti

If in a dream one sees a black man with black teeth, that man will kill him. Kauṣītaki-brāhmaṇa

Those who know dreams (*tad-vidaḥ*) say (*ācakṣate)* that the dream indicates good or bad results. Riding on an elephant indicates something auspicious will happen and riding on a donkey indicates something inauspicious. In smṛti it is described how one can obtain a mantra in a dream:

ādiṣṭavān yathā svapne rāma-rakṣām imāṁ haraḥ
tathā likhitavān prātaḥ prabuddho buddha-kauśikaḥ

Buddha-kauśika on waking in the morning wrote out the mantra called Rāma-rakṣā that

Śiva taught him in a dream. Rāma-kavaca

It is proven that dreams often predict future events truthfully and reveal mantras or medicines. And one hears of persons being killed by persons previously seen in their dreams (indicating that a real person was seen in a dream). Thus dream objects are real like objects in the waking state.

The author responds to the objection that dreams are sublated by waking experience.

Sūtra - 3.2.5

| | parābhidhyānāt tu tirohitaṁ tato hy asya bandha-viparyayau | |

Dreams disappear by the will of the Lord. This is not surprising since he is also the cause of bondage and liberation.

The dream objects disappear (*tirohitam*) by the will (*abhidyānāt*) of the Lord *(para).* They are not negated as in the case of mistaking shell for silver. This is because (*hi*) bondage and liberation (*bandha-viparyayau)* of the jīva *(asya)*

arise from the Lord *(tataḥ)*. *saṁsāra-mokṣa-sthiti-bandha-hetuḥ:* the Lord is the cause of bondage, subsistence and release in this world. (Śvetāśvatara Upaniṣad 6.16) The meaning of the sūtra is "It is not surprising that he how is the cause of bondage and liberation can remove dreams." One should understand that appearance and disappearance of the dream is caused by the Lord.

svapnādi-buddhi-kartā ca tiraskartā sa eva tu
tad-icchayā yato hy asya bandha-mokṣau pratiṣñhitau

The Lord alone is the creator and destroyer of perception of dreams since by his will the jīva attains bondage and liberation. Kūrma Purāṇa

Thus the objects of dreams are real and produced by the Lord.

Topic 3 (Sūtra 6)

Deha-yogādhikaraṇam - The waking state

The Lord is the cause of the waking state. In Kaṭha Upaniṣad 2.1.4 it is said:

svapnāntaṁ jāgaritāntaṁ cobhau yenānupaśyati
mahāntam vibhum ātmānaṁ matvā dhīro na śocati

Thinking of the great pervading ātmā by whom one sees within dreams and in waking state, the wise man does not lament. Kaṭha Upaniṣad 2.1.4

The doubt is this. Is the cause of the jīva waking in this verse the Lord (called *ātmā* here)?

(Pūrvapakṣa) It is not the Lord since we see that the waking state is dependent on time and other factors.

Sūtra - 3.2.6

| | deha-yogād vā so'pi | |

And the Lord alone is the cause of the waking state with its bodily connection.

And the waking state, by connection with the body (*deha-yogāt*) is caused by the supreme Lord alone *(so'pi)* because of the very verse quoted and because time is insentient. The word *api* indicates that the Lord is the agent during deep sleep and fainting conditions also, since it is said that the Lord is agent of all activities of the jīva.

Topic 4 (Sūtras 7 - 8)

Tad-abhāvādhikaraṇam - Deep sleep

Now the location of deep sleep is considered. Here are the śruti texts dealing with deep sleep. *āsu tadā nāḍīṣu supto bhavati*: the jīva then enters the *nāḍis.* (Chāndogya Upaniṣad 8.6.3) *tābhiḥ praty avasṛpya purī-tati śete:* entering by the membranes of the heart, the jīva sleeps near the heart. (Bṛhad-āraṇyaka Upaniṣad 2.1.19) *ya eṣo 'ntar hṛdaya ākāśas tasmin śete:* the jīva sleeps in the ether within the heart. (Bṛhad-āraṇyaka Upaniṣad 2.1.17) There are other texts also describing this. The word ether means Brahman. Thus the jīva rests in the *nāḍis*, or in the place near the heart (*purī-tat*) or in Brahman. Does the jīva sleep in any of the three places as options, or does he sleep in all three places?

(Pūrvapakṣa) There is an option of any of the three, since, in statements of equal strength when there is no dependence of one on another, there is choice. This is according to the logic *tulyārathas tu vikalperan*: where statements are of equal force, it indicates option.

Sūtra - 3.2.7

|| tad-abhāvo nāḍīṣu tac-chruter ātmani ca ||

The jīva's place of deep sleep is in the *nāḍis,* in the pericardium and in Brahman because of the śruti statement.

The word *ca* indicates that the jīva sleeps not only in the *nāḍis* but near the heart as well. The state of deep sleep with absence of waking and dreaming (*tad-abhāvaḥ*) takes place in the *nāḍis (nāḍiṣu)* and near the heart (*ca*) and in Brahman *(ātmani).* Why? Because it is stated in śruti (*tat-śruteḥ*) that the jīva sleeps in all three places. To make the places optional would refute the scriptural texts. The *nāḍis* and *prāṇa (*Paramātmā) are seen together during deep sleep.

tāsu tadā bhavati. yadā suptaḥ svapnaṁ na kaṇcana paśyaty athāsmin prāṇa evaikadhā bhavati

The jīva enters the *nāḍis.* When in deep sleep he does not see dreams. The jīva becomes one with the *prāṇa (*Paramātmā). Kauṣītaki Upaniṣad

The choice because of the logical principle does not apply because there is no equality in the statements. It is similar to the statement "Entering by the door, he sleeps in the place on a bed."Thus the jīva entering by the *nādīs,* sleeps on Brahman in the covering that surroundings the heart (*purītat*). Thus the three are taken collectively and Brahman is directly the place where the jīva resides during deep sleep. The *purītat* is the covering that surrounds the heart or pericardium.

Sūtra - 3.2.8

|| ataḥ prabodho'smāt ||

There, the jīva awakens from Brahman.

Since Brahman is the place of deep sleep for the jīva, the jīva awakens from deep sleep from Brahman (*asmāt*) through the gates of the *nādīs.* This is described in Chāndogya Upaniṣad. *satas cāgatya na viduḥ sata āgacchamahe:* coming from Brahman, we do not know that we came from Brahman. (Chāndogya Upaniṣad 6.10.2) If there were options then the text would say the jīva comes sometimes from the *nāḍis,* sometimes from the pericardium and sometimes from Brahman. But the text does not say that. Therefore Brahman is ultimately the resting place of the jīva during deep sleep.

Topic 5 (Sūtra 9)

karmānusmṛti-śabda-vidhy-adhikaraṇam - Karma, memory, scripture and injunctions

It was said that the jīva coming from Brahman does not know that it came from Brahman. There is another consideration in this statement. The doubt is this. Does the sleeping jīva arise from Brahman or does another jīva arise in its place?

(Pūrvapakṣa) Since it is impossible for the jīva associated with Brahman to have connection with the previous body, another jīva must arise.

Sūtra - 3.2.9

|| sa eva tu karmānusmṛti-śabda-vidhibhyaḥ ||

The same jīva awakens because he must resume unfinished karmas, because he remembers his previous identity, because scriptures testify this and because there are injunctions for liberation which would not be necessary if everyone who went to sleep got liberated.

The word *tu* refutes the doubt. The sleeping jīva arises and no one else. Why? Because the jīva must complete the remaining karmas started before deep sleep. Furthermore the jīva recollects himself (*anumsṛti*), thinking, "I who slept have woken up." Furthermore there are śruti statements (*śabda*) such as *iha vyāghro vā siṁho vā vṛko vā varāho vā kīṭo vā pataṅgo vā daṁśo vā maśako vā yad yad bhavanti tadā bhavanti*: whatever tiger, lion, wolf, pig, worm, insect, gnat or mosquito is here becomes that again. (Chāndogya Upaniṣad 6.10.2) Whatever bodies the jīvas had before sleep, the same jīvas attain those bodies again on waking. And furthermore there are injunctions *(vidhi)* like the following concerning liberation. *ātmānaṁ eva lokam upāsīta*: he must worship the Lord alone along with his abode. (Bṛhad-āraṇyaka Upaniṣad 1.4.15) If a different jīva appeared after sleep it would mean that the previous jīva, on going into deep sleep, had attained liberation (without worshipping the Lord in most cases).

The meaning is this. Just as a jar full of salt water with a covering on its mouth is thrown in the Gaṅgā and then pulled out, so the jīva covered by his impressions after attaining Brahman as a resting place during deep sleep, with suspension of sense activity, then rises again to enjoy. The jīva does not attain liberation which is devoid of impressions. This is because he still has karma.

Topic 6 (Sūtra 10)

Mugdhādhikaraṇam - State of Fainting

A related item is now considered. Does the jīva completely attain Brahman or partly attain Brahman when he faints?

(Pūrvapakṣa) The jīva completely attains Brahman because fainting is a type of sleep.

Sūtra - 3.2.10

|| mugdhe'rdha-sampattiḥ pariśeṣāt ||

In the state of fainting, the jīva only partially attains Brahman, because there is a trace of awareness in this state.

When in a fainting state (*mugdhe*), he partially attains Brahman. Why? He does not completely attain Brahman as in deep sleep because of some awareness-- pain (*pariśeṣāt*). Because he does not see objects he also is *not* in a state of non-attainment of Brahman as in the waking state. But because of some awareness he half attains Brahman.

hṛdaya-sthāt parāj jīvo dūrastho jāgrad eṣyati |
samīpasthas tathā svapnaṁ svapity asmin layaṁ vrajan |
ata evaṁ trayo'vasthā mohas tu pāriśeṣataḥ |
ardha-prāptir iti jñeyo dṛśsarva-mātraṁ prati smṛteḥ ||

When the jīva is distant from the Lord situated in the heart, he is in the waking state. When he is near the Lord, he dreams. When he is in deep sleep, he merges with the Lord. These are the three states. Fainting is half attainment of the Lord, because of a remainder of awareness, because of recollection of pain on recovery. Varāha Purāṇa

The jīva being situated far means being situated in the eye. Being situated nearby means being situated in the throat.

"Three states of the jīva situated in a body have been described: waking, dream and deep sleep. One does not see any other state. Therefore there is no separate state called fainting. It is included in one of the three states."

That is not so because it is a different state. It is not waking state because one does not perceive objects using the senses. It is not a dream state, because the person is unconscious. It is not deep sleep because the fainting person lacks a joyful face and the complete immobility of limbs seen in deep sleep. It is a separate state, which inferred because of the trace of awareness. This is well known in the world and in medicine.

The intention of this section is to show that the Lord alone is worthy of service, since he has greatness, being the agent of waking, sleeping and deep sleep.

Topic 7 (Sūtras 11 - 13)

Ubhaya-liṅgādhikaraṇam - Non-difference of the Lord's forms

The greatness of the Lord was shown by his controlling power over everything. Now, the author shows the Lord's possession of an inconceivable form which is such that, though it appears as many, does not give up it oneness with himself. Though the Lord's quality of having many avatāras was shown in 2.3.44 (*prakāśādivan naivaṁ paraḥ*), the perception of difference when the Lord simultaneously appears as many was not resolved. This is resolved here by showing his inconceivable nature. Śruti says *eko'pi san bahudhā yo'vabhāti*: though one he appears as many. (Gopāla-tāpanī Upaniṣad)

The doubt is this. Are the various forms of the Lord which are situated in various places different from each other or not?

(Pūrvapakṣa) They are different because the forms are situated in different places. Objects with the quality of being in different places cannot be the same object. The text stating that the Lord is one but many is only a general statement. Since the objects are different, this means that there are many Lords. This being so, because there are many objects, bhakti to one Lord is impossible.

Sūtra - 3.2.11

|| na sthānato'pi parasyobhaya-liṅgaṁ sarvatra hi ||

There are not different forms though they are in different places, because the Lord can be everywhere by his inconceivable power.

The Lord (*parasya)* does not have two forms (*ubhaya-liṅgam*) even though he is in different places (*sthānato' pi*). Though the places are different, the person located there is not different since (*hi*) the one form can appear simultaneously everywhere *(sarvatra)* because of his inconceivable power. That is what is stated in the quotation from Gopāla-tāpanī Upaniṣad. The places which are the shelter of the Lord's appearances become the places of his pastimes and are called Saṁvyoma. There are also many types of devotees. One form (*svarūpa*) appears in all these places, to many types of devotees.

Sūtra - 3.2.12

|| na bhedād iti cen na pratyekam atad-vacanāt ||

If you say the explanation is not logical because the forms are actually different, it is not so, because śruti states that all the forms are not different from the Lord.

"What was just said is illogical (*na*) because if one form appear in many forms essentially it means that the Lord is different in these forms (*bhedāt*)." That is not so. Why? Because śruti says that they are not different (*pratyekam atad-vacanāt*).

indro māyābhiḥ puru-rūpaḥ īyate yuktā hy asya harayaḥ śatādaśety ayaṁ vai harayo'yaṁ vai daśa ca sahasrāṇi ca bahūni cānantāni ca tad etad brahmāpūrvam anaparam anataram abāhyam ayam ātmā brahma sarvānubhūtir ity anuśāsanam

The Lord appears as many by his *śaktis.* He has a thousand forms, then thousand forms, many, unlimited forms. This Brahman is without compare, without difference, without exterior, spread everywhere, omniscient. This is the instruction. Bṛhad-āraṇyaka Upaniṣad 2.5.19

Sūtra - 3.2.13

// api caivam eke //

Moreover, one group of Vedic scholars teaches this.

Api ca means moreover. One branch (*eke*) say *amātro 'nanta-mātraś ca*: the Lord though devoid of difference has infinite forms of himself. (Māṇḍūkya-kārikā 29) They teach that though the Lord has infinite forms those forms are one. *Amātraḥ* means devoid of difference from himself. *Ananta-mātra* means unlimited forms of himself. Smṛti also describes this:

eka eva paro viṣṇuḥ sarvatrāpi na saṁśayaḥ /
aiśvaryād rūpam ekaṁ ca sūryavad bahudheyate //

The one supreme Viṣṇu is everywhere without doubt. By his power, the one form becomes many like the sun. Matsya Purāṇa

The meaning is this. The Lord is like the *vaidūrya* gem. Though one, the gem appears as many forms because of different viewers. The Lord is also like an actor. Though he displays many bhāvas or emotions in himself, he does not give up his oneness in himself though he appears to be many. Thus, though the Lord appears to be many because of difference in his resulting forms and differences in the emotions of the meditators, he does not give up his one form in himself.

maṇir yathā vibhāgena nīla-pītādibhir yutaḥ |
rūpa-bhedam avāpnoti dhyāna-bhedāt tathācyutaḥ ||

Just as a gem is endowed with blue, yellow and other colors in different parts, the Lord takes different forms because of different meditations. Viṣṇu-tantra

yat tad vapur bhāti vibhūṣaṇāyudhair
avyakta-cid-vyaktam adhārayad dhariḥ
babhūva tenaiva sa vāmano vaṭuḥ
sampaśyator divya-gatir yathā naṭaḥ

The Lord, whose body is eternally endowed with ornaments and weapons and is invisible to the world and who has a spiritual form, became visible. Then, in the presence of his parents, to please them, the Lord, like an actor whose actions are hard to understand, became Vāmana, a brāhmaṇa-dwarf, a *brahmacārī.* SB 8.18.12

The gem is the *vaidūrya. nataḥ* is an actor. Thus though the Lord is one, because of his inconceivable energy, he appears as many simultaneously, with forms that have contrary qualities. This is a good quality, since he becomes the particular object in differing minds in his devotees. This produces bhakti to the one supreme Lord endowed with inconceivable energy.

Topic 8 (Sūtras 14 - 17)

Arūpavad-adhikaraṇam - Non-possession of form

Now the form of the Lord as himself is established. "If his form is different from himself, with himself becoming secondary to the form, bhakti would take on a secondary nature." This is not so, because the devotee experiences bhakti as a primary element. The following are found in the Atharva-śiras. *sac-cid-ānanda-rūpāya kṛṣṇāyākliṣṭa-kāriṇe*: I offer respects to Kṛṣṇa, the form of eternity, knowledge and bliss, who performs actions without fatigue. (Gopāla-tāpanī 1.1) *tam ekaṁ govindaṁ sac-cid-ānanda-vigraham* : I satisfy that on Govinda with a form of eternity, knowledge and bliss. (Gopāla-tāpanī 1.29)

Does Brahman possess a form or not? This is the doubt.

(Pūrvapakṣa) He possesses a form because of designations like *viṣṇor mūrti* (form of Viṣṇu) and because the *bahuvrīhi* compound means "he who possesses a form of eternity knowledge and bliss."

Sūtra - 3.2.14

|| arūpavad eva hi tat-pradhānatvāt ||

The Lord does not possess a form since his form is his very self.

Brahman is not endowed with a form (*arūpavat*) or *vigraha*. The word *eva* indicates refutation of the opposing logic. Why? Because his form is himself (*tat-pradhānatvāt*). That form is itself the possessor of qualities like all-pervasion, knowing, and acting as the *antaryāmī.*

"By meditating on the entity Paramātmā who is knowledge and bliss, its opposite, *prakṛti*, with insentience and pain, should disappear. How can the author say that this Brahman who is knowledge and bliss accepts a form (which implies impermanence and suffering)?"

Sūtra - 3.2.15

|| prakāśavac cāvaiyarthyāt ||

The form of Brahman is not useless, as in the case of the sun.

The word *ca* indicates refutation of the doubt. *Prakāśavat* means "in being like the sun." Just as it is not useless for the sun to have a form though it is a single entity of light, so one can think of Brahman with a form for purpose of meditation, though it is actually pure knowledge and bliss. Otherwise meditation could not take place. *dhyāyati kāntaṁ virahiṇī*: the women in separation meditates on her lover. It is seen that meditation has a form as its object.

There is proof that one does not imagine a false form for that meditation.

Sūtra - 3.2.15

|| āha ca tan-mātram ||

And the scriptures say that the form is the Lord.

The word *mātra* indicates limitation (only). The scriptures say *(āha)* that the form *(tat)* is Paramātmā only *(mātram)*. That form is a proven fact. It is said:

sat-puṇḍarīka-nayanaṁ meghābhaṁ vaidyutāmbaram |
dvi-bhujaṁ jñāna-mudrāḍhyaṁ vana-mālinam īśvaram ||
... mukto bhavati saṁsṛteḥ

Meditating with concentration of two-armed lotus-eyed silent Kṛṣṇa, having the complexion of a cloud, with cloth flashing like lightning, wearing a garland, one becomes liberated from *samsāra.* Gopāla-tāpanī Upaniṣad 1.9

That form with qualities like having lotus eyes is identical with the Lord. Smṛti says *deha-dehi-bhidā caiva neśvare vidyate kvacit:* there is no difference at all between the Lord's body and himself. (Padma Purāṇa). This quotation means that difference between his body and he who possesses that body does not exist in the Lord. The body *is* the Lord.

Sūtra - 3.2.17

|| darśayati cātho api smaryate ||

Śruti shows the Lord and his form are non-different. Smṛti confirms this.

sākṣāt-prakṛti-paro yo'yam ātmā gopālaḥ kathaṁ tv avatīrṇo bhūmyāṁ hi vai: how has this Gopāla, who is beyond *prakṛti,* made his appearance on earth? (Gopāla-tāpanī Upaniṣad 2.22) Later in the text it is explained that the Lord is his form. The word Gopāla (cowherd) was previously explained in the same work as the chief entity, the Lord of all, dark in complexion, with most attractive face and feet. *gopa-veśam abhrābhaṁ taruṇaṁ kalpa-drumāśritam, sat-puṇḍarīka-nayanam*: the form of Kṛṣṇa wears the dress of a cowherd; he has the complexion of a cloud; he is youthful and sits under a desire tree. (Gopāla-tāpanī 1.8) Smṛtis also confirm that the form of the Lord is his self.

īśvaraḥ paramaḥ kṛṣṇaḥ sac-cid-ānanda-vigrahaḥ |
anādir ādir govindaḥ sarva-kāraṇa-kāraṇam ||

Kṛṣṇa is the supreme controller. He is the enjoyer of innumerable consorts, and the possessor of an eternal form of knowledge and bliss. Though, he is without origin, he is the source of all other forms of God, and is the cause of all causes. He is Govinda, the boy who cares for the cows. Brahma-saṁhitā 5.1

The word *athaḥ* indicates completeness. The last two sūtras indicate that the Lord's form and himself are interchangeable. The form is the self. The self is the form. The Lord's self being his form is proven, since it is not subject to logical argument, being inconceivable, understood only by scripture. This means that the bhakti directed to that form is supreme bhakti, not inferior.

That the Lord is his form though his self is knowledge and bliss, is understood from śruti, since the Lord is a non-material being. That the Lord is his form is understood by person having emotions of bhakti, just as the form of a *rāga* is perceived by the ear trained in music. Otherwise śruti descriptions of the Lord like *vijñāna-ghana* (solidified knowledge) or *ānanda-ghana* (solidified bliss) would be contradicted. The same may said of other qualities of the form like "entering all beings." Any other conception about this arises from illusion.

etat tvayā na vijñeyaṁ rūpavān iti dṛśyate
icchan muhūrtān naśyeyam īśo 'haṁ jagato guruḥ
mātrātma hy eśā mayā sṛṣṭā yan māṁ paśyasi nārada
sarva-bhūta-guṇair yuktaṁ naiva tvaṁ jñātum arhasi

This cannot be understood by you. It appears that I possess a form. In a second I, the Lord, guru of the universe, can by my desire make myself invisible. What you see, O Nārada, is only myself, created by my *māyā.* You cannot know me though I am endowed with all qualities and elements. Mahābhārata 12.326.42

naśyeyam means "I will be invisible."

Topic 9 (Sūtras 18 - 22)

Upamādhikaraṇam - Comparison with the sun

Now the difference between the worshiper and the worshipped is explained. Without that distinction bhakti will not arise. Bhakti cannot arise if one thinks oneself to be the object of worship with no difference between the Lord and the self. Although it has already been plentifully explained that the Lord is different from the jīva, this section refutes other types of knowledge from persons led astray by false scriptures, who maintain that Brahman and jīva are non-different.

bahavaḥ sūryakā yadvat sūryasya sadṛśā jale
evam evātmakā lokeparātma-sadṛṣā matā

Just as many reflections of the sun, with similarity to it, are seen in water, so in this world the jīvas are seen with similarity to the Lord.

The doubt is this. It was previous concluded that Paramātmā was a form of bliss and knowledge. Does Paramātmā under some condition become the jīva, or is Paramātmā different from the jīva?

(Pūrvapakṣa) The Paramātmā is the jīva because he alone becomes jīva when reflected in ignorance. The reflection and the original form are not different since it can be determined that where the form exists so does the reflection, and when the form does not exist, neither does the reflection. It is said:

darpaṇābhihitā dṛṣṭiḥ parāvṛttya svam ānanam
vyāpnuvaty ābhimukhyena vyatyastaṁ darśayen mukham

Looking way from the mirror one sees one's own face and turning towards the mirror one sees a reverse image.

Therefore in contact with ignorance, the Paramātmā becomes the jīva.

This idea is rejected in the next sūtra.

Sūtra - 3.2.18

|| ata eva copamā sūryakādivat ||

Because there is difference between the Lord and the jīva, comparison is made with the sun and its reflection.

Since the jīva is different from the Paramātmā *(ataḥ)* they are compared *(upamā)* to the sun and its reflection (*sūṛyakādivat*). The form and the reflection cannot be the same. If that were so, the shadow of a fire would cause burning and the shadow of a sword would cut. This does not happen because the reflection is not the same as the original form. The word *ca* indicates that there are other reasons for difference as well. Therefore Paramātmā is different from the jīva.

"Let that be. There is difference between the jīva and the Lord in the illustration of form and reflection. But it can still be accepted that the jīva is a reflection of consciousness (*cid-ābhāsa*) (even if they are different). Just as the reflection of the sun in water is called something resembling the sun, so the jīva is a reflection of the Lord in ignorance." This argument is refuted.

Sūtra - 3.2.19

|| ambuvad agrahaṇāt tu na tathātvam ||

There is no similarity because one does not see distance between the Lord and the jīva as one sees distance between the sun and water to cause the reflection.

The word *tu* indicates emphasis. *Ambuvat* has a possessive or locative meaning. There is no similarity (*na tathātvam*) because it is not seen (*agrahanāt*) to be like the reflection in water (*ambuvat*) of the sun which only occurs because the sun is at a distance. Paramātmā, since he is all-pervading cannot be compared to the sun which known to be at a distance from objects. The reflection of the sun in a limited form is seen on the medium of water at a distance from the sun. But this is not so for the Paramātmā since he is never limited or cut in pieces. Thus there is no similarity. Jīva is not a reflection of Paramātmā. Śruti says *alohitam acchāyam:* the Lord is without color, without reflection. (Praśna Upaniṣad 4.10) But the jīva has similarity to the Lord by being conscious. *nityo nityānāṁ cetanaś cetanānam:* the Lord is the chief eternal and the chief consciousness.

In this way, another comparison, that of the sky and its reflection, is also refuted. What is seen in the reflection is caused by some of the sun's rays in a particular portion of sky. If sky itself could be reflected (because it had a form) then one would see directions also. Sound and its echo (both having no form) also cannot be used as a comparison since echoes and reflections are not the same. Therefore the jīva is not a reflection of the Viṣṇu.

Now the sūtras are reconciled.

Sūtra - 3.2.20

| | vṛddhi-hrāsa-bhāktvam antarbhāvād ubhaya-sāmañjasyād evam | |

The comparison with the sun is accepted in the sense that it illustrates the nature of greatness of the Lord and dependence of the jīva, since this is included in the scriptural conclusion and harmonizes the elements of the comparison.

The example of the sun and its reflection given in the scripture quoted is not appropriate in the primary sense, but can be accepted in a secondary way to illustrate their greatness and smallness (*vṛddhi-hrāsa-bhāktvam*). It is metaphorical in that it illustrates that the jīva takes similar qualities, but as a dependent entity. Why? Because jīva as an *aṁśa* is the conclusion of scriptures (*antarbhāvāt*), and because in this way there is agreement of the object and the object to which it is compared (*ubhaya-sāmañjasyāt*).

The meaning is this. In the previous sūtra, because the proposal of a form and its reflection in the primary sense was refuted, the example is now accepted by accepting some similarity in the form and its reflection. It should be understood in this way. The sun partakes of increase: it does not partake of the qualities of water, the *upādhi*. It is independent. The small portions of the sun, the reflections, partake of decrease, being connected with the qualities of water, the reflecting medium, the *upādhi.* They are dependent. Similarly Paramātmā, all-pervading, is not affected by the qualities of *prakṛti* and is independent. His *aṁśas*, the jīvas, small particles, are affected by the qualities of *prakṛti* and are dependent. The example is acceptable in terms of similar qualities, dependence and difference, but not to show that jīva is a reflection of Brahman in ignorance. Paiṅgi-śruti says *nirupādhi-pratibimbo jīva*: the jīva is a reflection without a medium (*upādhi).*

sopādhir anupādhiś ca pratibimbo dvidheṣyate
jīva īṣasyānupādhir indraśapo yathā raveḥ

Reflections are of two types: with *upādhi* and without *upādhi.* The jīva is a reflection of the Lord without *upādhi* just as the rainbow is a reflection of the sun without an *upādhi.* Varāha Purāṇa

Sūtra - 3.2.21

|| darśanāc ca ||

Comparisons based on some similarity are acceptable because this is seen in the world.

One says, "Devatatta is a lion." Accepting partial similarity is seen in dealings in this world. Thus there is agreement of those texts with the ultimate conclusion by accepting them in a figurative or secondary sense.

It is not suitable that the jīva is a conscious entity like the Paramātmā. Jīva is reflection of him only, since Bṛhad-āraṇyaka Upaniṣad 2.3.1 forbids any substance except Brahman. The passage begins with *dve vāva brahmaṇo rūpe mūrtaṁ caivāmūrtaṁ* ca: there are two forms of Brahman, with form and without form. The five elements, divided into two groups (earth water and fire are in one group with form and air and ether in the other group without form), are consired to be forms of Brahman.

tasya haitasya puruṣasya rūpaṁ yathā māhārajanaṁ vāso yathāpāṇḍv-āvikaṁ yathendragopo yathā agny-arciryathāpuṇḍarīkaṁyathā sakṛd vidyuttam sakṛdvidyutteva havā asya śṛī bhavatiya evaṁ veda

What is the form of that person? He is like saffron dyed cloth, red like an *indragopa* insect, like the flame of a fire, like a white lotus, like a flash of lightning. One who knows his beautiful form becomes like a flash of lightning. Bṛhad-āraṇyaka Upaniṣad 2.3.6

Having described the forms of this *puruṣa,* the text then says:

athāta ādeśo neti neti na hy etasmād iti nety anyat param asti atha nāma-dheyaṁ satyasya satam iti prāṇā vai satyam teṣāṁ eṣa satyam

Now here is the teaching. Not so, not so. There is nothing superior. His name is the truth among all truths. *Prāṇa* is truth. He is true among them.

The meaning is this. After defining the world as having form or no form, it concludes that there is nothing at all excellent from knowing that. Then the instruction is given "Not so, not so." It should be understood that this is teaching about Brahman. The phrase is repeated in order to deny all other things whether mental or physical, material or conscious. The text gives the meaning of *neti* by saying *na hy etasmāt*: there is nothing other than Brahman. "Like the material world, Brahman can also be denied by that statement of *neti."* But that is not so. It means that there is the *svarūpa* of Brahman, existence itself *(sanmātram),* beyond all illusion, completely different from the visible material world. Therefore, because of denial of anything except Brahman, it is not correct to say that the jīva is a conscious entity different from Brahman. It is correct to say that Brahman alone is the form of the jīva reflected in ignorance.

You say that jīva and Brahman are different because jīva is atomic and Brahman is all-pervading, based on difference of qualities. But there is no difference, since it is only imagination. It is like the small sky in a pot and the great expanse of sky outside the pot.

Sūtra - 3.2.22

|| prakṛtaitāvattvaṁ hi pratiṣedhati tato bravīti ca bhūyaḥ ||

The passage denies that what was described concerning *prakṛti* is everything about Brahman. It says that Brahman is much more.

This śruti does not propound one Brahman without qualities while denying existence of anything else. Describing Brahman with qualities, the text denies that Brahman is only what was described. It rejects the idea that Brahman is limited to things with and without form as described. It does not deny the existence of these things. Later, after negative statements, again the text speaks emphatically of real names and form.

The meaning of the teaching is this. After describing the different forms, since Brahman is an immeasurable form, the instruction *neti neti* is given. The word *iti* indicates completion. The form of Brahman is not (*na*) just the quantity of what was previously described (*iti*). Brahman is not limited to that. Brahman is a form with the name "truth" etc. This is the meaning that śruti states with the phrase *na hy etasmād.*

The meaning is this. This is not the limit (*neti*). Beyond these things with and without form (*etasmāt*) is there is something higher (*param anyat*): his name is the truth of all truths. That name is the form of Brahman also. The word *satya* is explained. *prāṇo vai satyam*: *prāṇa,* meaning living beings or jīvas, are *satya*. Thus the Lord is the life of the jīvas (*teṣām eva satyam*).

The word *rūpa* means qualities. It is explained that Brahman is endowed with unlimited qualities both material and non-material. Thus the text does not deny things other than Brahman. The material forms are those with and without shape. The qualities like the color of saffron cloth etc. are non-material. *Prāṇa* or the jīvas are also called *satya* because they do not transform into something completely different *(svarūpānyathā*), like ether or other elements. But Brahman is *satya* more than the jīvas, since Brahman does not undergo transformation in the form of restriction or expansion of knowledge. Thus the jīva has eternal consciousness. Paramātmā, different from the jīva, is an ocean of unlimited auspicious qualities. This understanding gives rise to bhakti for the Lord.

If, in this passage, form in Brahman was denied-- by teaching about Brahma's remarkably colored form and then denying it--it would amount to utterances of a madman. The author of the sūtras by using the word *etāvattam* (this much) in the present sūtra would also be charged with lack of intelligence. He should have written *etad-rūpaṁ pratiṣedhati*: śruti denies a form of Brahman. Thus the explanation given is correct (being confirmed by the author of the sūtras).

Topic 10 (Sūtra 23)

Avyaktādhikaraṇam - The invisible Lord

Now the Lord as the inner self of all beings is established. Otherwise, if he were easily available like pots and other external objects, bhakti to him would not arise. Śruti describes that he has a form of eternity, knowledge and bliss.

The doubt is this. Does the supreme Brahman have a form perceivable by the senses externally or only perceived internally?

(Pūrvapakṣa) That form is perceivable externally because it is seen by *devatās*, demons and men.

Sūtra - 3.2.23

|| tad avyaktam āha hi ||

He is not visible to the material senses because this is stated in scripture.

Brahman (*tat)* by his nature is not visible (*avyaktam*) to the material senses. He is internal, because Kaṭha Upaniṣad says (*āha*) the following. *na saṁdṛśe tiṣṭhati rūpam asya na cakṣuṣā paśyati kaścanainam*: his form is not visible; no one can see him with the eye. (Kaṭha Upaniṣad 2.3.9) Another śruti says *agṛhyo na hi gṛhyate*: not perceived by the senses, he cannot be perceived. (Bṛhad-āraṇyaka Upaniṣad 3.9.26) Smṛti says *avyakto'kṣara ity uktas tam āhuḥ paramāṁ gatim*: that which I have described as eternal and unmanifest is called the supreme goal by the followers of *Vedānta* (BG 8.21)

Topic 11 (Sūtras 24 - 27)

Saṁrādhanādhikaraṇam - Intense bhakti

Now it is shown that though the Lord is internal, he can be attained by *jñāna*[66] and bhakti. If the Lord were completely unavailable, bhakti would not arise because of the devotee's despair. In Kaivalya Upaniṣad it is said *śraddhā-*

[66] Jñāna means knowledge of difference between jīva and the Lord.

bhakti-dhyāna-yogād avaiti: one meets the Lord by faith, bhakti and meditation. It appears that the faithful devotee attains the Lord by meditating on him.

The doubt is this. Is the Lord perceived by the mind or by the senses like the eye?

(Pūrvapakṣa) He can be obtained by the mind only for it is said *manasaivānudraṣṭavyam*: he should be perceived by the mind alone. (Bṛhad-āraṇyaka Upaniṣad 4.4.19) Only by the mind can he be perceived.

Sūtra - 3.2.24

|| api saṁrādhane pratyakṣānumānābhyām ||

When there is intense bhakti, the Lord can be perceived by the senses, since this is stated in śruti and smṛti.

The word *api* indicates censure. The objection is to be reviled. When there is intense bhakti (*saṁrādhane)*, the Lord is perceived by senses like the eye. Why? Because of śruti and smṛti (*pratyakṣanumānābhyām*).

parāñci khānivyatṛṇat svayambhūs
tasmāt parāṁ paśyatināntarātnam
kaścid dhīraḥpratyag ātmānam aikṣad
āvṛtta-cakṣur amṛtatvaṁ icchan

The creator created external senses. Therefore man sees external objects, not the inner Lord. A wise man, desiring immortality, turning his eyes inward, sees the Lord within. Kaṭha Upaniṣad 2.1.1

The Lord is seen by the knowledgeable devotee:

jñāna-prasādena viśuddha-sattvas
tatas tu taṁ paśyate niṣkalaṁ dhyāyamānaḥ

By the mercy of knowledge, a pure person on meditating sees the undivided Lord. Muṇḍaka Upaniṣad 3.1.8

nāhaṁ vedair na tapasā na dānena na cejyayā |
śakya evaṁ-vidho draṣṭuṁ dṛṣṭavān asi māṁ yathā ||

Not through the *Vedas*, not through austerities, not through charities, and not through performance of worship, is it possible to see me as you have seen me. BG 11.53

bhaktyā tv ananyayā śakya aham evaṁ-vidho 'rjuna |
jñātuṁ draṣṭuṁ ca tattvena praveṣṭuṁ ca parantapa ||

Only by *ananyā bhakti* is it possible to know me, see me, or become connected to me, O Arjuna. BG 11.54

Therefore it is proved that the Lord is perceived by intense bhakti. The senses become pervaded with bhakti. Thus he can be known by those senses. In that case, the word *eva* in *manasaivānudraṣṭavyam* does not mean "only" but "also."

Sūtra - 3.2.25

|| prakāśādivac cāvaiśeṣyāt ||

The Lord does not take a gross form to be visible to the eyes because there are no distinctions of gross and subtle qualities in the Lord as there are in fire.

The word *na* (not) is understood from sūtra 3.2.19. If one proposes that the Lord is invisible in his subtle form but visible in a gross form, like fire, the answer is "no." Why? Because he does not have subtle and gross qualities (*avaiśeṣyāt)* like fire *(prakāśādivat). asthūlam anaṇv ahrasvam:* the Lord is not gross, not atomic and not short. (Bṛhad-āraṇyaka Upaniṣad 3.8.8)

sthūla-sūkṣma-viśeṣo 'tra na kaścit parameśvare
sarvatraiva prakāśo 'sau sarva-rūpeśuajo yataḥ

There are no distinctions of gross and subtle in the Supreme Lord because the unborn Lord is manifest everywhere in all forms. Garuḍa Purāṇa

"Perceiving the Lord directly does not take place by intense bhakti since one does not see the devotees having such direct perception."

Sūtra - 3.2.26

|| prakāśaś ca karmaṇy abhyāsāt ||

The Lord appears by practice of devotional acts.

The word *ca* indicates a destruction of the doubt. By repetition of *arcana* or acts such as meditation (*karmaṇi abhyāsāt*), the Lord will reveal himself (*prakāśaḥ*), because it is said *dhyāna-nirmathanābhyāsād devaṁ paśyen nigūḍhavat*: by constant meditation, as if churning, one sees the Lord who is hidden within. (Brahma Upaniṣad) By practice or repetition one develops affection for the Lord. Then one can see him.

na tam ārādhayitvāpi kaścid vyaktīkariṣyati |
nityāvyakto yato devaḥ paramātmaā sanātanaḥ ||

One cannot make the Lord appear just by worship since the eternal Lord, Paramātmā, is eternally invisible. Brahma-vaivarta Purāṇa

This verse from Brahma-vaivarta Purāṇa refers to worship without affection.

"The Lord who is within (and invisible) making an appearance is a contradiction of terms since it would make *sādhana* to see him directly useless (if he were just invisible), and would destroy his nature of being inside and invisible (if he made his appearance)."

Sūtra - 3.2.27

|| ato'nantena tathā hi liṅgam ||

There is manifestation to the devotee by the infinite Lord because it is indicated in the scriptures.

Since there is proof *(ataḥ)* that one who meditates can see that Lord inside (unmanifest), the infinite, continuous, inner (unmanifest) Lord (*anantena*), appears to his devotees being pleased by their bhakti, because of his inconceivable *śakti.* Why is this said? Because of indications in śruti (*tathā liṅgam*). *vijñāna-ghana ānanda-ghanaḥ sac-cid-ānandaika-rase bhakti-yoge tiṣṭhati*: the form which is full of eternity, knowledge and bliss, resides in *bhakti-yoga*, which, like Kṛṣṇa, is filled with knowledge and bliss. (Gopāla-tāpanī Upaniṣad 2.78) He appears to the devotees by his mercy alone.

nityāvyakto'pi bhagavān īkṣate nija-śaktitaḥ |
tām ṛte paramātmānaṁ kaḥ paśyetāmitaṁ prabhum ||

Though the Lord is eternally unmanifest, he is seen because of his own *śakti.* Who can see the Paramātmā, the Lord, without that? Nārāyaṇa adhyātma

The Lord himself says this:

avyaktaṁ vyaktim āpannaṁ manyante mām abuddhayaḥ |
paraṁ bhāvam ajānanto mamāvyayam anuttamam ||

The unintelligent think that the impersonal *ātmā* has manifested an illusory form as myself. They do not know my transcendental existence with form and activities, which is eternal and most excellent. BG 7.24

Though he becomes visible by prema, his unmanifest nature is not destroyed, since his manifestation to his devotee is a function of his *svarūpa-śakti.* To persons without prema he appears in a reflected form (*ābhāsa-rūpa*) only. *nāhaṁ prakāśaḥ sarvasya yoga-māyā-samāvṛtaḥ*: being covered by my bewildering power of *māyā*, I am not visible to all these people.(BG 7.25) Thus the Lord with a form of the highest bliss appears as a terrifying form to them. He remains inside (unmanifest), unperceived by the senses to persons without prema.

Topic 12 (Sūtras 28 - 31)

Ahikuṇḍalādhikaraṇam - The snake coil

Now the non-difference of the qualities of the Lord from his *svarūpa* is established. If they were different, because they would be secondary to the Lord, bhakti to the Lord would also be secondary (since it depends on his qualities). This is not so, because these qualities are experienced in a primary manner.

The following statements are found. *vijñānam ānandaṁ brahma:* Brahman is knowledge and bliss. (Bṛhad-āraṇyaka Upaniṣad 3.9.28) *yaḥ sarvajñaḥ sarvavit*: the Lord is omniscient, the knower of everything. (Muṇḍaka Upaniṣad 1.1.9, 2.2.7) *ānandaṁ brahmaṇo vidvān*: one knows the bliss of Brahman. (Taittirīya Upaniṣad 2.2.9)

The doubt is this. Does the worshipable Brahman possess knowledge and bliss (as qualities), or is he knowledge and bliss itself (without qualities)?

(Purvapakṣa) Because both types of statements are seen, it cannot be decided.

Sūtra - 3.2.28

// ubhaya-vyapadeśāt tv ahi-kuṇḍalavat //

The Lord is both knowledge itself and qualified with knowledge, like a snake and its coils because scriptures say the Lord is both.

Brahman whose *svarūpa* is knowledge and bliss should be considered to have knowledge and bliss as his qualities, like the coils of a snake (*ahi-kuṇḍalavat*). The coil should be considered the quality of the snake, but the snake also has the coil as his very nature. Why? That is explained. Because both are described in the śrutis just mentioned (*ubhaya-vyapadeśāt*). The word *tu* indicates that this is understood only from scriptures. He is of this nature because of his inconceivable power. One cannot say that because both are stated in scriptures that his *svarūpa* is either one-- sometimes Brahman with no qualities and sometimes Brahman with qualities. Nor does Brahman have internal distinctions or parts (*svagata-bheda*).[67]

Sūtra - 3.2.29

|| prakāśāśrayavad vā tejastvāt ||

Because Brahman is knowledge itself, he can be defined as the shelter of knowledge.

Because Brahman's *svarūpa* is knowledge (*tejastvāt),* he can also be defined as the shelter of knowledge. The sun, whose nature is light, is the shelter of light. Similarly the Lord is knowledge itself and the shelter of knowledge. Light (*tejas*) is defined as the opposite of ignorance or the opposite of darkness.

Sūtra - 3.2.30

|| pūrvavad vā ||

Or the dual nature of the Lord can be compared to time, which is essentially one but has past, present and future.

Time is referred to as "past" etc. Just as time (*pūrvavat*), though one, appears to be divisible, and to cause divisions (of past, present and future), similarly knowledge and bliss should be understood to be both quality and the object in which qualities reside.

ānandena tv abhinnena vyavahāraḥ prakāśavat
pūrvavad vā yathā kālaḥ svāvacchedakatāṁ vrajed

[67] The quality cannot be separated from Brahman.

By being non-different from bliss, the Lord is like light (and the sun) or it is like time, which divides itself up into past, present and future (though it is one). Brahma Purāṇa

The later examples are more subtle than the previous ones in the sūtras (snake's coil, light and time).

Sūtra - 3.2.31

|| pratiṣedhāc ca ||

The Lord and his qualities are non-different because difference is rejected by scripture.

The word *ca* is for emphasis.

manasaivedam āptavyaṁ neha nānāsti kiñcana
mṛtyoḥ sa mṛtyum āpnoti ya iha nāneva paśyati

By the mind one can understand that there is no difference in the Lord. He who sees difference goes from death to death. Kaṭha Upaniṣad 2.1.11

yathodakaṁ durge vṛṣṭaṁ parvateṣu vidhāvati
evāṁ dharmān pṛthak paśyaṁs tān evānuvidhāvati

As water falling on mountains flows to inaccessible places, a man who sees the Lord's qualities different from the Lord flows into the material world of *saṁsāra*. Kaṭha Upaniṣad 2.1.14

nirdoṣa-pūrṇa-guṇa-vigraha ātma-tantro
niścetanātmaka-śarīra-guṇaiś ca hīnaḥ
ānanda-mātra-kara-pāda-mukhodarādiḥ
sarvatra ca svagata-bheda-vivarjitātmā

The Lord is a form with faultless, perfect qualities. He is independent. He is devoid of the qualities of the material body. His hands, feet, face and belly are all bliss. He is devoid of internal difference everywhere. Nārada Pañcarātra

The qualities of the Lord are not separate from his *svarūpa*. Difference between the quality and possessor of the quality is rejected in the Lord (according to scriptures as quoted above). The word Bhagavān is defined in terms of his qualities like knowledge.

jñāna-śakti-balaiśvarya-vīrya-tejāṁsy aśeṣataḥ
bhagavac-chabda-vācyāni vinā heyair guṇādibhiḥ

The word *bhagavān* means infinite, knowledge, śakti, strength, powers, potency and energy without base qualities. Viṣṇu Purāṇa 6.5.79

The Lord who is one entity is described as two (quality and possessor of quality), like water and waves, because of the function called *viśeṣa*.[68] He who is *rasa* itself is filled with the joy of rasa and has his own body of joy. That body is eternal since his actions (using the body) are defined as eternal.

Viśeṣa or distinction is a likeness of difference. Though difference is actually absent, for normal usage we make differences in terms of quality and the possessor of the quality. Otherwise common usages like "existence exists," "time exists all the time" and "space is everywhere" would be meaningless. "Existence exists" is not an error of intelligence since it is never negated, just like "the pot exists" is never negated. Nor is "existence exists" a figurative attribution like "Devadatta is a lion" for we never say "existence does not exist." (whereas we can say "Devadatta is not a lion.") This usage is not because it is natural to things like existence and time, which have no interior (substance), since naturalness requires *viśeṣa* to inhere in them. *Viśeṣa* is proved by the strength of the statement about water flowing down the hill and by *arthāpatti* (explained above).[69] In the verse naming the Lord's qualities, there is forbiddance of seeing difference between those qualities and the Lord. In the absence of *viśeṣa* or the semblance of difference, the relation of quality to possessor of the quality cannot be brought about even if there are many qualities. *Viśeṣa* is non-different from the object and is self-accomplishing. Thus there is no infinite regression. Non-difference of *viśeṣa* from the object and its self-accomplishing nature are proved by the fact that the Lord is the possessor of qualities (while being one inseparable entity).

Topic 13 (Sūtras 32 - 34)

Parādhikaraṇam - The Lord's bliss is different

---

[68] [68] *Viśeṣa* is the power of objects to distinguish their being from their qualities, though the object and its qualities are inseperable.

[69]*Arthāpati* is necessary supposition of an unperceived fact (like *viśeṣa*) which alone can explain a phenomenon that demands explanation.

Now the nature of the Lord as supreme bliss is described. Bhakti would not arise if that bliss were the same as the jīva's. The topic (*viṣaya*) is statements revealing the qualities of the Lord.

The doubt is this. Is the bliss of Brahman different or not from that of the jīva?

(pūrvapakṣa) It is not different since the common word "bliss" is used for the Lord and the jīva, just as the object denoted by the word "pot" is not different from a pot.

Sūtra - 3.2.32

|| param ataḥ setūnmāna-sambandha-bheda-vyapadeśebhyaḥ ||

The Lord's bliss is different from that of the jīva because in scriptures his bliss is designated as a bridge, and is described as immeasurable, with a relationship of jīva's bliss being dependent on the Lord's bliss, and as different from the jīva's bliss.

The bliss of Brahman is different (*param*) from that of the jīva. It excels in type and quantity. Why? Because the Lord's bliss is designated (*vyapadeśabhyaḥ*) as a bridge (*setu*). *eṣa setur vidhṛtiḥ:* the Lord is a bridge, a support. (Chāndogya Upaniṣad 8.4.1) The Lord's bliss is designated as immeasurable (*unmāna*). *yato vāco nivartante*: words cannot describe that bliss. (Taittirīya Upaniṣad. 2.8) The relationship of the two types of bliss is stated. *etasyaivānandasyānyāni bhūtāni mātrām upajīvanti*: other living beings depend upon the Lord who is bliss. (Bṛhadāraṇyaka Upaniṣad 4.3.32) The difference is expressed in the following:

anyaj jñānaṁ tu jīvānām anyaj jñānaṁ parasya ca
nityānandāvyayaṁ pūrṇam paraṁ jñānaṁ vidhīyate

The knowledge of the jīva is different from the knowledge of the Lord. The Lord is called superior knowledge, which is perfect and filled with eternal, immutable bliss.[70]

Since the Lord's bliss is described as a support for beings etc. it cannot be material.

---

[70] This is quoted in Bhagavat-sandarbha, and is found in Madhva's commentary.

"The object indicated by the word 'pot' is not different from pot."[71]

Sūtra - 3.2.33

|| sāmānyāt tu ||

The Lord's bliss is not material because the word implies similarity only.

The word *tu* destroys the doubt. Just as the word pot represents potness in general in various pots, a word like bliss represents general bliss--in both material and spiritual objects of bliss. It does not imply complete similarity in appearance.

para-jñāna-mayo 'sadbhir nāma-jātyādibhir vibhuḥ
na yogavān na yukto 'bhun naiva pārthiva yokṣyati

The Lord, having knowledge superior to the jīva, was not, is not and will never be touched by the names and types of matter. Viṣṇu Purāṇa

This verse says that the Lord has knowledge superior (*para-jñāna-mayaḥ*) to the jīva's knowledge.

"If the Lord is different from this world made of jīvas and matter, this contradicts the teaching *sarvaṁ khalv idaṁ brahma tajjalān iti śānta upāsīta*: everything is Brahman; everything arises from Brahman, lives in Brahman and merges into Brahman; the peaceful person should worship Brahman. (Chāndogya Upaniṣad 3.14.1)"

Sūtra - 3.2.34

|| buddhy-arthaḥ pādavat ||

Oneness of everything with Brahman is stated for easy understanding of the greatness of the Lord, like the word *pāda*.

This is an instruction so one can easily understand that everything belongs to Brahman. It is like the usage of the word *pāda* in referring to the universe. *pādo ṣya viśvā bhūtāni*: all the beings are his foot. (Ṛg Veda 10.90.3) The mind debased by hatred for others becomes inclined to the Lord (since everything is related to him). One will not maintain attraction for any object in the world

---

[71] Thus bliss applied to the human experience is the same as the Lord's.

because one will also understand the inferior nature of everything material (since it merges into him).

Topic 14 (Sūtras 35 - 36)

Sthāna-viśeṣādhikaraṇam - Difference in Place

The variegated appearance of the Lord who is worshipped by various types of bhakti has been described. Without this variety, bhakti would not appear. Variegatedness of appearance is eternally accomplished since the location of the qualities is without beginning. One Brahman in one place appears in various places, rather than having many forms appearing in various places, since it is said *eko 'pi san bahudhā yo vibhāti*: though one he appears as many. (Gopāla-tāpanī Upaniṣad)

The doubt is this. Will there be degrees of his appearance (showing more or less qualities) in these places?

(Pūrvapakṣa) There will be no degrees of his appearance because he is one substance, and is understood by the same words (of scripture) and intelligence.

Sūtra - 3.2.35

|| sthāna-viśeṣāt prakāśādivat ||

The Lord appears variously because of different places and devotees, like light.

Even though the *svarūpa* of Brahman is only one, his appearance will be various because of differences in the places of his appearance and the devotees (*sthāna-viśeṣāt*), with differences in degrees of the devotee's mood of *aiśvarya* or *mādhurya,* and *in śānti, dāśya sakhyā, vātsalya* and *mādhurya bhavas*. It is just like light and other things (*prakāśādivat*).

A lamp light appears differently in sparkle and hue in rooms made of crystal or ruby. One sound appears with different sweetness and sonority in a conch, drum, or flute. The meaning is this. Where there is appearance of the great powers of the Lord, at that place bhakti to the Lord is executed according to the rules. By that type of bhakti, the Lord's manifestation is sharp, like a light in a crystal room. Where there is manifestation of the Lord's sweetness, even though the Lord actually has all powers, bhakti for the Lord is executed with taste. By that type of bhakti, the manifestation is sweetness, like the light shining in a ruby room. Thus difference in bhakti has been demonstrated with different abodes and different devotees' moods.

Sūtra - 3.2.36

|| upapatteś ca ||

The Lord manifests variously, because it is reasonable according to the texts.

This being the case, the statement *yathā kratuḥ asmin loke puruṣo bhavati*: according to faith in this world a person becomes in the afterlife (Chāndogya Upaniṣad 3.14.1) is suitable. It is not otherwise. Thus it is reasonable that the Lord, though one, according to the place manifests himself with various degrees of manifestation of qualities (according to the desires of the various types of devotees).

Topic 15 (Sūtra 37)

Anya-pratiṣedhādhikaraṇam - Nothing higher

Now the supreme status of the Lord is described. If there is someone higher, bhakti will not arise. Śvetāśvatara Upaniṣad 3.8, starting with *vedāham etam,* describes the form of Brahman as the best among all. Then the same passage says *yad uttaratam*: beyond this there is a superior object.

The doubt is this. Is there something superior to Brahman, the object of worship or not?

(Pūrvapakṣa) From the self-evident meaning of the text, there is something higher.

Sūtra - 3.2.37

|| tathānya-pratiṣedhāt ||

Brahman is the highest because śruti denies anything higher.

Brahman is the highest of all. There is nothing superior. Why? Because śruti texts refute that there is anything higher (*anya-pratiṣedhāt*).

yasmāt paraṁ nāparam asti kiñcid
yasmān nāṇīyo na jyāyo 'sti kiñcit

There is nothing superior to him. There is nothing different from him. There is nothing smaller than him. There is nothing larger than him. Śvetāśvatara Upaniṣad 3.9

The meaning of the text in question is this:

vedāham etaṁ puruṣam mahantam
āditya-varṇaṁ tamasaḥ parastāt
tam eva viditvāti mṛtyum eti
nānyaḥ panthāḥ vidyate 'yanāya

I know this great person, shining like the sun, beyond darkness. Knowing him alone one surpasses death. There is no other path to tread.

This verse teaches that there is nothing higher than knowledge of the great person, who is the path to immortality. By saying that there is nothing superior or inferior, greater or smaller, his superiority is illustrated. The next verse confirms what was stated: there is nothing greater than the Lord.

tato yad uttarataraṁ tad arūpam anāmayam
ya etad vidur amṛtās te bhavanty athetare duḥkham evāpi yānti

Those who know that which is superior to the world, those who know that which has no material form, is devoid of suffering and become immortal. Others attain only suffering. Śvetāśvatara Upaniṣad

If the verse were to mean that there is something higher than Brahman, then the previous verses would be meaningless. The Lord himself says *mattaḥ parataraṁ nānyat kiñcid asti dhanañjaya:* O conqueror, there is nothing superior to me. (BG 7.7)

Topic 16 (Sūtra 38)

Sarva-gatatvādhikaraṇam - The Lord pervades everything

Now the pervasion of the Lord is described in order to describe the devotee's closeness to the Lord. If the Lord is not close, bhakti will weaken because of lack of enthusiasm. In śruti it is said *eko vaśī saravagaḥ krsṇa īḍyaḥ*: staying in one place Kṛṣṇa is everywhere. (Gopāla-tāpanī Upaniṣad 1.19)

The doubt is this. Is the Lord, the object of meditation, limited or all-pervading?

(pūrvapakṣa) Because he is realized in a medium-sized form, and because he must necessarily be separate from the material world (and therefore not pervade it), he is limited.

Sūtra - 3.2.38

|| anena sarva-gatatvam āyāma-śabdādibhyaḥ ||

The Lord is all-pervading with medium size because of statements indicating his pervasion, because of his inconceivable nature, and because of the logic of a previous sūtra.

By the Supreme Lord *(anena)* even though he is of medium size, pervading everything (*sarva-gatatvam*) takes place. The medium sized form itself pervades everywhere. Why? Because he pervades everything (*āyāma). Ādi* means endowment of the quality of inconceivability and logic which indicates this. And also scriptures say this (*śabdādibhiḥ*). Words indicating pervasion are *eko vaśī sarvagaḥ kṛṣṇa īḍyah.* Also it is said:

yac ca kiñcit jagat sarvaṁ dṛśyate śrūyate'pi vā |
antar bahiś ca tat sarvaṁ vyāpya nārāyaṇaḥ sthitaḥ ||

Nārāyaṇa, pervading everything, is situated inside and outside of whatever is seen or heard in the world. Taittirīya-āraṇyaka and Nārāyaṇa Upaniṣad 13

From these statements it is concluded that the Lord's size is medium. The Lord himself says he pervades everything though he has a medium sized form, which is greater than everything, because of his inconceivable *śakti.*

mayā tatam idaṁ sarvaṁ jagad avyakta-mūrtinā |
mat-sthāni sarva-bhūtāni na cāhaṁ teṣv avasthitaḥ ||

I pervade this whole universe by my form which is invisible to material eyes, and simultaneously all entities are within me. But I am not in them.

na ca mat-sthāni bhūtāni paśya me yogam aiśvaram |

And the living beings are not in me. See my inconceivable power. BG 9.4.-5

The Lord is not limited by the fact that the material world occupies some space (where the Lord should not pervade), since śrutis says he pervades inside and outside everything. He is said to be like the oil in the sesame seed or the ghee in yogurt. Thus it is proved that the worshipable Lord is all-pervading. This is also illustrated in the Dāmodara pastime. The reason for the Lord being of this nature was previously explained in sūtra 1.2.7.

Topic 17 (Sūtras 39 - 42)

Phalādhikaraṇam - Giver of results

Now the Lord as the giver of all results is explained. Bhakti would not arise if the Lord did not give anything or gave meagerly, displaying stinginess. *puṇyena puṇyaṁ lokaṁ nayati:* the Lord leads a person to a pious place because of the person's pious acts. (Bṛhad-āraṇyaka Upaniṣad in text, but Praśna Upaniṣad in actuality)

The doubt is this. Do the results like Svarga come from sacrifice or the Lord?

(Pūrvapakṣa) The results come from sacrifice because if the person does the act he goes and if he does not do it, he does not go.

Sūtra - 3.2.39

|| phalam ata upapatteḥ ||

The Lord alone gives the results because that is reasonable.

The Lord is the giver of all results (*phalam*) like Svarga. Why? Because that is reasonable (*upapatteḥ*). Ability to give results to all acts at all times is suitable for the Lord alone who is eternal, omniscient, endowed with all *śaktis,* most munificent, and worshipped by sacrifices etc. And it is not suitable for actions (sacrifices) which are destroyed in a moment and insentient.

Proof is given.

Sūtra - 3.2.40

|| śrutatvāc ca ||

The Lord is the giver of results because of śruti statements.

The following śrutis show that the Lord is the giver of good fortune. *vijñānam ānandaṁ brahma rātir dātuḥ parāyaṇam:* the Lord is knowledge and bliss, the give, the goal of the sacrificer. (Bṛhad-āraṇyaka Upaniṣad 3.9.28) *sa vā eṣa mahān aja ātmā annādo vasudānaḥ:* the great unborn Lord is eater of food and giver of wealth. (Bṛhad-āraṇyaka Upaniṣad 4.4.24) *Datuḥ* means the sacrificer. *Rātiḥ* means giving results.

A different opinion is given.

Sūtra - 3.2.41

|| dharmaṁ jaiminir ata eva ||

Pious acts give good results according to Jaimini.

Jaimini thinks that dharma comes from the Lord. The pious acts in dharma alone give results. The pious actions come from the Lord (the Lord does not directly give results), for śruti says *eṣa eva sādhu karma kārayati*: the Lord makes a person do good acts. (Kauṣītaki Upaniṣad 3.8) The Lord should not be accepted as the giver since by doing the good act one gets good results and by not doing the act there are no good results. The Lord ceases acting on generating the pious activity.

"Since actions are momentary, they cannot give results in the future. Something that has ceased to exist (action being destroyed immediately) cannot give rise to something." That is not so. Though action is destructible, action, when it appears, produces *apūrva* (karmic reaction) and then disappears. That *apūrva* will give results to the person at a later time according to his action. Thus action gives the result.

The author states his opinion.

Sūtra - 3.2.42

|| pūrvaṁ tu bādarāyaṇo hetu-vyapadeśāt ||

Bādarāyaṇa holds the view that the Lord is the giver of results, since he is designated as the cause of results in scripture.

The word *tu* removes the doubt. Lord Bādarāyaṇa says that the Lord as previously mentioned (*pūrvam*) is the give of results. Why? Because the Lord is designated as the cause of results in *puṇyena puṇyaṁ lokaṁ nayati* and action disappears on being performed. Scripture states the existence of action and its results (karma) depends on the Lord.

dravyaṁ karma ca kālaś ca svabhāvo jīva eva ca |
yad-anugrahataḥ santi na santi yad-upekṣayā ||

By connection with the Lord, matter, *karma,* time, *svabhāva* and the totality of *jīvas* can produce effects. Without his presence, they have no effect. SB 2.10.12

Thus it is proved that Brahman alone is the cause of action. The proposal that action, though destructible, gives the results is foolish since it is impossible that *apūrva* (karma), insentient like a stone or piece of wood, can give results and this idea is not approved by scriptures.

"Since one worships *devatās* during sacrifice, then the *devatās* who are worshipped are the givers of results." Put into action by the Supreme Lord, the *devatās* give results. This is accepted in the *antaryāmi-bṛahmaṇa.* Thus, the Lord bestows results. The lotus-eyed Lord himself says this:

yo yo yāṁ yāṁ tanuṁ bhaktaḥ śraddhayārcitum icchati |
tasya tasyācalāṁ śraddhāṁ tām eva vidadhāmy aham ||

I give those persons firm faith in those *devatās* whose forms they desire to worship faithfully.

sa tayā śraddhayā yuktas tasyārādhanam īhate |
labhate ca tataḥ kāmān mayaiva vihitān hi tān ||

Endowed with the faith given by me, that person worships the *devatā*, and attains his desired objects, which are actually given only by me. BG 7.21.22

It is said here that the Lord who is worshipped by sacrifices gives the auspicious results. Satisfied by bhakti however, the Lord will give everything, including *himself.* This will be explained later in sūtra 3.4.1.

Thus these two pādas of the third chapter have shown that a thirst for Brahman, along with disgust with everything not the Lord--caused by describing his many qualities like being the controller of everything and having a pure body of knowledge, and by glorification of his freedom from all faults, through describing the faults of the world filled sufferings like birth and death--is the cause of attaining him.

Section 3

parayā nirasya māyāṁ guṇa-karmādīni yo bhajati nityam |
devaś caitanya-tanur manasi mamāsau parisphuratu kṛṣṇaḥ ||

May Lord Kṛṣṇa with a body of consciousness, who, defeating *māyā* by his superiority, eternally partakes of qualities and actions, appear in my mind.

Topic 1 (Sūtras 1 - 5)

Sarva-vedānta-pratyayādhikaraṇam - Brahman is ascertained in all the Vedas

In this pāda, worship of the qualities of the Lord is shown. The method is as follows. Various eternal forms manifest eternally in the supreme Brahman, the Supreme Lord, who is fixed in his own form, like a *vaidūrya* gem. Understanding that this Lord, endowed with these many forms, is completely pure and perfect, a person who worships the Lord endowed with one favorite form among these forms, also gathers qualities mentioned in scripture concerning another of the Lord's forms, if those qualities are also mentioned in relation to his chosen form. Those who worship Brahman as the mind or other powers collects qualities found in other branches of the Vedas with various types of worship and accept those qualities which are found to agree with those in their chosen form, but they do not accept other qualities.

Others however have a different opinion. Brahman reveals various *bhāvas* which are situated in Brahman, just as an actor reveals *bhāvas* during a performance. He takes on various names, appears in various places, and reveals various qualities and actions. Thus it is possible to collect qualities from other śrutis and meditate on them in one's chosen form.

"How can one meditate on one form with qualities found in another form?" It is possible because the one Lord appears in these various forms.

"Because qualities like sweetness, grandeur, enjoyment, peace, austerity and cruelty are mutually contradictory, because meditating on a human form with horns, tail, mane and teeth, or a fish form with flute, conch, cakra and bow, would be disturbing to meditation; because it is contrary to smṛti scriptures; and because it is not supported by the realization of authorities, collecting qualities from different forms in one meditation is not proper. It is said:

yo 'nyathā santam ātmānam anyathā pratipadyate
kiṁ tena na kṛtaṁ pāpaṁ caureṇātmāpahāriṇā

Anyone who thinks of the Lord in another way than he really exists commits the worst sin, being a thief who tries to steal the Lord. Mahā-bhārata 1.68.26"

In answer to this, it should be said that collecting qualities of various forms in one worship is proper. One type of person meditates in his worship upon qualities mentioned in one form, along with qualities not mentioned in relation to it but in relation to another form. Another type of person merely acknowledges existence of those qualities in other forms but does not meditate on them. The first type of person is called *sva-niṣṭha* and the second type is called *ekāntika (pariniṣṭhita* and *nirapekṣa).* In the fourth section of this chapter, these three types of persons qualified for knowledge are shown. Among them the *svaniṣṭhas,* generally *devatās,* have equal affection for all forms. They collect all the qualities from all the forms. There is no conflict in meditation on many contrary qualities in one form since for one who sees equally, it is possible to accept within one form differences of form, just as they exist in a *vaidūrya* gem.

The *pariniṣṭhita* and *nirapekṣa* are both *ekāntikas,* and have unequal affection for the various forms. They meditate upon and see only the qualities revealed in their chosen form. Though they are aware of the existence of other qualities in the Lord, they do not meditate upon or see the qualities manifested in other forms because those qualities do not manifest to those devotees and they are not attracted to those qualities. This will be explained in another *adhikaraṇa.*

The verse from the Mahā-bhārata merely criticizes those who maintain that the Lord is merely consciousness itself with no qualities. The qualities of Brahman should be sought, according to *tasmin yad antas tad anveṣṭavyam:* one should seek out that which is within the heart. (Chāndogya Upaniṣad 8.1.1) *ānandaṁ brahmaṇo vidvān na bibheti kutaścana*: knowing Brahman as bliss, one fears nothing (Taittirīya Upaniṣad 2.4.1) By knowing Brahman's qualities, one becomes free of fear. Thus the purport of scripture is that Brahman has qualities.

The concept of the Lord's qualities being superimposed (*ānuvādika)* and conventional (*vyavahārika*) is imaginary, for it is impossible to attribute qualities to something that cannot be conceived by the mind, and the word "conventional" is not found in the scriptures. An objector may say the qualities may be imagined in the object of worship just as śruti says "Worship speech as a cow." (Bṛhad-āraṇyaka Upaniṣad 5.4.1) This is bad intelligence, for then even statements like *satyātmetyevopāsīta* (one should meditate on *ātmā*) could be classed as imaginary.

In commenting on sūtras 3.3.12 and 3.3.38, even these objectors accept the qualities of Brahman (bliss) as real, and accept non-difference between jīva and the Lord as real. When scripture says that Brahman is without qualities, it means Brahman has no material qualities. There can be no objection to this, since it is accepted that there is no difference between the quality and its possessor (the Lord).

Qualities suitable for meditation are of two types: some are intrinsic to the Lord and others are secondary. This will be made clear later. First, it will be established that the Lord is to be known by all the Vedas in order to facilitate collecting all his qualities. The subject *(viṣaya)* is all the statements concerning *sādhana*.

The doubt is this. Is Brahman to be known by teachings in one's own branch or by teachings from all branches?

(Pūrvapakṣa) Brahman is to be known by one's own branch since the meaning is different in each branch.

Sūtra - 3.3.1

|| sarva-vedānta-pratyayaṁ codanādy-aviśeṣāt ||

Knowledge ascertained in all the Vedas is Brahman because this is the common subject of injunctions in the Veda and logic.

Here the word *anta* means ascertainment or conclusion. That is ascertained from the following. *ubhayor api dṛṣṭo 'ntaḥ anayos tattva-darśibhiḥ*: those who see things in truth realize this conclusion *(antaḥ)* about both of these. (BG 2.16) The knowledge ascertained as the conclusion in all the Vedas (*sarva-vedānta-pratyayam*) is Brahman. Why? Because of the unity everywhere in scriptures *(aviśeṣāt)* of injunctions (*codana*) such as *ātmety evopāsīta* (one should worship the Lord) and the logic stated about this. The injunctions mentioned in the Mādhyandina branch are the same as those in the Kānva branch.

"Each branch speaks differently. One says *vijñānam ānandaṁ brahma*: Brahman is knowledge and bliss. Another branch says *yaḥ sarvajñaḥ sarva-vit*: he is omniscient, and knows everything. All the branches will not have one subject."

Sūtra - 3.3.2

|| bhedān neti cen nakasyām api ||

If one argues that there is not one topic alone because of conflicting statements, the answer is no. There is only one topic.

That is not so, because one sees the one Brahman described by all these words in one branch of the Vedas (*ekasyām*). Thus Taittirīya Upanisād say that athe Lord is truth, infinite knowledge (omniscience) and bliss: *satyaṁ jñānam anantaṁ brahma, ānando brahma* etc. Thus by all words in all scriptures, one Brahman is named. There is no contradiction.

Sūtra - 3.3.3

|| svādhyāyasya tathātvena hi samācāre'dhikārāc ca ||

There is one Brahman in all the Vedas because all followers are qualified for all actions in all the Vedas, and the instruction is given to all of them to study all Vedas.

All the Vedas give the same instructions (*tathātvena*) like *svādhyāyo 'dhyetavyaḥ*: one should study the Vedas. Smṛti says *vedaḥ kṛtsno 'dhigantavyaḥ sa-rahasyo dvijanmanā*: the brāhmaṇa should study all the Vedas including the esoteric portions. And everyone is qualified in ability for all karmas *(samācare 'dhikarāt*). Smṛti says:

sarva-vedokta-mārgeṇa karma kurvīta nityaśaḥ
ānando hi phalaṁ yasmāc chākhā-bhedo hy aśakti-jaḥ
sarva-karma-kṛtau yasmād aśaktāḥ sarva-jantavaḥ
śākhā-bhedaṁ karma-bhedaṁ vyāsas tasmād acīkḷpad

One should perform karmas daily according to the path stated in all the Vedas from which the result is bliss. The different branches arose because of inability to know everything. Because people were incompetent in doing all karmas, Vyāsa divided it into different branches with different karmas.[72]

Thus it is established that if a person is capable, Brahman is to be known by the *sādhana* mentioned in all branches.

An example is given by indirect reasoning.

Sūtra - 3.3.4

|| savavac ca tan-niyamaḥ ||

Rites like *sava* however are restricted to one group.

Sava refers to seven sacrifices starting from the *saurya* and ending with *śataudana* which are performed only by followers of the Atharva Veda since they use only one fire. However, in contrast to this, worship of Brahman can be done by all followers of the Vedas.

Instead of *savavat* sometimes *salilavat* is seen. The meaning is then "Just as, in the absence of obstacles, all water goes to the ocean, so all words describe Brahman." This rule to study all the Vedas is according to the ability of the person.

yathā nadīnāṁ salilaṁ śaktyā sāgaratāṁ vrajet
evaṁ sarvāṇi vākyāni puṁ-śaktyā brahma-vittaye

Just as water of rivers flowers to the sea with power, so all statements of the Vedas are suitable for indicating Brahman according to a person's ability. Agni Purāṇa

A text is quoted.

Sūtra - 3.3.5

|| darśayati ca ||

The text shows that the Lord is the goal of all the Vedas.

Śruti says *sarve vedā yat padam āmananti*: all the Vedas describe the Lord. (Kaṭha Upaniṣad 1.2.15) This shows that the Lord is to be known by all the Vedas. The word *ca* indicates "according to one's ability." One should worship Brahman with all the *sādhanas* mentioned in all branches of the Vedas,

---

[72] Found in Madhva's commentary.

according to one's ability. If one is unable to do this, then one should worship the Lord according to the practices mentioned in one's own branch. This was mentioned in sūtra 1.1.4, but now it is reiterated in another way for use in gathering the qualities of the Lord.

Topic 2 (Sūtra 6)

Upasaṁhārādhikaraṇam - Gathering qualities

It has been concluded that the Lord is to be known by all the Vedas, so that now the Lord can be revealed by collecting all his qualities from various portions of the Vedas. In Gopāla-tāpanī Upaniṣad (1.8) the *svarūpa* of Brahman is described: he has the form of a cowherd, is black like a *tamāla* tree, wears yellow cloth, has a Kaustubha jewel, wears a peacock feather, plays the flute, is surrounded by cows, cowherds and gopīs, and is the deity of Gokula.

In another scripture, the Lord is also described as the lord of Ayodhya, having Sītā on his left side, carrying a bow, killing Rāvaṇa.

prakṛtyā sahitaḥ śyāmaḥ pīta-vāsā jaṭā-dharaḥ
dvi-bhujaḥ kuṇḍalī ratna- mālī dhīro dhanur-dharaḥ

Accompanied by Sītā, peaceful Rama is dark in complexion, having two arms, wearing yellow cloth and matted locks, holding a bow, wearing a necklace and earrings. Rāma-tāpanī Upaniṣad

Elsewhere the Lord is described as Nṛsiṁha with ferocious mouth, frightening even to Śiva. The word "terrifying" is found in his mantra:

atha kasmād ucyate bhīṣaṇam iti. yasmād yasya rūpaṁ dṛṣṭvā sarve lokāḥ sarve devāḥ sarvāṇi bhūtāni bhītyā palāyante svayaṁ yataḥ kutaścin na bibheti.

Why is he called ferocious? Because on seeing his form all planets, all *devatās,* all beings became frightened and fled, because he is not afraid of anyone.

bhīṣāsmād vātaḥ pavate bhīṣodeti sūryaḥ.
bhīṣāsmād agniś cendraś ca mṛtyur dhāvati pañcamaḥ.

Out of fear of him the wind blows. Out of fear of him the sun rises. Out of fear of him fire, Indra and death, the fifth, run. Nṛsimha-tāpanī Upaniṣad 2

The Vedas describe Vāmana:

viṣṇor nu kaṁ vīryāṇi prāvocaṁ
yaḥ pārthivāni vimame rajāṁsi
yo askambhayad uttaraṁ sadhasthaṁ
vicakramāṇas tredhorugāya

I speak of the valor of Viṣṇu who created the earth and heaven, who established the worlds above and below, and with three great steps surpassed all. Ṛg Veda 1.1.54.1

Just as the sacrifice differs according to the difference in *devatā,* so the worship appears different according to the qualities of the Lord's form.

The doubt is this. In worshipping one form should one use the qualities gathered from another form?

One should not collect qualities from descriptions of other forms since the qualities mentioned for one form will be helpful in gaining knowledge, and there is no extra result in mixing up the qualities of other forms, and the qualities are also contradictory.

Sūtra - 3.3.6

|| upasaṁhāro'rthābhedād vidhi-śeṣavat samāne ca ||

Qualities from other forms can be collected if they indicate Brahman, since there is no difference of Brahman's qualities in any of the scriptures. It is just like collecting rules for sacrifice from various scriptures.

The word *ca* indicates limitation. One can gather together qualities mentioned elsewhere *(upasaṁhāraḥ*) only when the worship mentioned elsewhere is similar (*samāne*), that is, when the one pure Brahman is the object of worship. Why? Because there is no difference in any scripture concerning characteristics of Brahman, the object of worship *(arthābhedāt*).

An example is given. It is like supplementary rules (*vidhi-śeṣavat*). One should gather together the procedures for sacrifice mentioned in different places in the scriptures and the sacrifice is still one (though rule are scattered everywhere.) In worshipping Rāmacandra qualities of other forms like Matsya are gathered:

yo vai śrī-rāmacandraḥ sa bhagavān ye matsya-kūrmādy-avatārā bhūr bhuvaḥ svas tasmai namo namaḥ

I offer repeated respects to Rāmacandra, the Lord, who has avatāras like Matsya and Kūrma, who is bhūh, bhuvaḥ and svah. Rāma-tāpanī Upaniṣad

Rāma and others are included in Kṛṣṇa's worship in the following. *eko 'pi san bahudhā yo 'vabhāti:* though one, Kṛṣṇa appears as many. (Gopāla-tāpanī Upaniṣad) The same is true in the following statement, addressed to Kṛṣṇa. *namas te raghu-varyāya rāvaṇāntakarāya*: I offer respects to the best of the Raghus, the killer of Rāvaṇa. (SB 10.40.20)

Topic 3 (Sūtra 7)

Anyathātvādhikaraṇam - Non-collection of qualities

"But since scripture says *ātmety evopāsīta*: only ātmā should be worshipped (Bṛhad-āraṇyaka Upaniṣad), it appears that one should not gather elements from different forms in worship."

Sūtra - 3.3.7

|| anyathātvaṁ śabdād iti cen nāviśeṣāt ||

If one argues that one should not collect qualities of all the forms of the Lord because of scriptural injunctions, the answer is no, because there is no specific forbiddance concerning collecting qualities.

If one argues that there should not be a collection of qualities (*anyathātvam*) the answer is no. Why? Because there are no particular injunctions *(aviśeṣāt)* which say these qualities should not be used in worship. The word *eva* (only) indicates that one should exclude what is not ātmā, but does not exclude other qualities. If one says, "The king alone was seen" this does not exclude seeing the king's umbrella and other objects associated with him. Thus it is concluded that, according to one's ability, one should meditate on all the qualities of the Lord, collecting those qualities from various scriptures.

What is said is this. In the supreme Brahman there are many eternal forms, as in the *vaidūrya* gem. The Lord endowed with all those forms is complete and pure. Sometimes he reveals all the qualities and sometimes not all of them. The person in knowledge should meditate on qualities of all forms mentioned anywhere in various scriptures. This collation of qualities is for the *sva-niṣṭha* devotee.

Topic 4 (Sūtra 8)

Prakaraṇa-bhedādhikaraṇam - Different bhakti

Though the *ekāntīs* have studied many branches of the Vedas, they meditate on only the qualities of the Lord mentioned in their favored Upaniṣads, and not the qualities of the Lord mentioned in other branches. Thus, an exception to the above is now discussed. The subject (*viṣaya*) is Gopāla-tāpanī Upaniṣad.

The doubt is this. When the *ekantī* worships, should he collect the qualities found everywhere or not?

(pūrvapakṣa) He should collect all qualities as far as he is capable, because this is praised.

Sūtra - 3.3.8

|| na vā prakaraṇa-bhedāt parovarīyastvādivat ||

The *ekāntīs* do not gather qualities from many forms since their bhakti is superior. The worshippers of the Lord in the sun do not gather qualities mentioned in relation to worship of the Lord in ether such as his being *parovarīya.*

The word *vā* indicates certainty. Those who are attached to one form of the Lord (the *ekantīs*) do not gather qualities manifest in other forms. Thus a person attached to the form of Kṛṣṇa does not meditate on the qualities of ferocity, teeth and mane found in Nṛsiṁha. Similarly the devotee of Nṛsiṁha does not meditate on the qualities of peacock feather, cane and flute found in Kṛṣṇa. Why? Because of difference (*bhedāt*) in the excellent activity of bhakti (*prakaraṇam*). The *ekāntī* is superior to the *sva-niṣṭha* bhakta because of the depth of his attachment.

An example is given. The *ekāntī* worshippers of the golden person in the sun do not gather qualities such as *parovarīyas* found in the *udgītha. Parovarīyān* means "superior to the highest" and "best among the excellent." *Parovyarīyastva* means "the state of *parovarīyān* found in the *udgitha."*

Topic 5 (Sūtras 9 - 10)

Saṁjñāto 'dhikaraṇam – Sameness of all devotees

"Both are called worshippers of Brahman. Therefore the *ekāntīs,* like the *sva-niṣṭhas,* should meditate on all the qualities found in all the branches. For instance, everyone called *brāhmaṇa* worships *gāyatrī* without exception."

Sūtra - 3.3.9

|| saṁjñātaś cet, tad uktam, asti tu tad api ||

If one argues that the two have the same name, the answer is no. The reason has been stated previously. And there is an example of this.

The word *tu* indicates refutation of the doubt. One may say that gathering all qualities is proper since all the devotees are defined the same (*saṁjñataḥ*). But that is not correct *(tu)* because the devotees are different, as mentioned (*tad uktam*) in the last sūtra (*prakaraṇa-bhedāt*). The *ekāntī* is a particular member of the general definition of devotee. Because of his superiority, he does not meditate on all the qualities of the Lord. If he were to do otherwise, his superiority would be lost. The *ekāntī* is superior to the common *sva-niṣṭha* because of complete absorption in one form of the Lord. Even the *sva-niṣṭha* is incapable of gathering *all* the qualities of the Lord. *viṣṇor nu kam vīryāṇī prāvocam*: who can describe the glories of Viṣṇu? (Ṛg Veda 1.1.54.1)

nāntaṁ guṇānām aguṇasya jagmur
yogeśvarā ye bhava-pādma-mukhyāḥ

Even those who are masters of yoga and the *devatās* headed by Brahmā and Śiva cannot find an end to the spiritual qualities of the Lord who is without material qualities. SB 1.18.14

The author then shows that contents may be various even when two things have a common name. Even with accepted differences, as the *parovarīyas* and worshippers of the golden form in the sun, both have the same name--performers of *udgītha* worship (*asti*). Therefore the *sva-niṣṭhas* should collect all the qualities and worship. And the *ekāntīs* should worship with particular qualities only. This is the meaning of the last two *adhikaraṇas.*

The author now begins to gather qualities of the Lord such as infancy.

kṛṣṇāya devakī-nandanāya oṁ tat sat. bhūr bhuvaḥ svas tasmai vai namo namaḥ.

I offer respects to Kṛṣṇa, the son of Devakī. I offer respects to the three worlds, which represent his power. I offer respects to the *antaryāmī* of *prāṇa*. Gopāla-tāpanī Upaniṣad 2.86

The author of Nāma-kaumundī says *kṛṣṇa-śabdas tu tamāla-nīla-tviṣi yaśodā-stanandhaye rūḍhiḥ:* the word Kṛṣṇa by convention indicates the person who drinks milk from Yaśodā and has the complexion of a *tamāla* tree.

In the Rāma-tāpanī Upaniṣad it is said:

oṁ cin-maye 'smin mahā-viṣṇau jāte dāśarathe harau
raghoḥ kule 'khilaṁ rāti rājate yo mahī-sthitaḥ

When the Lord, Mahāviṣṇu, pure consciousness, is born to Dāśaratha in the dynasty of Raghu, Rāma shines *(ra)* and gives (*ra*) all things when he is situated on earth (*ma*)

In various śrutis one hears of the various qualities of Brahman, such as his infancy. This is also seen in the smṛtis. The doubt is this. Should one meditate on all of these qualities?

(Pūrvapakṣa) Meditating on all these qualities would give various sizes to the Lord's form. Because this contradicts the śrutis that state the Lord is unchangeable, one should not meditate on these qualities.

Sūtra - 3.3.10

| | vyāpteś ca samañjasam | |

Meditation on the Lord's form in various ages is proper because the Lord is all-pervading.

This meditation is proper (*samañjasam*) because the Lord is never subject to change (big, small etc. since he is all-pervading (*vyapteḥ*) -- though he has qualities of infancy etc. This was already concluded in sūtra 3.2.39. He does not undergo transformations like birth since it is said *ajāyamāno bahudhā vijāyate*: unborn, he is born many times. (Puruṣa-sūkta) Birth means simply a manifestation of the Lord who is devoid of birth. The word *ca* indicates that śruti also says the Lord is *rasa. raso vai saḥ*: the Lord is *rasa*. (Taittirīya Upaniṣad) By his inconceivalbe *śakti* the Lord manifests a particular form, by which devotee experiences *rasa* and *līlā.* These worshippers headed by *nityamuktas* are unlimited in numbers. This is proved by *tad viṣṇoḥ paramaṁ padaṁ sadā paśyantisūrayaḥ*: these devotees always see the supreme abode of Viṣṇu. The one Lord manifests simultaneously to all types of devotees in various ages. Some say he is like the syllable *da* given to *devatās*, humans and demons. They understood the syllable in three different ways.[73] Thus one should meditate on the infancy and other ages of the Lord since the Lord is unchanging because of his pervasion, though he appears in all these ages.

Topic 6 (Sūtra 11)

Sarvābhedādhikaraṇam - Non-difference of the Lord from his actions

"The actions of the Lord's infancy are eternal since they are qualities of the Lord. One should meditate on these eternal actions in conjunction with the various associates of the Lord connect with those actions. One among those associates should be related to many actions both previous and later. Since the previous action is eternal, one must say that there is an eternal relationship of the action with the associate involved in the action, otherwise the act could not be accomplished. But in that case, a later action involving that person would be impossible to perform. If one accepts his relation with the later action, the eternal nature of the previous action would be destroyed (since the associate would not be there). If the previous action is eternal, the later action must be performed by a different person. But this is contrary to experience and scripture. Moreover it is seen that an action has previous and later parts and each part is accomplished by having a beginning and end. Without that, the very nature of action could not exist. One could not experience *rasa* by the nonexistence of that nature. Thus, how can those actions be eternal? Eternity is perceived in something which never changes, like a picture.

One may argue, "If there are different manifestations of an action, there will be continuity because of the many actions in the series." But it is difficult to avoid the fact that with each beginning, there would be a different act. Without the perception "This is that action" how could one believe in the eternal nature of the act? Therefore it cannot be concluded that the actions of the Lord are eternal. The answer follows.

---

[73] For *devatās* the syllable *da* meant "be subdued." For men it meant "Give." For the demons it meant "Be merciful."

Sūtra - 3.3.11

|| sarvābhedād anyatreme ||

The Lord, his associates and parts of action at a later time exist in the previous action because there no difference between the Lord, his associates and the parts at various times.

One should accept that the Lord and his associates and the parts of the action which exist in the previous actions also will exist in the later action (*anyatreme*). Why? Because there is no difference in all these (*sarvābhedāt*)--of the Lord, his associates, and the parts of action, previous and later. The Lord has many forms, for śruti says *eko 'pi san bahudhā yo 'vabhāti:* though one, he appears as many. Smṛti says *ekāneka-svarūpāya*: I offer respects to the Lord with many forms. (Viṣṇu Purāṇa) The associate of the Lord also has many forms since this is stated in *bhūma-vidyā* in reference to the liberated souls. Bhāgavatam also says that the same associates were also present when Kṛṣṇa simultaneously married many queens at many weddings simultaneously. There is oneness of actions which are the same, though they appear different because of time. *Dviḥ pāko 'nena kṛto na tu dvau pākāv iti dvir go-śabdo 'yam uccarito na tu dvau go-śabdāu:* one can light the fire in the hearth twice, but there is only one fire, and one can say the word "cow" twice, but that does not mean there are two words to indicate a cow. Because of the many manifestations of the Lord, his associates and his abodes, they start and conclude actions with these distinctions. Because of this, there is oneness in each commencement of action. Thus, the eternal nature of acts is accomplished. This explains the manifestation of various *rasas* caused by experiencing this succession of action.

This is not without proof. *yad bhūtaṁ bhavac ca bhaviṣyac ca*: the Lord is the past, present and future. (Bṛhad-āraṇyaka Upaniṣad) *eko devo nitya-līlānuraktaḥ*: the one Lord is engaged in eternal pastimes. (*Māṭhara śruti*) The Lord says *janma karma ca me divyam*: my birth and actions are spiritual. (BG 4.9) This perception takes place by the mercy of the Lord.

yāvān ahaṁ yathā-bhāvo yad-rūpa-guṇa-karmakaḥ
tathaiva tattva-vijñānam astu te mad-anugrahāt

By my mercy, may you attain perfect realization of whatever dimensions, intentions, forms, qualities and pastimes I manifest. SB 2.9.32

Therefore the Lord's actions are eternal. Actions accomplished by his *cic-cakti* and his *svarūpa* are eternal. Actions accomplished by *prakṛti* and time, like creating Svarga, are temporary. If they were not temporary, this would contradict scriptural statements about their destruction at *pralaya.*

Topic 7 (Sūtra 12)

Ānandādy-adhikaraṇam - Collection of qualites like bliss

Now the following will be considered. In the Upaniṣads, the qualities of Brahman like full bliss are described.

The doubt is this. In all worship of the Lord, should all these qualities be gathered?

(Pūrva-pakṣa) Because there is no authority for collecting those qualities which were not in the same section of the Vedas, only those which are in one section should be collected. Because there is no rule to collect all qualities, it should not be done.

Sūtra - 3.3.12

|| ānandādayaḥ pradhānasya ||

Qualities like bliss in the Lord should be collected together for meditation.

The qualities like affection for the devotee, knowledge and full bliss of Paramātmā, who is the possessor of the qualities (*pradhānasya*) mentioned in śruti, should be collected together because they create thirst for the Lord.

Topic 8 (Sūtras 13 - 18)

Priya-śirastvādy-aprāpty-adhikaraṇam - Non-meditation on the bird

It is said in śruti that the *ānanda-maya* Lord has the quality of having a head of *priya* (joy). *Tasya priyam eva śiraḥ*: his head is joy. (Taittirīya Upaniṣad 2.5.2) Should such qualities be gathered together for meditation?

(Pūrvapakṣa) Because it is said that one should gather all the qualities like bliss from everywhere, and because these words in the Taittirīya Upaniṣad all mean bliss, all these qualities should be gathered for meditation.

Sūtra - 3.3.13

|| priya-śirastvādy-aprāpitir upacayāpacayau hi bhede ||

One should not collect qualities like "head of joy" because these indicate increase and decrease in bliss, and thus, internal difference in the Lord.

One should not collect the qualities like head of joy (*priya-śirastvādy-aprāptiḥ*), since Viṣṇu, made of bliss, in the form of a man, does not have the form of a bird whose head is joy (as described in the particular passage of Taittirīya Upaniṣad). Moreover, in that passage, increase and decrease of bliss (*upacayāpacayau*) is indicated by the words *pramoda* (great bliss) and *moda* (bliss). Increase and decrease become possible where there is difference. But there is no difference in the bliss of the Lord since scriptures deny internal difference in the Lord. Therefore these qualities mentioned in the Taittirīya Upaniṣad should not be combined in meditation on the Lord.

Sūtra - 3.3.14

|| itare tv artha-sāmānyāt ||

Other qualities mentioned elsewhere in the same Upaniṣad should be gathered for meditation, since they all contribute to liberation.

Other statements before and after the depiction of the head of joy, such as *tasmād va etasmāt, so 'kāmayata* and *bhīṣāsmād*, concerning the Lord's pervasion, knowledge and bliss, creatorship of the universe, and supreme powers, which are the qualities of the *ānanda-maya* Brahman found in the same scripture, should be gathered for meditation. Why? Because they all have the same goal, liberation (*artha-sāmānyāt*). Liberation is possible by meditating on the Lord's unique qualities of great power, his friendship with all, his giving shelter to all, and his ability to give liberation.

"What is the purpose of the comparison of the *ānanda-maya* Lord to a bird? One can see that the analogy of the charioteer comparing the worshipper's body to the chariot in *ātmānaṁ rathinam viddhi* (Kaṭha Upaniṣad 1.3.3) is for the purpose of controlling senses and body, which are instruments useful in worship. In the analogy of the bird one can see no such result. In not aiming at any result, the tendency of the Vedas to use analogy in this way is not proper."

The goal of this analogy is now stated.

Sūtra - 3.3.15

|| ādhyānāya prayojanābhāvāt ||

This analogy is made for meditational purpose since there is no other goal.

This analogy is made for meditational purpose (*ādhyānāya*) since there is no other goal (*prayojanābhāvāt). Ādhyānam* means complete concentration. The meaning is this. One Brahman mentioned in the statement *brahmavid apnoti param*: the knower of Brahman attains Brahman (Taittirīya Upaniṣad 2.1) is situated in two ways: as his *svayam-rūpa* and as *vilāsa* and other forms. *Svayam rūpa* is Svayam Bhagavān Kṛṣṇa and the other forms are Nārāyaṇa, Vāsudeva, Saṅkarṣaṇa, Pradyumna and Aniruddha. In *svarūpa*, qualities and name they are all-pervading forms of knowledge and bliss. This however is hard to understand for those of dull intelligence. Therefore the *ānanda-maya* Brahman is divided into forms like *priya* and *moda* and taught by metaphor as the head and wings of a bird so that these people can understand. When their intelligence is elevated they can directly meditate on Brahman as described in the Upaniṣads.

The analogy starts with the head and other parts of the *annamaya puruṣa* to elevate the intelligence. *tasyedam eva śiraḥ* etc. Metaphors are then made, using the limbs of a bird for the *prāṇamaya, manomaya* and *vijñāna maya puruṣas* with *tasya prāṇa eva śiraḥ* etc. Then in a similar way, the *ānandamaya puruṣa*, the Lord, different from the others, is described with *tasya priyam eva śiraḥ* etc.

Since these five limbs of the bird represent pure Brahman only metaphorically, they should not be gathered together for meditation. This has been established.

One should not protest that the five limbs of Brahman are without scriptural basis, for there are statements in other śrutis. *eko 'pi san bahudhā vibhāti:* the one Lord appears as many. (Gopāla-tāpanī Upaniṣad) *ekaṁ santaṁ bahudhā dṛśyamānam*: the one Lord appears as many.[74] *sa śiraḥ sa dakṣiṇaḥ*

[74] Quoted by Jīva in Bhāgavat-sandarbha. Brahmā Upaniṣad says ekaṁ santaṁ bahudhā yaḥ karoti.

pakṣaḥ sa uttara-pakṣaḥ sa ātmā sa pucchaḥ: he is the head, he is the right wing, he is the left wing he is the body and he is the tail. (Catur-veda-śikhā)

śiro nārāyaṇaḥ pakṣo dakṣiṇaḥ savya eva ca
pradyumnaś cāniruddhaś ca san deho vāsudevakaḥ

His head is Nārāyaṇa, his right wing is Pradyumna, his left wing is Aniruddha and his body is Vāsudeva.

nārāyaṇo 'tha san deho vāsudevaḥ śiro 'pi vā
puccham saṅkarṣaṇaḥ prokta eka eva ca pañcadhā

Or Nārāyaṇa is the body and Vāsudeva is the head. Saṅkarṣaṇa is the tail. In this way, one Lord is five forms.

aṅgāṅgitvena bhagavān krīḍate puruṣottamaḥ
aiśvaryān na virodhaś ca cintyas tasmin janārdane
atarkye hi kutas tarkas tv apramaye kutaḥ pramā

The Lord plays as the *aṅgas* and the *aṅgī.* Because of his powers, there is no contradiction in the Lord. How can one speculate about the Lord who is beyond logic? How can one prove he who is beyond proof? Bṛhat-saṁhitā

Sūtra - 3.3.16

|| ātma-śabdāc ca ||

The passage is metaphorical because it uses the word *ātmā* in describing the blissful bird.

The *ānanda-maya puruṣa* is called *ātmā*. Because the word ātmā is used, and it is impossible that *ātma* can have a tail like a bird, the passage is metaphorical only for easily understanding.

Sūtra - 3.3.17

|| ātma-gṛhītir itaravad uttarād ||

The word *ātmā* in this passage means the Lord because of other texts where *ātmā* means the Lord and because of the meaning of the sentence following the statement about *ātmā*.

"The word *ātmā* is used to indicate material bodies or the jīva in passages like *anyo 'ntara ātmā vā prāṇa-mayaḥ:* there is another interior *ātmā* which is made of *prāṇa.* (Taittirīya Upaniṣad 2.2) How then can it refer to the Supreme

Lord in the phrase *anyo 'ntara ātmānanda-mayaḥ:* there is another interior ātmā, which is made of *ānanda*? (Taittirīya Upahiṣad 2.5) This sūtra replies. In other places ātmā refers to Paramātmā as in *ātmā vā idam eka evāgra āsīt:* the Lord alone existed previously. (Bṛhad-āraṇyaka Upaniṣad.1.4.1) Why does ātmā mean the Lord in this case? Because of the next statement (*uttarāt*) concerning the *ānanda-maya ātmā.* This statement is *so 'kāmayata bahu syām:* he thought, "Let me be many." This statement would not be suitable if the *ānanda-maya ātmā* did not mean Paramātmā, since creating the universe is the work of the Lord and not others.

Sūtra - 3.3.18

|| anvayād iti cet, syād avadhāraṇāt ||

If you say ātmā refers to the jīva, the answer is no. It must refer to Paramātmā because of ascertainment from a previous statement.

"It is not possible to ascertain that *ātmā* means the Lord simply because of the next sentence, since previously the word *ātmā* referred (*anvayāt*) to material things like *prāṇa* and to the jīva." The word *ātmā* must certainly be *(syāt)* Paramātmā. Why? By using intelligence it is understood *(avadhāraṇāt*) to be Paramātmā from a previous statement *tasmād vā etasmād ātmanaḥ:* from that ātmā came ether. Otherwise the instruction to meditate on the *ānanda-maya puruṣa* would be nullified. What was previously ascertained, crossing over the other ātmās made of *anna, prāṇa, manas* and *vijñāna,* finds resolution in the *ānanda-maya puruṣa,* understood as Paramātmā, for after that, no other *ātmā* is defined. Taking shelter of the maxim of showing Arundhatī star through showing other stars, one finally understands that Paramātmā is the real ātmā, after rejecting the other ātmās one after the other. Thus, from the later sentence it is ascertained that *ātmā* means Paramātmā. Everything is without fault.

Topic 9 (Sūtra 19)

Apūrvādhikaraṇam - Thinking of the Lord in other ways

Now begins the topic of collecting qualities such as the Lord acting as a father. It is said in śruti that Nārāyaṇa is the mother, father, brother, house, shelter, friend and goal. In smṛti it is said:

pitā mātā suhṛd bandhur bhrātā putras tvam eva me
vidyā dhanaṁ ca kāmaś ca nānyat kiñcit tvaya vinā

You are my father, mother, friend, relative, brother and son, knowledge, wealth and love. There is nothing except you. Jitanta-stotra

janma-prabhṛti dāso 'smi śiṣyo 'smi tanayo 'smi te
tvaṁ ca svāmī gurur mātā pitā ca mama mādhava

O Mādhava! From birth I am your servant, student, and son. You are master, guru, mother and father. Jitanta stotra[75]

The doubt is this. Should one think of the Lord with a form and qualities of father, son, friend, or master?

(Pūrva-pakṣa) One should not think of the Lord in this way, since śruti says one should worship the Lord as ātmā only (*ātmety evopāsīta*).

Sūtra - 3.3.19

|| kāryākhyānād apūrvam ||

One should meditate on the Lord acting as father etc. since it is explained that this causes the Lord to come under the devotee's control.

Pūrvam means the previous qualities of the Lord like being full of bliss. *Apūrvam* in this sūtra means other similar qualities like the Lord acting as a father. The various devotees should think of the Lord in this way. Why? Because the result, the Lord coming under control by the various *bhāvas* of the devotees, is described (*karyākhyānāt*) in śruti statements like *bhāva-grāhyam anīdākhyam*: the Lord, said to be without a body, is attained by the devotee's *bhāva.* (Śvetāśvatara Upaniṣad 5.14) The Lord himself says:

yeṣām ahaṁ priya ātmā sutaś ca
sakhā guruḥ suhṛdo daivam iṣṭam

For the devotees, I am a lover, the *ātmā,* son, friend, elder, companion or worshipable deity. SB 3.25.38

---

[75] Jitanta stotra is often quoted by followers of Rāmānuja. It is a Pañcarātric text.

Therefore the devotees should think of the Lord as having qualities of father etc., just as he has qualities like being full of bliss. The statement *ātmety evopāsīta* has already been explained in sūtra 3.3.7.

Topic 10 (Sūtras 20 - 25)

Samānādhikaraṇam - Non-difference in the Lord's features

Now begins the subject of collecting qualities of the Lord indicating his form. One finds statements in śruti describing the Lord as *ātmā. Ātmety evopāsīta*: one should worship only *ātmā*. (Bṛhad-āraṇyaka Upaniṣad 1.4.7) *ātmānam eva lokam upāsīta*: one should worship ātmā. (Bṛhad-āraṇyaka Upaniṣad 1.4.15) We also find statements describing the Lord with a specific form:

tad u hovāca hairaṇyo gopa-veśam abhrābhaṁ taruṇaṁ kalpa-drumāśritam. tad iha ślokā bhavanti
sat-puṇḍarīka-nayanaṁ meghābhaṁ vaidyutāmbaram |
dvi-bhujaṁ jñāna-mudrāḍhyaṁ vana-mālinam īśvaram ||

gopa-gopī-gavāvītaṁ sura-druma-talāśrayam |
divyālaṅkaraṇopetaṁ ratna-paṅkaja-madhya-gam ||

kālindī-jala-kallola-saṅgi-māruta-sevitam |
cintayan cetasā kṛṣṇaṁ mukto bhavati saṁsṛteḥ ||

Brahmā spoke to them. The form of Kṛṣṇa wears the dress of a cowherd. He has the complexion of a cloud. He is youthful and sits under a desire tree. Meditating with concentration on two-armed lotus-eyed silent Kṛṣṇa, having the complexion of a cloud, with cloth flashing like lightning, wearing a garland, surrounded by cowherds, gopīs and cows, bedecked with shining ornaments, while sitting under a desire tree on a jeweled lotus, served by a breeze mixed with water drops from the Yamunā, one becomes liberated from *samsāra.* Gopāla-tāpanī Upaniṣad 1.8-11

The doubt is this. Does one obtain liberation by worshipping the Lord as merely *ātmā* or by worshipping him with a form?

(Pūrvapakṣa) One obtains liberation by worshiping the Lord as *ātmā* only because then there is only one object of concentration. It is said in scripture that one attains liberation by worship of *ātmā*, one object of concentration. One cannot attain liberation by worshipping the Lord with particular qualities like eye etc. which are mutually different, since that form has many objects of attraction.

Sūtra - 3.3.20

|| samāna evaṁ cābhedāt ||

Though there are differences because of the Lord's features, the Lord is still one entity, because his features are non-different from himself.

The word *ca* means "though." Even though (*ca*) there is an appearance of difference, with eyes etc., the Lord should be understood to be the same (*samānaḥ*), one entity *(ekarasa)*, like the features on a gold statue. Why? Because the features like eyes are not different from *ātmā (abhedāt).* Therefore one attains liberation by worshiping the Lord as *ātmā* with a form. Otherwise the statement from Gopāla-tāpanī that by such meditation one attains liberation would be contradictory. Smṛti also says that the Lord's form with various features is one (*ekarasa*). *satya-jñānānantānanda-mātraika-rasa-mūrtayaḥ*: these Viṣṇu forms were all eternal, unlimited , full of knowledge and bliss, and were one form *(ekarasa*). (SB 10.13.54) Though this topic was covered in 3.2.14 *(arūpavat eva hi tat-pradhānatvat)* it is again presented in another way. The merciful *ācārya* considers the difficult topic repeatedly so that it may be easily understood.

It has been explained that one should gather qualities from all the *avatāras* of the Lord, his direct forms, for meditation. Now the *āveśāvatāras,* who are jīvas are considered. It is said:

adhīhi bhagava iti hopasasāda sanatkumāraṁ nāradas taṁ hovāca ...taṁ māṁ bhagavān śokasya pāraṁ tārayatu

O Lord! teach me. Nārada approached Sanatkumāra and spoke to him. May the Lord make me cross over suffering. Chanḍogya Upaniṣad 7.1.1-3

The Kumāras and others, endowed with the Lord's own qualities like *jñāna-śakti*, are jīvas with empowerment by the Lord. Thus the word *bhagavān* is used for them.

The doubt is this. Should the devotees of these *āveśa* forms gather all the qualities of the Lord and apply them to these jīva forms?

The author gives alternatives. First the positive perspective is explained.

Sūtra - 3.3.21

|| sambandhād evam anyatrāpi ||

This applies to the *āveśa* forms also since they are invested with the Lord's powers.

All the qualities of the Lord should be gathered in meditating on the Kumāras and other *āveśa* forms (*anyatrāpi*). Why? Because they are related (*sambhandāt),* having being endowed with the Lord's powers like fire heating a piece of iron.

The negative side is explained.

Sūtra - 3.3.22

|| na vāviśeṣāt ||

The *āveśa* forms should not be worshipped with all the Lord's qualities since they are still jīvas.

One should not gather all the qualities of the Lord and apply them to the *āveśa* forms. Why? Because, though they are empowered by the Lord, they are no different from other jīvas in that they have the characteristics of jīvas. The word *vā* indicates "because they are given special respect, being dear to the Lord, one need not attribute all the Lord's qualities to them."

Sūtra - 3.3.23

|| darśayati ca ||

The text itself shows the difference between the *āveśa* forms and the Lord.

The śruti in which Nārada inquires from Sanatkumāra illustrates that Nārada, who is also an *āveśāvatāra*, is eager for knowledge (and thus not complete like the Lord). Therefore in meditating on the *āveśa* forms, one should not gather all the qualities of the Lord and attribute those qualities to the *āveśa* forms.

Sūtra - 3.3.24

|| sambhṛti-dyu-vyâpty api cātaḥ ||

The Lord's qualities of supporting everything and spreading everywhere should not be applied to the *āveśa* forms, since they are jīvas.

One should not gather the qualities of support (*sambhṛti*) and pervasion of the sky (*dyu-vyāpti)* in meditating on the *āveśa* forms. The reason has been given in the previous sūtra (*ataḥ*): these forms are only jīvas. The meaning is this. The following are found in the Eṇāyanīya texts:

brahma jyeṣṭhā vīryā sambhṛtāni brahmāgre jyeṣṭhaṁ divam ātatāna. brahma bhūtānāṁ prathamaṁ tu jajñe. tenārhati brahmaṇā spardhituṁ kaḥ.

Brahman, the eldest, supported and nourished all powers. Brahman, the eldest, in the beginning spread the sky. Brahman appeared previous to the living beings. Who can compete with Brahman? Taittirīya Brāhmaṇa 2.4.7.10

Here Brahman is glorified as the chief support and pervader of the sky. These qualities should not be used in meditating on *āveśa* forms since they belong to the Lord only.

Another reason for not gathering all the qualities in meditating on *aveśa* forms is now given.

Sūtra - 3.3.25

|| puruṣa-vidyāyām iva cetareṣām anāmnāt ||

The *āveśa* forms should not be endowed with all qualities of the Lord because they are not described with these qualities in the stories, whereas the qualities befitting the Lord are related in *puruṣa-sūkta* and other works.

In the stories concerning the Kumāras and other *āveśa* forms, since qualities like creating all beings, and controlling everything are not mentioned (*anāmnāt*) in relation to these forms, all the qualities of the Lord should not be gathered in meditating on them. An example is given by negation. In contrast (*iva*), in puruṣa-sūkta (*puruṣa-vidyāyām*) and other works like Gopāla-tāpanī (*ca*), these qualities are mentioned in relation to the Lord. They are not mentioned in stories of the *āveśa* forms.

Here is the meaning. There are two parts in these *āveśa* forms, like a hot iron ball. Those who see the Lord's portion, like fire, meditate on that *āveśa* having all the qualities of the Lord. Those who see the jīva portion, like the iron, meditate on the qualities of those forms as dear servants of the Lord. The Lord, pleased with their reverence for the Lord's servants, accepts those devotees. Bhāgavatam and other scriptures also used the term *bhagavān* in addressing these *āveśa* forms. And their jīva natures have been revealed in those scriptures by describing their lower qualities. The reconciliation of these two types of descriptions is the same as mentioned above.

Topic 11 (Sūtra 26)

Vedhādy-dhikaraṇam - Violence

It was said one should worship Brahman endowed with the qualities mentioned in one's branch of the Vedas. It has also been said that the person desiring liberation should not worship the Lord with some of the qualities mentioned there. Atharva Veda says *agne tvacaṁ yātudhānasya bhindi*: O Agni, pierce the skin of the Yātudhāna. *taṁ pratyañcam arciṣā bidhya marma:* pierce his organs with your flames as he approaches. (Atharva Veda 8.3.4, 17)

The doubt is this. Should one worship the Lord with qualities like piercing others?

(Pūrvapakṣa) The Lord should be worshipped with these qualities since he should punish the sinful.

Sūtra - 3.3.26

|| vedhādy-artha-bhedāt ||

The desirer of liberation does not meditate on qualities of violence in the Lord since the devotee's goal is different from violence.

The word *na* is understood from the previous sūtra. The Lord should not be worshipped with qualities like piercing. Why? Because that worshipper desires a different result (*artha-bhedāt*). He is has given up the quality of using violence. The Lord himself says:

amānitvam adambitvam ahiṁsā kṣāntir arjavam

Freedom from pride; lack of ostentation; non-violence; forbearance; sincerity are the methods of gaining knowledge. BG 13.8

nivṛttaṁ karma seveta pravṛttaṁ mat-paras tyajet

The person dedicated to me engages in *karmas* without desire and gives up *karmas* for material results. SB 11.10.4

Topic 12 (Sūtras 27 - 28)

Hāny-adhikaraṇam - Destruction of bondage

It is said in Śvetāśvatara Upaniṣad 1.11:

jñātvā devaṁ sarva-pāśāpahāniḥ
kṣīṇaḥ kleśair janma-mṛtyu-prahāniḥ
tasyābhidhyānāt tṛtīyaṁ deha-bhede
viśvaiśvaryaṁ kevala āpta-kāmaḥ

Having understood the Lord, one is free of all bondage, suffering, birth and death. By meditation on the Lord, on leaving the body, one goes to the third place filled with the Lord's powers and without *māyā's* influence, and is fully satisfied.

From knowing the Lord, one destroys bondage of attraction to body and house. Birth and death are destroyed because one is free from the sufferings created by birth and death. This scripture glorifies knowledge of the Lord. By constant meditation (*abhidhyānāt*) on the Lord after knowing him properly, the knower of the Lord destroys the body and, ignoring the worlds of the moon and Brahma, attains the feet of the Lord. What is that place? It is full of powers of the Lord. It is without material *māyā (kevalam)*. The person becomes full in his desires.

In this passage, it is said that the Lord is understood by scriptural knowledge. Is that contemplation on the Lord (discerning the truth) a rule or as one desires?

(Pūrvapakṣa) It is a rule because it causes absorption in the Lord by increasing steadiness.

Sūtra - 3.3.27

|| hānau tūpāyana-śabda-śeṣatvāt,
kuśā-cchandaḥ-stuty-upagānavat tad uktam ||

For a person who has severed bondage, meditation on the Lord's qualities as found in scriptures is optional, like optional praises after obligatory actions with *kuśa* in the hand, since the person is close to the Lord and this is the goal of all scriptural words.

The word *tu* refutes the opponents view. When bondage is destroyed (*hanau*) by knowledge of the Lord, the learned person with attraction for the Lord optionally meditates on the qualities of the Lord as told in the scriptures, like optional singing of hymns while holding a *kuśa* blade (*kuśācchandaḥ-stuty-upagānavat*). The student after doing compulsory study while holding *kuśa* may, by strong or weak desire (*ācchanda)*, chant or not chant praises. This is indicated by use of the word *abhidhyānāt* (because of absorption he attains the third place). The reason for his absorption is his closeness to the Lord (*upāyana*) or his attraction. *Śabda* means words which make it known. All statements are in accordance to (*śabda-śeṣatvāt*) this statement about closeness to the Lord. That is what is meant by the passage *tam eva dhīraḥ*: the wise man should not engage in words. (Bṛhad-āraṇyaka Upaniṣad 4.4.21)

pūrtena tapasā yajñair dānair yogaih samādhinā
brāhmaṁ niḥśreyasaṁ puṁsāṁ mat-prītis tattvavin-matam

The result that men attain by pious acts, austerity, sacrifices, charities, and concentration in *yoga* should be something that pleases me. This is the opinion of the knowers of truth. SB 3.9.41

Thus meditation is optional for one who has gained knowledge of the Lord. The meaning is this. Discerning the truth about the Lord is difficult by logic and śrutis whose meaning is difficult to fathom. This quest is performed by many branches of the Vedas with many subject matters. The devotee, because his heart has softened by thinking of the Lord with blissful form and because he is attracted to the Lord alone, does not indulge in this knowledge since it causes hardness in the heart. Coming out of his ecstasy, he may sometimes engage in contemplating the truth about the Lord according to scripture, to assist in his attraction to the Lord.

Proof and reason for this is given.

Sūtra - 3.3.28

|| sāmparāye tartavyābhāvāt tathā hy anye ||

The scripture says that when one has attained prema, this type of meditation and deliberation is not necessary since there is no bondage to overcome.

Sāmparāya means the Lord, since all things in existence lead (*samparayanti*) to him. Prema for the Lord is called *sāmparāya,* that which exists in the Lord, formed by the rule *tatra bhavaḥ* (Pāninī 4.3.53) When there is prema (*sāmparāye*), meditation on the qualities of the Lord is optional. Why? Because at that time there are no bonds to be cut (*tartavyābhāvāt*). The Vājaseyins (*anye*) say:

tam eva dhīro vijñāya prajñāṁ kurvīta brāhmaṇaḥ.
nānudhyāyed bahūn śabdān vāco viglāpanaṁ hi tat.

The wise brāhmaṇa, understanding the Lord, should worship him. He should not meditate on many words, which are mere weariness of speech. Bṛhad-āraṇyaka Upaniṣad 4.4.21

The Lord himself says:

tasmād mad-bhakti-yuktasya yogino vai mad-ātmanaḥ
na jñānaṁ na ca vairāgyaṁ prāyaḥ śreyo bhaved iha

Therefore, for a devotee engaged in *bhakti,* with mind fixed on me, the cultivation of knowledge and renunciation is generally not beneficial for *bhakti.* SB 11.20.31

Topic 13 (Sūtras 29 - 30)

Ubhayāvirodhādhikaraṇam - Permission to perform two types of bhakti

It has been said that one should meditate on the Lord possessing qualities. Two types of qualities are now shown. *tad u hovāca hairaṇyo gopa-veśam abhrābham*: Brahmā said: he wears cowherd clothing and is the color of a cloud. (Gopāla-tāpanī Upaniṣad) *prakṛtyā sahitaḥ śyāmaḥ:* dark complexioned Rāma is accompanied by his consort. (Rāma-tāpanī Upaniṣad) *sa vā ayam ātmā sarvasya vaśī sarvasyeśānaḥ*: this *ātmā* is the controller of all, the Lord of all. (Bṛhad-āraṇyaka Upaniṣad 4.4.22)

Sometimes *ruci-bhakti,* using knowledge of his sweetness, is seen as the cause of attaining him. Sometimes *vidhi-bhakti* is seen as the cause of attaining him, using knowledge of the Lord's power. Which of these is the cause of attaining him, since the two are different, caused by difference in the object of worship?

(Pūrvapakṣa) The person desiring progress will find it impossible to advance since the method cannot be determined.

Sūtra - 3.3.29

|| chandata ubhayāvirodhāt ||

By the will of the Lord, both paths of bhakti exist. There is no confusion about method, because of scriptural statements concerning both paths.

The word *na* (not) is understood from sūtra 3.3.22. Both types of bhakti exist for jīvas of either type, because of the will of the Lord (*chandataḥ*), arising by association with devotees of these types. Thus it is not true that it is impossible to have advancement. Why? Because permission is given in statements concerning these two methods (*ubhayāvirodhāt*).

The meaning is this. Worship of the Lord's eternal qualities of two types, starting from the groups of eternal associates, spreads to the *sādhakas* like the flow of the Gaṅgā from heaven to earth. When the jīvas of this universe get the chance to have devotee association (of one of these two types), the Lord, who relishes bhakti, desires to inspire these persons who have had devotional association to have attraction to his qualities. These jīvas follow the Lord by that particular path. The devotees who give mercy to the jīvas are understood to be the *madhyamas.*

īśvare tad-adhīneṣu bāliśeṣu dviṣatsu ca
prema-maitrī-kṛpāpekṣā yaḥ karoti sa madhyamaḥ

An intermediate or second-class devotee, called *madhyama-adhikārī,* offers his love to the Supreme Lord, is a sincere friend to all the devotees of the Lord, shows mercy to ignorant people who are innocent, and disregards those who are envious of the Lord. SB 11.2.46

Therefore one cannot accuse the Lord of being partial (since the devotee gives the mercy).

Sūtra - 3.3.30

|| gater arthavattvam ubhayathānyathā hi virodhaḥ ||

Both paths, containing the Lord, are suitable to attain him. Otherwise, scriptures would be contradicted.

Accepting this, both paths *(ubhayathā)* are for attaining the Lord (*gateḥ*). Because of having worship of the Lord with sweet qualities or because of having worship the Lord with qualities of great power, both worships contain the Lord (*arthavattvam*). *Artha* means the goal of mankind, the Supreme Lord. *Arthavattvam* means "something endowed with the Supreme Lord." If this is not accepted *(anyathā)* it will be contrary to scriptural statements (*virodhaḥ*). The word *hi* indicates that both are authorized processes. One should not say that a person should practice both methods by citing sūtra 3.3.6 which instructs one to gather all qualities of the Lord, since only the cherished qualities (either sweet or grand) will manifest to the *ekāntī.* This will be explained later (sūtra 3.3.56).

Topic 14 (Sūtra 31)

Upapannādhikaraṇam - The best bhakti

Now the superiority of *ruci-bhakti* will be established. The doubt is, which is best, the path of *vidhi* or the path of *ruci*?

(Pūrvapakṣa) The path of *vidhi* is superior because it is more honorable to follow the rules properly.

Sūtra - 3.3.31

|| upapannas tal-lakṣaṇārthopalabdher lokavat ||

***Ruci-bhakti* is best because by this one attains the Lord who is most attracted to such devotees, just as a king is most attracted to the citizen who serves with most attention.**

It is better (*upapannaḥ*) to worship the Lord by the path of *ruci* for there is reason for its superiority. Why? Because one attains (*upalabdheḥ*) the Lord with sweet qualities (*artha*)-- who has the quality of being devoted to his devotee who is attracted to his sweetness (*tad-lakṣaṇa*), bringing the Lord under his control. An example is given. In this world some person who acts solely for the benefit of the king who appreciates those who are loyal brings the king under his control and is praised. The devotee with *ruci-bhakti* is like that. There is no fault that the Lord becomes dependent, since it is a good quality of the independent Lord to be controlled by the affection of a follower.

The meaning is this. The Supreme Lord, relishing affection, revealing his sweetness to his *ruci* devotees, accepts them when they offer themselves to him out of attachment. He, being purchased, makes them more prominent than himself out of affection for them, so that they may experience him fully. Otherwise, they cannot experience him fully. Śrī Śuka says:

nāyaṁ sukhāpo bhagavān dehināṁ gopikā-sutaḥ
jñānināṁ cātma-bhūtānāṁ yathā bhaktimatām iha

The Lord, son of Yaśodā, is not easily available to materialists or to *jñānīs* with realization of *ātmā,* but is easily available to persons with devotion to the son of Yaśodā. SB 10.9.21

Though he is controlled by all devotees as a rule, he is most controlled by the *ruci* devotees. Thus, it is proved they are the best and following the path of *ruci* is best.

Topic 15 (Sūtras 32 - 33)

Aniyamādhikaraṇam - No rule to perfom all aṅgas of bhakti

Now the author shows two types of worship: using one *aṅga* of bhakti or many. Gopāla-tāpanī Upaniṣad defines the *svarūpa* of bhakti in the section beginning *oṁ munayo ha vai brahmānam ūcūḥ* and ending with *sakalaṁ paraṁ brahma*. Then it says *etad yo dhyāyati rasati bhajati, so 'mrto bhavati:* he who meditates, does *japa* and worships becomes immortal. (Gopāla-tāpanī Upaniṣad 1.6)

The doubt is this. Does a person practice for liberation by all the methods mentioned starting with meditation or does he practice one method?

(Pūrvapakṣa) One should perform all methods since after mentioning them all, it is said one attains liberation.

Sūtra - 3.3.32

|| aniyamaḥ sarveṣām avirodhaḥ śabdānumānābhyām ||

It is not obligatory to perform all *aṅgas* of bhakti as this would contradict other statements in śruti and smṛti.

There is no rule that one attains liberation doing all the items (*aniyamaḥ sarveṣam*). Each of them can be done separately. Why? Because then there is no conflict of this śruti with other śruti and smṛti texts (*śabdānumānābhyām avirodhaḥ*).

cintayaṁś cetasā kṛṣṇaṁ mukto bhavati saṁsṛteḥ

Meditating with the mind on Kṛṣṇa one becomes liberated from *saṁsāra.* Gopāla-tāpanī Upaniṣad 1.10

pañca-padaṁ pañcāṅgaṁ japan dyāvābhūmī sūryācandramasau sāgnī

Uttering these five parts of the mantra while thinking of their presiding deities-- sky, earth, sun moon and fire--one attains Brahman as Kṛṣṇa by this mantra. Gopāla-tāpanī Upaniṣad 1.12

kīrtanād eva kṛṣṇasya mukta-saṅgaḥ paraṁ vrajet

Simply by chanting about Kṛṣṇa, one can become free from material bondage and attains *prema.* SB 12.3.51

eko 'pi kṛṣṇāya kṛtaḥ pramāṇo
daśāśvamedhāvabhṛthair na tulyaḥ
daśāśvamedhī punar eti janma
kṛṣṇa-pramāṇī na punar-bhavāya

The purificatory rites performed during ten horse sacrifices cannot equal even one *praṇāma* offered to Kṛṣṇa. A person who performs ten horse sacrifices takes birth again. The person offering *praṇāmas* to Kṛṣṇa does not take birth again. Nārada Pāñcaratra, BRS 1.2.129

By taking the passage "he who meditates, relishes and worships" to mean each process gives liberation, there is then no contradiction with other śruti and smṛti texts which mention that one process gives liberation. The meaning of the passage is "He who meditates attains liberation; he who does *japa* attains liberation; he who worship attains liberation." If one does all the processes, so much more the result. The three processes mentioned are representative of the nine processes.

"Śruti says that after doing meditation one attains liberation. *ātmā vā are draṣṭavyaḥ: ātmā* should be seen (by meditation). (Bṛhad-āraṇyaka Upaniṣad 4.5.6) Why does it say that after doing *japa* and other actions one attains liberation?" *Japa* and other actions and meditation are mutually connected. In *japa* there is meditation and in meditation there is *japa* and other actions.

"It is not correct to say that on knowing Brahman one becomes liberated, because one sees that Brahmā, Śiva, Indra and others (having knowledge of the Lord) stay for a long time in the material world performing acts against the Lord."

Sūtra - 3.3.33

|| yāvad-adhikāram avasthitir ādhikārikāṇām ||

The jīvas holding posts in the universe remain as long as their term lasts (and later they attain liberation).

We do not say that all those knowers of Brahman become liberated with perfection of knowledge. Those who have perfected knowledge, who have destroyed accumulated karmas of acts in past lives *(aprarabdha)* by knowledge, who have dissolved karmas produced by their present bodies (*kriyamāna)* by knowledge and have destroyed the present body attained by karma *(prārabdha*) by enjoying it, attain liberation. But Brahmā and others, who hold positions, though they have destroyed or dissolved accumulated (*aprārabdha)* and present karmas (*kriyamāna)*, remain in the material world as long as their karma which has given them this position (*prārabdha*) is not destroyed. At the completion of those karmas which have started in this life, they become liberated and enter the supreme abode.

This should be understood. Those like Indra who have shorter periods of office, after their term is finished, go to Brahmā who holds office for longer. At the end of Brahmā's term, when he is liberated, they are liberated with him. This will be stated in sūtra 4.3.10 (*kāryātyaye tad-adhyekṣeṇa*).

When they act against the Lord, that is simply following the Lord's desire for nourishing his pastimes. It is not a fault on their part. Though they appear to be attached to material enjoyment, that is only a show, for they are fixed in knowledge of the Lord. Thus except for those holding posts, other knowers of the truth on knowing the Lord attain liberation. There is no doubt.

Topic 16 (Sūtras 34 - 35)

Akṣarādhikaraṇam - Worshipping akṣara-brahman

Now the author gathers qualities like "not gross." In śruti it is said:

etad vai tad akṣaram gārgi brāhmaṇā abhivadanty asthūlam aṇava-hrasvam

O Gārgī, the brāhmaṇas call this the imperishable. It is not gross, not long or short. Bṛhad-āraṇyaka Upaniṣad 3.8.8

ata parā yayā ad akṣsaraṁ adhigamyate yad adreśyam agrahyam agotram avarṇam acakṣuḥ-śrotram

By superior knowledge, the *akṣara* which is unseen, ungrasped, without family, without color, not known by eye or ear is known. Muṇḍaka Upaniṣad 1.5-6

The doubt is this. Should Brahman, described as *akṣara,* which forbids thinking of it as gross etc., be used in all worship or not?

(Pūrvapakṣa) One should not use these descriptions in worship of Brahman because it is impossible for them to exist in the Brahman, since what was described was worship of Brahman with a form in sūtra 3.3.20 (*samāna evaṁ cābhedāt*).

Sūtra - 3.3.34

|| akṣara-dhiyāṁ tv avarodhaḥ sāmānya-tad-bhāvābhyām

aupasadavat, tad uktam ||

The words used to describe *akṣara* should be gathered in all worship because the Brahman is only one in all scriptures and does not lack these qualities. It is like the use of mantras in sacrifice. This is mentioned by Jaimini.

The word *tu* refutes the argument. The conceptions of "not gross" etc. related to *akṣara* Brahman (*akṣara-dhiyām*) should be gathered *(avarodhaḥ)* for all worship. Why? Because everywhere in scripture only Brahman is described *(sāmānya*). *sarve vedā yat-padam āmananti:* I will teach what all the Vedas proclaim. (Kaṭha Upaniṣad 1.2.15) And because all these qualities like "not gross" exist in Brahman with a form.

The meaning is this. From knowledge one attains liberation. *jñātvā devam*: knowing the Lord all suffering is destroyed. (Śvetāśvatara Upaniṣad 1.11) Knowledge means knowledge of something extraordinary, not ordinary. Otherwise the statement would be an exaggeration. (It would mean that knowing anything gives liberation.) Thus knowledge will become extraordinary when Brahman, all-pervading, has a form non-different from knowledge and bliss and endowed with qualities like "not gross" since this distinguishes Brahman from all else. In this way a form devoid of all inferior qualities is indicated.

Gajendra prayed:

sa vai na devāsura-martya-tiryaṅ
na strī na ṣaṇḍo na pumān na jantuḥ
nāyaṁ guṇaḥ karma na san na cāsan
niṣedha-śeṣo jayatād aśeṣaḥ

The Lord is not a *devatā*, demon, human, animal, female, neuter, male or any other living being. He is not the *guṇas* or *karma.* He remains after everything is negated. May the unlimited Lord remain glorious! SB 8.3.24

The Lord, praised with qualities such as being devoid of grossness, made his appearance to Gajendra in his form (*harir āvirāsīt*)--with those very qualities. The Lord appeared in the form with the qualities that Gajendra requested. That is clear. Otherwise knowledge alone (without a form) would have arisen in Gajendra's mind from his prayer. In the verse, material *devatā* or human forms are negated. But the Lord has his *devatā* nature and *puruṣa* nature fixed in his *svarūpa* since he makes his appearance as *devatā* or human.

The word *aupasadavat* shows that the qualities follow the principal object. It is like the mantra used in ritual (*upasada*). The mantras (secondary) for offering cakes in the Jāmadagni rites, though from the Sāma Veda (in which the mantras are chanted loudly), are used by the *adhvaryu* priests of the Yajur Veda (but chanted softly according to Yajur Veda principles), since the priest must offer the cakes (principal). Thus the qualities like "not gross" are used everywhere along with the principle object *akṣara-brahman*. Those qualities follow Brahman.

In Vidhi-kāṇḍa it is said *guṇa-mukhya-vyatikrame tad-arthatvān mukhyena veda-saṁyogaḥ:* when there is a conflict between secondary and primary statements, there is a connection with the Vedas by the primary statement, and the secondary ones are useful for supporting the principal ones.

"Just as Brahman has qualities like having a form, it is said *sarva-karmā sarva-gandhaḥ:* Brahman is all action and all fragrances. One must meditate on Brahman as all action as well."

Sūtra - 3.3.35

|| iyad āmananāt ||

One should meditate on the qualities previously mentioned, since that meditation is recommended.

One must necessarily meditate on all that was previously mentioned *(iyat)*, the qualities like having a form. Why? Because that meditation is instructed there (*āmananāt*). Using all those qualities one should meditate on Brahman. "Being all action" only follows after Brahman which is the object of meditation. Thus meditation on such qualities is not a rule.

Topic 17 (Sūtras 36 - 37)

Antarādhikaraṇam – The meaning of "in the city of Brahman"

Now qualities like having an abode are gathered. It is said:

yaḥ sarva-jñaḥ sarva-vid yasyaiṣa mahimā bhuvi sambabhūva divye pure hy eṣa samvyomny ātmā pratiṣṭhitaḥ

He who is omniscient, knowing all, whose glory manifests on earth, is situated in the sky in a shining palace. Muṇḍaka Upaniṣad 2.2.7

The passage ends with *brahmaivedam viśvam idaṁ variṣṭham*: Brahman is this, everything and best. The doubt is this. Does that city of Brahman called *saṁvyoma* mean simply that Brahman has great powers and strength or does it mean a city with gates, walls and palaces?

(Pūrvapakṣa) It means the greatness of Brahman, since his possession of greatness is described in śrutis. His greatness is described as a city and is called sky or *saṁvyoma* because of its unlimited nature. "Brahman is everything" means that what is all pervading has no support. (It is independent.)

Sūtra - 3.3.36

|| antarā bhūta-grāmavat svātmanaḥ ||

In the city of Brahman, objects which seem to be made of the elements appear to the devotee.

In that city (*antarā*) everything appears to be made of groups of elements (*bhūta-grāmavat)* to the devotee (*svātmanaḥ*). *Svātmanaḥ* means "to the person whom the Lord has chosen as his own." *yam evaiṣa vṛnute tena labhyaḥ:* the person whom the Lord chooses can attain him. (Muṇḍaka Upaniṣad 3.2.3) Though everything there is Brahman, it appears to be made of elements like earth. The suffix *vat* (like) denies being made of material elements. Rather those objects are the Lord himself.

brahmaivedam amṛtam purastāt paścāc ca. brahma dakṣiṇataś cottareṇādhaś cordhvaṁ prasṛtam. brahmaivedaṁ viśvam idaṁ variṣṭham

This Brahman is eternal; Brahman is spread in the east and west. Brahman is spread in the south and north, down and up. Brahman is everything and most excellent. Muṇḍaka Upaniṣad 2.2.11

Just as a variety of hands, feet, nails and earrings appear in the Lord filled with knowledge and bliss for the devotee, so in that spiritual world, which is non-different from the Lord, earth and water appear in the Lord for the devotee. The one Brahman has variety, like colors on a peacock feather.

Sūtra - 3.3.37

|| anyathā bhedānupapattir iti cen, nopadeśāntaravat ||

If one objects that, because of non-difference, there can be no city supporting Brahman, the answer is no, since other śrutis show difference.

"In the absence of difference between Brahman and other things (*anyathā*), there can be no difference between the support and the supporter (and thus no city)." This is not a fault. Why? Because there are other teachings (*upadeśāntaravat*). Just as there are other statements like *ānandaṁ brahmaṇo vidvān (*he knows the bliss of Brahman), which teach non-difference, by the strength of *viśeṣa*, difference is accomplished.

Topic 18 (Sūtra 38)

Vyatihārādhikaraṇam - Lord and his abode are interchangeable

Next, it is indicated that the place of the Lord should be worshipped like the Lord.

Sūtra - 3.3.38

|| vyatihāro viśiṁṣanti hītaravat ||

The Lord and his planet are interchangeable just like the Lord and his form.

It is said *ātmānam eva lokam upāsīta*: one should worship the Lord as his planet. (Bṛhad-āraṇyaka Upaniṣad 1.4.15) Since śrutis specify that Paramātmā is the planet and that the planet is Paramātmā, they are interchangeable (*vyatihāraḥ*). Paramātmā is the planet and the planet is Paramātmā. Elsewhere *(itaravat)* other śrutis specify that the form is Paramātmā and the form is Paramātmā. For instance, there is the passage beginning *sat-puṇḍarīka-nayanam:* he has lotus eyes and concluding with *sākṣāt prakṛti-paro 'yam ātmā gopālaḥ:* the cowherd is directly the Lord, beyond matter. (Gopāla-tāpanī Upaniṣad) Similarly, the Lord with a form of bliss and knowledge appears in the form of his planet made attractive by his *acintya-śakti,* for his devotee and not to others. Like the Lord, his planet is the object of meditation.

Topic 19 (Sūtra 39)

Satyādhikaraṇam - Qualities like truth

This section commences in order to strengthen what was said. The subject (*viṣaya*) is texts giving specific qualities about the Lord.

The doubt is this. Are these qualities *māyā* or natural to the Lord?

(Pūrvapakṣa) *neha nānāsti kiñcana:* there is no variety at all. (Bṛhad-āraṇyaka Upaniṣad 4.4.19) *athāta ādeśo neti neti*: this is the teaching, not this, not this. (Bṛhad-āraṇyaka Upaniṣad 2.3.6) Thus these qualities are *māyā.*

Sūtra - 3.3.39

|| saiva hi satyādayaḥ ||

It is the Lord's *svarūpa-śakti* from whom qualities like truth arise.

Śvetāśvatara Upaniṣad (*parasya śaktiḥ*) and Viṣṇu Purāṇa (*viṣṇu-śakti parā proktāḥ*) describes the natural, superior *svarūpa śakti* of the Lord, like warmth of a fire, which is different from *māyā.* That *śakti (saiva*), though *māyā,* is related to his self since this *śakti* becomes truth and other qualities. The two reasons for the spiritual nature of these qualities like truth are given in the next sūtra: this *śakti* is all pervading and releases the devotees. Thus it is said "Not this, not this." The word *athāta* was previously explained. The word *ādi* stands for cleaniness, mercy, tolerance, omniscience, omnipotent, bliss and beauty. Thus Parāśara defines the word *bhagavān* as the Paramātmā with pure qualities of great power and then says the Lord from which arises total *(samaṣṭi)* and individual matter *(vyaṣṭi)* has qualities of supporting all and possession of all powers. He describes the qualities like unlimited knowledge.

śuddhe mahā-vibhūty-ākhye pare brahmaṇi śabdyate
maitreya bhagavac-chabdaḥ sarva-kāraṇa-kāraṇe

O Maitreya! The word *bhagavān,* means the cause of all causes, the supreme Brahman, who is pure and is called the great power.

sambharteti tathā bhartā bha-kāro 'rtha-dvayānvitaḥ
netā gamayitā sraṣṭā ga-kārārthas tathā mune

The syllable *bha* means the support of all and the maintainer. The syllable *ga* means the leader, creator and the cause of going to Vaikuṇṭha.

aiśvaryasya samagrasya vīryasya yaśasaḥ sriyaḥ
jñāna-vairāgyayos cāpi ṣaṇṇāṁ bhaga itīṅganaḥ

The six *bhagas* are all power, potency, fame, beauty, knowledge and renunciation.

vasanti yatra bhūtāni bhūtātmany akhilātmani
sa ca bhūteṣv aśeṣeśu vakārārthas tato 'vyayaḥ

The syllable *va* means the indestructible Lord in whom all beings dwell and who dwells in all beings.

The Lord's *śakti* is non-different from his *svarūpa.* Truth and other qualities come from this *śakti.* One should meditate on them as non-different from the Lord (*dharmī*).

Topic 20 (Sūtras 40 - 42)

Kāmādy-adhikaraṇam - The Lord's consorts

Now commences collection of the quality related to Śrī. *Śrīś ca lakṣmīś ca patnī*: Śrī and Lakṣmī are his wives. (Śukla Yajur Veda 31.22) Some say Śrī means Ramā and Lakṣmī means divine wealth. Other say Śrī is speech and

Lakṣmī is Ramā. *kamalā-pataye namaḥ ramā-mānasa-haṁsāya govindāya namo namaḥ*: I offer respects to the master of Lakṣmī, to Govinda, the swan in Ramā's mind. (Gopāla-tāpanī Upaniṣad) *ramādhārāya rāmāya*: I offer respects to Rāma, the support of Rāma. (Rāma-tāpanī Upaniṣad)

The doubt is this. Is Śrī temporary, being a material entity, or eternal because of being spiritual?

(Pūrvapakṣa) *athāta ādeśo neti neti*: the instructon is "not this, not this." Since any qualities are forbidden in the Lord, Śrī and others cannot be his qualities. The *viśuddha-sattva* form of the Lord, which has accepted *māyā,* is connected with Śrī, also influenced by māyā. That Śrī is temporary.

Sūtra - 3.3.40

|| kāmādītaratra tatra cāyatanādibhyaḥ ||

Śrī is the Lord's spiritual *śakti,* who spreads desire for *śṛṅgāra-rasa* in the spiritual and material worlds since she is all-pervading and gives liberation.

The words *sā eva* are understood from the previous sūtra. She is the spiritual *śrī.* In the spiritual sky untouched by *prakṛti (tatra)* and in the manifestation in the material world (*itaratra),* she displays conjugal desire (*kāmādi)* for her Lord. Thus the Lord eternally accompanies her. *Ādi* indicates other related qualities and service to him. Śrī is spiritual. Why? Because she is all-pervading (*āya*) and because she spreads (*tāna*) the bliss of liberation to the devotees. These two qualities are like truth and the rest. The word *ādi* indicates that Śrī is also one with the *parāśakti.* Because his *parāśakti* has been said to be non-different from him (*svabhāviki*) and natural to him, Srī is also of the same nature as his spiritual *śakti.* Since it is said that she is the form of knowledge and mercy, she also gives liberation. Since she is non-different from *parāśakti,* she has these qualities.

Smṛti says:

nityaiva sā jagan-mātā viṣṇoḥ śrīr anapāyinī
yathā sarva-gato viṣṇus tathaiveyaṁ dvijottama

O brāhmaṇa! The mother of the universe, Śrī, is eternally the consort of Viṣṇu. Just Viṣṇu is everywhere she is also. Viṣṇu Purāṇa 1.8.15

ātma-vidyā ca devi tvaṁ vimukti-phala-dāyinī

She is knowledge of *ātmā* and the giver of liberation. Viṣṇu Purāṇa 1.9.118

One cannot say that Śrī and the Lord are separate, being different persons, since this is against the scriptural proof. Smṛti also says that Śrī is one with the Lord.

procyate parameśo yo yaḥ śuddho 'py upacārataḥ
prasīdatu sa no viṣṇur ātmā yaḥ sarva-dehinām

May the pure supreme Lord Viṣṇu, who, though one, is called figuratively the lord of Lakṣmī,[76] and who is the soul in all bodies, be merciful to us. Viṣṇu Purāṇa 1.9.45

It is clear that Paramā means Lakṣmī in this verse. Because of being all-pervading and giving liberation, she cannot be *prakṛti.* She is different. Thus Śrī is spiritual and eternal.

"If Śrī is the *parā śakti*, it would be impossible for her to have bhakti (since she is one with the Lord). It is impossible to have bhakti for oneself."

Sūtra - 3.3.41

|| ādarād alopaḥ ||

Śrī's bhakti does not disappear, though she is one with the Lord, because of her adoration.

Though Śrī is non-different from him, her bhakti does not disappear because of her adoration of him, since he is the ocean of multifarious qualities and her very foundation. There is no branch which does not respect the tree and no ray which does not respect the moon. Her bhakti is indicated in the śrutis previously quoted. Smṛti says:

śrīr yat-padāmbuja-rajaś cakame tulasyā
labdhvāpi vakṣasi padaṁ kila bhṛtya-juṣṭam
yasyāḥ sva-vīkṣaṇa utānya-sura-prayāsas
tadvad vayaṁ ca tava pāda-rajaḥ prapannāḥ

Śrī, whose glance is sought after by the *devatās* with great endeavor, has achieved the unique position of always remaining on the chest of her Lord, Nārāyaṇa. Still, she desires the dust of his lotus feet, even though she has to

---

[76] Baladeva says that this viśeṣa. One entity can be perceived as two, though it is actually one.

share that dust with Tulasī-devī and with the Lord's many other servants. Similarly, we have approached the dust of your lotus feet for shelter. SB 10.29.37

"Desire for conjugal love can exist only if there is a difference in the two parties as *viṣaya* and *āśraya.* It is not possible where there is nondifference."

Sūtra - 3.3.42

|| upasthite'tas tad-vacanāt ||

Love between the Lord and his consort arises by their distinct presences, since this is stated in śruti.

Upasthite is a past participle form expressing a state (being near). Though there is no difference between Viṣnū and his *śakti,* desire arises when they are in proximity (*upasthite),* with Supreme Lord acting as the shelter of *śakti,* and *śakti* acting as the jewel of youthful beauty for fulfilling his nature as self-enjoying and complete. Why is this? Because of statements concerning that desire in Gopāla-tāpanī Upaniṣad.

yo ha vai kāmena kāmān kāmayate sa kāmī bhavati. yo ha vai tv akāmena kāmān kāmayate so 'kāmī bhavati

He who desires objects with desire to enjoy them is an enjoyer. He who desires objects without a desire to enjoy them is not an enjoyer. Gopāla-tāpanī Upaniṣad 2.21

The word *akāmena* means "something like desire, but not desire": prema, which is similar to *kāma.* The Lord's natures as self-enjoying and being complete in himself are not contradicted by his loving a person with prema which gives an experience of his very self. The great bliss he experiences from the touch of Śrī, who is himself, is like seeing his own beauty.

This is what has been said. When the supreme entity endowed with his *svarūpa-śakti* called *parā*, established in śruti and smṛti, manifests with himself in the predominant position, it is called Supreme Lord. When he is manifest with *parā-śakti* predominant, it is called his quality (*dharma*). *Parā* manifests as dharma in the form of knowledge, joy, compassion, majesty, sweetness. As sound, she takes the form of the name. As the earth, she is the form of the dhāma. Forms of Śrī like Rādhā are all called *parā* since they are all the jewel of youthfulness composed of *saṁvit* (consciousness), endowed with the essence of *hlādinī* (bliss).

Though Śrī is non-different from him, her desire for him is accomplished because of the appearance of difference of *āsraya* and *viṣaya* produced through the action of distinction, caused by *viśeṣa*. Her forms as quality etc. are not later creations but eternally accomplished. There is no fault at all in this manifestation. Therefore the devotees should meditate on the supreme Lord with Śrī, his consort.

Topic 21 (Sūtra 43)

Tan-nirdhāraṇāniyamādhikaraṇam - No rules regarding worshipping only Kṛṣṇa

In śruti the following is found. *tasmāt eva kṛṣṇaḥ paro devas taṁ dhyāyet taṁ raset taṁ*

bhajet taṁ yajet. iti. oṁ tat sat: therefore Kṛṣṇa is the supreme being; one should meditate on him, experience his sweetness, worship him and serve him. (Gopāla-tāpanī Upaniṣad 1.48)

The doubt is this. Is it a rule that one should worship the Lord with the qualities of Kṛṣṇa only?

(Pūrvapakṣa) Taking the literal meaning of *eva* (only), one must do this.

Sūtra - 3.3.43

|| tan-nirdhāraṇāniyamas tad-dṛṣṭeḥ pṛthag ghy apratibandhaḥ phalam ||

There is not rule to worship only Kṛṣṇa, since the śruti indicates that many forms can be worshipped. But worship of Kṛṣṇa is different for worship of others: it removes the idea that one must perform other worship.

There is no rule (*aniyamaḥ*) to worship the Lord as only Kṛṣṇa (*nirdhāraṇa*) and not other forms. Though Kṛṣṇa is the child who drinks Yaśodā's milk, he is certainly the entity of knowledge and bliss. (But other forms can be worshipped.) Why? Because it is seen in scriptures (*tad-dṛṣteḥ*).

yatrāsau saṁsthitaḥ kṛṣṇas tribhiḥ śaktyā samāhitaḥ
rāmāniruddha-pradyumnai rukmiṇyā sahito vibhuḥ
catuḥ-śabdo bhaved eko hy oṁkāras hy aṁśakaiḥ kṛtaḥ

There the powerful Lord Kṛṣṇa resides, situated with excellent pastimes, accompanied by Balarāma, Aniruddha and Pradyumna and by his *śakti* Rukmiṇī. It is declared that the four Vedas become one as *oṁkāra.* Gopāla-tāpanī 2.36-7

It is seen in these verses that Balarāma and others who are non-different from Kṛṣṇa are also to be worship. "Then the word *eva* (only) in the text would be useless." No. Because (*hi*) the result is different (*pṛthak).* What is that? His worship removes the obstacle *(pratibandhaḥ*) of other worship being superior (his worship makes one understand that it is superior to all other worship). If there is inclination and ability, one can worship them all. If not, then worship only Kṛṣṇa.

Topic 22 (Sūtra 44)

Pradānādhikaraṇam - Mercy of guru

Now starts the topic of the Lord's quality of being attained through a guru. This is stated in scriptures dealing with vidyā.

yasya deve parā bhaktir yathā deve tathā gurau
tasyaite kathitā hy arthāḥ prakāśante mahātmanaḥ

The meaning of scriptures is revealed to the great souls whose bhakti to the Lord is equaled by bhakti to guru. Śvetāśvatara Upaniṣad 6.23

Similarly it is said *ācāryavān puruṣo veda*: one who accepts guru knows the Vedas. (Chāndogya Upaniṣad 6.14.2) *tad-vijñānārthaṁ sa gurum evābhigacchet*: to gain knowledge of the Lord, one must approach a guru. (Muṇḍaka Upaniṣad 1.2.12)

The doubt is this. Does one gain the result from hearing through the guru or hearing along with the mercy of the guru?

(Pūrvapakṣa) It comes from hearing since the scriptures say that the result comes from hearing. What is the use of mercy?

Sūtra - 3.3.44

|| pradānavad eva tad uktam ||

It is stated in scriptures that mercy of guru is necessary to attain the goal, just as his mercy is necessary to get the means to the goal.

Just as the cause of attaining Brahman is the *sādhana* of hearing, given (*pradānavat*) by the pleased guru, so also the result, attainment of Brahman, is achieved by the pleased guru. It is not just by hearing. Mercy is necessary. Mercy of the guru directed to the disciple is stated in scriptures. The word *pra* indicates mercy. Thus *pradānavat* means "as in the case of mercifully giving *sādhana*." The Lord himself says *ācāryopasanam*: knowledge means approaching a guru. (BG 13.8) One attains the goal by hearing along with mercy of the guru.

Topic 23 (Sūtra 45)

Liṅga-bhūyastvādhikaraṇam - Mercy is stronger than effort

Which is the stronger influence for attaining the goal, one's efforts or grace of guru?

(Pūrvapakṣa) One's efforts are stronger influence because without effort, grace becomes insignificant.

Sūtra - 3.3.45

|| liṅga-bhūyastvāt tad dhi balīyas tad api ||

Because of indications in scriptures, mercy of guru is stronger. But hearing and other actions are also necessary.

Having heard about Brahman from devatās who has assumed forms of a bull, fire, swan and bird, Satyakāma then requested his guru *bhagavāṁs tv eva me kāmaṁ brūyāt*: O great respected guru, please speak this knowledge to me if you desire. (Chāndogya Upaniṣad 4.9.2) Similarly Upakośala who heard the knowledge from Agni then asked his teacher for the same knowledge. Because of many indications (*liṅga-bhūyastvāt*) concerning the mercy of guru seen in the Chāndogya and other Upaniṣads, mercy of guru is stronger.

But one should not think "That mercy is enough. Effort is not necessary." Hearing and other actions are necessary (*tad api*). *Yasya deve parā bhaktiḥ*: the person who has bhakti to the Lord has all the meanings of scripture revealed. (Śvetāśvatara Upaniṣad 6.23) It is also said *śrotavyaḥ mantavyaḥ*: one should hear and contemplate. (Bṛhad-āraṇyaka Upaniṣad 2.4.5) Smṛti says:

guru-prasādo balavān na tasmād balavattaram
tathāpi śravaṇādiś ca kartavyo mokṣa-siddhaye

Mercy of guru is strong. There is nothing stronger than this. However hearing and other actions must be performed to attain liberation.[77]

Topic 24 (Sūtras 46 - 47)

Pūrva-vikalpādhikaraṇam - *So 'ham* is bhakti[78]

It has been established that one will attain the result from worship of the Lord endowed with qualities with the mercy of guru. This conclusion is strengthened by reconciling the meaning of contrary statements such as the following. In Gopāla-tāpanī, Brahmā, on being asked by sages about the entity having qualities like being most worthy of worship, indicated Kṛṣṇa to have those qualities and taught bhakti as the cause of attaining him. Then it is said:

tasmād eva paro rajasa iti so 'ham ity avadhārya gopālo 'ham iti bhāvayet.
sa mokṣam aśnute sa brahmatvam adhigacchati sa brahma-vid bhavati.

Therefore one should understand that the Lord is beyond the *guṇas,* and one should identify one's interests with his using the mantra *so'ham*. One should thus meditate "I am Gopāla." He becomes free of ignorance. He attains a spiritual form. He knows Kṛṣṇa. Gopāla-tāpanī Upaniṣad 2.38-39

With the words *so 'ham*, one sees practice of seeing non-difference of the jīva and the Lord.

The doubt is this. Is this a meditation of oneness of the *svarūpa* of the Lord and jīva or is it a type of bhakti as previously taught?

(Pūrvapakṣa) Because of the direct meaning of the words, the cause of liberation is identifying jīva as identical with the Lord.

Sūtra - 3.3.46

|| pūrva-vikalpaḥ prakaraṇāt syāt kriyā mānasavat ||

---

[77] First line is quoted by Madhva and his followers.
[78] The words *so 'ham* indicate bhakti as previously mentioned, not the complete indentity of the Lord and the jīva

***So ham* means a type of bhakti because of the context. It is just like deity worship and meditation.**

So 'ham is an alternate form of the bhakti previously mentioned (*pūrva-vikalpaḥ*). Why? Because bhakti was previously stated in the same Upaniṣad and also at the end (*prakaraṇāt*).

bhaktir asya bhajanaṁ tad ihāmūtropādhi-nairāśyenāmusmin manaḥ kalpanam etad eva naiṣkarmyam

Bhajanam or service means devotional service to Kṛṣṇa. It is concentration of the mind on Kṛṣṇa without desires for enjoyment in this life or the next. It destroys all karma. Gopāla-tāpanī 1.14

sac-cid-ānandaika-rase bhakti-yoge tiṣṭhati

The Lord resides in bhakti, which is completely filled with eternity, knowledge and bliss. Gopāla-tāpanī 2.78

Because of this context (*prakaraṇāt*), the statement *so 'ham* in a middle text must be a type of bhakti. It cannot mean anything else. An example is given. It is like deity worship (*kriyā*) and meditation (*manasavat*). Just as these two are types of bhakti, meditating *so 'ham* is also a type of bhakti previously mentioned. The state of "I am that (*so 'ham*)" arises when, out of great attachment or fear, one becomes absorbed in an object. Out of attachment one may say "I am Kṛṣṇa." Out of fear one may say, "I am a lion."

What is said is this. In the first part of the Upaniṣad it was said *kaḥ paramo devaḥ*: who is the supreme deity? (Gopala-tāpanī Upaniṣad 1.2) The sages asked Brahmā about the supreme goal, most worthy of worship, which destroys *saṁsāra*, shelters all, and causes everything. Brahmā replied *śrī-kṛṣṇo vai paramaṁ daivatam*: Kṛṣṇa is the supreme deity. (Gopala-tāpanī Upaniṣad 1.3) He explained that Kṛṣṇa was endowed with the proper qualities. He then instructed the sages to meditate on Kṛṣṇa and when they asked about bhakti rendered to Kṛṣṇa, worthy of worship, Brahmā described Kṛṣṇa's *svarūpa* along with his associates. *te hocuḥ kiṁ tad-rūpam tad u hovāca hairaṇyo gopa-veśam abhrābham:* Brahmā said ,"He wears cowherd clothing and is dark like a cloud." He explained that Kṛṣṇa, the form just described, is to be attained by japa. *ramyām punā rasanam*: one should chant his mantra. After describing Kṛṣṇa as knowledge and bliss, he concluded by saying *tasmāc chrī-kṛṣṇa eva paro devaḥ*: therefore Kṛṣṇa is the supreme Lord. (Gopala-tāpanī Upaniṣad 1.48)

In the second part of the Upaniṣad, Kṛṣṇa when playing with the gopīs, was questioned by them. He ordered them to feed Durvāsā with food. Durvāsā was satisfied with them, and offered them a boon. They asked about Kṛṣṇa. Desiring to explain how Kṛṣṇa's pastime's were different from others' pastimes, starting with *ayaṁ hi śrī-kṛṣṇa,* he spoke about Kṛṣṇa being the cause of everything, his nature of being controlled by pure affection and his eternal love for his consorts. When asked about Kṛṣṇa's birth, activities and abode, Durvāsā told the story of Brahmā and Nārāyaṇa in order to describe the conclusion by repetition, starting with *sa hovāca taṁ hi* (Gopāla-tāpanī Upaniṣad 2.26) He explained that Kṛṣṇa is complete and gives liberation from *saṁsāra.* He described Kṛṣṇa's place, called Mathurā, which is Brahman, which holds the *cakra,* and which shines with many forests.

Then he stated *tasmād evam; paro rajaseti so 'ham* (Gopāla-tāpanī Upaniṣad 2.38), a statement of non-difference of the jīva and the Lord, in order that persons could attain liberation. Because of the context as stated, this identity of self and the Lord must be a type of bhakti which was previously taught. This particular state in which one says "I am he" is like weeping and fainting. A statement of non-difference, seen also in Taittirīya Upaniṣad in the statement *brahmāham āsmī*: I am Brahman, occurs only when there is actual difference between the Lord and the devotee. It occurs in persons completely overcome by love for the Lord. This was previous explained.

One should accept the state of *so 'ham* as a particular type of bhakti, not as an attempt to merge the jīva into the Lord. Another reason is given for this conclusion.

Sūtra - 3.3.47

|| atideśāc ca ||

***So 'ham* indicates a type of bhakti because there is a statement *(atideśāt)* that the Lord has affection for the devotee just as Brahmā has for his sons.**

It is said:

yathā tvaṁ saha putraiś ca yathā rudro gānaiḥ saha
yathā śriyābhiyukto 'ham tathā bhakto mama priyaḥ

Just as you (Brahmā) are affectionate to your sons, just as Śiva is affectionate to his associates, just as I am affectionate to Lakṣmī, so I am affectionate to my devotee. Gopāla-tāpanī 2.48

The word *ca* indicates another, later statement:

dhyāyen mama priyo nityaṁ sa mokṣam adhigacchati
sa mukto bhavati tasmai svātmānam ca dadāmi vai

Meditating in this way, he who is dear to me attains eternal liberation. He gives up material bondage. More than that, I give myself to him. Gopāla-tāpanī 2.73

Kṛṣṇa says that he is eternally affectionate to his devotee and gives himself to his devotee who has given himself to the Lord. Therefore oneness is not possible. Therefore *so 'ham* should be understood to be a type of bhakti. Statements of *so 'ham* in Rāma-tāpanī Upaniṣad should be understood in the same way. Therefore liberation is achieved by worship of the Lord (not identity with the Lord) along with mercy of the guru. There is no fault in this conclusion.

Topic 25 (Sūtras 48 - 50)

Vidyādhikaraṇam - Knowledge

Vidyā means worship of the Lord along with knowledge of scripture. To clarify that *vidyā* produces liberation a new topic begins. In *puruṣa-sūkta* it is said *tam eva viditvāti mṛtyum eti nānyaḥ panthā vidyate 'yanāya:* knowing the Lord one surpasses death; there is no other path for going. Another version has *tam eva vidvān amṛta iha bhavati*: knowing this, he becomes immortal.

The doubt is this. Is the cause of liberation, karma (ritual and sacrifice), a combination of karma and *vidyā,* or just *vidyā*?

(Pūrvapakṣa) Karma is the cause of liberation because of what will be said in sūtras 3.4.2-7. *Vidyā* is secondary. Or liberation is caused by a combination of *vidyā* and karma, not either alone because scripture states this.

ubhābhyām eva pakṣābhyāṁ yathā khe pakṣiṇo gatiḥ
tathaiva karma-jñānābhyāṁ mukto bhavati mānavaḥ

Just as the motion of a bird in the sky takes place by two wings, a man attains liberation by karma and *jñāna.*

Or *vidyā* alone causes liberation *tam eva viditvā:* only knowing him one attains liberation. (Śvetāśvatara Upaniṣad 3.8)

Therefore the cause of liberation cannot be determined.

Sūtra - 3.3.48

|| vidyaiva tu tan-nirdhāraṇāt ||

***Vidyā* alone leads to liberation because that is ascertained in scriptures.**

The word *tu* indicates a refutation of the doubt. *Vidyā* is the cause of liberation, not karma or the combination of *vidyā* and karma. Why? Because this is ascertained with statements like *tam eva viditvā*: knowing him one attains liberation. (Śvetāśvatara Upaniṣad 3.8) The word *vidyā* means bhakti after attaining *jñāna* (knowledge of the Lord). *vijñāya prajñāṁ kurvīta*: knowing him, one performs bhakti (*prajñam*). Smṛti also uses the word *vidyā* to mean both knowledge and bhakti. *vidyā-kuṭhāreṇa śitena dhīraḥ*: the wise man cuts ignorance with the sharp axe of knowledge. (SB 11.12.12) *rāja-vidyā rāja-guhyam*: bhakti is the king of *vidyā* and king of secrets. (BG 9.2) Therefore the word means both knowledge and bhakti. It is like the word *kaurava* which means the sons of Dhṛtaraṣṭra and the sons of Pāṇḍu. Similarly the word *mīmāṁsaka* means a knower of karma and a knower of Brahman.

Liberation means direct, external perception of the Lord by *vidyā.*

Sūtra - 3.3.49

|| darśanāc ca ||

Liberation is caused by seeing the Lord.

Muṇḍaka Upaniṣad says:

bidyate hṛdaya-granthiś chidyante sarva-saṁśayāḥ
kṣīyante cāsya karmāṇi tasmin dṛṣṭe parāvare

The knot in the heart is cut, all doubts are destroyed and all karmas are destroyed when one sees the Lord. Muṇḍaka Upaniṣad 2.2.8

This means that by seeing the Lord, one attains liberation.

"But this contradicts scripture which says one attains liberation by karma and one attains liberation by karma and *jñāna*."

Sūtra - 3.3.50

|| śruty-ādi-balīyastvāc ca na bādhaḥ ||

That *vidyā* alone is the cause of liberation cannot be annulled by other statements, because of the strength of the śruti statement, because of logic, and because of other descriptions and other statements.

The scriptural statement that *vidyā* is the cause of liberation cannot be annulled (*na bādhaḥ*) by these two claims. Why? Because of the stronger positive śruti statement (*śruty-ādi-balīyastvāt*) with the word *eva* (only) in *tam eva viditvā* (Śvetāśvatara Upaniṣad 3.8) The word *ādi* indicates that logic and other indications also show this. The indication is this:

indro 'śvamedhāc chatam iṣṭvāpi rājā
brahmāṇam īḍyaṁ samuvācopasannaḥ
na karmabhir na dhanair nāpi cānyaiḥ
paśyet sukham tena tattvam bravīhi

Indra, having performing a hundred horse sacrifices, approached Brahmā and spoke. One cannot see happiness by karmas, wealth or anything else. Therefore, please speak the truth.

The logic is *nāsty akṛtaḥ kṛtena*: one does not attain non-action by action. (Muṇḍaka Upaniṣad 1.2.12) The sūtras 3.4.2-7 supporting karma are refuted by the author in sūtras 3.4.8-14. The word *ca* in the sūtra indicates all statements saying that *vidyā* destroys all karma. The śruti *taṁ vidyā-karmaṇi samanvārabhete: vidyā* and karma take hold of the seeker (Bṛhadāraṇyaka Upaniṣad 4.4.2) is resolved by these same sūtras (particularly 3.4.11). Therefore it is certain that *vidyā* alone is the cause of liberation.

Topic 26 (Sūtra 51)

Anubandhādhikaraṇam - Insistence on worship of devotees

Now the quality of the Lord of being attained with the help of devotees is gathered. It is said *atithi devo bhava*: let the guest be treated as the Lord. (Taittirīya Upaniṣad 1.11.2)

The doubt is this. Does worship of the devotee produce liberation?

(pūrvapakṣa) Liberation is possible by worship of the Lord along with mercy of guru. What is the use of devotees?

Sūtra - 3.3.51

|| anubandhādibhyaḥ ||

Devotees are also necessary for liberation because the scriptures insist on it.

Anubandha means insisting on worship of great souls. *Atithi-devo bhava* means he should be worshipped like the Lord. Therefore by his mercy one attains liberation. Otherwise the statement would not be made. Smṛti also says the same:

rahūgaṇaitat tapasā na yāti
na cejyayā nirvapaṇād gṛhād vā
na cchandasā naiva jalāgni-sūryair
vinā mahat-pāda-rajo-'bhiṣekam

Without bathing in the dust from the feet of great devotees, one cannot realize the Lord through concentration of the mind, performance of sacrifices, distributing food, building shelters for the destitute, studying the Vedas, or performing austerities in the water, fire or the sun. SB 5.12.12

The Lord himself says:

na rodhayati māṁ yogo na saṅkhyaṁ dharma uddhava
na svādhyāyas tapas tyāgo neṣṭa-pūrtaṁ na dakṣiṇā
vratāni yajñās chandāṁsi tīrthāni niyamā yamāḥ
yathāvarundhe sat-saṅgaḥ sarva-saṅgāpaho hi mām

O Uddhava! Only by associating with my pure devotees one can destroy material attachment and attain me. One cannot attain me by *aṣṭāṅga-yoga,* distinction of *ātmā* from body, practice of nonviolence, study of the Vedas, austerity, *sannyāsa,* sacrifices, charitable projects, donations, vows, worship of *devatās*, secret *mantras*, holy places, or observing prohibitions and rules. SB 11.12.1-2

Personally instructing about himself, the Lord orders association with devotees. He reveals that this association is the secret of *sādhana.* The word *ādibhyaḥ* in the sūtra indicates that serving the *tīrthas* of the Lord and giving up criticism of persons other than the Lord (*devatās*) is included.

śuśrūṣoḥ śraddadhānasya vāsudeva-kathā-rucih
syān mahat-sevayā viprāḥ puṇya-tīrtha-niṣevaṇāt

O *brāhmaṇas!* Attraction for topics concerning Kṛṣṇa will arise by service to the great devotees and tīrthas, followed by faith, by surrender to the feet of the pure *guru*, and by the desire to hear. SB 1.2.16

harir eva sadārādhyaḥ sarva-deveśvareśvaraḥ
itare brahma-rudrādyā nāvajñeyā kadācana

The Lord of all the *devatās* should always be worshipped. But one should not neglect Brahmā, Śiva and others. Padma Purāṇa.

"Since guru and devotee association is caused by the Lord, the Lord's mercy is the cause of liberation. Good karma is not the cause of association with devotees or guru, since that also is caused by the Lord. The Lord is the cause of all actions as stated in sūtra 2.3.4. Therefore it is not proper to imagine that the mercy of guru or devotees is the cause of liberation."

Even though it is admitted that the mercy of guru and devotees is caused by the Lord, still that mercy is given to the guru and devotees to distribute. Therefore they are independent in giving mercy. When the devotees and guru give mercy to a person, the Lord follows and gives mercy to him. All statements have been reconciled and irregularities removed.

Topic 27 (Sūtras 52 - 53)

Prajñāntarādhikaraṇam - Difference in Knowledge and worship

There is a doubt concerning the passage *yathā kratur asmin loke purṣo bhavati tatheyaḥ pretya bhavati:* just as according to faith a man becomes what he is in this life, so after death he becomes according to that faith. (Chāndogya Upaniṣad 3.14.1) Does a person get results according to the degree of intensity of his worship of Brahman along with worship of guru?

(Pūrvapakṣa) Since one does not hear about differences in results in statements like *nirañjanaḥ paraṁ samyam upaiti*: the pure person attains the Lord with similarity (Muṇḍaka Upaniṣad 3.1.3), the intensity in *sādhana* is not a cause of the type of result. One cannot say that people going to a city by various paths see different cities.

Sūtra - 3.3.52

|| prajñāntara-pṛthaktvavad dṛṣṭaś ca tad uktam ||

Just as there is difference in knowledge, there difference in the worshipper and the result. That was stated in the scripture quoted.

In the passage *vijñāya prajñaṁ kūrvīta*: knowing the Lord one should practice knowledge, one sees two types of knowledge. One is based on sound (teachings) and the other is based on worship (*prajñam*). There is difference *(pṛthaktvavat*). Similarly, one will see different types of worshippers. In the passage quoted, the difference is stated. One sees the Lord according to the type of worship and then attains liberation of that type. The similarity to the Lord is according to the purity of the person.[79]

"Let that be. One cannot see the Lord without *vidyā.* One cannot have liberation without seeing the Lord. Both of these statements are incorrect because one can see the Lord without *vidyā,* when the Lord makes his appearance as *avatāra* and those who thus see him do not get liberation."

Sūtra - 3.3.53

| | na, sāmānyād apy upalabdher mṛtyuvan nahi lokāpattiḥ | |

This is not true. From seeing the Lord in a general way one does not get liberation, just as dying does not give liberation. One attains a higher planet by seeing the Lord without bhakti. This is not liberation.

The word *api* expresses limitation. Seeing (*upalabdheḥ*) the Lord in a general way (*sāmānyāt)* does not cause liberation, just as dying (*mṛtuvat*) is not the cause of liberation. What is the result of seeing the Lord (without bhakti)? They attain a higher planet (*lokāpattiḥ)* from seeing in a general way, like the Vidyādhara Sudarṣana or King Nṛga.

"Going to a higher planet is liberation." No (*na hi*), it is only elevation to a higher planet. Smṛtis confirm this. *sāmānya-darśanāl lokā muktir yogyātma-darśanāt*: from seeing the Lord in a general way one goes to a higher planet and from seeing him with qualification one attains liberation. (Nārāyaṇa-tantra).

The meaning is this. Seeing the Lord is of two types: where the Lord is covered and where the Lord is not covered. The first type arises by great piety and by its influence it makes one attain planets like Svarga. The second type, arising

[79] Different degrees of bliss will manifest according to the *sādhana.*

by making the Lord filled with knowledge and bliss one's dearest love, causes liberation on destroying the body by *brahma-vidyā*. Thus everything is resolved.

They say that some attained liberation by seeing the Lord when they were killed by him. This was caused by the destruction of their body by the power of the touch of his *cakra.* Thus one should understand that the cause of liberation is seeing him with affection. Otherwise there would be contradiction to many scriptural statements.

Topic 28 (Sūtra 54)

Tādvidhyādhikaraṇam - Choosing the devotee for his bhakti

Now begins confirmation of the fact that by seeing the Lord through *vidyā* one attains liberation. It is said in Muṇḍaka (2.2.23) and Kaṭha Upaniṣad (3.2.3):

nāyam ātmā pravacanena labhyo
na medhayā na bahunā śrutena
yam evaiṣa vṛṇute tena labhyas
tasyaiṣa ātmā vivṛṇute tanuṁ svām

The Lord is not attained by speaking, by intelligence or by hearing. He is attained by the person whom he chooses. The Lord shows his form to him.

The doubt is this. Does seeing the Lord arise from the Lord choosing the person or from the person's bhakti along with detachment from wealth?

(Pūrvapakṣa) It arises from the Lord's choosing since that is the direct meaning of the words.

Sūtra - 3.3.54

|| pareṇa ca śabdasya tādvidhyaṁ bhūyastvāt tv anubandhaḥ ||

The words indicating that the Lord chooses the person to whom he will reveal himself mean that he chooses the person because of his bhakti. His choice is mentioned as the only cause because it is most important.

The words (*śabdasya)* indicating that the Lord shows himself only to the person he chooses means that he reveals himself because of a person's bhakti (*tādvidyam*). This is understood from the next verse and other statements as well. Thus the verses do not indicate that only by the Lord's choosing is he revealed. It is said in the next verse in Muṇḍaka Upaniṣad:

nāyam ātmā bala-hīnena labhyo
na ca pramādāt tapaso vāpy aliṅgāt
etair upāyair yatate yas tu vidvān
tasyaiṣa ātmā viśate brahma-dhāma

The Lord is not attained by weakness of bhakti, uncontrolled senses, or austerity unsanctioned by scriptures. The Lord or *brahma-dhāma* appears to the wise man who endeavors by these methods of strong bhakti, controlled senses and approved austerity.

Etair upāyaiḥ means by strong bhakti, controlled senses and approved austerity. *Bala* means bhakti. The following statements give the same conclusion:

vaśe kurvanti māṁ bhaktāḥ sat-striyaḥ sat-patiṁ yathā

Just as a chaste wife controls her husband, my devotees control me. SB 9.4.66

puruṣaḥ sa paraḥ pārtha bhaktyā labhyas tv ananyayā

The Supreme Lord is obtained by pure bhakti. BG 8.22

The next verse in Kātha Upaniṣad says:

nāvirato duścaritāt nāśānto nāsamāhitaḥ
nāśānta-mānaso vāpi prajñānenainam āpnuyāt

A person who has not given up bad activities, who is disturbed, who has not controlled his senses, and who has not controlled his mind cannot attain the Lord by his knowledge. Kaṭha Upaniṣad 2.2.24

In this verse the *sādhana* is described: one who meditates on the Lord while having proper conduct and sense control realizes the Lord. Thus because of this later statement, it is understood that the Lord chooses a person because of his bhakti. The first verse states that the Lord is attained only by the Lord's choice. The Lord chooses the person he loves, not someone he does not love. He loves those who are devoted to him, not those who are without devotion. The Lord himself says:

teṣāṁ jñānī nitya-yukta eka-bhaktir viśiṣyate
priyo hi jñānino 'tyartham ahaṁ sa ca mama priyaḥ

Of these four types, the *jñānī*, who is constantly engaged in thinking of me, who is practicing pure *bhakti*, is the best. This *jñānī* loves only me, and I love only him. BG 7.17

It is also said elsewhere *śraddhā-bhakti-dhyāna- yogād avehi*: know the Lord through faith, bhakti, meditation and yoga. (Kaivalya Upaniṣad 2) To say that the Lord reveals himself *only* by his choice is contrary to these statements. It would admit prejudice on the part of the Lord as well.

"But why does the verse say only by the Lord's choice is he attained?" It is because of the greatness (*bhūyastvāt)* of the Lord's choosing to whom he will reveal himself. The word *tu* indicates "only." Because of being the immediate cause, it is indicated as most important. There is a sequence. Because of the person being dear by performance of bhakti, the person is chosen. Then the Lord reveals himself.

Topic 29 (Sūtra 55)

Śarīre bhāvādhikaraṇam - Worshipping the Lord in the body

Those having *dāsa, sakhya* or other *bhāvas* worship the Lord situated in the spiritual sky from the beginning of their worship and will see him there on perfection. Some with *śānta-bhāva* worship the Lord in the beginning in the stomach or other places. This is described in certain places in the śrutis. Should the Lord be worshipped in the stomach?

(Pūrvapakṣa) The lord should not be worshipped in the stomach since the Lord does not exist in the material stomach. He should be worshipped in the spiritual sky since he resides there eternally.

Sūtra - 3.3.55

|| eka ātmanaḥ śarīre bhāvāt ||

Some Vedic followers say that one should worship Viṣṇu in the various parts of the body, because he exists there.

Some members of branches of the Vedas (*eke*) say that one should worship Viṣṇu (*ātmanaḥ)* in various parts of the body *(śarīre)* such as stomach, heart and top of the head. Why? Because he is present even there (*bhāvāt*). *akke cen madhu vindeta kim arthaṁ parvataṁ vrajet:* if one can enjoy honey in the corner of the house why go to the mountain to get it? Being pleased, the

Lord will eventually give them his abode. That is what they intend to say. Smṛtis also says:

udaram upāsate ya ṛṣi-vartmasu kūrpa-dṛśaḥ
parisara-paddhatiṁ hṛdayam āruṇayo daharam
tata udagād ananta tava dhāma śiraḥ paramaṁ
punar iha yat sametya na patanti kṛtānta-mukhe

Among the followers of the methods set forth by great sages, those with less refined vision worship the *antaryāmī* in the region of the abdomen. The Āruṇis then worship him in the heart, which allows one to come close to the Lord. From there, O unlimited Lord, these worshipers raise their consciousness upward from there to Satya-loka and then to Vaikuṇṭha. They reach that place from which they will never again fall to this world into the mouth of death. SB 10.87.18

Topic 30 (Sūtras 56 - 58)

Tad-bhāva-bhāvitvādhikaraṇam - The Lord appears according to the devotee's bhāva

In statements like *yathā kratuḥ* (Chāndogya Upaniṣad 3.14.1) worship of the Lord with sweet and majestic qualities was described. Taking association of devotees with these *bhāvas,* by the will of the Lord, the jīvas develop inclinations to either sweet or majestic qualities of the Lord, and then attain the Lord and see the form endowed with those particular qualities. This was shown in sūtra 3.3.29.

The doubt is this. Does a person attain the form with the qualities which he meditated upon by his worship or does he attain a form with additional qualities?

(Pūrvapakṣa) Since the object of either type of meditation is ultimately one, he will attain a form with all the qualities.

Sūtra - 3.3.56

|| vyatirekas tad-bhāva-bhāvitvān, na tūpalabdhivat ||

The devotee does not see the Lord with other qualities, because the Lord responds to the *bhāva* of the devotee, just as knowledge of one form brings realization of that particular form.

The word *tu* destroys the doubt. The form realized is not one with additional qualities *(vyatirekaḥ na)*. Why? Because the Lord has the quality of revealing a form with the qualities corresponding to those employed by the meditator (*tad-bhāva-bhāvitvāt*). What was indicated in the meditation will be attained in liberation. Having known an object in a particular way (*upalabdhivāt*) and meditating on it, one sees that particular object in liberation. Though the knowers of the Lord are aware that the Lord has other qualities, those other qualities do not manifest when they see the Lord, since they did not meditate on those qualities. In this way there is no contradiction to the statement *yathā kratuḥ.*

By the will of the Lord, persons develop particular inclinations and by those inclinations they attain a particular form of the Lord. That is shown by an example.

Sūtra - 3.3.57

|| aṅgāvabaddhās tu na śākhāsu hi prativedam ||

Priests are assigned to certain roles and cannot perform all the actions of all the Vedas, because those roles employ particular Vedas.

The sponsor restricts all the priests in performing parts of the sacrifice to certain assigned activities (*aṅgāvabaddhāḥ*). *Avabaddhāḥ* means these persons are given certain names. "I select you to be the *adhvaryu.* I select you to be the *hotṛ.* I select you to be the *udgātṛ.*" Though they are qualified to perform all parts of the sacrifice, because of the assigned roles, they are qualified for one role, not all. This is the rule. Being of that nature, they cannot perform all actions prescribed in all branches of the Vedas *(śākhāsu)* because (*hi*) their actions at that time are restricted to a particular Veda (*prativedam*). The *hotṛs* chant from the Ṛg Veda. Adhvaryus chant form the Yajur Veda. The *udgātṛs* chant from the Sāma Veda. The *brahmas* chant from the Atharva Veda. Just as the will of the sponsor determines the particular action of the priests with difference in donation at the end, so the will of the Lord determines the particular worship of the jīvas with different forms of the Lord at the end.

Being dissatisfied with seeing the mixed *bhāva* of Uddhava and others, the author speaks another teaching.

Sūtra - 3.3.58

|| mantrādivad vāvirodhaḥ ||

The Lord's will to invoke different moods in different devotees is like a mantra which is used in different ways. Thus there is no contradiction in the Lord's will.

The will of the Lord to bring about bhakti to a particular form of the Lord is like a mantra *(mantrādivat*). Just as one mantra is used in a variety of actions, another mantra is employed in two acts only and another mantra is employed in one act only, so the Lord wills some jīvas to worship in several modes and others in one mode. The word *ādi* indicates that time and karma act in various ways like mantras. One time is the cause of flowers and leaves at a certain time, of no leaves at another time, of infancy at a ceratin time and youth at another time.

Thus (*vā*) there is no contradiction. Since the particular form with its particular qualities which was worshipped in *sādhana* manifests directly with those qualities in liberation, it is not a fact that one realizes qualities beyond what one used in meditation.

Topic 31 (Sūtra 59)

Bhūma-jyāyastvādhikaraṇam - Possessing many forms

Now the following will be considered. *eko 'pi san bahudhā yo 'vabhāti*: though one he appears as many. (Gopāla-tāpanī Upaniṣad) *ekaṁ santaṁ bahudhā dṛśyamānam*: being one he is seen as many. *atha kasmād ucyate brahma*: why is he called Brahman?

There are many different forms of the Lord, who is like a *vaidūrya* gem. Endowed with those forms, the one form is called many names. Because he has many forms through having many qualities, he is actually many.

The doubt is this. Should one meditate in all worship on the Lord's aspect as many forms and qualities, as stated in scriptures?

(Pūrvapakṣa) One should not meditate on the Lord's multiplicity since this contradcits his oneness stated everywhere, as in sūtra 3.3.12.

Sūtra - 3.3.59

|| bhūmnaḥ kratuvaj jyāyastvam, tathā hi darśayati ||

Possession of many forms is the best quality of the Lord, pervading everything like the sacrifice. This is also stated in śruti.

Since his having many forms is the best among all qualities, this should be the object of meditation at all times just as the sacrifice remains in all conditions. Just as the superiority of the *jyotiṣṭoma* continues in all its parts from initiation until the final bath, so the Lord's capacity for having many forms continues to be present in all his forms and qualities. Proof is given to show this (*tathā hi darśayati*). *yo vai bhūmā tat sukham nālpe sukham asti bhūmaiva sukham:* his possession of many forms, not scant forms, gives happiness. (Chāndogya Upaniṣad 7.23.1) It shows that without this quality of being many, bliss will not arise. This means that meditating on this quality should be done all the time. If this quality of having many forms is not accepted, then the eternity of the Lord's actions cannot be accomplished.

Topic 32 (Sūtras 60 - 61)

Śabdādi-bhedādhikaraṇam - Difference in mantras

Is the worship of many forms of one type or many? This is the doubt.

(pūrvapakṣa) The worship is of one type because the form worshipped is one only.

Sūtra - 3.3.60

|| nānā śabdādi-bhedāt ||

The worship is different because of difference in mantras, forms and actions.

There are various types of worship (*nānā)* of many forms. Worship of each form is different. Why? Because of difference of mantras for the particular deities like Nṛsiṁha (*śabda*), and because of difference of forms and actions.

kṛtaṁ tretā dvāparaṁ ca kalir ity eṣu keśavaḥ
nānā-varṇābhidhākāro nānaiva vidhinejyate

In Satya, Treta, Dvāparā and Kali the Lord takes different colors and names and is worshipped in various ways. SB 11.5.20

Thus the worship is different for the different forms.

It was said that the worship of various forms of the Lord like Nṛsiṁha was of various types. Should the worshippers combine all worships or is that optional?

(Pūrva-pakṣa) All worships should be done since there is no reason for it to be optional.

Sūtra - 3.3.61

|| vikalpo'viśiṣṭa-phalatvāt ||

Worshipping many forms is optional, since seeing the Lord and liberation is the same for every type of worship.

Performing all worship is optional (*vikalpaḥ*). One must perform worship which was received by the will of the Lord, following association of a particular devotee and not other worship. Why? Because the result, seeing the Lord and liberation, is the same (*aviśiṣṭa-phalatvāt*) in all the types of worship. If one gets perfection by one type of worship, why perform other types? Though it has been said that all worshippers of Brahman attain the Lord,[80] it is not a fault to repeat the fact since it strengthens the exalted position of the *ekāntī*.

Topic 33 (Sūtra 62)

Kāmyādhikaraṇam - Worshipping with desires

It was said that the *ekāntīs* must always do worship of their particular deity like Nṛsiṁha which gives liberation as a result. Bṛhad-āraṇyaka Upaniṣad describes worship of Brahman for attaining fame, conquering others, and wealth.

The doubt is this. Should such worship be optional or combined with one's personal worship?

---

[80] *tad-viduṣām* is mentioned, but perhaps this refers to sūtra 3.3.54 with the words *tādvidyām:* the Lord chooses to reveal himself to a person who has bhakti.

(pūrvapakṣa) Worship of different forms is optional as with the previous question since the worship of Brahman in any form gives the same result.

Sūtra - 3.3.62

|| kāmyas tu yathā-kāmaṁ samucchīyeran na vā pūrva-hetv-abhāvāt ||

Worship for particular desires may or may not be performed by persons with desires, since the result of that worship is different from the main worship.

Worship for results other than seeing the Lord, like fame (*kāmyaḥ),* may or may not be combined (*samucchīyran na vā*) with one's worship by the worshippers who have desires (*yathā-kāmām*). Why? Because of different results (*pūrva-hetv-abhāvāt*). All worships can be done if one has desire for those particular results. If one does not have desires, then one does not have to perform the other worship.

The intention of the statement is this. If a person desiring liberation has another desire, then he worships only the Supreme Lord and not any *devatā.*

akāmaḥ sarva-kāmo vā mokṣa-kāma udāra-dhīḥ
tīvreṇa bhakti-yogena yajeta puruṣaṁ param

The person desiring destruction of all desires, the person with all desires, and even the person with an intense desire for liberation, if he has good intelligence, will worship the Supreme Lord with pure *bhakti.* SB 2.3.10

This is also explained in relation to worship using the ten syllable mantra. The reasoning in the sūtra did not take into account another qualifier (desiring to see the Lord).

Topic 34 (Sūtras 63 - 68)

Yathāśraya-bhāvādhikaraṇam - The qualities in the Lord's limbs

Having explained the qualities of the Lord himself, now the author commences to describe qualities of his limbs. At the end of the first part of Gopāla-tāpanī Upaniṣad Brahmā promised to please Govinda with his praises. He then praised Kṛṣṇa with verses and described his qualities like having a soft smile and merciful glance in his various limbs like face and eyes.

The doubt is this. Should one meditate separately on the qualities of his limbs such as face or not?

(pūrvapakṣa) One should not meditate separately upon these features since one derives no additional benefit by separate meditation, since one gains the goal just by meditation the qualities of the person possessing the limbs.

Sūtra - 3.3.63

|| aṅgeṣu yathāśraya-bhāvaḥ ||

One should meditate on the qualities of his limbs.

One should meditate (*bhāvaḥ)* on the qualities (*yathāśraya*) in the limbs (*aṅgeṣu*). One should meditate on his soft smile and pleasing words in his mouth. One should meditate on the merciful glance in his eyes.

Sūtra - 3.3.64

|| śiṣṭeś ca ||

Meditation on the qualities in the limbs should be done because Brahmā taught this.

At the end of his prayers, Brahmā says to his students, the sages:

atha haivaṁ stutibhir ārādhayāmi tathā yūyaṁ pañca-padaṁ japantaḥ
kṛṣṇaṁ dhyāyantaḥ samsṛtiṁ tariṣyatha

Just as I have worshipped with prayers, chant this mantra of five parts, meditate on Kṛṣṇa, and you will cross *saṁsāra.* Gopāla-tāpanī Upaniṣad 1.46

One should meditate on the qualities in his limbs because Brahmā teaches (*śiṣṭeḥ*) meditation on these.

It is said *yathā kapyāsaṁ puṇḍarīkam evam akṣiṇī*: his eyes are like fully blossoming lotuses. (Chāndogya Upaniṣad 1.6.7) This mentions only his merciful glance and nothing else.

Sūtra - 3.3.65

|| samāhārāt ||

Nothing is deficient because all qualities are gathered in one quality.

The word *na* is understood from three sūtras later and is also understood in the next sūtra. There is nothing lacking because by this single description all other qualities are gathered (*samāhārāt*).

Someone proposes that one should meditate on every limb having all the qualities. The next sūtra is a *pūrva-pakṣa.*

Sūtra - 3.3.66

|| guṇa-sādhāraṇya-śruteś ca ||

One should meditate on any limb having all the qualities since all qualities are in all limbs according to śruti.

sarvataḥ pāṇi-pādaṁ tat: everywhere are his hands and feet. (Śvetāśvatara Upaniṣad 3.16, also in BG 13.14) Since all qualities are in all the limbs according to śruti (*guṇa-sādhāraṇya-śruteḥ*), one can meditate on each limb having all the qualities of other limbs. The word *ca* indicates that smṛti also says that all qualities are in all limbs:

aṅgāni yasya sakalendriya-vrttimanti
paśyanti pānti kalayanti tathā jaganti
ānanda-cinmaya-sad-ujjvala-vigrahasya
govindam ādi-puruṣaṁ tam ahaṁ bhajāmi ||

I worship the Supreme Lord Govinda whose individual limbs, possessing the functions of all the senses, are forever creating (by seeing), maintaining and annihilating the worlds, because those attractive limbs are made of eternity, knowledge and bliss. Brahma-saṁhitā 5.32

This is now refuted.

Sūtra - 3.3.67

|| na vā tat-sahabhāvāśruteḥ ||

This is not correct because it is not stated in scriptures that the qualities of one limb coexist with the qualities of other limbs in the same limb.

The word *vā* indicates emphasis. One should not meditate on all qualities in each limb. Why? Because it is not stated in scripture that the qualities in one particular limb (*tat-saha-bhāvah*) exist with other qualities. Thus one should not meditate in this way. Rather one should meditate on the qualities with the particular limb. Statements like *sarvataḥ pānī* indicate that all the śaktis of the Lord are everywhere. That is the meaning.

Sūtra - 3.3.68

|| darśanāc ca ||

One should not medittate on all qualities in one limb because descriptions of qualities of one limb and not other qualities are seen in scripture.

One sees descriptions in scriptures of a soft smile on the mouth. Because of seeing this *(darśanāt)* one should not meditate on qualities of other limbs in one limb.

Section Four

śraddhā-veśmany āstṛte sacchamādyair
vairāgyodyad-vitti-siṁhāsanāḍhye |
dharma-prākārañcite sarva-dātrī
preṣṭhā viṣṇor bhāti vidyeśvarīyam ||

The goddess of knowledge, consort of Viṣṇu, giver of all things, shines in the abode of faith, spread with a covering of pure sense and mental control, on a throne of intelligence elevated by detachment, surrounded by walls of dharma.

Topic 1 (Sūtras 1 - 14)

Puruṣarthādhikaraṇam - Vidyā produces all goals

In the previous part, vidyā, meaning meditation and worship directed to Brahman, the Lord, along with vidyā's assistants, was described. Now in this section, the independence of vidyā (bhakti), its having karma as its *aṅga*, and the three types of practitioners and other facts are revealed.

Persons desiring vidyā are of three types because of different faith. Some, desiring to see the variety of planets, practicing *varṇāśrama dharma* with intensity, are called *svaniṣṭhas.* Some however who practice the same dharmas only to teach the population are called *pariniṣṭhitas.* Both of these types have *āśramas.* Others however, who are purified by truth, austerity, *japa* etc and qualities attained from previous births, are called *nirapekṣas.* They have no *āśrama* in practicing vidyā. These three types will be described later. First the independence of vidyā will be discussed.

Statements like the following are found. *tarati śokam ātmavit*: the knower of *ātmā* surpasses lamentation. (Chāndogya Upaniṣad 7.13) *brahma-vid āpnoti param*: the knower of Brahman attains the supreme. (Taittirīya Upaniṣad 2.1.1.) *etad dhy evākṣaraṁ jñātvā yo yad icchati tasya tat*: knowing the *akṣara,* one attains whatever he desires. (Kaṭha Upaniṣad 2.16)

The doubt is this. Is vidyā the cause of liberation or Svarga?

(Pūrvapakṣa) Vidyā is the cause of liberation only because the wise have no other desire.

Sūtra - 3.4.1

|| puruṣārtho'taḥ śabdād iti bādarāyaṇaḥ ||

Bādarāyaṇa says that vidyā produces all results because that is stated in śruti.

Lord Bādarāyaṇa says that all human goals (*puruṣārthaḥ*) arise from vidyā (bhakti). Why? Because this is stated in śruti (*śabdāt*). The Lord, satisfied by vidyā, gives himself to his devotee. If a devotee like Kardama has some desire, the Lord gives what he desires because of vidyā alone, karma (material objects) being its attendant.

Jaimini objects to this.

Sūtra - 3.4.2

|| śeṣatvāt puruṣārtha-vādo yathānyeṣv iti jaiminiḥ ||

Because vidyā is subordinate to karma, the results of vidyā stated in scripture are exaggeration, like the praises given to objects, purification and rites in sacrifice. This is the opinion of Jaimini.

After understanding the essential relation of the worshipper with Viṣṇu, the object of worship, the jīva by himself engages in actions whose essence is worship of the Lord, as previously described. Destroying impurities by those actions, he enjoys results in the form of liberation or Svarga through *adṛṣṭa* (fate or karma). Since vidyā is subordinate to karma (*śeṣatvāt*), praise for the results of vidyā is exaggeration meant to inspire humans (*puruṣārtha-vadaḥ*). It is exaggeration of results like the praises of objects, purification rites and certain rituals (*yathānyeṣu*). For instance it is said:

parṇa-mayī juhūr bhavati na sa pāpaṁ ślokaṁ sṛṇoti

If one uses a ladle made of *palāśa* wood one does not hear bad words. Kṛṣṇa Yajur Veda 3.3.5.7

yadāṅkte cakṣur eva bhrātṛvyasya vṛṅkte

He covers the eyes of his enemies with the ointment used to cover his eyes during purification. Kṛṣṇa Yajur Veda 6.6.1.1

yat prayājānūyājā ijyante varma vā etad jyajñāsya kriyate varma
hyajamānāya bhrātṛvyābhibhūyai

When he performs *prayāja* and *anuyāja* rites, he makes armor out of this rite for the sacrificer to overcome his enemies. Kṛṣṇa Yajur Veda 2.2.6.1

This is Jaimini's opinion. *dravya-saṁskāra-karmasu parārthatvāt phala-ś*rutir *artha-vāda*h *syād:* the praises mentioned in relation to objects, purification and actions are exaggeration because they are dependent on other acts. (Jaimini sūtras 4.3.1)

Śruti says that one who develops sense and mental control from performing sacrifices of the householder throughout life attains Brahman. *ācārya-kūlād vedam adhītya.. brahma-lokaṁ abhisaṁpadyate na can punar āvartate:* after studying the Vedas in the family of a teacher, he attains Brahma-loka and does not return. (Chāndogya Upaniṣad 8.15.1) Smṛti says:

varṇāśramācāravatā puruṣeṇa paraḥ pumān |
viṣṇur ārādhyate panthā nānyat tat-toṣa-kāraṇam ||

The supreme Lord Viṣṇu should be worshipped by a person performing *varṇāśrama.* There is no other way of pleasing him. Viṣṇu Purāṇa

There are other verses as well. Statements about renunciation are for the lame and blind, unable to do karmas (sacrifices).

He speaks of *ātma*-vidyā as a mere *aṅga* of karma for another reason.

Sūtra - 3.4.3

|| ācāra-darśanāt ||

Vidyā is subordinate to karma because persons who had vidyā engaged in sacrifices in order to attain perfection.

Vidyā is subordinate to karma because one sees performance of karmas by even the best of learned men (Janaka and Āśvapati in the following examples). *janako ha vaideho bahu-dakṣiṇena yajñe neje:* Janaka of Videha performed a sacrifice with profuse gifts at the end. (Bṛhad-āraṇyaka Upaniṣad 3.1.1) *yakṣamāṇo ha vai bhagavanto'ham asmi*: O lords, I will perform a sacrifice. Chāndogya Upaniṣad 5.2.5) These learned men would not have endeavored to perform karmas if they had attained perfection just by vidyā. Why go to the forest when there is honey in the corner of the house?

Sūtra - 3.4.4

|| tac-chruteḥ ||

Vidyā is subordinate to karma because of a śruti statement.

Chāndogya Upaniṣad 1.1.9 says *yad eva vidyayā karoti śraddhayopaniṣadā tad eva viryavattaraṁ bhavati:* karma alone, which is done with vidyā, faith and knowledge, is powerful. This shows that vidyā is a subordinate element to the action.

Sūtra - 3.4.5

|| samānvārambhaṇāt ||

Vidyā is subordinate to karma because of the passage in Bṛhad-āraṇyaka Upaniṣad 4.4.2 starting with the word *samanvārabhete.*

The following shows that both vidyā and karma act together in the final result. *taṁ* vidyā-*karmaṇī samanvārabhete pūrva-prajñā ca*: vidyā and karma as well as previous knowledge take hold of him. (Bṛhad-āraṇyaka Upaniṣad. 4.4.2)

Sūtra - 3.4.6

|| tadvato vidhānāt ||

Vidyā is subordinate to karma because a knower of Brahman is apponted as a priest in karma rites.

It is said *brahmiṣṭho brahmā darśapaurṇamāsayos taṁ vṛṇīte*: the knower of Brahman is chosen as the *brahma* priest for the *darṣa* and *paurṇamāsa* rites. (Taittirīya-saṁhitā) Vidyā is an *aṅga* of karma because of the act of choosing (*vidhānāt*) a person who knows Brahman as the *brahma* priest. Since a knower of Brahman is made into a priest (performing karma) vidyā is shown to be an *aṅga* of karma.

Sūtra - 3.4.7

|| niyamāc ca ||

Vidyā is subordinate to karma because karma is prescribed throughout life.

In Īśopaniṣad it is said:

kurvann eveha karmāṇi jijīviṣec chataṁ samāḥ |
evaṁ tvayi nānyatheto'sti na karma lipyate nare ||

Performing prescribed actions without attachment while living in the world, you can aspire to live for a hundred years. There is no other method than this for you or any human being to become free of contamination. These actions do not contaminate you.

This verse says that for one's whole life one who knows *ātmā* must engage in karma. From this it is understood that though person may argue that karma could be optional because of statements recommending giving up karma, this is not correct. The statements about detachment are for lame and blind people, incapable of doing the karmas. The Taittirīya statement criticizes renunciation. *vīrahā vā eṣa devānāṁ yo'gnim udvāsayate:* the person who gives up the fire of the *devatā* is destroyed. (Kṛṣṇa Yajur Veda 1.5.2)

The idea that vidyā is not independent in giving its result since it is an *aṅga* of karma is now refuted.

Sūtra - 3.4.8

|| adhikopadeśāt tu bādarāyaṇasyaiva tad-darśanāt ||

Vidyā is not subordinate to karma, because teachings about vidyā are stronger, because this is the teaching of Bādarāyaṇa, and because this is shown in the scriptures.

The word *tu* rejects the *pūrva-pakṣa.* Vidyā is not subordinate to karma, because vidyā is indicated to be superior to karma (*adhikopadeśāt*). Vidyā must be considered the principal element. Why? Because of Bādarāyaṇa's teachings. His teaching cannot be uprooted because it is shown in śruti (*tad-darśanāt*).

tapasā śraddhayā yajñenānāśakena caitam eva viditvā munir bhavaty etam eva pravrājino lokam abhīpsantaḥ pravrajanti

Knowing the Lord by austerity, faith sacrifice and fasting, one becomes a sage. Desiring the world of the Lord, the renounced people wander about the world. Bṛhad-āraṇyaka Upaniṣad 4.4.22

This text shows that karma leads to vidyā, and when vidyā arises, karmas are then given up. The result is greater than the means, since karma becomes useless in the next world.

It was argued that karma is superior because even men having vidyā did karmas. That argument is now refuted.

Sūtra - 3.4.9

|| tulyaṁ tu darśanam ||

Equally, texts show that vidyā is not an *aṅga* of karma.

The word *tu* indicates a refutation of the idea that vidyā is subordinate. There is equal evidence in scripture to show that vidyā is not an *aṅga* of karma.

etad dha sma vai tad-vidvāṁsaḥ āhur ṛṣayaḥ kāvaṣeyāḥ kim-arthā vayam adhyeṣyāmahe, kim-arthā vayaṁ yakṣyāmahe, etad dha sma vai tat pūrve vidvāṁso'gnihotraṁ na juhavāñcakrire[81]

The knowledgeable sages of Kavaṣa's lineage said, "For what purpose should we study? For what purpose should we perform sacrifices? Those in knowledge previously did not offer sacrifice.

etaṁ vai tam ātmānaṁ viditvā brāhmaṇaḥ putraiṣaṇāyāś ca vittaiṣaṇāyāś ca lokaiṣaṇāyāś ca vyuttāyātha bhikṣācaryaṁ caranti

After knowing the Lord, brāhmaṇas reject desire for sons, wealth and elevation to higher planets. They become mendicants. Bṛhad-āraṇyaka Upaniṣad 3.5.1

Because these texts show that persons with vidyā renounce karma, there is no unanimous support for karma. Men with vidyā performing karmas does not negate vidyā's superiority, since those men performed karmas for purification of their existence and teaching others.

The argument presented in sūtra 3.4.4 is refuted.

Sūtra - 3.4.10

|| asārvatrikī ||

The statement mentioned in sūtra 4, that vidyā is subordinate to karma, is not concerning all vidyā.

The statement that a person performs karmas with knowledge and faith (Chāndogya Upaniṣad 1.1.8) as subordinate elements is not a universal statement. It does not apply to all vidyā since it refers to having knowledge of the *udgītha* only. Thus, all vidyā is not subordinate to karma.

---

[81] Taken from Shankara's commentary, original source untraced.

Sūtra - 3.4.11

|| vibhāgaḥ śatavat ||

Vidyā and karma give different results, like the division of a hundred coins received on selling a cow and goat.

One should see a division of results of performing vidyā and kārma in the Brhad-āraṇyaka Upaniṣad 4.4.2. statement in sūtra 5 which describes that both vidyā and karma act together in the final result. Vidyā produces one result and karma produces another result. An example is given. When a man sells a goat and cow and receives a hundred coins, he gets ninety coins for the cow and ten coins for the goat. Similarly the results of vidyā and karma are different.

Sūtra - 3.4.12

|| adhyayana-mātarataḥ ||

The person is chosen as a *brahma* priest, not because he knows Brahman, but because he is just fixed in studying the Vedas.

The person is chosen as a *brahma* priest, not because of knowing Brahman, but because he is just fixed in studying the Vedas (*adhyayana -mātrataḥ*). Therefore, it is not proper to say that vidyā is an *aṅga* of karma. *Brahma* in the phrase *brahmiṣṭhaḥ* means fixed in the Vedas, not fixed in the highest realization of Brahman, since it is said in scriptures that a person truely fixed in Brahman would give up all karmas. One who, knowing the Vedas of unchanging words, studies them alone and does not desire anything material from that study, is called *brahmiṣṭha.* Some say that the suffic *iṣṭa* indicates the person is to be regarded as *brahma* but is actually not a knower of Brahman. He is permitted to be a *brahma* priest as a knower of Brahman, but it is only for praising karma. (He actually does not know Brahman.)

"Since it is impossible to do karmas with ignorance of the Vedas and studying the Vedas ends in understanding the meaning of the Vedas, and therefore the person will have knowledge of *ātmā* by studying the Upaniṣads in the Vedas, this makes vidyā an *aṅga* of karma."

One who knows the words is not a knower of Brahman. One who realizes Brahman is the knower of Brahman. By simply understanding the words "honey is sweet" one does not become a knower of honey's sweetness. If it were so, then merely by those words a person would have the effects, such as intoxicaton. But that does not take place. When Sanatkumāra asked Nārada to tell what he knew, Nārada said he had studied the Ṛg-veda and other scriptures. Then he said *so'ham mantravid evāsmi nātmavit*: I know the mantras but I do not know the *ātmā*. Therefore worship is different from knowledge of the words. Vidyā means realization arising from *bhakti*. This is the cause of the highest goal, liberation. In Taittirīya Upaniṣad it is said:

vedānta-vijñāna-suniścitārthāḥ
sannyāsa-yogāt yatayaḥ śuddha-sattvāḥ |
te brahma-loke tu parānta-kāle
parāmṛtāt parimucyanti sarve ||

All those who have discerned Brahman and realized it through the Upaniṣads, who have endeavored and purified their existence by renunciation, live on Brahma-loka and at its end they are liberated from *prakṛti*.

Thus knowledge of the words, like renunciation, are simply accompanying factors of vidyā.

tac chraddadhānā munayo jñāna-vairāgya-yuktayā |
paśyanty ātmani cātmānaṁ bhaktyā śruta-gṛhītayā ||

The seriously inquisitive student or sage, well equipped with knowledge (of the words) and detachment, realizes that Absolute Truth by rendering devotional service after hearing from guru. SB 1.2.12

"Bhakti consists of actions of the body, voice and mind. Realization arises from mental meditation. How can one develop realization from *japa* or *arcana* which are actions of the body and voice?"

Bhakti is *saṁvit-śakti* endowed with the essence of *hlādinī-śakti*. *saccidānandaika-rase bhakti-yoge tiṣṭhati:* the Lord resides in bhakti, which is completely eternity, knowledge and bliss. (Gopāla-tāpanī Upaniṣad 2.78) If it were not so, it could not bring the Lord under control. Because it is of this nature, bhakti, manifesting identity with the actions of the body, voice and mind of the devotee, takes the form of action. Logic is useless in things which are inconceivable, since it is said *śrutes tu śabda-mūlatvāt*: the defects of the agent do not apply to Brahman because of scriptural statements, which are the only proof concerning inconceivable subjects. (sūtra 2.1.27)

Now sūtra 7 is refuted.

Sūtra - 3.4.13

|| nāviśeṣāt ||

There is no injunction to perform karmas for the whole of life, since such statements are not for everyone.

It is impossible to make a rule from the scripture quoted that the knower of Brahman must perform karmas for his whole life. Why? Because that is not specified in the verse quoted. Taittarīya-āraṇyaka 10.5 says *karmaṇā prajayā dhanena tyāgenaike amṛtatvaṁ ānaśuḥ:* not by karmas, sons or wealth, only by renunciation, can one attain immortality. Two statements are provided for different *āśramas.*

Having refuted the first meaning of the Īśopaniṣad verse, the author gives the real meaning.

Sūtra - 3.4.14

|| stutaye'numatir vā ||

Permission is given to perform karmas in order to praise vidyā.

Vā indicates "only." In order to praise vidyā, performing karmas throughout life is permitted. This is understood from the context. Vidyā is so powerful that though one performs karmas, the man of knowledge is not contaminated by that karma. In this way vidyā is praised. This is the meaning of the last line of the verse quoted *evaṁ tvayi nānyatheto 'sti:* there is no alternative for you; action does not bind the man who performs work with knowledge. (Īśopaniṣad 2) Thus the proposal that vidyā is an *aṅga* of karma has been refuted.

Topic 2 (Sūtras 15 - 22)

Kāma-kārādhikaraṇam - Acting as you please

Having defined vidyā's independence in this way (by refutation), now the author does so by showing vidyā's great superiority. In Bṛhad-āraṇyaka Upaniṣad 4.4.23 it is said *eṣa nityo mahimā brāhmaṇasya na karmaṇā vardhate no kanīyān:* the eternal greatness of the knower of Brahman does not increase or decrease by karma (sacrifices etc.).

The doubt is this. Will persons with vidyā act as they please or not (not according to rules of karma)?

(pūrvapakṣa) They will not act as they like, because by giving up prescribed rules they commit sin.

Sūtra - 3.4.15

|| kāma-kāreṇa caike ||

One branch of the Vedas says that the knower of Brahman can act as he wishes.

One branch of the Vedas (*eke*) says to the verse quoted means that the knower of Brahman has no relationship with good or bad by performance of karmas according to his will (*kāma-kāreṇa*), since the good results he mercifully bestows to others and no sin is incurred by not performing the karmas. This is the meaning of *nityo mahimā* in the verse according to the followers of this branch of the Vedas. *Brāhmaṇa* means a person who has realized Brahman. In performing karmas, he does not incur piety, and in not performing karmas, he does not incur sin, since karmas such as sacrifices do not cling to him, as water drops slide from a lotus leaf, and since sins are burned to ashes, like a handful of grass in a fire. This is the great power of vidyā.

The meaning is clarified.

Sūtra - 3.4.16

|| upamardaṁ ca ||

Karmas are destroyed by vidyā.

All karmas (reactions) are destroyed by vidyā. This is shown in the following śruti and smṛti texts.

bhidyate hṛdaya-granthiḥ chidyanate sarva-saṁsayāḥ
kṣiyante cāsyakarmāṇi tasmin dṛṣṭe parāvare

The knot in the heart is cut, all doubts are destroyed and all karmas are dissipated when one sees the Lord. Muṇḍaka Upaniṣad

yathaidhāṁsi samiddho 'gnir bhasma-sāt kurute 'rjuna |
jñānāgniḥ sarva-karmāṇi bhasma-sāt kurute tathā ||

As a blazing fire burns to ashes all fuel wood, the fire of realization turns to ashes all karmas. BG 4.37

Because of this, vidyā is greater than karma. If vidyā can destroy even half-experienced *prarabdha- karma,*[82] it is not surprising that there is no fault in giving up prescribed duties after realizing Brahman.

"It cannot be accepted by knowers of scripture that karmas of the present body (*prārabdha-karmas*) are destroyed. They must be experienced." Even though vidyā is capable of burning up *all* karmas, karmas of the present body are not burned up (he continues with his body with a pattern of karma) by the will of the Lord, in order that the person who has realized the Lord preach the *sampradāya* teachings. Like a piece of burned cloth (traces of karma), the karmas accompany the knower of Brahman. In this way, the statement that *prārabdha- karmas* must be experienced is fulfilled. This will be further explained in sūtra 4.1.15.

Sūtra - 3.4.17

|| ūrdhva-retaḥsu ca śabde hi ||

Vidyā is independent of karma because the renunciate acts as he desires, according to scriptures.

Vidyā is independent of karma because the *yatis* or *sannyāsīs* (*ūrdhva-retaḥsu*), special *pariniṣṭhita* devotees, with great realization, are allowed to perform karmas as they wish, as stated in scripture (*śabde*). The scriptures are as follows:

tasmād brāhmaṇaḥ pāṇḍityaṁ nirvidya bālyena tiṣṭhāset bālyaṁ ca
pāṇḍiyaṁca nirvidyatha munir amaunaṁ ca maunaṁ ca nirvidyātha
brāhmaṇaḥ sa brāhmaṇaḥ kena syād yena syāt tenedṛśaḥ

Therefore a renounced knower of Brahman, having heard about Brahman, should desire to contemplate with a pure heart. Having heard and contemplated, he becomes absorbed in meditation. Having heard, contemplated and meditated, how should he be situated? Having renounced

---

[82] *Aprārabdha-karmas* are all destroyed. Present actions do not incur karma. Only the *prārabdha-karmas* remain. Those *prārabdha karmas* now being experienced (half-enjoyed) are also destroyed.

all karmas, he is equal to one who has performed all karmas. Bṛhad-āraṇyaka Upaniṣad 3.5.1

Bu a householder pariniṣṭhita devotee should act as follows:

saktāḥ karmaṇy avidvāṁso yathā kurvanti bhārata |
kuryād vidvāṁs tathāsaktaś cikīrṣur loka-saṁgraham ||

Just as the ignorant people work with attachment, O Bhārata, the wise, desirous to teach the people, should perform work without desire for results. BG 3.25

Thus the power of vidyā is such that a person is not touched by sins, even if he acts as he likes (not doing karmas).

Jaimini gives a different interpretation of the text.

Sūtra - 3.4.18

|| parāmarśaṁ jaiminir acodanā cāpavadati hi ||

According to Jaimini, the knower of Brahman should also do karmas, since renunciation of karmas is criticized and there is no rule allowing renunciation of karmas.

Śruti says that the knower of Brahman must do the actions which are prescribed as rules in the manner he chooses (but still does them) because (*hi*) śruti criticizes (*apavadati*) giving up karma and recommends (*parāmarśam)* karma even for the knower of Brahman. There is no rule (*acodana*) for the knower of Brahman to give up karmas.

The meaning is this. Śruti says *kurvann eveha karmāṇi:* one should do karmas in this world. (Īśopaniṣad) This says karma must be done. Other śrutis criticize giving up karma. *vīrahā vā eṣa devānāṁ yo'gnim udvāsayate:* the person who gives up the fire of the *devatā* is destroyed. (Kṛṣṇa Yajur Veda 1.5.2) Thus there is no rule to give up karmas since one cannot simultaneously perform and give up karmas (by following some statements that apparently advise giving up karmas). Statements that allow renunciation of karmas are not without a subject: they are meant for incapacitated persons like the lame. Therefore the knowers of Brahman should perform karmas mentioned in śruti and smṛti, doing them somehow or other (his meaning of *kena syāt*). That is the meaning of *kāmacāraḥ* (doing as one likes) and not anything else. This is the opinion of Jaimini.

Having stated Jaimini's opinion that the passage means that the knower of Brahman should perform karmas, the author shows that the passage permits the knower of Brahman to do as he pleases.

Sūtra - 3.4.19

|| anuṣṭheyaṁ bādarāyaṇaḥ sāmya-śruteḥ ||

Bādarāyaṇa says that the person in knowledge should perform karmas, omitting some as he likes, since the passage indicates that even by acting in this manner he is equal to a person who does all karmas.

Bādarāyaṇa says that one should only perform karmas one prefers, doing some and not doing some. Why? Because the śruti says that the man of knowledge even partially doing the karmas (*kena tenedṛśaḥ*) is equal to someone doing them fully (*sāmya-śruteḥ*). According to Jaimini's interpretation in which the man of knowledge still performs all karmas, the statement that his actions are equal is redundant, since the man of knowledge is obviously equal in doing all the prescribed karmas. In not performing some karmas, equality is accomplished as a unique feature, since it expresses negation of the inequality of incomplete karmas of the *jñānī (*person having vidyā*)* compared to complete karmas of the other person.

Recommending karmas for everyone including the knower of Brahman is a statement for those attached do doing karmas, and the warning that not doing karmas destroys sons and strength is in consideration of persons ignorant of Brahman. In this way, the injunction against renunciation of karmas is dismissed. The statement that renunciation of karmas is only for invalids is not correct, since there is no śruti to support this statement, and since renunciation of karmas is recommended-- because karmas are not conducive for liberation. This is made clear in the statement *na karmaṇā na prajayā*: not by karmas, not by progeny.

Sūtra - 3.4.20

|| vidhir vā dhāraṇavat ||

Or the text may be taken as an injunction for the knower of Brahman to perform karmas like the injunction that all three *varṇas* should study theVedas.

Kena syāt yena syāt could be understood (*dhāraṇavat*) as a rule (*vidhiḥ*) for the *jñānī* (knower of Brahman). Just as there is a rule that all three *varṇas* should study the Vedas, there is a rule that the knowers of Brahman who are *pariniṣṭhitas* and not others, should do the karmas, but by his own will (*kena syāt*) .

śaucam ācamanaṁ snānaṁ na tu codanayā caret
anyāṁś ca niyamāñ jñānī yathāhaṁ līlayeśvaraḥ

Just as I, the Supreme Lord, execute regulative duties by my own free will, similarly, the *jñānī* should maintain general cleanliness, perform *ācamana,* take bath and execute other regulative duties not by force, but by his own free will. SB 11.18.36

This proposal is attacked and a conclusion is reached.

Sūtra - 3.4.21

|| stuti-mātram upādānād iti cet, na, apūrvatvāt ||

If one argues that the statement is just praise for the *jñānī,* the answer is no, since the statement is an original rule.

"The passage is thus glorification of the *jñānī* (devotee), not an injunction that the realizer of Brahman can do whatever he wants. One may praise a person one likes by saying, 'Do as you like' but this does not mean the person should perform any action whatsoever. Similarly in saying the *jñānī* can do as he wishes it is just praise because even the *jñānī* follows the injunctions."

In responses to this, the answer is no. Why? It is not just praise since the statement that the realizer of Brahman does as he likes regarding karmas is actually an original rule (*apūrva-vidhi).*

Sūtra - 3.4.22

|| bhāva-śabdāc ca ||

The knower of Brahman performs only some karmas because śruti indicates that he is absorbed in prema.

The following statement indicates a person with bhāva:

prāṇo hy eṣa yaḥ sarva-bhūtair vibhāti
vijānan vidvān bhavate nātivādī

ātma-krīḍa ātma-ratiḥ kriyāvān
eṣa brahma vidāṁ variṣṭhaḥ

The Lord is he who appears with all beings. Knowing this, the wise man ceases useless talk. He plays with the Lord, enjoys with the Lord, performs activities with the Lord and is the best of knowers of the Lord. Muṇḍaka Upaniṣad 3.1.4

The knower of Brahman performs karmas as he wishes because of a statement showing that he has *bhāva.* The word bhāva means *rati* or *prema.* The meaning is this. Because the *pariniṣṭhita* devotee is absorbed in the Lord, he performs only some karmas in some way, and only in order to teach others. Thus *brahma*-vidyā is independent of karma.

Topic 3 (Sūtras 23 - 24)

Pāriplavādhikaraṇam - Mere stories

Another doubt is raised and resolved.

Sūtra - 3.4.23

|| pāriplavārtho iti cen, na, viśeṣitatvāt ||

If one argues that the stories in the Upaniṣads depicting *brahma*-vidyā are merely *pāriplava,* the answer is no, since *pāriplava* stories are specified as such.

There are many stories in the Upaniṣads describing *brahma*-vidyā:

atha ha yājñavalkyasya deva bhārye babhūvatur maitreyī ca kātyāyanī ca

Yājñavalkya had two wives, Maitryeī and Kātyāyanī. Bṛhad-āraṇyaka upaniṣad 4.5.1

bhṛgur vai vāruṇiḥ varuṇaṁ pitaram upasasāra adhīhi bhagavo brahmeti

Bhṛgu, approached Varuṇa his father and said "O father! Teach me about Brahman." Taittirīya Upaniṣad 3.1

pratardano ha vai daivodāsir indrasya priyam dhāmopajagāma

Prataradano son of Divodāsa came to the beautiful abode of Indra. Kauṣītaka Upaniṣad 3.1

jānaśrutir ha pautrāyaṇaḥ śraddādeyo bahu-dāyī bahu-pākya āsa

Jānaśurti Pautrāyaṇa was full of faith, generous, cooking food for distribution. Chāndogya Upaniṣad 4.1.1

Are these stories merely interludes in the sacrifice, in order to praise *brahma*-vidyā?

(Pūrvapakṣa) They are understood to be interludes (*pāriplavārthaḥ*) since it is said *sarvāṇy ākhyānāni pāriplave*: all the stories are interludes (not really true). In recitation, because the words take prominence, real knowledge is secondary. *Brahma*-vidyā related in the stories is like exaggeration used in mantras and cannot lead to liberation. The strories cannot speak of karma being secondary to vidyā. Thus their importance is dismissed since they do not prove anything about vidyā.

This is not so. Why? Because *pāriplava* stories are specifically mentioned as such (*viśeṣitvāt*). Related to the *pāriplava* recition it is said, "On the first day one should recite the story of king Vaivasvata Manu. On the second day one should recite the story of Indra, son of Vaivasvata. On the third day one should recite the story of Yama, son of Vaivasvata." If all stories in the Upaniṣads were *pāriplava,* the injunction to recite certain stories on certain days would be meaningless. The statement that all stories are *pāriplava* means all stories in the particular section are *pāriplava*. Thus the stories in the Upaniṣads are not for use as *pāriplava.*

Sūtra - 3.4.24

|| tathā caika-vākyopabandhāt ||

The stories are suitable for illustrating vidyā since they harmonize with the vidyā taught.

Since the stories in the Upaniṣads are not for *pāriplava* purposes, they are suitable to confirm vidyā connected with the story. Why? Because the stories are related by having the same meaning as the vidyā taught. *ātmā vā are draṣṭavyaḥ śrotavyaḥ:* the Lord should be seen and heard. (Bṛhad-āraṇyaka Upaniṣad 4.5.6) This is connected with the story of Yājñavalkya and his two wives. The story starting with *so 'rodīt* (he wept) is for praising the injunctions of karma being discussed. The story is not for *pāriplava.* Similarly, the stories in the Upaniṣads are for the purpose of praising vidyā described next to them.

The meaning is this. Vidyā, the cause of liberation, is independent. Thus many great sages endeavor with effort for that vidyā. Vidyā is taught through stories because the stories make vidyā easy to understand and are filled with excitement. *ācāryavān puruṣo veda:* a person who accepts a teacher knows the Vedas. (Chāndogya Upaniṣad 6.14.2) The śruti is merciful (in giving the method of understanding the meaning). Thus vidyā is independent of karma.

Topic 4 (Sūtra 25)

Agnīndhanādhikaraṇam - Sacrifices

Sūtra - 3.4.25

|| ata eva cāgnīndhanādy-anapekṣā ||

Since vidyā is independent, it does not need sacrificies to yield its result.

Because it has been concluded that vidyā is independent *(ata eva),* it is not dependent (*anapekṣā*) on karmas such as sacrifices (*agnīndhanādi*). Thus the proposal that *jñāna* and karma should be performed together is refuted.

Topic 5 (Sūtras 26 - 27)

Sarvāpekṣādhikaraṇam - Other practices in the beginning

Having described the power of vidyā *(*bhakti), and its independence, now the author begins to describe the person qualified for vidyā (bhakti). *tam etaṁ vedānuvacanena*: one should try to know him by study of the Vedas, sacrifice. (Bṛhad-āraṇyaka Upaniṣad 4.4.22) *tasmād evaṁ-vic chānto dānta uparatas titikṣuḥ samāhito bhūtvā 'tmany evātmānaṁ paśyati*: knowing this, endowed with peace, control of the senses and mind, and tolerance, he sees the Lord in the self. (Bṛhad-āraṇyaka Upaniṣad 4.4.23) Sacrifices and sense control etc. are understood to be secondary to vidyā. Are both sacrifices and sense contro necessary to practice or not?

(Pūrvapakṣa) They are not necessary to practice because it is proved that bhakti starts by serving a guru.

Sūtra - 3.4.26

|| sarvāpekṣā ca yajñādi-śruter aśvavat ||

Vidyā is dependent on sacrifice and other factors in the beginning, since that is stated in the verses quoted, just as a horse is necessary to go to the village, but is unnecessary after arriving.

Though vidyā is independent in revealing its results, it is dependent on all dharmas such as sacrifices etc. (*sarvāpekṣā*). Why? Because it is stated in the śrutis quoted above that sacrifices and sense control etc. are necessary for vidyā. An example is given. In order to go to a village, a horse is necessary, but having arrived there, it is not necessary.

"If one can perfect vidyā by sacrifices etc. why is sense control etc. necessary?"

Sūtra - 3.4.27

|| śama-damādy-upetaḥ syāt tathāpi tu tad-vidhes tad-aṅgatayā teṣām avaśyānuṣṭheyatvāt ||

Sense and mental control should be practiced since the verses quoted say they should be necessarily performed as secondary items.

The word *tu* serves to indicate certainty and refuting the doubt. Though sacrifices etc. purify a person so that vidyā arises, a person desiring vidyā should also have sense control etc. (*sama-damādy-upetaḥ*) Why? They should necessarily be performed since they are stated to be *aṅgas*, secondary principles (*tad-aṅgatayā*). Both sets of rules should be followed because there are śruti statements recommending both. Sacrifices etc. are external and sense control etc. is internal. The word *ādi* indicates other qualifications previously mentioned like truth. (sūtra 1.1.1)

Topic 6 (Sūtras 28 - 31)

Sarvānnānumaty-adhikaraṇam - Permission to eat all food

The author excludes forbidden actitivies for the knower of Brahman. It is said *yadi ha vā apy evaṁ vin nkhilaṁ bhakṣayitvaivam eva sa bhavati:* if a knower of Brahman eats any food he still remains the same (pure).

The doubt is this. Is this an injunction to eat all food or merely permission?

(pūrvapakṣa) This is an injunction to eat all food, since eating all food cannot be inferred otherwise.

Sūtra - 3.4.28

|| sarvānnānumatiś ca prāṇātyaye tad-darśanāt ||

This is permission to eat all food only when the body must survive, since that is seen in the scriptures.

The word *ca* indicates limitation (only). It is only (*ca)* permission to eat all food (*sarvānnānumatiḥ*) in times when the person must get food when there is danger to his life (*prāṇātyaye*). Why? Because it is seen in scriptures. In the behaviour of Cākrāyaṇa the following conduct is seen. *mātācīhateṣu kuruṣu.... na vā ajīviṣyam imān akhādann iti hovāca kāmo na udapānam*: without eating these beans I could not live, whereas drinking water is not so, depending on my desire. (Chāndogya upaniṣad 1.10.4)

This is the story. The sage Cākrāyaṇa ate the left over, impure food of Ibhya. But when Ibhya offered him water, he did not accept it for fear of contamination and because it was readily available elsewhere. Then the next day he ate his own stale left overs. Other stories can be similarly explained.

Sūtra - 3.4.29

|| abādhāc ca ||

Any food was permitted since it did not impede the sage's knowledge.

In times of need, permission is given to eat all food since his knowledge was not impaired *(abādhāt)* by that eating. It did not contaminate his heart.

Sūtra - 3.4.30

|| api smaryate ||

Smṛtis also state the same.

It is said:

jīvitātyayam āpanno yo 'nnam atti yatas tataḥ
lipyate na sa pāpena padma-patram ivāmbhasā

A person under danger to his life who eats food from here or there is not contaminated by sin, just as a lotus leaf is not touched by water. Manu-smṛti 10.204

In dangerous situations only, but not at all times, everyone can eat any food. Thus the śrūti statement is permission only and not a rule, since it is forbidden in scriptures to eat all types of food.

Sūtra - 3.4.31

|| śabdaś cāto'kāma-kāre ||

Scripture also says that in normal conditions one cannot eat anything he pleases.

Because only in times of danger one is permitted to eat any food, the knower of Brahman should not act as he pleases (*akāma-kāre)* at other times. Śruti (*śabdaḥ*) forbids acting whimsically. *āhāra-śuddhau sattva-śuddhiḥ, sattva-śuddhau dhruvā smṛtiḥ smṛti-lambhe sarva-granthīnāṁ vipramokṣaḥ:* from pure food arises pure consciousness; from pure consciousness arises fixed meditation; firm meditation leads of liberation from all knots.(Chāndogya Upaniṣad 7.26.2) Since only in danger does one have permission to eat any type of food, in normal situations one must follow the injunctions of scripture.

Topic 7 (Sūtras 32 - 33)

Vihitatvādhikaraṇam – Prescription of karmas for the sva-niṣṭha devotee

In the previous section, three types of devotees were shown. Now the question of whether these types of devotees should follow *varṇāśrama* when they have attained vidyā is discussed. First the *sva-niṣṭha* devotee is examined.

paśyann apīmam ātmānaṁ kuryāt karmāvicārayan yad ātmanaḥ suniyatam ānandotkarṣam āpnuyāt

Seeing this Lord, one should perform karmas without discrimination since he will positively attain the highest bliss. Kauśārava-śruti.

The doubt is this. Should the *svaniṣṭha* perform karmas or not when he has attained vidyā?

(Pūrvapakṣa) He should not do karmas since it is seen that *sādhana* ends on attaining the result, and he has attained the result, vidyā.

Sūtra - 3.4.32

|| vihitatvāc cāśrama-karmāpi ||

The *svaniṣṭha* should perform *varṇāśrama* duties since this is prescribed in the scriptures.

The word *api* indicates that *varṇa* actions should be included with *āśrama* actions. He should to the actions of his *varṇa* and *āśrama.* Why? Because these actions are prescribed *(vihitatvāt)* for him to increase the vidyā.

"Since karma is prescribed even after atttaining vidyā, is not performing *jñāna* and *karma* together then approved?" This is denied in the next sūtra.

Sūtra - 3.4.33

|| sahakāritvena ||

Karmas do not produce liberation because karmas are done only as an accompanying activity.

Karmas should be done along with vidyā, but not as a cause of liberation since scripture factually states the nature of vidyā. *tam eva viditvā*: knowing Brahman one attains liberation. (Śvetāśvatara Upaniṣad 3.8) What is said is this. The *svaniṣṭha* in the beginning performs his karmas with Paramātmā as the goal. By making the Lord the goal of those karmas, vidyā (realization in bhakti) aimed at the Lord arises like the fine threads within the lotus stem. He performs karmas even after vidyā has arisen in order to increase vidyā by them. Vidyā does not destroy those karmas performed after vidyā arises, since they are not contrary to vidyā. Vidyā keeps them, so that the person can experience the varieties of Svarga. *nā hāsya karma* kṣīyate: his karma is not destroyed (Bṛhad-āraṇyaka Upaniṣad 1.4.15) These karmas are not for fulfilling personal desires since they are performed for realization of the Lord. Since they are not performed with material desire, the *svaniṣṭha* devotee, knowing the Lord, attains the Lord and realizes Svarga as secondary effect. It is like touching grass. In going to the village one touchs grass. Vidyā gives the experience of Svarga through his execution of accompanying karmas and gives the attainment of Brahman by vidyā itself to the *svaniṣṭha* devotee who desires to attain Brahman, while experiencing the bliss of Svarga. Śruti indicates this with *taṁ* vidyā-*karmaṇī samanvārabhete pūrva-prajñā ca*: vidyā and karma as well as previous knowledge take hold of him. (Bṛhad-āraṇyaka Upaniṣad. 4.4.2) In this way the determination of the *svaniṣṭa* devotee should be understood.

Sometimes in order to test the *nirapekṣa* devotee's complete detachment, vidyā itself makes him go to Svarga. *sarvaṁ ha paśyaḥ paśyati*: the sage who sees Brahman sees everything. (Muṇḍaka Upaniṣad 3.3.) This is not contrary to the reasoning that persons go to Svarga by karmas, since now the reasons are different, for persons other than svaniṣṭḥas. For the *svaniṣṭha* devotee, vidyā destroys all karmas except the results of pious karmas of this life and *prārabdha-karmas* from acts of previous lives which will take the *svaniṣṭhā* to Svarga. For the *pariniṣṭhita*[83] and *nirapekṣa* devotees, vidyā destroys all except *prārabdha-karmas.* Thus vidyā (bhakti) is independent in giving results and karma is merely an assistant.

Topic 8 (Sūtras 34 - 35)

Sarvathādhikaraṇam – Necessity of performing bhakti

Now the *pariniṣṭhita* devotee is examined. *ātma-krīdā ātma-ratiḥ kriyāvān*: the devotee plays with the Lord, enjoys with him and acts with him. (Muṇḍaka Upaniṣad 3.1.4) The *pariniṣṭhita* devotee performs *varṇāśrama-dharma* for the people and performs *bhagavad-dharma* in the form of hearing and chanting, out of love for the Lord. Does he perform both *varṇāśrama* and bhakti simultaneously, or one after the other or does he give up *varnāśrama-dharma* completely and perform only *bhagavad-dharma*?

(pūrvapakṣa) Because it is impossible to do both simultaneously and it is a fault to give up *varṇāśrama-dharma* , it cannot be determined what to do.

Sūtra - 3.4.34

|| sarvathāpi ta evobhaya-liṅgāt ||

The pariniṣṭhita devotee must perform bhakti, even at the expense of varṇāśrama duties, since this is indicated in śruti and smṛti.

Api indicates emphasis (indeed). Even not giving respect to his dharmas (*api*), the *pariniṣṭhita* must perform *bhagavad-dharma (sarvathā).* He performs his

---

[83] The actions of the present life give mild results to the *pariniṣṭhita* devotee. The *nirapekṣa* devotee obtains only *prārabdha-karmas.*

dharmas to some degree, at minor times. Why? Because this is indicated in two ways--śruti and smṛti *(ubhaya -liṅgāt*). *tam eavikaṁ jānatha*: know the Lord alone. (Muṇḍaka Upaniṣad 3.2.5)

mahātmānas tu māṁ pārtha daivīṁ prakṛtim āśritāḥ |
bhajanty ananya-manaso jñātvā bhūtādim avyayam | |

Those of profound mind, taking shelter of my spiritual *svarūpa*, serve my human form with no distractions, knowing that my human-like body is the cause of all things, that it is indestructible and fully spiritual.

satataṁ kīrtayanto māṁ yatantaś ca dṛḍha-vratāḥ |
namasyantaś ca māṁ bhaktyā nitya-yuktā upāsate | |

Having strict vows, desiring to be my associates, diligent to understand my Nature, they worship me at all times with devotion, through singing, offering respects, and other devotional acts. BG 9.13-15

Another reason confirms this.

Sūtra - 3.4.35

| | anabhibhavaṁ ca darśayati | |

The śruti shows that the *parninişṭhita* devotee does not incur sin by neglecting *varṇāśrama* duties.

It is said:

naimaṁ pāpmā tarati sarvaṁ pāpmānaṁ tarati nainaṁ pāpmā tapati saravam; pāpmānaṁ tapai

Sin does not ovrecome him; he overcomes all sin. Sin does not burn him; he burns up all sin. Bṛhad-āraṇyaka Upaniṣad 4.4.23

This passage shows *(darśayati)* that the *pariniṣṭhita* devotee is not overcome (*anabhibhavam*) by faults arising from not performing his *āśrama dharma* because of performing bhakti. Giving up performance of dharma, he performs *bhagavad-dharma* (bhakti). The verse from the Viṣṇu Purāṇa indicates that a person who performs *varṇāśrama* pleases the Lord by also worshipping the Lord:

varṇāśṛamācaravatā puruśeṇa paraḥ pumān
viṣṇur āradhyate panthā nānyat tat toṣa-kāraṇam.

A person performing *varṇāśrama* duties should worship the supreme Lord Viṣṇu. There is no other way to please him.

The absorption of King Bharata in the Lord is described also in Viṣṇu Purāṇa:

yajñeśacyuta govinda mādhavānanda keśava
kṛṣṇaviṣno hṛṣīkeśa vāsudeva, manostue te
iti rājāha bharato harer nāmāni kevalam
nānyaj jagāda maitreya kiṇcit svapnāntare 'pi ca
etat padaṁ tad-arthaṁ ca vinā nānyad acintayat
samit-puṣpa-kuśādānaṁ cakre deva-kriyā-kṛte
nānyāni cakre karmāṇi niḥsaṅgo yoga-tāpasaḥ

O Yajña, Acyuta, Govinda, Mādhava, Ananda, Keśava, Kṛṣṇa, Viṣṇu, Hṛṣīkeṣa, Vāsudeva! I offer respects to you. In this way King Bharata spoke the names of the Lord only. O Maitreya! He did not speak anything else at all, even in his dreams. He did not think of anything except the Lord. In worshipping the Lord he offered fire wood, flowers and kuśa. Endowed with yoga and austerity, he did no other activities. Viṣṇu Purāṇa 2.13.9-11

Topic 9 (Sūtras 36 - 38)

Vidhurādhikaraṇam - Those without āśrama

Having shown vidyā and the conduct after attaining it for persons in *āśrama (gṛhaṣṭha* and *sannyāsī)* now the author shows vidyā and consequent conduct for *nirapekṣas*, without *āśrama.* Gārgī, a knower of Brahman without *āśrama,* is described in the śrutis. *atha vācaknavy uvāca--brahmaṇā bhagavanto hantāham enaṁ yājñavalkyaṁ dvau praśnau prakṣyāmi:* Gārgī said, "O great brāhmaṇas, I will ask Yājñavalkya two questions." (Bṛhad-āraṇyaka Upaniṣad 3.8.1)

The doubt is this. Will vidyā arise in a person with no *āśrama* ?

(pūrvapakṣa) It will not arise because they lack *āśrama* which is said to be the cause of vidyā arising according to the scriptures.

Sūtra - 3.4.36

|| antarā cāpi tu tad-dṛṣṭeḥ ||

Vidyā arises in persons without *āśrama* since this is seen in scripture.

The word *tu* dismisses attachment to formalities of karma. The word *ca* indicates certainty. Without *āśrama (antarā)* vidyā arises in those persons purified by truthfulness, austerity, *japa* and other acts performed in previous births, and who in this life show natural detachment. Why? Because it is seen that Gārgī possessed knowledge of Brahman. The meaning is this. Because some persons gave up their bodies in a previous life before the fruits of previously practiced dharma could manifest, they could not experience the results. In the next life however, vidyā (bhakti) appears with detachment in these persons already purified, just by association with devotees.

Vidyā *(*bhakti) arises with the destruction of impurities by devotee association, which is powerful.

Sūtra - 3.4.37

|| api smaryate ||

This is also described in the smṛtis.

It is said:

pibanti ye bhagavata ātmanaḥ satāṁ
kathāmṛtaṁ śravaṇa-puṭeṣu sambhṛtam |
punanti te viṣaya-vidūṣitāśayaṁ
vrajanti tac-caraṇa-saroruhāntikam ||

Those who drink the sweet pastimes of the Lord and his devotees held in the cups of their ears clean their hearts of all contamination and attain the lotus feet of the Lord for service. SB 2.2.37

rahūgaṇaitat tapasā na yāti
na cejyayā nirvapaṇād gṛhād vā
na cchandasā naiva jalāgni-sūryair
vinā mahat-pāda-rajo-'bhiṣekam

Without bathing in the dust from the feet of great devotees, one cannot realize the Lord through concentration of the mind, performance of sacrifices, distributing food, building shelters for the destitute, studying the Vedas, or performing austerities in the water, fire or the sun. SB 5.5.12

The word *api* indicates that qualities like truthfulness etc. (besides *āśrama* duties) are also favorable for vidyā*'s* appearance.

Vidya (bhakti) arises very easily in the *nirapekṣa* who has had devotional association, because of the special mercy of the Supreme Lord.

Sūtra - 3.4.38

|| viśeṣānugrahaś ca ||

The *nirapekṣa* receives special mercy from the Lord.

It is said:

mac-cittā mad-gata-prāṇā bodhayantaḥ parasparam |
kathayantaś ca māṁ nityaṁ tuṣyanti ca ramanti ca ||

With minds absorbed in me, completely dependent on me, mutually informing each other about me and speaking about me, they continuously experience satisfaction and enjoyment.

teṣāṁ satata-yuktānāṁ bhajatāṁ prīti-pūrvakam |
dadāmi buddhi-yogaṁ taṁ yena mām upayānti te ||

To those who constantly desire to be with me and worship me with great love, I give the intelligence by which they attain my direct association. BG 10.9-10

It is seen in these verses that the *nirapekṣa* devotee receives special mercy. The status of *nirapekṣa* is evident because they are absorbed in the Lord *(satata-yuktānām)*.

Topic 10 (Sūtras 39 - 43)

Itarādhikaraṇam - Superiority of persons without āśrāma

It has been shown that persons with *āśrama,* like Yājñavalkya, and persons without *āśrama* like Gārgī possesssed vidyā. The doubt is this. Is the person with *āśrama* or the person without *āśrama* superior?

(Pūrvapakṣa) The persons with *āśrama* are better because they follow the rules of Vedic *āśrama* and are absorbed in Brahman.

Sūtra - 3.4.39

|| atas tv itaraj-jyāyo liṅgāc ca ||

The person without *āśrama* is better than the person with *āśrama* because this is indicated in śruti.

The word *tu* removes the doubt. The word *ca* indicates exclusion. The person without *āśrāma (itarat)* is better (*jyāyaḥ*) than the person with *āśrama (ataḥ)* regarding praciticing vidyā. Why? Because of indications (*liṅgāt).* Gārgī attained great vidyā (bhakti). *āśramas* are prescribed in the scriptures in order to diminish material tendencies of jīvas having those tendencies without beginning. The purpose is not their performance but only diminishing the material tendencies. These tendencies are an obstacle to attaining attraction to Brahman, the Lord. Those who have developed attraction to the Lord, and have had their material tendencies already destroyed, obtain no results from practicing the *āśramas*. Thus being without *āśrama* is superior.

The Jābāla Upaniṣad, after recommending passing through the *āśramas* in sequence, says that the detached person can avoid the *āśramas.* The person absorbed in Brahman such as Sāmvartaka rejected *sannyāsa.* [84] Though there are texts like *anāśramī na tiṣṭheta dinam ekam api dvijaḥ:* the twice born should not remain without an *āśrama* for one day, this is a general statement.

Let that be. It has been stated that the person without *āśrama,* the *nirapekṣa* devotee is superiorbecaue of being absorbed only in Brahman. This is not correct since it is possible that they again become dependent on *āśramas* (they fall). As per the rules, it is criticized to again accept an *āśrama* of a householder etc. The superiority of a person with no *āśrama* is negated because scripture condemns reverting to a lower *āśrama* which had not been experienced, because one gives up what was accepted according to rules, and because it would be impossible to be remain concentrated on Brahman after his accepting an *āśrama* which would be distracting, and which he accepted because of developing faith in the *āśramas,* praised for being Vedic. On the other hand the *svaniṣṭha* and *pariniṣṭhita* devotees, purifing their existence by practicing the rules of their *āśrama,* have no obstacles, because they meditate on the Lord without break with greater and greater intensity.

Sūtra - 3.4.40

|| tad-bhūtasya tu nātad-bhāvo jaiminer api niyamāt atad-rūpābhāvebhyaḥ ||

---

[84] It is said that they reject the signs of *sannyāsa* such as the *daṇḍa* and water pot. Jada-bhārata is mentioned among them.

The *nirapekṣa* devotee, absorbed in the Lord, cannot fall from that position, because his senses are absorbed in the Lord, all desires other than the Lord have been destroyed, and there are examples like Gārgī. This is the opinion of Jaimini and Bādarāyaṇa.

The word *tu* refutes the doubt. The *nirapekṣa,* absorbed in Brahman (*tad-bhūtasya*), could not fall from his attraction to the Lord (*na atad-bhāvaḥ*). That is the opinion of Jaimini and of Bādarāyaṇa also (*api*). Why? Because his senses are restricted (*niyamāt*) to a thirst for Brahman and because of the destruction (*abhāvebhyaḥ)* of all desires *(rūpa)* other than Brahman *(atad*) and because of the exampleof Gārgī and others who did not accept household life. Smṛti also says this:

kāmādibhir anāviddhaṁ praśāntākhila-vṛtti yat
cittaṁ brahma-sukha-spṛṣṭaṁ naivottiṣṭheta karhicit

When one's consciousness is uncontaminated by material lusty desires, when it is peaceful in all activities and is touched by the happiness of Brahman, the consciousness does deviate at any time. SB 7.15.35

Though Jaimini is inclined to karma sometimes he thinks in this way since he is afraid of strong śrutis concerning the position of the *nirapekṣa* devotee. He admits that some people, purified by karmas undertaken in previous life, are of this status of absorption in Brahman in this life.

Next the superiority of the *nirapekṣa* over the *svaniṣṭha* devotee is shown.

"It is said *sarvaṁ ha paśyaḥ paśyati:* the knower of Brahman sees everything in the universe. (Chāndogya Upaniṣad 7.26.2) Since by vidyā one attains Svarga and other planets in the universe, the *nirapekṣa* devotee, by becoming attached to the enjoyment of Svarga that he attains, will lose his concentration on Brahman."

Sūtra - 3.4.41

|| na cādhikārikam api patanānumānāt tad-ayogāt ||

The *nirapekṣa* never desires the post of a *devatā* or worldy enjoyment since he remembers that one falls from that position and has no desire for such a position from the beginning.

The word *ca* is for emphasis. The word *api* indicates inclusion of worldly happiness. They never desire the post of a *devatā (adhikārikam*) or happiness on earth (*api*). Why? Because he remembers (*anumānāt*) that one falls from those positions (*patanānumānāt*). *ā brahman-bhuvanāl lokāḥ punar-āvartino 'rjuna*: O Arjuna, from all planets including Brahma-loka one must return. (BG 8.16) And because from the beginning, the *nirapekṣa* devotee has no desire for such enjoyment (*tad-ayogāt*). Smṛtis also should be seen in this regard. Though by the power of vidyā he consents to accept these places, his concentration on the Lord is not disrupted by that place because he has no desire for enjoyment. Thus the conclusion is without refutation.

The *nirapekṣa* is superior to the *pariniṣṭhita* devotee.

Sūtra - 3.4.42

|| upapūrvam api tv eke bhāvam aśanavat tad uktam ||

The followers of the Atharva Veda say that the *nirapekṣa's* worship and his prema are full of taste.

The word *api* is for emphasis. The word *tu* removes the opposite opinion. One group, the followers of the Atharva veda, say that the *nirapekṣa* devotee's worship of the Lord (*upapūrvam*) and his perfected *bhāva* are tasty like his food (*aśanavat*). *bhaktir asya bhajanaṁ tad ihāmutra*: bhakti is worship of the Lord in this world and the next. (Gopāla-tāpanī Upaniṣad 1.14*) sac-cid ānandeka-rase bhakti-yoge tiṣṭhati*: the Lord resides in bhakti composed of eternity, knowledge and bliss. (Gopāla-tāpanī Upaniṣad 2.78) Some devotees, wherever they worship the Lord, experience him like the bliss in the spiritual world. *so śnute sarvān kāmān*: the jīva experiences all enjoyments. (Taittirīya Upaniṣad 2.1.1) One will find smṛtis saying this also.

The *nirapekṣas,* without endeavor, attain *sālokya, sāmīpya* and other types of liberation. Other reasons are given.

Sūtra - 3.4.43

|| bahis tūbhayathāpi smṛter ācārāc ca ||

The nirapekṣa devotee is beyond the material world because it is described in smṛti that he is united with the Lord and because the Lord acts on behalf of the devotee.

The word *tu* is for emphasis. Though the *nirapekṣas* are situated in the material world, they should be considered to be outside *(bahiḥ)*. Why? Because smṛti describes the union of the Lord and his servant to be like gold and jewels, in which both are attracted to each other (*ubhayathā smṛteḥ*):

visṛjati hṛdayaṁ na yasya sākṣād
dharir avaśābhihito 'py aghaugha-nāśaḥ
praṇaya-rasanayā dhṛtāṅghri-padmaḥ
sa bhavati bhāgavata-pradhāna uktaḥ

He who binds the lotus feet of the Lord by ropes of love, and whose heart the Lord, destroyer of heaps of sin, does not leave, even if beckoned accidentally, is called the best of devotees. SB 11.2.55

And because of the Lord's conduct with his devotees (*ācārāt*). The Lord himself says:

nirapekṣaṁ muniṁ śāntaṁ nirvairaṁ sama-darśanam
anuvrajāmy ahaṁ nityaṁ pūyeyety aṅghri-reṇubhiḥ

I always follow the footsteps of my pure devotees, who are free from all personal desire, are rapt in thought of my pastimes, are fixed in me, without any feelings of enmity, and are equal to all conditions of the world. Let me be purified by the dust from their feet! SB 11.14.16

For these two reasons (smṛti statements and conduct of the Lord), the union of the Lord and the n*irapekṣa*, with the Lord existing internal and external to the devotee, is established. Opposition to the Lord is the cause of *saṁsāra* and by its destruction the devotee attains liberation in this form.

Topic 11 (Sūtras 44 - 46)

Svāmy-adhikaraṇam - Maintenance by the Lord

It has been stated that the *nirapekṣa* devotee has no attaction for the happiness of any material place including Brahma-loka. Now it is stated that these devotees have no attraction to the happiness of the present world. *bhartā san bhriyamāṇo vibhāti*: the maintainer, the Lord, is served by the devotees. (Taittirīya Āraṇyaka 3.14.1)

The doubt is this. Does the *nirapekṣa* maintain his present body by his own endeavors or by the endeavor of the Lord?

(pūrvapakṣa) They maintain themselves by their own efforts since they do not want to make the Lord put forth efforts on their behalf.

Sūtra - 3.4.44

|| svāminaḥ phala-śruter ity ātreyaḥ ||

Their bodies are maintained by the Lord since the śruti states this. This is the opinion of Dattātreya.

Their bodies are maintained by the Lord (*svāminaḥ*). Why? Because śruti states that the Lord maintains them. This is the opinion of Dattātreya (*ātreya*).

ananyāś cintayanto māṁ ye janāḥ paryupāsate |
teṣāṁ nityābhiyuktānāṁ yoga-kṣemaṁ vahāmy aham ||

But I carry the burden of supply and maintenance of those who desire constant association with me, and who, thinking only of me, worship only me. BG 9.22

darśana-dhyāna-saṁsparśair matsya-kūrma-vihaṅgamāḥ
svāny apatyāni puṣṇanti tathāham api padmaja

The fish nourishes its offspring by seeing, the turtle by meditation, and the birds by touch. I nourish my devotees with similar affection, O Brahmā. *Padma Purāṇa*

From these statements it is understood that thinking that the devotee should not engage the Lord in supporting him is a material conception, since the devotee never desires maintenance and the Lord does not make endeavor, since everything is accomplished by his will. Simply by serving the Lord, their bodily maintenance is achieved. Thus the passage quoted says the Lord is simply served by the devotees (*bhriyamānah).*

The Lord's devotion to maintaining his devotees is illustrated with an example to make it clear.

Sūtra - 3.4.45

|| ārtvijyam ity auḍulomis tasmai hi parikriyate ||

Auḍulomi compares the Lord to a priest who is purchased by the devotee for maintaining his body.

The word *iti* means "like." The Lord's support of the *nirapekṣa* devotee is like (*iti*) the work of a priest (*ārtvijya*), because he is purchased (*parikriyate*) by the devotee for maintaining his body *(tasmai*).

tulasī-dala-mātreṇa jalasya culukena ca
vikrīṇīte svam ātmānaṁ bhaktebhyo bhakta-vatsalaḥ

The Lord, affectionate to the devotee sells himself to the devotees by their offering merely a *tulasī* leaf and a drop of water. Viṣṇu-dharma

The sponsor of the sacrifice purchases the priest by a donation to do the sacrifice with its *aṅgas.* Auḍulomi explains bhakti improperly (like a purchase) because he is a proponent of impersonal Brahman. The *nirapekṣa* devotee is superior to this.

Sūtra - 3.4.46

|| śruteś ca ||

The devotee's body is maintained by the Lord because this is stated in śruti.

The priest asks the sponsor what blessings he wants. *tasmād u haivaṁ vid udgato brūyāt kaṁ te kāmam āgāyāni:* therefore the *udatṛ* priest who has knowledge should say, "Which of your desired objects should I produce by singing?" (Chāndogya Upaniṣad 1.7.8-9) This shows that the sacrificial acts performed by the priest go to the sponsor. The Lord, supporting his devotee, is compared to the priest supporting the sponsor.

Topic 12 (Sūtra 47)

Sahakāryantara-vidhy-adhikaraṇam - Secondary rules for the nirapekṣa

Now the author shows the activities of the devotees after acquiring vidyā (bhakti). *tasmād evaṁ vic chānto dāntaḥ:* knowing this, he becomes peaceful, controlling his senses. (Bṛhad-āraṇyaka upaniṣad 1.4.23) *Ātmā vā are draṣṭavyaḥ*: one should see the Lord. (Bṛhad-āraṇyaka Upaniṣad 2.4.5) These passages describe the activities of one who desires the Lord to be controlling the mind, meditation etc.

The doubt is this. Should the *nirapekṣa* devotee perform control of the senses and mind, ending with meditation or should he simply remember the form, qualities and activities of the Lord.

(pūrvapakṣa) One who has acquired vidyā will not develop steadiness without control of the senses and mind etc. Therefore the *nirapekṣa* should perform all these activities.

Sūtra - 3.4.47

|| sahakāry-antara-vidhiḥ pakṣeṇa tṛtīyaṁ tadvato vidhy-ādivat ||

Control of senses and mind are activities for devotees having an *āśrama*, but the main activity of the *nirapekṣa* devotee is meditation on the Lord's form, to be done like a rule.

Control of the mind and senses etc. (*sahakāry-antara*) were included as assisting elements along with sacrifices in causing vidyā to arise. (sūtra3.4.26) These rules (*vidhiḥ*) should be accepted as unique statements (*apūrva*) for the *svaniṣṭha* and *pariniṣṭhita* devotees (*pakṣeṇa*) but as naturally occuring in the *nirapekṣa* devotee (and therefore not a rule). Rather he should remember the Lord's form, qualities and activities. The *nirapekṣa* devotee who desires only the mercy of the Lord, should perform mental activities, the third method (*tritīyam tadvataḥ*). *manasaivedam āptavyam:* the Lord is attained by the mind. (Kaṭha Upaniṣad 2.1.11) This means he should meditate without physical or vocal actions. An example is given to show that this is necessary. It is compulsory like the *sandhya* rites, which are a rule (*vidhyādivat)* of those having an *āśrama.* Therefore the *nirapekṣa* who has had vidyā manifest must meditate on the form, qualities and activities of the Lord. He is not restrained from doing *japa,* deity worship etc. since these are attained by meditation itself. Or since meditation is most prominent among the elements, it alone is mentioned. Thus the three types of devotees and their actions have been described.

Topic 13 (Sūtras 48 - 49)

Kṛtsna-bhāvādhikaraṇam - Household āśrama contains all āśramas

The acquisition of vidyā by the three types of devotees has been described. Now begins a discussion of how to make vidyā steady.

ācārya-kuād vedam adhīyta yathā-vidhānaḥ guroḥ karmātiśeṣe;abhisamāvṛtya kuṭumbe śucau deśe svādhyāam adhīyāno dharmikān vidadhad ātmani sarvendriyāṇi sampratiṣṭhāpya ahiṁsan sarvāṇi bhūtāny anyatra tīrthebhyaḥ | sa khalv evaṁ vartayan yāvad āyuṣaṁ brahma-lokam abhisampadyate na ca punar āvartate

Having studied the Vedas in a family of teachers, he should return home after satisfying the guru according to the rules and recite the scriptures in a clean place in his house (after marriage). Acting righteously, establishing all the senses in the Lord, being non-violent to all beings except for sacrifices, he should pass his life. He will then attain Brahman and never return. Chāndogya Upaniṣad 8.15.1

Because this description mentions only the householder, others cannot attain vidyā. Though sometimes śruti speaks of renunciation in order to praise Brahman, these passages simply mean that one should try to give up everything for Brahman since Brahman is so great. But only the householder acting as described can attain Brahman, as this is stated in the text.

Sūtra - 3.4.48

|| kṛtsna-bhāvāt tu gṛhiṇopasaṁhāraḥ ||

Because the household *āśrama* contains rules of all *āśramas,* it alone is mentioned in the passage concerning realization of Brahman.

The word *tu* removes the doubt. The conclusion (*upasaṁhāraḥ*) describing the householder attaining liberation does not mean that he alone attains liberation. Rather, because the household *aśrama* includes all rules for all *āśramas (kṛtsna-bhāvāt),* it alone is described. The rules of *āśṛama,* which are many for the householder, and which require effort to perform, are listed here as obligatory. The rules of other *āśramas,* such as non-violence and control of the mind, also must be performed to the best of their ability. Thus, since the rules of all *āśramas* are contained in the household *āśrama,* it is not wrong to say that the household *āśrama* attains Brahman.

Smṛti also says:

bhikṣā-bhujaś ca ye kecit parivrāḍ brahmacāriṇaḥ |
te'py atraiva pratiṣṭhante gārhasthyaṁ tena vai paraḥ ||

The *vanapraṣṭhas, sannyāsīs* and *brahmacārīs* are situated in the household *āśrama*. Thus it is the supreme *āśrama*. Manu-smṛti

Since other *āśramas* are mentioned in the scriptures, the household *āśrama* is often mentioned at the end, because it contains all *āśramas*. This is expressed in the next sūtra.

Sūtra - 3.4.49

|| maunavad itareṣām apy upadeśāt ||

All *āśramas* can attain liberation because of scriptural statements of the other *āśramas* attaining liberation as well, after the mention of *mauna* in the Chāndogya Upaniṣad.

Maunavat means attaining the position of a sage (*muni*). Previous to this, in the Upaniṣad it is said:

trayo dharma-skandhāḥ | yajño 'dhyayanaṁ dānaṁ prathamas tapa eva dvitīyo brahmacārya-kula-vāsī tṛtīyo'tyantam ātmānam ācārya-kule'vasādayan sarva ete puṇya-lokā bhavanti brahma-saṁstho'mṛtatvam eti

There are three branches of dharma. The first is sacrifice, study of the Vedas, and charity (householder). The second is austerity (*vanapraṣtha*). The third is living in the house of the guru practicing *brahmacārya*, undergoing difficulties of the body in the guru's house. All these attain pious worlds. Fixed in Brahman they attain immortality. Chāndogya Upaniṣad 2.23.1

evam eva viditvā munir bhavaty etam eva pravrājino lokam abhīpsantaḥ pravrajanti

Knowing the Lord, one becomes a sage. Desiring the world of Brahman, the sannyāsī wanders the world. Bṛhad-āraṇyaka Upaniṣad 4.4.22

Others also attain liberation because of the statements mentioning other persons who are steady (*gṛhastha, vanaprastha* and *brahmacārī*) and the *sannyāsi* attaining Brahman (*itareṣām upadeśāt*). Thus mentioning the household *āśrama* being qualified for liberation includes all *āśramas*. The plural is used in *itareṣām* to indicate the four divisions of each *āśrama.*

Jābāla Upaniṣad describes four *āśramas.*

brahmacaryaṁ samapya gṛhī bhavet gṛhiṇāṁ bhūtvā vanī bhavet, vaṇī bhūtvā pravrajet, yadi vanerathā brahmacayād eva pravrajet gṛhād vā vanād vā | atha punar avratī vā vratī snātako vāsnātako votsan nāgnir anagniko yā yad ahar eva virajyet tad ahar eva pravrajet

After completely *brahmacārī* life one becomes a householder. Having finished household life one becomes a *vanaprastha.* Having completed *vanaprasthā*, one becomes a *sannyāsī.* Or he may become a *sannyāsī* after *brahmacārī* life, or after household life. He may perform sacrifices or not. He may complete his *brahmacārī* life or not. He may maintain the fire or not. Whenever he becomes detached, he may take *sannyāsa. Jābāla Upaniṣad 4*

The *nirapekṣa* is later described in the same Upaniṣad after the words *paramahaṁsānām.*

Thus the household *āśrama* is alone mentioned only because it includes many rules of dharma. Since it is specifically mentioned that one can renounce household life when one attains detachment, the idea that only the householder attains liberation is defeated. Everywhere it is stated that a person with attachment enters household life and one who is detached renounces household life. Thus it is concluded that vidyā arises in the person without *āśrama (*the *nirapekṣa),* who is suitable ornamented with control of the senses, mind etc.

Topic 14 (Sūtra 50)

Anāviśkārādhikaraṇam - Not teaching vidyā

Now the secret nature of vidyā is explained. Śvetāśvatara Upaniṣad says:

vedānte paramaṁ guhyaṁ purā-kalpe pracoditam |
nāpraśāntāya dātavyaṁ nāputrāyāśiṣyāya vā punaḥ ||

The supreme secret in Vedānta, spoken in a previous *kalpa,* should not be given to a person who is not peaceful, to a person without a son, and to a person who is not a disciple. Śvetāśvatara Upaniṣad 6.22

The doubt is this. Should vidyā be taught to everyone?

(Pūrvapakṣa) Vidyā should be revealed by the compassionate teacher to all, since it would be contradictory to his compassion to discriminate who is qualified and who is unqualified.

Sūtra - 3.4.50

|| anāviṣkurvann anvayāt ||

The teacher should not reveal vidyā to the unqualified person, since that is directly stated in śruti.

He should teach without revealing vidyā *(anāviṣkurvan).* Why? Because this is seen in the teachings of the scripture quoted (*anvayāt*). The lotus-eyed Lord says this:

idaṁ te nātapaskāya nābhaktāya kadācana
na cāśuśrūṣave vācyaṁ na ca māṁ yo 'bhyasūyati ||

This is not to be spoken to a person lacking control of his senses, to a person without true devotion, to a person who is unwilling to hear, or to a person who envies me, thinking that I am material. BG 18.67

The Lord instructs this because vidyā gives results to qualified persons, and not to the unqualified. Śruti also makes similar statements like *yasya deva parā bhaktiḥ*: the meaning of scriptures is revealed to a person who has the highest devotion to the Lord. (Śvetāśvatara Upaniṣad 6.23) In Chāndogya Upaniṣad, Indra and Virocana both heard the same teachings, but Virocana could not understand the meaning. Thus, vidyā should be taught to the qualified and not to the unqualified. The qualified person is the person with faith who can understand the meaning of what is said in scriptures.

Topic 15 (Sūtra 51)

Aihikādhikaraṇam - Bhakti in this life

Now the author considers when vidyā will arise in a person. The subject *(viṣaya)* is Vāmadeva and the stories of Naciketa and Jābāla.

The doubt is this. Does vidyā produced by the means previously described[85] arise in the very life in which the person performed those acts, or in some other birth?

(Pūrva-pakṣa) Vidyā arises in the same life in persons who perform the *sādhana,* since people are inclined to the process with the aim of achieving it in this life.

---

[85] The sādhana to attain bhakti is association and mercy of devotees, practice of sense control, study of Vedas and other scriptures mentioned in sutra 3.4.26.

Sūtra - 3.4.51

|| aihikam aprastuta-pratibandhe tad-darśanāt ||

Vidyā appears in this life if there are no obstacles, since that is seen in scriptures.

When there are no obstacles (*aprastuta-pratibandhe*), vidyā arises in this life (*aihikam*). If there are obstacles it appears in the next life. Why? Because it is seen (*tad-darśanāt*).

mṛtyu-proktāṁ naciketo'tha labdhvā
vidyām etāṁ yoga-vidhiṁ ca kṛtsnam |
brahma-prāpto virajo'bhūd vimṛtyur
anyo'py evaṁ yo vidadhyātmam eva ||

Attaining all vidyā and rules of yoga spoken by Yama, Naciketa, becoming pure, attained Brahman and immortality. Anyone else who knows *ātmā* attains Brahman. Kaṭha Upaniṣad 2.3.18

This śruti shows vidyā can arise in one life. Vidyā can arise in the next life because it arises from *sādhana* spread into the next life. Vāmadeva obtained vidyā in the womb. (His practice to get vidyā must have been done in a previous life.)

This is what is said. When obstacles are destroyed because of special, strong *sādhana* against some weak obstacles, vidyā will arise in this life. This is the case of Naciketa and King Rahugana. If the obstacles are strong, vidyā, though manifest with the assistance of sacrifice, charity, austerity, sense and mind control practiced, will actually appear only in the next life, when the obstacles have been destroyed.

ayatiḥ śraddhayopeto yogāc calita-mānasaḥ |
aprāpya yoga-saṁsiddhiṁ kāṁ gatiṁ kṛṣṇa gacchati ||

O Kṛṣṇa, what is the destination of one who, though having faith, does not fully endeavor, because of unsteady mind, and does not attain the goal of *yoga*—seeing ātmā? BG 6.37

prayatnād yatamānas tu yogī saṁśuddha-kilbiṣaḥ |
aneka-janma-saṁsiddhas tato yāti parāṁ gatim ||

That *yogī*, striving with more effort than in his previous life, becoming purified of his faults, and reaching full perfection after many births, finally attains liberation with a vision of *ātmā* and Paramātmā. BG 6.45

It is not a rule that one seeks out what can be attained in this life only, since one sees people who say "Let the result of my efforts come in this life or the next." Thus it has been proved that vidyā (realization) may arise in this life or the next, whenever the obstacles have been destroyed.

Topic 16 (Sūtra 52)

Mukti-phalādhikaraṇam – Rule for attaining liberation

The author shows that with the acquisition of vidyā, liberation will necessarily follow. Śruti says *tam eva vidvān amṛta iha bhavati:* knowing (realizing) the Lord one attains immortality in this life. (Bṛhad-āraṇyaka Upaniṣad 4.4.17) *tam eva viditvātimṛtyum eti*: knowing the Lord, one surpasses death. (Śvetāśvatara Upaniṣad 3.8)

The doubt is this. Will liberation occur when leaving this body in which vidyā arose, or will it occur in the next body?

(Pūrva-pakṣa) He will obtain liberation in this life after leaving the body since the effect must follow the cause.

Sūtra - 3.4.52

|| evaṁ mukti-phalāniyamas

tad-avasthāvadhṛtes tad-avasthāvadhṛteḥ ||

There is no fixed rule when liberation will occur, since it depends on the remaining *prāradbha-karmas.*

It is not a rule that the person desiring liberation, who is equipped with *sadhāna* to attain vidyā, will attain vidyā in this life. It will happen after the destruction of the obstacles. (That was just explained.) Similarly, it is not a rule that a person who has attained vidyā will attain the result, liberation, in this life when he leaves the body. It will occur after the destruction of *prārabdha-karmas*. If there are no *prārabdha karmas*, then when he leaves this body (the last *prārabhda-karma*) he will attain liberation. If there are remaining *prārabdha-karmas* then he will obtain liberation in the next life.

Liberation cannot play favorites. Why? Because the condition of liberation (*tad-avasthā*) for the realized persons is determined (*avadhṛteḥ*) to be after the destruction of *prārabdha-karmas.* (*tad-avasthāvadhṛteḥ)*

ācāryavān puruṣo veda tasya tāvad eva ciraṁ yāvan na vimokṣye atha sampatsye

One who has a teacher knows the truth. As long as he has karma, he will not be liberated. With the exhaustion of karmas, he achieves the result. Chāndogya Upaniṣad 6.14.2

Smṛti says:

vidvān amṛtam āpnoti nātra kāryā vicāraṇā |
avasannaṁ yad ārabdhaṁ karma tatraiva gacchati |
na cet bahūni janmāni prāpyaivānte na saṁśayaḥ ||

One should not doubt that a person who knows the Lord will attain him. When the *prārabdha-karmas* are finished he will attain the Lord. If his *prārabdha karmas* are not finished, after many births he will attain the Lord. There is no doubt about this. Nārāyaṇa ādhyātmā

It has already been said that even though all karmas will be destroyed by vidyā, by the will of the Lord some portion of *prārabdha* may remain. This will also be explained later. The last words are repeated to indicate the end of the chapter.

May the Lord who creates detachment, binds the devotee to his qualities and gives delight to the devotee, and, who, bound by ropes to his devotee, is attracted to his devotee, be my friend.

Chapter Four

Table of Contents (Chapter 4)

Section One

dattvā vidyauṣadhaṁ bhaktān
niravadyān karoti yaḥ
dṛk-pathaṁ bhajatu śrīmān
prītyātmā sa hariḥ svayam

May the Lord, full of affection, who cures the devotees by giving them the medicine of vidyā, become visible.

Topic 1 (Sūtras 1 - 2)

Āvṛtty-adhikaraṇam - Repetition of sādhana

This chapter considers the results of vidyā (bhakti). Though from the beginning many sūtras dealt with *sādhana*, this is called the chapter of the results because the results of *vidyā* are most prominent in this chapter. *ātmā vā are draṣṭavyaḥ*: one should see the Lord. (Bṛhad-āraṇyaka Upaniṣad 4.5.6)

The doubt is this. Should one repeat hearing and other prescribed processes?

(Pūrvapakṣa) There should be no repetition since one should see the Lord by once performing hearing etc. just as one attains Svarga by once performing an *agniṣtoma* sacrifice.

Sūtra – 4.1.1

|| āvṛttir asakṛd upadeśāt ||

***Sādhanas* should be repeated since the scriptures teach that one must engage many times.**

Repetition (*āvṛttiḥ*) is necessary. Why? Because scriptures say *(upadeśāt*) that the processes should be done many times (*asakṛt*). Śvetaketu was told nine times about the Lord. *sa ya eṣo 'ṇimā, aitadātmyam idaṁ sarvaṁ, tat satyaṁ, sa ātmā, tattvam asi:* the Lord is very subtle, and all this has the Lord as its essence: he is the ātmā, and the you are dependent on him. (Chāndogya Upaniṣad 6.8.7) Though it is said that the meaning of scripture is stated once, such repetition is not a contradiction to this. The injunction to state something once is related to results which cannot be seen in this life. Since the result of *vidyā* (bhakti), seeing the Lord, is a result that can be seen in this life, hearing and other processes should be repeated till the result is attained, just as one repeatedly beats rice till the rice is visibly free of the husk.

Sūtra – 4.1.2

|| liṅgāc ca ||

Repetition is required because of indications in scripture.

This is proved by the indications of repetition in the example of Bhṛgu. *tad vijñāya punar eva varunāṁ pitaram upasasāra:* Bhṛgu again approached his father Varuṇa for understanding about the Lord. (Taittirīya Upaniṣad 3.2) Repetition is required because of the existence of offenses.

Topic 2 (Sūtra 3)

Ātmatvopāsanādhikaraṇam - Worshipping the Lord as ātmā

Another topic is considered. Should one worship the Lord while thinking of him as the Lord *(īśvara)* or while thinking of him as *ātmā*?

(pūrvapakṣa) One should worship the Lord thinking of him as the Lord, for śruti says *juṣṭaṁ yadā paśyaty anyam īśam*: one sees the other person, the worshipped Lord. (Śvetāśvatara Upaniṣad 4.7)

Sūtra – 4.1.3

|| ātmeti tūpagacchanti grāhayanti ca ||

Knowers of truth worship the Lord as *ātmā* and teach this to their students.

The word *tu* indicates emphasis. The Lord should definitely be worshiped as the self (*ātmeti*) because the knowers of truth approach (*upagacchanti*) him as *ātmā. yeṣām no 'yam ātmāyaṁ lokaḥ:* the Lord is realized by us as ātmā. (Bṛhad-āraṇyaka Upaniṣad 4.4.22) They teach this to their students as well. *ātmety evopāsīta*: the Lord should be worshipped as ātmā. (Bṛhad-āraṇyaka Upaniṣad 1.4.7)

The word *ātmā* should be understood to mean the all-pervading Lord with a form of knowledge and bliss having a human shape. Others say that ātmā means that the Lord is also the individual self since he gives the individual self its existence. Thinking of the Lord as oneself in the sense that the jīva freed from ignorance becomes Brahman is wrong, since this idea was previously refuted.

Topic 3 (Sūtra 4)

Pratīkādhikaraṇam - Lord is different from mind

In Chāndogya Upaniṣad 3.18.1, it says *mano brahmety upāsīta*: one should worship the mind as Brahman.

The doubt is this. Should one worship, thinking the mind is *ātmā* as one thinks of the Lord as *ātmā?*

(Pūrvapakṣa) One should think of the mind as *ātmā* since Brahman and mind are non-different according to the śruti.

Sūtra – 4.1.4

|| na pratīke na hi saḥ ||

One should not think of the mind as the Lord because the Lord is different from the mind.

One should not think the mind (*pratīke*) as ātmā (the Lord) because *(hi*) the Lord (*saḥ*) is not the mind. Rather he is the support of the mind. Smṛti says:

khaṁ vāyum agniṁ salilaṁ mahīṁ ca
jyotīṁṣi sattvāni diśo drumādīn
sarit-samudrāṁś ca hareḥ śarīraṁ
yat kiṁ ca bhūtaṁ praṇamed ananyaḥ

A person devoted only to the Lord should bow down to ether, fire, air, water, earth, the sun and other luminaries, all living beings, the directions, trees and other plants, the rivers and oceans, seeing them as the body of Kṛṣṇa. SB 11.2.41

The meaning the śruti statement is "Worship Brahman in the mind." The word *manaḥ* stands for *manasi (*in the mind).

Topic 4 (Sūtra 5)

Brahma-dṛṣty-adhikaraṇam - Lord as Brahman

Seeing the Lord as ātmā was advised but seeing the mind as the *ātmā* was forbidden. The doubt is this. Should the Lord be seen as Brahman or not?

The subject is a number of texts that indicate Brahman is the Lord.

(Pūrvapakṣa) The Lord should not be seen as Brahman because previously the Lord was to be seen as *ātmā.*

Sūtra – 4.1.5

|| brahma-dṛṣṭir utkarṣāt ||

The Lord should be seen as Brahman since this is best for meditation.

Seeing the Lord as *ātmā* and as Brahman should always be done. Why? Because of the excellence of this meditation, since this helps one remember that Lord is the abode of unlimited auspicious qualities. Śruti indicates that the Lord is both *āṭmā* and Brahman. *ayam ātmā brahma sarvānubhūtiḥ*: the Lord is ātmā and Brahman, full of all knowledge. (Bṛhad-āraṇyaka Upaniṣad 2.5.19) This is also illustrated in *atha kasmād ucyate brahmeti bṛhanto hy asmin guṇāḥ:* why is he called Brahman? In him are infinitely expanding qualities. (quoted by Madhva BS 1.1.1)

Topic 5 (Sūtra 6)

Ādityādimaty-adhikaraṇam - Lord's limbs as the sun

It is said:

candramā manaso jātaś cakṣuṣaḥ sūryo 'jāyata
śrotrād vāyuś ca prāṇaś ca mukhād agnir ajāyata

The mind gave birth to the moon. The eyes gave birth to the sun. The ears gave birth to Vāyu and *prāṇa.* The mouth gave birth to Agni. Ṛg Veda10.90.19

Here it appears that one thinks of the Lord's eyes and other organs as the cause of the sun etc. The doubt is this. Should one think in this way or not?

(Pūrvapakṣa) One should not think in this way since it is improper to impose fierce qualities on the Lord's limbs which are most tender. The limbs are compared to lotuses.

Sūtra – 4.1.6

|| ādityādi-matayaś cāṅga upapatteḥ ||

One should think of the Lord's limbs as the cause of the sun etc. because this demonstrates the excellence of the Lord.

The word *ca* indicates a refutation of the opponent's view. One should think of the sun etc. as the Lord's limbs such as the eye. Why? Because these demonstrate the Lord's excellence (*upapatteḥ*) as the cause of the sun etc. The Lord should be accepted as the cause of these objects because it is stated in scriptures and because it illustrates the Lord's inconceivable nature.

Topic 6 (Sūtras 7 - 11)

Āsīnādhikaraṇam - Sitting for meditation

In the Śvetāśvatara Upaniṣad (2.8) it is said:

trir-unnataṁ sthāpya samaṁ śarīraṁ
hṛdīndriyāṇi manasā sanniveśya
brahmoḍupena pratareta vidvān
srotāṁsi sarvāṇi bhayāvahāni

Situating himself with straight body, with erect head, neck and chest, concentrating the senses along with mind in the heart, the wise man should cross over all fearful currents by the boat of Brahman.

The doubt is this. Must one use this posture or not?

(Pūrvapakṣa) It is not necessary because any particular body posture is not suitable for remembering, which is a mental action.

Sūtra – 4.1.7

|| āsīnaḥ sambhavāt ||

One should mediate while in a seated posture because then meditation becomes possible.

One should remember the Lord while in seated in this posture *(āsīnaḥ)*. Why? Because meditation becomes possible in this posture (*sambhavāt*). Meditation is impossible while lying down, standing or moving about because distraction of the mind cannot be avoided in those positions.

It is said *te dhyāna-yogānugatā apaśyan*: those who are devoted to meditation and yoga have seen the Lord. (Śvetāśvatara Upaniṣad1.3) This shows that those desiring the Lord perform meditation. This possible is in a seated posture and not otherwise.

Sūtra – 4.1.8

|| dhyānāc ca ||

One must be seated because meditation is possible only then.

Meditation means exclusive contemplation without the interruption of extraneous thoughts. Meditation is not possible while lying down, standing or moving. Thus one must be seated.

Sūtra – 4.1.9

|| acalatvaṁ cāpekṣya ||

Meditation implies being motionless.

The word *ca* means "only." In the Chāndogya Upaniṣad (7.6.1) the word *dhyāyati* is used, and this is related to being motionless. *Dhyāyatīva pṛthivī:* the earth (being motionless) seems to meditate. Thus by indication, one should be seated. In common language also it is said, "The woman in separation meditates (sitting is implied) on her lover."

Sūtra – 4.1.10

|| smaranti ca ||

Smṛti confirms this also.

Smṛti also says that the meditator should be motionless in body, senses and mind:

śucau deśe pratiṣṭhāpya sthiram āsanam ātmanaḥ
nāty-ucchritaṁ nāti-nīcaṁ cailājina-kuśottaram
tatraikāgraṁ manaḥ kṛtvā yata-cittendriya-kriyaḥ
upaviśyāsane yuñjyāt yogam ātma-viśuddhaye
samaṁ kāya-śiro-grīvaṁ dhārayann acalaṁ sthiraḥ
samprekṣya nāsikāgraṁ svaṁ diśaś cānavalokayan
(praśāntātmā vigata-bhīr brahmacāri-vrate sthitaḥ |
manaḥ saṁyamya mac-citto yukta āsīta mat-paraḥ ||)

Establishing his own solid *āsana* in a clean place, not too high and not too low, he should prepare a sitting place, by spreading *kuśa* grass, then placing a deer skin and cloth over it. Sitting on the *āsana*, concentrating his mind on one point, and controlling the activities of the mind and senses, he should engage in yoga for purification of the internal organ. Keeping the body, head and neck straight and motionless, having firm determination, gazing at the tip of the nose, without looking in other directions, with peaceful mind, fearlessness and celibacy, he should sit, withdrawing his mind from sense objects while meditating on Me, with Me alone as the goal. BG 6.11-14

Being motionless is not possible without sitting. Thus one should meditate while sitting.

In statements like *ātmā va are draṣṭavaḥ*: one should see the Lord (Bṛhad-āraṇyaka Upaniṣad 4.5.6) something else should be considered.

(doubt) In this worship are there rules concerning direction, place and time?

(Pūrvapakṣa) Since one sees rules in Vedic activities, there should be rules for worship also, since the rules apply to all Vedic actions.

Sūtra – 4.1.11

|| yatraikāgrato tatrāviśeṣāt ||

One should perform worship wherever the mind can concentrate, since specific rules are not given in the scriptures.

In whatever condition that one develops concentration on the Lord *(yatraikāgrataḥ)*, one should worship the Lord. There is no rule for direction, place and time. Why? Because scripture does not give specific rules for this as it does for other Vedic practices. Smṛti confirms this:

tam eva deśaṁ seveta taṁ kālaṁ tām avasthitim
tān eva bhogān seveta mano yatra prasīdati
na hi deśādibhiḥ kaścid viśeṣaḥ samudīritaḥ
manaḥ-prasādanārthaṁ hi deśa-kālādi-cintanam

One should worship the Lord in that place, time, or condition, and with those items when the mind is soothed. There are no specifics enjoined concerning place, time or condition. One considers these factors only for calming the mind. Varāha Purāṇa

"But there are rules for time and other factors mentioned in the following:

same śucau śarkara-vahni-vāluka-
vivarjite śabda-jalāśrayādibhiḥ
mano-'nukūle na tu cakṣu-pīḍane
guhā-nivātāśrayaṇe niyojayet

One should practice in clean and even place, devoid of stones, fire, sand, noise and water bodies, a place favorable for the mind, which does not pain the eyes, a cave without wind. Śvetāśvatara Upaniṣad 2.10

This verse states that using a sacred place is a cause of liberation. Therefore rules are necessary. "

That is true. If there are disturbances to the mind in particular places, those places cannot be used for worship. If there is no disturbance there, then they are most suitable for worship. It is said in the verse that the place should be favorable to the mind.

Topic 7 (Sūtra 12)

Āprayāṇādhikaraṇam - Worship up to liberation

It is said *sa yo haitad bhagavan manuṣyeṣu prāyaṇāntam oṁkāram abhidhyāyīta katama vāva sa tena lokaṁ jayati:* O Lord, what world is attained by the person, most qualified among men, who utters *oṁkāra* after liberation? (Praśna Upaniṣad) In Nṛsiṁha-tāpanī Upaniṣad (2.4) it is said *yaṁ sarve devā namanti mumukṣavo brahma-vādinaś ca*: all the *devatās,* persons desiring liberation and persons established in Brahman, offer respects to the Lord. In Taittirīya Upaniṣad (3.10.5) it is said *etat sama-gayann āste:* singing the *sama,* they remain seated. In the Ṛg Veda (1.22.20) it is said *tad viṣṇoḥ paramaṁ padaṁ sadā paśyanti sūrayaḥ*: the devotees always see the highest abode of Viṣṇu. In these passages it is mentioned that a person worships up to liberation and after liberation.

The doubt is this. Should a person worship only up to liberation or even after liberation?

(Pūrvapakṣa) One should worship the Lord only up till liberation, since the result of worship is liberation.

Sūtra – 4.1.12

|| ā prāyaṇāt tatrāpi hi dṛṣṭam ||

One should worship the Lord up till liberation and also after liberation because that is stated in scriptures.

One should worship up till liberation (*āprayāṇāt)* and after liberation also (*tatrāpi).* Why? Because (*hi*) it is seen in śruti. Those texts have been quoted. What is said in those texts is also stated in the following. *sarvadainam upāsīta yāvad vimuktiḥ muktā api hy enam upāsate:* one should worship the Lord until attaining liberation and the liberated person also worships the Lord. (Sauparṇa-śruti)

"The liberated person should not worship because there is no rule or result for that." That is true. Though there is no specific injunction to worship in the liberated state, it takes place because of the intense beauty of the object of worship. After being cured of *pitta* disease by taking sugar a person still takes sugar, because of its sweetness. Thus it is proved that the worship of the Lord takes place at all times.

Topic 8 (Sūtra 13)

Tad-adhigamādhikaraṇam - Attainment of Brahman

Having discussed the *sādhana* of *vidyā,* the author now discusses the results. It is said *yathā puṣkara-palāśa āpo na śliṣyante evam eva vidi pāpaṁ karma na śliṣyate:* just as water does not stick to the lotus leaf, sinful karma does not stick to the knower of Brahman. (Chāndogya Upaniṣad 4.14.3) In the Chāndogya Upaniṣad (5.24.3) it is said *tad yathaiṣīkā-tūlam agnau protaṁ pradūyetaivaṁ hāsya sarve pāpmānaḥ pradūyante*: just as a clump of reeds is burned in fire, all sins are burned for the person in knowledge who performs sacrifice.

The doubt is this. Are the sinful reactions accrued by actions in this life and previous lives destroyed by experiencing them or do they become ineffective and destroyed by the power of *vidyā*?

(Pūrva-pakṣa) According to the following smṛti they are destroyed by experiencing them.

nābhuktaṁ kṣīyate karma kalpa-koṭi-śatair api
avaśyam eva bhoktavyaṁ kṛtaṁ karma śubhāśubham

Unexperienced karmas are destroyed only by millions of *kalpas.* One must experience the karmas both pious and sinful created by oneself. Brahma-vaivarta Purāṇa

In that case śrutis stating total destruction of karmas are meant as mere praise for the knowers of Brahman.

Sūtra – 4.1.13

|| tad-adhigama uttara-pūrvārdhayor aśleṣa-vināśau tad-vyapadeśāt ||

With attainment of Brahman, present sinful actions have no effect and previous karmas are destroyed since that is indicated the śruti.

When there is the attainment of Brahman, *brahma-vidyā (tad-adhigame),* there is no effect of sins committed in this life (*uttara aśleṣa*) and destruction (*vināśau*) of previously accrued karmas (*pūrvārdhayoḥ*). Why? Because these actions are indicated in the two śruti texts quoted above. It is not possible to diminish the meaning of śruti. Statements like those of the Brahma-vaivarta Purāṇa are suitable for ignorant people (who do not know Brahman).

Topic 9 (Sūtra 14)

Itarādhikaraṇam - Previous pious acts

In Bṛhad-āraṇyaka Upaniṣad (4.4.22) it is said *ubhe u haivaiṣa ete tarati*: the knower of Brahman surpasses both sin and piety. (Bṛhad-āraṇyaka Upaniṣad 4.4.22) This śruti states that both piety and sin are overcome.

The doubt is this. Just as all present sins and sinful karmas from previous lives are ineffective and destroyed, do the present pious acts give no future effect and are the karmas arising from pious acts of previous lives also destroyed?

(Pūrvapakṣa) The pious acts of this life and pious karmas of previous lives should not be ineffective or destroyed because they are not contrary to *vidyā,* and since those acts follow Vedic injunctions. They will be destroyed by experiencing them (on higher planets). Since there are still obstacles in this body in the form of these pious acts, statements concerning immediate liberation are exaggeration.

What was previous stated is now enlarged.

Sūtra – 4.1.14

|| itarasyāpy evam asaṁśleṣaḥ pāte tu ||

Pious acts give no effect and karmas from pious acts of previous life are destroyed. On exhaustion of *prārabdha-karmas* the person attains liberation.

Like the sins, pious acts of this life do not produce karma and previous karmas caused by pious acts in previous lives *(itarasyāpi)*[86] are destroyed *(asaṁśleṣaḥ)* by *vidyā* (bhakti). One cannot say there is no conflict of pious acts and *vidyā* with the argument that pious acts are recommended in the Vedas, since the results of piety (heavenly planets) are obstacles to the results of *vidyā* (liberation).

Pious acts are not actually pure. *sarve pāpmāno 'ato nivartante:* all sins turn from him (Chāndogya Upaniṣad) The word "sin" here indicates pious acts also. It is said *yathaidāṁsi samiddho' gniḥ:* just as fire destroys wood, the fire of vidyā destroys all karma. (BG 4.37) This verse states that all accumulated karmas (sinful or pious) are destroyed. Thus it is proved that both sinful and pious karmas are destroyed. Then the sūtra says *pāte tu. Tu* indicates certainty. With the destruction (at death) of *prārabdha-karmas*--reactions to sin and piety to be experienced in this life, the person attains liberation. The statement is not useless or exaggeration.

Topic 10 (Sūtra 15)

Anārabdha-kāryādhikaraṇam - Destruction of aprārabdha-karmas

The body should be immediately destroyed by *vidyā* since the karmas of piety and sin which created this body have been destroyed. Then there would be no one to teach *vidyā* in the world. To refute this doubt, a new topic begins. The accumulated sinful and pious karmas are of two types: *anārabdha (aprārabdha)* and *ārabdha (prārabdha).* Are both types destroyed or are only the sinful and pious results of the *anārabdha* destroyed?

(pūrvapakṣa) Since no distinction was made in the śruti statement quoted above *ubhe u haiva,* both types are destroyed, since *vidyā* acts equally on both.

---

[86] These are *aprārabhda-karmas*, acts committed in the past but which will give effects in next life not this life.

Sūtra – 4.1.15

|| anārabdha-kārya eva tu pūrve tad-avadheḥ ||

The *anārabdha-karmas* are destroyed but the *prāradbha-karmas* remain, because that is the conclusion of śruti.

The word *tu* indicates refutation of the doubt. The *anārabdha* effects, of prevous sin and piety (*pūrve*), not designated to appear in the present life, are destroyed. The *ārabdha* effects of sin and piety give their results in this life. Why? Because of the conclusion of śruti (*tad-avadheḥ*). *tasya tāvad eva ciraṁ yāvan na vimokṣye:* as long as the body lasts, he is not liberated. (Chāndogya Upaniṣad 6.14.2) Smṛti says:

tvad-avagamī na vetti bhavad-uttha-śubhāśubhayoḥ
guṇa-viguṇānvayāṁs tarhi deha-bhṛtāṁ ca giraḥ

When a person realizes you, he no longer cares about his good and bad fortune arising from past pious and sinful acts, since it is you alone who control this good and bad fortune. SB 10.87.40

The above verse indicates that the body continues to exist until the *prārabdha- karmas* are destroyed (by experiencing), by the will of the Lord.

What is said is this. *Vidyā,* being most powerful, burns up all karmas without distinction just as a blazing fire consumes all types of fuel. Though this is seen in the scriptures, by the will of the Lord who desires to spread the teachings, the *ārabdha-karmas* remain, since we see those who have realized Brahman remaining in their bodies. There is no fault if *vidyā* does not burn all karmas. It is like a fire which, though capable of burning everything, is counteracted by gems.

Some say that *vidyā* cannot arise without taking shelter of the stock of *ārabdha* results (happiness and distress in the body). Having taken shelter of karma, *vidyā* becomes dependent on the force of karmas, which is like the turning of a potter's wheel. *Vidyā's* appearance depends on the destruction of that force. Just as the wheel stops turning when the force is dissipated by itself, *ārabdha-karmas* are destroyed when their results are experienced.

That proposal is not true. There can be no obstacle to *vidyā* since it is most powerful, able to uproot all karma. It uproots everything except the will of the Lord. The potter's wheel cannot move if a heavy stone is dropped on it. Thus what was previously stated is true.

Topic 11 (Sūtras 16 - 18)
Agnihotrādy-adhikaraṇam - Fire sacrifices

It has been concluded that the previous pious results of the person in knowledge were destroyed. The results of daily rites (*nitya-karma*) should also be destroyed just as knowledge destroys the results like *kāmya-karmas*. This idea is now refuted.

The dout is this. Does *vidyā* destroy the results of daily rites like fire sacrifice as it destroys the results of *kāmya-karmas*?

(pūrvapakṣa) The results of daily rites are destroyed like those of *kāmya-karmas* since the inherent power of *vidyā* cannot be destroyed.

Sūtra – 4.1.16

|| agnihotrādi tu tat-kāryāyaiva tad-darśanāt ||

The results of daily acts like sacrifice yield effects as *vidyā* since that is seen in scriptures.

The word *tu* destroys the doubt. Daily rites like sacrifice *(agnihotrādi)* performed before the appearance of *vidyā* yield results *(tat-kāryāya)* in the form of *vidyā*. Why? Because that is seen (*tad-darśanāt*) in statements like *ta etam vedānuvacanena*: they know him through study of the Vedas, sacrifice etc. (Bṛhad-āraṇyaka Upanisād 4.4.22) Thus the meaning of *itarasya* in sūtra 4.1.14 is that results of previous pious acts *other than daily rites* like sacrifice are destroyed. The results of daily actions are not destroyed since they give *vidyā* as their result. Like grains damaged but not destroyed when a house is burned down, these karmas remain. But the portion which should take the person to Svaraga--which is described in a statement like *karmaṇā pitṛlokaḥ:* by pious acts one goes to Pitṛ-loka (Bṛhad-āraṇyaka Upaniṣad)---is destroyed.

It has been shown that by the will of the Lord the *prārabdha-karmas* of the man with knowledge (realization) remain so that teaching *vidyā* continues. It is now shown that the *prārabdha* of some *nirapekṣas* is destroyed without their having to experience the sinful or pieous results.

It is said *tat-sukṛta-duṣkṛte vidhunute tasya priyā jñātayaḥ sukṛtam upayānty apriyā duskṛtam*: his pious and sinful reactions are destroyed --his pious results go to his dear friends or relatives and the sinful results got to the sinful. (Kauṣītaki Upaniṣad 1.4) *tasya putrā dāyam upayanti suhṛdaḥ sādhu-kṛtyāṁ dviṣantaḥ pāpa-kṛtyām:* his children receive his inheritance, his friends receive his pious results and his enemies receive his sinful results. (Sāma-veda-jaiminiya-brāhmaṇa 1.18.27)

The doubt is this. Can both types of *prārabdha*, from sin and piety, be destroyed without experiencing them?

(Pūrvapakṣa) The *prārabdha-karmas* will not be destroyed since it is their very nature that they should be experienced.

Sūtra – 4.1.17

|| ato'nyāpi hy ekeṣām ubhayoḥ ||

For some *nirapekṣa* devotees both types of *prārabdha-karmas* are dissolved because this is stated is some śrutis.

The sinful and pious *prārabdhas* both (*ubhayoḥ*), without having to experience them, are dissolved for some *nirapekṣas* who are absorbed in Brahman and are most anxious for the Lord, because (*hi)* other śrutis (*anyāḥ*) of some branches of the Vedas *(ekeṣām)*--the Kauṣītaki Upaniṣad and the Sāṭyayanis say this, as opposed to the śrutis which say that by the will of the Lord the *prārabdha-karmas* remain.

The meaning is this. One must consider that the conflicting statements have different persons (some *nirapekṣas* in this case) in mind in order to reconcile the above statements (in which the person's *prārabdhas* are transferred to others) with śrutis saying that karma is destroyed by knowledge *(aprārabdha)* and enjoyment (*prārabdha*).

Kāmya-karmas performed in this life never become transferred karmas, since all karmas sinful or pious except *prārabdha-karmas* (ie. all *aprārabdha-karmas* and actions performed in the present life) are destroyed according to sūtras 4.1.3 and 4.1.14 and one would not perform *kāmya-karmas* to receive sinful results (to be given to an enemy).[87]

What is said in this *adhikaraṇa* is that the Lord, unable to tolerate delay in meeting the dearest devotees, who long to see him, brings the devotees to him after giving the *prārabdhas* to his sons or relatives. Since the karmas should be experienced, the Lord's arrangement remains intact by having the sons or relatives experience the pious results.

"It is not correct to say that the results get transferred to another person, because pious and sinful reactions do not have a concrete form that can be given to another person, and others would receive results for which they performed no action." This is not so because the Lord, by his power, can make other arrangements for karmas. Thus for some *nirapekṣas,* the *prārabdha-karmas* get dissolved without having to experience them.

The objection that the karmas of a *nirapekṣa* devotee cannot go to other person is refuted.

Sūtra – 4.1.18

|| yad eva vidyayeti hi ||

Karmas can be transferred to another person because śruti says that whatever is done using *vidyā* is powerful.

It is said *eva vidyayā karoti śraddhayopaniṣadā ted eva viīryavattraṁ bhavati*: whatever one does with *vidyā,* with faith and knowledge, becomes extremely powerful. (Chāndogya Upaniṣad 1.1.10) This shows that great power from a jīva's knowledge in relation to karma. *Hi* means "because." It is not astonishing that the great effect of nullifying *prārabdha-karmas* without experiencing them sometimes appears in a jīva by the great mercy of the supreme Lord, with *vidyā* using its power to destroy all obstacles.

---

[87] The text describes that the bad effects of karmas go to the enemies. There are no bad effects from *kāmya-karmas* since one performs them only for having personal comforts. Therefore the text cannot refer to effects from *kāmya-karmas.*

Topic 12 (Sūtra 19)

Itara-kṣapaṇādhikaraṇam - Giving up both bodies

Then what happens?

Sūtra – 4.1.19

|| bhogena tv itare kṣapayitvā sampadyate ||

Having given up the gross and subtle bodies, he attains a body of an associate of the Lord for enjoyment.

Giving up (*kṣapayitvā*) the gross and subtle bodies, different *(itare*) from the body of an associate which will be attained, a body of an associate of the Lord is accomplished (*sampadyate*) with enjoyment (*bhogena*) after attaining it. *so 'śnute sarvān kāmān*: he enjoys all pleasures. (Taittirīya Upaniṣad 2.1)

Section Two

mantrād yasya parābhūtāḥ parā bhūtādayo grahāḥ |
naśyanti sva-lasat-tṛṣṇaḥ sa kṛṣṇaḥ śaraṇaṁ mama ||

I surrender to Kṛṣṇa, eager to protect the desires of his devotees, from whose mantra the strong senses, mind and *prāṇas* which cover the jīva's *svarūpa*, after being brought under control, flee away.

Topic 1 (Sūtras 1 - 2)

Vāg-adhikaraṇam - Speech

With a desire to discuss the path of *devayāna* in the third section of this chapter, in the second section the author discusses how the person in knowledge (bhakti) leaves the body.

In the Chāndogya Upaniṣad (6.8.6) it is said:

asya saumya puruṣasya prayato vāṅ-manasi sampadyate manaḥ prāṇe prāṇas tejasi tejaḥ parasyām devatāyām

O gentle one! When the person leaves the body, speech enters mind, mind enters *prāṇa, prāṇa* enters fire and fire enters the supreme deity.

The doubt is this. Do the functions of speech enter the mind or does speech itself enter the mind?

(Pūrvapakṣa) The functions of speech alone enter the mind since mind is not the material cause of speech and the functions of speech alone depend on the mind.

Sūtra – 4.2.1

|| vāṅ-manasi darśanāc chabdāc ca ||

Speech enters mind because that is stated in śruti and it is seen that mind operates when speech ceases.

Speech itself enters the mind. Why? Because one sees (*darśanāt*) that mind functions when speech ceases its functions and the śruti (*śabdāt*) says *vaṅ manasi sampadyate*: speech enters mind. (Chāndogya Upaniṣad 6.8.6) To give another meaning would contradict the meaning of the words. And there is no scriptural statement to say that the functions of speech alone enter into the mind.

"Since mind is not the material cause of speech, then speech should not enter the mind. Rather the functions alone should enter the mind since one sees that the functions of fire enter water, though water is not the material cause of fire." Speech unites with the mind but does not merge with it. Speech itself joins with mind, though mind is not its material cause.

Sūtra – 4.2.2

|| ata eva sarvāṇy anu ||

All the senses enter the mind after speech enters.

Since speech enters mind, not fire, it should be understood that all the senses (*sarvāṇi)* like the ear enter the mind, after (*anu)* speech enters the mind.

tasmād upaśānta-tejāḥ punar-bhavam indriyair manasi sampadyamānair yac cittas tenaiṣa prāṇa āyāti

When energy is exhausted, he again takes birth. With senses in the mind, according to his desire he enters into *prāṇa.* Praśna Upaniṣad 3.9

yathā gārgya marīcayo 'staṁ gacchato 'rkasya sarva etasmiṁs tejo-maṇḍale ekī-bhavati tāḥ punar udayataḥ pracaranty evaṁ ha vai tat sarvaṁ pare deve manasy ekī-bhavati

Just as the rays become one with the globe of the setting sun and again spread out when the sun rises, all the senses become one with the superior, shining mind. Praśna Upaniṣad 4.2

Topic 2 (Sūtra 3)

Mano 'dhikaraṇam - The mind

Now the mind entering *prāṇa* is considered. Does the mind enter the moon or *prāṇa*?

(pūrva pakṣa) The mind enters the moon since it is said *manaś candram*: the mind is the moon. (Bṛhad-āraṇyaka Upaniṣad 3.2.13)

Sūtra – 4.2.3

|| tan-manaḥ-prāṇa uttarāt ||

Mind enters *prāṇa* because that is mentioned later in the same passage.

With all the senses, the mind enters *prāṇa:* Why? Because of the statement later in the text *manaḥ prāṇe*: mind enters *prāṇa.* (Chāndogya Upaniṣad 6.8.6) There is the statement *yatrāsya puruṣasya mṛtasyāgmiṇ vāg apy eti*: the speech of the dying man enters fire. (Bṛhad-āraṇyaka Upaniṣad 3.2.13) But Bādarāyaṇa has said in sūtra 3.1.4 that this statement must be taken metaphorically, not literally.

Topic 3 (Sūtra 4)

Adhyakṣādhikaraṇam - Jīva, the controller

Now *prāṇa* entering fire is considered. Do *prāṇa* with mind and the senses enter fire or the jīva?

(Pūrvapakṣa) *Prāṇa* enters into fire since that is what is said in the text.

Sūtra – 4.2.4

|| so'dhyakṣe tad-upagamādibhyaḥ ||

***Prāṇa* enters the jīva since this is seen in the scriptures.**

Prāṇa (saḥ) enters into the jīva, the controller (*adhyakṣe*) of the senses and body. Why? Because that is understood:

tad yathā rājānaṁ prayiyāsantam ugrāḥ pratyenasaḥ sūtā grāmaṇya abhisamāyanty evaṁ haivaṁ ātmānam antarāle sarve prāṇā abhisamāyanti. yatraitad ūrdhvocchvāsī bhavati.

Just as warriors, officials, charioteers and leaders of armies gather around the king when he leaves the palace, so all the *prāṇas* gather around the *ātmā* when the person is about to die. Bṛhad-āraṇyaka Upaniṣad 4.3.38

It is stated here that the *prāṇas* along with the senses go with the jīva. This does not contradict the statement that the *prāṇa* enters fire since it can be said that joining with the jīva, *prāṇa* later enters fire just as one says that the Yamunā goes into the sea, when it actually merges with the Gaṅgā which then enters the sea.

Topic 4 (Sūtras 5 - 14)

Bhūtādhikaraṇam - Elements

Now the jīva entering fire is considered. The doubt is this. Does the jīva with *prāṇa* enter fire or into the collective elements?

(Pūrvapakṣa) Jīva enters fire because that is stated.

Sūtra – 4.2.5

|| bhūteṣu tac-chruteḥ ||

The jīva enters all the elements because this is stated in śruti.

The jīva enters all the five elements not just fire. Why? Because śruti *says jīvasyākāśamayo vāyumayas tejomaya āpomayaḥ pṛthivīmayaḥ*: the jīva is endowed with ether, air, fire, water and earth. (Bṛhad-āraṇyaka Upaniṣad 4.4.5)

Moreover, the following should be said.

Sūtra – 4.2.6

|| naikasmin darśayato hi ||

The jīva does not enter fire alone but enters all the elements since this is stated in śruti.

It should not be thought that jīva enters only fire (*ekasmin*). Because (*hi*) this is concluded in the questions and answers (*darṣayataḥ)* in Chāndogya Upaniṣad 5.3-10. It was also established in sūtra 3.1.1. Moreover it has been established that *prāṇa* enters into all the elements including fire by means of the jīva.[88]

In the previous passage of śruti, something else must be considered. Does the passage out of the body occur for the ignorant jīva or for the knower of Brahman also?

(Pūrvapakṣa) That description applies only to the ignorant person since the person in knowledge, having attained immortality, is not described as leaving in that way. In Bṛhad-āraṇyaka Upaniṣad (4.4.7) it is said:

yadā sarve pramucyante kāmā ye 'sya hṛdi sthitāḥ
atha martyo 'mṛto bhavaty atra brahma samaśnute

---

[88] This means that the elements, prāṇa, the mind and senses go with the jīva.

When a person is free of all desires in the heart, the person attains immortality and enjoys Brahman in this state.

Sūtra – 4.2.7

|| samānā cāsṛty-upakramād amṛtatvaṁ cānupoṣya ||

The ignorant person and knower of Brahman leave the body in a similar way before entering the *nāḍīs.* The immortality of a living person refers realization while still connected with the body.

The first *ca* indicates emphasis. Leaving the body is the same *(samānā)* for the ignorant and the knower of Brahman, up to the point of entering the *nāḍīs (āśrty-upakramāt)*. There is difference when entering the *nāḍīs*. The ignorant person goes through one of the hundred *nāḍīs* and the person in knowledge goes through the hundred and first *nāḍī.*

śataṁ caikā ca hṛdayasya nāḍyas tāsāṁ mūrdhānam abhiniḥsṛtaikā.
tayordhvam āyann amṛtatvam eti viśvag anyā utkramaṇe bhavanti

There are a hundred and one *nāḍīs* of the heart and chief one goes to the top of the head. Going through this *nāḍī* one attains immortality. The others are for going out of the body (into another body).

The statement *tasya haitasya hṛdayasāgram* indicates that the knower of Brahman goes through the upward *nāḍī.* Others, the ignorant, go through the other *nāḍīs.* When the text says that the person attains immortality here (*iha*), it means realization while connected with this body (*prārabdha-karma*). This immortality (*amṛatatva*) means that *aprārabdha* karmas have been burned up completely and acts of this life have been weakened (*anupoṣya*).

This is further explained.

Sūtra – 4.2.8

|| tad ā-pīteḥ saṁsāra-vyapadeśāt ||

Immortality while in the body refers to a person without sin, since *saṁsāra* is said to exist until one meets the Lord.

The immortality *(tat)* of a knower of Brahman while still with a body refers to his condition of being without sin. Why? Because *saṁsāra* is said to be connection with the body (*saṁsāra-vypadeśāt*) until the jīva directly meets the Lord (*āpīteḥ*). That meeting takes place by treading the *devayāna* path and going to the spiritual world. This is well known in Vedānta.

Sūtra – 4.2.9

|| sūkṣma-pramāṇataś ca tathopalabdheḥ ||

The passage relates to a person in the body because there is proof that the subtle body remains at that time. Scripture shows that the subtle body exists even on higher planets.

The relation with the body is not destroyed in this world for the person in knowledge since the subtle body still remains (*sūkṣma*). Why? Because of proof (*pramāṇataḥ*). The existence of the body is seen (*upalabdheḥ)* in the conversation between the moon and the departed person travelling on the *devayāna* path. *taṁ prati brūyāt satam; brūyāt*: one should speak to him the truth. (Kauṣītaki Upaniṣad 1.3) Thus the immortality described in the passage of Bṛhad-āraṇyaka Upaniṣad is related to a person still with his body.

Sūtra – 4.2.10

|| nopamārdenātaḥ ||

Because of this, the text does not speak of immortality in the sense of destroying a relationship with the body.

Because of this reason (*ataḥ)* the text in question does not say that a person is immortal in the senses of destroying connection with the body (*na upamārdena*).

Sūtra – 4.2.11

|| tasyaiva copapatter uṣmā ||

The subtle body is responsible for warmth in the body, since this is reasonable and supported by scripture.

The warmth *(uṣmā*) felt on touching the gross body before death is the quality of the subtle body, not the gross body. Why? Because it is reasonable *(upapatteḥ)* that the warm comes from the subtle body, since there is warmth when the subtle body is in the living body and there is no warmth when the gross body is dead and the subtle body has separated from it. The word *ca* indicates another reason--scriptural statements. Thus, the man in knowledge also goes out of the body with the subtle body, and this is inferred by the departure of warmth.

A doubt is raised and resolved.

Sūtra – 4.2.12

|| pratiṣedhād iti cen, na, śārīrāt ||

If one argues that the *prāṇas* of a man of knowledge do not go out because scripture indicates this, the answer is no, because the passage indicates only that the *prāṇas* do not leave the jīva.

The man of knowledge does not go out of the body like others. It is said:

athākāmayamāno yo 'kāmo niṣkāma āpta-kāmo na tasya prāṇā utkramanti brahmaiva san brahmātyeti

For person with no desires, whose desires are all fulfilled already, his *prāṇas* do not go out of the body (or do not leave him). Being Brahman, he goes to Brahman. Bṛhad-āraṇyaka Upaniṣad 4.4.6-7

This is not so. The quotation does not mean that the *prāṇas* do not go from the body, but rather the *prāṇas* do not leave the jīva. It is seen that the *prāṇas* leave the body of the man of knowledge also.

Sūtra – 4.2.13

|| spaṣṭo hy ekeṣām ||

This interpretation is correct because in one recension it is clearly stated that the *prāṇas* do not leave the jīva.

There should be no argument about this interpretation because (*hi)* in the Mādhyandina recension *(ekeṣām*) one clearly (*spaṣṭaḥ*) sees that the *prāṇas* do not leave the jīva. *na tasmāt prāṇā utkramanti. atravaiva samavalīyante brahmaiva san brahmātyeti:* the *prāṇas* do not leave the ātmā; they merge with Brahman; becoming Brahman, he attains Brahman. (Bṛhad-āraṇyaka Upaniṣad 4.4.6) The words *atraiv*a mean "in Brahman alone, which is present before the jīva."

"In the Kāṇva recension, Ārtabhāga asks Yājñavalkya if the *prāṇas* of the man in knowledge leave the body, and Yājñāvalkya says they do not."

It should be understood that this is the case of an intensely devoted person (who directly goes to the Lord, without travelling on the *devayāna* path with the subtle body).

Some explain that the case of the subtle body not leaving the body refers to a person who meditates on merging into the impersonal Brahman, but that is a foolish argument since that meaning cannot be derived from the words of the text and Brahman without distinction of a jīva does not exist.

Sūtra – 4.2.14

|| smaryate ca ||

This is also stated in smṛti.

In the Yājñavalkya-smṛti (3.167) it is said:

ūrdhvam ekaḥ sthitas teṣāṁ yo bhittvā sūrya-maṇḍalam
brahmalokam atikramya tena yāti parāṁ gatim

The jīva, after going through the sun and surpassing Brahmaloka, goes to the supreme destination by that one *nāḍī* situated in the head, among all the *nāḍīs*.

The smṛti explains that the man of knowledge goes by the *nāḍī* situated in the head. Thus it is established that the man of knowledge also leaves his body with the *prāṇas* (and goes by *devayāna* with the subtle body.)

Topic 6 (Sūtra 15)

Para-sampatty-adhikaraṇam - Entering the Lord

It has been said that the jīva accompanied by the senses and *prāṇa* enters into the subtle elements. It was objected that this does not take place for the person in knowledge, but that objection was refuted. Now the following should be considered.

Do the *prāṇas* (senses) like speech and the elements of the body in subtle form enter into their causes (the elements) or into Paramātmā. This is the doubt.

(Pūrvapakṣa) They enter into the elements because the śruti passage starting with *yatrāsya puruṣasya mṛtasyāgmiṇ vāg apy eti*: the speech of the dying man enters fire (Bṛhad-āraṇyaka Upaniṣad 3.2.13) says that they do.

Sūtra – 4.2.15

|| tāni pare tathā hy āha ||

Fire and all the senses and *prāṇa* enter into the Supreme Lord since this is stated in śruti.

It is said *tejaḥ parasyām*: fire enters the supreme Lord (Chāndogya Upaniṣad 6.8.6) It is understood from that passage that fire, including all the sense like speech and *prāṇa* (*tāni)*, enter into Brahman, the *ātmā* of all beings *(pare)*, since he is the material cause of everything. Why? Because (*hi*) śruti says this, as mentioned above (*tathā āha*). The passage from Bṛhad-āraṇyaka Upaniṣad is metaphorical, as explained previously.

Topic 7 (Sūtra 16)

Avibhāgādhikaraṇam - Elements merging into the Lord

Another doubt is raised concerning this topic. Is the merging of the *prāṇas* etc. of the person in knowledge into Paramātmā like merging of speech into mind, merely joining together or is it a complete identity of everything with Paramātmā, just the rivers flowing into the ocean and becoming one with it? This is the doubt.

(Pūrvapakṣa) It is just joining together (without loss of qualities) since that is the direct meaning of the śruti quotations given and there are no particular statements saying that all things completely merge their identities.

Sūtra – 4.2.16

|| avibhāgo vacanāt ||

The elements merge completely because this is stated in śruti.

Prāṇa and other elements become completely one (*avibhāgaḥ*) with Paramātmā. Why? Because of statements saying so.

evam evāsya paridraṣṭur imāḥ ṣoḍaśa-kalāḥ puruṣāyaṇāḥ puruṣaṁ prāpyās taṁ gacchanti bhidyete cāsāṁ nāma-rūpe puruṣa

The sixteen elements, going to the Lord, attaining the Lord, enter the Lord. Their names and forms are destroyed in the Lord. Praśna Upaniṣad 6.5

The text says that the elements like *prāṇa* enter the Lord and their names and forms are destroyed. The person then becomes immortal.

The meaning is this. When the jīva leaves the gross body, the subtle body of the person in knowledge follows the jīva, but withered away by vidyā, like a pile of burned dung. When the jīva surpasses the shell of the universe, he merges that withered subtle body into prakṛti, the eighth layer (śakti of the Lord). Pure, the jīva, having attained a body of Brahman, joins with Brahman which is the shelter of prakṛti.

Topic 8 (Sūtra 17)

Tad-oko 'dhikaraṇam - Lighting up the heart

Now begins the description of the details of how the person in knowledge leaves the body, as was promised. It was said that the person in knowledge goes by the hundred and first *nāḍī* whereas the person in ignorance goes by the other *nāḍīs*. The doubt is this. Is this a set rule or not?

(Pūrvapakṣa) It cannot be a rule because it is impossible for person who has no discriminating power (when dying) to understand, since the *nāḍīs* are numerous and very fine. *tayordhvam āyann amṛtatvam eti* means that if by chance a person goes by the hundred and first *nāḍī* he attains immortality.

Sūtra – 4.2.17

| | tad-oko'gra-jvalanaṁ tat-prakāśita-dvāro vidyā-sāmarthyāt tac-cheṣa-gaty-anusmṛti-yogāc ca hārdānugṛhītaḥ śatādhikayā | |

The person in knowledge can recognize the hundred and first *nāḍī* because he obtains mercy from the Lord in the heart, power through worship, and memory of the method of leaving from his previous knowledge. The Lord lights up his heart so that the path is revealed.

The person in knowledge leaves by the *suṣumnā,* the hundred and first *nāḍī (śatādhikayā).* It cannot be said that this person cannot distinguish this *nāḍī* because he receives mercy from the Lord in the heart (*hārdānugṛhitaḥ*), he obtains the ability from his worship *(vidyā-sāmarthyāt*) and he has memory (*anusmṛti-yogāt*) of how to attain the Lord (*gati*) with the assistance of *devatās,* as a result of worship *(tad-śeṣa).* When the jīva desires to leave along with the senses, the heart (*okaḥ*) lights up at its tip *(agra-jvalanam).* This means that the jīva can recognize the particular hundred and first *nādī* because the jīva has the path lit up by the Lord (*tat-prakāśita-dvārā*). Thus the method of leaving of the person in knowledge is correct.

Topic 9 (Sūtra 18)

Raśmy-anusārādhikaraṇam – Following the rays of the sun

In the Chāndogya Upaniṣad (8.6.5) it is said:

atha yatraitasmāt śarīrād utkramaty etair eva raśmibhir ūrdhvam ākramate.
sa om iti vā hodvā mīyate sa yāvat kṣipyen manas tāvad ādityaṁ gacchaty
etad vai khalu loka-dvāraṁ viduṣāṁ prapadanaṁ nirodho 'viduṣāṁ

When he leaves the body, he goes upward by the rays of the sun. Saying *oṁ*, he dies. As fast as the mind travels, he goes to the sun. This is the door for reaching Brahman. Those who are ignorant are forbidden.

It is understood from this that the person in knowledge goes by the hundred and first *nāḍī* and follows the rays of the sun to the sun.

The doubt is this. The person dying in the daytime can follow the rays of the sun. What happens at night?

(Pūrvapakṣa) Since there are no rays at night, the person dying at night cannot follow the rays.

Sūtra – 4.2.18

|| raśmy-anusārī ||

He follows the rays of the sun even if he dies at night.

Whenever the person in knowledge dies, he follows the rays of the sun and attains the sun since it is never said in scriptures that the person in knowledge does not attain the sun.

Topic 10 (Sūtra 19)

Niṣādhikaraṇam - Night

Sūtra – 4.2.19

|| niśi neti cen, na, sambandhasya yāvad-deha-bhāvitvād darśayati ca ||

It cannot be said that the person dying at night cannot attain the rays of sun since as long as the body exists there is a connection with the nāḍī.

"The person dying at night cannot follow the rays of the sun (*niśi na*) since the rays do not exist at night." This is not so *(na)*. Why? Because as long as the body exists there is a connection of the rays with the *nāḍī (sambandhasya yāvad deha-bhāvitvāt)*. Whenever a person dies he can follow those rays. Because of those rays, heat can be observed in the body in summer and winter. If those rays were not present, a person would become cold in winter. Thus, this is not just a logical proposition. The śruti also states this (*darśayati*).

amuṣmād ādityāt prayānte tathāsu nāḍīṣu sṛptā ābhyo nāḍībhyaḥ prayānte te amusminn āditye sṛptāḥ

From the sun the rays go to the *nāḍīs*. From the *nāḍīs* the rays go and enter into the sun.

Chāndogya Upaniṣad 7.6.2

Another śruti says:

saṁsṛṣṭā vā ete raśmayaś ca nāḍyaś ca naiṣāṁ vibhāgo yāvad idam śarīram ataḥ etaiḥ paśyaty etair utkramate etaiḥ pravartate

The rays and the *nāḍīs* are connected and never separated as long as the body exists. Through these rays he sees, goes out and enters into activity.

Thus it is a rule that the man in knowledge goes by the rays of the sun.

Topic 11 (Sūtras 20 - 21)

Dakṣiṇāyanādhikaraṇam - Southern course of the sun

Now the following is discussed. Does the man in knowledge dying during the southern course of the sun attain the results of his *vidyā* (bhakti) or not?

(Pūrvapakṣa) He does not attain the results, since one sees in śruti and smṛti that one goes to the spiritual world by dying during the northern course of the sun, and this is seen in the case of Bhīṣma and others.

Sūtra – 4.2.20

|| ataś cāyane'pi dakṣiṇe ||

The person in knowledge, even dying during the southern course of the sun, attains the results.

If the person in knowledge dies during the southern course (*āyane dakṣiṇe*) he still attains the results since all obstructing karmas were destroyed by *vidyā* and *vidyā* does not play favorites in giving its results (*ataḥ*). The proposition of the opponent is foolish since the word "northern course" means the *devatās* who assist the jīva on leaving his body (and not a particular time). Bhīṣma waited from the northern course in order to show that the boon given by his father (to die at will) was effective and to follow proper behavior (in common understanding).

yatra kāle tv anāvṛttim āvṛttiṁ caiva yoginaḥ
prayātā yānti taṁ kālaṁ vakṣyāmi bharatarṣabha...

...śukla-kṛṣṇe gatī hy ete jagataḥ śāśvate mate
ekayā yāty anāvṛttim anyayāvartate punaḥ

O best of Bharata's line, I will now explain about the paths by which the *yogīs* return or do not return... These two paths, of light and dark, are accepted in this world as being without beginning. By one path, one does not return, and by the other path, one returns. BG 8. 23, 8. 26

Since time is emphasized in these verses of the Gītā, the verses indicate that for liberation particular times must be chosen.

(Pūrvapakṣa) Liberation cannot take place if a person dies at night or during the southern course of the sun.

Sūtra – 4.2.21

|| yoginaḥ prati smaryate smārte caite ||

These items are explained for the person who is fixed in Brahman. The two paths should be remembered by him.

In the Gītā it is explained (*smaryate*) that for the person fixed in Brahman (*yoginaḥ*) attaining the moon is inferior and attaining the light is superior. These two facts should be remembered (*smārate ete*) since it is said *naite sṛtī pārtha jānan yogī muhyate kaścana*: Knowing these two paths the *yogī* is never bewildered. (BG 8.27)

Thus there is no rule of time when the person in knowledge should die to receive the results. The topic is not time, since fire and other things mentioned for the dying person are not related to time. All these words do not refer to time at all, but to the *devatās* ruling those times (including time).

The supreme Lord, author of the sūtras will also explain this in sūtra 4.3.4. There are statements like the following:

divā ca śukla-pakṣaś ca uttarāyaṇam eva ca
mumūrṣatāṁ prasastāni viparītaṁ tu garhitam

Daytime, the phases of the waxing moon, and the northern course of the sun, are best for those who are about to die. The opposite times are not recommended.

But these statements are for the ignorant. The person in knowledge, wherever and whenever he dies, attains the Lord.

Section Three

yaḥ sva-prāpti-pathaṁ devaḥ sevanābhāsato'diśat |
prāpyaṁ ca svapadaṁ mamāsau śyāmasundaraḥ ||

Because I have performed a shadow of service, may I attain Śyāmasundara, who has shown the method of attaining him.

Topic 1 (Sūtra 1)

Arcir-ādy-adhikaraṇam - The light

In this section, the path to attain the world of the Lord and the *svarūpa* of Brahman to be attained are described. It is said:

atha yad u caivāsmin śavyaṁ kurvanti yadi ca nārciṣam evābhisambhavaty arciṣo 'har aha āpūryamānam āpūryamāna-pakṣād yan sad-udaḍḍeti māsān tān samebhyaḥ samvatsaraṁ

samvatsarād ādityam ādityāc candramasaṁ candramaso vidyutaṁ tat puruṣo 'mānavaḥ. sa etān brahma gamayaty eṣa deva-patho brahma-patha etena pratipadyamāna imaṁ mānavam āvartaṁ nāvartante

Whether his final rites are performed or not, he who knows the Lord goes to the light. From the light he goes to the day. From the day he goes to waxing phase of the moon. From there he goes to the six months when the sun travels in the north. From the six months when the sun travels in the north he goes to year. From the year he goes to the sun. From the sun he goes to the moon. From the moon he goes to lightning. From there a divine person leads him to Brahmā. This is the path to the Lord, the path to the Supreme Lord. Those who travel this path do not return to the world of human beings. Chāndogya Upaniṣad 4.15.5

Light is first on the path according this passage. In Kauṣītaki Upaniṣad however, fire is first.

sa etaṁ deva-yānaṁ panthānam āpadyāgnilokam āgacchati sa vāyulokaṁ sa varuṇalokaṁ sa indralokaṁ sa prajāpatilokaṁ sa brahmalokam

Having attained the *devayāna,* he goes to the planet of fire, the planet of air, the planet of water, the planet of Indra and the planet of Prajāpati and the world of Brahmā.

In Bṛhad-āraṇyaka Upaniṣad 5.10.1, air is first.

yadā ha vai puruṣo 'smāt lokāt praiti sa vāyum āgacchati tasmai sa tatra vijihīte yathā ratha-cakrasya khaṁ tena ūrdhva ākramate sa ādityam āgacchati

When the person leaves this planet he goes to air. The air makes an opening for him like space in the wheel of a chariot. From there he proceeds upwards and goes to the sun.

Bṛhad-āraṇyaka Upaniṣad 5.10.1

Muṇḍaka Upaniṣad says sūrya-dvāreṇa te virajāḥ prayānti: those who are pure go by the sun. In other passages of śruti other versions are given.

The doubt is this. Are there various paths to Brahman or is there one path beginning with light?

(Pūrvapakṣa) There are various paths, since different situations are described, and the word *eva* (only) limits each path.

Sūtra – 4.3.1

|| arcir-ādinā tat-prathiteḥ ||

Persons in knowledge start the ascension with light since that is understood in scriptures.

All persons with knowledge (bhakti) go to Brahma-loka by the path starting with light (*arcir-ādinā*). Why? Because that is understood (*tat-prathiteḥ*). *tad ya ittham vidur ye ceme 'raṇye śraddhāṁ tapa ity upāsate te arciṣam abhisambhavanti*: those who know in this way worship with faith and austerity in the forest and go to the light. (Chāndogya Upaniṣad 5.10.1) This passage from the section dealing with knowledge of fire first teaches going to the Lord by the path starting with light for persons with other *vidyā.*

dvāv eva mārgau prathitāv arcir-ādir vipaścitām
dhūmādiḥ karmiṇāṁ caiva sarva-veda-vinirṇayāt

There are two paths known, concluded from all the Vedas: for the knowers of Brahman the path starting with light and for the performers of karmas the path starting with smoke.

Brahma-tarka

Thus, where different paths are described, the details have been summarized, and some parts, though not mentioned, should be gathered from elsewhere and included, for the knowledge is one, though expressed differently in different passages. The word *eva* is used simply to indicate going first to light, not to exclude other paths.

Topic 2 (Sūtra 2)

Vāyv-adhikaraṇam - Going to air

Now gathering information from other texts which start with air etc. and adding it to the list starting with light is shown. *sa etaṁ deva-yānaṁ panthānam āpadyāgnilokam āgacchati sa vāyulokam:* attaining the *devayāna* path he goes to the planet of fire, then the planet of air. (Kauṣītaki Upaniṣad 1.3) Should air and other details be added to the path starting with light?

(Pūrvapakṣa) They should not be added because that order is not mentioned there and no options are mentioned.

Sūtra – 4.3.2

|| vāyum abdād aviśeṣa-viśeṣābhyām ||

Air should be inserted after the year because its place is unspecified in Kauṣītaki Upaniṣad and specified in Bṛhad-āraṇyaka Upaniṣad.

Air (*vāyum*) should be inserted after the year (*abdhāt*) and before the sun. Why? Because all detailsof order are not given *(aviśesā)* in the Kauṣītaki text. The text merely says "He goes to the planet of air." Bṛhad-āraṇyaka Upaniṣad 5.10.1 however gives a specific sequence (*viśesābhyām*): leaving this world he goes to air, and then to the sun. In Bṛhad-āraṇyaka Upaniṣad 6.2.15 it is said *māsebhyo deva-lokam deva-lokāt adityam*: from the months he goes to *devaloka* and from *devaloka* to the sun. *Devaloka* here means the planet of air since it is said *yo 'yaṁ pavana eṣa eva devānāṁ gṛhaḥ*: air is the house of the *devatās.* Others say that *devaloka* refers to a specific part of the path, not air. This *devaloka* should be inserted after the year and before the air. It cannot be inserted between the month and the year since the relationship of month and year is well known. Thus *devaloka* and air are inserted after the year and before the sun.

Topic 3 (Sūtra 3)

Taḍid-adhikaraṇam - Lightning

Now the author examines the text *sa varuṇalokaṁ sa indralokaṁ sa prajāpatilokam*: he goes to the planet of water, the planet of Indra and the planet of Prajāpati. (Kauṣītaki Upaniṣad 1.3)

The doubt is this. Should the planet of water be inserted in the sequence beginning with light or not?

(Pūrvapakṣa) It should not be inserted since like air, there are no indications in the text to do so.

Sūtra – 4.3.3

| | taḍito'dhi varuṇaḥ sambandhāt | |

Water should be placed after lightning, because of the relationship between them.

It was said *candramaso vidyutam*: from the moon he goes to lightning. (Chāndogya Upaniṣad 4.15.5) Water (*varuṇaḥ)* should be placed after (*adhi*) lightning (*taḍitaḥ*). Why? Because of the relationship (*sambandhāt*) between lightning and water. Where there is lighting rain falls. When profuse lightning and rumbling thunder dance in the belly of the clouds and water fall people say *vidyotate stanayati varṣayati vā*: there is lighting, thunder and it will rain. (Chāndogya Upaniṣad 7.11.1) The relationship of water (*varuṇa)* with lightning is well known since Varuṇa is the deity controlling rain. Indra and Prajāpati should be inserted after water since they cannot be inserted elsewhere and the text of Kauṣītaki places them in that order. Thus it is proven that there are twelve or thirteen steps (if *devaloka* is taken separate from air) starting from light and ending with Prajāpati before attaining the world of Brahman.[89]

---

[89] The thirteen are light, day, waxing fortnight, northern course of the sun, year, Devaloka, air, sun, moon, lightning water, Indra-loka and Prajāpati-loka.

Topic 4 (Sūtras 4 - 5)

Ātivāhikādhikaraṇam - Presiding deities

After discussing light etc., what do these terms mean? Are they marks on the path, are they personified elements or are they guides for the knowers of Brahman?

(Pūrvapakṣa) They are marks on the path. That is understood because one indicates a path by showing landmarks. People give directions like "Going from the city, go to the river, then to the mountain, then to the cowherd village." Or they could be persons since the names can be taken literally.

Sūtra – 4.3.4

|| ātivāhikās tal-liṅgāt ||

They are *devatās* appointed by the Lord, because of the specific description.

Light etc. are *devatās* appointed by the Lord (*ātivāhikāḥ*). They are not marks or just personified elements. Why? Because there are descriptions of their guiding those who go to Brahman. At the end of the list, a specific person who guides and assists is described. *tat puruṣo 'mānavaḥ sa etān brahma gamayati*: that person, not a human, leads them to Brahman. (Chāndogya Upaniṣad) Light and the others on the list should also be understood to be persons acting with the same function.

It should be accepted that they are not mere marks or persons with the elements personified.

Sūtra – 4.3.5

|| ubhaya-vyāmohāt tat-siddheḥ ||

The words refer to *devatās* since the first two options have been discounted and the third option has been described in scriptures.

They cannot be marks on the path because if a person dies during the night he could have no relationship to light, and thus the mark of light on the path would not be permanent. As well they cannot simply be elements acting like persons since the light etc. are insentient, and could not guide. Because both of the other propositions are untenable, and scripture indicate the third option, the light etc. are deities who act as guides.

Topic 5 (Sūtra 6)

Vaidyutādhikaraṇam - Lightning

Does the non-human appointed by the Lord come down to the light and lead the worshippers, or only down to lightning?

(Pūrvapakṣa) He comes down to light since Ajāmila and others were led by associates of the Lord, who came down to earth.

Sūtra – 4.3.6

|| vaidyutenaiva tatas tac-chruteḥ ||

The person is taken by the non-human guide who comes down to lightning, because that is mentioned in śruti.

The knower of Brahman is taken to the Lord by the associate of the Lord who comes to lightning (*vaidyutena*), after the devotee has come up to lightning. Why? Because of śruti statements. *candramaso vidyutaṁ tat-puruṣo 'mānavaḥ sa etān brahma gamayati*: they go from the moon to lightning and then the non-human takes the devotees to Brahman. (Chāndogya Upaniṣad 4.15.5) This is accomplished with the help of Varuṇa, Indra and Prajāpati (who are placed after lightning). This is the usual method of their going to Brahman. There are unusual cases because we see a special case where Ajāmila was taken from earth itself.

Topic 6 (Sūtras 7 - 9)

Kāryadhikaraṇam – The jīva goes to kārya Brahmā

Having described the path, the goal of the path is described. *sa enān brahma gamayati*: he leads them to Brahman. (Chāndogya upaniṣad 5.15.50) This is the text in question. Bādari's opinion is explained first.

The doubt is this. Does the non-human take the person to the supreme Brahman or to four faced *kārya* Brahmā (the creator of the universe)?

(Pūrvapakṣa) Since the principle meaning of Brahman is the supreme Brahman and the goal is immortal, the person goes to the supreme Brahman.

Sūtra – 4.3.7

|| kāryaṁ bādarir asya gaty-upapatteḥ ||

Bādari says that the non-human takes the person to four-faced Brahmā since one can attain him.

Bādari says that he goes to *kārya brahman (kāryam)* Why? Because, since *kārya brahman* is situated in one place, one can attain that goal (*gaty-upapatteḥ*). Since the supreme Brahman is situated everywhere, one cannot attain him.

Sūtra – 4.3.8

|| viśeṣitatvāc ca ||

The person attains four-faced Brahmā because that is mentioned in śruti.

The nonhuman takes the person to *kārya brahman* since details are mentioned in the Chāndogya Upaniṣad 8.14.1. *Prajāpateḥ sabhāṁ veśma prapadye*: I attain the meeting hall of Brahmā.

Sūtra – 4.3.9

|| sāmīpyāt tu tad-vyapadeśaḥ ||

It is stated that they do not return from the planet of Brahmā because they are very close to attaining the Lord.

In the Bṛhad-āraṇyaka Upaniṣad (4.2.15) it is said:

sa etya brahmalokān gamayati tu teṣu brahmalokeṣu parāḥ parāvanto vasanti. teṣām iha na punar āvṛttir asti

Having come to lightning, the non-human associate of the Lord takes them to planet of Brahmā. Surrendered to the Lord's superior *śakti,* these excellent devotees live on this planet. They do not return to this world.

The statement that they do not return *(tad-vyapadeśaḥ*) indicates their closeness to the Lord (*sāmīpyāt*). Having attained the planet of Brahmā, they attain the supreme Brahman from whom they are not separated and are very close, along with Brahmā. Then they do not return.

Topic 7 (Sūtras 10 - 14)

Kāryātyayādhikaraṇam – The destruction of Brahmā's planet

When does this happen?

Sūtra – 4.3.10

| | kāryātyaye tad-adhyakṣeṇa sahātaḥ param abhidhānāt | |

Along with four-faced Brahmā, the devotee attains the Lord, when the universe is destroyed, because that is stated in śruti.

When the whole universe up to Brahmā's planet is destroyed (*kaṛyātyate*), the person along with *(sahātaḥ)* four-faced Brahmā (*tad-adhyakṣena*) attains the person superior (*param*) to Brahmā. Why does he attain the Lord with Brahmā? Because that is stated *(abhidhānāt)*. *brahmavid āpnoti param... so 'śnute sarvān kāmān saha brahmaṇā:* the knower of Brahman attains the supreme and enjoys all pleasures along with Brahmā. (Taittirīya Upaniṣad 2.1.3) *Saha brahmaṇā* means "along with four-faced Brahmā."

Sūtra – 4.3.11

| | smṛteś ca | |

That the devotee goes to the Lord when Brahmā goes is correct because of smṛti statements as well.

brahmaṇā saha te sarve samprāpte pratisañcare
parasyānte kṛtātmānaḥ praviśanti paraṁ padam

Those who are on Brahma-loka with exalted status at the time of dissolution go directly to the supreme abode, along with Lord Brahmā. *Kūrma Purāṇa* 1.11.284

The Bādari concludes that the *devatās* of light etc. take the devotee to Brahmā.

Sūtra – 4.3.12

| | paraṁ jaiminir mukhyatvāt | |

Jaimini says that the non-human leads the devotee to the supreme Brahman since that is the main meaning of the word Brahman.

Jaimini says that the non-human takes the meditators to the supreme Brahman, not Brahmā. Why? Because the word Brahma primarily means (in neuter gender) the supreme Brahman. One cannot say that the supreme

Brahman, being all-pervading, cannot be goal since the Lord mercifully permits the devotee to attain him in order to make it known that the devotee attains him after destroying his material body.

Sūtra – 4.3.13

|| darśanāc ca ||

The devotee attains Brahman, because that is shown in śruti.

In the *dahara-vidyā* section of Chāndogya Upaniṣad (8.12.3) it is said *eṣa samprasādo 'smac charīrāt samutthāya param jyotir upasaṁpadya svena rupeṇābhiniṣpadyante*: the peaceful persons, rising from this body, attains the supreme light, and are endowed with their own forms. This describes that the devotees attain Brahman since the goal, Brahman, is described there as being immortal, and the persons going there appear with their forms *(svarūpa*). All this is not appropriate to four-faced Brahmā, nor is Brahmā the topic of this particular section of the Upaniṣad. The topic is the supreme Brahman. The supreme Brahman as the goal is also described in the Kaṭha Upaniṣad 2.3.16. *śataṁ ca...tayordhvam āyan amṛtatvam eti:* going upward he attains immortality (Brahman). In this passage it is indicated that the person attains Brahman, who is immortal. The same Upaniṣad starting with *anyatra dharmāt* (1.2.14) explains about attaining Brahman.

Another reason is given.

Sūtra – 4.3.14

|| na ca kārye pratipatty-abhisandhiḥ ||

The person with knowledge would not desire to achieve material Brahmā.

Pratipatti means knowledge. *Abhisandhiḥ* means desire. A person in knowledge would not desire to go to *kārya-brahman* since that is not the highest goal. He would desire to go the supreme Brahman. Since the devotee makes the Lord his goal, he attains the Lord, according to the reasoning of *yathā kratuḥ*: as one mediates upon Brahman in this world he attains Brahman after departing from this world. (Chāndogya Upaniṣad 3.14.1) Jaimini concludes that the non-human leads the worshippers to the Supreme Lord (not four-faced Brahmā).

Topic 8 (Sūtra 15)

Apratīkālambanādhikaraṇam - Indirect worship

The author gives his view.

Sūtra – 4.3.15

|| apratīkālambanān nayatīti bādarāyaṇa ubhayathādoṣāt tat-kratuś ca ||

Bādarāyaṇa says that the non-human leads those who do not worship name or other objects, because the other two views are contrary to scripture. According to the worship one attains the result.

Lord Bādarāyaṇa says that the non-human leads *(nayati)* all those who worship Brahman, such as the v*saniṣṭhas, pariniṣṭhitas* and *nirapekṣas,* who do not worship name, speech etc (*apratīkālamanān*), to the Lord. He does not accept that the non-human leads the only worshippers of four-faced Brahmā (Bādarī's view) to Brahmā or only the worshippers of the supreme Brahman (Jaimini's view) to Brahman. Why? Because there are contradictions to both views (*ubhayathā-doṣāt*).

Bādarī's view that the non-human leads the devotees to four-faced Brahmā is contradicted by the statement that they reach the highest light or *paraṁ jyotiḥ* (Chāndogya Upaniṣad 8.12.3). Jaimini's view that only worshippers of Brahman attain Brahman is contradicted by the fact that those with knowledge of five fires (not Brahman) go by the path of light to Brahman. (Chāndogya Upaniṣad 5.10)

The reasoning of *tat-kratu* shows the real meaning. Those who worship name etc.[90] (Chāndogya Upaniṣad 7.1.3) do not attain the supreme Brahman, going by the path of light, since that would contradict the rule that they attain what they worship. Rather they attain skill in names--meaning words, scripture etc. *sa yo nāma brahmety upāste yāvan nāmno gataṁ tatrāsya kaṁa-cāraḥ:* A person who worships the name as Brahman becomes expert at the name. (Chāndogya Upaniṣad 7.1.5)

---

[90] Those who worship four-headed Brahmā would not automatically go to the spiritual world when Brahma goes there.

Those who have knowledge of the five fires, going by the path of light, attain Satya-loka (planet of four-faced Brahmā) because they meditate on their own *ātmā.* There they perfect knowledge of Brahman, the Lord, since those on higher planets also worship the Lord (sūtra 1.3.26). (They then attain Brahman.) Thus this agrees with the statement that those who go on the path of light do not return to this world.

Topic 9 (Sūtra 16)

Viśeṣadhikaraṇam – Exceptional cases of going to the Lord

Now it is explained that the Lord personally takes some *nirapekṣa* devotees to his abode.

etad viṣṇoḥ paramaṁ padaṁ ye
nityodyuktāḥ samyajante na kāmān
teṣām asau gopa-rūpaḥ prayatnāt
prakāśayed ātma-padaṁ tadaiva

Kṛṣṇa in his cowherd form reveals his own abode to those persons who constantly worship Kṛṣṇa in the *pīṭha* and who have no other desires.

oṁkāreṇāntaritaṁ ye japanti
govindasya pañca-padaṁ manuṁ tam
teṣām asau darśayed ātma-rūpaṁ
tasmān mumukṣur abhyasen nityaṁ śantyai

He shows his form to those who utter the five part mantra of Govinda enclosed at both ends by *oṁ*. Therefore those who have give up all other desires repeatedly chant this mantra for eternal bliss. Gopāla-tāpanī Upaniṣad 1.22, 24

The doubt is this. Do the *nirapekṣas* go to the Lord's abode by the guidance of *devatās* or by the guidance of the Lord himself?

(Pūrvapakṣa) Since it is described that there are two paths and that the knowers of Brahman go by the path of light, the *nirapekṣas* also enter the Lord's abode by the guidance of *devatās.*

Sūtra – 4.3.16

|| viśeṣaṁ da darśayati ||

In exceptional cases, the Lord takes the devotee. This is shown in scripture.

The normal method is that the knowers of Brahman attain the Lord through the devatās. The exceptional case (*viśeṣam*) is that the Lord himself takes some *nirapekṣas* who have intense longing for the Lord, since they cannot tolerate separation from him. The śrutis quoted above show this. Smṛti also states this:

ye tu sarvāṇi karmāṇi mayi sannyasya mat-parāḥ
ananyenaiva yogena māṁ dhyāyanta upāsate
teṣām ahaṁ samuddhartā mṛtyu-saṁsāra-sāgarāt
bhavāmi na cirāt pārtha mayy āveśita-cetasām

But for those who, having surrendered to me, having given up all activities in order to attain me, meditate on me and worship me with *ananya-bhakti-yoga*, I quickly become the deliverer from the ocean of repeated birth and death, O son of Pṛthā. BG 12.6-7

The word *ca* indicates that simultaneously these devotees give up their material bodies and gain a spiritual body (*tanu*). One cannot say that the *nirapekṣa* devotee cannot go to the Lord except by the path of light for it is said:

nayāmi paramaṁ sthānam arcir-ādi-gatiṁ vinā
garuḍa-skandham āropya yathеccham anivāritaḥ

Putting the devotee on the shoulders of Garuḍa, by my will, without obstacles, I take the devotee to the supreme abode without going by the path of light. Varāha Purāṇa

Thus what has been said is correct.

Section Four

Topic 1 (Sūtra 1)

Sampady-āvirbhāvādhikaraṇam - Manifestation of jīva's svarūpa

akaitave bhakti-save 'nurajyan
svam eva yaḥ sevakasāt karoti
tato 'ti-modaṁ muditaḥ sa devaḥ
sadā cid-ānanda-tanur dhinotu

May the joyful Lord with body of knowledge and bliss, who becomes dependent on his servants, being attracted to the nectar pure bhakti, always nourish their intense bliss.

In this pāda of Chapter Four, after the author defines the *svarūpa* of the jīva, the enjoyment and powers of the liberated souls are described. It is said:

evam evaiṣa samprasādo 'smāt śarīrāt samutthāya paraṁ jyotir upasampadya svena rūpeṇābhiniṣpadyate sa uttamaḥ puruṣaḥ.

Receiving mercy, rising from his body, he attains the supreme light and manifests with his own form. The Lord is the supreme person. Chāndogya Upaniṣad 8.12.3

The doubt is this. In manifesting this form, is there a relationship of the *ātmā* with this body like that of a *devatā's* body, as a result of *sādhana,* or is it manifestation of what is naturally present in the *ātmā*?

(Pūrvapakṣa) It arises as a result of *sādhana* since the word used is *abhiniṣpatti*: to attain. Otherwise this word would be meaningless. The scriptures dealing with liberation would not be teaching a goal, for if this form were naturally related to the *ātmā,* being a manifestation only, there would be no attainment, since the natural *svarūpa* would have been previously present. Thus the form must be achieved by practice.

Sūtra – 4.4.1

|| sampadyāvirbhāvaḥ svena-śabdāt ||

The jīva manifests his *svarūpa* on attaining the Lord since the word "his own" is used.

It is said in the text that when the jīva has attained (*sampadya*) the supreme light (the Lord) by bhakti, which is served by *jñāna* and *vairāgya*, there is a manifestation (*avirbhavaḥ*) of a particular situation characterized by the arousal of his *svarūpa* endowed with eight qualities when he is freed from the bondage of karma.[91] Why is this the meaning? Because of the word *svena,* which modifies *rūpena.* This indicates his natural form. If he were to receive a new form, the word would have no meaning, since having his own form can only be accomplished by not obtaining a new form. The word *abhiniṣpadyate* is not meaningless since it means "manifested" in sentences like *idam ekaṁ suniṣpannam:* this one has appeared nicely.

One cannot argue that because this form existed previously it cannot be recognized as a goal of human life, for it had not previously made its appearance in this special condition of showing eight qualities. The method of attainment is not useless because it become successful in producing the manifestation of these qualities.

Some say that the jīva, being self-illuminating consciousness alone, on attaining the supreme light, manifests merely a state of destruction of all suffering caused by the superimposition of *prakṛti.* But that is not so, because śruti states that one attains intense bliss. *rasaṁ hy evāyaṁ labdhvānandī bhavati*: the jīva, attaining the Lord who is *rasa,* becomes blissful. (Taittirīya Upaniṣad 2.7)

Topic 2 (Sūtra 2)

Muktādhikaraṇa - Liberation

"How is liberation to be understood for the jīva who has approached the supreme light?"

Sūtra – 4.4.2

|| muktaḥ pratijñānāt ||

Liberation means manifestation of jīva's svarūpa, because that is promised.

---

[91] Manifesting his *svarūpa* means manifesting spiritual qualities inhered in the jīva. The appearance of a particular form for service, for instance with two or four arms, is mentioned later.

Liberation is manifestation of the jīva's svarūpa. Why? Because this is promised (*pratijñānāt*). Prajāpati had promised to explain the jīva, starting with *ya ātmā*, which is liberated from the three conditions of waking, dream and deep sleep, free of the body produced by karma causing happiness and distress. He makes the final promise *etaṁ tv eva te bhūyo 'nuvyākhyāsyami*: I will explain again to you only this, the true self. He then explains in the passage quoted above about the jīva manifesting his own form. Therefore liberation is manifestation of the jīva's *svarūpa,* a natural state of the *svarūpa* freed from the body produced by a relationship with karma.

Topic 3 (Sūtra 3)

Ātmādhikaraṇam - The Lord as light

It is stated that after approaching the supreme light one's *svarūpa* manifests. Something should be considered here. The doubt is this. Is that supreme light the sun globe or the supreme Brahman?

(Pūrvapakṣa) It is the sun globe for it is said that after piercing the sun glove one attains Brahman. The sun was mentioned on the path starting with light.

Sūtra – 4.4.3

|| ātmā prakaraṇāt ||

The supreme light is the Lord since that is understood from the context.

The supreme light is the Lord *(ātmā)* not the sun globe. Why? Because of the context. Though the word "light" is a general term, it means the Lord in the particular context just as in the sentence "The lord knows my mind" the word "lord," a general term, means "you." The word *ātmā* means the all-pervading one whose form is knowledge and bliss. Etymologically *ātmā* means "that which goes or manifests *(atati)*." Thus *ātmā* means he who is approached by the liberated souls. *Ātmā* also means "he who pervades everywhere." Like the word *upaniṣad, ātmā* has many meanings. One should understand that this *ātmā* has a human form (*puruṣa*) since the passage ends with the words *sa uttamaḥ puruṣaḥ:* he is the supreme person. That supreme light which is approached is the supreme person, the Lord.

Topic 4 (Sūtra 4)

Avibhāgādhikaraṇam - Intimate association

Now something else should be considered. Does the liberated jīva on attaining the supreme light situated in the city called Saṁvyoma simply dwell on the same planet *(sālokya)* as the Lord or does he join with him intimately (*sāyujya*)?

(Pūrvapakṣa) He resides on the same planet as the Lord, as one sees a person enter the king's city and reside there.

Sūtra – 4.4.4

|| avibhāgena dṛṣṭatvāt ||

The jīva and the Lord attain *sāyujya,* intimate association, since that is seen in the scriptures.

One should understand that the jīva on attaining the Lord remains united with him *(avibhāgena*). Why? Because that is seen *(dṛṣṭatvāt*).

yathā nadyah syandamānāḥ samudre
astaṁ gacchanti nāma-rūpe vihāya
yathā vidvān nāma-rūpād vimuktaḥ
parāt paraṁ puruṣam upaiti divyam

Just as flowing rivers, giving up name and form, disappear in the ocean, so the man in knowledge freed from name and form attains the supreme, shining person. Muṇḍaka Upaniṣad 3.2.8

Sāyujya means coming together.

ya evaṁ vidvān udag-ayane pramīyate devānām eva mahimānaṁ
gatvādityasya sāyujyaṁ gacchati

The wise man who dies during the northern course of the sun, going to the great devatās, attains *sāyujya* with the sun. Taittirīya Upaniṣad, Mahā-nārāyaṇa Upaniṣad

Though there are other types of liberation (*sālokya, sārṣṭi, sārūpya,* and *sāmīpya),* these are special types of *sāyujya.* This state of *sāyujya* is not lost during separation from the Lord since the Lord is with the devotee internally by his great power. One should not think that the *svarūpa* of the Lord and the jīva are identical by citing the example of the rivers flowing into the sea, since internally there remains difference in the water though the water has become one. Otherwise there would not be an increase in the water when the rivers entered the ocean.

Topic 5 (Sūtras 5 - 7)

Brāhmādhikaraṇam - Eight qualities of Brahman

The author will describe the enjoyments of the liberated jīva, but first he will determine the spiritual form (*vigraha*) with an aggregate of qualities like *satya-saṅkalpa*, which are the cause of his enjoyment. In this description, first the qualities will be defined. Does the jīva who attains the supreme light (the Lord) somehow manifest a *svarūpa* endowed with many qualities or is the jīva's svarūpa simply consciousness itself (*cinmātra*), or does the jīva manifest a *svarūpa* of qualities *and* pure consciousness, since there is no contradiction between the two? Jaimini's opinion follows.

Sūtra – 4.4.5

|| brāhmeṇa jaiminir upanyāsādibhyaḥ ||

Jaimini says that the jīva manifests the eight qualities of Brahman because these qualities are mentioned in śruti.

The jīva manifests with many qualities (*brāhmeṇa*-- that which is produced by the Lord) starting with freedom from sin and ending with accomplishing whatever it wills.[92] Why? Because Prajāpati mentions these qualities of the jīva (*upanyāsa*). *Ādibhiḥ* indicates actions of the liberated jīva related to those qualities such as eating and playing. Because of these scriptural statements, Jaimini believes that the *svarūpa* of the liberated jīva simply manifests with endowment of these qualities. Smṛti also says:

yathā na kriyate jyotsnā mala-prakṣālanān maṇeḥ
doṣa-prahāṇān na jñānam ātmanah kriyate tathā

Just as by washing away dirt, light is not created in a jewel, so by destroying faults knowledge is not created in the jīva.

---

[92] The eight qualities are freedom from sin, freedom from old age, freedom from death, freedom from lamentation, freedom from hunger, freedom from thirst, *satya-kāma* and *satya-saṅkalpa.*

yathodapāna-khananāt kriyate na jalāntaram
sad eva niyate vyaktim asataḥ sambhavaḥ kutaḥ

Just as water is not created by digging a well, an existing thing becomes manifest. How can something not existing appear?

tathā heya-guṇa-dhvaṁsād avarodhādayo guṇāḥ
prakāśyante na jānyante nitya evātmano hi te

Similarly by destruction of bad qualities, the obscured qualities, which are eternal in the *ātmā,* manifest and are not created. Viṣṇu-dharma[93]

Sūtra – 4.4.6

|| citi tan-mātreṇa tad-ātmakatvād ity auḍulomiḥ ||

Attaining Brahman, the jīva manifests his svarūpa as pure consciousness alone, since this is stated in śruti. This is the opinion of Auḍulomi.

When ignorance is destroyed by knowledge of Brahman, a person becomes liberated and, attaining Brahman, pure consciousness (*citi*), manifests as consciousness alone (*tan-mātreṇa*). Why? In the second story of Maitreyī in the Bṛhad-āraṇyaka Upaniṣad 4.5.13, it is said *sa yathā saindhava-ghano 'nantaro 'bāhyaḥ kṛtsno rasa-ghana evaṁ vā are ayam ātmānantaro 'bāhyaḥ kṛtsnaḥ prajñāna-ghana eva*: just as a mass of salt has not interior or exterior and is completely consisting of taste, so the ātmā has no interior or exterior and is completely consisting of knowledge alone. It is understood from this that the *ātmā* is consciousness alone (*tad-ātmakatvāt*). Thus it is understood that the *svarūpa* of the jīva is consciousness with no qualities. The words describing eight qualities starting with absence of sin should be understood to be placed in the passage merely to exclude the qualities like change and material happiness which arise from *avidyā.* This is Auḍulomi's opinion.

Now the author's view is given.

Sūtra – 4.4.7

|| evam apy upanyāsāt pūrva-bhāvād avirodhaṁ bādarāyaṇaḥ ||

[93] This was quoted in 2.3.26. The text here says *hrīyate* instead of *krīyate* but this seems to be a mistake.

Though the jīva is pure consciousness, this is not contrary to the śruti stating that the jīva has eight qualities. This is the view of Bādarāyaṇa.

Though the jīva's *svarūpa* has been defined as pure consciousness *(evam api)*, this is not contradictory (*avirodham*) to the jīva's *svarūpa* having eight qualities. This is the view of Lord Bādarāyaṇa. Why? Because of proof (*upanyāsāt*) in the form of Prajāpati's words used by Jaimini, in first opinion (*pūrva-bhāvāt*), which proved that the *ātmā* manifested eight qualities. The conclusion is that the jīva has both forms because the proofs given by Jaimini and Auḍulomi are of equal strength, since the statements are not qualified in any way. Because śruti says the jīva is *prajñāna-ghana eva*, consciousness, Bādarāyaṇa accepts that the jīva's *svarūpa* is consciousness without qualities because he says this view (*evam api*) is not contradictory (*avirodham*) to the jīva having eight qualities. The word *prajñāna-ghana eva* does not mean "only consciousness and nothing else." It is clear from the passage that the intention of the word *eva* is only to deny insentience (*jaḍatā*) absolutely in the jīva which is self-illuminating.

The jīva having eight qualities, understood from the other śruti, is not contrary to the jīva being pure consciousness. Qualities like hardness and form perceived by the eye or other senses are not contrary to the salt being full of taste. Therefore in the liberated state the jīva manifests as a *svarūpa* of knowledge, endowed with eight qualities.

Topic 6 (Sūtra 8)

Saṅkalpādhikaraṇam - Fulfillment of will

Now the ability of the liberated jīva to will anything to happen (*satya-saṅkalpa*) is discussed. In the Chāndogya Upaniṣad (8.12.3) it is said *sa tatra paryeti jakṣan krīḍan ramamāṇaḥ strībhir vā yānair vā jñātibhir vā*: the liberated jīva moves, eats, and plays, enjoying with women, vehicles and relatives.

The doubt is this. Does his attaining relatives etc. take place by making efforts or by his will alone which makes it happen?

(Pūrvapakṣa) He attains these things by his will assisted by his efforts, since one sees that there is dependence on effort of kings or others to fulfill their will even though they are said to be *satya-saṅkalpa*.

Sūtra – 4.4.8

|| saṅkalpād eva tac chruteḥ ||

The liberated jīva attains things by his will alone, since that is stated in śruti.

The liberated jīva attains these things by will alone (*saṅkalpāt eva*). Why? Because of statements to that effect in śruti (*tac-chruteḥ*). In the Chāndogya Upaniṣad

(8.2.1) it is stated that he attains various persons by his will alone. It is said *sa yadi pitṛloka-kāmo bhavati saṅkalpād evāsya pitaraḥ samuttiṣṭhanti. tena pitṛlokena sampanno mahīyate:* if he desires persons from Pitṛloka, those persons arrive; endowed with Pitṛloka he is happy. If it were not so, the word *eva* (only) in the phrase *saṅkalpād eva* would be contradicted. In the phrase *prajñāna-ghana eva* of Bṛhad-āraṇyaka Upaniṣad, the word *eva* has a different meaning since there are statements in Chāndogya Upaniṣad stating the eight qualities. In the present case however, we do not see other statements which make the will dependent upon effort.

This type of liberation, predominated by one's own happiness and powers however is not desired by devotees who are greedy for the taste of *rasa* in service. Thus there are statements condemning this type of liberation.

Topic 7 (Sūtras 9 - 12)

Ananyādhipaty-adhikaraṇam - Control by others in a liberated state

The author now shows that the liberated jīva with the quality of *satya-saṅkalpa* depends on the Lord alone.

The doubt is this. Is the liberated jīva controlled by anyone except the Lord?

(Pūrvapakṣa) He is controlled by others, not the Lord, since he goes to someone else's place, for if one goes to the king's palace, one is ordered by persons other than the king. Similarly, in going to the Lord's abode, one is ordered by the Lord's associates.

Sūtra – 4.4.9

|| ata eva cānanyādhipatiḥ ||

Because of the Lord's mercy and the jīva's nature of *satya-saṅkalpa*, the liberated jīva has no master except the Lord.

Because of the manifestation of the Lord's mercy and because of the jīva's *satya-saṅkalpa* nature alone (*ata eva*), the liberated jīva has no other master than the Lord (*ananyādhipatiḥ*). Taking shelter of the Lord alone, he plays. Otherwise, if he had another master, he would be in a situation similar to that in the material world. Though the jīva's nature of *satya-saṇkalpa* exists within himself (*svātma-bhūtam*), it manifests because of his worship of the Lord. Thus the devotee enjoys while at the same time recognizing the mercy of the Lord full of unlimited bliss, who is affectionate to those who take shelter of him. The Lord also gives bliss to the liberated jīva. That will be explained in sūtra 4.4.20. Since the jīva is an *aṁśa* of the Lord (dependent on him) his nature of being an agent and enjoyer comes from the Lord alone. That was previously shown.

Another meaning is as follows. Because the liberated jīva has *satya-saṇkalpa (ataḥ),* he has no other master: he is not restricted by injunctions or prohibitions. The injunctions and prohibitions would destroy his nature of *satya-saṅkalpa.*

The author now shows the acquisition (*yoga*) of a spiritual body (*divya-vigraha*) by the liberated jīva.

The doubt is this. Does the liberated jīva, with attainment of the highest light (the Lord), have a body (*vigraha*) or not: or by his choice, can he have or not have a body?

Bādari's opinion on the matter is given.

Sūtra – 4.4.10

|| abhāve bādarir āha hy evam ||

Bādari says the liberated jīva has no body, because śruti states this.

Bādari thinks that the liberated jīva has no body (*abhāve*). Bodies are produced by karma. Since the liberated jīva has no karma, he cannot have a body. Why? Because (*hi*) Chāndogya Upaniṣad 8.12.1 states (*āha*) this (*evam*). *na ha vai sa-śarīrasya sataḥ priyāpriyayor apahatir asti aśarīraṁ vāva santaṁ priyāpriye na spṛśataḥ*: when he is in the body the jīva cannot rid himself of happiness and distress and when devoid of a body happiness and distress do not touch him. Having described suffering because of having a body, the state of not having a body is then described. *asmāc charīrāt samutthāya param jyotir upasaṁpadya*: rising from that body, the jīva attains the supreme light. (Chāndogya Upaniṣad 8.12.3) Smṛti also confirms this. *dehendriyāsu-hīnānāṁ vaikuṇṭha-pura-vāsinām*: the inhabitants of Vaikuṇṭha have no body and senses. (SB 7.1.35)

Sūtra – 4.4.11

|| bhāvaṁ jaiminir vikalpāmananāt ||

According to Jaimini, the liberated jīva has a body because of statements indicating the jīva can choose various bodies.

Jaimini says that the liberated jīva has a body (*bhāvam).* Why? Because in the *bhūma vidyā* section of Chāndogya Upaniṣad (7.26.2) various options for bodies are described for the jīva (*vikalpa-āmananāt*).

sa ekadhā bhavati dvidhā tridhā bhavati pañcadhā saptadhā navadhā caiva punaś caikādaśa smṛtaḥ. śataṁ ca daśa caikaś ca sahasrāṇi ca viṁśatiḥ

He becomes one. Then he becomes two, three, five, seven, nine and eleven. He becomes one hundred and ten. He becomes one thousand and twenty.

Without having bodies, the jīva, which is *aṇu* (indivisible), could not become many forms as stated. One cannot infer that this description is not factual since it is in the section on liberation. That being the case, when śruti speaks of the jīva being without a body *(aśarīram*) it means that the jīva is devoid of a body produced by karma. This is proved by smṛti which will be quoted after the following sūtra.[94]

The author gives his view.

Sūtra – 4.4.12

|| dvādaśāhavad ubhaya-vidhaṁ bādarāyaṇo'taḥ ||

Because of his nature as *satya-saṅkalpa*, the jīva can have or not have a body just as the twelve day sacrifice can have one sponsor or many.

---

[94] *vasanti yatra puruṣāḥ mūrtayaḥ sarve vaikuṇṭha.*

Because of having the nature of *satya-saṅkalpa (ataḥ)* the liberated jīva can either have a body or not have a body (*ubhaya-vidhim*). This is Bādarāyaṇa's view because both statements are made in the śruti. He accepts that the jīva in his liberated state can exist with a body or without a body. It is like the twelve day sacrifice (*dvādaśāhavat*). By the desire of the sponsor the sacrifice can be a *satra* with many sponsors or it can be *ahīna* with only one sponsor, and there is no contradiction. Similarly the liberated jīva can by his will have a body or not have a body.

The meaning is this. The liberated jīvas, having destroyed all suffering by Brahma-vidyā, manifest their *satya-saṇkalpa* nature. Those among them who desire a body, by their will, have a body. Thus śruti says *sa ekadhā*: he manifests one body. (Chāndogya Upaniṣad 7.26.2) Those liberated jīvas who do not want a body do not manifest a body. Thus, śruti says *aśarīram vāva*: he is without a body. (Chāndogya Upaniṣad 8.12.1)

For those who desire to serve the Lord eternally with a spiritual body, that body made of the *cic-cakti* manifests.[95] Eternally possessing that body they serve the Lord.

Śruti says:

yatra tv asya sarvam ātmaivābhūt tat kena kaṁ paśyet

When all the senses of the liberated jīva become filled with the Lord's *śakti*, how does he see and what does he see: he sees the Lord by senses endowed with the Lord's *śakti*. Bṛhad-āraṇyaka Upaniṣad 4.5.15

sa vā eṣa brahma-niṣṭha idaṁ śarīraṁ martyam atisṛjya
brahmābhisampadya brahmaṇā paśyati brahmaṇā śṛṇoti brahmaṇaivedaṁ
sarvam anubhavati

The person fixed in Brahman, leaving his material body, achieves the Lord and sees by the Lord, hears by the Lord and experiences everything by the Lord alone. Madhyandinañana śruti

Smṛti says:

vasanti yatra puruṣāḥ sarve vaikuṇṭha-mūrtayaḥ

---

[95] Since the satya-saṅkalpa of the jīva is under the Lord, Lord manifests this spiritual body, which should be eternally within the Lord.

In that place all men reside with forms like the Lord. SB 3.15.14

The decision of the jīva to have a body or not have a body should be understood to be determined from the time of *sādhana* since it was previous said *yathā kratu:* as one mediates upon Brahman in this world he attains Brahman after departing from this world. (Chāndogya Upaniṣad 3.14.1) As well smṛti as previously quoted says *gacchāmi viṣṇu-pādābhyāṁ viṣṇu-dṛṣṭyānudarśanam*: I move by the feet of Viṣṇu, I see by the eyes of Viṣṇu (Bṛhad-tantra).[96] Smṛti also confirms this with *muktasyaitad bhaviṣyati:* such *sādhana* will result in the liberated jīva attaining that status.[97]

Topic 8 (Sūtras 13 - 14)

Tanv-abhāvādhikaraṇam - In the absence of a body the jīva can enjoy in the spiritual world

The qualities of the liberated jīva and the attainment of a spiritual body (*divya-deha*), causes for enjoyment, have been described. The enjoyment is proved by śruti such as *so 'śnute sarvān kāmān*: he enjoys all pleasures. (Taittirīya Upaniṣad 2.1.1) It will be explained in this section that the jīva can enjoy either with a body or without a body.

The doubt is this. Can the liberated jīva enjoy or not?

(Pūrvapakṣa) Since he does not have a body or senses, enjoyment is impossible. If he is considered a yogī, since he would be full of bliss already, he would not develop desires for enjoyment. Thus enjoyment in liberation is not proper.

Sūtra – 4.4.13

|| tanv-abhāve sandhyavad-upapatteḥ ||

Even without a body, the liberated jīva can enjoy, since it is reasonable as in the dream state.

---

[96] The commentary indicates this was previously quoted, but the verse is not found anywhere else in the commentaries. The sūkṣma ṭika says this is from Bṛhad-tantra.

[97] This seems to be a quote from somewhere, but untraceable.

Even without a body (*tanv-abhāve*), he can enjoy, because it is reasonable (*upapatteḥ)* as in a dream *(sandhyavat*). *Sandhya* means a dream. In a dream, without having a body, one enjoys. Thus even without a body the liberated jīva can enjoy.

If the jīva has a body, the enjoyment is more.

Sūtra – 4.4.14

|| bhāve jāgradvat ||

The liberated jīva, if he has a body, enjoys as in the waking state.

With a body (*bhāve*) the jīva can enjoy (more intensely) as in the waking state. The argument that the liberated jīva has no desire is not proper because *rasa* which is to be enjoyed become desired by the jīva, since it is the mercy of the Lord.

Though the Lord is satisfied in himself, he has desire to enjoy because of the desire of the devotee (to give him enjoyment). However the liberated jīva has desires for enjoying what is given as the mercy of the Lord, because of his bhakti to the Lord (accepting it to please the Lord).

Topic 9 (Sūtras 15 - 16)

Pradīpādhikaraṇam - Knowledge like a lamp

The author shows that the liberated jīva has all knowledge.

In the Chāndogya Upaniṣad (7.26.2) it is said *na paśyo mṛtyuṁ paśyati na rogaṁ nota-duḥkhitaṁ sarvaṁ hi paśyaḥ paśyati sarvam āpnoti sarvaśaḥ:* the liberated jīva does not see death, sickness or suffering; seeing everything, he sees and obtains everything in all ways. This states that the liberated jīva has knowledge of all things.

The doubt is this. Is this true or not?

(Pūrvapakṣa) It is not true since Bṛhad-āraṇyaka Upaniṣad 4.3.21 states that he does not have all knowledge. *na bahyam kiñcana veda*: he does not know anything externally.

Sūtra – 4.4.15

|| pradīpavad āveśas tathā hi darśayati ||

Like a lamp, the jīva's knowledge enters many places. That is shown in śruti.

Just as a lamp enters many places by its rays, so the liberated jīva enters many objects (becomes aware of any objects) by its consciousness which spreads out. *prajñā ca tasmāt prasṛtā purāṇī*: because of the Lord, the jīva's eternal knowledge spreads out everywhere. (Śvetāśvatara Upaniṣad 4.18) From the Lord (*tasmāt*) the jīva's eternal (*purāṇī*) knowledge spreads (*prasṛtā*).

"It is not correct that the liberated jīva has all knowledge because particular knowledge is denied in the śruti beginning with *prājñenātmanā.*" [98]

Sūtra – 4.4.16

| | svāpyaya-sampatyor anyatrāpekṣyam āviṣkṛtaṁ hi | |

The text quoted does not forbid particular knowledge of the liberated jīva. It refers to other conditions of the jīva--deep sleep and dying. These conditions do not refer to the liberated jīva because śruti reveals that the jīva is free of sleep and death when liberated.

The text quoted does not forbid particular knowledge of the liberated jīva. It refers to other conditions--deep sleep and dying (*svāpyaya-sampatyoḥ*). *svam apīto bhavati tasmād enaṁ svapītīty ācakṣate:* the senses merge in the self, and thus they say he sleeps. (Chāndogya Upaniṣad 6.8.1) *vāṅ manasi sampadyate*: speech merges into the mind.(Chāndogya Upaniṣad 6.15.1) Because (*hi*) śruti reveals *(āviṣkṛtam*) that the jīva is free of sleep and death when liberated. Thus he has all knowledge.

In the text, the state of unawareness in deep sleep is first described:

nāhaṁ khalv ayam evaṁ sampraty ātmānaṁ jānāty ayam aham asmīti no evemāni bhūtāni vināśam ivāpīto bhavati. nāham atra bhogyaṁ paśyāmi

He does not know himself at that time. He is not aware of "This is I." He is not aware of other beings. He has entered sleep as if he were destroyed. I do not see any enjoyment there.

After this, the liberated jīva is described as having omniscience:

---

[98] *prājñenātmanā sampariṣvakto na bāhyaṁ kiñcana veda nāntaram:* the jīva, embraced by the omniscient *ātmā* (Brahman) does not know anything outside or inside. (Bṛhad-āraṇyaka Upaniṣad 4.3.21)

sa vā eṣa etena divyena cakṣuṣā manasy etān kāmān paśyan ramate ya ete brahmaloke

With spiritual eyes seeing attractive objects in the mind, he enjoys in the spiritual world.

Chāndogya Upaniṣad 8.12.5

The non-liberated jīva's lack no awareness due to death is described elsewhere. *etebhyo bhūtebhyaḥ samutthāya tāny evānuvinaśyati:* rising from all elements, he does not see (is not aware of) those elements. (Bṛhad-āraṇyaka Upaniṣad 2.4.12) *Vinaśyati* means "he does not see." Thus the liberated jīva is omniscient.

Topic 10 (Sūtras 17 - 21)

Jagad-vyāpāra-varjādhikaraṇam - Jīva cannot create universes

In Chāndogya Upaniṣad (8.1.6 and 8.2.1) it is said:

atha ya iha ātmānam anuvidya vrajanty etāṁś ca satyān kāmāṁs teṣāṁ sarveṣu lokeṣu kāma-cāro bhavati

Those who depart from here while knowing *ātmā* and true desirable objects wander at will in all worlds. Chāndogya Upaniṣad 8.1.6

sa yadi pitṛloka-kāmo bhavati

If he desires Pitṛ-loka, the Pitṛs come to him. Chāndogya Upaniṣad 8.2.1

The doubt is this. Can the liberated jīva create a universe or not?

(Pūrvapakṣa) He can, since it was said he is *satya-saṅkalpa* and is very similar to the Lord.

Sūtra – 4.4.17

|| jagad-vyāpāra-varjaṁ prakaraṇād asannihitatvāt ||

The liberated jīva cannot create universes, because of express statements indicating that the Lord only does this and these statements do not apply to the jīva.

Since it was said if he desires Pitṛloka the Pitṛs come to him, the liberated jīva can create some worlds (pitṛloka). But excluded (*varjam)* is the creation, maintenance and destruction of the universe (*jagad-vyapara*), which can be done only by the Lord. Why? Because there are passages (*prakaraṇāt*) stating that everything comes from Brahman. *Yato vā imāni bhūtāni:* from him arise all these beings. One cannot take statements concerning the Lord and the jīva and mix them. Since the topic in the passage *yato va imāni bhūtāni* is not concerning the jīva (*asannihitatvāt*), one cannot conclude that the liberated jīva can create universes by those two statements quoted above. If the jīva could create universes the author would not have defined Brahman with *jamādy asya yataḥ*: Brahman is that from which universes are created. If there were many creators (jīvas becoming God) it would amount to complete disorder in the universe. Therefore the liberated jīva is not the creator of universes.

"In Taittirīya Upaniṣad 1.5.3 it is said *sarve 'smai devā balim āvahanti*: all the *devatās* offer tribute to that liberated jīva. In Chāndogya Upaniṣad 7.25.2 it is said *sa svarāḍ bhavati tasya sarveṣu lokeṣu kāma-cāro bhavati:* he becomes independent, wandering in all the worlds as he pleases. The liberated jīva should have power to create universes since he is worshipped by the *devatās* and it is said that he has great powers."

Sūtra – 4.4.18

|| pratyakṣopadeśād iti cen, na, adhikārika-maṇḍalasyokteḥ ||

If you say there are direct statements in śruti to show that the liberated jīva has the power to create universes, the answer is no, because those statements only indicate that the liberated jīva visits the *devatās* by the mercy of the Lord.

If you say that it is not correct to say that the liberated jīva cannot create universes because of direct statements in śruti (*pratyakṣupadeśāt*) the answer is no. Why? The text merely says *(ukteḥ)* that the liberated jīva, by the mercy of the Lord, can go to the planets of Brahmā and the *devatās (adhikārika-maṇḍalasya)* and enjoy those pleasures. The smṛtis tell us that the Kumāras and Nārada without obstruction go to these places and are welcomed by their rulers. The liberated jīva by the Lord's mercy enjoys those pleasures in the world which is the Lord's effect and which express the Lord's powers. Because this is the meaning of those texts, the liberated jīva does not create universes.

"If the liberated jīva enjoys the pleasures within the material world he is no different from the conditioned souls since these pleasures are temporary."

Sūtra – 4.4.19

| | vikāra-varti ca tathā hi sthitim āha | |

The liberated jīva is situated in Brahman, devoid of material changes, because this is stated in śruti.

The liberated jīva, is situated in the perfect *svarūpa* of Brahman endowed with its qualities and *dhāma* etc., in which the material world does not exist (*vikāra-avarti*). There he experiences Brahman after having destroyed the coverings of ignorance by *vidyā* (bhakti) directed towards the Lord. He is in no way contaminated by the world, because (*hi)* Kaṭha Upaniṣad speaks (*āha*) of his situation (*sthitim*) in this way (*tathā*).

puram ekādaśa-dvāram ajasyāvakra-cetasaḥ
anuṣṭhāya na śocati vimuktaś ca vimucyate

Situated in the body with eleven gates belonging to the unborn omniscient Lord, the liberated jīva does not lament and is free of illusion. Kaṭha Upaniṣad 2.2.1

The meaning of the phrase *vimuktaṣ ca vimucyate* is "The person, knowing Brahman, freed from things covering Brahman's svarūpa (*vimuktaḥ*), becomes free (*vimucyate*) from the things covering Brahman's qualities." Free from the two types of obstruction to experiencing the Lord, he remains directly seeing Brahman, enjoying the imperishable goal. The covering is like a covering produced by clouds, affecting the vision of the jīva.

vilajjamānayā yasya sthātum īkṣā-pathe 'muyā
vimohita vikantthante mamāham iti durdhiyaḥ

The ignorant *jīvas*, bewildered by *māyā* who is ashamed to stand in sight of the Lord, boast about "I" and "mine." SB 2.5.13

The Lord, who is like the sun, is not covered by clouds of *māyā.*

"Since the goal is to realize the *ātmā* whose *svarūpa* is bliss and knowledge, endowed with qualities like *satya-saṅkalpa,* why endeavor for seeing Brahman, the Lord?"

Sūtra – 4.4.20

|| darśayataś caivaṁ pratyakṣānumāne ||

Śruti, smṛti and logic as well show that the liberated jīva attains additional bliss by relating with the Lord.

Though the liberated jīva is endowed with knowledge and bliss as described above, he does not possess unlimited bliss, since he is very small. He should realize Brahman because he can experience unlimited bliss by that realization. Śruti and smṛti (*pratyakṣanumāne*) show this (*darśayataḥ*). *rasaṁ hy evāyaṁ labdhvānandī-bhavati*: attaining the Lord who is *rasa*, the jīva attains full bliss. (Taittirīya Upaniṣad 2.6.1) *Ānandī* means full bliss.

brahmaṇo hi pratiṣṭhāham amṛtasyāvyayasya ca
śāśvatasya ca dharmasya sukhasyasikāntikasya ca

I become the ultimate, affectionate shelter of the *jīva* who has attained his *svarūpa*, who is beyond death and possesses unchanging devotion to me, for I am the shelter of eternal qualities and extraordinary *rasa* for that *jīva*. BG 14.27

The word *ca* indicates that logic also demonstrates this: taking shelter of a wealthy man, a poor man becomes rich.

"According to the statement *nirañjanaḥ paramaṁ sāmyam upaiti*: the jīva attains similarity with the Lord (Muṇḍaka Upaniṣad 3.1.3), the liberated jīva is equal to the Lord. Then what is the use of the Lord? Being small refers to material intelligence of the jīva and does not really mean that the jīva is small (*aṇu*). "

Sūtra – 4.4.21

|| bhoga-mātra-sāmya-liṅgāc ca ||

The jīva is not equal to the Lord because there are indications that equality refers only to their enjoyment.

The word *ca* means "only." The word *na* (not) is understood from sūtra 4.4.18. It is said *so 'śnute sarvān kāmān saha brahmaṇā vipaścitā*: the jīva enjoys all delights with omniscient Brahman. (Taittirīya Upaniṣad 2.1) The liberated jīva is like the Lord only in enjoying. The statement from Muṇḍaka Upaniṣad does not mean that their *svarūpas* are identical, since there are indications of differences. That the jīva is not atomic has been refuted previously (sūtra 2.3.19). By the present sutra, the last one defining the *svarūpa* of the jīva, which shows that the jīva and Brahman are similar only in their enjoyment, the author is thus pointing out their real difference in the capacities of their *svarūpas.*

Topic 11 (Sūtra 22)

Anāvṛtty-adhikaraṇam – Not returning to this world

Now the author explains that the liberated jīva is at all times close to the Lord. The statements dealing with attaining the planet of the Lord are the subject.

The doubt is this. Is liberation, the characteristic of attaining the Lord, temporary or permanent?

(Pūrvapakṣa) It is temporary because one can fall from there as one falls from Svarga, since it is just another planet.

Sūtra – 4.4.22

|| anāvṛttiḥ śabdāt anāvṛttiḥ śabdāt ||

There is no return from the Lord's abode, because of scriptural statements.

For the person who has attained the Lord's planet, by understanding him through worship, there is no return from there (*anāvṛttiḥ*). Why? Because of scriptural statements.

Śruti says:

etena pratipadyamānā imaṁ mānavam āvartaṁ nāvartante

Those who go by this path do not return to the world of men. Chāndogya Upaniṣad 4.15.5

sa khalv eva vartayan yāvad āyuṣam brahmalokam abhisampadyate na ca punar avartate.
Living his life in this way, he attains the world of Brahman and does not return. Chāndogya Upaniṣad 8.15.1

Smṛti says:

mām upetya punar janma duḥkhālayam aśāsvatam
nāpnuvanti mahātmānaḥ samsiddhiṁ paramāṁ gatāḥ

Attaining me, those noble-minded souls do not again take material birth, which is filled with suffering and is temporary. They attain me, the highest goal.

ā-brahma-bhuvanāl lokāḥ punar āvartino 'rjuna
mām upetya tu kaunteya punar janma na vidyate

O Arjuna, all those including the inhabitants of Brahma-loka take birth again. But having attained me, O son of Kuntī, a person does not take birth again. BG 8.15-16

One should never worry that the supreme Lord would desire to make the jīva who is dependent on him fall from his planet and that the devotee would ever desire to give up the Lord, since scripture describes their mutual affection for each other:

priyo hi jñānino tv artham ahaṁ sa ca mama priyaḥ

Of these four types, the *jñānī*, who is constantly engaged in thinking of me, who is practicing pure *bhakti*, is the best. This *jñānī* loves only me, and I love only him. BG 7.17

sādhavo hṛdayaṁ mahyaṁ sādhūnāṁ hṛdayaṁ tv aham

The pure devotee is my very heart: what pains him pains me. I am the heart of the pure devotee: what pleases him pleases me. SB 9.4.68

ye dārāgara-putrāptān prāṇān vittam imaṁ param
hitvā māṁ śaraṇaṁ yātāḥ kathaṁ tāṁs tyaktum utsahe

Since pure devotees give up their homes, wives, children, relatives, riches and even their lives simply to serve me, without any desire for material improvement in this life or in the next, how can I give up such devotees at any time? SB 9.4.65

dhautātmā puruṣaḥ kṛṣṇa- pāda-mūlaṁ na muñcati
mukta-sarva-parikleśaḥ panthāḥ sva-śaraṇaṁ yathā

The person with a pure heart does not give up the root of the feet of Kṛṣṇa. He is like a traveler, who, giving up all sufferings after earning wealth, does not leave his house. SB 2.8.6

The Lord can never let his devotees fall because smṛti says the devotees have exclusive devotion to him and the Lord is determined never to give them up, and because the Lord is without faults like cruelty or miserliness and the devotees are without fault, having devotion exclusively for the Lord.

This is what is said. The supreme Lord, an ocean of affection for those who take shelter of him, true to his word (*satya-vāk*) and having all his desires accomplished (*satya-saṅkalpa),* destroying *avidyā,* the cause of turning away from him, in his devotees who have given up everything for him, brings these devotees, his most dear *aṁśas* close to him and never gives them up.

The jīvas, seeking happiness at all costs, though attracted to insignificant material objects for a shadow of pleasure for unlimited births, having understood their source by special good fortune, by the grace of guru, becoming completely purified by service to him and desiring no one else, having attained their master, the best friend, the most merciful, the form of unlimited bliss and knowledge, never desire to leave him. This is what is understood from scriptures (not from logic). Those who are completely surrendered to scripture must have firm faith in this.

The sūtra is repeated to indicate the completion of the work.

samuddhṛtya yo duḥkha-paṅkāt samuktān
nayaty acyutaś cit-sukhe dhāmni nitye |
priyān gāḍha-rāgāt tilārdhaṁ vimoktuṁ
na cecchatv asāv eva sujñair niṣevyaḥ ||

Acyuta, who is served by the intelligent, and who, delivering his devotees from the mire of suffering, leads them to his eternal abode of knowledge and bliss, never desires to separate those dear devotees from their deep attachment to him for even a second.

śrīmad-govinda-padāravinda-makaranda-lubdha-cetobhiḥ |
govinda-bhāṣyam etat pāṭhyaṁ śapatho'rpito'nyebhyaḥ ||

This Govinda-bhāṣya should be studied by those persons greedy for the honey of Govinda's lotus feet. A curse is offered to others.

vidyā-rūpaṁ bhūṣaṇaṁ me pradāya khyātiṁ
ninye tena yo mām udāraḥ |
śrī-govindaḥ svapna-nirdiṣṭa-bhāṣyo
rādhā-bandhur bandhurāṅgaḥ sa jīyāt ||

May generous Govinda, with beautiful limbs, the friend of Rādhā, who, giving me the name Vidyābhūṣaṇa, ordered this commentary in a dream, be victorious.

About the Author-Translator

His Holiness Bhanu Swami maharaja was born in Canada on the 26th December 1948 to the most fortunate Japanese parents. HH Bhanu Swami Maharaja is one of the senior disciples of His Divine Grace A.C Bhaktivedanta Swami Srila Prabhupada, founder acharya of ISKCON, the International Society for Krishna Consciousness. He holds a BA Degree in Oriental fine arts history from the University of British Colombia. He joined the Hare Krishna movement in India in 1970. Initiated in 1971 by Srila Prabhupada, he took sannyasa vows in 1984. Bhanu Swami was personally instructed in the art of Deity worship by Srila Prabhupada, and within ISKCON he has become an authority on the topic. He is a great inspiration for many devotees around the world and he preaches Krishna consciousness in Australia, Japan, Malaysia, Russia and India.

HH Bhanu Swami Maharaja met the disciples of His Divine Grace A.C. Bhaktivedanta Swami Srila Prabhupada in 1971 in Tokyo, just after his graduation in history. Srila Prabhupada was about to set on his India tour with his Western disciples and Bhanu Maharaja joined with them.

By 1972, His Holiness Bhanu Swami maharaja already earned credit from Srila Prabhupada for his exact Sanskrit pronunciation, expertise in cooking and excellence in deity worship. He also began to translate Srila Prabhupada's books into Japanese.

He continues with this translation service to this day, giving us the nectar from the Bengali and Sanskrit works of the previous Vaishnava acharyas to enhance our understanding of the Gaudiya Vaishnava philosophy. He is also a member of the Governing Body Commission of ISKCON.

His other works are listed here - https://www.amazon.com/HH-Bhanu-Swami/e/B01F1JK6W6